Kentucky

Portrait in Paradox, 1900–1950

To my parents

Kentucky

Portrait in Paradox, 1900–1950

by James C. Klotter

Kentucky Historical Society
Frankfort, Kentucky

The Library of Congress has cataloged the hardcover edition as follows:

Klotter, James C., 1947–
        Kentucky: portrait in paradox, 1900–1950 / by James C. Klotter.
             p.   cm.
        Includes bibliographical references and index.
        ISBN 0-916968-24-3
        1. Kentucky–History–1865– . I. Title.
F456.K57   1996
976.9'04–dc20

Paper ISBN 10: 0-916968-34-0
Paper ISBN 13: 978-0-916968-34-2

This book is printed on acid-free recycled paper meeting
the requirements of the American National Standard
for Permanence in Paper for Printed Library Materials.

Manufactured in the United States of America.

Contents

My Old Kentucky Home

The sun shines bright in the Old Kentucky Home
'Tis summer, the people are gay,
The corn top's ripe and the meadow's in the bloom
While the birds make music all the day,

The young folks roll on the little cabin floor,
All merry, all happy and bright
By'n by hard times comes a-knocking at the door,
Then my Old Kentucky Home, good night.

CHORUS
Weep no more, my lady,
Oh weep no more today.
We will sing one song
For the Old Kentucky Home
For the Old Kentucky Home, far away.

– Stephen Collins Foster, revised version

The generational disconnection that affect us:
All times, we assume, are different; we therefore
have nothing to learn from our elders, nothing to teach our
    children.
Civilization is thus reduced to a sequence of last-minute
    improvisations,
desperately building today out of the wreckage of yesterday.

– Wendell Berry

"United We Stand, Divided We Fall"

– State Motto

Tell me a story
In this century, and moment, of mania,
Tell me a story.
Make it a story of great distances, and starlight.
The name of the story will be Time
But you must not pronounce its name.
Tell me a story of deep delight.

– Robert Penn Warren

Preface

The Kentucky state song, officially adopted in 1928, says much about the commonwealth in this era. "My Old Kentucky Home" begins with images of happy adults in a lush agricultural setting, listening to birds "make music all the day." Around them are laughing children, "happy and bright." Then the mood changes and "hard times comes a-knocking." In the chorus, the spirit is both melancholy and hopeful, for the people should weep no more and sing instead of a nostalgic place, a Kentucky home, "far away."

Stephen Collins Foster was writing about a different century and of the slaves who lived in it, but the themes, looked at in terms of the first half of the twentieth century, were still appropriate. In 1900, Kentuckians chiefly lived in agrarian settings and looked back to their nostalgic past. The state, while not at the level nationally that it had been earlier, still was an important one. At the beginning of the twentieth century, Kentucky, statistically, stood high compared to the rest of the South. It had promise, even yet.

But by 1950, there were few categories that Kentuckians could point to with pride, even compared to the region. Overall, the actions taken, the roads chosen, the decisions made, had not been ones that allowed Kentucky to keep pace. Some reasons for the change lay outside of the commonwealth's power to change. But some did not.

This is an account of what happened *in* Kentucky and *to* Kentucky in that time. It focuses on the process and the possibility of change, and how the people sought to adjust and to balance the positives of their past with the promise of their future. To understand the options they had requires a broad overview of various parts of the state, not just its political system, but also its situation regarding people's everyday lives, their economy, their culture, their educational system, and more. Obviously, such state studies provide the building blocks for constructing a larger national picture. Yet, in their detail, they offer the opportunity for an in-depth examination of the evolution of a specific entity — in this case a commonwealth — in that system. To know better what happened between 1900 and 1950 requires a study of not only the formal actions taken, but also the irony of actions, the presence of paradoxes, and the quieter things that shaped the state's character, its essence, its heart, and its soul.

There are dangers in that approach. First of all, it may simply not be done properly. Second, in attempting to cover so much, it may be that little is covered well. The detail needed may overwhelm the themes. And, finally, such books are exploratory, not definitive in nature, are designed to stimulate further research, and are aimed at both a scholarly and general reading public. As David Thelen noted in a recent *Journal of American History* article, historians must produce a literature that is not "detached from life, beyond human reach and comprehension." They must connect history with a public purpose. They must challenge.

There are strengths to be gained from an in-depth study of broad coverage. Previously unseen interconnections become clear. New relations between actions are revealed. Fresh perspectives appear. The use of personal recollections from all classes of people, oral histories, forgotten county histories, literary works with special insights, all reveal the past from a variety of outlooks, not widely applied to Kentucky's history previously. Some of the very questions broached — such as the decline of the commonwealth in many areas — are seldom raised by investigators of the state's past. In short, problems exist with the approach chosen, but the possible benefits make the risk worthwhile.

This book closes in 1950, for at mid-century, Kentucky was re-examining itself. A whole series of studies had identified what had occurred previously. Problems were noted and presented. At both the state and national level, serious concerns still existed. But there seemed an atmosphere conducive to change, and the various studies offered ways to accomplish that. After a half-century of decline, Kentucky still believed it could reverse that process. It did not want to be an urbanized, industrial giant, for there were positive aspects of the state that the people did not want to sacrifice for that. Yet it could be something better than it was in 1950. The work closes with a people once more on the brink, ready to make — or not make — decisions that would shape them into the twenty-first century. Would their image of the future commonwealth be realized, or would that view of their Old Kentucky Home remain elusive and "far away"?

Acknowledgments

Research on this book began more years ago than I like to recall and was interrupted several times by other projects taking precedence. Since the work covered an extended period, the names of those to be thanked has grown long. After a public plea for materials, for instance, I found my mail filled with items from strangers, eager to help make the story as full as possible. Others told me informally over the years about their memories and how they interpreted them. Because of that process and the numbers involved, many who deserve recognition as being a part of this book may not be mentioned, but they all should know that each recollection given, each memory shared, helped shape this work and my judgments.

Two decades ago, little secondary writing covered Kentucky history in the twentieth century. Since that time a sizeable number of articles and books has appeared, and each made my task easier. All those authors cannot be recognized but I owe a great deal to those who blazed the historical path before me.

Much of my own original research was done in a score or more of research institutions, both inside and outside of Kentucky. The seventy or so manuscript collections cited cover a dozen libraries and archives; perhaps that many more provided background information and are not specifically mentioned, but their staff aided as well. Within Kentucky, William J. Marshall, Terry L. Birdwhistell, William Cooper, Claire McCann, and others at Special Collections of the University of Kentucky provided materials, encouragement, and good cheer. The same could be said of virtually all who call research libraries home and who help those who visit: Riley Handy, Nancy Baird, Penny Harrison, and Pat Hodges at the Kentucky Library, Western Kentucky University; Charles C. Hay III at Eastern Kentucky University; Keith M. Heim at Murray State University; Thomas L. Owen and William J. Morison of the University of Louisville; Nelson L. Dawson and James J. Holmberg of The Filson Club; Gerald F. Roberts of the Berea College Library; and numerous people at the Kentucky Department for Libraries and Archives, headed by James A. Nelson. Staff at the Library of Congress, the National Archives, the University of Virginia, and West Virginia University all helped, as did archivists at numerous other out-of-state places. Financial support from an American Association for State and Local History grant and from the Kentucky Historical Society made much of that research possible.

For those of us toiling in what is sometimes termed the public history field, institutional support for research is not always a given. It has been at the Kentucky Historical Society. Working there has brought me in contact with so many people who have been, and are, both knowledgeable and helpful, no mean combination. The late William R. Buster, Robert B. Kinnaird, the late Hambleton Tapp, William Chescheir, James E. Wallace, and Helen Prewitt all assisted. In the library, Anne J. McDonnell, Mary E. Winter, Nathan Prichard, Mary Margaret Bell (now at the University of Louisville), and others provided support, while in the area of publications, Melba Porter Hay, James Russell Harris, and Mary Lou Madigan contributed more than they know. Kim Lady Smith and Enoch Harned aided in the oral history field. A special thanks goes to Thomas H. Appleton Jr. for excellent editing, and to Glenda Harned, who put my prose into readable form. Some of the material used within appeared previously in my articles in the *Journal of American History*, the *Register of the Kentucky Historical Society*, the *Filson Club History Quarterly*, and the *Journal of Kentucky Studies*.

So many other people, some of them now deceased, also assisted by giving bibliographic references, or by providing source materials, or by sharing their work and ideas. They include Walter Baker, Helen Congleton Breckinridge, Scott D. Breckinridge, Louise Combs, Kyle Ellison, James Fallin, Jack Foster, Arthur Kelly, Judy Lyons, Henry C. Mayer, Sally Meigs, John W. Muir, Edward F. Prichard Jr., Sheryl G. Snider, E. I. "Buddy" Thompson, Gregory A. Waller, John Fred Williams, Ruby Yancy, and Frances Zane. Cheryl Conover, David Dalton, Paul Newman, and Dave Withers gave needed research support to the project.

Among other historians, the grand man of Kentucky history, Thomas D. Clark, as well as Forrest C. Pogue Jr., James Larry Hood, and George C. Wright all aided the cause, as did so many others across the state. Anyone who has published knows the gratitude an author owes to those who read his or her manuscript and offer supportive criticism, ideas, and advice. My already long-standing debt on that score is deepened to Tom Appleton, Terry Birdwhistell, Donald Carmony, William E. Ellis, Melba Porter Hay, and John David Smith. They always do better than I deserve.

But my greatest debt is owed to family. Freda and I have three children, now all young adults. Focusing on them and what their future will be in the twenty-first century helped me to think about what the Kentucky they grew up in could have been, had the first half of the twentieth century unfolded differently. That in turn emphasized again to me the importance in my own life of two people born in the first quarter of this century — my parents. To them this work is dedicated, with love and many thanks.

Signs of prosperity and poverty stand side-by-side at Altro, Ky., on the North Fork of the Kentucky River in Breathitt County, ca. 1920.

1

"The Sun Shines Bright in The Old Kentucky Home"

The City

She was a poor widow with five children, living in the slums of turn-of-the-century Louisville. Her alcoholic husband had died; their rural home had burned, driving her to the city on a cold January night. She found her rent past due, her coal supplies gone, her food stores reduced to beans and potatoes. Then her eldest child, a fifteen-year-old boy, died, literally working himself to death trying to meet family needs. In those dark, difficult days, a young society girl, Lucy Olcott of Terrace Park, entered her life, first bringing a basket of food. A friend of Miss Lucy's found jobs for two of the children — one as an office boy and the other a tile worker. Even though the family remained poor and still resided in the slums, they were ever-optimistic amid their poverty. The mother summed up their philosophy, saying, "Looks like ever'thing in the world comes right, if we jes' wait long enough!"[1]

At nearly the same time, another family faced a different problem in a nearby Kentucky county. On the porch of a mansion Colonel Lloyd would sit — alone except for his servants. Dressed in a white suit, with a white goatee, he had never forgotten the Civil War that had cost him an arm and his only son. Then, against his wishes, his daughter Elizabeth had married a northerner, Jack Sherman, and the Colonel had vowed never to speak to her again. He was a lonely man.

His daughter's husband had lost his wealth and had gone west to regain his fortune. As a result, Elizabeth had sold their elegant New York home and moved with their daughter back to a small family cottage in Kentucky, physically near her father, but far from him emotionally. But the grandchild, in a chance encounter, had met Colonel Lloyd, and the bright, innocent girl captivated him. He eagerly awaited her visits and the freshness she brought into his life. But when his son-in-law returned, ill, and the Colonel refused to help, even the newly beloved granddaughter turned on him. Shamed by her, his conscience challenged, the Colonel finally went to his daughter, found that his son-in-law's investments had prospered, and they all reconciled. The reunited family could say, as did the young granddaughter, "Isn't this a happy mawnin'?"[2]

Such happy endings often exist only in novels. In this instance, that was the case as well, for the woman in the Louisville slum was the fictional *Mrs. Wiggs of the Cabbage Patch*, while the granddaughter bringing her family together was *The Little Colonel*. Both novels became tremendous best sellers – *Mrs. Wiggs* having sales of over 650,000 in a hundred printings, while *The Little Colonel* series reached the two million mark by mid-century.[3] Both books voiced the same philosophy — that individuals could solve any problem. Both works offered positive solutions to the real-world issues of poverty and family division — the one suggesting patience and optimism for the poor, the other offering upper-class love and tolerance as the answer. And both reflected perfectly the viewpoints of the class that produced them and the society that read them, both in Kentucky and in America.

The authors of the two books comprised part of an exceptionally talented literary and cultural elite that called Louisville home in the first decades of the twentieth century. That group knew each other intimately; they socialized frequently; they shared views constantly. At that moment in time, in that one city, conditions produced a kind of regional writer's colony. It did not represent the naturalism of a Theodore Dreiser, whose novel *Sister Carrie* was suppressed in 1900, nor the powerful muckraking views of Upton Sinclair and his *The Jungle* of 1906. The poets and novelists of Louisville instead reflected a happier mood where the problems of modern America could be solved. They focused on a kinder, more humane life and world, one where racism and poverty were conquered. Not for another two decades would Kentucky writers begin to deal realistically with the darker side of the commonwealth. Like Kentucky, they did not face the state's real self, nor the new century. Their stories had happy endings. That was the way they wanted life to be.

With that outlook, this group of people enjoyed their Louisville. A small Authors Club, for instance, featured Alice Hegan Rice, the author of *Mrs. Wiggs*; Annie Fellows Johnston, producer of *The Little Colonel* series; George (Georgia) Madden Martin, writer of another best-seller, *Emmy Lou*; plus the book review editor of the respected Louisville *Courier-Journal*; the internationally known geographer Ellen Churchill Semple; and numerous others. All together, club members published over seventy books. Composed only of women, meeting in residences, the group read each other's works, commented on them — by rule only constructively — and seemingly just delighted in being together.[4]

It was Martin, for instance, who penned, in the time of Einstein, the limerick which went:

> There once was a lady named White
> At figures exceedingly bright
> She went out one day
> In a relative way
> And came back on the previous night.

To which Rice responded, quoting another limerick:

> I wish I was a moron,
> He doesn't give a damn.
> I wish I was a moron . . .
> My God! perhaps I am.

But these women *did* care about the world around. Martin, for example, became very active in the fight for black rights and chaired the Association of
Southern Women for the Prevention of Lynching, while Rice's *Calvary Alley*
pictured southern housing conditions in such a way as to influence reform
legislation in that area.[5]

Yet, in the end, they could never really break free from their past. Rice, a
compassionate, caring woman who did philanthropic work and invited young
neighbor girls into her childless home and read with them, chiefly presented a
world of warm hues. Martin, described as an "intensely feminine woman"
who always chose masculine roles in Authors Club plays, would criticize society regarding education or blacks, yet was reluctant to embrace woman suffrage or equal rights. Even Annie Fellows Johnston — who had been widowed
after only four years of marriage and had struggled to raise three stepchildren
— never focused on the problems women of her era encountered. Witty, deli-
cate, attractive, with "a kind of spiritual aristocracy," she instead wrote senti-
mentally about sheltered lives. Her readers learned nineteenth-century values, while they faced a twentieth-century world.[6]

The talent in Louisville extended to the male side as well, for the city became home for extremely important leaders and produced others who made
their fame elsewhere. Abraham Flexner, born in Louisville one year after the
Civil War's close, helped reform America's educational thinking, particularly
in regard to medical training. Louis Brandeis, another native of the city, at
nearly the same time would receive his acclaim as the "people's attorney,"
eventually becoming an associate justice of the U.S. Supreme Court.[7]

But while they both eventually left the Falls City, many of the talented remained. Foremost among those was journalist Henry Watterson, who had
become the spokesman for the New South and had a national following in the
Courier-Journal. Among the other talented newsmen was Arthur Krock, who
eclipsed Watterson and won four Pulitzer Prizes. Such men found very satis-
factory literary company in Louisville, for the best-selling novelist, Charles
Neville Buck, also lived there, as did Alice Hegan's poet-husband, Cale Young
Rice. Even the city's business elite was generally well educated and progressive, while numerous attorneys displayed their considerable skills in the courtroom and on the political hustings.

While on the surface cosmopolitan in travel and tastes, the leadership class
of the city usually returned to Louisville in the end, and to the comfortable,
safe, and satisfying existence of their cloistered world. There they produced
an intimate relationship between the political leadership and the arts, one
symbolized by St. James Court.

Once a marshy area owned by the Louisville branch of the duPonts, the few
blocks of land between Fourth and Fifth Streets had been the site of the 1883

Kentucky Historical Society

View down St. James Court, Louisville, ca. 1903.

Southern Exposition, then had been developed into the exclusive St. James Court after the exposition's close. Statues of lions guarded an entrance to this tight little residential island, one shaded by linden and chestnut trees. An atmosphere of elegance was everywhere, from the large stone and brick homes with their heavy hand-carved doors, lace curtains, and wine cellars, to the carriages with uniformed coachmen waiting on call. (The court would be long undisturbed by noise from gasoline engines, for only electric automobiles or horses were, for a time, allowed within the confines of this protected world.) After 1904, nearby Central Park provided a play area for children, or a place simply to stroll and enjoy the varieties of plants or the sounds of swallows circling at twilight.[8]

In this small area at St. James Court in 1902, lived a former congressman, a former mayor, novelist Buck, and many other prominent figures. On adjacent Fourth Street stood the homes of a former Kentucky governor and a future one as well as residences of wealthy patrons of the arts, such as the Belknaps; Robert Worth Bingham, later ambassador to Great Britain; Milton Smith, the powerful railroad president; the Bullitts, Castlemans, Haldemans, Helms, and other prominent families; several judges and city officials. *Mrs. Wiggs'* Alice Hegan, who would marry poet Cale Young Rice that year of 1902, also lived on Fourth Street. She and her husband moved to St. James Court three years later. In short, when "receiving day" came and the upper class visited each other (usually on Tuesday), they almost all lived within walking distance. It was a very close, tight-knit group in this city of nearly a quarter-million people.[9]

In summer the situation changed somewhat and newspapers would run stories telling when prominent families were leaving their homes to retire to cooler summer residences in the nearby countryside. Yet even there similar gatherings took place. Annie Fellows Johnston purchased "The Beeches" in 1911 and lived in Pewee Valley where, she wrote, "I felt as if I had stepped back into a beautiful story of antebellum days. Back into the time when people had leisure to make hospitality their chief business in life, and could afford for every day to be a holiday." Bingham and others had summer residences there for a time as well. Between 1900 and 1920, suburbs like Glenview, Harrod's Creek, Prospect, Nitta Yuma, and the tree-lined Anchorage where Martin lived were connected conveniently to the city by the interurbans which provided an umbilical cord between city and country elite. Despite its size and the dual homes, Louisville was, as Alice Hegan Rice wrote, "'an intimate city.' The majority of men and women in social life have known each other from childhood and an easy camaraderie exists between them."[10]

These people of St. James Court and Fourth Street did not live in a perfect world, but, for them, it may have seemed nearly so. Their class did not rule Kentucky government, but did not need to. On matters of importance their voice would be heard, and often heeded. They preferred, in large part, to let others dirty themselves in the soiled rags of politics. Instead, the Louisville elite focused on social and cultural matters, and on everyday life and conventions. In conversation they spoke of new books, the problems with servants, trips to spas, springs, or seashores, or the latest petty scandal among them. Concerned with dress and etiquette, they moved quietly yet extravagantly through their world, knowing their place, confident about it, and only occasionally noting uncertainties around them.

They were not unaware of poverty or new reform movements, such as women's rights. But their response seldom varied from that expected of those of their station. That meant supporting charitable efforts for the poor, perhaps helping settlement houses; it could even mean taking a liberal stand on suffrage for "the ladies." But they almost never stepped over the reform line to radicalism.

In social clubs and literary gatherings, they might discuss new movements and old problems, but their world was carefully shielded from life's harsher aspects by mists of nostalgia. Reality became a blurry image observed from afar. Their self-created world, safe in clouds of perceptions, seldom required them to confront the world beyond. Only later would their generation face — or have to face — the revealing breezes the modern world brought.[11]

In their turn-of-the-century city another world instead prevailed, one built on an attitude and atmosphere of southernness. Even though Louisville had been as much, if not more, Union in sympathy than Confederate during the Civil War, even though its wealth came in large part from its use as a Federal supply depot in that conflict, the city had looked to Dixie after the war and had become a supplier for the devastated South. As Kentucky turned more and more sympathetic to the Lost Cause in the last decades of the nineteenth century, so had Louisville. Ex-Confederates became the predominant postwar leaders, even though Kentucky had furnished more soldiers who wore Union blue than Rebel gray.[12]

The state's increasing love affair with the Lost Cause mythology continued into the twentieth century. In 1902, a Confederate Home was established for Southern veterans and was located, appropriately, in *The Little Colonel*'s home of Pewee Valley. That same year the legislature appropriated funds to mark Confederate graves at the Perryville battlefield. Eight years later, the general assembly presented the United Daughters of the Confederacy with enough money to finish a statue of General John Hunt Morgan. At this statue's unveiling in Lexington in 1911, some ten thousand cheered the memory of "The Thunderbolt of the Confederacy." A year later, the legislature set up pensions for indigent and disabled Confederate veterans and their widows, then appropriated money to secure the Kentucky birthplace of Jefferson Davis. Similarly, in 1926, Robert E. Lee's birthday would be made a legal holiday; the same year, as Confederate veterans gathered in Lexington, that city inaugurated its first automatic traffic signals. For Kentucky, the symbolism of Confederates riding in horseless carriages seemed altogether fitting. They wanted to carry Old South traditions into the new century.[13]

Louisvillians did not seem to differ from their fellow Kentuckians regarding devotion to the Lost Cause. From the national gathering of Confederate veterans which met in Louisville in 1900 throughout the next several decades, the prosouthern view dominated. General Morgan's principal lieutenant, Basil Duke of Louisville, served the Louisville and Nashville Railroad as its chief lobbyist for years until his death in 1916, while other ex-Confederates held numerous positions of power. When a young girl refused to sing "Marching Through Georgia" in the city's school system, she was cheered and eventually honored at the 1902 state convention of Confederate veterans. All ages seemed imbued with the spirit.[14]

The Union men did not capitulate completely. Historian Hambleton Tapp recalled that the Filson Club in Louisville long avoided Civil War topics for their historical meetings because of the hard feelings still prevalent. Not until the 1930s would that situation change. Yet, philosophically, the Union admitted defeat, for the heroic southern cavalier image had won out. No Civil War monument was erected in Louisville for the Union cause, but on Third Street an imposing monument honored the Confederate soldier. Ironically, Kentucky had no need for a religion based on the Lost Cause, nor for a way to overcome the psychology of a tragic defeat — as did southerners generally — because most Kentuckians, and the state itself, had been on the winning side. Yet, they still wholeheartedly embraced the mythology and the moonlight and magnolia image. The South *had* won.[15]

Yet, while looking nostalgically backward to an agrarian southern ethos, the Louisville elite remained part of an urban, modern, almost northern, environment. While less than 20 percent of Kentuckians resided in cities, 55 percent of those who did lived in the Louisville environs. Almost literally, Louisville was urban Kentucky.[16]

In cities across America in 1900, social lines solidified, and the resulting elite often sought a stable society. The Falls City was no different. A decade earlier a traveler had praised the area's growth, prosperity, and "cheerful appearance," while noting that "family and pedigree have always been held in . . . high esteem." Abraham Flexner, part of a small but dynamic Jewish community in the city, stressed in his memoirs how the hometown of his youth was cosmopolitan in many ways, yet was "distinctly stratified" in its society. The

Kentucky Historical Society

Col. "Dick" Redd on his horse "Major," in front of the John Hunt Morgan home in Lexington, ca. 1931. Colonel Redd and "Major" regularly attended Confederate reunions.

elite, he recalled, "lived beyond their means, smoked, drank, [and] gambled." For those of that class, Flexner concluded, "Louisville was a delightful place in which to live in comfort and abundance." But perhaps the best analysis of Louisville came in the 1918 book, *The Sunny South and Its People*, which said that people of the city were "happy, comfortable, and in a measure contented, hence conservative."[17]

The upper class did, indeed, seem content with their city and their way of life. In fact, they lived a fairly consistent and patterned existence as a result of that satisfaction. A comment made about a slightly later time in Louisville reflected that sameness: "To be someone in the city you had to be born in Jewish Hospital, be a member of the Louisville Country Club and the Pendennis Club, die at Norton's Hospital, and be buried in Cave Hill Cemetery." Such a definition would limit membership in the elite, for the country club in 1902 had only 130 families as members. But their names told of the prominence achieved – Atherton, Belknap, Bingham, Bullitt, Bruce, Churchill, Helm, Heyburn, Norton, Speed, and numerous other important families.[18]

For children of the elite, education might begin in one of the city's nationally known kindergartens directed by Patty Smith Hill, then continue in the fine private schools, generally limited to one sex (such as Miss Semple's School for Girls). High school – again divided by sex – would be at Male High or Female High, with their excellent curriculum and faculty, followed by college – chiefly for the young men – at such places as Washington and Lee or the University of Virginia, or more northern ones such as Princeton or Yale.[19]

After schooling came marriage announcements (delivered by carriage), weddings, then careers. For the women that still meant work as wife and mother, though philanthropy and various reform causes often took them from the home. Men would generally go into business or law, often in family-connected firms. It was a time when attorneys proudly listed the corporations they represented and little stigma was attached to such associations with "big business."[20]

Married, respected, honored in their community, the elite moved in similar social circles, sharing entertainment with others of their class. If the Country Club was restricted, the prestigious Pendennis Club, founded in 1881, had a somewhat larger membership, including a Flexner. Many other specialized clubs provided attractive meeting places as well, ranging from the Authors Club to the Conversation Club to the Dramatic Club, to heritage-oriented groups such as the Colonial Dames to the all-male and exclusive Salmagundi Club, to the all-female Whist Club. But club life was only one facet of their social setting. Carriages might take people to picnics in a fine system of parks, designed in part by Frederick Law Olmsted, or, after 1909, to the new Seelbach Hotel with the city's first roof garden. Other diversions might be a moonlight trip on the river, a visit to Macauley's Theater, where national companies stopped, or a winter sleigh ride in the snow with a party and hot chocolate afterward.[21]

If carriages did not provide transportation to such entertainment, electric street railroads and interurban railways did. Their hundreds of miles of track brought rich and poor alike to the central core of the city. As the years progressed, automobiles, with more mobility and no fixed track to follow, would alter traffic patterns away from downtown. But by 1909, only some 656 automobiles and motorcycles contested in Louisville with the horse and electric trolleys for supremacy.[22]

Still, despite the club life, and downtown society, men's and women's lives centered on their homes. Outside, in the street, peddlers would cry out "umbrellas to mend," or call for knives to be sharpened, while others sang songs offering their pots and pans for sale. Herds of cattle and sheep might fill Broadway with their cries as they were driven to market. But in the Victorian-Era home, insulated from this, upper-class families depended on servants — and Louisvillians ranked high in the number of servants — to do daily chores. Workers, usually Irish or African Americans, would start fires, cook, clean, wash, iron, run errands, and care for the children. That allowed the upper class enough leisure time to play golf or tennis, or to do charity work, or to engage in a myriad of other activities. Their lives appeared comfortable and placid.[23]

Yet, there was another side of Louisville life, one far removed from the sitting rooms of St. James Court. Did the elite know of that world and ignore it, or were they simply ignorant of it? Or did they feel guilt about what they knew and their reaction to that knowledge? Various sides of Louisville life simply did not match the image many had of their progressive, modern city. By 1900, for example, one of every five Louisvillians was black, but the main contact the leadership had with those 39,000 citizens was in a master-servant relationship. Segregation prevailed with few exceptions, and practically no one in the white community sought to change that condition. As a result, the talented black poet Joseph S. Cotter, who made his living as a principal of a "colored" school in Louisville, would not be welcome in the numerous gatherings of the galaxy of literary talent in the city. Even though he would be listed in *Who's Who* in 1919, the only black Kentuckian so acknowledged, he remained isolated from other writers and poets. Both races — and literature — likely lost as a result.[24]

A shadow world of saloons, prostitutes, and tenement houses likewise existed outside the realm of polite society's conversation. Some seven hundred saloons, open all days of the week, dotted the urban landscape, and competed for male attention with over a hundred houses of prostitution, including those of Madame LaRoy, Lizzie Long, and Mother Mack. Violence flourished in both saloon and brothel, as evidenced in 1893 when Alfred Victor duPont was shot and killed in a Green Street bordello. But the elite were protected: Louisville newspapers simply said he had died from a heart attack and printed nothing about a shooting or a house of prostitution.[25]

But even more widespread problems, in a sense, existed in slum housing. By 1900, one-fifth of the city's population lived in dwellings of more than eleven people; one-third of all families lived in dilapidated tenements. The situation was so bad that a commission was finally formed in 1909. Its report pointed to places where, in pre-Civil War Louisville, one family had lived but now up to eight families occupied. Another district's name, Bug Alley, "graphically suggests the local conditions and standards." Even drinking water presented problems, for until a filtration plant was built in 1909, water from the Ohio River was dark-colored, muddy, and unfiltered. Pumps on street corners, where many slum families got their water, were often further polluted by open sewage. Typhoid epidemics broke out periodically. Smoke pollution

Kentucky Historical Society

Regulars at the Quinn Saloon in the Portland area (Louisville), 1910.

and filthy streets — a thousand horses in eight hours deposited some "five hundred gallons of urine and ten tons of dung" — added to the blight, and throughout the city, open privies, plentiful germs, ill-ventilated rooms, crowded quarters, and abundant drugs all combined to make life miserable and dangerous for a large part of the forgotten people of Louisville.[26]

For much of her life, Alice Hegan Rice helped those ignored Louisvillians by telling their story and revealing their conditions in her widely read novels. But she did more, for there was a real Cabbage Patch only seven blocks from her St. James Court home. The slum had no paved streets, no lights, no sewers, but did have abundant saloons. It was a place, Rice remembered, where "boys and girls ran wild through the muddy streets and dark alleys." There she and other concerned citizens started and supported a settlement house, which later had a second-hand clothing store, a wholesale grocery, a cooking and sewing school, and an employment agency, all operated by a paid staff and a hundred volunteers. But there was even more reality to the *Mrs. Wiggs* story than that. One day Rice spoke to a "dirty and improvident" woman who had stopped by her back door asking for food. From the stories told by this Mrs. Mary Bass of the Cabbage Patch, the fictional Mrs. Wiggs emerged in Rice's mind.[27]

Ironically, while matters end on a positive note in the novel, the non-fictional outcome was very different. Bass, alias Mrs. Wiggs, later brought suit against Alice Hegan Rice, claiming injury to her good name as a result of the "scandalous, malicious, and defamatory libel" set forth in *Mrs. Wiggs of the Cabbage Patch*. The defendant later wrote in her autobiography that the suit was "thrown out of court, and the lawyer disbarred." But apparently Rice actually settled out of court and paid Bass one thousand dollars plus additional fees. No kind-hearted, pleasing Mrs. Wiggs, satisfied with her fate, was her real-life counterpart.[28]

In fact, that represented the contradiction for those of Rice's generation and class. They were exceptionally talented people who individually helped the less fortunate. They sought to do what was right, and, in part, did. They deservedly won praise. Yet the writers' tame, sentimental prose almost operated to counter their individual, progressive actions. A critic wrote of another Rice book in 1903, "Here we have a picture of the poor as we would like them to be." The reviewer pointed out that the popularity of the book came because "it is comforting to think of the poor as such happy people." Rice, Johnston, Martin, all of them, knew better. But their prose seldom indicated that very strongly. As a result, the attitudes fostered by the books did little to help those in Louisville's slums. Reform remained limited to traditional change. The upper class found it very difficult indeed to break the hidden cultural ropes binding them so firmly to a dying ethos.[29]

Nowhere was that more evident than in the person of another Louisville literary figure, Madison Julius Cawein. Born in the city near the end of the Civil War, he spent much of his youth with his German-speaking father hunting herbs in rural areas. Cawein soon developed a love of nature, which, when combined with his mother's spiritualism, resulted in a strain of imaginative poetry.[30]

Cawein's world was a divided one. Poor in his youth, he graduated from Male High School, then worked for years in a pool room and betting establishment, often not returning home until nine or ten at night. But in the early mornings, before his workday began, Cawein put aside the mundane life of struggle and wrote fine poetry. During his lifetime, some 1,500 original poems in thirty-six volumes were presented in places far removed from his gambling establishment job. His verses instead told of a world of elves, gnomes, and fairies: of mythological creatures; of a nature of fantasy and beauty. "I am a pagan, always and always," he wrote an acquaintance in 1908, and other friends recalled a Cawein who loved to play a flute, to visit graveyards, to search for quiet woods and fresh streams.[31]

Early on, Cawein's *Blooms of the Berry* attracted the favorable attention of William Dean Howells of *Harper's* and the "Kentucky Keats" soon gained international acclaim. English critics named him one of America's best poets, while others called him the Southland's greatest writer of verse. The resulting modest financial success allowed Cawein to abandon the pool room for the muse; "the Kentucky Woodland Thrush" moved to St. James Court in 1907, joined the exclusive clubs, and received widespread praise. But his modest investments failed and the family faced a return to near-poverty. Amid great

Kentucky Historical Society

Looking north from the Seelbach on Fourth Street, Louisville, ca. 1916.

personal depression, Cawein died of apoplexy in 1914 at the age of only forty-nine. The Boston *Transcript* noted, on his dying, that he had "a kind of spiritual nostalgia which made him feel that he was born out of his age in a materialistic environment," while a Louisville paper concluded that "the old legends came to him trailing clouds of glory and lived again." And so this man who had known the hardships of life, who had known firsthand the struggles of the lower class, even he died without writing about the realities of the world. Like the novelists, Cawein chose another path and wrote of a Kentucky free of the ills of the world, a Kentucky which chiefly existed in the imagination. As Cawein affirmed:

> The path that winds by wood and stream
> Is not the path for me to-day
> The path I take is one of dream
> That leads me down a twilight way.[32]

Louisville itself existed in a twilight world, one of paradox. To Kentucky it represented progress and the promise of the new century; it had a cultured, educated, even progressive elite; it symbolized modernization and change. Yet, beneath all that was a city limited by its past. Its satisfied society worshipped at the shrine of the Lost Cause, even as they proclaimed a New South; they read books, written by their own, that presented a gentle picture of the world around them; they memorized a nature poetry of Cawein's which further removed them from reality. Perhaps the leadership class had to deal with life that way in order to preserve what they held dear in such a rapidly changing era. Perhaps they consciously chose an optimistic positivism. For whatever reason, they sat back, basking in their sunshine of satisfaction, and calmly waited for the twentieth century to affect them. As a result, the commonwealth's major urban center would not be a real modernizing force until after World War II.

Very different in many ways from the rest of the state, Louisville was Kentucky, but it also was not Kentucky.

The Mountains

Some one hundred miles to the southeast, another world existed, one far removed in more than distance from the upper-class society of Louisville. The eastern Kentucky mountains — Appalachia — were to many Kentuckians like Louisville in only one sense: they too were often viewed as "different" from the rest of the state. "Discovered" by outside observers in the last decades of the nineteenth century, the region had quickly been stereotyped, and its resultant image varied as day and night from Louisville's.

The city on the Ohio was urban; the mountains of Kentucky were rural, with no interior incorporated town exceeding 6,000 people in 1910. Louisville had a large immigrant and black population; Appalachia in 1910 had few members of either group — blacks made up 5 percent of the population of eastern Kentucky and the foreign-born under 1 percent. The Falls City was perceived nationally as a cultured, learned, literary place, at the forefront of modern America; the Highlands to the east were seen as an ignorant, uneducated, unlettered area where people lived as rough frontiersmen had centuries earlier. Louisville had a southern ethos; Appalachian Kentucky still honored

"Main Street, Hyden, Leslie Co., Kentucky," ca. 1928.

its Union ties. The city projected an image of superb mansions, excellent transportation systems, and fine culinary delights; the mountains received a stereotyped view featuring dirty log cabins, impassable roads, and inedible food. It seemed the only other feature common to both places was the fact that they belonged to the same political entity, Kentucky.[33]

Those people of the eastern part of the state, if asked, probably would have had a difficult time articulating exactly what they were, other than Kentuckians. Most who left records certainly did not speak of themselves as southern, nor, for that matter, northern. While they might say "I'm from the mountains," at the same time they did not generally consider themselves part of a larger, interstate region called Appalachia — although many others might. They were Kentuckians, but they were separate. Isolated and ignored for a long period of the state's history, they had only recently begun to receive attention, much of it unwanted. With that attention came great change, as well as confusion and uncertainty. Louisville had transformed slowly and could embrace change without such trauma, still keeping its traditions and outlooks. But in the mountains, when modernization arrived it usually came rapidly, in some cases literally overnight, and people had to adjust immediately, if at all. The Highlanders wanted to retain old values but also to adopt new ways. Yet they had little time to balance the two. Trauma would be the result.

Few adequately voiced those problems of the mountains, but novelist John

Fox, Jr., tried to do so in his enormously popular *Trail of the Lonesome Pine*. His first major success, *The Little Shepherd of Kingdom Come*, had joined Rice's *Mrs. Wiggs* and her *Lovely Mary* as one of the ten best-selling books of 1903. Now, five years later, he had literary good fortune once more, as he described Appalachia and made the annual best-seller list again. Like so many who wrote about the region, Fox was not native to the mountains. He had been raised in the central Bluegrass, had graduated with honors from Harvard, and had written for the New York press. But his home state drew him back. As he looked at Kentucky, Appalachia intrigued him, and, unlike many authors writing about the mountains, Fox spent much time in the larger region. He observed it well. He portrayed it honestly.[34]

The result was a readable book which Cratis Williams called "the best fictional interpretation of mountain life ever achieved." Despite some stereotypes and improbable plot turns, Fox presented a rarity — a reasonably realistic story about the Highlands. The tale of John "Jack" Hale, an outsider, and young June Tolliver, daughter of feudist "Devil Judd," symbolized the struggle taking place between the forces of industrialization and tradition in the mountains. In the end, June and Jack Hale, like the region itself, try to retain a part of the old and adopt some of the new. Unlike the region, however, they live happily ever after.[35]

By the time he was writing his book in 1908, Fox — like all writers concerned with the mountains — had to deal with stereotypes. In fact, images already prevalent in the American popular mind would haunt Appalachia throughout the rest of the century. Its demon was itself.

While an Appalachian image, a stereotype, had developed in American writing in the half-century after 1880, it was a decidedly divided picture in many ways. Various accounts pointed to the prevalence of feuds or gun-toting moonshiners, yet others uniformly described the friendly, hospitable people of the mountains. Some authors told of a land that the present had by-passed, only recently awakened from its "Rip Van Winkle sleep" so it could now leave behind its frontier, eighteenth-century lifestyle. Yet, others revealed a land rooted not in early America but in Elizabethan England, a place where people sang the ballads and spoke the Queen's English of an earlier era. Certain writers looked at the virgin forests and the unspoiled beauty of the hills and praised the natural majesty, while others appraised the same vistas and depicted a land rich in hidden mineral wealth just waiting to be tapped. Were Appalachian Kentuckians, then, violent hillbillies or hospitable homeowners? Were they living like Americans of the eighteenth century or the English of the sixteenth? Were they in a place to be preserved for its beauty or to be mined for its minerals? Were they the opposite of America or the essence of America? Or were they really something different from any of that? America had a hard time explaining Appalachia.[36]

If confusion existed about parts of the stereotype, on certain other things most writers agreed. And that conformity shaped an image that had become amazingly widespread as early as 1910. Americans in the several decades before then had seen great shifts take place: urban areas mushroomed; "un-Americanized foreigners" poured into the nation, bringing different ideas, religions, and lifestyles; life changed. To those who felt threatened by all that, to those who wanted to preserve the old America, the "discovery" of Appalachia seemed a godsend. Here lived a rural people of the "purest Anglo-Saxon stock," untouched by the "evils" of recent immigration. Here lived original Americans, held in reserve by their isolation, now ready to fight "in defense of Protestantism." Here lived America's hope.[37]

And, to some observers, the Appalachian people represented even more. For northerners, these mountain people had appeal, because they had supported the Union and had been "uncontaminated with slavery." They could become, as the president of Berea College suggested, "the New England of the South," bringing a civilizing influence to what some saw as an unrepentant, race-baiting region. So Appalachians, including those in Kentucky, furnished the stuff of future dreams for various parts of America.[38]

Yet there remained the troubling reality of the present. The multitude of writers agreed that the land had a long way to go to achieve the Utopian promise portrayed by its new-found advocates. In the stereotypical view that prevailed, Appalachia was a place where scraggly, unkempt, bearded mountain men armed with moonshine jug and squirrel gun would leave the house to fish and hunt — sometimes for human prey. Behind in a dark log cabin or run-down shack in a "holler," the hard-working wife, once attractive but now mother to too many children, would start the chores that would prematurely age her. If strangers arrived at the home, they would be welcomed and invited to eat. Food would be scanty, fried, and seldom tasty. The guests would hear a strange form of English spoken by the family, if, indeed, much was said at all. Overall the people, according to the stereotype, lived in a world of fatalistic religion, primitive superstitions, and sweeping illiteracy.[39]

A few positive characteristics surfaced in such accounts. These were "Shakespeare's people," natives who preserved the pure English of the Bard's time. While isolation had stopped their development, it had also protected rich traditions. In another similar version, the mountain people, cut off from the outside world, had stagnated in a kind of retarded frontier, but, as a result, had retained characteristics of that earlier time — honesty, individuality, courage, and loyalty. And, in a third view, the beauty of the area was emphasized. Even in such melodramatic, feud-oriented films as Kentuckian D. W. Griffith's *The Mountaineer's Honor* (1909) and *A Feud in the Kentucky Hills* (1912), the region was presented idyllically; as one historian noted, Griffith's Dixie was "homey in the highlands."[40]

But was the stereotypical view accurate? A few writers questioned the emerging image, but with little success. Kentuckian Henderson Daingerfield, speaking to the American Social Science Association in 1901, noted that "it is easier to assume that all Appalachian America is inhabited by feudists and moonshiners than to inform one's self of the true character of the people." A letter-writer from the mountains told the president of Berea College that, based

Louisville Courier-Journal & Times

John C. C. Mayo's mansion in Paintsville stands in contrast to the image of poverty in Kentucky's mountains.

on accounts he had read, reporters must have been ordered to present "lurid" and "sensational" copy in order to please the editorial staffs. Two decades later, similar criticisms continued to appear. A Kentucky congressman from the hills angrily attacked fiction writers who constantly made a universality out of an isolated Appalachian incident. The same year a Louisville *Herald* reporter admitted, "most of the stuff written about Kentucky mountaineers is mythical, makes good reading, but is what is commonly known as 'bunk.'" John C. Campbell, after his long study of the area, summarized the situation best. This was a land, he wrote, "about which perhaps more things are known that are not true than any part of the country."[41]

One of the most common errors concerned class differences, according to some critics. All too often the mountaineers were pictured as belonging to a single social and economic class, one not far advanced on the scale. Not so, said a 1901 *New England Magazine* article: "very great differences exist among the people." A decade and a half later still another writer reminded his readers that all grades of society comprised the mountain population. Certainly there were the poor, sometimes living in squalid conditions. But a middle class and even an upper one, wealthy by mountain standards, also resided there. Few, if any, wrote their stories. In fact, when well-bred out-of-state women went into the region as workers for the Frontier Nursing Service in the

1920s and 1930s, they discovered something surprising. Mary Breckinridge wrote a friend that "mountain people, like lowlanders, are just people, men, women and children — not so different in essentials the world over." A New Hampshire woman recalled that she made a similar find: "mountain people don't differ particularly from one area to another." In fact, her new Kentucky people seemed more aware of the outside world than the mountain people of New Hampshire.[42]

Were the stereotypes simply a result of the urban provincialism of the writers describing the land? Was there some truth to the accounts? On certain questions, the image and the reality did not far diverge. Appalachian Kentucky, for example, did not have very many blacks or immigrants; it was a native, Protestant, predominantly Anglo-Saxon population, as pictured. Nor was the region very well educated. While the state as a whole had a white illiteracy rate of 13.9 percent, eastern Kentucky's rate was 23.5 percent. Of some thirty-six Appalachian counties studied in 1908, only three had a public high school. Furthermore, the mountains were, in some places, not well-off economically. A 1903 article pointed out that, excluding buildings, mountain farms had an average value of $482; farms in the rest of Kentucky averaged $1,548, over three times as much. In 1911, of the Kentucky counties, only sixteen had land whose average value was under six dollars per acre; all sixteen were in Appalachia. The disparity between Rowan County's $3.31 average paled in comparison to Fayette County's (Lexington) $80.07 figure.[43]

Other parts of the typical accounts of eastern Kentucky also contained a large element of truth. For instance, roads were abysmal — if they existed at all. Often a creek-bed furnished the only route of travel. And that was far from an easy trek, as author Horace Kephart found out in 1913: "the only roads," he wrote, "follow the bed of tortuous and rock-strewn water course, which may be nearly dry when you start out in the morning, but within an hour may be raging torrents. There are no bridges. One may ford a dozen times a mile." What roads that did exist were dirt, and few of them well made. Rough and rocky, they filled the air with dust in the heat of summer and quickly turned into quagmires when wet. When Franklin D. Roosevelt visited family-held lands in the Kentucky mountains in 1908, he wrote back to Eleanor, contrasting the "horrible conditions of the roads" with the beautiful country he saw.[44]

Such circumstances made travel extremely difficult for all people of the region. Rivers — and railroads where they existed — allowed some mobility. But for most of the region's people their world was limited by the hills and the lack of roads. Letcher County got its first automobile only in 1911; nearby Knott County had only one registered car as late as 1924. And the lack of vehicles was not limited to motor-powered ones. A person who migrated to Leslie County in 1921 could recall no more than one wagon in that locale. As one historian noted, Appalachia in the 1930s "was the only part of the United States where the automobile was not common." An ox or a mule would be a far more likely sight than a Model T.[45]

Isolation did result from such conditions. Numerous outside observers, as well as those born in that region, pointed out whole families who had ventured only a few miles from their home in their entire lives.[46] E. L. Noble, growing up on a farm in Breathitt County, did not even see his county seat — a maximum of twenty miles away — until he was seventeen years old. Later, another person recalled that one man near him never ventured farther from his home than a nearby creek, "and only then if it didn't rain." The scattered, rural population meant that the closest home, the nearest family, might frequently be over a mile away. That isolation hindered change from the outside and developed a culture heavily tied to land, family, and friends. Self-sufficient farms on poor soil might not produce great wealth for many, but the people did own their land and had almost total independence. The strong individualism growing out of that lifestyle had another side, however, for those families placed great stress on kinship ties and, for the larger group, on supportive networks. "We seemed to have an obligation to each other," an eastern Kentuckian remembered. "We are kinfolks. If we were cousins we were all same as brothers and sisters." As a result, a curious mix of strong family ties and an equally strong individualism emerged.[47]

But the effects of isolation on the mountains should not be exaggerated. Eastern Kentucky contained 30 percent of the state's land area in 1900, and only 20.9 percent of its people, suggesting underpopulation. Yet, given the hills and the amount of uninhabitable and unfarmable land, the number of inhabitants was not that small. In fact, as early as 1921, knowledgeable observers were questioning whether the region was already overpopulated. Two decades later a journalist concluded that eastern Kentucky's chief problem could be easily summarized: "there are too many people on too few acres." And even if some exaggerated isolation did exist, that was not so different than elsewhere. All across rural America people lived what one historian has termed "a narrow, isolated, and restricted existence . . . many families never traveled out of their home county or beyond the nearby village." In that context, the "different" mountain people did not seem so unusual after all.[48]

Other parts of the stereotypes regarding Appalachian Kentucky coincided somewhat with reality, yet also varied considerably from the truth in other ways. Almost invariably, for instance, mountain homes were described as cabins with mud between the logs and a plank porch in front. Consisting of one or two rooms, the houses might have a small window and perhaps a stone fireplace and chimney. Newspapers or pages from magazines provided the wall coverings, while sparse home-crafted furniture and several beds partially masked the rough-hewn wood, or even dirt, floor.[49]

Yet, as in other areas, the picture was incomplete. Yes, the walls might be covered with magazines and catalogue pages — for which the inhabitants would be ridiculed by outside observers — but that provided insulation and color to otherwise drab wood. Moreover, many of the coverings were carefully selected and placed so that young children might read the poems or view the pictures in leisure moments. Log cabins were also often very clean, despite

Kentucky Historical Society

Interior of a mountain home on Bullskin Fork, Hell For Certain Creek, Leslie County. Most people outside Appalachia saw images of ramshackle cabins, rather than comfortable homes such as this one.

the stereotype. But even more than that, homes built of other materials and of very different size existed across the region. Ballad collector Cecil Sharp found remote Clay County in 1917 to be "quite sophisticated," with frame homes "the rule" around its creeks. A Baptist minister voiced the same thoughts: "You may picture almost any kind of home you wish and I will undertake to find a home in the mountains of Kentucky to fit it. There are well-to-do and even wealthy people all through the section . . . principally about the towns. . . ."[50]

If homes varied across the region, so did those towns and villages. No large urban area could be found in the inner reaches of the mountains. In more remote parts, county seat towns generally were not unlike Hyden in Leslie County. People who lived there and who visited that place in the 1920s particularly remembered its muddy unpaved streets, "full of enormous holes," and the pigs running freely through town. A few strategically placed stones allowed people to leave the plank sidewalks and cross the "slop hole" of a street. A silent movie made in 1927 shows the town's dirty, uneven Main Street, full of horses, all of it looking remarkably like the set for a film about the Old West.[51] The courthouse dominated the town, and the few merchants, without electricity and not on the railroad, either had to haul groceries by four-day wagon trip from Laurel County or had to have supplies brought upriver by flatboat from Beattyville. That downriver town, in fact, brought forth descriptions remarkably like Hyden's. Paul Blazer, so responsible for the growth of Ashland Oil Company, visited Beattyville on business in 1919 and recalled that it was a place without roads: "the streets were just mud wallows. Even the pigs preferred the sidewalks; there were plenty of pigs." While Pikeville, on the railroad, might be praised for its brick streets, excellent schools, and "handsome residences," it was the exception. Small, rather rough mountain towns were the rule.[52]

Most Appalachian Kentuckians lived in an agrarian setting, however. A study of three hundred households in a rural part of Pike County indicated that in 1900, some 90 percent of the people there had been born in Kentucky. All were white; three-fourths were farmers; and over one-third could not read or write. By the time they were twenty-four years of age, 76 percent of the males and 84 percent of the females were married. The mostly nuclear families (three-fourths of them were nuclear) had a median household of 6.4 persons. That statistical profile was not unusual for rural parts of the region.[53]

But numbers did not tell Appalachia's story. Memories do. Some recalled the hard life. An Owsley County teacher remembered her childhood in a log cabin, with five other children and poorly educated parents. She had one change of clothes and her mother had made that: "I have seen her shear the wool, pick out the burs, wash, card, spin, dye, weave, knit and work up the yarn into clothes." From that background the child grew to be a teacher, raised money, and built a community school. In neighboring Breathitt County, a man recounted in third person how in his youth "there were no books to read; no newspapers to engage his leisure hours; no magazines to instruct the curious mind . . . ; so all he could do was sit by the fireside and be instructed and entertained by old witches (so-called). . . ." As an adult, he wrote a four-volume study of that county. Deprivation certainly existed in this land where the average person purchased thirty-four cents of postage in a year. But many did not view their situation as so bad, and some overcame the problems and achieved. Yet, voiceless others, who left few recollections, faced a bleak, hard existence.[54]

Others remembered a more positive life. They explained that with people growing most of their food, few needed much income, except to buy coffee, salt, candy, or flour from a country store. "Back then everybody knowed each other," as one person noted, and that supportive, communal network provided physical, psychological, or financial support when needed. Whether it was killing hogs, clearing fields, or stringing beans, local cohesiveness helped achieve the task. And while memories often tend to favor the best parts of the past, these people's reminiscences ring true. The folk beauty of the hills, for them, transcended technology. A Harlan County man, one of eight children, lived in a world of feather beds and quilts, handmade furniture, and a cashless economy. But he most remembered the beauty of the land, with streams "filled with fish" and abundant game. In a neighboring county, a person's youth there included memories that "the land was a part of the man and both became partners with God. If the rains didn't come so be it, there was a bad year. . . ." That outlook reinforced "that the man was not the master." The Leslie countian concluded, "I don't remember ever seeing a Van Gogh or

Rembrandt . . . but I remember beauty. . . . There was natural beauty enough to fill the eyes and the soul." It is easy to ignore the real poverty, hunger, and unhappiness and paint an idyllic picture of a self-sufficient, agrarian way. Yet, at the same time it is equally easy to look at the surface, simple life and its hardships and draft too harsh a pen-sketch of that world. Like Louisville, like Kentucky, like America, Appalachia had its problems — and its strong points.[55]

In this preindustrial, rural society, people had few ways to earn money to buy necessities, or even pay their meager taxes. Their chief opportunity to do so depended on the forest around them. As one recalled, "If we needed a little money for something, we would just cut enough for a small raft [of timber] and then float it to Frankfort. . . ." A great timber boom began in the mountains in the last decades of the nineteenth century, one helped in part by expanding railroads and by large firms buying sizeable tracts of land to clear. In 1910, the Mowbray-Robinson Timber and Land Company, for instance, purchased 15,000 acres on the North Fork of the Kentucky River at Quicksand in Breathitt County. Employing some five hundred men, building a narrow-gauge railroad, sawing trees at 100,000 board feet per day, it became known as the largest hardwood producer in the world.[56]

But many Appalachian families had a more intimate, more direct involvement in the business. From nearby forests, they individually cut the oaks, walnuts, maples and other dense trees, as well as the lighter poplars, pines, and others. Family members, and perhaps neighbors, formed a small group that hauled the trees to a nearby water course. There logs would lie until high water ("tides"), usually in the spring, would float them to a larger body of water, such as the Kentucky, Licking, or Big Sandy Rivers. Now they were ready to be "run" downstream for sale. Huge log rafts, with the buoyant lighter logs tied to heavier ones, filled the rivers. Often well over a hundred feet in length, these rafts would consist of logs pinned or lashed together, with long oars fore and aft, and a small platform for the crew. When this boat-like mass began its voyage it was an impressive sight. The raftsmen might sing out, as one song went:

> We're floatin' down Big Sandy
> We're floatin' with the tide
> A hundred yeller poplar logs
> Oh Lordy, how they ride.[57]

However, for those involved in maneuvering the raft to its destination, their task was risky and dangerous. A "run" from Beattyville, where the forks converged to form the Kentucky River, to Frankfort might take five days or more. Along the way, hidden rocks, snags, or rapids could damage or break up the raft, throwing men into the river. Lives were lost. Nor were those the only problems. Near Catlettsburg, a chief timber market on the Big Sandy, the frozen river could create a log-jam, with dozens of rafts held by the ice. When the thaw came, often with a flood of water, the logs would be forced together violently, throwing the wood into the air, tearing apart the loosely constructed

Logging in Kentucky.

This post card of "Logging in Kentucky" captures the timber boom which led to depletion of eastern Kentucky virgin forests.

rafts, crushing the timber into splinters. Lost logs resulted, and that meant lost income. Those long hours of cutting and hauling trees, done at a sacrifice, taking time from farm work, might go for naught in such situations.[58]

But if the trip went well, if few logs were lost, the results might make the difference between a meager existence and an adequate one. On the Kentucky, the destination for many of the rafts was Frankfort and its sawmills. There they would sell their logs at prices ranging from $5 to $11 per thousand feet. With full pockets, they often hesitated briefly before heading home. In the rough area of the city known as "The Craw," the mountaineers found little law, numerous bars, plentiful prostitutes, and abundant gambling houses. For the men it represented the big city and they partook of its offerings before starting back. Some would finally go home by train, but others simply walked. A group returning to Leslie County after a ten-day river trip took a train from Frankfort to Lexington, then a wagon for a time, before walking the final sixty miles. A Clay County man recalled, "my father went all the way to Frankfort and they would have to walk from Lexington back. Took them about three days. About 80 miles."[59]

But the timber that provided needed personal income did not last. As Albert Cowdrey has noted, "Poverty is no friend to natural resources, which typically are devoured piecemeal to sustain existence." Both large concerns and individuals cut virgin forests without much worry about reforesting. The huge Mowbray-Robinson Company at Quicksand had depleted the area around it by the early 1920s. Its mills idle, its tracks rusty, and its task ended, the company moved out, the village was abandoned, and the land was donated to the University of Kentucky as an experimental station. Across the region, the story was repeated. A 1905 state report found almost all accessible areas of eastern Kentucky "denuded of the best timber." Less than a half-decade later a study of forest conditions in the state depicted a "suicidal" cutting pattern which left under 1 percent of the land in virgin forest. The report predicted that the resulting bare soil would leave the eastern part of the state particularly vulnerable to flooding, while if unchecked, the lumbering would exhaust *all* timber resources in the state within eighteen years. By 1930, the Bureau of Agriculture, Labor, and Statistics concluded that five-sixths of the state's original lumber supply had been exhausted and at least a million acres would need to be planted with new, second-growth trees to replenish the species.[60]

Such conditions ended the "boom." Using 1904 and its 568 million board feet as the index year (100.0), the peak production after that came in 1909 (860 million, an index of 107.6), then a steady decline began. Production rose briefly during World War I (to 84.3), then fell drastically after that to a 29.9 level in 1927. By then, a land rich in timber resources had to depend on other states for 84 percent of the lumber used in Kentucky. It was a sad situation, one that revealed the cost of environmental recklessness. The last timber raft floated from Clay County in 1923; much of the infamous "Craw" in Frankfort was, symbolically, virtually washed away by the great 1937 flood and a different neighborhood emerged. The old one had lived and died by the river. Soon the end of the timber era came, quietly. The start of another era had already begun and had done so with much less tranquillity.[61]

King Coal's long reign had opened. It had all started quietly enough, in the previous century, with small mines operated by few people. In fact, the western part of the state would produce more coal than the eastern fields until 1912. But the symbol for the metamorphosis of eastern Kentucky was a native Kentuckian riding up to individuals' homes and persuading them to sell their mineral rights. The act seemed simple and the results limited. It was neither.[62]

John C. Calhoun Mayo represented the forces of change transforming Appalachia. While many pictured gullible farmers being duped out of their mineral rights or land by shrewd northern capitalists, that was not necessarily the case. First of all, for many of the landholders, they knew what they were doing, and the dollars received, though limited, loomed large in a near cash-less economy. Certain parts of the land even turned out to be worthless to the speculator. But some sellers also were not told all the ramifications of their actions and they were, indeed, deceived by the purchaser. Yet, as often as not, that buyer spoke not with a northern accent, but with a southern, or Kentucky, one. A study of forty-eight "coal barons" in Kentucky found only one-fourth were northerners; half were non-mountain southerners; one fourth were, in fact, from southern Appalachia. J.C.C. Mayo was one of those.[63]

Born in Pike County in the eastern corner of Kentucky, just a few months before the Civil War ended, Mayo had a rather typical mountain childhood with education coming at a log schoolhouse. But the boy desired more, and, with the help of a father who mortgaged the farm to help finance his son's higher education, Mayo eventually graduated from Kentucky Wesleyan College, then located at Millersburg. After a stint as a teacher, he practiced law, married, and began doing meticulous research into land records. Mayo equipped his wife with a specially made dress that had pockets inside the skirt, where they placed gold coins, and they began their treks in search of wealth.[64]

Having already searched the title books, Mayo would make the hard trip to some rural farmer's distant cabin, introduce himself and his wife, chat for a time, and then offer the landholder a small sum for an option to buy the mineral rights of the land. Mrs. Mayo would appear with the gold coin and the agreement would be sealed. If the option was taken later, the farmer would further receive a slightly higher (though still modest) payment. Mayo was not the first to use the Mayo, or "broad-form," deed, for New Yorker Richard M. Boas, among others, had earlier purchased land on similar terms at a dollar an acre. But the careful and hard-working Mayo went beyond that. His charming manner, his piercing eyes, his friendly face (often wrapped in cigar smoke) — all made him successful both in prying land from people in the mountains and in making deals in corporate board rooms. After several false starts, he had by 1907, reportedly accumulated leases or land totalling between 500,000 and 700,000 acres. Through his influence, the 1906 legislature's new tax laws further protected the sometimes dubious claims involved in certain leases. That so-called "squatters rights" law was sustained by both the state and national judiciary by 1911, and Mayo's claims became even more valuable. Already called eastern Kentucky's first millionaire, he remained in his mountains at Paintsville, and built a church, a bank, an office, and a huge columned mansion, complete with marble, mahogany, and many paintings. Having made his own fortune by accumulation of and selling the region's mineral wealth to outside, absentee control, Mayo rested on his laurels as economic empire builder.[65]

On a smaller scale, many local entrepreneurs had also encouraged corporations to come to their areas and buy land. Some of those would-be Kentucky capitalists did make some money. But in large part their economic enthusiasm yielded only short-term personal gains. The region's wealth chiefly went to financial forces outside the state and a kind of colonial economy emerged. An angry college graduate in a 1913 thesis confessed, "I think one of the saddest tragedies . . . is the fact that we have slept, lo these many years, and allowed 'outsiders' to come in, and get possession of our land for a mere pittance . . . . We . . . through ignorance allow foreign capitalists to reap a rich reward from resources naturally our own." That lament would be heard for the rest of the century.[66]

Now corporations bearing names such as Northern Coal & Coke, or Consolidated Coal Company, or Elk Horn Coal Corporation, began working with railroads to develop the huge tracts of land they controlled. Companies whose parent corporations included International Harvester, Ford, and U.S. Steel adopted the viewpoint presented openly in the first issue of *Mountain Life &*

Work: "The mountains [are] a region of vast resources that [has] been blocked out of the wild by a great people and held in trust . . . for the modern capitalist to develop and utilize."[67]

The result was a tremendous coal boom. Counties totally rural and almost completely free of coal production changed seemingly overnight. Neither Perry nor Letcher County produced any commercial coal in 1911. Four years later they mined almost three million tons. By 1920, that tonnage had risen to over twice the amount of only a half-decade earlier. Adjoining Harlan County experienced the same industrial transformation. Together the three counties doubled in population from 1910 to 1920. After the arrival of railroads and mining, the number of Harlan's residents rose sixfold, from ten thousand in 1910 to over sixty-four thousand twenty years later. Variations of that story were repeated in coal counties across the region.[68]

With the increased coal production — from over five million tons in Kentucky in 1900, to thirty-one million in 1918 — came additional problems, not the least of which involved mine safety. Going underground had always been a dangerous occupation, as candles, then burning oil, and then carbide, lighted a miner's way through a dark and dangerous cut, one that went deeper and deeper under the earth's surface as the century progressed. Ventilation of the shafts remained difficult, even after motor-driven blowers arrived on the scene. Neglected timbering of roofs for support, coal and rock falls, and mishandled explosives continued as dangers. Tardy safety legislation and higher production formed conditions which resulted in increased mine fatalities. In the fifteen years before 1902, some 165 Kentucky miners died. But in the ten years after 1910, 754 fatalities occurred; the next decade saw 1,614 men lose their lives. In the western coal fields, 34 miners died in a 1910 explosion at Browder Mine in Muhlenberg County, and in 1917, in Webster County, 62 men perished in a similar disaster. Nor did it end with those losses: the 84 Kentucky fatalities in 1911 also left behind 45 widows and 94 orphans. Death touched many. It is little wonder that a miner who started work in the mines at age sixteen remembered those days as a time when "there was someone killed every day. All the time somebody was getting killed."[69]

Yet, despite the dangerous conditions, people flocked to mining camps. Some believed they had few options: "I didn't have any choice. I had a family. They had to eat. There wasn't anything else to do. The timber was practically all gone in the county by then. . . . We didn't have anything else to work at." For others, the choice may not have been as desperate, but rather simply made financial sense. At a time when farm laborers received between fifty and seventy-five cents, plus board, for a day's work, a person working in the mines could earn at least two to four dollars a day. A man who became a county judge started his working career as a fourteen-year-old mine worker in 1919, making $2.88 a day. It seemed a fortune. More experienced hands garnered even higher wages. And even though hidden expenses and deductions often reduced the take-home pay considerably, most miners still made much more than they had previously. For some the move, then, from farm to mining was a studied decision, one where those involved knew the various advantages and disadvantages. Others considered little about consequences; the promise of more money was all they needed to hear.[70]

Exemplary company towns, such as Jenkins and Lynch, made the move even more appealing. In Letcher County, near the Virginia line, a single mountain cabin sat within a quiet valley. Then the railroad inched into the area, and the town of Jenkins appeared literally only days later. Consolidated Coal Company built a model town, with over a thousand dwellings, a school, a library, a park, a hospital, an electric plant, and several churches. Water, sewage, and garbage systems were set up, as were sawmills, brick factories, and kilns. In 1919 a woman suffrage leader visiting there expressed her surprise at finding clay tennis courts, movie theaters, an "excellent" school, five children's playgrounds, and reading rooms in the still-new town. The company-owned store, bakery, and butcher shops seemed to her "sanitary models that larger cities . . . may envy."

A little over a decade after its founding, the town was praised for its concrete sidewalks, white frame houses (repainted every four or five years), and vegetable gardens. At the same time another observer called it "very attractive" with paved roads, good schools, and recreational facilities.[71]

Lynch, Kentucky, in neighboring Harlan County, brought forth similar descriptions. Begun in 1917 at a site where almost no one lived and named for the president of U.S. Coal and Coke, the town had a payroll of 1,500 men on hand within four months. A spur line connected it to major railroads and its population soon numbered 6,500. Schools, churches, a hospital, a power plant, tennis and bowling teams, a hotel, ten miles of paved streets — all were quickly established. A 1920 study of coal towns presented Lynch as a carefully planned place, with "good" buildings, newly plastered homes, and conveniently located public services. Overall, its appearance was "very pleasing." The next year the State Board of Health praised sanitary conditions at Lynch. Four years after that, the town had two hundred single houses, four hundred double ones, and five boarding houses. According to the company's figures, 80 percent of the workers received more than the $6.30 per day minimum wage. Out of their monthly wage they paid $2 a month for room rent, $.75 per month for water, and $.30 monthly for electricity. The three-story company commissary, or "Big Store," was open six days a week, thirteen hours a day, and employed some one hundred clerks to help workers find further ways to spend those wages. Despite its monopoly, the store had prices which were competitive with outside concerns.[72]

Nor were Lynch and Jenkins the only company towns attracting favorable descriptions. A black coal miner, while remembering a few negative aspects of his life in Wheelwright in Floyd County after Inland Steel purchased it in 1930, also recalled low prices at the company store, good paved roads, "clean and orderly" streets, freshly painted homes, and fine public facilities, including an Olympic-size swimming pool and golf course. Another man of the first generation born in coal camps had strong memories of the "feeling of neigh-

Kentucky Historical Society

The Consolidation Coal Company maintained a neat interior in this recreation building at Jenkins, Ky., ca. 1916. (The sign on the column warns, "Please don't spit on the floor.")

borliness" in the Blue Diamond community of his youth: "Everybody felt a common kinship . . . there was even a companionship between the mine operators and the men at one time, before the Great Depression." High wages made workers feel they were in "paradise" in his Perry County town. The presence of good schools, the prospect of a regular income, the availability of modern housing, the convenience of a large store, the expectancy of a feeling of community, the promises of a new life — all made camps attractive to rural Appalachians. Thousands responded to the hope offered and an exodus resulted from farm to mine.[73]

Unfortunately, model camps like Lynch and Jenkins were not the norm. Physically, mining towns varied widely. A 1920 survey noted that if the company was benevolent, conditions exceeded the surrounding countryside and might even be termed good. But, "if there is ignorant or unscrupulous management, the situation may be unspeakably bad." Both extremes existed. For every camp with freshly painted homes, electric lights, and vegetable gardens, there were camps with poorly constructed shacks of unpainted, monotonous likeness. Typically, a coal company house was twenty-eight feet square with two bedrooms, kitchen, and living room. No plaster, no closets, no indoor plumbing, no gardens, and much dirt and grime from the mines represented more usual descriptions of coal town homes. For every camp with its carefully planned streets and houses, there were others with mud holes and garbage, towns which developed haphazardly and spread all over the countryside. For every good town there was a bad one.[74]

A study of the mountain region, just as the Depression of the 1930s was starting, described a typical coal camp town. Hard times had come to even the best places and living conditions had declined since the boom days of the 1910s. Now,

> all the way along stand little square gray houses, for the most part crowded close to the road . . . but also in tiers on the hillsides wherever the slope is not too steep. Between the houses lie dirt, tin cans, broken automobile parts, heaps of garbage; and flies, pigs, chickens and cows make themselves at home around the cabins. . . . There are no fences and no flowers. Outdoor pumps each serve a number of neighboring houses. Unpleasant smells rise from the creek, which is the only sewer; and the odor of coal gas comes from high, burning piles of waste coal. The air is full of smoke and coal dust.[75]

For thousands, economic reality destroyed the bright optimism they had brought to the camps. For them the future seemed as dark as the coal they mined.

There had always been a somber, unpleasant, often unspoken side to company towns. Violence, for instance, was widespread, and election fraud commonplace. Justice's blindfold did not keep her from favoring one side over the other. A miner recalled that "the courts were run by the coal companies and they had the power to elect whoever they wanted." While paternalism did operate in some places to create a unity of feelings, more often than not strong class differences existed. White-collar employees, often living high on hills overlooking the shacks below, maintained a social and physical distance from the miners. And with the working force itself, social distinctions existed from the beginning.[76] Coal camps had their own segregated areas, where blacks lived apart from whites, and then areas where native whites stayed separate from immigrant whites. Those living in places with names such as "Little Poland," or "Hunkieville," or "Niggertown" faced a more hostile world than did the native white workers or those on "silk-stocking row." Both immigrants from the North and blacks from the South had likely been recruited by agents and shipped to the camps to work. Both retained a sense of identity, one, in fact, almost forced on them by segregation. Hungarians, for example, started their own foreign-language newspaper in Martin County while the immigrant population growth in Harlan — from 12 in 1910 to 1,269 a decade later — caused groups there to band together in lodges and churches. Consisting of diverse ethnic groups, coal camps across the region were little melting pots of cultural pluralism, but ones where assimilation had limits. The most realistic statement of conditions came at death, when both groups were buried in cemeteries segregated by race and place of national origin.[77]

Yet all workers shared several things equally. They all were exposed to

Alice Lloyd College Archives

Coal camp at Red Ash, Whitley County.

black lung disease and the physical dangers involved in digging coal. They all had sums deducted from each month's paycheck for company-sponsored medical care (of varying quality), for company-sponsored teachers (generally good), and for a company-sponsored burial fund. They likewise had Company Store charges taken from the check given them. If the prices were fair — as many were — then few questions arose. But investigators found some places had charges 10 percent to 100 percent higher than those in non-company towns in the same area. Such conditions bred dissatisfaction, particularly when the times of prosperity passed. Workers then began to feel as one miner expressed it, that companies "didn't care nothing about nothing but some coal."[78]

The chief problem of the coal camps was not physical, nor social, but rather psychological. For a people who valued their independence; who had previously worked at their own pace, and when they wished; who, for decades, had never been part of an industrialized society — for them the camps' requirement for conformity and a set schedule created conflicts. One worker felt "too hemmed up" and left. Like him, some would return to their old homes but found it hard to go back to that way of life, willingly left earlier. Others enjoyed the material benefits of the camp, despite problems, and stayed on. But when cracks developed in the system, those same people might strike out against it.[79]

The company that owned and ran each coal town was a small kingdom unto itself. The company owned the miner's home; it employed him; it sold him his groceries; it doctored his family and educated his children; it gave him entertainment. The miner had little input into his working conditions or the government of the community in which he lived. Insulated from the outside world, uprooted from the past, not yet established in the present, the miner and his family lived in a system which rendered them dependent and seemingly powerless. The physical change from rural cabin to coal tipples, company housing, schools, and stores was a hard enough adjustment. The move from a farming economy to a technological, consumer one in itself would be very difficult.[80] The transference from a homogeneous, tight-knit small community to a place, as one author wrote in 1920, "with as cosmopolitan a group of people as may be found in any industrial center of the country" would alone create vast problems of adjustment. Add to that the suddenness of it all, plus the even greater mental metamorphosis required, and the problems faced by Appalachians in the early twentieth century were almost overwhelming. The battle between old traditions and new forces would be fought, long and hard, for decade after decade.[81]

Appalachia, then, in the first years of the twentieth century was full of contrasts or paradoxes. There was a rural Appalachia and a quasi-urban one, an agrarian place and an industrial one, an isolated area and a more cosmopolitan one. The eastern mountains had people of many social classes, from many nations and races; they also had overall homogeneity as well. There were rural areas of great poverty and distress, and others of solid beauty and strength. There were coal towns which offered people real hope for a better future in their lives, and other camps of sadness and despair. Eastern Kentucky was an unchanging land in places; it was a land of revolution in other locales.[82]

The contrasting images of Appalachia were personified in the lives of two women. Jean Ritchie, born in 1922 in Viper, Kentucky, was the fourteenth child her then-forty-four-year-old mother had to raise. Their home had been built by hand by her father and friends, and her earliest recollection concerned story-telling and ballad-singing as the family gathered around a fire. Her descriptions of growing up in a rural area abound with nostalgic accounts of bountiful dinners of fried chicken, fresh beans, cornbread, and molasses, or rewarding work with the farm animals, or hickory-nut hunts, or fodder-pulling time. When the radio arrived, with it came modernization and, for a time, the family did not sing the old songs as before. But the spell of restlessness cast by the radio soon wore off, and her family once more began to take up the traditional ballads. Ritchie went on to graduate Phi Beta Kappa from college and became famous for singing and preserving the folk songs of her past.[83]

If Ritchie's world was one filled with pleasant memories of traditional ways, Loretta Webb Lynn's life contained very separate remembrances and followed a much different course. Born in a log cabin in Butcher Hollow, near Van

Lear, Kentucky, she was one of eight children born to a coal-mining father who "kept his family alive by breaking his own body down." They were poor and isolated; Loretta Webb never had a dress until she was seven years old, slept on the cabin floor until she was nine, and never rode in an automobile until she was twelve. She recalled winters "where all we ate for weeks was bread dipped in gravy." By age fourteen Loretta Lynn had left that world, married, and become a mother. By the time she reached age twenty-nine, she was a grandmother. But a few years earlier Loretta had begun a singing and song-writing career, one not rooted in mountain ballads but rather in the country music she had heard on the radio. Where Ritchie preserved the traditional tunes, Lynn created new ones, born out of the conditions of her own life and of those around her. Her recognition as country music "Entertainer of the Decade" in 1980 was hard-earned, just as Ritchie's own success was. They each came from Appalachian roots which, if different in part, also matched closely the contrasting parts that composed that region. Ritchie and Lynn both represented Appalachia.[84]

Very different in some ways from the rest of the state, Appalachia was still Kentucky — just as it was not Kentucky.

The State

Throughout the twentieth century, three areas of the state would receive almost all the national attention directed to Kentucky. Appalachia became the focus of more print than any other region, followed by Louisville, then the central Bluegrass region of horse farms. But almost no one wrote of northern Kentucky, often viewed as an appendage of Cincinnati; or the Jackson Purchase in far-west Kentucky where the people lived closer to Memphis or St. Louis than Louisville; or the Ohio River cities such as Owensboro; or Bowling Green and south-central Kentucky. They remained almost ignored, except at election time. They were the forgotten majority.

A virulent regionalism infected the entire state, and, when combined with a widespread spirit of localism, made unity of action and thought very difficult indeed. Part of the problem was simply geographical. The people in the easternmost county of the state could reach the shore of the Atlantic Ocean quicker than they could travel the four hundred miles to west Kentucky. Citizens of the northern part of the commonwealth lived nearer Canada than the Jackson Purchase area of their own state. Students attending the regional university at Murray, Kentucky, were closer to the University of Mississippi than the University of Kentucky.[85]

But it was more than distance separating Kentuckians. It was also a spirit, one in which each place felt itself treated differently than the rest of the state. Such attitudes were not unique to Kentucky, of course, nor to the time. But that did not make the slings and arrows any less hurtful. Nor was any locale free from that spirit. Urban, well-educated Louisvillians, according to a 1906

"Covington, the Gateway." The orientation of this photo implies that Covington serves as the gateway to Cincinnati, rather than to its own state of Kentucky.

account, "are more provincial than the citizens of any village in Kentucky. They think Louisville is the state." And more than any other large urban area in Kentucky, Louisville would continue to be viewed by many as something separate from the rest of the state. Its success, population growth, and urbanity distanced it from the small-town, rural Kentuckian who so long typified the commonwealth.[86]

Everywhere prevalent, however, was what a Pike countian in the eastern mountains called "piteful [*sic*] sectionalism." That 1925 letter-writer complained that west Kentucky and Appalachia and the central Bluegrass region knew almost nothing about each other. Since there could be no unity, no vision, in such a situation, he asked "Is it possible that Kentucky's zenith was of yesterday?" Over a decade later, another writer commented how much "hostility and misapprehension" existed between sections. A similar sentiment was voiced in 1940 by a Bell County lawyer who went to Knoxville or Huntington or Cincinnati to shop: "We don't like Louisville one bit better than it likes us." Another man from the mountains told the same reporter that he disliked the Bluegrass because "they're the proudest set of people in Kentucky and they've

Lancaster, the seat of Garrard County.

got less to be conceited about." Even novelists took up the theme as the widely read Kentuckian James Lane Allen had one of the Bluegrass upper class admit that people in that section were ignorant of other regions of the state, while John Fox, Jr., explained in a 1903 novel that a Kentucky aristocrat "knew as little about the [mountain] people as he knew about the Hottentots, and cared hardly more."[87]

Yet, despite the sectionalism, a unity of sorts did exist. Louisville and Appalachia constituted only 36 percent of Kentucky's population in 1900. The other regions of Kentucky — where almost two of every three Kentuckians lived — really more represented what Kentucky was — and was not. Regionalism splintered the state, but the core remained, a center chiefly composed of rural, native-born people.[88]

In terms of numbers, these people comprised an important state. Kentucky's 2,147,174 citizens in 1900 made it twelfth among the states in population. But the figures spoke troubling words. As had been true every decade since 1820 — and would be true, with one exception, throughout the next seventy years — Kentucky's rate of growth fell behind that of the United States (15.5 percent to America's 20.7 in 1900). Moreover, the relative decline was accelerating. The 2,289,905 population a decade later represented only a 6.6 percent increase; the U.S. average represented a 21.0 percent growth, well over three times the Kentucky figure. Kentucky's rate was the lowest in the South and third lowest in the nation. In fact, for the next sixty years, the commonwealth never had double-digit population growth in any decade. America, on the other hand, experienced such increases every decade but one. Once the eighth most populous state (in 1880), Kentucky fell to fourteenth in 1910. That process would continue throughout the century. The situation was graphically evident in various ways. The large, powerful nineteenth-century commonwealth that produced numerous presidential nominees and vice-presidents, and twelve cabinet officers, furnished in the next century only one vice-president and a single cabinet member calling the state home. Kentucky was in obvious decline in power, population, and prestige.[89]

But what one paper called "Kentucky's Humiliation" of low growth did not apply to all areas of the commonwealth. In the decade after 1900, almost all mountain counties experienced sizeable population gains, due chiefly to the coal boom and transportation explosion. Three of the four counties containing the state's largest urban areas also grew by more than 10 percent. On the other hand, of the thirty-six high-growth counties, only seven were west of Louisville. Between 1910 and 1920 every county, save one, that was in the western coal field lost population, as that region was eclipsed by the new eastern fields. In fact, the Appalachian area's 21.1 percent increase in that decade exceeded the national figure. Growth there and in most urban centers was offset, however, by only small increases in west Kentucky and nonurban parts of north-central Kentucky. Population change thus came to Kentucky selectively, slowly, and, in some locales, not at all.[90]

Who were the Kentuckians of 1900, then? Some 13.3 percent of them were black, but that part of the state's population was proportionally declining. Twenty years later the percentage would be 8.7 and would generally decrease after that. Between 1900 and 1910 the black population suffered a real loss of 7,000 people, to 473,000, and Kentucky was the only southern state to have such a change. From 1920 to 1930 the Negro population in the commonwealth decreased 4.2 percent, while the Caucasian rose 9.5 percent. At the same time, the nation's black citizenry increased by over 13 percent, and, even in the South where significant black out-migration was taking place, the overall black population also went up. In short, Kentucky blacks were leaving the state faster than elsewhere, and few immigrants of the same race were taking their place.[91]

Those black Kentuckians who remained lived increasingly in urban areas. In 1900, some 40 percent of the state's black citizens resided in cities and made up significant portions of many urban populations. While the two northern Kentucky cities of Covington and Newport had very few black inhabitants, the other two largest cities — Louisville and Lexington — were just the opposite. Lexington's population in 1900, in fact, was 38.4 percent black, the twelfth largest percentage among the nation's urban areas. Louisville's 39,000 blacks made up 19 percent of that city's census.[92]

Three decades later, by 1930, blacks had moved to town even more as over half now lived in urban environs. Smaller cities had sizeable percentages — Hopkinsville (37.0 percent), Madisonville (25.8), and Paducah (20.1) in west Kentucky, and Richmond (29.2), Shelbyville (27.8), and Danville (26.7) in the central region. Lexington's black population, which still made up almost 28 percent of that city's population, would continue its statistical decline; Louisville's 15 percent would fluctuate more but remain near that figure for a half-century. Outside the urban landscape, blacks lived chiefly in central and west Kentucky farming counties such as Bourbon and Woodford in the Bluegrass, or Fulton, Todd, and Trigg in the west — all over one-fifth black. But the large percentages of blacks in some areas was misleading. In many parts of rural Kentucky almost no blacks lived. One-fourth of the counties of the state

Although log homes were often associated with Kentucky's mountainous region, this one, purported to be one hundred years old in 1920, was located in western Kentucky near Mexico, Crittenden County.

reported a black population of under 2 percent, and two counties each had only one black resident. Ten counties in chiefly non-coal producing parts of eastern Kentucky all were under 0.4 percent black, with those ten counties totalling a minority population of only 232. Generally, then, Kentucky had a sizeable black population in some places and an almost nonexistent one in others. But no matter where the locale, overall the proportion of blacks to Kentucky's population was declining.[93]

Whatever the race, the average Kentuckian in 1900 was, statistically, a native of the state. Nine of every ten citizens — black or white — had been born in Kentucky and that figure had changed but slightly a decade later. In 1910, only four other states outranked the commonwealth in the percentage of people who still resided in their native state. Such statistics indicate that population growth chiefly came from within. And, given the state's small rate of increase, it was also evident that out-migration was sizeable and steady. Of those born in Kentucky but residing elsewhere in 1900, over 40 percent lived in Missouri, Indiana, or Illinois. Even when Kentuckians left, then, they did not go far away. But leave they did. By 1930, reports indicated some 965,000 native

Kentuckians lived outside the commonwealth, while only 295,000 people born in other states called Kentucky home. The state was losing the migration battle.[94]

Kentucky's population was increasingly homogeneous due not only to a declining black percentage and little immigration by native Americans, but also because of a very limited foreign immigration. In 1900 only 50,000 foreign-born — 2.3 percent of Kentucky's population — lived within the state's borders. And at a time when large numbers of immigrants were arriving in America from eastern Europe, Kentucky had almost no influx from that quarter. Instead, over half of the state's foreign-born were German immigrants; three-fourths were either German or Irish. The presence of numbers of these "Old Immigrants," and the 15 percent decrease in Kentucky's foreign-born over the previous decade, suggest that most foreign-born may have arrived even before the Civil War and were an elderly population in 1900. Certainly the state attracted few of the young "New Immigrants," except in small numbers to the coal camps. Those immigrants who did live in Kentucky made up a sizeable bloc in urban areas along the Ohio River, and overall 10.5 percent of the population of cities in the state was foreign-born. In Louisville, some churches conducted services only in German in the first decade of the century, while the *Anzeiger*, which still had 7,000 subscribers in 1930, continued to publish until 1938, on the eve of World War II. Similarly, the *Kentucky Irish American*, with its lively and cutting commentary, was, when it closed in 1968, one of the last three newspapers of its kind in the nation. But outside the cities, only 1 percent of the population of rural areas were immigrants. Novelist Harriette Arnow expressed the attitude concerning "foreigners" in that family-oriented, agrarian world of her Kentucky youth: "I do recall once I heard talk of a foreigner. He dealt in meat and his speech was strange; . . . worse, nobody had so much as seen his father or even knew he had been born. . . . In any case he was not one of our people." For rural Kentucky — except in coal mining areas — the cultural diversity that immigrants brought to their new homes was something those Kentuckians would only hear or read about.[95]

By 1910, one-seventh of all the inhabitants of the United States had been born abroad. In Kentucky, on the other hand, fewer than one in fifty was foreign-born (1.8 percent). Despite the massive immigration from eastern Europe to America, nearly 70 percent of the Kentucky foreign-born still hailed from Germany or the British Isles. The only sizeable non-western European element came from some 3,000 Russians (8 percent of the total). But from whatever country, the census recorded only 6,000 new foreign immigrants entering the state during the decade. By 1930, the United States' foreign population percentage was fourteen times that of Kentucky's. Obviously, the state — like the South — diverged considerably from national population trends.[96]

A similar deviation took place regarding the commonwealth's rural-urban ratio. In 1910, the United States was nearly 40 percent urban; Kentucky was under 20 percent. Within a decade America would become more urban than rural, but Kentucky's population would not become so until a half-century

Kentucky Historical Society

Bird's-eye view of Burkesville, Cumberland County.

after that, in 1970. The commonwealth's rate of urbanization also fell behind that of the South, which in 1930 was 34 percent urban. Nationally, only ten states had a smaller percentage of their citizens living in urban areas than did Kentucky. People of the state did follow the well-worn path from farm to city, but they walked that road at a much slower pace than did most of their fellow Americans.[97]

A large portion of those who did reside in urban parts of Kentucky lived in Louisville, really the state's only sizeable city at the time. Its 204,000 people ranked it as the nation's eighteenth largest city in 1900. The next three largest urban areas of the commonwealth — Covington (43,000) and Newport (28,000), both across the river from Cincinnati, and Lexington (26,000) — when combined did not have even half the Falls City's population. A decade later the situation had changed only slightly. All four cities had grown faster than had the state overall and Louisville's 224,000 people comprised 40 percent of all the commonwealth's urban dwellers. But a 33 percent increase in Lexington's population had made it Kentucky's third-largest city. The two northern Kentucky centers of Covington and Newport would change little in population over the next seventy years, but already other locales were growing closer to them — the west Kentucky cities of Paducah (23,000), Owensboro (16,000), and Henderson (11,000) had almost doubled in twenty years and now ranked as the commonwealth's next largest cities. Still, only thirteen places in the entire state exceeded 6,000 in population. Urban centers, while growing, still comprised a limited commodity in early twentieth-century Kentucky.[98]

When urban areas did exist, they usually varied a great deal in their composition from the rest of the state. In Louisville in 1910, for example, almost half of the population consisted of either blacks, immigrants, or those of foreign or mixed parentage. The other three largest cities had similar statistics, either as a result of the presence of a sizeable number of blacks or of immigrant families. In a state whose population had generally small percentages of both, the city — any sizeable city — seemed very different indeed from the rural, white, native-born, Anglo-Saxon countryside.[99]

The composite Kentucky family, rural and urban combined, did not fit an often-expressed stereotype that the state had large families. While slightly larger in size in 1900 than the average American family — 4.9 to 4.7 — the variance was not great and was declining. A decade later a rapid decrease in the mean size of Kentucky families had taken place, and they nearly approximated the United States average. Overall, in the first part of the century, Kentucky had a higher birthrate than the nation, had more males than females (103 to 100), and had a younger population than the United States. Generally, the life-course of men and women followed a nineteenth-century pattern that would remain stable until the World War II era, with women marrying in their early twenties to men about three years older. Children followed fairly rapidly, though the number and timing changed over the decades.[100]

Health Care

Disease greatly affected those families and their offspring. Tuberculosis (TB) was a major crippler and taker of life, and Kentucky ranked second highest among the states in its death rate from that disease. In Hopkinsville in 1916, one of five deaths resulted from TB; places with large black populations particularly suffered since blacks contracted the disease twice as often as whites. And despite the increased presence of pasteurized milk, deaths by tuberculosis continued. By 1942, over 1,800 citizens died, making it the sixth leading cause of death in the commonwealth. For that disease, the state's death rate exceeded the nation's by 50 percent. Earlier, in 1910, one Kentucky governor had vetoed a "tuberculosis bill" as too expensive. Two years, and numerous deaths, later, the bill passed, and a start was made toward eradication. But real progress came only after a 1944 act set up sanitaria across the state. Within a decade the rate had fallen drastically, and, where 1,748 had died in 1943, only 77 deaths were attributed to TB thirty years later. By then, one feared disease threatened few of Kentucky's children.[101]

Kentuckians experienced health problems out of proportion with the rest of the nation in several other areas. Hookworm was one of those. When the

Rockefeller Sanitary Commission examined some five thousand people in one Appalachian county, 42 percent were found to be infected. Poor sanitation extended all across the state, however, and, of the 450,000 Kentuckians eventually tested by the commission, one-third had hookworm. Similar conditions in the commonwealth helped spread trachoma, an eye disease, as well. The practices of sharing the same towel or same beds meant whole families would be affected. In some regions, one of every four persons had the disease. Statewide, at least 8 percent of the mountain children and around 4 percent of urban ones experienced the contagious inflammation that could leave them blind. Through the efforts of doctors like Joseph A. Stuckey and a strong-willed reformer, Linda Neville, who organized a trachoma crusade, great strides were made rather rapidly. By 1936, one study proclaimed the disease virtually eradicated.[102]

Open privies, sewage-polluted rivers, poor personal sanitation — all these contributed to very high death rates from diarrhea, dysentery, and typhoid as well. Lexington's health officer noted in 1916, for example, the presence of over 3,000 unhealthy and open outdoor toilets in that city, while a Louisvillian recalled that during that same era, home sewage ran down his alley to Beargrass Creek, then to the river. But some places did not even enjoy an outdoor privy. More than one school had arrangements for its children like those recalled by a mountain boy. When they felt nature's call, "the boys went up the creek . . . while the girls went down the creek." In fact, modern sewers came at very different intervals to Kentucky. One eastern Kentucky county seat received its first lines as late as 1969, while several rural counties had under 5 percent of their population connected to such systems in the 1980s. Public drinking wells with public cups (until prohibited by state law in 1912) added to health problems. Given such conditions, it is little wonder that the state's diarrhea and dysentery death rates in 1916 doubled the national average. Kentucky in 1921 also ranked first in morbidity rate for typhoid fever. Low-lying Paducah located on the Ohio River was particularly hard-hit, placing second highest in death rate due to typhoid fever among all of the cities of the United States, and the third highest rate of malarial fever deaths in 1900. Its overall death rate exceeded the national figures by 50 percent.[103]

Yet, in time, those rates and others declined drastically, so a 1945 report could conclude that in the last quarter-century, Kentucky's diptheria death rate had fallen to one-tenth its former figure, and its typhoid fever rate to one-fifteenth. The one-time major health problem — smallpox — was now only "a medical curiosity," the study announced. Such advancements in health resulted in longer lives for Americans — from an average life expectancy of 47 in 1900 to almost 60 in 1930 — and for Kentuckians as well. But perhaps more important, the increased freedom from disease and illness further removed one source of anxiety from the people and increasingly replaced it with a spirit of hope.[104]

But for some Kentuckians, hope still came in a bottle. Widely available patent medicines often contained dangerous drugs or large percentages of

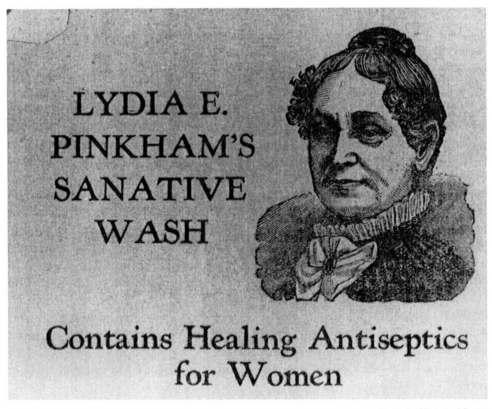

LYDIA E. PINKHAM'S SANATIVE WASH

Contains Healing Antiseptics for Women

This advertisement touted the new four-ounce size costing 50 cents per bottle, as well as the one-and-a-half ounce at 30 cents.

alcohol. While some were more innocuous, their very presence caused people to place their faith in them and delay seeing a physician, causing further problems. Yet the cures offered by these medicines seemed all-pervading and even miraculous. Advertisements in the widely read *Courier-Journal* for 1903 told of Dr. Radway's Sarsaparillian Resolvent which cured tuberculosis, syphilis, ulcers, sore eyes, ringworm, "female complaints," "night sweats," and "nocturnal losses," all for one dollar a bottle. California Fig Syrup Company provided a laxative, while Wine of Cardui relieved "pangs of menstrual disorders, bearing-down pains or ovarian troubles." Swamp-Root was a remedy for kidney, liver, and bladder problems, and Mother's Friend was a "scientific liniment" which prevented morning sickness and "toughens and renders pliable all the parts and assists nature in its sublime work" of childbirth. Numerous advertisements filled even small-town newspapers with promises of cures from Peruna and Lydia E. Pinkham's (both of which were reportedly over 20 percent alcohol), Carter's Little Liver Pills, and Black Draught (for "malaria, headache . . . , indigestion, rheumatism, pimples, blotches . . . etc."). Such notices illustrated the real health concerns of large numbers of citizens, problems not yet solved by medical science. Others, both in Kentucky and across the country, found relief through the health "readings" and clairvoyant predictions of Edgar Cayce of Hopkinsville. Between 1901 and his death in 1945, this "Sleeping Prophet" became a national phenomenon. For desperate people, such approaches and various medicines offered them optimism, a scarce commodity in the health field at that time.[105]

Soon national reform movements helped control the content of the worst patent medicines. But, for some, certain problems continued. The Lexington ordinance in 1901 that prohibited the sale of cocaine and opium without a doctor's prescription indicated the widespread and open use of narcotics in a society which only slowly recognized the effects of such use. When morphine was similarly restricted in 1910, Lexington police collected "dozens" of boxes of the drug. A young boy in Livingston, Kentucky, recalled how "vagabond dopers" would come up to his physician father and desperately ask for the drug laudanum. The problem of drug addiction was not hidden. Newspaper advertisements offered home drug cures, "permanently and painlessly" administered, if the reader would but send money to the person listed. The editor of the Hazel Green *Herald* openly reported his 1910 return from an Indiana sanitarium where he had tried to "kick" his morphine habit. And what Kentuckians experienced, so too did other Americans. In 1935 the United States Public Health Service opened a narcotics hospital outside Lexington. It represented an open reminder to the commonwealth of a long-standing concern.[106]

State and federal action took place in another health problem area — food adulteration. And while Kentucky tended to follow the national trend regarding drug and medicinal restrictions, it played a leading role in the pure food reform movement. The state had similar problems as elsewhere: a 1908 inspection found "horrible" conditions in slaughterhouses. Hogs and buzzards sifted through the offal in the mornings, while flies "alternated between indescribable filth and the fresh meat." Workers trod on ground "soddened with the blood and filth of years," as they went on with their chores. A Louisville inspector found "barbaric" workplaces with food prepared by unwashed hands, hung on uncleaned hooks, and left in uncovered areas where flies quickly coated the meat.[107]

Such conditions had sparked state action. A Pure Food Law was enacted in 1898, revised two years later, then strengthened considerably in 1908. Through the initial efforts of Melville A. Scovell, first director of the state's agricultural experiment station, and Robert McDowell Allen, significant actions began. Allen, the son-in-law of a Pennsylvania U.S. senator, was made secretary to the food control division, supervised by Scovell, when he was only twenty-three. That same year of 1902, some 453 food samples were tested in Kentucky, and 256 were found to be adulterated. Allen reported violators to local county attorneys for action; of the 210 reported, only 2 were found not guilty. In 1910, under the new law, the experiment station examined 3,410 foods and drugs and named 1,004 adulterated or mislabelled, a number that rapidly declined thereafter. Allen, meanwhile, had also become secretary of the National Association of State Dairy and Food Departments and used that forum and his very considerable publicity skills to work for a national law. He led a delegation that met with Theodore Roosevelt twice in 1905, and the president recommended such a bill soon thereafter. Publication of *The Jungle* the next year, as well as a national report critical of the meat-packing industry, aided Allen's efforts and the ensuing Pure Food Law went into effect in 1907.[108]

The state had taken similar positive steps in the field of public health care. The State Board of Health had been set up in 1878, making it the third such organization established in the United States. Poorly funded for a long period following its origin, the board nevertheless made great strides under the leadership of its long-time secretary, Dr. Joseph N. McCormack (who was very active also in national health reform), and his son Dr. Arthur T. McCormack. Legislative actions strengthened the licensing of physicians and dentists in 1904 and set up a Board of Examiners for Trained Nurses a decade after that. A 1918 law gave the board a great deal more funding ($75,000 versus $2,500 the year before) and supported aid to county medical centers. As a result, Kentucky established in 1908 the nation's first full-time county health departments.[109]

The same era also saw important changes enacted regarding the training of medical doctors. As the State Board of Health reported, Kentucky at one time "was probably the worst quack ridden state in the Union." An 1874 law requiring graduation from a medical school had resulted in the establishment of so-called medical institutions for training physicians which were, in the report's words, little more than "headquarters for ignorant vampires, usually with criminal records." By 1893 that situation changed somewhat, but at least seven medical schools still existed as late as 1906. Various mergers left only the one operated by the University of Louisville in existence by 1911. For a half-century that private school became the state's only medical institution. Initially, it too faced problems, for the 1910 Flexner report on medical education criticized its low admission standards (less than a high school education and the largest enrollment of any medical school in the nation), its "inadequate" labs, and its large classes. But reform followed and the medical department provided solid education for the state's doctors.[110]

By 1930, the problem with medical service in Kentucky was not in its training, or in its statewide support, but rather in the distribution of physicians. The U.S. average was one doctor per 753 people; Kentucky's figure was one per 879, which placed it still in the mid-range of the states. But the extremes hurt — while Lexington led with one per 281, Elliott County had only one doctor for 7,705 people. Some one-fourth of the counties and one-seventh of the population, according to a study, had no suitable medical care. The poorer the county, the fewer the physicians. Kentucky particularly suffered from a lack of hospital care, ranking in the bottom ten among the states in that regard. Leitchfield residents, for example, had a sixty-five-mile trip by railroad to the nearest hospital; the sick from Columbia had to go over fifty miles by road to get such care. And the inequity of numbers meant some rural physi-

Kentucky Historical Society

The gross anatomy class at the University of Louisville Medical School used dissecting tables designed by a Louisville resident, Louis G. Gutermuth Sr., ca. 1930s.

cians had to travel a great deal to remain faithful to their Hippocratic oath. Dr. Archibald M. Glass of Owsley County had three horses which he rode in rotation day after day. In a three-year period from 1904 to 1906 he traveled over 15,000 miles on horseback — a daily average, including Sundays, of nearly 14 miles. Not surprisingly, he died a worn-out man, a decade later, when only fifty-three years of age. Death was a constant for all Kentuckians.[111]

The Kentucky Mind in a New Century

Officially, the new century began on 1 January 1901, but Kentuckians, seldom ones to pass up the opportunity, celebrated both then and earlier, on New Year's Day, 1900. Such revelry generally took the form it did at Hopkinsville. That last night of the nineteenth century, people danced till midnight, then the town clock chimed, whistles blew, firebells rang, and fireworks exploded. Church services welcomed the twentieth century in a quieter fashion.[112]

Many of the earlier, divisive issues seemed to have died with the old century. The money question, the tariff issue, the fiery anger of the Populist Party — all had faded and more national unity followed the Spanish-American

War. Certain broad questions remained, however, as people still debated localism versus centralism, individualism versus collectivism, or laissez-faire versus state intervention. Often the discussion only took new forms, however.
Should the nation, for example, be involved in world affairs — in the immediate case, the Philippines — or remove itself entirely from any questions of im-
perialism? For Kentuckians that was a question directly affecting them, as a
one-hundred-thousand-man American army eventually fought in the Philip-
pine Insurrection. Deaths resulted in that colonial war, and local newspapers
recorded the September 1900 death of a Green County youth, the February
1901 burial of a Clark County officer, the March 1901 demise of another officer, from Lexington, and other deaths. Hot and homesick soldiers wrote
home, as did one Adair County man, complaining about "a God forsaken"
place where the chief exports were rice, hemp, sick soldiers, and war bulletins.
The general removal of that issue around 1902 only put the debate off center
stage for a time. The first editorial of the Lexington *Herald* in the new century
had predicted the rise of the United States as a world power, but the exact
form of that prophecy would be long debated.[113]

Other, newer issues continued to intrude on the consciousness of Kentuckians in the 1900s. Urban values competed with agrarian ones and worried
commentators questioned such competition. Kentucky's superintendent of
public instruction wrote in 1915 that migration to the city and the resulting
adoption of urban ideas would, in the end, lead to "national decay and dis-
honor." Old ways of conducting business similarly found their antithesis in
spirit with the adoption of scientific management and efficiency engineering
ideas. The handmade warred with the machine-made, the farm with the factory, the spiritual with the material. For much of the century, the battles
generally went to the urban army, yet there always remained that part of the
traditional past, one that would later reemerge, in modified form, with new
force.[114]

The clearest mixture of the new and the old appeared in newspapers, and
the stories of 1901 illustrated the variety of questions and problems awaiting
Kentuckians in the new century. The assassination of President William
McKinley brought in the new, dynamic Teddy Roosevelt. Queen Victoria's
death in England the same year marked, in some ways, an end to the era that
bore her name. Closer to home, in Louisville in 1901, a person was charged
with abortion, an anti-poolroom ordinance was passed, automobiles were allowed in city parks for the first time, the women's clubs refused to admit black
members, and some 870 saloons were licensed. Across Kentucky that year the
Baptist state convention denounced divorce, one hundred people were indicted
for bootlegging in Laurel County, a feud was raging in Clay County, lynchings
of blacks were widespread, toll roads were destroyed, and a Fulton, Kentucky,
druggist was recorded as selling a hundred dollars' worth of cocaine per week,
on the average. And there was much more.[115]

Given the uncertainties of the twentieth-century future that was unfolding
before them, many Kentuckians — like many other Americans — looked nostal-

gically to their past. Author Robert Penn Warren remembered his Kentucky youth as a time when people who were descended from Virginians still thought of themselves as Virginians, despite having never been in that state themselves. Even for those who had not retreated so far into history, their world was shaped by golden visions of yesteryear. As Thomas D. Clark and Albert D. Kirwan wrote, "the ghost of the past stalked the land trying to reincarnate itself." Novelist John Fox, Jr., spoke for that skewed remembrance of the past in his *The Little Shepherd of Kingdom Come*. He presented an antebellum Bluegrass where "there were the proudest families, the stateliest homes, the broadest culture, the most gracious hospitality, the gentlest courtesies, the finest chivalry, that the State has ever known. . . . There were as manly virtues, as manly vices, as the world has ever known." Such presented and recollected images of a world that really never was sometimes joined with visions of progress to shape the state's future course; at other times, those same images drew people away from future change, for it seemed too disruptive, too unstable, too strange.[116]

As a result, the agrarian ethos still kept a strong hold on Kentucky, even as urbanism made its inroads. Farming had been a noble profession to nineteenth-century minds, but now the business ideal seemed to be ruling supreme nationally. People spoke of the "rural problem" and the agrarian world appeared more uninviting. Yet that world still dominated in the commonwealth. It was a different vision than the nineteenth-century one, for rural Kentucky wanted the benefits of the wonderful century's inventions, while keeping the traditions of the past. The 1905 book *Country Estates of the Blue Grass* combined that outlook, as it criticized the corruption and "conventionalities" of the city and praised the country as the best hope for the future. But it was a kind of urbanized countryside the authors sought, "where one may find every convenience that is found in the city" — daily newspapers at the door, morning mail, running water, telephone lines, grocery consignments, and periodic ice delivery.[117]

That, however, was a vision long delayed. More often, the country farmer lived in isolation, an isolation that often fostered static conservatism. The agrarians' future went little further than a single crop season; their world seldom extended beyond the county seat. A like-mindedness resulted, one which wanted low taxes, little change, and general governmental inertia. Yet there was another strand in the agrarian web, a more positive one, often overlooked by critics of the rural landscape. The agrarian life, with its own pace, let neighbors work together and enjoy leisure time in what has been called "a distinctive form of rural civility." Moreover, these land-oriented people developed intimate relationships with nature. They knew where various trees were located, where each stream could be crossed, where each hill could be scaled. As essayist Wendell Berry has noted, such farmers cared about their land because they had not only economic but also hereditary and traditional ties to it. They valued their sense of place.[118]

This became particularly evident in June 1906 when the commonwealth

COURT HOUSE, NICHOLASVILLE, KENTUCKY.   HOME-COMING DAY, JUNE 20, 1906.

Kentucky Historical Society

Jessamine County residents flock to the Nicholasville courthouse on Home-coming Day, June 20, 1906.

held a "Home-coming" celebration. Over thirty thousand native Kentuckians returned home and joined the state's citizens in a four-day fête. On the first day, the entire front page of the *Courier-Journal* featured an illustration of a goateed gentleman standing before his white-columned mansion, with his wife on the steps, and two black servants standing to the side. He greets those returning to the Bluegrass State; the visitors are in modern clothes. The accompanying stories stressed that "the love of home is as much of the Kentuckian's being as his blood and brawn."

While interrupted periodically by rain, the pageantry over the next days featured innumerable singings of "My Old Kentucky Home," band concerts at night, unveilings of statues to Stephen Collins Foster and Daniel Boone, a floral parade, a reenactment of the attack on Boonesborough in frontier times, and almost endless addresses. The new Louisville Armory, decked in bunting, electric lights, and Liberty bells, provided a place where each county had a register for visitors to sign and where various speakers and singers held forth. On the last day, festivities moved to Frankfort where the cornerstone was laid for the new capitol. Then, for those who desired, individual counties had their own welcoming ceremonies all across the state. Kentuckians became aware of the influence the state had exerted, through the important figures who had left, but they also learned that many of the commonwealth's hopes had departed with them.[119]

Kraemer Art Company, Cincinnati, created a collage of "Kentucky's Fame" in a postcard proof, ca. 1910, featuring derogatory images which suggested "Kentucky's Infamy" instead.

2

"Divided We Fall": Violence in Kentucky

The Troubling Image

Kentucky entered the twentieth century under a cloud which never lifted. The state's dark image of violence severely hindered development, retarded growth, and limited the commonwealth's every effort. Citizens seemed in a constant state of siege from without and deeply divided within.

The stereotype associating Kentuckians with violent, lawless actions stood firmly in place by the first days of the new century. It had developed gradually, growing out of the pioneer period, maturing with the duels and military struggles of the antebellum era, then emerging full blown when individual actions and feuds resulted in bloodshed before the public eye. A justice of the state's highest court was fatally shot in 1879; various political quarrels were settled violently before and after that time. Then in 1900, in the midst of a contested gubernatorial election, one claimant to the office was assassinated in front of the capitol. Before his death four days later, he was named governor, thus becoming the only state chief executive in the nation's history to die in office as a result of assassination. The death of William Goebel propelled Kentucky headlong into national headlines. Newspaper reporters wrote of the state's "seeming disregard for human life and . . . semi-barbarous ways of settling arguments." Even five years later, as trials concerning the murder dragged on, the Cleveland *Plain Dealer* worried about such dangerous and "un-American" practices in Kentucky.[1]

But by then the violent image was already firmly planted in the American mind. Deaths due to extensive feuds in the mountain regions of Kentucky had brought forth strong words from newspaper writers for decades. The New York *Times* in 1879 had indicated that Kentucky was a delightful place to live, "if one enjoys anarchy and mobocracy, relieved by personal affrays and personal assassinations." Six years later the same paper had not changed its opinion of these "unreclaimed savages" who were "a horrible disgrace to civilized communities." The Chicago *Tribune* that year said the state's civilization "has been tested and found to be barbarism." Numerous others joined in — novelists, essayists, sociologists, and seemingly anyone capable of lifting a pen. By the start of the twentieth century, Kentucky was viewed as a dangerous place to live — or even visit.[2]

Goebel

The death of William Goebel in February 1900 left Kentucky in what *Harper's Weekly* called "the greatest political crisis in any state of the United States since the days of 1877" (when a contested presidential election occurred). Democrats claimed the governor's chair for Goebel's successor, his lieutenant governor; Republicans supported their governor who had been inaugurated two months earlier. Each side had its own militia force, its own army. Neither recognized actions by the other as legal. Civil war, this time along party lines, threatened the state, and a stray shot could have exploded the conflict into a bloody war. Luckily, calm actions prevailed and the parties agreed to let the courts decide the issue. In the wake of the assassination, the Democratic legislative majority had declared enough ballots illegal to make Goebel the victor. Now the courts — all the way to the U.S. Supreme Court — allowed that action to stand, and, four months after Goebel was shot, the Democrats reclaimed the office of governor in May 1900. The Republican claimant, under indictment as an accessory to murder, fled the state.[3]

Unfortunately for Kentucky, the Goebel Affair did not end quickly. It continued for some twenty years, and, each time another trial or another court action or another pardon took place, the whole matter was relived again in the national press. In an era when numerous international political leaders were killed, the Goebel example was also constantly cited. It was an albatross around Kentucky's neck that long hung there.[4]

Three men were eventually convicted: the Republican secretary of state, Caleb Powers, said to be the mastermind; Henry Youtsey, an attorney in the Auditor's office who supposedly supplied the weapon; and James Howard, a former feudist who was pictured as the man who pulled the trigger. But the judicial pattern which evolved did not honor Justice. Juries were "packed" with Democrats, and judges were partisan (indeed, one was a former Democratic lieutenant governor). When Howard and Powers appealed their first convictions, a high court that was 4-3 Republican reversed the decisions. Only the emotionally unstable Youtsey declined to appeal. Eventually Howard went through three trials before a court confirmed his life sentence; he lost in his U.S. Supreme Court appeal in 1905. Powers, a clever and articulate person, wrote his memoirs while he served eight years in jail as he went through four trials. Three juries found him guilty; thrice the higher court overturned the decision. Finally, a fourth trial in 1908 ended with a deadlocked jury. With a Republican governor sitting in Frankfort, Howard and Powers were pardoned that year. Later, six other men, including the former Republican governor (at that time living in Indiana), were also granted pardons from standing indictments. When Democrats regained the governorship, Youtsey, who had turned "state's evidence," was granted parole and then was pardoned in 1919. After two decades, the Goebel Affair finally seemed over at last.[5]

Two of the three men — Youtsey and Howard — returned to private life for most of their days. Powers defeated the incumbent in a 1910 primary and then was elected to Congress that fall. He won reelection enough times from his Republican-dominated constituents so he could say he served as many years in Congress as he had in jail. He died in 1932. By then various people had written about the assassination, and different ones pointed to disparate villains. In answering the question, "Who killed Goebel?" one author wrote: "The evidence is simply too contradictory and the people involved were too partisan to allow any definitive answer." What is known is that the assassination and the ensuing trials deeply divided the state and added to Kentucky's dubious legacy of violence.[6]

"Bloody Breathitt"

By the beginning of the twentieth century, feud violence was fading. Most of the major family-oriented and business-oriented "wars" had ended, some a decade or more earlier. The best-known (though not the bloodiest), the Hatfield-McCoy feud had generally concluded by 1890. One of its leaders, "Devil Anse" Hatfield, lived quietly in West Virginia, experienced a religious conversion, and died of pneumonia at the age of eighty-six. His nephew, a physician, was elected Republican governor of West Virginia in 1912. On the other side, Jim McCoy served as sheriff of Pike County, Kentucky, while his enemy, Elias Hatfield, was named chief of police of Logan, West Virginia. In Hazard, Kentucky, site of the French-Eversole feud, bullet holes in store walls and numerous orphans were the chief bequests of a conflict that had killed an estimated thirty to sixty people. Other mountain feuds had also ended with similar results.[7]

But it was too late. The violence in these and other locales had already left its mark, and commentators had already begun to explain it. One study even pointed to sixteen different causes, including drunkenness, "hot tempers," the consequences of the Civil War, politics, boredom, and a code of honor. A 1902 article in a national journal told of visiting this land "where the sun set crimson and the moon rose red." Feuds, the author found, resulted from poor transportation, in-breeding, and a "savage idea of the meaning of honor." A year later another article saw the people's "lust for human blood" as the chief explanation, together with isolation, consanguineous marriages, and politics. In a 1906 book "the old feeling of blood kin," the effects of war, and a "tribal spirit" were emphasized. Later works also stressed the family aspect, the prevalence of firearms, and the miscarriages of justice. Most early accounts saw the feuds originating from problems of the Appalachians themselves.[8]

In more recent times, two different schools of thought have arisen to explain the feuds. One argument, with several variations, focuses less on family and more on community and economic rivalries. It suggests that societal changes created conflict between competing forces. Feuds resulted when outside, urban, industrial, national economic forces disrupted rural preindustrial, traditional ones. In one explanation, a citizenry faced with a loss of control

At the informal "Court at Asher" in Leslie County, ca. 1940, the judge, seated at center, and the accused woman, seated at right, hear testimony of a witness, seated with back to camera.

over their lives struck out with weapons against their enemies. In another view, those who caused violence were the modernizers who perceived the mountaineers as barriers to a "new" Appalachia built on coal and railroads. They let violence cleanse the land of the old "savages." In contrast to earlier studies, then, here the heroes are the Appalachian people or at least those living in traditional societies.[9]

A second recent explanation suggested that, yes, certain somewhat unique conditions did exist in the region, but that feud violence, in a sense, was a kind of rational reaction in a society without adequate forms of legal redress. Often, simply no law existed. As a Kentucky poet wrote:

> . . . There were
> No plaintiffs and no judges: each one
> Carried his court in his own hands

In such cases, the church (for more minor transgressions) and business alliances or the family (for more major ones) policed the community. Isolated areas had long accepted extralegal violence as part of their moral code. But the problems extended beyond that. When law did exist in Appalachian Kentucky, it all too often favored one side over the other. Justice smiled on certain families or factions. A corrupt jury system could free those brought to trial, a local court system favored certain claimants, and a state government allowed its governor to pardon, often only for political reasons, those who were convicted. All this suggested to feudists that justice could not be received within the system. Then, as one mountaineer explained, "Our only retaliation . . . is the muzzle of our guns; when all else fails us we at least have that left us." Such attitudes created a form of family vigilantism and a bloody chapter in Appalachian history.[10]

One of the most violent, and one of the last, parts of that story was still being written as the new century opened. On the North Fork of the Kentucky River in Breathitt County, feuds had been occurring for decades. As in most cases, leading citizens were involved, and a county judge had been assassinated. Now, after a brief lull, the "war" began again with James Hargis leading one group, James B. Marcum the other. Hargis, a wealthy, contentious, and physically strong man, had numerous coal, timber, and business interests. He and his brother had ties to the Democratic state administration, and he himself had been elected county judge. Marcum, on the other hand, had ties with Republicans and had been appointed a trustee at the state university. A talented lawyer, he did not shrink from struggle either.[11]

The feud origins went back years, but the assassination of Marcum's uncle in the 1890s had left harsh feelings. Then, in an election, questions arose over the results, and Judge Hargis and sheriff-elect Ed Callahan were questioned by attorney Marcum. When depositions were being taken, an angry Callahan cursed Marcum; Marcum accused him of murdering his uncle, but nothing further occurred. In February 1902, however, Hargis's youngest brother, Ben, met Marcum ally Tom Cockrill in a saloon fight which left both men wounded. Ben Hargis never recovered. With the aid of Marcum and young doctor B.D. Cox, Cockrill's trial was moved to another county, and he was found not guilty. Another contributing incident years before involved another Hargis brother. John ("Tige") Hargis had made an enemy of Jerry Cardwell in matters concerning Cardwell's sister. The two men fought on a train and Tige Hargis had been killed. Cardwell, convicted of the murder, had been pardoned by the Republican governor.[12]

Vengeance now came. Dr. Cox, who had helped Tom Cockrill go free, by this time had also married into the Cardwell family. To Judge Hargis, then, Cox had ties to both shootings of his brothers. In April 1902, as County Judge Hargis and Sheriff Callahan watched, Dr. Cox was shot and killed. His grief-stricken wife died soon thereafter. Then three months later, town marshal James Cockrill, brother of the man who had killed Ben Hargis, was fatally shot from the courthouse. That night the building in which Ben Hargis had been shot was burned to the ground. Cockrill died the next day. Three men, including Curtis Jett (a kinsman of Judge Hargis and a deputy jailer under Callahan), had been the assassins of Cockrill. But no action was then taken.[13]

A reign of terror commenced. In the years 1902 and 1903, "the waters of the North Fork ran red with blood." Estimates of the number killed in Breathitt County ranged from twenty-seven to thirty-eight.[14] Cockrill allies fled the townof Jackson, and the streets of the once-prosperous city on the railroad were deserted. Marcum remained, but seldom ventured into public without a young child in his arms, knowing that even his enemies would not risk killing a baby. Then, in May 1903, not far from where Cockrill had fallen, an unescorted Marcum was shot once in the back, then, at close range, a second time in the head. Tom White, who had recently been pardoned and freed from prison by the governor at the behest of Judge Hargis, and Curtis Jett were those immediately responsible for the ambush; Hargis and Callahan, once more, watched. Marcum's niece gathered in a newspaper her uncle's brains, scattered by the gunshot blast. Marcum's young wife, her dark eyes showing "ineffable sorrow," tried to console her five children.[15]

Belatedly, the governor sent in troops, and eventually trials took place. The first Marcum murder trial, presided over by Hargis ally Judge D. B. Redwine, ended in a hung jury. A second attempt, after a change of venue, brought a guilty verdict and a life sentence for Jett and White in August 1903. A month later, Jett was also found guilty of the Cockrill murder. He served some fifteen years in jail, was paroled, then pardoned, and became a minister in Harlan County. Sheriff Ed Callahan, who had years before killed a Deaton and had not been convicted, went into seclusion, fearing revenge from either Deaton, Marcum, or Cockrill relatives. In April 1904, a nephew of Marcum's was killed by a cousin of Callahan's. The next month, a witness at one of the trials was shot from ambush on Troublesome Creek. Callahan barricaded his home and store, stayed armed, and avoided open areas. But on the anniversary of Marcum's death, Callahan answered a phone call and stood near a store window. He was shot and killed. A Deaton was among the convicted, who were later pardoned.[16]

Retribution came to Judge Hargis in even more horrible form. Found not guilty in a May 1907 criminal trial, he did lose a civil suit instituted by Mrs. Marcum but seemed to have survived the feud. Then, in February 1908, the forty-three-year-old Hargis was shot five times by his only son. The twenty-year-old "Beach" Hargis had been knocked down and beaten by his father days earlier and, harboring that resentment, he had gotten drunk, had taken the judge's pistol, and had emptied it into his father's body. On receiving news of the tragedy, Hargis's daughter, then on her honeymoon, broke down and sat with a "listless, dazed, . . . vacant stare." The widow undertook a strong defense of her son and engaged, among others, a former governor as counsel. "Beach" tried suicide through an overdose of morphine but failed. After a hung jury initially, he was found guilty, unsuccessfully tried suicide once more, and then served eight years in jail, until paroled in 1916. He violated his parole, joined the Canadian Army in World War I, and, then, in the words of one who knew him, "disappeared."[17]

"Bloody" Breathitt's and Kentucky's problems did not vanish so easily, however. The Washington *Post* in 1903 had proclaimed that the unfortunate county had received more unfavorable attention in the last months "than any other section of the world." And a local newspaper letter-writer in 1909 reacted to

Kentucky Historical Society

This peaceful scene at the Forks of Long's Creek, Breathitt County, ca. 1920, belies the violence which took place a few years earlier. The Crockettsville post office and store *(second from left)* **was the scene of Ed Callahan's death.**

the statement that the mountain people "see God in the clouds," saying, "If they see God in the clouds above 'Bloody Breathitt' . . . they've got to do it with one eye while the other is kept busy watching for a shot from the bush." A singer remarked of another county's violence that it was "the worst I ever seen for guns. . . . I can see how to walk by the light of pistols." Such attitudes about feuds, according to a 1927 Louisville *Courier-Journal* story, "did more than anything else to give Kentucky a bad name and retard its material development." With the death of Callahan in 1912, feud violence had virtually ended. Its memories, and its effects, however, lived on.[18]

Night Riders

The assassination of Goebel in 1900 had been followed by the sensational Breathitt County feud accounts, starting in 1902. No pause in violence or the nation's awareness of it followed, for soon another "war," in the tobacco-growing areas of Kentucky and Tennessee, once more focused attention on the

Bluegrass State.

Across west Kentucky a massive movement embraced much of the populace as they sought to defeat an economic monopoly. Thousands upon thousands gathered and cheered at huge parades; large numbers pledged their support. But when not all joined in, masked bands began destroying the property of their enemies. Troops were sent, trials took place, and acquittals followed. All that was the Black Patch War, named for the region growing "dark" tobacco, in contrast to the new, lighter burley grown elsewhere. Greater than the feuds, this "war" included extensive parts of the population and, much more so than the family vendettas, it represented an angry society's attempt to strike back at outside forces.

The immediate impetus was economic. Tobacco farming was — and is — difficult. A labor intensive crop, tobacco was sown in seed beds in cold weather, re-sown by hand later, and then had to be plowed and hoed fairly often. Buds had to be nipped to control flowering (topping) and secondary shoots had to be removed (suckering). Each plant had to be examined individually and any worms pulled off by hand. Days of often blistering work in dusty fields were followed by cutting the tobacco — with knives — then hanging the heavy leaves in a hot barn. Finally came the wait to see what price the crop, in its hogshead barrels, would bring. Would it be a profitable season? Would it bring enough to "get by" for one more year? Or would it all be a loss?[19]

At the beginning of the twentieth century, one estimate indicated that farmers needed a price of six cents per pound of tobacco just to recover their costs for the season. Prices in much of the late nineteenth century had been over ten cents a pound, and many farmers had abandoned other crops for the profits of tobacco. But from 1900 to 1902 the price was only six cents a pound overall, and often less than that in the dark-tobacco areas of the Black Patch. Others calculated that it cost forty-two dollars an acre to raise tobacco, while returns were only averaging twenty-eight dollars an acre in that period. By whatever standard, Kentucky farmers were not prospering.[20]

Debt-ridden small farmers, with little hope given for the future, joined with larger farm producers, who also felt the economic hard-times, and agreed on the enemy — the "tobacco trust." J. B. "Buck" Duke's 1890 merger of major companies into the American Tobacco Company resulted in an entity that by 1910 controlled some 86 percent of American cigarette sales and similar shares of the plug, smoking tobacco, and snuff markets. Overseas groups, chiefly the Imperial Tobacco Company of Great Britain and the Italian "Regie," seemed to cooperate with the American Tobacco Company in such a way so as not to challenge each other. Global competition disappeared before the corporations. Farmers had few options other than to sell to a single buyer at the price offered. And when prices fell — the Hopkinsville market averaged only 3.5 cents a pound in 1904 — then producers perceived an obvious villain. In actuality, numerous other factors had contributed to lowered prices, including increased production, a decline in foreign demand, and a higher federal tax which reduced domestic consumption and company profits. But the actions of the so-called "trust" had been a major factor as well, and when federal corrective responses were not forthcoming, angry agrarians chose to take matters into their own callused hands. In their view, it was a question of the monopoly or them.[21]

Farmer revolts were not new to the area or the era. West Kentucky had been a center of dissent, ranging from the Greenback Party of the 1870s to the Grange and Farmers Alliance to the Populist Party of the 1890s. Numerous other groups across America challenged corporations in the early 1900s. Now, in September 1904, at Guthrie, Kentucky, a new organization sought to answer the trust with a monopoly of its own, a farm one. What would be called the Planters' Protective Association (or P.P.A.) was formed as a cooperative, where farmers would "pool" their tobacco and hold it off the market until given a fair price. If they controlled the crop, the trust would have to deal with them, thus raising prices and profits. In 1906, the Kentucky legislature made such pooling legal (an action declared unconstitutional by the U.S. Supreme Court eight years later). Leading the P.P.A. was Felix G. Ewing, a wealthy Tennessee farmer who raised a quarter-million pounds of tobacco and lived in a large white mansion.[22]

In the enthusiasm of the Guthrie meeting, some five thousand signed the Association pledge. Eventually, perhaps thirty thousand joined the P.P.A. In central Kentucky the overlooked Burley Tobacco Society, headed by Clarence LeBus, and other similar organizations elsewhere enlisted sizeable numbers. West Kentucky political leaders, such as influential congressmen (later senators) A. O. Stanley and Ollie James eagerly supported their voters, while many local banks lent money to the P.P.A. to help it give farmers at least a partial advance on their pooled crop. In the first year, some 70 percent of the area's dark tobacco was placed, and when the 1905 crop sold a year later, it garnered seven cents a pound. Success seemed assured.[23]

But not all had entered the ranks. Some farmers did not pool because their immediate money needs so dictated. These so-called "Hillbillies" represented a threat to the cooperative, for the Trust eagerly purchased their tobacco, at high prices, not only to fill allotments but also to lure others away and break the P.P.A. Future uncertainty could not compare to ten-cent-a-pound tobacco now. Debt motivated them as well. While many merchants cooperated with the P.P.A. and extended further credit, not all did. Certain financiers still called for payment of loans and hesitated to provide new ones. Some small farmers also simply did not fully trust the motives of the generally wealthy planters who ran the organization. But to their neighbors in the "pool," those who did not join them were traitors. The presence of these "Hillbillies," the continuing resistance of the "trust," the economic hard times resulting from the waiting — all combined to cause dissatisfaction with the pace of the protest. Out of that came violence; out of that came the Night Riders.[24]

Angry farmers, calling themselves "Possum Hunters," met in Tennessee in 1905 and passed resolutions which expressed the attitude of the extremists. Christian County, Kentucky, farmers repeated those sentiments. Because the tobacco trust, in their eyes, broke the laws, it had no rights worth respecting. Any man aiding it was an accomplice and a criminal, "beyond the pales of honor," subject to prosecution by their group. Warnings had not been enough, and the idea spread throughout the region. The "Silent Brigade" — known more commonly as Night Riders — was formed in 1906. Members joined lodges, took oaths of secrecy, learned passwords, paid dues to assist in any trial expenses, and became part of a military-like force.[25]

At its inception, the Silent Brigade represented a desperate people's attempt to defeat what seemed to them a powerful giant. Hunger and want existed in the Black Patch already, and the future seemed even bleaker — unless they won. And so many good people joined an organization that operated beyond the law. Others remained quiet and tacitly approved. Yet, as with most such groups, the original purpose often became sublimated to other, baser ones, and some forces degenerated into lawless attempts at personal vengeance or moral and racial control. Instead of unifying the region, the Night Riders bitterly divided it.[26]

Initially, the Silent Brigade focused on those individuals, of all classes, who remained outside the pool. These "Hillbillies" would be warned, often with a message tied to a bundle of sticks thrown in front of their house. One such caution read, "If you want to save your back and that little tobacco of yours, you must have it in the Association by Monday night, or you will get hell on your back and your barn burnt." Beatings and barn-burnings combined with "scraping" young plant beds, whippings, and even shootings as methods of intimidation. As one author wrote, "To join the Night Riders was both fire and life insurance."[27]

Important leaders appeared to approve such violence. Demagogic congressman James paraded with known Night Riders and proclaimed that "upon the side of the farmers would be their poverty, their hungry families, their thatched roof, their mortgaged farms, and their wrecked hopes." Representative Stanley, a friend of the leader of the Silent Brigade, would eventually take a more moderate view, but in 1908 he appropriated the Kansan Mary Lease's quote, telling farmers that if the trusts go after corn next, "raise oats, If trusts are found on all cereals, raise h____." In the Bluegrass, where farmers conducted a successful "cut-out" of the entire 1908 crop, congressman J. Campbell Cantrill also suggested that force should be acceptable in such a just cause.[28]

Encouraged by all this and by the inaction of Democratic governor J.C.W. Beckham — who cited constitutional reasons but seemed more concerned with political ones, as he refused to send troops to a region dominated by his party — the Night Riders grew in power and numbers. Most estimates placed the strength of their "army" at ten thousand. In many counties, law enforcement officials either joined as members, sympathized with the Silent Brigade, or feared it. The police judge in Eddyville, the county attorney of Lyon County, and others were physically beaten when they stood opposed. With little legal support, "Hillbillies" had to defend themselves. Homes across the region, on both sides, became arsenals.[29]

Leading the Night Rider army in 1907 was David A. Amoss, a stocky fifty-year-old Caldwell County physician who did not farm. A lay pastor and a man with military school training, "General" Amoss joined with his friend and second-in-command, farmer Guy S. Dunning, to mold the Silent Brigade. These "possum hunters" soon focused on bigger game than individual "Hillbillies."[30]

The last huge Association meeting at Guthrie in September 1906, brought some 25,000 supporters to town, but that surface success masked serious problems within the organization. Time operated against the P.P.A., for the trust was only purchasing part of the pooled crop. And money concerns caused farmers to wonder whether "pooling" was enough. Critics questioned Ewing's leadership. Despair and doubt brought more support to the Night Riders, who were, after all, Association members (though not all members of the P.P.A. were Night Riders). More people argued that rather than trying to force all farmers in, perhaps the best strategy would be to destroy the monopoly's power, and, particularly, its tobacco.[31]

The new targets of this paramilitary vigilante force, the Night Riders, were tobacco company warehouses and factories. It now became almost a war of rural against urban, for towns housed these buildings. At first the efforts were small and limited. In December 1905 a warehouse was burned in Todd County, and, in November of the next year, a warehouse in Lyon County was destroyed. But that was just the start. On the night of 30 November 1906, three hundred men on horseback, in a well-conceived raid, seized virtually the entire town of Princeton in Caldwell County. They cut telephone and telegraph wires, took over the fire department, drove away any guards, then burned two large warehouses containing 400,000 pounds of Trust tobacco. Over the next year more individual violence occurred, and further bloodshed resulted. Then, in December 1907, the Night Riders made their boldest attack. A band of three to five hundred masked and well-drilled men took Hopkinsville. The 2:00 A.M. raid followed the earlier pattern, as all communications were seized, then warehouses were burned. Losses totaled $200,000 and blazes illuminated the whole town. Several other buildings caught fire, various windows were broken, and the newspaper office was partially destroyed. An estimated 175 bullet holes marked the city judge's office. A buyer for the British was beaten and another man shot.[32]

As the confident band left, singing "The Fire Shines Bright on My Old Kentucky Home," the citizens of Hopkinsville began organizing a posse to pursue the raiders. They attacked part of the Night Riders force and, in the exchange of shots that followed, several of the Silent Brigade were wounded and at least two died. Either during the raid or later, "General" Amoss was himself wounded. But the resistance there was not typical, and other raids generally encountered little opposition. In January 1908, Russellville was attacked, two factories were destroyed, and two merchants were wounded. The next month three hundred or more Night Riders took Eddyville, shot some thousand rounds, and whipped as many as a dozen people. Eight blacks were ordered to leave town. That same month Amoss's home county saw masked

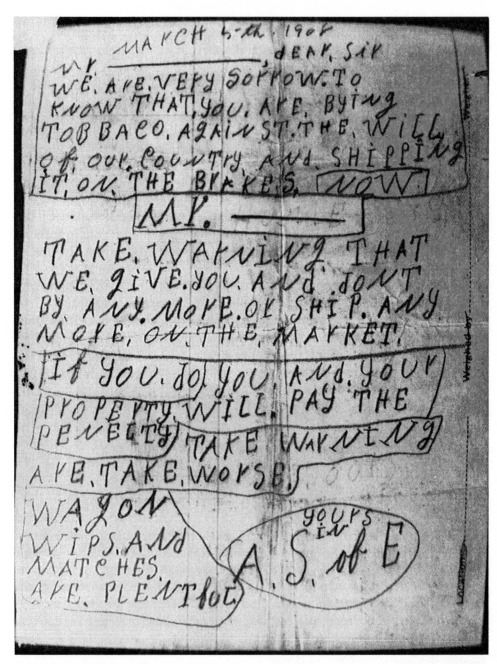

Kentucky Historical Society

Night riders threatened those who bought and shipped tobacco with "wagon w[h]ips and matches."

men destroy a tobacco factory and barn and 45,000 pounds of leaf. In the burley belt, raids in Bath, Owen, Fleming, Woodford, Scott, Kenton, and other counties in 1908 destroyed warehouses and hundreds of thousands of pounds of tobacco there.[33]

At the same time, the movement began taking its ugly turn to racism. Even though one thousand blacks had marched in the first Guthrie parade, and many black farmers supported the Association, Night Riders began to initiate Ku Klux Klan-like tactics designed to remove blacks from various areas. While some violence was directed toward blacks simply because they were "Hillbillies" or because they aided the Trust as workers, most incidents appeared to be more racially motivated. Following a Christian County whipping of a white man whose sin was staying in a black hotel, the Owensboro *Inquirer* praised the Night Riders. In March 1908 a hundred men attacked black houses at Birmingham in Marshall County. When the defenders returned the fire, a raider was wounded; eventually a black man and his granddaughter were killed and six others in the house were wounded. Marshall County witnessed another Night Rider or "Whitecap" attack on five blacks. All were wounded, including a two-year old. Numerous other blacks were whipped. A sign posted in the county seat read, "All Negroes must leave Benton." A steamer took some black families away that year. Overall, between 1900 and 1910, the county's black population fell from 348 to 135. By 1960, no blacks were listed as living in the county. In October 1908, masked men in Fulton County, on the Mississippi River, raided the home of a black man accused of cursing a white woman. When he resisted and killed one of the attackers, they set fire to his house and shot the family as they emerged, one by one, from the burning building. The husband and two children, one of them five years old, died; his wife was severely wounded, as were other children. Outnumbered, with virtually no immediate recourse to legal authorities, blacks from across the region fled to towns or left the state entirely.[34]

The vicious attacks on blacks represented only one sign that the Night Rider movement was in trouble. Their destruction of warehouses drove companies from the area, creating financial shortfalls for banks which, in turn, had to call on farmers for repayment of loans. The Association's board of directors in July 1907 formally repudiated the Night Riders and requested their dissolution. The Silent Brigade had become a threat to a parent who no longer could control it. Hopkinsville set up a Law and Order League of some two hundred men following the raid there, and other towns followed suit. Now two extralegal forces existed.[35]

Soon, a new element entered the fray as well — the Commonwealth of Kentucky. The new governor inaugurated in December 1907 was A. E. Willson, a Louisville Republican who had promised to bring law and order to the state. He was deluged with letters from fearful Kentuckians — "Bracken Co., and Mason Co. are being overrun by outlaws"; "the people of this city [Hopkinsville] are absolutely dominated by fear of invasion"; "we are practically without the protections of law in this county" [Carlisle]. If Willson acted on such complaints, he risked being branded an ally of the trusts (he had been a lawyer on two occasions for the American Tobacco Company). His party would also have to answer Democratic charges that Republicans relied on military force too often.[36]

Willson quickly called out the militia, however, and encouraged groups to set up Law and Order Leagues, saying "All our homes are nothing if the ghost of fear rides over them." In August 1908, the governor created considerable controversy when he stated that pardons would be given to those who killed a Night Rider — and then followed up his words with action. Some Democratic papers approved; others saw his decree as an invitation to more lawlessness. Willson even sent spies into the Black Patch to determine which local officials sided with the Silent Brigade.[37]

The State Guard forces sent in by Willson never numbered more than three hundred and, while helpful, were not a major factor. The courts, once totally impotent in bringing justice to Night Riders, now began to record at least some convictions. Even though Dr. Amoss, after apparently perjuring himself, went free in his trial, as did the murderers of a man who testified against Amoss, a federal court had awarded damages in 1908 to a woman wounded in a Night Rider raid, while a black whipped in a 1908 attack later received a $24,000 judgment.[38]

But the excesses of the Night Riders, and the decline in community support, killed the Silent Brigade more than did the militia and the reappearance of the judicial system. Besides, success, of a temporary and limited sort, made their existence less necessary. Fortunately for the P.P.A., which had suits against it regarding its management, tobacco prices did rise due to its efforts. Moreover, A.O. Stanley received credit for getting an oppressive tobacco tax removed in Washington, while the U.S. Supreme Court in 1911 ruled the tobacco combine to be in violation of the Sherman Anti-trust Law. The enemy seemed beaten. The old P.P.A. lingered on, without much success, a year longer. In the Bluegrass, the Burley Tobacco Society officially died in 1914, and the Night Riders erstwhile leader, David Amoss, supported the Socialist Party briefly before his death in the same year as the Association's.[39]

What, then, was the effect of the entire movement? On the positive side, it showed that Kentuckians could unite, especially on economic issues. But it also demonstrated that such community consensus remained elusive and hard to maintain. More often, the state's citizens helped each other individually rather than collectively.

The tobacco fight also ended, positively, with higher tobacco prices. The per-pound average for 1907 pooled tobacco had risen to 10.5 cents. A new innovation begun in that decade, loose-leaf warehouse sales, also aided farmers. But with good times the cooperative died, while the basic problems facing tobacco growers still remained, only dormant until the next crisis.[40]

As peace seemed to return to the region as well, optimistic observers praised the prosperity brought by higher prices — new fences, available money, abundant crops. But it was a false hope, for the violence had driven many citizens from the state and very likely had convinced others not to come in the first place. The ill-will, the beatings, the threats, the deaths, would not easily be forgotten within Kentucky, nor would violence, once loosened, end over night. And even with its decline, the image remained, as a poet of sorts now added more lines to the Breathitt County saga:

> The hand of Judge Hargis directs the machine,
> And his victims are shot from ambush, unseen.
> From Big Sandy's banks to the Purchase, man's blood
> Flows red as it flowed in the days of the Flood;
> The Farmers at night are shot down at their door,
> And the 'Night Riders' redden our soil with their gore.

As a Paducah paper accurately predicted in 1908, "It will be a long, long time before Kentucky will be able to rise from the ashes of these deeds . . . deeds that will leave a trail of darkness behind them."[41]

Racial Violence

In April 1911 citizens of the small west Kentucky town of Livermore seized Will Porter, a black man accused of a barroom-brawl murder, and placed him on the stage of the local opera house. Some accounts indicate that people were then charged admission to the "event." Most descriptions, however, agree on what happened next. The audience, on signal, began emptying their pistols at Porter. Over fifty shots were fired. As Porter lay dead, the mob finally left. Given national and even international attention — the Paris, France, *Le Petit Journal* ran an illustration of the event — the murder brought an unusual outcry for justice. Surprisingly, eighteen men were indicted by the McLean County grand jury. Not so unusual, all were easily acquitted.

Five years later, in October 1916, a crowd of 5,000 to 10,000 people in Paducah watched a lynching. A mob had broken into the jail, and, even though they took one to five hours (accounts differ) to break into the cell, no one interfered. They had taken a black man accused (but not indicted or tried) of assault and robbery. Another black man, probably trying to stop the mob, was seized as well. A judge sought to halt the group, but to no avail. The two black men were spirited away, hanged before the huge crowd, then shot, and finally burned beyond recognition. Done in broad daylight, with numerous officials present, including the judge, the lynching was carried out by "unknown persons," according to official reports. No grand jury investigated. The Lexington *Herald* noted, "the law itself . . . has been murdered."[42]

Such scenes were repeated in Kentucky throughout the first decades of the twentieth century as they unfortunately had been in earlier years. Injustice based on race and violence directed toward blacks did not disappear with the close of the Black Patch War. Prejudice still replaced justice, passion still overcame reason, and the lynch mob's rope still symbolized the era for Kentucky blacks.

The entire racial climate of the early twentieth century portended few sunny days for African Americans in their Kentucky home. Nationally, segregation was increasing and racial clashes growing. Sectional reconciliation brought with it more acceptance by both North and South of the arguments of southern demagogues. "Scientific" thought often appeared to favor racial discrimination. Historical writings presented an increasingly benign view of slavery. Blacks in America, then, had to fight just to retain current rights, such as they were, rather than seek fairer ones. Often, they had to struggle simply to avoid the hangman's rope.

In his book on racial violence in Kentucky, George C. Wright found evidence that seventy people — sixty-one of them black — were lynched in Kentucky in the twentieth century. Forty-four of those died between 1900 and 1909. And other lynchings remain hidden in obscure sources, if reported at all. In short, mobs killed dozens of blacks in that era. But why? With slavery's end, one race's control over another now could be challenged. Violence had resulted in an attempt to maintain that past dominance. As new generations grew to maturity without much intimate contact with other races, "these men feared each other with the fear of ignorance. They saw each other dimly, at a distance." Resulting actions taken against one individual black were designed to control an entire people. Viewed as a lower, savage race by the white mobs, Negroes, so the argument went, should not expect the same justice meted out to Caucasians. Unspoken were the fears of a white society that only seldom doubted aloud whether they might be wrong or questioned the rightness of segregation. Any action by blacks, even as slight as refusing to step aside and let whites pass, might indicate they did not accept a second-class status. Such threats to the status quo resulted in lynchings. Troubled white consciences erupted into violence.[43]

Lynchings could not occur without substantial community approval, and the resulting mobs often included the "best people." Over one-fourth of the commonwealth's counties — thirty-two — lynched blacks in the twentieth century, and the trail of murder extended across the entire state. Multiple lynchings generally, but not exclusively, occurred in the more southern-like part of Kentucky — in the west Fulton County had ten deaths; Ballard, Todd, Trigg, and Logan Counties had four each. But central Kentucky counties, such as Shelby, with four lynchings, and other locales killed blacks illegally as well.[44]

Most of the time, the mobs justified their actions citing crimes of murder and rape that were allegedly involved. Yet whites committing the same crimes — including rapes of black women — were not similarly punished in large part. The attitude, the pervasiveness of white fears, comes through clearly in the writings of a respected Frankfort attorney in his 1912 book, as he described a Franklin County lynching: "A merited punishment was sternly and speedily administered . . . which ought to be sufficient warning to the negro [sic] race. . . . During the half century which the negro has been free, not one of them has ever been tried in Franklin County by a legally constituted court . . . and doubtless during the next half century not one of them will be tried." Such viewpoints showed little concern, even by members of the legal profession such as he, over whether justice was served. Guilt was assumed if the skin color was not white. And the lynchings went on until the last one in Hazard, Kentucky, in 1934. The blinders of racism shut out compassion and sympathy and concern.[45]

Blacks who escaped the mob often found that the courtroom held little hope for full justice. First of all, the faces in the jury box were all white. Blacks had occasionally served on juries in Kentucky in the latter parts of the nineteenth century, but by 1900 that practice had virtually ended. State courts ruled that commissioners could not discriminate against blacks in jury selection but did not have to select them. As a result, none did. Finally, in 1937, in *Hale* v. *Commonwealth*, the United States Supreme Court, in a unanimous decision, struck down a Kentucky ruling and overturned that practice. Defense attorneys had shown that in Paducah, where at least 8,000 of the 48,000 residents in the county were black, no member of that race had served on a jury in the last thirty years or even longer. The court cited such "systematic and arbitrary exclusion of Negroes" as a denial of rights under the Fourteenth Amendment and ordered a new trial. Discrimination would still occur in jury selection, but it would be less blatant.[46]

More troubling, in many ways, were the uses of the court for the purposes of the mobs. What happened differed little from the hangings by lawless groups; the only change was that the forms of the law were followed. Legal lynchings resulted. In case after case, community leaders would forestall a mob by promising that the intended victim would be dealt with speedily through the court system. Between 1900 and 1934 at least 151 people, 85 of them black, would be legally executed in Kentucky. Of those, many had only a farce of a trial.

In the west Kentucky town of Mayfield in July 1906, a black man accused of rape was returned for a trial and found a scaffold already constructed. He arrived in town at 6:58 P.M. The jury began deliberations twelve minutes later, found him guilty, sentenced him to death, and the judge ordered the sentence to be carried out immediately. By 7:40 P.M. he was hanged and by 8:00 his body was being taken through the streets. The defendant had no recourse for appeal to a higher court or for a plea of clemency from the governor.

The general assembly soon mandated a thirty-day delay between sentencing and execution to allow such legal rights. But that mattered little. In 1909, citizens of the northern Kentucky town of Dry Ridge threatened to lynch a black awaiting trial. The circuit judge called for calm, then promised that the defendant would be found guilty and given the death penalty. At his trial, the teenage boy was, in fact, declared guilty and his court-appointed attorney did not appeal the death sentence. Exactly thirty days later the youngster was executed.[47]

A 1910 law sought to reduce the spectacles of public hangings witnessed by thousands. It required executions by electric chair within the state penitentiary. But racial feelings rang strong, and a decade later the statute was amended to require hanging within the county where the crime was committed, but only for one crime: rape. Since no white man received the death penalty for committing that crime against blacks in that era, the target was obvious. While the first execution under that exception came in 1925, and the well-publicized hanging of Ed Harris took place the next year, the Rainey Bethea hanging in Owensboro in August 1936 focused attention on Kentucky as the last state conducting public hangings. Found guilty in a brief trial, after a four-minute jury deliberation, Bethea was executed amid a carnival atmosphere, with "hanging parties" at homes and street vendors hawking ice cream, popcorn, and drinks to a crowd of twenty thousand. Finally, the next year the legislature abolished hanging and returned all executions to the state penitentiary. Lynchings — legal and otherwise — seemed a thing of the past.[48]

But transgressions against blacks did not always end in death. During the Night Rider era, many blacks fled the state following beatings, burnings, and threats of further violence. Racial antagonism often combined with economic motivation to create such occurrences. In Corbin in eastern Kentucky in 1919, for example, blacks holding well-paying railroad jobs there created resentment among whites. Rumors of stabbing were enough for a crowd which had gathered to hear a political candidate. Becoming an armed mob, they forced an estimated two hundred to three hundred blacks to flee the town. Many were searched, others were attacked; virtually all were forced to leave behind most belongings, were placed on trains, and were told to go to Tennessee. Similar actions, for like reasons, forced blacks from Estill and Bell Counties in the 1920s.[49]

For blacks in Kentucky in that era, the pages of their recent history revealed few causes for optimism. Instead, segregation, injustice, and a violent second-class status seemed the rule. But a few chapters in the story promised some hope. The governors of Kentucky, particularly Republican ones in whose ranks black voters resided, generally spoke out and acted with more force than did most of their fellow whites. An anti-lynching bill emerged during the term of Republican W.O. Bradley and included a provision in which officials could forfeit their office if they did not resist mobs. But in 1902, under Democratic governor Beckham, that section was eliminated. Eighteen years later, with a Republican governor again in office, a similar provision was included in new legislation. Both houses passed the measure without a dissenting vote. When a jailer in a county adjoining the capital did not attempt to halt a mob which lynched a black man in 1921, Governor Ed Morrow acted and removed the official. The same thing occurred the next year, also in a county adjacent to Franklin, and in 1926, with the same results. After the last illegal lynching, in 1934, a Democratic governor took similar actions.[50]

In one particular case, a Kentucky governor personally faced a lynch mob. Democratic governor A.O. Stanley was far from a racial egalitarian — in 1908 he wrote his wife, "I am glad he shot the nigger — he needed it." But in 1917 in Murray in west Kentucky, a mob held the circuit judge and prosecutor as virtual hostages as the crowd sought the return of a black man on trial for murder. Stanley went to Murray, confronted the mob, told them the law must prevail, and they soon dispersed. Later that year, Stanley performed a similar duty and prevented another lynching. Yet, the governor's actions seemed motivated more by his determination to uphold his oath of office than by any

Transylvania University

Guards on the Fayette County court house steps braced against the assembling mob during the Will Lockett trial.

humanitarian reasons. Later, as senator, he would oppose a federal anti-lynching law, for instance. But ironically, he became well known nationally as the southern governor who faced a lynch mob and won.[51]

In other instances, force, not persuasion, turned mobs away. Guards rebuffed a Fleming County lawless group in 1901, and the next year a militia force, complete with Gatling gun, successfully protected a black man held in that same county. In Lincoln County in 1911, armed blacks guarded members of their race held in jail there, while the jailer even gave his prisoners weapons for protection. The expected lynching never materialized. Best known of all the confrontations, however, was the so called "Second Battle of Lexington."[52]

What has been called the first forceful suppression of a lynch mob by local and state officials in the South occurred in Kentucky in 1920. Will Lockett, a black World War I veteran, had been arrested for murder and, without benefit of counsel, had confessed. His trial was scheduled for the morning of 9 February in Lexington. The police force, supplemented by nearly a hundred members of the National Guard sent by Governor Morrow, protected the courthouse. Within, the trial took thirty minutes. Lockett's attorney made no defense, and the jury, in finding Lockett guilty, never left the jury box. Outside stood a mob of several thousand curious onlookers. One report indicated a cameraman urged the crowd to "shake your fists and yell" for the camera; when some obliged, other, more serious members of the crowd began to react angrily and in earnest. The roaring mob broke through a restraining cable and surged forward. The commanding general of the Guard forces signaled for his men to fire and their volley left bodies everywhere. Five members of the mob died of their wounds that day and a sixth died later. An undetermined number — probably as many as fifty — were wounded. Survivors ransacked pawnshops seeking weapons in order to retaliate, but by mid-afternoon a sizeable detachment of veteran U.S. soldiers, with flags flying and bayonets fixed, marched to the courthouse as reinforcements. Martial law was declared and no further violence erupted. A month later, Will Lockett was executed in the penitentiary at Eddyville.[53]

Yet, when the counting was done, the actions of the governors, the anti-lynching laws, the occasional protection from mobs, and the cases where justice did prevail, all paled in comparison to the toll extracted from blacks by lynchings, legal lynchings, beatings, forced removals, and the like. With the state ranking high in violence directed toward blacks, it is little wonder that the state's black population fell so drastically in the early years of the twentieth century.[54]

The Violence of Anger

Deaths connected with elections, moonshining, and general crime continued to fuel the commonwealth's image of violence. Politics, for instance, created ill-will in various feuds, while fights — even shootings — at election time seemed almost commonplace. The bloodiest of those affrays was the so-called "Battle of Clayhole." The voting precinct of that name on Troublesome Creek in "Bloody Breathitt" witnessed a virtual gun battle after a woman's right to vote was challenged there in 1921. When the smoke cleared, twenty-one people were shot, and up to nine died of their wounds. On election day, 1933, seven people died and four more were wounded in conflicts across Kentucky.[55]

Nor were prominent citizens immune. Beside Goebel's assassination and the Marcum murder, in 1900 two leading editors of Richmond, Kentucky, papers met and, after a struggle, one died of bullet wounds. The county judge of a mountain county was assassinated in 1902. In 1937, Henry H. Denhardt, an attorney, former lieutenant governor, and former adjutant general of the state, went on trial for killing his fiancee. After the first trial ended in a hung jury, Denhardt was released on bail pending another court date. But the victim's brothers did not wait; the three Garr brothers confronted Denhardt on Main Street in Shelbyville. Of the seven bullets they fired, three hit Denhardt, all in the back of his body. He fell and was shot in back of the head. His attorney went to the ground and then saw one of the Garrs pointing a gun at him. Another brother yelled, "Oh, hell don't bother with him; he ain't nothing but a lawyer." The Garrs left. Widely supported in the community, they went free. A ballad soon proclaimed:

Kentucky Historical Society

Harry Walker and Will Smith jokingly brandish pistols at Crisco, Carter County, ca. 1908, spoofing the violent image.

> Oh, the harvest moon was shinin'
> On the streets of Shelbyville
> When General Henry Denhardt met his fate
> The Garr boys was a waitin'
> They was out to shoot and kill
> Death and General Denhardt had a date.[56]

Death has made many stops over the years as it rode its pale horse across the state. And the spectre of Kentucky violence cast deep shadows over the commonwealth for years. But was that violent image really deserved? For the first third of the twentieth century, the answer was "Yes."

For any rural people of that era, killing was part of their everyday life. Chickens might be killed for food almost daily, hogs would be slaughtered every winter, and game would be hunted frequently. Knives and weapons were needed in such situations, and people knew how to use them. But the presence of such weapons did not mean they had to be turned against humans. Other regions and other states did not match Kentucky's dubious record. In fact, a subculture of violence existed, one that produced aggressive behavior which found few restraints in a state where a folk system of justice often condoned such violence. Robert Penn Warren remembered that in the Kentucky of his youth, "There was a world of violence that I grew up in. You accepted violence as a component of life. . . . You heard about violence, and you saw terrible fights . . . the violence of anger, what sociologists call status homicide. . . . There was some threat of being trapped into this whether you wanted to or not. . . ." He escaped. Others could not and did not.[57]

Further support for the presence of such a subculture as an explanation of violence comes from studies which suggest that when Kentuckians left the state and settled in other areas — in other cultures — they did not continue their violent ways to the same extent. One group of migrants to an Indiana town from a once-violent south-central Kentucky area appeared remarkably law-abiding in that new locale.[58]

But what about back in Kentucky? Did the statistics support the image of violence which developed over time? First of all, it should be noted that statistics regarding violence, particularly in the early years of the century, are not reliable and must be used carefully. Given that, certain trends still result. From 1900 to 1945, the state's homicide rate placed it consistently in the top ten nationally. A Chicago newspaper's highly questionable 1901 figures indicated Kentucky had the sixth largest number of murders over the previous decade. By 1933, the percentage of convicts in Kentucky's jails for murder and manslaughter (27 percent) was the second highest in the nation; the commonwealth's murder rate that year (14.5 per 100,000 offenses) was eighth highest among the states. At the end of World War II, Kentucky still stood ninth.[59]

But a rather consistent decline in Kentucky's homicide rate and its ranking began in the late 1940s. After having 602 murders in 1933, the state had only 204 in 1955. The commonwealth's homicide rates in 1960 placed it fifteenth nationally; in 1976 it stood eighteenth; in 1983, twenty-third. Using the broader overall crime index, Kentucky also stood very low, ranking forty-fifth among the states in 1976. In short, Kentucky, comparatively, became an increasingly safe place to live as the century progressed.[60]

However, the image of violence that became so clear in the early part of the twentieth century long haunted Kentucky. The lawless activities slowed growth greatly and made prosperity difficult to achieve. A Philadelphia paper noted in 1911, "Kentucky is not growing in population, because all her good men are killed or get out early." The next year a history of the state noted that, contrary to many, "The Kentuckian does not go about with . . . a revolver in his belt, breathing forth threatenings and slaughter." Still, as humorist Irvin S. Cobb wrote in 1924, the image remained. The state seal, he pointed out, had two men grasping each other by the right hand. "The intent of the picture," he solemnly intoned, "is plain. So long as they hold hands, neither can reach for his hardware."[61]

Cobb was not alone in invoking Kentucky's seal to satirize the Commonwealth's violent image. This adaptation, labeled "Seal of Kentucky--Revised," appeared after the Goebel assassination, in the February 1, 1900, Minneapolis *Journal*.

A parade of fashionable Kentuckians includes a turn-of-the-century "tacky party" mocking nineteenth-century garb at Wickliffe, Ballard County; "the smart set" in Laurel County, ca. 1912; 1920s women from the Louisville area; and a General Shoe Company model in Frankfort, 1940.

3

"All Happy and Bright": Life in Kentucky

The Home

Waking in a feather bed, filled with goose feathers, provided a warm and cozy reason to stay there — Alben Barkley considered it "the only thing fit to sleep on." But even for those sleeping on a mattress filled with corn shucks and supported by ropes, the promise of a cold, perhaps even unheated, house made the warmth of their bed even more attractive. One central Kentucky man remembered that in his youth the stone house in which his family lived had no heat for the two rooms upstairs. At night, "Claude and I would prepare for bed downstairs by the fire, run up, and jump in bed." The race was reversed in the morning. In other counties, memories were similar, and a Boone County person recalled only two warm spots in his house — by the kitchen and living room stoves. Yet, numerous variations occurred. Journalist Arthur Krock grew up in a middle-class home in Glasgow that featured a fireplace in every room. But even then, fires would die out and someone — often a small child — would have to get up in the cold and re-start them. Many poorer families, unable to afford the luxury of matches, had to keep a fire going all the time. If not, they had to do as Barkley recalled doing as a child: he ran over to a neighbor's house, some distance away, and brought back smoldering coals to rekindle the fire. While some compelling reasons existed for leaving the beds — a mountain resident recalled that "Everyone got fleas but there wasn't any way to get rid of fleas. You just scratched. Everyone got bed bugs . . ." — still the cold that was awaiting caused pause.[1]

Some of the homes had no windows, or only shuttered ones without glass, which, when open, could let in not only light but insects in the summer or rain and cold in the winter. One of the first of the realistic novelists of twentieth-century Kentucky, Elizabeth Madox Roberts, tells of the people of these homes — a people of limited geography, of lives of wandering. When her heroine moves at last into a snug house, Roberts writes that she "had never before known this detachment from the immediacy of the weather." On the other hand, different homes, occupied by people at the other end of the economic spectrum, would be well-lit with gas or, later, electricity and would, by the 1930s, perhaps even have a rare home air-conditioning unit. From the stereotypical homes of Appalachia to the glamour houses of St. James Court, a wide gap existed.[2]

But what was typical? While Metcalfe County in south-central Kentucky may not have been the norm for rural Kentucky (which was most of the state), it was not far from that. Those who died and whose estates were inventoried in the first year of the twentieth century left a clear record of their homes and what they contained. And if the story did not involve great wealth, it did show differences in self-sufficiency. The average value of the items inventoried fell under $420, ranging from under one hundred dollars to over twelve hundred dollars. The smallest estate, that of one David Wade, had only a $59 value on all goods, but included most basic items for living. A literate farm laborer who had died at eighty-two, Wade had for his kitchen a few plates, tumblers, pitchers, and bowls, plus a set of knives and forks, tea kettle, molasses jug, muffin pan, and sugar chest. A widower, he owned 2 bedsteads and 3 feather beds, along with 11 quilts (several would be needed for warmth), a dresser, a candleholder, a clock, and 2 mirrors. A bookcase, a Bible, and 16 other books indicated reading limits, while 2 chests, 6 chairs, and 2 kerosene lamps filled the rest of his space. A saw, a posthole digger, a mowing blade, and 2 buckets represented the remaining estate. Over one-third of the $59 value lay in the bedsteads ($3), the feather beds ($12), and the quilts ($6.35).[3]

In some respects, the estate of the wealthiest person to die in Metcalfe County did not vary greatly from that of the poorest. Farmer Charlie C. South, at his death soon after he reached the age of fifty, left behind a wife, eight children, and many items similar to Wade's — 4 beds, 2 dressers, a mirror, a table, knives and forks, chairs, and the like. The difference in the two homes was obvious, however; South's family had a sewing machine, a washing machine, a churn, a stove, a cupboard — all absent in the poorer estate. But the greatest change came outside, where South owned a mule, a mare, 2 cows, 47 hogs, a wagon, and a surrey — valued together at over $240, four times that of Wade's entire estate. Moreover, while Wade left behind only a bushel of salt worth $.25 among significant perishables, South had stored 1,500 pounds of millet, 35 barrels of corn (worth $105), 100 pounds of bacon, and 64 pounds of lard. At one level, the differences between the two estates may have only seemed a matter of degree, but to Wade that likely appeared to be a significant inequality, even in his agrarian society.[4]

No matter what the divergence in income or standard of living in the rural areas — where four of every five Kentuckians lived in 1910 — certain patterns of living prevailed. Waking in the morning, a youngster would dress quickly and leave the house for an outdoor privy. (A Russellville resident recollected "very few bathrooms of any kind" in that town, and even a Louisvillian recalled that no one around them had indoor facilities in the early 1900s.) Returning, the youth might wash outside, or on a porch near a well, and would likely use homemade soap, made from lye prepared from "cracklings" and wood ashes. A young family member would then prepare to enter a world built on community networks, kinship ties, and self-sufficiency.[5]

Harriette Arnow remembered small-town Burnside of her youth as a place where "everybody knew where everybody lived and where the stores and businesses were." Neighbors would help each other by jointly burning bushes and clearing land, by stringing beans and peeling apples, by killing hogs and baling hay. As a worker recalled, "In those days you could depend on your neighbors. . . . Why, you had to: There wasn't anyone else you could depend on." And the toil in the fields often mixed with social gatherings, so the differences were not clear. Later generations made those distinctions between work and play much more explicit. In the early twentieth century, though, such community work ties, reinforced by social contacts, produced what was often a supportive atmosphere, a trusting place, a place of unlocked doors and helping hands. But such intimacy could also produce conflict which, in such a closed setting, might be reinforced daily. Almost every personal action, positive or negative, would be known in that atmosphere. The good and the bad both lived in rural and small-town Kentucky.[6]

More than community, however, the family represented the basic focus of both home and work. While at one level, it was simply a labor force which would support effort either in the fields or in the business arena, it also provided a different kind of comfort. Robert Penn Warren related how "the burden of genealogy lay lightly over the summer gatherings at the farm . . . but it was there that I sensed the meaning of family." That could be a tangible meaning, as was the case in a Perry County circuit court in 1912. In *Jent* v. *Combs* (Jent's mother was a Combs), the judge, the two attorneys, the sheriff, and the stenographer all either had a Combs as mother or were related to Combses. Most of the jury were named Combs; all the witnesses were. Kinship connections could prove useful — or complicating. But more important, in one sense, was the psychological comfort these close ties could provide. In emotionally or financially difficult times, families could expect support from these kinship connections. It was not always there, of course, and it was not always sought. But people placed great importance on those ties, and the record of numerous visits among relatives shows that. Those family memories remained even after death, for the Louisville *Courier-Journal* and other papers ran an "In memory" column where children acknowledged their debt and love to deceased parents. A 1903 column, for instance, had items for fathers and mothers dead from one to six years. As in the past, family remained an important part of the makeup of Kentuckians.[7]

Many of those families lived in an almost self-sufficient world. Across the state, for example, numerous people still sheared sheep, washed the wool, painfully got the burrs out, then either spun it into thread on a spinning wheel, or sent it to a mill somewhere and had it done. Blankets or cloth might be made from that, or even knit stockings, dyed with berry juice. Other wearing apparel was made at home as well.[8]

Increasingly, however, clothes came from stores. For young boys their early apparel differed greatly from that of adults: From a poor family, Barkley wore short pants until he was twelve, while the son of a Bowling Green College teacher remembered his youthful dress as "a freshly washed and starched white sailor suit with short pants, low red, white, and blue socks to match the stripes on the collar of the middy-blouse, and a new pair of black patent-leather shoes. I still had bobbed hair with bangs cut straight across the forehead."[9]

Adult males wearing wide-brimmed straw hats (sometimes called buckeyes) or, if wealthier, Derby hats or Panama hats would also be outfitted in 1900 in a dark wool suit (no difference existing in winter or summer outfits), a starched, detachable collar and cuffs, and heavy socks. Sunday dress included a vest, perhaps with a watch fob in the pocket. Low-cut shoes, at first used only in summer, had begun to replace those with tops. But for most Kentucky men, their daily dress differed greatly. Boys would be barefoot in the summer, except for "high days and holidays," while older males wore brogans or leather boots; jeans or denim, rough shirts, and no underwear in summer (or flannels in winter) represented more typical daily work-clothes patterns.[10]

Attention on women's fashions tended to focus on middle- and upper-class dress. At the top of the body, hair styles traversed almost the whole gamut from 1900 to 1930. High, elaborate styles at the beginning of the century gave way to more modest forms, then the highly controversial "bobbed" hair of the 1920s. One female student recounted that "About the worst thing any of my friends did was to cut their hair, for which you got expelled. . . ." Short hair brought forth denouncements from the pulpit and in print, but, in modified form, remained. Since fashionable clothes at the turn of the century still included numerous petticoats, tight-laced corsets, tight-sleeved, high-necked blouses, and bell-shaped skirts dragging the ground, it was little wonder that a Lexington belle complained of "very dirty" dress trains.[11]

That situation was one factor that brought about a change in the length of skirts, something that was upsetting for many Kentuckians. A man described the time he grew to maturity as one when "women were legless. . . . If they had them they never mentioned them and never exhibited them." Another observer recalled a farmer's wife "who liked to cross her limbs while driving to and from town in her runabout. . . . This practice provoked severe comments from the more demure dames of the neighborhood." Yet the hemlines went up, first a few inches in the so-called "rainy days skirts," then by 1920 to the knees and above. Silk stockings increasingly replaced those made of cotton. But, for most Kentucky women, the usual dress might be something made by them from purchased cloth, or a simple, functional outfit such as the so-called "'Mother Hubbard', which . . . covered everything but touched nothing." Like life itself, the variety of clothes marked the differences — economic and otherwise — among Kentuckians.[12]

Once youngsters got dressed in the morning, whether in homemade, mail-order, or "storebought" clothes, they then moved to one of the busiest places in the house — the kitchen. While dress styles changed over the years, so too did the amount of clothes that were made by hand; in the area of food, a similar shift took place as Kentuckians became generally less self-sufficient over the years. But, at the same time, diets — unlike dress styles — did not change a great deal.

Food preparation methods varied with the economic spectrum, ranging from cooking over an open fireplace to simple stoves to more elaborate ones. Similarly, the percentage of food purchased increased, as a rule, with family income. Self-sufficiency came, after all, at a high price — long hours of work, hard labor in the fields, times of uncertainty, and much else. Economic security allowed people to move away from that toil — but at the price of dependence on others. Still, many Kentucky homes gave the appearance of miniature villages, with henhouses, fruit cellars, smokehouses, cribs, and barns scattered around. Chickens furnished meat and eggs; cows, milk and butter; sheep, wool for clothes; and hogs, meat. Hog-killing in particular became important. Taking place in cold weather after the first hard freeze, the event brought neighbors together and the end-product was shared communally — often some of it at that killing time. As one boy noted, "Unless you have tasted sausage made on the farm, you have never tasted sausage." The remaining pork would be taken to a dirty smokehouse "to take the salt," then the hams, bacons, and home-ground sausages might be placed in corn shucks or cloth bags and cured by hickory smoke (to prevent invasion by worms). Later, chemicals replaced the smoking process. Gardens yielded vegetables which would be used various ways: sweet potatoes and cabbage were "holed in" by putting them in a straw, or board-lined, hole in the ground, or were kept in a cool cellar. Later the cabbage could be ground into sauerkraut. Green beans, peppers, and other vegetables could be dried and eaten later; tomatoes, beets, blackberries, and other items could be placed in jars, covered in fat, then sealed and stored in cellars. Fortunate families with orchards could supplement their diet with fruit — apples, for instance, could be eaten raw, fried with meals, made into apple butter, or dried.[13]

Not everyone, of course, had access to such. For some, scattered game from the forest or fish from streams might be the main meat available. The result was an array of descriptions of what people ate. Some poorer rural families tended to have coffee with every meal, with molasses as a sweetener for the food. Salt bacon and other meat, "swimming in grease," appeared frequently, with cornbread or biscuits. Beans, apples, potatoes, and wild greens might supplement the meals at various times. Other families provided more variety. One mountain boy arose to the smell of coffee being ground, then went to a breakfast of hot biscuits, gravy, sausage, fried apples, strawberry and peach preserves, homemade butter, and "good creamy buttermilk." Urban meals would not surpass that. Across Kentucky, many people ate well, both in city and country; some did not. One mountain woman remembered, "I have been hungry many times for more nourishing food." Another was asked if she ever went hungry in the 1920s. "Yes, many a time . . . ," she answered. "Some mornings we had just enough meal in the house to make one hoecake. . . . And we had to divide that ten ways."[14]

Even the most self-sufficient family usually had to make periodic purchases of other foodstuffs. One Leslie County man recalled that most people in his mountain community made an annual trip by wagon to another county to sell chickens or other goods and, in turn, buy flour, sugar, and salt for the rest of the year. As an eleven-year-old, another Highlander would get in a wagon and alone make an all-day trip to the county seat to purchase similar supplies. Western Kentuckian Barkley told of going to town twice a year, to sell crops, pay off debts, and then buy new staples for the next months. As the century wore on, such trips became shorter, the frequency greater, and the purchases larger.[15]

Liquid nourishment took many forms. Drinking directly from streams or larger bodies of water occurred frequently, even in urban areas, and, for a time, river water was sent, without filtering, directly to homes or to open pumps on street corners. Both there and in wells, communal dippers added to the chance of disease. Many homes had a system that caught and stored rain water in barrels or cisterns, while others had deep wells. Supplementing water were alcoholic beverages, legal and illegal. In cities, beer was often delivered directly to homes, while moonshine found its way to many rural tables. A widespread alternative was milk, often from the person's own farm, but also purchased from daily deliveries. Unpasteurized, but usually boiled before being drunk, the milk was often kept cool by placing it in a container in a spring, in a "well house" or cellar, or in an icebox, if available. Before electricity, ice plants made daily deliveries for those iceboxes. People would place cards in their windows indicating the number of pounds of ice desired for that day (usually ranging from ten to a hundred pounds). Doors would be left un-locked, the iceman would bring his product to the kitchen, and then leave. That routine would be repeated day after day. But for many areas of the state no such luxury as daily ice deliveries existed; not until electricity made its way to those isolated areas (usually after World War II) did they have anything other than primitive refrigeration.[16]

Those delivering milk or ice were not the only merchants or vendors call-ing on homes, even some of the most isolated ones. Salesmen, with literally a pack on their back, would go door-to-door in rural areas selling women's cloth-ing, or curtains, or assorted goods. In more urban locales, homes might be visited by those delivering groceries or by street vendors offering vinegar, or fresh vegetables (not usually stocked in stores), or umbrellas, or scissor sharp-ening, or tin pan repairs, or much more. At a time when women would be spending time washing clothes by hand, ironing them with irons heated on stoves, placing them to dry in air often filled with soot from fireplaces; at a time when housewives might be hoeing a garden when they were not cooking over a hot fire; at a time when men still worked from daylight to dusk in good weather, if on farms, or at least ten hours a day, six days a week, if in the city, such street diversions were welcome.[17]

In rural Kentucky, there were only a few other interruptions to the daily routine, as a rule, and most of those even centered on work. Such labor-oriented social events as logrolling and houseraising, bean stringing and hull-ing, corn husking, and quilting all accomplished tasks while providing welcome opportunity to be with other families and friends. While such activities were in decline by the 1930s, many lingered on for decades more.[18]

But, in the end, life still focused, day in and day out, on the home. There, at the end of a day in the fields, or after finishing the last meal in the evening, parents and children gathered to enjoy whatever simple pleasures their existence afforded them. For the literate, reading was a favorite entertainment, at all social levels, and in urban and rural homes alike. In agrarian Kentucky, rural free mail delivery was a reality by the first decade of the twentieth century, and that brought newspapers and journals more readily to isolated areas. For some, such as poet Cale Young Rice, the choices were more limited, since the only book in his house when he was growing up was the Bible. But for others, parents might take turns reading aloud to children a whole variety of things, from children's books, to poetry, to adult works, as they got older. While English and French authors still had great appeal, American writers and American journals were increasingly popular.[19]

The practice of the family reading together began to decline with the advent of electricity and what it brought — the radio. At first that was not the case, for the electric lights saved many eyes accustomed to reading by dim lamps. The timing of electricity's arrival varied. Most rural county-seat towns had electric lights between 1890 and 1910, but some places remained isolated much longer. (Hyden received the first system in its county as late as 1934.) Rural areas remained in the dark much longer all across Kentucky. But for those places that had access to electricity, and for those homes that used huge batteries to furnish power, the change was drastic. As one Ohio County woman declared, "Electricity . . . just changed everything." The recollections of others all sound the same theme: "You put away those kerosene lamps. You put away a lot of labor. You had to fill the lamp at least once a week, and you had to clean those glass chimneys. . . . [Now] we had the light we could read by. . . ." "I remember when we turned those lights on. . . . You just couldn't believe it was the same place. We thought we were living in New York! It was something we never dreamed of."[20]

Electricity, among other things, brought the radio and its effect on home life for Kentuckians. They put aside books to listen to the new invention. In fact, a Kentuckian had played an early role in the development of that medium, for Nathan B. Stubblefield of Murray had been a pioneer in wireless telephony as early as 1892. Public demonstrations had been made a decade later; patents were secured in 1907. A personally distrustful and depressed man, Stubblefield received little acclaim and no wealth, dying of starvation, in obscurity.[21]

Ironically, the state partially responsible for radio was among the last seven in the nation to have a commercial station. That was remedied at 7:30 P.M. on 18 July 1922 when WHAS radio in Louisville went on the air. WLAP in Lexington, WPAD in Paducah, and WFIW in Hopkinsville followed within the next eight years. But for five decades, WHAS, owned by the Bingham family, functioned as the state's chief radio station. Its "clear-channel" power, its

Kentucky Historical Society

A group is entertained at the Pine Ridge radio listening center in the Alvan Drew School, Wolfe County.

University of Kentucky connection, and its state-based programming gave it that status. Additionally, even though Kentucky led the South in 1930 in radio ownership — with 18 percent of families possessing one — it lagged far behind the nation. Elliott County had only eight radios, and across the state, only 7 percent of farm families owned them. WHAS and the University cooperatively set up forty listening centers, starting in 1933, to try to bring the new innovation to more people. These radios, powered by battery and placed in stores and community centers, met the need until electricity and prosperity brought the radio to almost all homes. By 1946, nineteen radio stations operated in Kentucky; by 1957 over a hundred did. For three decades — the 1920s through the 1940s — it ruled supreme.[22]

The radio, like books, could allow people to live vicariously, to imagine other parts of the world, to be free of their daily existence, if just for the moment. But the reality of life made for a contrasting existence. Youngsters learned quickly about life and death. Farm animals openly procreated around them, while among their own species, many aspects of reproduction could not be easily hidden. For the family who all slept in one room, or perhaps two, little privacy existed, either for husbands and wives, or children. In public, babies were often breast-fed openly, while newspaper advertisements explained (for those who could read) more of life's facts. In notices across Kentucky, products promised cures for venereal diseases and other problems while others, such as "Gerstle's Female Panacea" or "Wine of Cardui," told how the medication established a "painless natural menstrual flow."[23]

Death and violence remained very real to Kentucky youngsters as well. On farms, chickens might be killed by wringing their necks, and hogs might be slaughtered annually (by shooting or by axing) then their throats slit and the blood drained out. Yet among some classes, little of this was known. They lived a sheltered life, where women and men dressed in such style that, for a time, a glimpse of a female ankle was almost scandalous. Nature's realities seldom reached them except scientifically. Ironically, that same class, in "the roaring twenties," would move far away from that past and much closer to the openness more characteristic of others. As Mark Sullivan wrote of the twenties: "What had once been shocking, such as talk about sex, was now accepted; what had been taboo, such as smoking for women, was now general; what had been authoritative, such as permanence of marriage, was now ignored or questioned; . . . what had been universal custom, such as grace at meals and family prayers, was now rare; what had been concealed, such as women's legs, was now visible." Those words applied more to urban America than rural Kentucky, but the changes, in subtler form, and the knowledge of larger change elsewhere caused trauma, nevertheless, across the state.

Still, even those on farms, or in small towns, remained sheltered in many ways as well. A central Kentuckian wrote, "We grew up as though wrapped in cellophane — hermetically sealed against contact with the world that surrounded us." Knowledgeable about some parts of life, such people also lived an isolated existence that left them ignorant about many other things. A Muhlenberg County woman told of "my summer of first things," as she rode a train for the first time and arrived as a young high school graduate in Lexington in 1902: "I experienced in the next six weeks, the first brick paved streets I ever saw, first electric lights, first gas lights, first bath rooms and toilet, first boarding house, first concrete walks, first street car, first florist shop, first movies, first Chautauqua, . . . first pipe organ, first tunnel, first X-ray machine, first love." For others never making that trip, they knew what was around them, what was near, but the larger world remained as far away as a distant universe.[24]

It is easy to portray the strengths of those first decades of the twentieth century — the simpler life, the strong family ties, the community support — and the traits from that time that live on. Stories of people sitting around a fireplace eating popcorn and sorghum cakes, drinking sugar water, and pulling taffy, or other accounts of swimming parties at some "Big Rock" at a stream or river — these project pictures painted in warm hues. One man remembered his log-cabin youth: "No electric, no telephone, no radio, no television, nothing. . . . We all enjoyed life. . . . There was plenty of walnuts. . . . We would gather around that big coal grate every night and crack walnuts. . . . Our . . . father was a pretty good hand at singing. He would sing a lot of old-timey songs to us." Such memories were of pleasures real and important. Living close to the land, intimately aware of local ridges and rivers, people felt what a later author called "the intense, almost physical bond that ties the Southerner to his place." That sense of interdependence of earth and people combined with a "web of traditions" to give Kentuckians, even in the poorest families, a feeling of dignified independence.[25]

But such a community portrait must not glow with nostalgia, for that world was also one of death, disease, poverty, hard work, and inequality. A former resident of a small place in far-west Kentucky recalled it as "an ingrown and unexpansive town where an unambitious and leisured close existence had bred ... its factions, its gossip, its scandal," and where family divisions still centered on "the War" or on "people marrying out" of their class. Another writer, after remembering his small-town Kentucky youth, dealt with the dangers of thinking back. His critics, he wrote,

> say the ole swimming hole was really only a mud hole, the houses we lived in were only shacks, ... the well-to-do families were not charitable, the businessmen made dishonest profits, the railroads charged excessive rates and paid lowly wages, the schoolhouse was a firetrap, ... the food serving places were not sanitary, the bootleggers sold poison whiskey, the river and creek were being polluted by sewage. ... The blacks were mistreated and exploited, ... and the churches were not really interested in the poor-poor. Perhaps. ... But, this does not change my love for the town of my childhood.

Even as he pointed out the hypocrisy of that place — where farmers sold corn to the distillery but shouted for prohibition, or ministers preached of brotherhood but supported racial segregation — he still could not forget the strengths of his hometown. His recognition of both the positive and the negative in his past is unusual. But out of such places, scattered across Kentucky, and out of backgrounds with similar strengths and weaknesses grew to maturity the Kentuckians of the twentieth century.[26]

Social Life Outside the Home

For many Kentuckians, days passed in a long succession of routine work. But for all, varieties existed that provided pleasant interruptions in such daily toil. Probably the most typical break came on Sunday, when people flocked to what might be the only unifying social institution in their locale — the church. Physically, the building was the community center, where school exhibitions, political oratory, temperance lectures, weddings, and funerals all took place. The regular — or in some isolated places, irregular — services brought people together in what were not only spiritual but also social gatherings. It is easy to forget, however, that religion played an enormously important role in the lives of Kentuckians of all races and both sexes. Even a cursory reading of diaries and letters shows that the lives, actions, and thoughts of a large number of the commonwealth's citizens revolved around the teachings of the Bible and their local minister. One man remembered indelibly the preachers of his youth in an Appalachian county: "They'd have voices just like a lion. You could hear

Kentucky Historical Society

Robert Burns Stone of the Faith Mission Band noted that Brother James Walters baptized "Old Regular Baptists" at Flax Patch, Knott County. It was necessary to break the ice for this wintertime baptism.

their voices ringing against them mountains, just like a freight train hollering." The educated and uneducated, the liberal and conservative, the strong speakers and the weak — all characterized the ministry across the state. But no matter how presented or how worded, the message given was heard by thousands each Sunday, as they sought solace.[27]

Yet, for some, as important as the spiritual support given was the social opportunity offered. For people isolated by distance, or class, or race, Sunday brought them into regular contact with others — neighbors, friends, relatives, even strangers. Walking to church, riding a mule, or traveling in an often-dirty wagon, people arrived and entered doors that were seldom locked. Family members might hear a minister read songs a verse at a time, while his congregation — many of whom might not be able to read or who did not have scarce songbooks — would then sing out what they had heard. For people without phonographs or, later, radio, this was the only music they might hear. In many churches, the sexes would be segregated, males on one side, females on the other, each with their own entrance. One man remembered a variation to that theme, for his church had a middle row where "courting couples" could sit. There they listened to talks which offered hope for spiritual intervention in daily problems, such as poor health, or for a better life in a divine hereafter. While conservative in theology overall, many churches did encourage and even get involved in Progressive Era movements, seeing those as reforms for God's cause on Earth, bringing nearer the millennium. But disillusionment following the death and destruction of the Great War, and the failure of the crusades to bring anticipated change, brought many to retreat once more into the quiet world of their own church. Social activities such as card-playing, dancing, or the new "movies" rather than the larger social ills around them now brought denunciations. Not until the 1960s would religious bodies again be as socially active as in the century's first decades.[28]

Still, for many, particularly the young, theological discussions took second place to social ones at religious gatherings. Meeting those of the opposite sex, flirting, courting, talking, perhaps visiting the other's home for a meal after church — these were the opportunities Sunday services offered them. Older adults likewise used the time to talk, to enjoy the company of others, to put aside daily toil for a restful interlude. The bell tolling the start of church meant many things to Kentuckians, but for those attending, the institution played a dominating role in their lives, intellectually and socially. That role would be increasingly replaced by others as the century continued.

The one other institution that had a widespread influence on rural Kentuckians was the country store. The building itself seemed to overwhelm people's memories. Reminiscing about a Muhlenberg County store, a writer recalled:

> One of the lasting impressions of visiting Cohen's store . . . came through a person's sense of smell. There was a fragrance which one wasn't apt to forget. It was a mellow aroma of long remembrance. Considering that its make-up consisted of interesting components such as "oil cloth" used for table cloths, "coal oil" which was used on the floor to keep down the dust, twist and plug tobacco that was cut into five and ten cent slices, roots and herbs, hung at random, patent medicines, Wisconsin hop cheese, Grandmas soap, lots of leather harness hanging here and there and perhaps one of the most delicious items in the potpourri, freshly ground coffee beans.
>
> Add to all this the earthy smell of farmers fresh from the plowed fields. . . . The list would not be complete without mention of horehound candy, sauerkraut, poultry feed, gun oil and rubber boots.
>
> In the wintertime this was all laced with a heavy layer of tobacco smoke produced by those who bailed hay, suckered tobacco, and caught real fish around the stove that made the place such a cold weather hangout in the first place.

Similarly, Harriette Arnow remembered "the tobacco smoke and juice, new overalls, bananas, new leather, oranges, freshly cut ham, cheese" of her nearby store, while a central Kentuckian noted the "blend of cigar smoke, dried fruit, cheese, and a hint of kerosene, with the distinct scent of chewing tobacco predominant."[29]

Aided by poor transportation, such stores provided the only realistically close place to buy supplies, many of which were brought by wagon from the nearest railroad or river. There, behind sturdy wooden counters and glass showcases, goods enticed the purchaser with their variety. Hardware sat in

Kentucky Historical Society

"Morley's Tasteless Chill Syrup" is advertised over the entrance to this eastern Kentucky general store, ca. 1902.

the rear of the store; a post office might be there as well. At a time when many goods, such as pickles, flour, or crackers, were not prepackaged, large barrels all around offered various products to shoppers. In addition to their economic value, country stores — like churches — provided a place for socializing. The ever-present pot-bellied stove, often with a cinder-box nearby for tobacco-chewers' use, attracted the populace, almost magnetically. It became a community meeting place, often for men and women of both races. Conversations covered diverse topics, and a young boy recalled learning much about adult life and "the shady side" of his town by listening to such talk. And while rural free delivery and mail-order catalogues, together with better roads and railroads, took people away from the country store, its decline did not mean an end to those learned discussions over the hot stove. Whether at a small-town restaurant or service station, or a large-town donut shop or senior citizen center, comparable conversations would continue throughout the century. A need was being met.[30]

A similar kind of sense of playfulness and, at the same time, continuous camaraderie took place with regularity at court day, which in some places brought more people together in a county than any other gathering. All across Kentucky farmers on the second Monday of the month, or some like time, would drive their wagons to town, hitch the team at the square, and then shop and socialize. Later, automobiles would fill towns as court day came. While wives sampled the somewhat wider variety of stores available at the county seat, husbands might trade horses, knives, or guns, or simply chew tobacco, swap stories, and perhaps sample local liquor. As the century progressed, as the automobile replaced the horse, as farmers began to arrive dressed as well as "city folk," social distinctions lessened, but the folk-gathering aspects remained.[31]

Even larger urban areas kept the court-day tradition. At Lexington's Cheapside, observers saw for sale "worn out stoves, broken-down furniture, plow gear, buggy harness, farming implements, homemade baskets, household utensils, jars of pickles and preserves and molasses by the gallon." People would bring ducks and hens for sale, or garden produce, and as one upperclass Lexingtonian remembered, "Old friends passed the time of day and a good time was had by all." Hundreds, or thousands, of people would crowd the small area around the massive stone courthouse, occasionally spilling over to the some 140 saloons in town. But such a mass of humanity, involved in a rural-oriented pastime, did not fit the image of a progressive urban community, and, in February 1922, court day ended at historic Cheapside. Across Kentucky, it continued — in Laurel County, for instance, it went on until World War II — and aspects of it, such as the day of stockyard sales, live on.[32]

Less widespread than court day, which occurred in virtually every agrarian county, but often wider attended were the chautauquas. Perhaps more middle or upper class in orientation, the chautauquas, nevertheless, attracted large numbers of people interested in community betterment, self-improvement, and good entertainment. In Owensboro, for example, a company organized there in 1901, and opened a park that included a large lagoon, landscaped walks, a bowling alley, a library, a dining hall, cottages, a 12,000-seat auditorium, and other buildings. For a dollar a day for room (or an additional dollar a day for board) families could stay in more permanent dwellings or could rent tents as large as fourteen by sixteen feet in size, for up to six dollars a week. Tickets to the two-week session in 1907, excluding lodging, cost $2.50. People attended classes in the morning, concerts or lectures in the afternoon, then the main program at night. Featured speakers over the years included Henry Watterson on (in a strange choice for him) "Money and Morals" and the quintessential lecturer William Jennings Bryan on "The Value of an Ideal." Such gatherings became not only a place of entertainment and enlightenment, but also social events, where whole families stayed for the run of the show, meeting other families, making further connections. A Paducah chautauqua in 1909 drew some three thousand people and included the ever-present Bryan speaking on "The Prince of Peace" and against Darwinism, plus singers, the Chicago Ladies Orchestra, and various animal acts.[33]

Such semipermanent chautauquas were fading as the century progressed, however. By 1909, for instance, Owensboro's had closed. But traveling tent shows, also called chautauquas, soon filled the void. Sponsored by national companies, such as Redpath out of Chicago, these scaled-down versions of the older forms contained many of the same elements — lecturers, plays, impersonators, dramatic readings, singing, and the like. A Russellville couple remembered those of the 1920s as "really rather literary" and less social-oriented than the earlier, larger ones. But they could not long compete with newer forms of entertainment, as motion pictures brought greater actors and different interests to patrons. The last chautauqua in Richmond, in central Kentucky, came in the Depression year of 1932, the same date as the final one performed in Owensboro. The automobile, radio, theater, and changing tastes ended those summer visits. The century that witnessed the birth of dramatic forms of entertainment and education also saw the death of worthy older ones, caused, in part, by those same new forces.[34]

People in small towns across Kentucky had access to various strands of entertainment, some of them, like the chautauquas, dying, others being modified, and still more remaining unchanged throughout the era. All along large rivers, for example, showboats offered a kind of traveling show for citizens. Calliopes would herald their impending arrival, and people would yell out, "Showboat's coming!" Evening performances, complete with band, chorus, and actors, would draw large crowds, although as one Maysville woman remembered, "Nice people did not go," due to the burlesque quality of some dances. After a show the group would pack up and move on downriver to another show at another town.[35]

If that represented the passing nineteenth century, another form of entertainment symbolized the new era. While vaudeville with its burlesque and minstrel shows continued in small-town theaters for many more decades, and while what was called "legitimate theater" still played in the almost innumerable opera houses, both were being displaced by the new marvel, the motion picture. By 1896, four motion picture projectors had been set up in Lexington; in the century's first decade, nickelodeons were widespread. By 1910 accessible medium-size places, such as Maysville, Mt. Sterling, and Carlisle, had full-fledged theaters. Traveling motion picture shows filled a void for small towns for a time. In some fourteen isolated mining camps surveyed a decade later, three had "movies" available for miners (complete with segregated balcony for blacks). The three-reeler silent film, with its cheap prices, did not immediately win out over vaudeville, for both coexisted. In 1910, for instance, some theaters in Louisville still focused on the established ways — the Buckingham advertised its "Advanced burlesque" while Macauley's promised minstrels and musicals — while others, such as the Gayety and the Mary Anderson, already concentrated on "movies" for fifteen to fifty cents admission. Not all accepted the changes without complaint, for "A Parent" in Lexington in 1916 criticized the new "immoral pictures" which "support things that you would never think of."[36]

Such critics fought a rear-guard action, for motion pictures advanced rapidly across Kentucky, despite the lack of sound and the use of subtitles, which illiterates could not read. Many of the one-reel films focused on the commonwealth itself, including several versions of *Uncle Tom's Cabin*, early 1904 titles *Kentucky Squire* and *The Moonshiner*, *A Kentucky Feud* (1905), and then in 1908, *The Kentuckian*. As time passed, horses and Appalachia seemed to be the only subjects which interested filmmakers, and popular pictures, such as the racing-oriented *In Old Kentucky*, went through various remakes (1909, 1920, 1927, and as a "talkie" with Will Rogers in 1935). The Appalachian theme appeared early, then was refined in features such as *The Trail of the Lonesome Pine* (1914, 1916, 1923, 1936, with Henry Fonda). The frontier emphasis developed slower with such films ranging from *Daniel Boone* (1907) and *A Frontier Hero* (1910) to John Wayne's 1949 *The Fighting Kentuckian* and Burt Lancaster's 1955 *The Kentuckian*. But in almost all cases, for the larger audience who viewed such motion pictures, the commonwealth usually appeared one dimensional and meant either frontier fighting, mountain feuds, or horse farms. Celluloid Kentucky changed little.[37]

Outside activities, especially in warm weather when theaters were less appealing (until air conditioning), continued to attract. The Fourth of July, once chiefly a black holiday in parts of the South, as well as in a few parts of Kentucky, was by the twentieth century widely celebrated among all races and classes, with picnics, ball games, swimming, band music, and, of course, fireworks. In organized form, it still was more an urban-oriented event, however.[38]

More widespread across all but the most isolated parts of Kentucky were summer carnivals and fairs. The State Fair, established by law in 1902, led the way, and numerous county fairs represented scaled-down versions of that midway and its connected events. The Montgomery County Fair of 1909 typified others of that era, as it had a merry-go-round and ferris wheel, as well as a saddlehorse show, mule and pony races, a pacing derby, and a two-day fox hunt. Soon after 1910 "airships" piloted by "great aviators" made their appearance at such events all across Kentucky. Seeing people fly in those early biplanes literally attacked established concepts and made the possibilities of a positive, limitless future seem even more real. As much as anything, airplanes caused Kentuckians to realize they were moving into a new century, almost a new world.[39]

To some, carnivals represented one aspect of the other side of that order, as they traveled throughout Kentucky as well. Small affairs with games of chance, a few acts, and some scantily clad women, they did not bring much contemporary favorable attention. With drinking and fighting often present, the events also were criticized as "a menace to the community," being mere "traveling bawdy houses." Such comments only suggested the presence of the darker side of Kentucky life, a side seldom spotlighted in public forums or in print. Often the problems were more perceived than real — a Madisonville ordinance outlawed chewing gum machines in 1911. But others were considered more serious, if less discussed. Just a perusal of the Kentucky *Acts* indicates the concerns — a 1910 law fixed a penalty for criminal abortion; a 1914 one prohibited selling cigarettes to youths; a wartime 1918 statute placed stricter controls on "houses of lewdness, assignation, and prostitution"; a 1934 act prohibited the sale of "marihuana, sometimes called 'loco weed' or any derivative of the drug carnibus indica." What some saw as their own brand of recreation, and what others saw as actions dangerous either to the person involved, or to the community, would continue to clash as the decades wore on.[40]

In fact, debates over morality did not suddenly arise in the "Roaring Twenties." Each passing generation seemed to have grave doubts about the morals of its youth. Questions concerning dancing illustrated that perfectly. Certain religious denominations had long frowned on dancing of any sort; the "dance craze" of the first decades of the century caused them positively to grimace in pain. As early as 1901, a Rockcastle County correspondent told a local paper, "there is a hop every night, the boys and girls seem to have devil in their heels, but nothing in their heads." The bunny hop, turkey trot, fox trot, tango, and "hesitation waltz" brought forth further denunciations and some attempts at formal restriction. In 1915, the secretary of the Winchester Purity League cried out against the "dance-mad" youth of her "sin-crazed age," those young people who, instead of reading, were dancing the fox trot and "other twists and squirms." One Louisville student, shocked at what she had seen her teacher do, confided to her diary, "Miss Parker danced the Fox-trot!!" Even in a supposedly objective 1919 study of child welfare in Kentucky, the author's personal feelings came through clearly: "At some of the dances attended by the writer, improper postures and movements were observed. Objectionable up-to-date styles of dancing like the 'shimmy' were in vogue in most [dance] halls." And that was all before the outcry generated by the Charleston, the black bottom, and other dances of the next decade. Such attitudes caused what is now Western Kentucky University to prohibit dancing between the sexes in any form until the late 1920s. Yet, despite the denouncements, the dances continued, particularly in urban areas and, later, in rural "road houses," while older, traditional dance forms, such as the Virginia reel, remained popular in large parts of agrarian Kentucky.[41]

But the debate concerned more than just the form of dance. It also had much to do with control of one generation over another, with rebellion, with changing patterns of life, with new communication channels, including radio and motion pictures, and with tradition. The passage from youth to maturity was being modified even quicker — a condition that would accelerate throughout the century — and some adults adapted with anger or uncertainty. What had seemed givens — that young people, at least in certain classes, would conduct their courtship at home or at church, or with a chaperone present — now was challenged. By the 1920s, in some parts of Kentucky, dating became a system initiated more by youths and less by adults; automobiles introduced a whole new factor in the equation, one that would further alter the dating formula. The change taking place in the century's first decade was only the beginning.[42]

As if to strike back at the blows falling on traditional ways, adult society seemed to go club-mad. The formalization of ancestral ties begun in the 1890s

through the Daughters of the American Revolution (cofounded by Kentuckian Mary Desha) and by other groups made the ancestral ties that had been
quietly discussed in private now a public badge of honor. The more informal
groups — sewing circles, church groups, and the like — continued, but a whole
band of new societies formed as well. Nor was the trend restricted to women.
Male-only associations (at the time) organized and spread sporadically over
the state. The first Rotary Club in the state began in 1912, the first Kiwanis in
1916. Lions Clubs and, later, Jaycees added to the available groups. By the
1920s and early 1930s most medium-size towns had their own local branches
of at least one of these groups. They formed a supportive network, often
helpful in business activities, and one in which, in part, a formal organization
replaced the more informal ones of earlier periods. Clubs provided security
amid change.[43]

But other activities also allowed Kentuckians to maintain ties in a changing
age. Parties filled the social columns of newspapers, for instance — ice cream
socials, theme-oriented Japanese luncheons, lawn parties, tea parties, and the
seemingly numberless card parties (euchre, whist, rummy, and rook). Even
simple acts, such as going to check the mail in the evening, became social
occasions where young girls and boys could meet and talk. And, of course,
visiting from home to home remained commonplace, whether the visitors
were friends or relatives. As one person remembered, "You just went visiting
when you took a notion. . . . They welcome you, you know." Of course, a
negative side, largely unspoken, existed to all that. A Woodford County woman
cried out in June 1914: "I am so thankful to be without company, I can't tell.
Not a day since I came from Florida on the 15th of April without some one in
the house to be thought of and provided for. . . ." Two months later she wrote,
exasperatedly, "I was sewing and giving thanks in my heart that no company
was here . . . when up came a buggy and two women! . . . There was Cousin
Susie and Lucy!!! Lucy with bag and baggage! Valise & basket of medicine &
Susie telling how I must treat Lucy and talked as if the[y] had come for good
and all. Lucy went up stairs and went to bed — Susie talked me blind!"[44]

Yet more prevalent were positive memories of sitting with family, talking
and relaxing, living in a slower, quieter world. A Maysville woman recounted
how they would promenade after dinner, then gather with neighbors on their
porch, "telling jokes, gossiping, the men smoking, the ladies fanning, telling
the men to blow the smoke their way to keep off the mosquitoes." The conversation wandered over diverse topics:

> "I hope the Reed house is not sold to those Mayslick people. . . . Our
> cousin tells me their house is like a hurrah's nest. . . ."
> "This cake's scrumptious, Mary. I must have the recipe."
> "The Ladds say they're putting most of their land in tobacco next year."
> "They'll be sorry. Ruins the soil."
> "Any more talk about Night Riders starting up?"
> "I haven't heard any. . . ."
> "[That] baby came yesterday. . . . Why on the name of sense did she have

to have a big church wedding. Now everybody can fix the date. . . ."

"I don't know what's happened to the young folks today."

And the conversation continued into the night.[45]

All those elements of social life combined to offer the well-to-do a plethora of activities. Margaret W. Preston of Lexington, for instance, kept a diary of her youthful life. After going to school in the mornings, she typically read, "which I dearly love to do," practiced the piano, went for a drive in the carriage (in summer), played croquet, cards, parchesi, golf ("I liked it very much"), lawn tennis, or ping-pong at parties, and in the evenings went to the theater or another party. In February 1900 she thought of the future: "that I would be in love only once . . . , would like my husband very well but would not be wild over him . . . , that he would not be rich when I married him, but that I should be quite rich before I died."[46]

By 1907 she now took "motor-car" rides, or interurban transportation, to parties, had a beau (but also had forty-two callers one Sunday), attended political rallies and football games, and lunched frequently at the country club. Three years later, Preston still enjoyed sampling new activities, including "that common Blue Grass Amusement Park," with its roller-coaster, merry-go-round, and dance floor. Motion pictures, dancing that included the Turkey Trot, and automobile rides with dust choking her were all part of 1912. Visiting New England two years after that, she declared that Fayette County beaus were far superior, for the northern men "all seem so cold and unaffectionate and . . . so very unchivalric in their attitude to women. . . . Most of them seem to fancy themselves mightily, as we say in the South." And so the "modern" woman, active in reform causes, still reflected her upper-class life, one she felt comfortable living, one which she seldom doubted.[47]

As Preston's diary indicated, better transportation had expanded her range of social activities. Railroads became the "life-blood" of even medium-sized Kentucky towns, such as Madisonville, where over a dozen passenger trains left daily. Arnow wrote that those near the railroads could travel the 180 miles from her home to Cincinnati far easier than they could go 5 miles into the interior of the county. Out of that situation, excursions became another diversion of the upper and middle classes. Resorts, such as those at Natural Bridge, had special trains and rates (one dollar from Lexington) which brought visitors for a day's picnic or a longer stay at the L Park Hotel, the dance pavilion, or the riding stables. Longer trips to more distant ocean or mineral spring resorts hastened the death of similar places in Kentucky.[48]

Transportation

Transportation, in fact, modified many ways Kentuckians did things in the first third of the century. Not all changed quickly, of course. In 1909 a homesick family traveled the long miles from Texas to Marshall County in a covered wagon; six years later the last stagecoach line in the state, from Burnside to

Monticello, made its final run. Both events symbolized a dying era. But for many, many Kentuckians, the horse or mule still provided their chief means of transportation. An affinity often developed between the animal and the person, one that would be lovingly remembered and haltingly ended. Trust abounded: "We would almost always tie up the reins and sleep when driving homeward at night, as the horse usually knew the way." In rural Washington County, one resident recalled, horses far outnumbered automobiles in 1921; a decade later, however, few wagons traveled those same roads. But in the Kentucky mountains, the change came later. A person in an agrarian county there noted that in the 1930s "very, very few had buggies or a spring wagon," much less an automobile. They thought little of traveling a dozen miles in some horse-drawn fashion to attend a pie supper or ball game. Such conditions caused almost every small town to have a blacksmith shop and livery stable well into the century.[49]

Older, mechanical forms of transportation still offered increased mobility to those on rivers or near railroads. Steamboats operated on the Cumberland River as late as 1932, while the larger Ohio continued to provide support to those on its banks even longer. Railroads dominated the commonwealth, however, in the first three decades of the century. Although some 15 percent of the state's counties had no rail lines in that era, most places had such transportation at least within a day's ride by horseback. While not free of danger — forty-eight were killed and that many more injured in a December 1917 wreck near Shepherdsville, for instance — and while not always comfortable — cinders might fly in open windows, while people might feel almost suffocated if the windows were closed — trains still offered fast movement, as rails covered 4,062 miles of the commonwealth in 1929.[50]

A similar mobility existed for city dwellers and aided the growth of suburban commuting. Most medium- and larger-sized cities had their streetcar, or trolley, systems, powered first by mules (Louisville's last mule-drawn car was discontinued in 1901), then by electricity. In Lexington for a nickel (up to 1917), citizens could ride from their homes to their workplaces on the electric lines. The story was repeated across Kentucky, until the automobile and bus lines began to erode the numbers. Barbourville's horse-drawn cars stopped in 1919; Somerset's electric street railway closed in 1923, the same years as Henderson's in west Kentucky. Other locales held on longer — Catlettsburg in eastern Kentucky ran an electric railway into the 1930s, as did Lexington.[51]

Interurbans suffered a similar fate. Larger cars, operating on the same principle, ran, perhaps hourly, from various smaller and nearby cities to large urban areas. Between 1901 and 1908, lines connected Lexington to five satellite cities, including Frankfort. Commuters from bedroom communities outside Louisville traveled interurbans daily to the Falls City for work. Henderson and Evansville, Indiana, were similarly connected from 1912 to 1928. An important service that deserved continuation, the interurbans, like the street railways, died before the onslaught of the gasoline-powered "machine."[52]

Unquestionably, the automobile — even more than the railroad earlier —

In an attempt to combat Kentucky's reputation as "the detour state" plagued with poor roads, a 1930 billboard advertises "Route 35 over the Wilderness Road, the Shortest Way to the South . . ." through Lawrenceburg, Harrodsburg, Danville, Stanford, Crab Orchard Springs, and Mt. Vernon.

changed lives drastically. It helped end provincial isolation, allowed greater mobility for play and work, promoted consolidated schools, changed vacation habits, helped the development of suburbs and factories away from the city center, and simply offered a sense of freedom to the individual. Some results were negative — the increasing death tolls — and others unanticipated. In rural areas, for instance, the lack of mobility had caused small communities to develop a diversity of services and stores. With the automobile age and, eventually, better roads, citizens would drive elsewhere for such specialized services, thus limiting the need for a variety of offerings in the local area. Cars also allowed fewer courtship restrictions (bringing the Hazard *Herald*'s 1926 editorial against "road-side petting parties," which hurt road-building support!) and resulted in other social changes. And, finally, the automobile tended to produce, eventually, a more homogeneous society by narrowing differences between sections of Kentucky.[53]

The arrival of that automobile age varied considerably across the state. Commercially produced "machines" (as they were called) reached the larger cities and communities nearby around 1900 and 1901. More distant but still reasonably accessible towns marked the automobile's first appearance from three to eight years later. Some locales proved harder to reach, particularly in the mountains. Still, in most places, a steady growth in numbers took place from early in the century. In west Kentucky, the city of Mayfield had one car for every twelve people in 1920, while the entire central Kentucky county of Anderson had a 1:17 ratio two years after that. In fairly isolated Cumberland County, in the south-central part of the state, there were 180 automobiles at the beginning of World War I, 869 at the start of the next conflict. Overall, statewide automobile registration went from 19,500 vehicles in 1915 to 90,000 four years after that, to 127,000 in 1921, to 300,000 by 1928. The rare had become commonplace, almost a necessity.[54]

Kentucky would develop almost a mania about building roads for those automobiles. Admittedly, the commonwealth had a long way to go, and a 1922 newspaper verse all-too-accurately described a common condition:

> There's mud on Benton's Broadway,
> There's mud on Main Cross Street
> There's mud around the courthouse of Marshall's county seat.
> It's old Kentucky mud of which we now relate,
> And Marshall county mud's the stickiest in the state . . .
> There's mud in every household, friend wife is in despair
> There's mud upon the porches and mud upon the stair.
> There's mud upon the carpets, the mud is everywhere,
> There's mud on children's feet, there's mud on ladies' shoes.
> We take our daily walks in quivering gobs of ooze.
> East side and west side and all around the town,
> The mud is ankle deep in tawny shades of brown.

Some Kentucky cities varied from this formula with streets of brick or wood block (which absorbed animal waste and smelled), or, more commonly, of macadamized construction. The crushed limestone of macadamized streets would become a pasty mess in wet weather and, conversely, would be very dusty in the summer, when streets might be sprinkled, or later, oiled. After 1900, asphalt had begun to be used for city streets, but many places long remained paved in the nineteenth-century style.[55]

The state soon became involved in the entire process, as between 1906 and 1917 all southern states set up highway commissions. In 1912, Kentucky established an advisory Department of Public Roads whose commissioner promptly noted that the commonwealth had already fallen from fourth to tenth nationally in the miles of improved roads. Two years later, in 1914, a public state highway system, consisting of roads connecting each county seat, was finally authorized and a road tax established. But after a decade, the results, according to an Efficiency Commission report, were "pathetic," since one mountain county had no gravel or hard-surfaced roads at all, and another had only one and one-half miles. As late as 1931, Leslie County still had no paved roads. Yet overall, Kentucky then ranked sixth nationally in the miles of surfaced roads. The problem centered on the isolated areas of the state. They remained almost ignored.[56]

Despite the condition of the highways, daring drivers began to speed down the thoroughfares in horseless carriages, including the Kentucky-made "Ames," "Dixie Flyer," "Lexington," and "Bowman." In 1904, a prominent citizen went from Louisville to Lexington in the "record-breaking time" of three hours and forty-five minutes. By 1906 smaller communities, such as Mt. Sterling, were already arresting those driving too fast. The state, in response to the problem, had set up a 15 m.p.h. limit, with 6 m.p.h. for curves and bridges, in 1904. Additionally, detailed rules on what to do when approaching and passing horses had been included. By 1910, the limits were 20 m.p.h. on open roads (8 on curves) and 10 m.p.h. in business portions of the cities; the same act set up requirements for registration, brakes and lights, and licenses. Weight limits on vehicles — fifteen tons initially — were instituted in 1918.[57]

Just as the automobile began to dominate Kentucky transportation, the sound of a biplane flying overhead warned that still greater changes would come as the century progressed. While the editor of the Paducah paper had predicted in 1908 that there was "no doubt" that dirigibles had more promise for "aerial navigation" than airplanes, which fell to earth "when the machinery stops," that prophecy proved false. By 1926, the Yellow Taxi Airline Company was flying passengers from Kentucky's largest city to Cincinnati. Louisville's Bowman Field, first used in 1919, had a terminal in 1929 and concrete runways by 1938. A state board, whose members were to be "male, white," and over twenty-five years of age, governed air activities after 1926; by 1937 it had certified 88 pilots in Kentucky. Within three years, the number had grown to 273. Airplanes still affected few people directly by then, but the future was already clear.[58]

Sports

Although sports-oriented activity may have taken place virtually from the time the first humans entered the region, the twentieth century would witness the great growth of organized sports and widespread participation and observation by both sexes and all ages. Expanded leisure time, improved mass communication channels, better transportation, and, simply, more individual interest all contributed.

That is not to say that Kentuckians had not had such interests before. Some activities whose roots went back to the first decades of Anglo-American settlement — such as cockfighting — continued throughout the century, for all classes, albeit in a more clandestine fashion. Other actions, such as hunting and fishing, had been necessities for people needing food on their tables. As that need lessened, a trip to the woods or the riverbank became more a form of recreation, a pleasant diversion from daily cares. Often it would be as part of a group, sometimes supplied with a "generous" supply of bourbon whiskey or

Kentucky Historical Society

"Black" Lou Bullock of Orangeburg, Mason County *(above)* **represented the average Kentucky hunter more accurately than the rarefied image of the Iroquois Hunt Club.**

Kentucky Historical Society

moonshine, as they chased foxes or raccoons. ("Nowhere in the South," wrote an author, "is the sport more popular than in Kentucky.") Whether on horseback or on foot, the hunters would harken to the "music of the dogs," all the while telling stories and enjoying the company around them. Formal hunt clubs, with members in fine dress and on quality horses, represented the upper-class version. Individual hunting or fishing forays continued throughout the years as well. But excesses and declining game populations caused limitations to be imposed; by 1902 acts protecting game had been passed. Two years later the office of fish and game warden, appointed by the county judge, was established. Finally, in 1912, a Game and Fish Commission was created and funded. It issued the first state hunting license the next year, and the first resident fishing license in 1928. With support from a League of Kentucky Sportsmen, organized in 1935, the Division of Game and Fish was made a separate agency of state government in 1944. In that operational format, the group continued to monitor those activities which formed a bridge across the centuries.[59]

Other sports, whose origins lay in the nineteenth century and which were individual-oriented, such as croquet, bowling, skating, and golf, remained popular or grew in popularity in the new century. By 1900 leading papers carried a "Golf Notes" section, while a 1919 cartoon's portrayal of "The Golf Widow" indicated the growth of that pastime. Similarly, bowling alleys spread across the state. A 1907 state directory listed only six such locales, but a perusal of county histories indicates many more were already in existence by then. Skating rinks had a like proliferation, and small towns, such as Drakesboro with two hundred people, even had such facilities before 1910. Tennis and croquet, which required less formal places to play, were enjoyed by large numbers of people, particularly among the middle and upper classes.[60]

But already team sports were pushing the individual ones off the pages of newspapers, and that trend would grow. Baseball and football received more attention nationally than basketball and Kentucky reflected that same focus, initially, but its sporting tastes would change. Yet from 1900 to 1930, baseball and, second, football were the chief sports that attracted widespread interest in the state.

Almost every locale seemed to field an amateur or semi-professional baseball team. From mining camps in the mountains to places in the Purchase, communities built diamonds and large numbers of fans cheered their favorite teams. At the professional level, the state's largest city had a major-league team as late as 1899, but by 1902 the Louisville Colonels operated at the highest minor-league level. Across the state, low-level minor-league ball was played in a sizeable number of towns, with teams in organizations like the Bluegrass League or the Kitty (K.I.T.) League. A reader of Hopkinsville newspapers in 1911 would barely know that a National or American League existed, for reports told instead of the nearly two thousand in attendance at the Kitty League's opening day there. Larger "baseball-mad" cities like Louisville had scoreboards outside newspaper offices so people could follow their favorite major-league teams, inning by inning. By the 1930s through the 1950s fans could chronicle the actions of native sons like Hall of Famers Earle Combs and Harold "Pee Wee" Reese. But it really was the lower professional leagues or the amateur, town-connected clubs that made baseball so popular. It gave those communities a unity at a time when rural areas had few high schools. Only later would sports at that level begin to provide the same kind of community cohesiveness, and then chiefly in a different sport.[61]

More controversial than baseball but almost as popular in its season was football, basically at the college level. By 1904, games garnered favorable front-page attention in newspapers, as well as supportive editorials, such as the Lexington *Herald* one in 1904: "It is a good game, a manly game. . . . One learns to stand punishment without a whimper: to accept defeat without a murmur: to bear victory without boasting. No craven can play it." That attitude represented one viewpoint, that of those who saw the sport as greater than the controversy surrounding it. But other forces were widely criticizing the college game as it existed. The "unseemly violence" and large numbers of deaths — twenty-three nationally in 1905 — was one cause. But it went beyond that. Across America rules were vague and ignored; the same was true in Kentucky. The best team in the state for the second two decades of the century was Centre College, which had a 53–7–1 record from 1917 to 1924, under coach Charlie Moran. That success culminated in 1921 with one of the century's acknowledged greatest upsets when the "Praying Colonels" beat an undefeated Harvard team by a 6–0 score. Betting was commonplace among coaches, players, and fans, as it was elsewhere at the time.[62]

Less successful, but better documented, and more symbolic of the problems across Kentucky and the United States, were the State College (present-day University of Kentucky) teams. A 1901 game with Kentucky University (Transylvania) had been cancelled because of "unfriendly feeling" between the two Lexington schools. After a turnover in personnel, the new coach at State College brought with him in 1903 a whole team of "ringers"; that is, professionals who had played elsewhere. A committee investigated the resulting 6–1 season and found it "a very disgraceful affair." Rules had been openly violated; players had been paid out of gate receipts (3,500 had attended the Kentucky University game that year); faculty and students had bet on outcomes of the contests. The school's president, long-opposed to the sport, would continue to attack football for making it "utterly impossible" to have Saturday classes and for the sport's "violent, spasmodic, and abnormal exertions." The new coach in 1904 went 9–1; the next year appropriations for the team increased over threefold. Three years after that, a not atypical team averaging five feet nine inches in height and 163 pounds in weight won eight and lost one, a record exceeded in 1909, after the (new) coach did away with nose and shin guards because of their excessive weight. In 1915, the team spent $59.84 for scouting other teams and $135.06 for doctor's bills. By then, organized sports had become a major college concern, particularly the need for increased safety. In 1912, the committee governing football rules had added a fourth down to make ten yards, removed the twenty-yard restriction on forward pass completions (although passes had to be thrown from five yards behind the line until 1954), increased a touchdown to six points, and reduced a field goal to three points. Helmets (which were not required until 1943) began to be available after World War I and, together with the freer rules, made a safer game. More secondary schools took up the sport as a result, but the question of priorities continued to trouble. One person grumbled in 1912 at the attention given an athletic victory over a speech contest — "The contrast is disgusting. Misplaced emphasis. . . . Athletics on the top of the pedestal! Intellectual and scholarly achievement provoke hardly a riffle!" — while a legislator told the president of Eastern Teachers College, in the 1930s, that the educator needed to catch the public eye if he wanted a new building. "What do you mean . . . by having an A-plus rating in all departments?" the president asked. "Naw," replied the politician, "get a winning football team." A historian of one high school wrote, "A wonderful team at Mayfield . . . had to be wasted due to a football armistice during the first World War."[63]

Basketball, a sport that would later become dominant in the state, did not have such popularity early in the century. In fact, the sport was often viewed as a brief wintertime activity, more for young women than men. At State College, the women's team played a full schedule a year before the men's, which started in 1903. Four years later each sex's first-year players competed against each other, with the men winning 17–11. In short, there were few perceived sexual differences regarding basketball (except that only females could watch the women's team play, attired as they were in bloomers). At the high-school level, the "girl's" teams often were also organized before the "boy's" and not infrequently received at least as much attention as their male counterparts. But for a variety of reasons — one coach indicated that it was thought girl's basketball was "too strenuous" — the sport of basketball was closed to young women at the University of Kentucky in 1924 and in high schools in the 1930s. Not for over three decades would that change. But before that and at whatever level, the young sport began to gain adherents. In 1918 and 1921, the boy's and girl's high school tournaments began. By 1928 the sport's popularity brought over four thousand spectators to watch Ashland defeat Carr Creek 13–11 in a twelve-minute overtime game that decided the boy's championship. Beginning in the 1920s, when colorful E. A. Diddle started coaching at present-day Western Kentucky University, and furthered when Adolph F. Rupp took over an already successful University of Kentucky program in 1930, college basketball began to displace baseball and even football as the spectator sport of choice for Kentuckians. By the end of their careers, Rupp stood first in college victories, Diddle third. What has been called "the prototypical modern sport" was eagerly accepted by a traditional people, so much so that the Encyclopedia of Southern Culture would conclude later, "If there is . . . one region of the South that is most noted for its basketball it is Kentucky."[64]

Just as major changes were taking place in basketball and football, so too were they occurring in one of the oldest of Kentucky's pastimes and one of the best attended — horse racing. Perhaps the greatest change, and attempted change, took place away from the track. Before 1906 betting was carried out by bookmakers who set odds, a situation that caused many to decry the influence of gamblers. Moreover, many of the state's tracks were not prospering under the system. To remedy that, the 1906 general assembly established a State Racing Commission to regulate the sport. Two years later, parimutuel betting machines, which set odds based on money wagered on the race, had replaced the now-prohibited bookies. Latonia Race Track (opened in 1883) challenged the law and lost; a 1916 order setting up minimum purses was appealed by Douglass Park (opened in 1906), but it too received the state court's approval. At the commonwealth's most famous race track, Churchill Downs, the changes there resulted less from laws than promotional flair, as personified in Matt J. Winn. Under his leadership, the Kentucky Derby went from a 1900 purse of $6,000 to a $50,000 added by 1921. Attendance soared, but more than money and the numbers was the publicity, especially after the 91–1 longshot Donerail raced to victory in 1913, and the filly Regret won in 1915. By the 1920s, the Derby had become a national event, drawing attention across America, so that humorist Irvin S. Cobb could proclaim, "Until you go to Kentucky and with your own eyes behold the Derby, you ain't never been nowheres and you ain't never seen nothin'!" At a time when horse racing was under attack, the Derby's success as well as the attention given horses like Man o' War helped insure the survival of the sport.

But racing still faced problems in a state which tried mightily to reconcile a religious tradition and a gambling heritage. Despite the prominence of the thoroughbred in Kentucky life and legend, many still did not approve. Yet, the opening of a new track, Keeneland, in 1936 indicated the people's continuing support for "the Sport of Kings."[65]

The Grandstand and Lagoon, Latonia Race Track, Covington, Ky.

This bucolic view of Latonia Race Track in Covington was issued on a post card by the Kraemer Art Co. in nearby Cincinnati, Ohio.

How to Make a Living

Food class, Clay High School.

Department store girls learning salesmanship, Louisville.

Adult clothing class, Lewisport High School.

Right: Office practice class of young ladies.

Kentucky Progress Magazine in 1932 featured a two-page spread on "Learning to Live and Learning How to Make a Living." Men were instructed on soils, field selection of seed corn, mining safety, and using linotype equipment. In contrast, women were shown learning cooking, sewing, salesmanship, and secretarial skills.

4

"Weep No More, My Lady": Majorities and Minorities

Women in Kentucky Life

The state's motto, "United We Stand, Divided We Fall," did not always reflect the prevalent mood of the commonwealth's citizens. A people divided by the Civil War and, more recently, the Goebel Affair of 1900, had lived constantly with divisions in their society. But most white, male Kentuckians, if asked, would likely have answered that as far as social and domestic relations went, their Kentucky was of a united mind. A male-dominated world, in which men set policy, earned income, conducted public affairs, and led the state, was, they said, accepted as the way things should be.

A kind of schizophrenic outlook confused the image regarding women, however. In one view, females were expected to be totally subservient to the adult males around them. Such attitudes came forth clearly when women served men the meals, perhaps shooed away flies from the table, and cleared off the dishes, all before eating separately or with the children. Conversations in which women addressed their husbands as "Mr. Morris," or letters signed "Your loving wife, Mrs. E.G. Young," expressed both a pride by the spouse in the public person in the household and a view in which she saw herself more as an extension of her spouse rather than an individual in her own right. One woman recalled how her father opposed women's gaining the vote because it would make no difference: He said "the women would vote just as the husbands told them."[1]

But the subservient woman who existed as a helpmate, chiefly as a quiet appendage to the household, was not the only existing feminine image. At another level, that outlook was modified so that women, while still secondary to men, also existed above them. The cult of noble womanhood had left women chiefly in the home, but gave them almost a place of moral superiority over the males occupying that home. This view, called by some "woman-worship," resulted in a kind of pedestal woman, standing above the crude public world, uplifting parts of the society, educating children in higher morals, living a life of purity and perfection. Such an image allowed for outside-the-home activities, within limited spheres. It gave stature, where the subservient life did not.[2]

Both perceptions promoted the idea of a clear division between the duties and lives of men and women. Both accepted the view that women's goal should be an early marriage (the minimum age of consent for women was then twelve), fruitful child-bearing, and a happy home life. In a crude form that dichotomy was presented in a 1914 Kentucky Department of Education *Bulletin* which explained that "Every school should begin to teach farmer boys the whys of the farm, and farmer girls the whys of the kitchen." In more polished form, it emerged in an editorial in a Stanford paper: "The bluegrass girl," the writer intoned, "is more than equal to a poet's dream. . . . The sweetheart of a gallant boy, she grows to be a true wife of noble man and soon has blossomed into motherhood to make the brain and brawn of old Kentucky richer in her progeny."[3]

It should not be forgotten in all this, of course, that in the home many men and women may have existed in a coequal situation, one mutually agreed-upon, and one in which each helped the other. A division of labor to make home life successful did not necessarily mean acceptance of the view that one sex was not equal to the other. Loving arrangements based on reciprocal respect did exist. But it was the other situations that began to create cracks in the pedestal's façade. The lack of options, the pressured inequality, the arrogance of power — all brought forth increasing attacks on the reality and the image. Kentuckian Josephine Henry had already criticized women "too ethereal to be troubled," whose lives centered on social prestige and family power, who did nothing to transcend the limits set by men. Her cry that "Liberty regards no sex, and justice bows before no ideal," and the voices of even more vocal equal rights leaders grew louder as the years progressed.[4]

All of that created divisions in the supposedly divided spheres but united social world of early twentieth-century Kentucky. Congressman A. O. Stanley wrote his wife Sue in 1905, criticizing women's rights: "I am . . . thinking of a diviner type of woman — she leads no ism — leads no sects and I hope will never be the object even of interest to strong minded women and hysterical old maids. Her life work is in her home." Similarly, political leader Ollie James asserted that "woman should remain in her sphere." Editor Henry Watterson praised women as "Keeper of the World's Sanctuary — the Moral Light of the Universe," while blasting changes which resulted in women's appearing "half-naked in the dance rooms and I do not dare describe how they appear on ocean beaches." In 1913, he attacked the "he-women" who led the suffrage movement, calling them failures in the home and "immoral" influences on society. By 1920, an attorney wondered if the "dangerous experiment" of giving the women the vote would not destroy "their supremacy amongst men." The debate over the role of women in Kentucky society incurably divided the people.[5]

But, in one sense, the reality of women's lives and work did more to stimulate change than did debate over image and policy. Kentucky author James Lane Allen had written in the 1890s not only about women who married well, adorned a home, and received praise but also the "crushed and silent women"

Kentucky Historical Society

Gussie Konen and Ada Kline make a daring appearance near Newport on the Ohio River.

of the state. Nowhere was that second class better described than in the voluminous writings about eastern Kentucky; scarcer records suggest that what was present there existed elsewhere in the commonwealth as well.[6]

Much of what was written about Appalachian women told of particularly hard lives. A writer concluded in 1916: "The modern woman movement hardly has penetrated into the hills. . . ." Females' lives in the region were controlled by the absence of choices. Unless a member of an already prosperous family, the unmarried woman had few options other than migration or matrimony. A few might teach — if they could overcome still-existing objections to their being in a classroom — but in a scattered, rural society with a limited cash economy, that occupation was the chief outlet. Most simply married and continued in the sexually segregated world of their youth. As a writer noted in 1912, "The women . . . still wear sunbonnets, and they still ride behind, horseback . . . ; still stand waiting at the table while their lords and masters eat." An outside observer who later lived in the region recalled, "When I first came here women were literally chattels," and another remembered, "when I first came in here . . . the man had to make the final decision."[7]

While both the size of mountain families and the youthful age at which marriage occurred have been exaggerated, an attitude still existed as expressed by a Letcher County man in the 1930s: "What more could a man want? The more children I have the more land I can tend." With still-sizeable families, many years were spent in childbearing and childrearing. One boy noted that his mother had nine children and no washing machine: "She would take [clothes] to the creek with home-made soap. She would wet them . . . then she would put then on a rock or log and I would beat them . . . until they would come half-way clean. Mother would have to patch our overalls over and over. . . . She would mend our shoes with leather from a ground hog hide. . . . Mother would knit socks . . . and sometimes mittens or a sweater. She didn't have much time left." One nurse heard a woman tell how she had borne twelve children — "eight ones are here and four are better off." For some, death did seem a happier option than the harsh promise any future offered.[8]

Large families, hard field work, time spent cooking, sewing, and cleaning all took a toll. Numerous commentators mentioned how wives aged quickly. A 1906 article, for example, praised the "buxom" young women "with the bloom of health written all over them," but concluded that the "burden of womanhood and excessive work and care . . . rob them of their maidenly charms." A Morehead newspaper blamed Appalachian women's grave and retiring dispositions on their "deplorable" place in the region's social caste. With horizons bounded by home, family, and neighbors, the mountain woman could easily feel enslaved by poverty, illiteracy, and what one person called "men without vision."[9]

But that story did not just exist in Appalachia. Across Kentucky, Monday might be a day for washing, Tuesday for ironing, Wednesday for sewing and mending, Thursday for canning, Friday for housecleaning, Saturday for shopping, Sunday for church, with all the other chores continuing almost each day. While many of the same problems were faced, still, a few more options appeared. Women worked in factories where available. In 1903, in west Kentucky, the Henderson Cotton Mills employed 638 people, 392 of them either women or younger girls; the Louisville Continental Tobacco Company had 1,614 workers, 10 percent of them female. Women in Henderson earned $.84/day versus the men's $1.05. A labor inspector's report two years later indicated that, statewide, women received $.87 per day while men averaged

$1.63, although in organized trades, wages were nearly equal. Almost a decade and a half later, the same office found a "tendency toward discrimination between men and women in the rate of pay for identical work." Given the fact that nationally, by 1930, almost nine of every ten married women remained outside the organized work force, such options — even discriminatory ones — were important first steps.[10]

Jobs outside the home were not the only modifications taking place. The social winds of change that people expected a new century to bring blew harder than many expected, or than some desired. One of the most obvious changes came in the area of divorce, which became easier and fairer as the decades passed. In 1900, Kentucky had been one of only three states which kept provisions allowing judicial divorce decrees for any cause deemed improper. Two decades later, men and women received generally equal treatment under divorce laws, except that men — and not women — had a legal duty to support their spouse, and only women could be divorced for "lewd behavior" indicating "bad character." One act of infidelity could be grounds for divorcing a woman, while men had to have a pattern of such action. By 1936, when laws changed once more, the chief remaining difference was that women could be divorced, without proof of adultery, if "lewd, lascivious behavior on her part proves her to be unchaste." In 1950 another revision let stand that language. Barriers to divorce had fallen over the years, but the double standard, if battered, still remained.[11]

But if victory could be won on the highly symbolic issue of suffrage for women, then it was expected that all the other efforts to provide full legal equality would be eventually successful over time. The vote was the all-important first step. It was not an easy one, for the cause's leaders found that they did not have the united support of women in the commonwealth, since significant numbers did not back the effort to secure votes for their sex. Others favored the cause but were too absorbed in making a living, or caring for children and the home, to be able to help. Yet, over time, growing numbers of women became advocates. For them the crusade was not so radical as it was pictured by opponents. In the main, they were middle- and upper-class women who saw the issue less as an attack on society and tradition than as a right that was deserved. Some saw the vote as a way to cleanse politics of fraud and corruption. Others saw it simply as an inalienable right, as an action that meant they would no longer be second-class citizens, behind even black males, who could vote. In short, while the reasons for supporting suffrage varied, the movement united behind the issue for one simple reason — justice.[12]

Leading the suffrage movement were two forceful and extraordinary women, Laura Clay and Madeline McDowell Breckinridge, both of Lexington. Clay, with the aid of her sisters, pioneered the movement in the nineteenth century. A daughter of the fiery antislavery leader Cassius Marcellus Clay, Laura Clay became committed to women's rights after the unfair treatment her mother received during her bitter divorce. In 1888, Clay led in the formation of the Kentucky Equal Rights Association (KERA) and served as its president for twenty-four years. By the 1890s, Clay was the leading southerner in the National American Woman Suffrage Association (NAWSA) and served as its auditor for fifteen years. Religiously devout, hard-working, and aristocratically dignified, she commanded attention as she spoke eloquently for the cause across the nation. In Kentucky, she had secured victories in the 1890s, but as late as 1906, only two people belonged to the Frankfort Equal Rights Association. Much remained to be done in the twentieth century, for the greatest prize — the vote — remained an elusive goal. But Clay's efforts had made suffrage a respectable, almost fashionable, cause and had given it the possibility of success. For those reasons, her course over the decade after 1910 was a sad one. Convinced that states and not the national government should be the avenue taken to secure the vote, and worried over federal involvement on the racial issue, Clay broke with the NAWSA, supported the southern group led by the more racist Kate Gordon, and became isolated from the women and forces she had organized. In the crucial decade, Kentucky's leadership would have to come from elsewhere.[13]

Madeline McDowell Breckinridge seemed the perfect choice to take the suffrage issue to the next level. Like Clay, she came from an established family — Henry Clay was her great-grandfather — and she solidified that standing by marriage to Lexington *Herald* editor Desha Breckinridge. Aided by his sister Sophonisba, a national leader in social work at the University of Chicago, they used the paper's columns to support various Progressive Era causes, but woman suffrage in particular. Thin and fragile-looking, "Madge" Breckinridge was tougher than she looked. Those large brown eyes concealed a very self-disciplined soul. When young, she lost part of a leg to tuberculosis of the bone. Later she suffered numerous illnesses and some unhappiness in her private life, but none of that kept her from being very active and quietly aggressive. An excellent speaker, she advocated numerous other causes — social settlement work in Appalachia, playground and kindergarten movements in urban slums, a state tuberculosis sanatorium, and juvenile court reform. But in 1912, she took her friend and distant cousin Laura Clay's post as president of the KERA, and the next year was named vice president of the national organization. From those posts, she led the fight, both in Kentucky and in America.[14]

In her sharp and sarcastic talks, Breckinridge examined male-led Kentucky, with its poor educational standing, its reputation for violence, and its faction-laden politics, and suggested that the question was not whether women were fit for suffrage, but whether men were. When she wrote to a governor, asking his support, she noted that "Kentucky women are not idiots — even though they are closely related to Kentucky men." That humor, plus her ability to organize and to use new tactics such as suffrage marches, helped bring new supporters into the fold. Between 1913 and 1915, formal membership in the Kentucky association went from 1,779 to over 10,500. Informal support was much more widespread, and all that translated to political gains: In 1912, women, both black and white, were given the right to vote in school elections. Two years later, Clay and Breckinridge addressed a joint session of the general

Gov. Edwin Morrow signs Kentucky's bill ratifying the Nineteenth Amendment, as members of the Kentucky Equal Rights Association look on. Madeline McDowell Breckinridge stands behind Morrow (left of the woman leaning on chair).

assembly on the suffrage question. In 1916, a state suffrage bill passed the senate, but failed in the house. By 1919, Breckinridge had to oppose, openly and reluctantly, Clay's stand against federal action and instead vigorously pushed for Kentucky's approval of what became the Nineteenth Amendment. On 6 January 1920, Kentucky became one of the four southern states to support that suffrage amendment. With its ratification, effective 26 August 1920, Kentucky women had reached legal equality in the voting booth. Other fights lay ahead.[15]

"Madge" Breckinridge would not live to fight them. On 25 November 1920, she died at the age of forty-eight. Breckinridge had voted in one election. A fruit vendor's comment on hearing the news of her death said it simplest and best: "She will be much missed." Clay would live on for two decades, remaining politically active until her death at the age of ninety-two, in 1941. But Clay and Breckinridge had only been the most visible parts of the story, for numerous other women had aided greatly, including Sallie Clay Bennett, Mary B. Clay, Josephine K. Henry, Christine Bradley South, and Lida Calvert Obenchain.

Those contributions, and the support of nameless others, often risking much, had brought final success to the suffrage movement.[16]

That had only been one phase of the equal rights campaign. Women had already begun to make inroads into professions previously denied them. By 1900, the state had three female attorneys; twenty-two years after, Mary Elliott Flanery of Boyd County sat in the Kentucky house, and she became the first woman elected to a southern legislature. In 1924 Emma Guy Cromwell was elected secretary of state; four years following that, Kathleen Mulligan of Lexington became the state's first justice when she was appointed a municipal judge. In more traditional "women's areas," such as education and health care, real individual good was done as well. By 1907, at least twenty women served as superintendents of county school districts, and at the college level, school after school became coeducational. Cora Wilson Stewart's work with illiterates, Linda Neville's trachoma crusade, Mary Breckinridge's 1925 Frontier Nursing Service with its pioneering nurse-midwife emphasis, and the settlement school work in Appalachia of Katherine Pettit, May Stone, Alice Lloyd, Ethel deLong, and others, all made a difference.[17]

Massive modification in women's lives took place away from the legal arena as well. The middle- or upper-class, urban "New Woman" did not leave her pedestal far behind, but stepped off more and more to expand the separate and accepted woman's sphere into new and less accepted areas. Voluntary groups, including women's clubs, began to become involved in broader societal concerns. At the same time, revolutions in the world of women — with industrial jobs, new kitchen appliances, automobiles, and the like — began to have an effect on social conventions. In mostly conservative Kentucky, the changing mores were evident even before the 1920s. Sometimes the result was confusion — a rural legislator in Frankfort in 1914 wrote his wife, "the women I wish you could see some of them, they have got a new kind up here to any I have seen any where and I can't describe them" — and often the result was shock — "My mother started wearing pants in the early 1920s. And, oh it was bad when she started riding her horse astride instead of side-saddle." In 1933 a Kentucky Birth Control League was formed. Freer clothing, the continuing equal rights debate, more frequent divorces, drinking and smoking by females, the whole expansive attitude of jazz and the flappers of the 1920s — all these challenged the past and created seemingly endless forecasts of future disaster, even though a large portion of Kentucky's women had personally experienced little of that change.[18]

The real difference regarding women's lives was not necessarily in clothes or manners, but rather in outlook. Now Kentucky women had more options, more choices, and more opportunities to excel. A teenage girl in her diary expressed a sentiment in 1914 that would grow over the decades: "Oh, I hope I'll do something really worth while. I want to be great *so bad*." The changes taking place in her lifetime allowed her to dream, to expect greatness, and to seek it.[19]

The Black Community

Between 1900 and 1950, Kentucky blacks had few expectations that their futures would be as bright as that young woman's. The crucial difference was that she was white; they were not. For even when women had limited rights, they still could mix and mingle socially with those opposing them. They still had many of the same opportunities; they could shop the same places; they could live where they pleased; they could expect courteous treatment. Not so with blacks in Kentucky. As Lyman Johnson, a black teacher and leader who would challenge segregation, pointed out, no matter what one's education, "a black man . . . is still black. Just like in slavery days, it was a badge he couldn't shake off." When Johnson visited a restaurant in rural Kentucky, he was not served in the dining room. Instead they shuttled him in the side door, offered a backroom table, and set out what turned out to be good food. As he noted, "They gave us everything but respect." The black world was a world apart, a place white Kentucky cared not to see, a life hidden and ignored, and, most of all, a community apart. Black Kentuckians grew up being told by law, custom, and word that they were not equal, that they were inferior, that they were second-class citizens. Whitney Young, Jr., who would later lead the National Urban League and whose father was a respected educator, remembered how they went to a theater and had to sit in the balcony while ill-dressed and uneducated whites always had better seats on the main floor. "Even at the age of five," Young recalled, "I recognized the hypocritical nature of it, the inconsistency of it."[20]

Everywhere a black youth turned, segregation appeared — at the water fountain, at the restrooms, at the schools, at the library, at the hospitals. In 1911, a black man, struck by a train, was refused admission to the white hospital in Frankfort and was taken to the workhouse to die instead. Sports teams, even amateur ones, were generally segregated; some, such as the Lexington Hustlers baseball club, did occasionally play white teams, but that was rare. When they did, the news would appear in a separate section of the newspaper under "Colored Notes." In racing, the grandstands at the Louisville tracks had been closed to blacks as patrons since the 1880s, although, ironically, black jockeys rode fifteen of the first twenty-eight Derby winners. Both races did mix in the Churchill Downs infield. But, as in other areas, increasing segregation in the first third of the century meant that after 1902 no black jockey rode a Derby winner; after 1911 none rode at all.[21]

In some ways, the inconsistencies perplexed as much as the overt segregation. In public transportation, for instance, the picture was mixed. Kentucky had required segregated railroads since the early 1890s, and that law would be upheld by the U.S. Supreme Court again in the 1920s. The Louisville and Nashville (L & N) Railroad supported that policy, for in 1904 the chairman of the board told President Milton Smith that they had to do all they could "in keeping darkies off the sleeping cars." Subsequently, a vice president told superintendents and conductors not to refuse blacks "outright" on interstate

Kentucky Historical Society

The Green Mill Service Station, Frankfort, maintained segregated facilities in 1930.

travel, but "to avoid feeding them in dining cars by various means," nevertheless. On interstate routes, he ordered them "to refuse absolutely to serve negroes [*sic*] in our dining cars." All agents were instructed not to sell blacks tickets for sleeping cars but to do so by "evasion without outright refusing." In short, in the absence of formal action, subterfuge could segregate just as effectively.[22]

Yet, on street railways, a different situation existed, at least in some areas. Ever since an 1871 court test, the streetcars of Louisville had been open to both races.[23] Attempts to modify that condition by ordinance and by legislative enactments failed on several occasions in the early 1900s. At the same time, however, Louisville taxi cabs refused to take black passengers. Not until 1929, when a separate company was organized to serve the black community, did that change. The interurbans that operated out of Lexington and the trains from Paducah both had separate waiting rooms for each race, as well as separate restrooms, but a common ticket office. Money was accepted equally.[24] While city government in Louisville had failed to segregate streetcars, it was more successful in regard to the park system. Up until 1914, blacks and whites apparently used the same swimming pools, tennis courts, picnic areas, and ball fields in the public parks. But that soon changed. In 1921, black baseball players were barred from the parks; then the next year a small new park was opened, to be used solely by blacks. By 1924 the Park Board resolved that it was "not desirable" for the two races to use the same parks and pools. Separate (though not equal) facilities resulted, and the once-integrated system became segregated.[25] In Henderson, the separation came in 1903, when one area of the city park was "reserved" for blacks; in Lexington, the parks were segregated in 1916. By then, that condition seemed almost everywhere. Blacks went to their own "Colored Fair" and were usually prevented from attending white-based ones. If hearing impaired or blind, they went to state-supported institutions with fully segregated "Colored Departments." Those unfortunate enough to be imprisoned would find, by 1900, separate chapel services and, eleven years later, segregated dining areas. Even in death, blacks would usually lie in graves separated from the white section, or in their own cemetery.[26]

It had not always been thus. Under slavery, blacks and whites had lived together, or nearly so. In the period immediately following the Civil War, blacks entered the cities in great numbers, and a more segregated pattern developed though considerable variations remained. Laws restricting blacks' rights had been passed almost immediately, but the strong statutes regarding segregation had not come forth. In short, by the late nineteenth and early twentieth century Kentucky still had a choice. It could follow a growing national tide of acceptance of restrictions on blacks and flow with the South into full segregation, or it could resist such currents and build a more unfettered and freer society.[27]

Most of the actions suggested that white Kentucky differed little from the South. Segregation laws did appear, particularly in regard to railroad coaches and both public and private education. Violence resembled forms and levels prevalent elsewhere. Local ordinances and customs usually followed the segregation theme, chapter and verse. And perhaps most important, personal attitudes were not often enlightened. No outcry resulted when the state's best-known editor, Henry Watterson, wrote about "a plump little nigger," or when lieutenant-governor candidate South Trimble in 1907 publicly termed African Americans "the meanest, blackest, slimiest of the earth." In a 1912 *History of Kentucky*, the author praised the "charming" slavery days and termed conferring the vote on blacks "a mistake." Increasingly racist terms and cartoons appeared in state newspapers at the same time. A Hopkins County school superintendent, after praising the Separate Coach Law, then complained of the mingling of the races when both black and white school teachers came to his office on payday: "Such conditions are quite embarrassing. . . ."[28]

Those attitudes reflected views prevalent over a wide spectrum of the white community. To such people (and obviously in varying degree), blacks were seen as an inferior race whose very touch contaminated — whether it be a library book, the water in a fountain, a seat in a theater, or a house in a neighborhood. Such people would not have respect enough to call blacks "Mr." or "Mrs.," would demand that Negroes step aside on sidewalks to let Caucasians pass, would further restrict blacks. That does not mean that such attitudes were directed solely at blacks. In an age that spoke of the superiority of the (white) American, English, and Anglo-Saxon culture, various groups were branded inferior, including the Irish, Orientals, and eastern Europeans. But those racial taunts and cartoons, in the end, did differ in degree.[29]

Given such conditions, Kentucky could easily have gone further down the road to segregation than it did. For those blacks who had to live in that world in Kentucky, the path followed went far enough. They were barred from many places, might have limited access to others (as in some restaurants where they could order carry-out only), or have totally separated facilities as the only choice. Yet, as with streetcars and parks for a time, they sometimes had an almost integrated situation. To live black in such a world required learning various rules on what could or could not be done without reprisal. Whites did not have to discover those rules.[30]

Yet, despite all that, Kentucky never took the final and, in some ways, the key step. It never disfranchised blacks. While all the other southern states did so, it did not. Undoubtedly the smaller percentage of blacks in its population was a factor, for blacks posed less of a threat to white dominance. Part of the reason may simply have been that while political leaders used the race issue in campaigns, it really never was made a crucial point around which major contests revolved. But some of the credit must also go to individuals, black and white, who spoke out against further restrictions.[31]

Among the whites, few were racial egalitarians; some were fully creatures of their age, with its prejudices; but many also believed in fairness and justice and presented those thoughts to fellow Kentuckians. An eloquent voice was stilled in 1911 when Supreme Court Justice John Marshall Harlan of Kentucky died. His famous dissent — "Our Constitution is color-blind" — spoke for the better side of the state. But others took up the call. Desha Breckinridge, the editor of the Lexington *Herald*, for instance, received praise from the national black press for his stand against the rising segregation of the national government under Woodrow Wilson. His editorial that "The door of hope is shut" to Negroes when segregated was applauded by *The Crisis* in 1913, while two years later his words that all races should be treated as equal before the law brought a black writer in the *A.M.E. Church Review* to say that no paper was more outspoken on the issue than the *Herald*.[32]

In the black community, the cautious but still influential actions of people like the Rev. Charles Parrish, the president of State (Simmons) University, or William H. Steward, the editor of the *Kentucky Baptist*, kept some opposition alive, while moderates such as James Bond, who had a column in major city newspapers, helped as well. But even more forceful actions came from a new wave of outspoken leaders: Albert E. Meyzeek, the principal of Central High School in Louisville, I. Willis Cole, the editor of the Louisville *Leader*, and William Worley.[33]

Worley played an important role in one of the major breaks made in the segregation wall by Kentucky blacks. In 1914 the Louisville city council, then the board of aldermen, and then the mayor all approved, without a dissenting vote, and in order to prevent "conflict between the white and colored races," a segregation ordinance on housing. Neither race could move into or build homes in a neighborhood predominantly settled by the opposite race. The ordinance became a model for cities across the South as well as a focal point for black opposition. Ministers preached against it, then Louisville organized a branch of the National Association for the Advancement of Colored People (NAACP). Nationally, a wealthy Kentuckian, William E. Walling, had been more responsible for setting up the NAACP than perhaps any other person. Now, in his home state, the newly formed branch tested the law, citing the restrictions on people's right to sell property. William Worley would eventually lose his job at the post office because of his role in what became *Buchanan v. Worley*, but in November 1917 the U.S. Supreme Court upheld his position and declared the Louisville law unconstitutional. It was a major national victory, at a time when blacks made few such gains.[34]

As perceived at the time, two partial victories came, surprisingly, in the field of entertainment. When the play *The Clansman* played in Kentucky in early 1906, reviewers pointed out how it built the audience "up to a fever heat of enthusiasm." Based on the Thomas Dixon novel of the same name, the play, like the book, presented a very prosouthern and anti-Negro view of Reconstruction. Future governor A.O. Stanley wrote after watching it that it showed "the horrible wrongs" of giving political equality to blacks. But in March of that year the general assembly passed a law prohibiting the performance of any play "that excites race prejudice." While a noble-sounding action, the statute may simply have been an attempt to quell *any* disturbances in the status quo. It could also be aimed at *Uncle Tom's Cabin*. Four years later, for instance, cities across Kentucky prohibited the showing of films of the Johnson-Jeffries heavyweight fight, in which the black fighter won, for the same reasons. In 1918 the Louisville NAACP successfully stopped the showing of D.W. Griffith's *Birth of a Nation* (in essence a film version of *The Clansman*) after only a two-day run. That made Louisville one of eight cities across the nation that barred the controversial film between 1915 and 1918.[35]

What, then, did all that mean? Was a visitor correct in 1918, when he said that, other than being "doomed" if under the judicial system, blacks were treated better "than in any other southern state I have visited"? Was the state that inspired the nineteenth-century Jim Crow character really very far removed from the other segregationist Jim Crow laws of the twentieth century? Probably not. After all, violence, law, and everyday actions continued to tell blacks that their place in the hierarchy of things was at the very bottom.[36]

Still, they could vote and wield some power in the political field. A black man sat on the Hopkinsville City Council until at least 1907, for instance, while blacks were selected as councilmen in Harrodsburg and Winchester a half-decade after that. In Mt. Sterling one or two African Americans served in similar positions through 1918. After a period of segregation across Kentucky, by the 1940s the earlier patterns began again. In 1945 a black was elected for the first time to the board of aldermen in Louisville. The fact that blacks made up a large percentage of the Republican Party in Kentucky (26,500 of 59,000 in Louisville), and that the Republicans did win important local and statewide elections between 1900 and 1950, meant that blacks could not be ignored — although white Republicans often tried to do just that. The dangers of such a tactic became clear in Louisville's November 1920 vote on a million-

A crowd endures rain outside a Frankfort newspaper office, eagerly awaiting the outcome of the Johnson-Jeffries heavyweight fight.

dollar bond issue for the University of Louisville. The black community was split as younger leaders called for rejection of the issue, because blacks would pay taxes and receive nothing in return. Requiring a two-thirds majority, the bond issue failed as the black voting wards went against it by 12,000. Defeat of the issue brought about an important victory for Louisville blacks, for in 1925 white leaders this time consulted the black community, included substantial funds for black schools in a bond proposal, and won by a four-to-one margin. In that instance, blacks gained from their having the vote. And when attempts were made in the Kentucky legislature to enact a disfranchisement law, they all failed, usually with little attention. While the effect should not be overestimated, the vote did make a difference for blacks in Kentucky.[37]

Yet it did not, could not, wipe away the ignominious effects of segregation on the lives of a people, of Kentuckians of color. Blacks might at times choose institutions peopled chiefly by blacks, as they did in churches, but in most cases they had no choice. They could not sit and eat where whites did; they could not meet them as equals; they could not expect to advance in many professional areas. As a result, they had to retreat to a world chosen in large part for them, one whose physical boundaries would be hard to cross but whose psychological ones were often even more difficult.

In the job market, for instance, fewer and fewer blacks lived on farms. The 1910 census indicated 35 percent of blacks were agricultural workers; by the end of World War II only one in five would be. As a result, existence for most blacks meant an urban setting. Rural blacks, often voiceless and isolated, may have experienced greater or lesser hardships than their urban cousins; the story has not yet been told, except in the coal fields where blacks labored early, but whose numbers dropped over the years. But in the towns and cities, a clear pattern emerged. In Louisville in 1920, for example, 90 percent of all janitors, railroad porters, and waiters were black. Barbers, sewer workers, livery stable operators, simple laborers — these were the common occupations for black men. While many of the same mindsets operated regarding black women as white females — that they should live happy lives as contented wives — economic necessity forced more black women into the marketplace, usually as cooks or laundresses. In Richmond in 1900, for example, of black working women, 286 were cooks, 141 laundresses, 71 house servants, and 26 nurses. In Louisville in 1920, blacks comprised 90 percent of the laundresses. Yet many jobs remained virtually closed: in Louisville in 1910 of 346 telephone operators, 1 was black; of 1,037 clerks, 8 were black — .008 percent of the clerks in a city 18.0 percent black.[38]

C. Vann Woodward has noted that the black ghetto created by segregation "served as a kind of tariff wall to protect a monopolized market." As a result, a form of a black upper class did emerge, one partially dependent on a segregated market. In examining biographies of black leaders in Kentucky in the early part of the century, it becomes clear that physicians, ministers, educators, attorneys, and undertakers dominate the lists — and all depended on a segregated clientele. No matter what the cause, a prosperous black community developed in towns with large populations. In Lexington in 1907, black businesses included artists, attorneys, bankers, blacksmiths, carpenters, dentists, druggists, grocers, hotel operators, music teachers, opticians, plasterers, photographers, plumbers, physicians, shoemakers, tailors, undertakers, and "wealthy land owners." Nor were all blacks tied solely to the black community for their business: contractors for the Fayette County courthouse and for a major white school were both black.[39]

All across Kentucky blacks created their own positive worlds out of the negatives of segregation. Some blacks became wealthy: in Christian County a black there left a $500,000 estate; others thrived in creative ways. In Louisville at Tenth and Chestnut and at Sixth and Walnut Streets, black life flourished. Walnut became almost the Falls City's equivalent to Beale Street, as people like Sylvester Weaver, the first black guitarist to record, and blues singer Sara Martin made their mark. Ohio County native Arnold Schultz, another talented black instrumentalist, played on riverboats and with white bands as well, displaying an unusual style. When the bandleader was questioned about his guitarist's color, he answered, "You don't hear color, you hear music." While

Dr. T. T. Wendell, seated in his office at 349 W. Short St., ca. 1905, provided medical services to the black community in Lexington. Photo by Neighbors of Lexington.

Louisville-born Lionel Hampton gained musical fame elsewhere, blacks in his hometown enjoyed other artists, as they strolled Walnut, with its ice cream parlors, theaters, restaurants, public halls, beauty shops, and night clubs. In Lexington, the Dewees Street area met a similar need, while other towns had their own smaller — but often no less vibrant — versions. And, as in the white world, churches were a center of community social and religious life.[40]

While urban blacks still did not live in totally segregated areas, it was becoming more that way. In Louisville, where 73 percent of black families were native Kentuckians and 46 percent owned their own homes in 1930, two of the four "black" city wards remained virtually stable in the percentage of blacks living there between 1900 and 1920. But one ward went from 44 percent black to 69 percent in that same time. That increasing concentration of black families would continue.[41]

The world of blacks and whites did not remain totally apart. When U.S. Senator John Sherman Cooper recalled playing as a boy with the black children living behind their house, he was expressing a not uncommon memory.

A white Lewisburg man remembered, for example, that "one of my dearest little playmates was a little Negro boy. We used to be inseparable." They ate together and became "pretty good buddies" — for a time. Then, at some moment, it was made clear, as one person explained it, "where the line between white and colored should be drawn." Segregation rose to change the relationships. But even then, the two races could not escape each other. An upperclass white woman explained that when she wrote, "Negroes and their doings and sayings were . . . woven into the texture of all our lives."[42]

Yet, despite that, blacks knew they were expected to be different, to be inferior. A man who later would be a respected college professor wrote of that growing awareness: "Through a veil I could perceive the forbidden city, the Louisville where white folks lived. . . . On my side of the view everything was black: The homes, the people, the churches, the school, the Negro park. . . . I knew there were two Louisvilles and in America, two Americas. I knew, also, which of the Americas was mine."[43]

VOL. I   NO. 3

KENTUCKY
PROGRESS MAGAZINE

NOVEMBER
1928

OFFICIAL PUBLICATION OF THE KENTUCKY PROGRESS COMMISSION

5

"The Corn Top's Ripe":
Agriculture, Industry, and Labor

The Economy

Kentucky remained essentially an agrarian state in the first third of the twentieth century. But all around it and, indeed, within it, cries for industry and urbanism challenged the agrarian idea and agricultural dominance. In the state's cities and larger towns, urban boosterism praised progress, promoted prosperity, and promised commercial success through corporate growth. An urban-industrial ethos was winning in America and was challenging agrarianism in Kentucky.

That fight, however, would continue throughout the rest of the century, and supporters of the agrarian ideal retreated very slowly in the state. The urban-industrial juggernaut never won a decisive victory in its struggle for the minds of Kentuckians. Agrarianism would remain an important force in the commonwealth throughout the twentieth century.

Farm Life

"Farming was not just an occupation. It was a way of life that colored all our days from birth till death," declared author Harriette Simpson Arnow. Both as a way of life and an occupation, farming had both positive and negative aspects. It could be, for instance, a hard life. As Jack Temple Kirby notes, even in the winter, fences had to be fixed, buildings repaired, livestock cared for, hogs killed, meat cured, and tobacco beds readied. The spring brought planting; the summer, cultivation; the fall, harvest. Hoeing a garden, digging potatoes, "suckering" tobacco, milking a cow, gathering fodder — the variety of jobs on a farm seemed, to some, almost endless. Youngsters might have to clean and oil harnesses, polish the brass, feed the animals, in addition to simple — but hot — tasks, such as picking beans and corn. Later they would learn to plow — "Every country boy knew the feel of the plow handle," said one reporter. While men and women both worked the fields at times, women chiefly prepared the food, did the canning and storage, and supervised or did the

Kentucky Historical Society

Hog killing day in Bracken County, ca. 1900.

daily household tasks. As the children got older, in some parts of Kentucky the young men would earn extra money by becoming a kind of itinerant laborer, following wheat binders across the Midwest, or going north to shuck corn. Then, as they reached maturity, they would have to make the decision made by their parents: Do I farm or not?[1]

The lives of individual farmers suggest what such a life could be like. In 1908, on the fringes of Appalachia, in Rockcastle County, William Ransome "Ranse" Coffey at age twenty-three bought half of his father's 225-acre farm. Later, when his father died in 1927, he added the rest of the acres. Living at first in a self-made two-room frame house, he built a smokehouse, and a wash house, both on concrete foundations. For nearly five decades, Coffey varied little in the way he farmed that land. He planted twelve to fifteen acres in corn, six to eight in wheat, four in tobacco, an acre or two in oats, and ten to twenty acres in hay. The remainder of the land housed hogs for slaughter and up to twenty cattle and thirty lambs. His mechanical aids included a one-horse corn drill, mowing machine, disk harrow, hay rake, four-horse wheat binder, and, after 1930, cultivating plow with three shovels. Coffey purchased his first automobile in 1922 and began fencing with wire in the 1930s. Other than changes such as those, his life was lived in much the same way as his father's.[2]

A not dissimilar life was that of Henry Clay Northcott, an elderly minister living in Hillsboro in northeastern Kentucky. In a two-week period in January 1905, for example, he got up early, fed and watered his fowls, milked a dozen cows, cleaned out stalls, hauled feed, and loaded coal, resting only on Sunday. In early spring, in addition to his usual tasks, Northcott was also hauling away manure, planting potatoes, repairing hen nests, pruning his vineyards, and celebrating his sixtieth wedding anniversary. The first two weeks of June 1905 saw him set out some 100 tomato plants and 109 sweet potato plants, gather peas, onions, and beets, fix his fences, clean out his melon patch, hoe his crops, feed and milk the cows, and more. He also purchased a rheumatism remedy. But whether as an individual like Northcott or as a group, Kentucky farmers worked not at a steady pace, with the same hours every day, but rather at a natural one, dictated by weather, the animals, and Nature's needs. As a young girl wrote, "You pray for the rain to come and if too much comes, you pray for it to stop. It keeps you busy all summer praying and hoeing."[3]

The hard work on a farm resulted in a life that combined self-sufficiency and cooperation. Many farmers could at least live on their own resources, with water from rain barrels and wells, milk from cows, meat from various animals, fruits from orchards, and vegetables from gardens. Cash crops, such as tobacco, provided money for lesser necessities. Yet, at the same time, a cooperative spirit still operated in many of the same communities. Often people from various farms would go around and weed the fields as a group, or would help gather the crops when the time came. Other activities, such as building a new house or simply shelling corn, brought about the same results. One observer noted, "Every thought and every act was bound up in the concept of helping one another." That spirit, when combined with the natural rhythms of farm life, provided a sustaining form of neighborliness, of rural civility, of support.[4]

Add to that what some saw as the joys of working the land, and farming could provide many positives. Alben Barkley recalled, for example, that "there is a sort of thrill that comes to a barefoot boy when he plows up the ground, turns it over, and steps into the fresh furrow with his bare feet. There is a good feel and a good smell to the earth." Those real pleasures, and others on the farm, had to be balanced, of course, by the often long hours, the hot work, the uncertain rewards, the vagaries of Nature, and the hard life. As late as 1940, some 97 percent of Kentucky farms had no indoor plumbing; in 1926 in Christian County, over one-third of rural boys worked four months a year in the tobacco fields. The story was repeated across the state. Nonetheless, the positive aspects remained.[5]

The problem for farmers, however, was often less physical than emotional — America and, to a lesser degree, Kentucky seemed to be less inclined to praise that lifestyle as the century progressed. Once held up as the ideal for a republic, small farmers were being ridiculed as "rubes," or "bumpkins," or "hayseeds." About the only agrarians exempt from such characterizations were the "business-like" farmers on large farms, the horseowners, or, perhaps, those viewed as "modern" farmers. The first statewide Kentucky State Farmers Institute was held in 1906 to overcome what the commissioner of the State Bureau of Agriculture said was farm opposition to "scientific investigation." Within five years, every county had held institutes in their locale. Extension agents spread across the state, bringing new ideas and methods. But change came slowly, for capital was weak, old habits were strong, and a mindset for modification was often absent. As a result, the glitter of the city continued to challenge youth to leave the agricultural life for another lifestyle. Many harkened to the siren's call, for Kentucky's rural population grew by only 3.3 percent, 2.8 percent, and 1.8 percent in the years 1910, 1920, and 1930, respectively, while urban growth was 18.8 percent, 14.1 percent, and 26.1 percent in the same period. Public officials still would praise and support the agrarian ideal, even long after its dominance in the commonwealth had passed. Yet each year saw increasing attacks on the agrarian mindset.[6]

Farms and Crops

Between 1900 and 1940, two trends continued from the previous century: the number of Kentucky farms increased and the average size decreased. In 1900, the state had 234,667 farms, a figure that grew and peaked at 270,626 in 1920. But, with one exception, the numbers would consistently decline thereafter. In some ways, then, 1919 with its flush times left by World War I, yet before the agricultural depression of the 1920s, marked the apex of agriculture in the state in the new century.[7]

Yet even those large numbers of farms masked the problems, for the average size of the farms declined — from 93.7 acres in 1900 (about the same as Indiana and Tennessee) to 79.9 in 1920 to 78 twenty years after that. Over one-fourth of all Kentucky farms in 1900 were between 50 and 100 acres; only 558 farms exceeded a thousand acres in size. The World War II decade and the agricultural prosperity of that time, together with more people leaving farming, reversed the declining average size of farms.[8]

Those farms were operated in a variety of ways by a variety of people. Tenants ran almost one-third of the farms in 1900, and that figure changed little over the next four decades. But at a time when nearly half of southern farms were operated in such a fashion, that meant, comparatively, more Kentuckians operated their own farms than did those elsewhere. Nearly four of every five tenants operated on a share basis, and those farms averaged 49 acres. Cash tenants ran operations of 79 acres on the average; owners averaged 112 acres in 1900. Unlike the deeper South, blacks in Kentucky did not make up a sizeable portion of the tenant population. In 1900, under 8 percent of all tenants were black. Of those who owned farms, some 4 percent were black. Over three decades after the Civil War, they had finally averaged 40 acres; whites averaged 96 acres per farm. But most owners, white or black, had farms free of mortgages, for in 1910 only 15 percent were under that form of debt.[9]

Statistically, Kentucky farms were not very valuable. Their $2,059 average value in 1900 was only half the national figure. Black farms, averaging $975, exceeded the national average of $669 for blacks and represented the highest for any southern state, even though only half the figure for white farms. Two decades later the state had fallen even further below the national statistics, for all Kentucky farms then averaged $4,587 in value, versus the U.S. figure of $12,084. The state ranked forty-one out of forty-eight states. Across Kentucky, the numbers varied widely. A 1911 newspaper reported that while the state average was $14.50 per acre, the range went from Fayette's $80.07, Jefferson's $75.00, and Bourbon's $61.86 per acre to Rowan's $3.31, Martin's $4.20, and Menifee's $4.56.[10]

Yet for all the small farms, the tenantry, and the low value of farms, Kentucky still remained an important agricultural state. The value of its farm products in 1900 — over $123 million — ranked it highest in the South, except for Texas. Among those crops grown on farmland, roughly half of the some six million acres of harvested cropland was in corn. In 1904, for example, the 3.2 million acres of corn produced 86,816,000 bushels, some 27 bushels per acre. The wartime year of 1917 produced the still-record high in the acres of that crop harvested. But within seven years, production had dropped to some 63 million bushels.[11]

Other crops went though similar variations. What had once been Kentucky's chief cash crop — hemp — still was grown in some locales, but was a dying industry. Wheat remained an important crop, but reached its peak production in 1899. By the next year, some 12 million bushels were produced, but by 1909 Kentucky's wheat crop took up fewer than 50 percent of the acreage of a decade earlier and produced almost 40 percent fewer bushels — some 8.8 million. Similarly, oats — which had been grown on twice as many acres as tobacco in 1889 — continued to fall from farmers' favor. By 1909, the number of acres producing oats had dropped 45 percent in ten years. Apparently some of that change in emphasis made hay a more valued crop, for in that same period, hay acreage increased over 40 percent and production went from 655,000 to 957,000 tons.[12]

But for most Kentucky farmers tobacco still remained king and still dictated the degree of success they achieved. Grown in an era where the same fields were often recultivated year after year, where soil erosion might be commonplace, where fertilizer was inconsistently used — "We didn't have the fertilizin' stuff. . . . We didn't have the money to buy it. . . . So we just didn't fertilize. We just let it grow" — tobacco offered high returns on limited acreage. It also offered hard work for that reward.[13]

Plowing the ground, sowing the tobacco beds, covering the seeds, weeding, re-setting the developing plants, cultivating the new field, "topping" the blooms from the plants, crushing the worms, suckering the plants, cutting the tobacco, placing it on sticks, hanging the sticks in the barn, curing it, stripping the leaves, sorting the tobacco into grades, taking it to a warehouse for sale — all that was tobacco growing, and all of it was labor-intensive. Putting so much

Kentucky Historical Society

Cutting tobacco on the Ijames family farm, Henderson County, 1916.

effort into the crop, depending on its price so much, Kentucky farmers made or lost money depending on small changes in price. As one Hopkinsville woman recalled, "If it [tobacco] was selling well, church assessments and doctor bills were paid, merchants beamed, and bankers took a small payment and renewed the note. Life limped or cakewalked to the tune of the tobacco market."[14]

It played inconsistent notes. By 1900, and until 1929, Kentucky led the nation in the amount of tobacco grown. The problems in the first decade of the century had culminated in the Black Patch War, with its pooling, "cutouts," and other tactics. But by 1909, production had stabilized and the state's 470,000 acres produced nearly 400,000,000 pounds of leaf — two and a half times the crop of five years earlier. Real prosperity came, however, with the Great War. Prices soared as World War I raged; one study listed prices per hundred pounds in that locale as going from $9.09 in 1915 to $17.41 in 1917 to $28.47 in 1919. Statewide, tobacco brought an unprecedented $34.00 that last year. In fact, more pounds of tobacco were produced in 1919 than at any time, before or since, in Kentucky's history. Following what a congressman called "unusually good" crops in 1918, the 1919 results convinced farmers to plant still more tobacco. Even though not all parts of the state were receiving high prices — dark tobacco in west Kentucky still was low — overall the promise of wealth outweighed caution.[15]

The 1920 crop was a disaster. A poor harvest, a glutted market, and a decline in overseas demand all were factors. While the overall 13.4 cents per pound average really marked more of a return to prewar levels, it looked pitiful compared to the previous year's figure, almost three times higher. What would 1921 bring? Would Night Riders once more march across the state? Would Kentucky's violent image be reemphasized?[16]

In January the market opened, and national headlines proclaimed "Bottom Drops Out of Tobacco Market." Congressman J. Campbell Cantrill, a Scott County tobacco grower and one of the spokesmen for farmers, received telegrams and letters from across the state. In Georgetown: "Great Disatisfaction [sic]"; in Proverb: "the tobacco situation is very serious . . . the people are stirred up as never before"; in Lexington: "Tobacco situation is alarming." At Carlisle, knives were drawn and buyers threatened. Quickly, Kentucky leaders in and out of agriculture moved to ward off violence while dealing with the problem. A Burley Tobacco Growers Cooperative Association was formed through the efforts of men like Cantrill, Ralph M. Barker of Carrollton, Samuel H. Halley of Lexington, Stanley Reed of Maysville, and others, including the two editors of the Lexington papers. Key financial support came from James B. Brown of Louisville and particularly Robert Worth Bingham of the *Courier-Journal*. The two joined with a Cincinnati bank to pledge $3 million to help finance arrangements. Bingham, one of the key leaders, also arranged for California attorney Aaron Sapiro to help organize a pool. Seeking to get farmers to pledge to sell only to the cooperative, the association received commitments from 80 percent of the burley growers. While a few instances of Night-Riding occurred, the overall process was peaceful. Pooling brought 1922 prices up to 28.4 cents per pound. But, as before, impatient farmers, often strapped for money, could not remain united. The next year the percentage in the pool fell to 71 and prices declined to 21 cents. By 1926, a majority of farmers remained outside the association; the crop brought only 12.5 cents. Five years later, the price of 8.2 cents was the lowest in a quarter-century. More and more farmers turned to burley tobacco, which went from under 50 percent of the total crop in 1919 to 85 percent in 1943. But it was all to no avail. Until the New Deal, tobacco farmers still remained hostage to the auctioneer.[17]

Livestock

The value of livestock in Kentucky in 1900 — $70.5 million — placed Kentucky second in the South to Texas, which was second in the nation. The commonwealth continued to be a leading livestock producer. In 1900, it had almost two million swine, over 700,000 sheep, 425,000 horses, and 170,000 mules, with Paducah having one of the largest mule markets in the South.[18]

But changes were taking place. In Appalachian Kentucky the number of sheep fell from 175,000 in 1900 to only 73,000 thirty years later. The availability of cheap cotton goods and growth of coal towns lessened people's dependence on home-grown wool. A similar decrease took place in the number of hogs on mountain farms. Cattle, on the other hand, benefitted from better

Kentucky Historical Society

"Driving 400 Bronze Turkeys to Campbellsville for shipment east."

disease-control methods and improved breeding techniques. World War I stimulated meatpacking industries in Kentucky as well, so that by 1920, cattle made up one-fourth of the $85.5 million livestock evaluation in the state. Yet agricultural problems of the 1920s, together with hard times due to drought and depression in the 1930s, brought down prime prices per hundredweight for cattle from $5.90 in 1925 to $3.05 in 1933. The number of beef cattle was at a record low in 1930. Finally, growth again occurred in the 1930s, and Kentucky farms were home for 1.5 million head in 1940.[19]

Yet, as modern market techniques and changing patterns of production marked those years, the old, almost frontier, ways still lived on in some places. Open-range grazing continued through World War I at locales across the state and, as late as the 1930s, on the Cumberland Plateau. Cattle drives from small mountain counties to Bluegrass or West Virginia markets went on into the 1920s. A Jessamine County youngster remembered how turkeys, hogs, sheep, and cattle all were driven by his home, while a youthful Perry County boy drove 1,700 geese from his mountain county to Mt. Sterling, over ninety miles away. He traveled around four or five miles per day, reaping an eventual profit of over $400. As in other agricultural areas, Kentucky livestock were in a transitional stage, not yet free of the past century, not yet committed to the ways of its present one.[20]

The Industrial World

An often-stated comment in present-day Kentucky is that the commonwealth has always been — or at least in the twentieth century has been — a second-class state economically, that it has always lagged behind most of the South and the nation as well. But that view is incorrect.

In 1900 Kentucky's value of manufactured products — $154,166,000 — ranked it best in the entire South and eighteenth in the United States. It stood in good stead as the new century began. But Kentucky's decline in that area chiefly took place over the next three decades. As McConnell points out in a good study of manufacturing in Kentucky, between 1904 and 1929 Kentucky's general index of manufactures increased 65 percent; the South's went up 171 percent. Broken down in smaller time periods, from 1904 to 1909 only two southern states grew more slowly than did Kentucky; in the next five-year period, Kentucky again was twelfth in growth among fourteen southern states studied. During the war years of 1914–1919, a huge gap appeared as Kentucky manufacturing declined 4.1 percent, while the South, overall, increased 27.5 percent. Only between 1919 and 1923 did Kentucky do better than its sister states in the South — a 17 percent increase to their 10.7 percent. But slower growth followed once more to 1929.[21]

Using 1904 as the base, Kentucky went from a manufacturing index of 100 that year to 165.5 a quarter of a century later. Without comparing themselves to others, citizens could — and did — boast of great growth. Yet the South, overall, went from 100 to 271 in that same time. North Carolina grew from 100 to 405, Texas to 387, Tennessee to 280. From a position of being number one in the South in 1904, Kentucky could have used that status to grow and dominate. Yet between 1904 and 1929, it tied with Arkansas as the southern state growing least in that period. Why?[22]

Why was Kentucky losing the industrial race in the first three decades of this century? Different commentators provided varied answers. Robert Worth Bingham later pointed to the state's reputation for violence as one cause, noting that he personally knew that the Goebel problem caused a $10-million plant to be built elsewhere. A legislator in 1906 explained that he could not get a railroad company to build in his locale due to feud stories: "It is almost impossible to get the ear of outside capital with conditions as they are." The Black Patch War added to those concerns in the century's first decade.[23]

Others pointed to the state's particular manufacturing make-up as a problem. A strong carriage-making industry and a hemp-producing one were dying; the lumber industry went into decline in that time; the liquor industry, which, as McConnell notes, contributed 37 percent of the total value added by manufacture and employed nearly 5 percent of all wage earners in the state, was, of course, restricted by Prohibition in the 1920s. That was a severe blow.[24]

Still other observers focused on more specific causes, such as the railroads. A Columbia University study of railroads in the South in 1916 concluded that "there is probably no state railroad commission in the entire United States

TABLE 5.1

Growth in Volume of Manufactures, 1904–1929

	Kentucky	Other 13 Southern States
1904	100	100
1909	121.7	134.8
1914	125.1	149.4
1919	120.0	190.5
1923	140.4	210.9
1929	165.5	270.9

Source: Joseph L. McConnell, "Growth of Manufacturing in Kentucky, 1904 to 1929" (Master's thesis, University of Kentucky, 1932)

with jurisdiction and powers more circumscribed than the railroad commission . . . of Kentucky." Given more powers during the railroad reform following Goebel's death, the commission often had still been ineffective, due to long legal litigations, with few clear-cut victories. In 1906, for instance, it found that railroads operating north of the Ohio River charged much lower rates than in Kentucky and produced a schedule of rates to correct what they saw as unreasonable fees. The railroads appealed, the case went to the United States Supreme Court, taking three years to decide overall, and the commission's actions were overruled in the end. Legislators, often tied closely to the L & N, did not strengthen the commission over the years, as other states were doing, and it remained generally weak. Members of the general assembly continued to accept free passage or reduced fare — Kentucky's was one of only two southern legislatures allowing that.[25]

In 1930, Kentucky Attorney General J. W. Cammack blamed the railroad situation for Kentucky's decline. Pointing out that fifty years earlier Kentucky had stood first in the South in population and was now fifth and falling, he said high freight rates for the interior of the state were a major factor in that decline. First-class travel from Louisville to Bowling Green, a distance by rail of 114 miles, cost more than a trip from Louisville to St. Louis, a 280-mile journey. To ship mining tools from Pittsburgh to Hazard cost Kentuckians a $.61 rate; the same goods going that distance to a northern state cost $.355. Steel shipped from Ashland to Danville within Kentucky went the 158 miles at a $.34 rate; the same product shipped from Ashland 450 miles north into Ohio cost the same amount. Cammack argued that it was often more economical for Kentucky businesses to ship raw materials out of the commonwealth than to ship them within the state for production. Given the nearness of the northern states, the "southern system," with its rate discriminations, hit Kentucky hard.[26]

But perhaps the best answer to Kentucky's relative decline was seldom spoken and then usually in the heat of a political debate. As much as anything else, Kentucky's leadership failed, both at the state political level and the private business one. There was no major reason why Kentucky could not grow as did other southern states — a 1927 study indicated growth in the South came from lower labor costs, an agricultural depression, favorable tax laws, nearness to raw materials, the closeness of fuels, and available sites. Kentucky had all that, including the agricultural depression. The state gave new businesses tax-exempt status for a period of years, and the Kentucky Progress Commission in 1929 pointed out that only one state had a lower county and state tax rate than Kentucky. Chambers of commerce and booster clubs voiced the industrial line, as did many political leaders.[27]

Yet, in the end, when major questions needed to be decided, the agrarian viewpoint usually won out. Bold, well-articulated visions, together with strong, well-conceived political plans to carry them out, seldom appeared. Leaders did not take the steps necessary to keep Kentucky in the position of strength it held in 1900. Instead, the state limped along, proud of its growth, only slowly reacting to the fact that the manufacturing world around it was changing more rapidly than it was. Almost in a panic, leaders then had to face a dilemma the South also had: If the decision is made that industry is needed for long-term economic security for the commonwealth, how far can — or should — the state go in giving such industry special advantages? Balancing worker rights with profit motives, environmental concerns with financial ones, would prove difficult and controversial.

The manufacturing wealth of the state, such as it was, was clearly concentrated on the Ohio River. In 1929, some 86 percent of the total value added by manufactures in the state was along that waterway — and 55 percent of the total was in or near Louisville. Its key industries were printing, foundry and machine shops, baking, and tobacco plants. (In 1900 it was said to have had the largest tobacco market in the world.) At one time the banking center of the South, Louisville was still strong in that area, as well as in the production of varnish, "Kentucky jeans," soap, and distilled spirits. (Kentucky stood second, behind Illinois, in the production of liquor in 1914.) Beginning in 1913, Ford produced automobiles, then trucks at various Louisville plants. All along the river, manufacturing had sprung up — at Covington and Newport, at Owensboro (which had the second largest wagon factory in the South in 1904), at Paducah (with the state's tallest office building in 1910), and elsewhere.[28]

One other river city later became the headquarters for one of the state's business success stories. In 1918, a Kentucky crude-oil producing group was organized, six years later a small refining company was formed, and Ashland Refining Company began a rapid growth. It grew in assets from $250,000 in 1924 to $8 million in 1940 to $175 million by 1956. Much of the credit for that success was due to its chief executive, Paul G. Blazer. Born in Illinois, majoring in social sciences before he dropped out of college in the World War I era, Blazer became a self-taught refining specialist, moved up the corporate ladder, and began purchasing smaller refineries and pipelines at bargain prices. When he retired as chairman of the board of Ashland Oil in 1957, he left behind a strong organization.[29]

But large in-state companies of such scope were all-too-few. Like the South generally, Kentucky suffered in part from a colonial economy, where much of the ownership and the profits lay outside the commonwealth. The state had unskilled labor, underdeveloped resources, and inadequate capital, which brought out-of-state control of much of the mining, industrial, and transportation properties. Of the directors of the L & N and the C & O Railroads in the century's first decade, only two of the twenty-two were from Kentucky. Ford Motor Company owned 45,000 acres in Clay County. The ownership situation in the coal companies was similar and, as a result, much of the state's wealth left its borders. Decisions shaping the state's economic life were made in corporate boardrooms outside Kentucky. As historian Thomas D. Clark noted, little tobacco, timber, or mineral money was used to endow hospitals, libraries, museums, historical societies, or schools. Once gone, it seldom returned.[30]

On another plane, dissatisfaction with "outside" involvement in Kentucky economic affairs spilled over into a full-fledged legislative debate. Small retailers increasingly complained about the growing number of chain stores in the commonwealth, particularly in the grocery area where A & P, Foltz, Kroger, and Piggly Wiggly were making an impact. By 1930, chain stores accounted for 15 percent of all retail sales in the state.

Reacting to what was perceived as a threat to local businessmen, who feared they could not compete, Danville had enacted a measure regulating such stores through a license fee. One of the first municipal laws of that kind in the United States, it was overturned by the state's highest court in 1925. The scene then shifted to legislative chambers where in 1930 a speaker said "foreigners" (chain-stores) were "slowly draining the life blood out of these country merchants." An anti-chain-store bill passed, but it too was overturned, this time in the U.S. Supreme Court, with Louis D. Brandeis dissenting. Other laws, in 1936 and 1940, took a different approach, but the Kentucky Court of Appeals found both unconstitutional as well. Fueled by localism, fears of outside ownership, and concerns about monopolies, the anti-chain-store movement in Kentucky finally failed because, as one historian wrote, "Kentucky was the prisoner of its own constitution."[31]

Minerals

In contrast to the state's overall industrial sluggishness, the coal industry was booming during the first two decades of the century. In 1900, the state did not stand high, nationally, in coal tonnage produced. The 123 commercial mines yielded but 5,020,000 tons, mostly in the Western Kentucky field. Of that figure, 60 percent was still sold in the state.[32]

But massive changes were underway as the new eastern fields began operating. By 1912, those fields were outproducing the western ones in total tonnage, and, two years later, Pike County in the east surpassed Muhlenberg in the west as the state's leading coal producer. Within five years, Pike alone was taking out almost as many tons as the entire state had produced in 1900. Mechanization, though of a primitive sort at first, began to have an impact as well. In 1904, for the first time, more coal was produced by crude machine than by hand; by 1916 some 84 percent was machine-influenced.[33]

The result of all that was a huge increase in coal tonnage from Kentucky mines:

TABLE 5.2

Coal Production in Kentucky, Selected Years, 1900–1920

Year	Tonnage (Rounded)
1900	5,020,000
1907	10,753,000
1912	16,491,000
1914	20,383,000
1916	25,394,000
1918	31,530,000
1920	38,892,000

Source: Willard R. Jillson, "A History of the Coal Industry in Kentucky," *Register* 20 (1922): 21–45, and Inspector of Mines Reports.

In two decades, coal production had grown over sevenfold. The state's overall value of mineral productions jumped from $12.1 million in 1909 to $98.5 million a decade later to $132.7 million in 1929. That elevenfold growth far exceeded the national increase, which quadrupled in that same era. From a state that was the eighth-leading producer of coal in 1905, Kentucky had become the third-leading producer in 1929. As the inspector of mines had noted in 1901: "The business world says 'Coal is King,' and so it is."[34]

For a time many thought increasing oil production might yield a royal rival to King Coal, but the oil industry seemed particularly oriented to cycles of boom or bust. Almost every rural county in the eastern half of the state had one such oil boom and an influx of "wildcatters" between 1900 and 1920. Discoveries of new "pools," such as Ragland in Bath County in 1900, or Campton in Wolfe County in 1903, or Big Sinking in Lee County in 1918, brought a new attack of "oil fever." From 62,000 barrels in 1900, production went to 1,214,000 barrels in 1906, but fell to under a half million by 1915. The war stimulated production, which soared to over nine million barrels in 1919, only to fall under seven million by 1925. Still, oil continued to be an important, if secondary, resource for Kentucky. The state also remained the national leader in the production of fluorspar and native asphalt in the 1920s. Kentucky's coal and other mineral wealth had slowly become a major part of the state's economic picture.[35]

Kentucky Historical Society

Loading coal onto barges on the Green River, Ohio County.

Labor Conditions

Increased industrialization came at a price — a human one. Boosters would worry that any criticism, any restriction, would drive away industry, while others worried that too much of a laissez-faire attitude would ignore the working conditions of those who labored. Those two different viewpoints would periodically clash throughout the century, sometimes ending in good discussion and productive action, sometimes concluding in harsh words and violent conduct.

Meeting in Louisville on 25 January 1900, forty delegates created the Kentucky Federation of Labor and elected James McGill as president. With lobbying money raised by a bazaar, organized labor had major success in the 1902 legislature. As the pro-labor *Kentucky Irish American* explained, laborers "have broken the ice in Kentucky." A child labor law, an act making Labor Day an official holiday, and a law creating a labor inspector resulted. The first inspector used the child labor law provisions — children under the age of fourteen could work only with a parent's approval — and investigated conditions. He often found poor work conditions with locked doors and dangers of fire, as well as some 1,900 underage children laboring without permits. Yet nearly

650 more had such permits and worked in conditions similar to those he found in Maysville: "They go to work at 5:45 in the morning and quit at 6:15 at night, with half an hour for dinner. Their pay is twenty-three cents a day." A compulsory education law in 1904 required school attendance for all children under the age of fourteen, ending the permit question, and the child labor law itself was amended in the next two sessions. By 1914, when it was further changed, it was being hailed as one of the best in the nation.[36]

The labor inspector's tours in 1902 and 1903 gave him a good overview of the situation. Laborers worked on the average a ten-hour day, with men averaging between $1.59 and $1.66 in daily wages (depending on region) while women averaged $.86 to $.90. Of the 869 factories visited, 102 were unionized. In comparing union workers and non-union, he indicated the 12,000 union laborers worked forty minutes less per day but earned wages almost a dollar higher.[37]

Such concrete rewards brought more active demands for unions, and that, in turn, did not always meet a friendly reception. Strikes occurred every year, and the ten in 1904 showed the diversity of union membership. Work stoppages took place among the meat cutters, carpenters, cigar makers, bricklayers, garment workers, and iron molders in Louisville, the leather workers in Paducah, and the iron and steel workers of Covington. The Kenton County area, in fact, would be a labor battleground for some time. Giving more votes to the Socialist Party in 1912 than anywhere else in Kentucky, the workers of Kenton and Campbell Counties had bitter fights with management. In one of the more serious conflicts, strikers and guards clashed at the Andrews Steel plant in Newport in 1919, and at least four people were shot.[38]

The Newport nightmare grew worse in January 1922. Iron, steel, and tin workers at the mills had organized, but management would not recognize their right to do so. The strike that followed grew increasingly bitter, and the militia was sent in. Unfortunately, its commander, Henry H. Denhardt, sought headlines more than peace. Operating at a time when memories were still fresh of the "Red Scare" that swept America after World War I, Colonel Denhardt told reporters that "red agitators of the worst type" were behind the trouble. Union leaders, far from free of inflammatory language either, compared the presence of troops to a Russian dictatorship. Early in January, Denhardt ordered his troops, including a machine-gunner, to fire into strikers; over a hundred rounds were shot. The next month, tanks and four hundred more National Guard troops were sent to Newport after a personal visit by the governor failed to resolve the impasse. When strikers attacked mill workers crossing their picket lines, the troops responded with more gunfire and clubs. Ten strikers were injured; more shots and more arrests followed before the unhappy situation ended. In Paducah that same year railroad violence resulted in three bombs exploding in homes, while in Corbin a policeman and a railroad worker were killed in labor problems in 1923. In fact, between 1900 and 1933, over seventy strikes were directed at railroads in Kentucky.[39]

Employees of the Ashland Iron & Mining Co. foundry, 1906.

Laborers in the coal fields were often not included in the statistics on union workers; they were viewed as a different group. Yet their problems were similar — low pay, poor conditions, unresponsive management — and the story line all too familiar. As the United Mine Workers of America (UMW) began to organize across the western Kentucky coal fields, strikes followed. In reporting a Hopkins County strike that began in November 1900, the militia officer dispatched to the scene gave an unusually dispassionate report. Both sides were armed and "in a state of hostility." The county was virtually lawless with shots randomly fired both in Madisonville and at the mines. The troops sent there left in October 1901; the next month "several" lives were lost in a battle between the two contending sides. The State Guard went back and calm followed. In evaluating the conditions, the military leader said only one side's view — that of the mine owners — was being given in newspapers, though both had good arguments. Both also had rights which must be protected, and that is where problems arose, he wrote. The situation left him with no answers.[40]

Others had problems resolving such conflict as well. The inspector of mines in 1903 found many mines "in a deplorably bad condition." Yet, if attempts to change that, or just to unionize generally, were met by total opposition, did that give strikers the right to wreak violence on the mines? Did the owners have the right to hire private armies for protection and make the mines little armed camps? It was a troubling situation and got no clearer.[41]

The problems continued. In 1901, for example, a clash near Hopkinsville between strikers and mine guards ended in gunfire and a dead deputy. When faced with a UMW strike, a Sturgis company hired strikebreakers, barricaded the mines, put up spotlights, and added a "rapid fire gun." Little wonder that near Christmas 1906, striking miners in the county fought with guards, and two union men and one guard died. In 1930, an airplane dropped bombs on a Providence mine during a strike there. And the episodes went on, in other west Kentucky locales, at other times, with variations on the outcomes. But the attention of the media focused on the problems of another area of Kentucky, a place where the term "war" was applied once more to a Kentucky action.[42]

The Harlan County Coal Wars

Harlan County had been affected more by the coal boom in eastern Kentucky in the first two decades of the century than perhaps any other part of the region. Its population tripled between 1900 and 1920, its rural landscape was transformed by a "whirlwind industrialization," and its people's lifestyle changed almost overnight. In a transitory situation, with newcomers — many of them blacks and immigrants — with new ways of doing things, and with new conflicts, non-union violence broke out. In the five years before 1925, the county's murder rate was nearly 8 per 10,000. It was a situation rife with more potentially dangerous problems.[43]

Initially, labor unions had done well in those boom years and, by 1912, some 19,000 workers statewide belonged to the United Mine Workers of America (UMW). Overall, Harlan miners prospered and wages rose from an average of $578 in 1922 to $1,235 in 1929. But unfriendly courts, failed strikes in 1922 and 1924, an abundance of strike breakers, and bad decisions all hurt labor in the 1920s. Then the "golden age" of coal ended as a slump in the coal economy became a depression at the end of the decade. As early as 1925, the Lexington *Herald* reported that "mine after mine has been closed and those operating now are only playing for time." That hand soon ended as the entire nation suffered the pangs of economic despair. The coal industry had too much equipment, too little demand, and too many workers. Between 1927 and 1932, one-third of Harlan County's mines closed; in the decade before 1932, unionized mines' share of the nation's coal production dropped from 70 percent to 20 percent. The UMW membership in Kentucky fell to 1,000. Unions had several problems and were almost dead; mines were in trouble and were closing. In that atmosphere, where there were few easy, or even right, answers, both sides erred.[44]

The once-proud company towns now became shabby. Lacking funds, the companies could not keep up the repairs. Paint began to peel from buildings, and the whole infrastructure developed problems. Companies' vaunted paternalism failed when they could not keep wages high — and they fell 60 percent from 1929 to 1931. Already dangerous work conditions got no better.

Soon layoffs became commonplace, and jobless miners, without funds, prospects, or any place to go, were evicted from their homes. The community cohesion so desired was replaced by community conflict. Class feelings became stronger and more openly displayed. And with the coal companies the only job in town, and their authority and dominance so complete, few options seemed available. Desperate, hungry people began inching to the edge of starvation. It was no longer a question of a job; it was a question of survival.[45]

"Bloody Harlan" was the result. The county was an armed camp, waiting to explode. Coal companies, fearful of violence on their properties, paid for well-armed special deputies, whose chief duties were to guard their mines and equipment and disrupt union organizing rallies. Unfortunately, those selected frequently had criminal records themselves and their rough tactics earned them their title of "gun thugs." By 1932, the sheriff had 170 of those deputies, all but 6 paid by the coal companies. In the operators' control as well was the commonwealth's attorney who served after 1934. He received thousands of dollars in coal company retainers every year, while the circuit judge from 1928 to 1933 was married to one of the owners of a mine. Locally, the forces of law seemed to be totally controlled by the coal barons. Added to that was the tendency of the governor to call out the National Guard to oppose the miners. All in all, then, Justice appeared blind only to labor's concerns, and workers armed to provide their own version of the justice denied them through regular channels.[46]

Facing a depressed industry and with few other options, coal operators reduced wages further in February 1931. Relief efforts for the unemployed were stopping. Workers were angry. At that time, the UMW held an organizing rally in nearby Bell County. The next day, Harlan operators began firing hundreds of those who had attended. Discharged workers moved to Evarts, a non-company town whose population jumped from 1,500 to nearly 5,000. Soon, some company store commissaries in the region were looted. The UMW district president warned President Herbert Hoover that these "very, very hungry" people were on the verge of "riot and bloodshed" if something was not done. The result was a local restraining order forbidding the union's organizers from talking to certain coal company employees. By April, deputies were arresting some unionists when another person fled. In an exchange of gunfire, the suspect was wounded and a deputy killed. Soon, a dynamite blast closed a mine entry, robberies grew more frequent, then sixteen empty company houses were destroyed by arson. On 5 May 1931, a three-car motorcade escorting a company truck passed near Evarts. A barrage of rifle and shotgun fire struck the vehicles, and, before it all ended, a thousand rounds had been exchanged between ambushers and deputies. In the thirty-minute "Battle of Evarts," three pro-company men were killed, and at least two more wounded; one miner lay dead as well. Virtual anarchy ruled now, and almost all Harlan miners went out on strike. The governor quickly sent almost four hundred National Guard troops to the area, and they remained for two months. They did have a calming effect, but also halted picketing. The military occupation,

Tension in the Harlan coal fields.

the local indictments followed by mass arrests of labor leaders, and the need for funds and food ended the strike and the 1931 attempt to organize. But the Harlan County "coal wars" had just begun. Choices had to be made, as a protest song of the decade indicated:

> If you go to Harlan County
> There is no neutral there
> You'll either be a union man
> or a thug for J. H. Blair
>> Which side are you on?
>> Which side are you on?[47]

Over the next eight years, Harlan County became a symbol. For those supporting labor, it could be presented as a perfect conflict pitting stubborn, reactionary capitalists and "gun thugs" against starving workers. For those supporting business, it could be viewed as a testing ground where radicals and communists sought through violence to take the scant profits and destroy legitimate businesses. Supporters of labor from outside the state made the march to Harlan, both to help the cause, as they perceived it, and to garner publicity for it. Nationally known writers and others, such as Theodore Dreiser, John Dos Passos, Waldo Frank, Edmund Wilson, and Malcolm Cowley, found themselves often beaten or indicted as a result. Their angry writing aroused more passions and attracted more attention. (One Kentucky editor wrote that if Dreiser's mind "were reduced to printed form it would be banned from the mails under the law prohibiting the transmission of obscene matter.") In turn, coal operators resented the "outside" actions, refused to compromise, and condoned suppression tactics that only added to the problem. In an eight-year period, six miners were killed and thirteen wounded; five deputies and two Guardsmen died, and three more were wounded. Compared to many other industrial strikes, or even the high non-union death rate in the country, that was not a high toll. Yet "Bloody Harlan" it became in the national consciousness.[48]

By 1931, the UMW had virtually deserted the Harlan coalfields, and into that void stepped the Communist-oriented National Miner Union (NMU). It set up some needed soup kitchens to help the hungry and made some initial inroads. But, as John Hevener noted, "The Communists' atheist, interracial, collectivist, and pro-Soviet views, once known, directly affronted the Harlan miners' fundamentalist religion, racism, individualism, and patriotism." In a sense, the miners were too American to support the NMU. In February 1932, the Dreiser group published *Harlan Miners Speak*, a pro-NMU work that gained national attention. But more balanced reports such as one by Henry Bullock of Lexington garnered less publicity. He found many operators were indeed working hard to aid miners, particularly through the extension of credit, but he did note that blacklisted miners and their families "are in want" and faced real hardship.[49]

Away from the printed page of reports, the violence continued. In May 1932, the head of the American Civil Liberties Union and several lawyers were refused entrance into Bell County. In December, an unemployed miner killed a deputy who had struck him with a revolver; in February 1933, a teen-age NMU organizer was murdered by a mine guard; in March, two hundred out-of-state students were stopped at Cumberland Gap, and, when they failed to post $1,000 peace bonds, were ordered out of the state; the next month, some visiting teachers and students were whipped and sent away. In 1933, the UMW started a membership drive, the church of a pro-union minister was bombed, a union leader's car was riddled with bullets, and that same organizer's apartment was later bombed twice. The next year, another pro-union minister found a bomb under his house and later had ten shots fired at that same house. Snipers fired on a miner's rally and a worker was pistol-whipped by deputies in 1934 also. Politics began to be a factor as Governor Ruby Laffoon sent in his adjutant general, Henry H. Denhardt, to study conditions. The Denhardt Commission concluded that the sheriff was in league with operators and that "there exists a virtual reign of terror. . . . Free speech and the right of peaceable assemblage is scarcely tolerated." But it was believed that Laffoon wanted a pro-union report to get labor's endorsement of his candidate in the 1935 Democratic primary for governor, and not much resulted from that study. In September 1935, the reform-minded county attorney Elmon Middleton was killed when a huge bomb destroyed his automobile, sending a part of the engine a quarter-mile away. Bombs destroyed two union organizers' cars in January 1937, and that same month snipers shot at a union leader and his wife as they were out walking. On 9 February 1937, three cars drove up in front of that organizer's home and fired a barrage of some twenty-five shots into the house. His wife and a son were slightly wounded. Another son, an innocent teenage boy, was killed — an event that angered the whole area. Yet, still no peace came to Harlan. An anti-operator court witness was assassinated in June; then, with the National Guard called in as a result of a strike, in 1939 the "Battle of Stanfill" resulted. Two pickets died and two guardsmen were injured as well. It was little wonder a woman remembered of the time: "Before they got organized . . . Harlan County blood ran like water."[50]

But by then, events outside the county were influencing a peace. Passage of the Wagner Act, and its approval by the U.S. Supreme Court in August 1937, guaranteed unions collective bargaining rights and outlawed blacklists, yellow dog contracts, and many other employers' tactics. It was a New Deal for labor. At almost the same time, the La Follette Civil Liberties Committee focused on Harlan and in 1937 issued a scathing report entitled *Violations of Free Speech and Rights of Labor*. Although confronted by lapses of memory and probably some perjury, the committee concluded that county officials were close allies of the coal operators and benefitted financially from that arrangement. They deplored the terroristic acts perpetrated by the deputy sheriff's "gun thugs" group and concluded that basic liberties of speech, press, and assembly were being denied. In September, sixty-nine companies, operators, and peace officers were indicted for conspiracy to "intimidate certain citizens" and to restrict their rights to bargain collectively. The resulting two-and-a-half-month trial ended in a deadlocked jury, but the signs were clear to the operators. The miners now had allies in government. In 1938 the company-paid deputy system was abolished by the state legislature. That same year a seven-month agreement was signed between the operators and 12,000 miners. After a strike the next year, a new two-year contract was ratified on 22 July 1939, one covering all the county's mines and workers. Many, many miners agreed with one worker's conclusion: "This was the greatest thing that ever happened." With that the "war" ended, and industrial peace came at last to the coalfields.[51]

It proved an uneasy truce, for in April 1941 another strike followed the expiration of the contract. There were more shootings and, at the "Crummies Creek Massacre," more deaths. The difference was that discussion, not more violence, resulted this time, and a new contract followed. By 1945, the homicide rate for the county was one-third the figure of two decades earlier. More and more often, deaths in Harlan did not take place on a deserted hill, or in an ambushed car, or in a picket line, but inside the still-deadly mines themselves. Labor victory had been won; the fight for industrial safety still was being fought.[52]

Cynthiana boasted a modern school, ca. 1931.

6

"The Young Folks": Education

At one level, Kentucky schools seemed adequate in 1900. Of the thirteen southern states, Kentucky stood fourth in expenditures per pupil, and its per capita funding more than doubled the figures of Alabama, North Carolina, and South Carolina. The average length of school term — over 115 days — ranked third in the South, only slightly behind the leaders and far ahead of North Carolina's 71-day average.

The problem was that support for southern schools was terrible, compared to national figures. Kentucky's per pupil expenditures came to only one-half the national norm; its school term stood thirty days behind the United States average. The state's schools had a long way to go. In the first decade of the twentieth century, major reforms took place in an attempt to remedy that situation. Important changes occurred. But what were hailed as solutions to the commonwealth's problems turned out to be cruel mirages of hope.[1]

The System

Many of the concerns about the educational system focused on its administrative make-up. Usually those worries did not center on the persons heading up the system, the popularly elected state superintendents of public instruction. Despite the fact that the office had no special educational requirements and a one-term limit, it attracted a generally respectable group of officeholders. While one had problems with drink, drugs, and nepotism, that was the exception. Overall, the state superintendents had good schooling and a background in education — the first three in the century had held positions as county superintendent, college professor, and city school superintendent, respectively. Yet, once in office, all the superintendents found their power limited and their position often little more than a fund-distribution center. They could, and did, voice their concerns and provide leadership, but the real power still resided at the local level.[2]

County superintendents composed the next rung in the educational ladder. An elective office since 1884, with only a limited educational requirement, the position was often viewed more as a part-time supervisory or even clerical one than as a post of educational leadership. The limited salary did not suggest that the office was very important. In 1902, the minimum was set at $400 and as late as 1920, the average was only $1,065. The low salary, limited educational requirements, and restricted duties often did not attract the best candidates. Of ninety-six county superintendents reporting in 1920, eight had only an elementary education and twenty-seven more had never finished high school.[3]

Yet the evidence is clear that in many cases, educated, excellent people filled that position, despite the problems, and did provide good leadership given the restrictions under which they operated. The county superintendent's job also provided women in Kentucky rare access to some power and to a politically elected office. In 1887, a woman was elected to fill her deceased husband's term as county superintendent. From that beginning, by the first decade of the new century women regularly held some twenty superintendent slots each year, spread across the state. The irony was they could be elected to office, but could not vote. Two exceptions existed: in 1838 widows with children and then fifty years later all widows and single women taxpayers received suffrage rights in school matters. Between 1894 and 1902, all women in second-class cities could cast ballots in education-oriented elections as well. Since schools were viewed as women's sphere, such actions were not as threatening to the established way. But even the urban suffrage right was rescinded, and not until a decade later, in 1912, could all Kentucky women vote even on limited educational matters. For most of the time, the female county superintendents were selected chiefly by a male vote.[4]

But whether male or female, county superintendents still did not comprise the centerpiece of the system. The troublesome trustee system did. Until 1909, school districts in each county were created per one hundred school-age children and were directed by three trustees. Each of those small districts had the power to fix local school taxes, set salaries, and select teachers, which gave trustees the key role in the entire system. Power resided in their hands, which often meant that school elections for trustees brought forth more interest — and more friction — than any other race before the electorate. As one mountain resident recalled: "Those elections were hotter than the President's because there were so many teachers that didn't have any jobs. The ones that had the largest number of votes and relatives that could vote in their behalf [would] get the school." After one such election at Prather Creek in 1933 left five dead and three wounded, the legislature changed the viva voce system still in effect in those races. The intensity continued, however.[5]

Requirements for the position remained minimal, and, as a result, many districts chose trustees not for their educational interest or expertise, but rather for their promise to keep taxes low or to favor certain people in the teacher-selection process. It could be a lucrative job. One woman recalled that "My daddy bought my first school job for me. Paid a trustee for it. The trustee told him, '. . . give me fifty [dollars] and it's yours.'" By law, the trustees qualified for the office if they were over twenty-one years of age, were of good moral character, and were, "when not impracticable," literate. Apparently, impracticability ruled supreme across the commonwealth, for in 1914, according to one state superintendent, over 5,000 of the trustees could not read or write.[6]

In 1907, county superintendents were asked to evaluate the trustee system with its 200 trustees (on the average) per county, its 8,000 trustee districts, and its 25,000 trustees — 1 in 80 people in Kentucky served as a trustee. The chief virtue of the system was that it was certainly democratic. Otherwise, the superintendents found little to praise. In Cumberland County, said the report, "many trustees are densely ignorant and very unscrupulous in their dealings," while the McLean County superintendent called the system "a farce and almost a total failure." Over and over, the same themes appeared, causing the state superintendent to conclude that the arrangement primarily promoted community feuds and rewarded ignorance.[7]

Problems with Kentucky education did not begin and end with the trustee system, however. Textbook selection, for instance, was frequently controversial. At the turn of the century, each little trustee district chose its own books, which meant that in one county potentially dozens of different books could be used for the same class. In 1904, that situation changed when a county textbook commission was established to provide countywide uniformity. Even after a state commission was given powers for statewide adoption, debate focused on whether its decisions were fair and unbiased. The 1919 adoption process, for example, was thrown out by the state's highest court. The problem of making books available to students seemed solved by a 1928 act providing for free textbooks through grade eight, but funding for that act became an issue for years to come.[8]

Even in an area where the state had taken something of a regional leadership role, debate continued on extending that lead. By 1900, Kentucky was the only southern state with a compulsory education law. In 1904, truant officers had been approved for urban areas, to strengthen the statute. Four years later, all children aged seven through fourteen were required to attend school, and a 1912 compulsory education act further strengthened the system. The same situation occurred on the length of the school term. Kentucky lengthened the school year from five to six months in 1904 and continued to rank high regionally in that regard. In 1912, the state stood fourth among sixteen southern states in length of term, and in 1914 extended its term to seven months. Yet in both areas, every time a change occurred, a minor hue and cry went up from Kentuckians who saw their labor force being taken away from them more and more. By the time Kentucky set its minimum school term at nine months in 1952, it had lost any leadership role it once held.[9]

Finances, of course, continued to be a problem. As with the South generally, Kentucky had less wealth to tax to raise funds. To garner the same resources as richer states required higher tax rates. But the problem went beyond that, for at the state level support of education was not meager. The deficits chiefly came locally, particularly in rural areas. In 1901, a professor pointed out that fifteen cities in Kentucky raised $600,000 per year for their school population of 150,000. All the rest of the state (with four times the students) raised $250,000, less than half the urban amount. Six years later, the state superintendent of public instruction made the same point, arguing that less money was generated by local taxation in Kentucky than in any other state. Some counties did well in raising funds; most did not. But the differences were often staggering: In 1919 the school rate varied from a low of $.06-2/3 in Hopkins County to $.50 in Washington County, yet the two places were not greatly different. Across Kentucky, schools called out for more money but often heard only a dim echo of support in return.[10]

When in 1902 a Kentucky governor declared that the state was "exceedingly generous" toward its schools, in one way he was not wrong. That year over 44 percent of the commonwealth's funds went to education, and, two years later, that increased to 53 percent. Over a decade after that, the state superintendent concluded that only seven states gave more from state taxes to schools than did Kentucky. But the poor support of the local level brought the system down. In 1919, the state ranked twelfth in state funds distributed, but thirty-second in overall money per student allocated to education.[11]

All of these problems — the trustee system, the apathy, the finances — when combined with low average daily attendance (60 percent in 1907) and a still-high illiteracy rate (12 percent in 1910) meant that the system had difficulties. Kentucky, when compared to the rest of the South, might stand statistically high, but most observers could see that major problems existed. They decided to do something about that.[12]

The Whirlwind Campaigns

An atmosphere for change was present in Kentucky by 1907, and Richmond lawyer and legislator J.A. Sullivan told the governor, "There is a stronger sentiment for education in Kentucky today than ever before. It amounts to almost a demand that progress be made." Over the mountains in Virginia an educational campaign in 1905 had been followed by a law the next year creating high schools across the state. Other southern states were making similar advances and providing like models.[13]

Yet, attitudes for change did not automatically translate into action. It required a dynamic leader to accomplish that, and such a person was the new superintendent of public instruction, forty-two-year-old John Grant Crabbe. Ohio born and educated, Crabbe had first taught Latin and Greek at a normal (teacher training) school in Michigan, then had been city school superintendent in Ashland, Kentucky, for some eighteen years. Elected with the Republican slate in 1907, he told the state's chief executive that he sought to change his office from a clerical place to a "clearing-house for educational ideas." A system, not a patchwork of laws, should be instituted for the schools, he wrote, so that real good could be done. Admittedly, his plan would produce a more centralized system with more control by professionals.[14]

The 1908 Kentucky General Assembly took his advice and passed laws which earned it the title "The Education Legislature." Some of the acts were more cosmetic, though still symbolic, such as changing names from State College to State University and Kentucky University to Transylvania University. But it also appropriated additional funds to State University, to Kentucky Normal and Industrial Institute for Colored Persons, and to the regional normal schools (Eastern and Western) created two years earlier.[15]

But the real emphasis focused on the elementary and secondary schools. It required a united effort to gain passage of legislation on that subject, and the Kentucky Federation of Women's Clubs provided much of the lobbying effort. Even after the general assembly enacted a law, the governor considered vetoing it because of the cost. Superintendent Crabbe and the Federation delegation persuaded him to sign and he did so at midnight. As passed, the School District Law, known as the Sullivan Bill, totally reorganized the system and made the county, not the small trustee units, the key taxing authority. The old trustee system could not be eradicated easily, however, and each county school still retained one trustee, who had to be literate. In combination, those sub-district trustees composed a "school division" which selected teachers, and the various chairmen of these made up the county board of education. It set salaries and distributed money. As it turned out, that somewhat complicated compromise system did not work well either and would be changed in twelve years.

More lasting was a passage in the Sullivan Bill requiring each county to establish a high school within a two-year period. Systems were given the authority to consolidate schools and levy a minimum school tax. That last provision alone increased funding in local districts from $180,000 in 1907–8 to $1 million. Other laws strengthened compulsory attendance, regulated child labor, and, to keep the reforms moving, formed an Educational Improvement Commission to make recommendations to the next general assembly.[16]

Crabbe realized that the brief reform flurry of the 1908 legislature could be viewed by the populace as having met all of education's needs. Yet he and others knew that much remained to be done and, as a result, began a series of meetings known as "The Whirlwind Campaigns." Designed, in Crabbe's words, as a "continuous cyclone bombardment against illiteracy and ignorance," the first publicity effort lasted for nine days in November and December 1908, as nearly thirty speakers gave three hundred public addresses in that time period. An estimated 60,000 heard the talks in person; thousands more read about them in the newspapers. In the summer of 1909, a second campaign involved even more speakers (some one hundred) and aimed particularly at rural schools, "to put new life and vigor" in them. It all was an impressive effort: "The meetings were held in schoolhouses, court-houses, opera houses and country stores. . . . Each one addressed three audiences a day and they were whirled from place to place by every sort of conveyance — train, wagon, and automobile, and in the mountains they went on horseback." This outpouring of interest made educators hopeful that what had been started in

1908 would continue, and that brighter days did indeed lie ahead for Kentucky education.[17]

Forty Years of Stagnation, 1910–1950

In some ways, much progress was taking place after the 1908–9 educational efforts concluded. Public high schools, for instance, increased in number from 54 in 1910 to 134 in 1915 to 202 in 1919, and the number of high school graduates went up over 600 percent between 1911 and 1928. As schools consolidated, students often had longer distances to travel, and, in 1917, the courts held that local school boards could pay for such transportation. Mason County, the pioneering consolidating county, employed twenty-nine buses and eight horse-drawn wagons for their students in 1923. By 1938 all but seven of Kentucky's counties were furnishing vehicles for such purposes. The legislature that year also required for the first time that the State Board of Education adopt regulations governing school bus design and operation.[18]

Funding levels to support schools and school buses increased as well. The 1918 general assembly not only passed legislation accepting federal support for vocational schools but also raised the maximum school tax levy for all schools by 50 percent, which gave education $8.6 million that year. Eight years later the maximum rates were increased another 50 percent to $.75 per $100. Some success even occurred in changing the Kentucky constitution, which required that educational funds be distributed only on a pupil-census basis. An equalization law passed by the 1930 legislature was ruled unconstitutional, so in 1941 voters approved a constitutional amendment that allowed the state to dispense up to 10 percent of school funds in another fashion. A similar amendment, passed in 1949, raised the figure to 25 percent. All that gave the state more flexibility in supporting poorer school districts.[19]

The administrative system continued to undergo needed change as well. The County Administration Law of 1920 established a school board elected from the county at large. That board, in turn, appointed the superintendent and selected the teachers. Four years later another act required county superintendents to have at least two years of college. But the old local trustee idea, vampire-like, sucked vitality for the system and would not die. In 1922, the County Administration Law was modified so that county board members would be elected from a district, rather than countywide. Two years later, the old subdistrict trustee was revived, with the power to recommend teacher selection. A 1932 law created three trustees per subdistrict, and the county superintendent's office was made an elective one once more. Finally, in 1934, the stake was driven through the heart of the old trustee system, and it was mercifully killed off in a sweeping revision of the school code. More high schools, better funding for education, reforms in administration — all seemed to say to Kentuckians that they were doing the right things. And in some ways they were. They simply were not doing enough, however, and dark clouds

Christian County pupils head for school, ca. 1912.

continued to hover on the educational horizon.[20]

Statistics did not tell the whole story. Historian Dewey Grantham's figures show that Kentucky's expenditures per pupil increased 238 percent between 1900 and 1920. Those years of reform, whirlwind campaigns, and tax increases for education had resulted in significant expansion in funding for Kentucky's schools and schoolchildren. Citizens congratulated themselves on what they had accomplished.

But they often did not look far enough outside their own areas. True, Kentucky's per capita funding had drastically increased, but even at that the commonwealth's growth fell behind both the region's and the nation's. In funding, the state had increased 238 percent in twenty years, but the United States average went up 345 percent. Kentucky had stood fourth of fourteen southern states and territories in 1900; by 1920 it stood eleventh. Its 1900 per capita average was one-half the national average; twenty years later it had fallen to about one-third that average. Kentucky had walked forward toward reform, while all those around it were running.[21]

In 1921, two reports appeared which showed the problems. Citing a professor's study based on ten factors, the superintendent of public instruction indicated that Kentucky, which had ranked thirty-sixth in education among the states in 1900, ranked forty-fifth in 1918. A state-funded survey by the Kentucky Education Commission argued that "the handicaps under which Kentucky suffers . . . are man-made and can be removed by man." It called for better support of rural schools, where those in one-room schools (three-fourths of the rural students) "are really two and a half years behind city children" in achievement tests. Its call for an equalization fund was rejected by voters in 1921 when they defeated a constitutional amendment on that subject. Only two decades later would a similar amendment pass. Until then, districts like Magoffin County, with an average of $545 in taxable property, would have had to have a tax rate almost fourteen times that of wealthy Bourbon County, with its $7,615 average, in order to produce similar school revenue. Inequality continued to plague the system.[22]

Study after study appeared, all bearing the same message and the same bad news. The 1924 report of the Efficiency Commission of Kentucky showed how poorly the state fared when examined under the microscope of comparative studies. A sociologist's look at the South in 1936 found Kentucky standing low nationally in many areas, including expenditures per pupil (41st) and in percentage of the population registered as library borrowers (45th). A 1943 *Courier-Journal* report showed Kentucky ranked 40th in the percentage of income spent on education, and at about that level in most other categories. The Postwar Advisory Planning Commission two years later pointed out that in 1940 the commonwealth stood alone and last in average length of school term and in the percentage of high school graduates.[23]

From the time of the Whirlwind Campaigns to mid-century, education had to compete with other demands on state funding, such as transportation and social welfare issues. While more funding did go to education in those years, it was not enough to keep support levels high, as the statistics show:

TABLE 6.1

Year	Percentage of State Funds Devoted To Education
1910	44.7
1920	38.1
1926	26.6
1930	27.9
1934	21.5
1940	24.9
1950	22.3

A leader of southern education in the nineteenth century, the commonwealth had fallen far from that status by 1950. Filled with promise, in the end, it had been a bad half-century for Kentucky's education.[24]

The Segregated System

On 12 January 1904, Democratic representative Carl Day of Frozen Creek in Breathitt County introduced House Bill 25, "An Act to prohibit white and colored persons from attending the same school." A nephew of Jim Hargis (of feud fame), Day said his legislation would prevent "the contamination of the white children of Kentucky." The act made it illegal for any school to operate with both races present, with fines for teachers, students, and schools that broke the law. A branch school could be established to serve one race's children, but even then it had to be twenty-five miles away. Supported by the state superintendent of public instruction and not opposed by the governor, the

Berea College

Integrated classes at Berea College fueled the passage of the Day Bill.

bill sailed through committee and passed the house 73–5, with four eastern Kentucky Republicans and one mountain Democrat in the minority. (None of the five would be returned to the house in 1906.)[25]

The so-called Day Bill was aimed at only one school in Kentucky, since separate public schools for blacks and whites had long been the law in the state. But privately supported Berea College remained integrated, the last institution of higher education in the South to do so. Established by abolitionists in the 1850s, the school had been devoted to interracial education from the start, and, in its early decades, the student body had typically been over 60 percent black. Since 1892 new president William G. Frost had turned the school's focus more to Appalachia and less to interracial education, but it still continued to serve both races. In 1903, blacks constituted 16 percent of Berea's students.[26]

Kentucky legislators apparently could not accept even small numbers of blacks and whites in the same school, for the Day Bill easily passed the state senate 28–5 and was signed by Governor J.C.W. Beckham in March. Berea College filed suit and engaged as counsel a Kentuckian who had been Speaker of the U.S. House. At the circuit-court level, the judge upheld the legality of the law, calling it "a blessing to Berea College." The state's highest court, in a 1906 opinion written by a future Republican gubernatorial candidate, struck down the twenty-five-mile section of the law but allowed the rest to stand.

Only future University of Kentucky president Henry S. Barker stood in opposition among the justices. In presenting the state's case before the U.S. Supreme Court, Attorney General James Breathitt used not only legal arguments but also stressed that the Anglo-Saxon race's superiority was "innate and God-given." The conservative court's 1908 decision supported the law's constitutionality — with one dissenting voice. Ironically, it was a Kentucky justice, John Marshall Harlan, who spoke out in opposition: "Have we become so inoculated with prejudice of race that an American government . . . can make distinctions between such citizens in the matter of . . . meeting for innocent purposes because of their respective races?" The answer was all too obvious.[27]

A defeated Berea College raised funds to establish a new school for blacks, but the 1910 legislature passed a law requiring three-fourths of a county's voters to approve the location of such a school. The Court of Appeals did strike down that action, and in 1912, Lincoln Institute opened in Shelby County. Particularly under the leadership of Whitney Young, Sr., who in 1935 became the first black to lead the school, Lincoln Institute developed into a strong center for black education. But with the closing of Berea College as an interracial school, Kentucky education was a totally segregated affair for over four decades.[28]

That segregated school system constituted one of the chief problems confronting education in the commonwealth. Not a wealthy state to begin with, Kentucky had to fund a dual and often duplicate system. As the head of the Division of Negro Education stated in 1927: "Kentucky has deliberately chosen the more costly policy of separate schools." That meant a separate administrative system for both races, a separate group of school buildings, and a separate teacher corps. Since the system, theoretically, was to be both separate *and* equal, that meant that in areas with a small black population, such as in the eastern mountains, a school would have to be set up for only a few black students, or else they would be transported to another county — either way, not a cost-effective way to operate.[29]

But was the system equal? In most respects the evidence suggests it was not. Three separate studies between 1920 and 1939 found, in general, second-class school buildings which were "old and in very bad condition." If the typical white one-room school was "inadequate," the black schools were even worse. Nor did things get better inside the structure. Books often did not meet the test of equality either. One student noted later, "I cannot recall getting a new book at all. The books that we would get would be the books that came from the white schools where they had changed or had been torn or written into."[30]

Aside from the physical situation of the schools themselves, students simply had very limited access to any school. In 1919 only twenty-eight counties had a black high school, and, eight years later, half of the black school children still lived in counties without a high school for them. Additional financing from outside Kentucky, through the John F. Slater Fund, the Jeanes Fund, and the Rosenwald Fund, helped change that situation somewhat: between 1915 and 1929 the number of blacks in high school increased fourfold so that about the same percentage of eligible blacks attended high school as did whites. Yet, even then, only one-third of Kentucky's counties provided a high school for blacks.[31]

But if the physical conditions of the schools and the numbers of them were not adequate, the teachers in them were more than adequate. As opposed to the white community, where teaching was still not highly valued as a profession, in the black community education attracted some of the best and the brightest. For one thing, the pay scale was generally equitable. While in 1905, some seventy-five counties paid white teachers more than blacks, sixteen counties paid blacks, on the average, more than whites. A 1916 Department of the Interior study on Negro education found that black teachers in Kentucky were paid, per child, an average of $8.53, while white teachers averaged only $8.13. Because pay at that time was based on the number of students, and because white teachers had more students on the average, their overall annual salary was $323 versus $310 for blacks. Rufus Atwood, the president of what became known as Kentucky State University, concluded in 1939 that salary discrimination "has almost disappeared" in the county districts, although it was still present in the independent urban ones. A black Lexington teacher's first job in 1929 paid him roughly $25 less per month than white teachers made. That system did change, however. Louisville equalized its salary scale, for example, in 1944 at a cost of $65,000 a year.[32]

Training was one of the reasons black teachers' pay did not greatly vary from that of white teachers. From the 1910s on, black teachers were generally as well educated, or better-educated, in terms of years in college, than were whites. A 1919 study found twice as many black teachers had completed one year of college compared to white teachers. Almost half of the black high school teachers were college graduates in 1919; a decade later 53 percent had completed four or more years of college. In 1936, virtually the same percentage of white and black teachers in Lexington — 76 percent — held college degrees. All this meant that black students had well-trained, reasonably paid educators who often were strongly dedicated to their profession. It is little wonder that one Lexington student remembered "super, super, super, superb teachers."[33]

That kind of teaching may have caused black students to make extra efforts to go to school, even when their economic condition might dictate otherwise. But for whatever reason, an important segment of the black school population attended school — 68 percent in 1900, which was the second highest average among sixteen southern states. (The white average of 78 percent was sixth highest.) And where schools were readily available and easily accessible, as in urban areas, the averages for both races were virtually identical. High schools might not exist in some places, but when blacks could get to those schools and when they did graduate, a larger percentage (44.5 percent) went to college in 1922 than did their white counterparts. By 1940, some 85 percent of Kentucky blacks aged ten to fourteen attended school; only 63 percent of white

Kentucky Historical Society

**President Rufus Atwood *(front row center)* posed with graduates of the Kentucky
State Industrial College in 1931.**

students did. Indicative of the decline in Kentucky schools, both figures were
near the bottom of the sixteen southern states surveyed.[34]

Black high school graduates faced perhaps the most discrimination of any
element of the school population. The closing of Berea College's doors to the
black population of the state left a void not quickly filled. The 1916 survey of
education indicated that no real public college-level instruction for blacks was
provided in the state. Founded thirty years earlier, Kentucky Normal and
Industrial Institute for Colored Persons in Frankfort trained a few teachers,
but basically offered only high-school-level classes. The Department of Interior study found the Frankfort school with a divided board, "unsatisfactory"
discipline, and students ready to revolt. When the state's Efficiency Commission evaluated the school in 1924, it called the entire educational procedure
"highly unsatisfactory" and its accounting system "lax." The school would receive needed stability when Rufus Atwood became its president in 1929. Enrollment jumped from 200 in that year to 590 less than a decade later. The
course of what became known after 1926 as Kentucky State Industrial College
for Colored Persons was firmly established at last. Still it operated after 1934
without its own board and instead was governed by the white State Board of
Education. In short, Kentucky State was grouped with high schools and voca-

tional schools, and its president, alone of the state colleges, did not sit on the newly created Council on Public Higher Education. All publicly funded white colleges and universities had their own boards, and the double standard was obvious. The State Board also governed another state-funded "college" for blacks. In 1918 the commonwealth had taken control of West Kentucky Industrial College in Paducah, but its problems had continued. Evaluations of it in 1921 and 1924 both recommended it be closed; in 1938 it was finally made a vocational school and any collegiate functions were transferred to the school in Frankfort.[35]

Probably the best black college in Kentucky and the only real one for part of the century was located in Louisville. Opened in 1879, the privately supported Simmons University not only offered college-level instruction, but for a time also graduate work in law, medicine, and theology. In 1931, under terms of an agreement regarding a city bond issue, the city purchased the school property and made it a municipally supported, though segregated, branch of the University of Louisville. Known as Louisville Municipal College, it received four-year college accreditation in 1932, and a Class A rating from the Southern Association four years later (three years before Kentucky State did). Until it merged in 1951 into the main university, after segregation partially ended, Louisville Municipal College provided good liberal arts instruction for Kentucky's blacks.[36]

But black students usually had no access to law schools, medical schools, or Ph.D.-level work within the Kentucky system. To try to forestall black arguments that they were denied an equal education, and to keep blacks out of white colleges of law and medical schools, the general assembly in 1936 appropriated $5,000 a year to be used to underwrite tuition costs for blacks forced to attend out-of-state schools for their advanced degrees. The Anderson-Myer State Aid Act provided up to $175 per student for that purpose. By 1948, Kentucky increased the funding pool to $40,000, but the action could not stop the segregation wall from crumbling. By then, "separate but equal" was in its death throes.[37]

The first symptom of its demise came about in higher education. As early as 1939, a black student had applied for admission to law school at the University of Kentucky; two years later another student sought to attend the engineering school. Both were turned away on technicalities. But on 15 March 1948, Lyman Johnson sought admission to the university's graduate program in history. Well-educated and a school teacher in Louisville, Johnson stood ready for a court case. In March 1949, Judge Church Ford ruled in Johnson's favor, calling attempts to provide instruction at Kentucky State "makeshift" and unequal. After a heated discussion, with the governor and the school president asking the university's board not to appeal the decision, the group finally agreed. That summer Johnson and other blacks integrated Kentucky's system of higher education for the first time in forty-five years. The next year, the old Day Law was modified further and several colleges began to admit blacks to undergraduate classes. By 1950, it seemed only a matter of time before full integration would take place. But, throughout the educationally segregated part of the century, Kentucky blacks had coped with inadequate financing, poor buildings, insufficient equipment, and sometimes unequal salaries. The physical and statistical inequalities were difficult enough, but the hardest burden to bear may have been what Pete Daniel has called the "spiritual deprivation" of a segregated society. The dual system of schools may have hurt the state financially, but most of all it hurt the human spirit of a significant portion of the commonwealth's people. Still, in the end, blacks operated within the system and learned under good teachers, while all the time working to destroy the divisive segregation that they had quickly learned could never be equal.[38]

Teaching in the System

Teachers, whether black or white, were equal in several ways — most were poorly paid, underappreciated, and without adequate facilities. A new teacher facing his or her first job typically began in a one-room school. In 1917, of 8,115 schools in Kentucky, 7,025 (87 percent) were one-room facilities; nearly three decades later, of 5,914 schools, 3,838 (65 percent) were still only one-teacher schools. While log buildings remained plentiful early in the century (1,238 in 1901), their numbers declined rapidly, to 123 in 1917. The majority of schools in Kentucky, then, were one-room frame buildings even as late as 1950.[39]

Memories of those one-room schools are surprisingly consistent. The frame walls were generally unpainted (not until 1921 were half of them not in that state); they stood on stone pillars (which allowed cold winds to blow underneath the floors); and they had a roof that frequently leaked. A 1919 study described a Muhlenberg County school as a mile and a half from the nearest farm, located on a road that was "almost impassable" in winter. "The windows are broken and stuffed with rags. . . . Benches which accommodate three or four children are broken and the teacher's desk is minus one leg. . . . There are no blackboards; one side of the wall is painted black and used for that purpose." Similarly, the study told of a Barren County school which had large cracks in the clapboard, allowing rain and wind to sweep in. There the children used soap boxes for tables. Across Kentucky the story was the same, as seats ranged from backless benches to homemade affairs to manufactured ones. None was described as comfortable. Usually schools had one or two blackboards, perhaps with sheepskin erasers, and a few maps or a globe, but little else in the way of teaching aids.[40]

Students usually arrived at those buildings between 8:00 and 8:30 A.M. and left around 4:00 P.M. In between they had mid-morning and mid-afternoon recesses and an hour-long lunch at noon. Warm weather and dry roads produced good attendance in the early months of school, starting in July, but the cold, the muddy roads, and the distance combined to limit the numbers by

December when many terms ended. A 1921 study found around 80 percent of the students in school in July; only 20 percent regularly attended in December. By 1940, teachers could expect an average of twenty-three pupils in daily attendance.[41]

Teachers had to spend part of their time with students simply providing necessities. They, or a student they paid, were the janitors, and started the fires in the morning. Since heat was typically provided by a single, centrally located pot-bellied stove, problems arose. One account said such heating "almost demoralized the school" as youngsters fought to be near the warmth. A student remembered putting her lunch in a far-off corner of the room and finding it frozen by mealtime.[42]

Providing drinking water posed another problem. By 1920, one-half of such schools had a well; the other half had to bring water from the closest creek, which could be some distance away. One person recalled carrying a two-gallon bucket over a half-mile to replenish the water supply. Students then all used the same "community dipper" to drink. Sanitation problems were compounded by the toilet facilities, or usually the lack of same. Some places had outdoor facilities, generally described as dirty and poorly located. (One study said the "boys' toilets are filthy and offensive beyond belief.") Other locales simply sent children into the woods.[43]

Given such conditions, critics abounded. One superintendent looked at the situation in the first decade and wrote, "Hundreds of farmers in Kentucky have more comfortable barns in which to shelter their stock than they have school-houses in which to train the minds and mold the characters of their children." Nearly three decades later another educator complained to a newspaper: "I drove by a $500 schoolhouse on a $1,000,000 highway. . . . No bargain roads, but bargain education everywhere."[44]

That same philosophy extended to teachers, who found that the commonwealth provided poor support not only to buildings but to people as well. As a result, the profession had difficulty attracting, and retaining, the best candidates. Many young people started as teachers and moved to other fields within a few years, thus creating considerable turnover. In 1907, a county superintendent said of his schools: "About 95 percent are in the hands of young, inexperienced and untrained teachers. We can not hope for better conditions with the present salaries, which are not even equal to that of the common laborer." A west Kentucky county at the same time reported the average age of teachers there as twenty-three for women, twenty-five for men, while the situation elsewhere brought the summation that "most of the teachers of Pendleton County are boys and girls trying to teach boys and girls." A decade later the turnover still continued as some 15 percent of the teachers each year were young newcomers.[45]

Three things contributed to that turnover — the better pay elsewhere, the view (particularly by men) that teaching was only a transitory job and not a career, and the fact that many women ceased teaching once they were wed. Few married women thus comprised the teaching corps — in McCracken County in 1907 only three of thirty women teachers in the county schools were married and in Hickman five years later only one of sixteen females was. That situation would evolve, over time, as women moved into professional jobs more and more, and as both sexes saw teaching in more favorable terms. But change came at a different pace in various locales. In the century's first decade, for example, while women made up almost two-thirds of all teachers, they comprised very few of the teachers in the mountains. Yet they filled most of the instructor jobs in the urban and central Kentucky areas. Rural parts of west Kentucky had a more mixed force. Did the fact that men made up fifty-nine of a mountain county's sixty-three teachers mean that women simply did not want to enter the profession there, or that they were not encouraged to receive education enough to do so, or that the community opposed women working professionally? Or did the fact that urban Henderson had seventy-five female teachers to ten males mean that such communities saw teaching as women's work, and not men's, or that they had few other options for the growing lists of educated women? (A woman elsewhere said, "My sister's [sic] and I were all teachers. That was about all that a girl could do.") Whatever the reason, great variances existed initially. Those differences would lessen as time passed, though elementary teaching continued to be chiefly the preserve of women.[46]

War also added to the instability in teaching. After World War I a state superintendent pointed to a shortage of over two thousand teachers, since men had gone into the service and "the strongest women teachers" had entered government work. Many never returned to their old jobs. Again in World War II, similar shortages forced the system to grant emergency certificates to people not fully qualified to teach, and one in four teachers in 1943 fell into that category. Two years later, of 5,000 such hires, 1,400 had taken no college courses. Peacetime reduced the use of emergency certificate teachers to under 15 percent by 1953.[47]

Of course, the lack of a college education had long been no barrier to teaching. Not until 1935 were high school teachers in Kentucky required to hold such a degree, and it would be another twenty-five years before elementary teachers had the same requirement. Between 1936 and 1939, the percentage of Kentucky teachers who were college graduates increased from 25 to 40 percent. By 1950, over one-half were.[48]

More of Kentucky's better educated citizens might have gone into teaching earlier in the century had the system been different. But before 1920, teachers could be certified at the county level, and for part of that time such powers resided with the ever-present trustees. To receive a basic certification required passing a test, but for those who might have difficulty there was always the "question peddler." Trustees, or their friends, would offer the answers to prospective teachers so that even the poorest prepared could pass. What was termed a "considerable" traffic in questions resulted, and the state superintendent even sent out detectives in an attempt to end it.

Teachers might not only pay for the test answers, but also be required to "kick back" a large percentage of their salary to the trustees. They would also be expected to be politically supportive at election time — and, if they were not, they could be dismissed without cause. On the other hand, some prospective teachers apparently initiated the process themselves and bribed trustees in order to secure a teaching contract. Even after certification power went to the county boards of examiners, the county superintendents in some places continued to grant certificates as payment for political services. Patronage and politics thus became so ingrained in the system that moving the certification of teachers to a central system in 1920 only meant that different tactics might be used locally. As a state superintendent noted in 1921, "Unless the people demand that merit and the rights of children alone, and not kinship . . . and not political or personal influence, shall determine the employment of teachers . . . , we can not hope to have good schools." That would be an elusive goal, long-sought.[49]

The system did become more professional as time passed. Membership in the Kentucky Education Association went from 470 in 1907 to 2,156 just five years later. Attendance at their annual convention surpassed that, with 3,000 present. But beyond membership in a professional organization, teachers began to see their jobs treated more and more with respect, attention, and protection. In 1940, a teacher retirement system began, and two years later an act strengthened teaching by requiring reasons for dismissal and setting up specified pay periods. Not until 1954, however, would teacher tenure be adopted.[50]

The greatest problem in attracting and keeping teachers was their pay. It is surprising people fought and bribed their way into the profession, for its financial rewards were slim indeed. Statewide, the average salary was $215 in 1900 and $337 a decade later. Not until 1912 was there a minimum wage, which started at $35 per month for six months and went to $75 by 1920. Before that 1912 law, numerous salaries fell below that minimum of $210. Later novelist Elizabeth Madox Roberts taught a full term ending in 1906 for total wages of $198.03. The next year the *average* salary in Gallatin County was under $26 per month. (Farm laborers' wages at that time might range from $15 to $18 monthly.)[51]

On the upper end of the wage scale were the urban schools and those in company towns. In the latter, the coal companies often supplemented county and state funds in order to attract better teachers and sometimes even provided free textbooks. But the real salary disparity came in the larger cities where salaries stood much higher than in rural locales. Louisville in 1918, for example, paid elementary teachers an average wage of $722; the entire state average only two years earlier had been but $364. And while the differences declined over time, they still remained: by 1943 rural teachers averaged $12.71 per week, while urban ones statewide averaged $17.53 — some 38 percent more. At that, however, the pay remained a pittance. Even the city teachers made only about one-fourth the government wages in a wartime world. Despite a 94 percent increase after the 1944 legislative session, teacher salaries still only averaged $1,325 per year. By 1951 that had increased, in a time of some inflation, to $2,350 — still under the average for the South by several hundred dollars. Money obviously was not the reason most people became teachers. Money *was* a chief reason why they left Kentucky for greener educational pastures. As people remarked at the time, Kentucky's greatest export was not bourbon or tobacco or thoroughbreds but teachers.[52]

Those who remained behind to teach made up an underpaid but often dedicated corps, one that as Thomas D. Clark noted, provided Kentuckians with "far more educational returns and dedication . . . than they have ever been willing to pay for." Poor teachers remained a part of that system; so too did political-minded administrators. But out there also were teachers who labored long and hard — and well. Robert Penn Warren recalled his instructors as "remarkably good teachers," for example. Recollections of others who went through the one-room schools, or the better brick ones, are alike in that most recall that one person who inspired them amidst that special "school smell of chalk, children, and oiled floor boards." Despite the fact that there could have been, should have been, much more offered; despite the underfunding, the politics, the patronage, the poor pay; despite the system's general failure; still, individuals overcame all that and were superb teachers.[53]

Special Schools

In urban settings, but even more commonly in eastern Kentucky rural ones, settlement schools became a key part of the educational system. Often funded by forces beyond the region, the private schools were designed to offer educational opportunities to populations without such promise. Generally their efforts aimed at the urban and mountain poor.

In Appalachia, such settlement schools proliferated. At times they might offer the only available instruction. In other instances, they provided better educational offerings than other schools in the area, and the students sometimes travelled long distances to attend. What they found in each place was generally similar. Usually the schools had been set up by women, often with connections outside Kentucky. Alice Lloyd, for instance, left her Bostonian background and brought her Radcliffe College degree to Appalachia, where she established a high school and junior college at Pippa Passes. There her students lived a regulated life, one that prohibited meetings with those of the opposite sex, but there also they learned. At Hindman in 1902, Kentuckians Katherine Pettit and May Stone founded a school under the auspices of the Women's Christian Temperance Union, and it featured both regular academic instruction and manual labor courses. At Pine Mountain Settlement School, founded in 1913, Ethel de Long of New Jersey joined with Pettit in providing similar work. The problem with some of the schools was that they needed the support of philanthropists in order to survive. That often meant that, ironically, they had to present the worst picture in order to get the most money. Whether willingly or not, they strengthened the negative stereotype of Appalachia, while at the same time doing real good in the educational field.[54]

Berea College

Pupils focus on their studies at the Hindman Settlement School.

Motivated by a northern missionary impulse, coming out of a women's college background, convinced that the area needed the instruction they provided, the teachers saw what they were doing as an extension of women's traditional roles. They may have been too narrow in their focus and too limited in their ambitions; they may have favored, or even advocated, the quaint, the old traditions, while rejecting the people's own interest in new forms; they might have been too romantic in their expectations; they might have been blinded, at times, by urban provincialism. Yet, in the end, those teachers did provide good instruction where little had been before. Impressed by the beauty all around them — Helen Dingman of New York wrote in 1917 of the hills: "There is something intoxicating about their beauty" — and attracted by the generosity of the people, they sought to change a situation where children had sometimes sought knowledge and had not been able to find it.[55]

That searching did not end with childhood. The census of 1900 showed that 16.5 percent of Kentucky's population was illiterate, including at least one-fourth of the voters. The state's prisons had 60 percent of their population in that category. Literacy was a problem in the commonwealth.[56]

Efforts to combat that situation had long existed and continued. In 1903, for example, A. H. Payne operated a night school for some 600 blacks in Louisville. Since public schools limited attendance to age twenty or younger, the students paid ten cents each to defray costs of their continuing education.[57]

But such sporadic work was soon supplemented by a systematic effort, in the form of the "Moonlight Schools" of Cora Wilson Stewart. A former teacher, a two-term school superintendent in Rowan County, and the elected president of the Kentucky Education Association in 1911 (the first woman to hold that post), Mrs. Stewart had been deeply involved in regular educational activities for some time. Then in 1911 she organized classes for illiterates, to be held on moonlit nights, and found a large outpouring of interest. From that beginning, the forceful Stewart appealed to the governor and legislature for regular state appropriations so the schools could be spread across Kentucky. In 1914, the Kentucky Illiteracy Commission was funded at $5,000 and received expanding state support for the next six years. Heading what she called "the first Illiteracy Commission in history," Stewart received cooperation from the State Federation of Women's Clubs, other civic and business organizations, and various individual volunteers. She wrote textbooks for adult new readers and spoke across the nation, becoming recognized as the leading authority on illiteracy. Still, problems plagued her efforts. Not particularly diplomatic, Stewart alienated some in the way she brought attention to the problem in the first place. Others criticized her speaking tours, the personification of the crusade in one person, and her statistics of success (in which she claimed in 1920 that 130,000 of the state's 208,000 illiterates had been taught to read and write). Stewart's base of support was eroding and in 1920, with the governor and state superintendent of public instruction in agreement, the general assembly ended the existence of the commission. She continued to speak for the cause and helped found the National Illiteracy Crusade, but back in Kentucky no lasting solutions had been found. Once the pioneer in the illiteracy fight, Kentucky found by 1940 that only one state had a higher illiteracy rate than did the commonwealth. The crusade had failed.[58]

Colleges and Universities

In January 1922, Lexington *Herald* editor Desha Breckinridge penned an editorial entitled, "What of the Future?" He wondered if in twenty-five years, politics would be governed not by partisan concerns, but rather by questions of ability; if there might not be a woman U.S. senator from Kentucky; if there would not be continuous legislative sessions. Amid his "fancies of the future" was one more — that Kentucky's various colleges would unite as part of the "great University," a school that would rival Oxford or Cambridge.[59]

Like many of his predictions, the one concerning education never came close to reality. Not only was there a philosophical debate about "one great University" or several more democratic ones, there was also no money given for either view. In 1904, Kentucky provided State College (later the University of Kentucky) appropriations in the sum of $36,380. Wisconsin furnished its university with $471,500 that year. A few years later a similar comparison

Western Kentucky University's hill-top headquarters dominates an aerial view of "Normal Heights and Bowling Green," ca. 1929.

indicated that the renamed State University of Kentucky realized $130,000 in annual income; Ohio State University garnered $700,000; and the universities of Wisconsin and Illinois, $1.1 million each. In 1912, the city of Louisville devoted more dollars to Male High School than the Commonwealth of Kentucky did to its one state-supported university. The funds necessary for one strong university simply were not allocated.[60]

Nor was the will. A perusal of biographical directories of the era shows that most Kentucky leaders attended good private in-state schools such as Centre College or Kentucky University (Transylvania University after 1908), or such out-of-state schools as Princeton University, the University of Virginia, Bethany (West Virginia), and Cumberland University (in Lebanon, Tennessee). The commonwealth's chief state-funded school only slowly drew alumni support from legislators. By the time that occurred, the regional teachers' colleges had become stronger and began fighting in earnest for a bigger piece of the higher education pie. Despite the strong leadership of President Frank L. McVey, who served from 1917 to 1940, the University of Kentucky could not overcome decades of underfunding and academic apathy. A professor commented in 1912 that the atmosphere at State University "tends strongly toward the side-tracking of the undergraduate students . . . into some vocational course." Near the time McVey became president, the school had but 36,000 volumes in its library and only 54 out-of-state students. It granted its first Ph.D. only in 1929, the twelfth southern university to do so. And when the funding began to get better, the Depression struck in 1930. Two years later, the state appropriation to the university had fallen nearly 50 percent, and not until 1946 would the support get back to that 1930 level.[61]

By then, the idea of giving adequate funding to insure the existence of one strong university seemed to be better accepted. Earlier rival Transylvania University had adopted a more limited stance as it closed its medical school in Louisville in 1908 and its law school four years later. Other private schools such as Georgetown College, Kentucky Wesleyan (then at Winchester), and Berea College provided good instruction but never sought to rival the University of Kentucky. The municipally supported University of Louisville offered the state's only medical school, plus the one other College of Law, but aside from those areas, its strengths were few. In short, by 1950, the state university was poised for the growth envisioned by Breckinridge decades before.

The role the regional public colleges would play on the educational stage remained uncertain. A national 1930s study had asked, "Does Kentucky need four state teachers colleges in addition to a state university?" But if that answer seemed clear to the writer, Kentucky had a different response. It supported all. The four white regional colleges — Eastern and Western, both established in 1906, and Morehead and Murray, formed in 1922 — had originally been envisioned as teacher training schools. Their missions expanded over time and they grew in size. But several regional college presidents, such as Western's H.H. Cherry, who twice sought the governorship, played major roles in state politics. That could be beneficial, or it could create problems, as it did in 1946 when a Republican governor allied with a friendly board to reject a new contract for the Democratic president of Morehead State Teachers College. That action resulted in the loss of accreditation for the school from the American Association of Teachers Colleges. By mid-century, then, the regional schools stood as unknowns. Would they expand in size and financial strength, or would they remain secondary players in the game?[62]

No matter what the answer to that query would be, it was clear by 1950 that more people attended Kentucky colleges and universities than ever before. Some forty institutions of higher learning offered college classes, but the question of both quality and quantity remained.

TABLE 6.2

Enrollments	1930	1940	1950
Univ. of Kentucky	3,245	4,202	8,476
Western	2,739	1,854	1,833
Eastern	1,179	1,541	1,861
Murray	902	1,294	1,665
Morehead	846	931	824
Kentucky State	138	682	716
	9,049	10,504	15,375

Still, Kentucky's appropriation to colleges was the lowest of any of the states surrounding the commonwealth, and its percentage of college graduates consistently ranked near or at the bottom of all states.[63]

At whatever level — elementary, secondary, collegiate — Kentucky was not meeting its responsibilities to the populace. Politics continued to be a factor in every system, money was never adequate, and the strong will to do better proved to be seldom present. Predictable results followed, and education lost. The state limped to mid-century, carrying with it some shabby educational baggage.

The insider's view of Kentucky life has been portrayed eloquently by such writers as (*clockwise from top left*) James Lane Allen, John Fox, Jr., Elizabeth Madox Roberts, Robert Penn Warren, Harriette Simpson Arnow, and Jesse Stuart.

The printing graphic "for art and truth" appears on the title page of Madison Cawein's One Day & Another. *Warren photo, Center for Robert Penn Warren Studies, Western Kentucky University. Stuart photo, Jesse Stuart Foundation. All other photos, Kentucky Historical Society*

7

"We Will Sing One Song": Kentucky's Cultural Milieu

Literature

A historian told one Kentucky author, "You have picked out the one state in which an author is absolutely certain to starve to death." Another chronicler of the state's traditions wrote in 1939, "In plain language we as a people do not care much for our own writers. . . . May the good God love them, because no one else does." Others noted the sad state of readership as seen in libraries in the commonwealth: the state university had but 10,000 volumes in its library in 1910; at the end of World War II, almost two-thirds of the population still had no access to a local library. Still others moaned about the violence, the poor educational level of the people, and the failings of the school system. Poor Kentucky. To some, it seemed a place of little literary promise, a barren field.[1]

Yet, as in other instances, that image and the reality did not coincide. In fact, the state produced major literary figures throughout the century and developed a strong tradition in that area. In 1903, for instance, *Publisher's Weekly*'s top-ten best-seller list featured five books written by Kentuckians — quite an achievement for one state. And the authors ranged widely in subject matter, some producing works with only popular appeal, some with only positive critical acceptance, and some combining both. Over the years, certain writers remained in Kentucky while others left — but even those who moved away still generally made the homeland the subject of much of their work. The place, the land, the people penetrated their consciousness and produced a fertile literary output indeed.[2]

The state's role in literature was already clear by the beginning of the century, for the person who was arguably Kentucky's first great author was firmly established by that time. He had a national readership, strong critical acclaim, and a reputation as one of America's major writers. In some ways, he also mirrored perfectly the conflicts within the Kentucky character.

James Lane Allen represented the antebellum mind as it struggled with the morals of modern America, a nation seemingly adrift from the old concepts citizens had once cherished. He wrote of honor, of chivalry, of duty, of faith.

But he also sought to confront and explain parts of his changing world. Like Kentuckians generally, he had difficulty doing both.

Born near Lexington in 1849, Allen grew to be an attractive physical person — tall, slim, handsome, a man whose graying mustache and nose glasses gave him the aura of the Victorian gentleman. The impeccably dressed, well-mannered Allen seldom let down his reserves, however, and seemed to acquaintances — he had few friends — almost too elitist and too removed from the coarse and rough life around him. As the Gilded Age and its crassness threatened the genteel life he had known, or at least idealized, as a child, he began to write of a time when nobility and purity had prevailed. And to protest against recent "downward-moving fiction" that belittled the past, Allen began to use his Kentucky settings to portray, in nostalgic ways, an earlier time of innocence, yet one which also had its share of tragedy as well.[3]

His first book, *Flute and Violin*, appeared in 1891, and its fine collection of stories combined hope and tragedy, love and duty. In the sensitive and sympathetic "Two Gentlemen of Kentucky," for example, an old aristocrat cannot adapt to a New South where "the rich had grown poor; the poor had become rich. . .the whole vast social system of the old regime had fallen. . . ." Old Colonel Romulus Field's mind "turned from the cracked and smoky mirror of the times and dwelt fondly upon the scenes of the past." Eventually his only solace is a former slave who becomes a friend, both "ruined landmarks on a fading historic landscape." The two are buried beside each other.[4]

Other books quickly followed – *The Blue-Grass Region of Kentucky* (1892), *John Gray* (1893), the popular *A Kentucky Cardinal* (1894), *Aftermath* (1895), the bold *Summer in Arcady* (1896), and then his acclaimed *The Choir Invisible* (1897). A historical novel that was highly praised by critics, *The Choir Invisible* tells the story of schoolmaster John Gray's unfulfilled love for the married Mrs. Falconer, "the first great awakening of his life in a love that was forbidden." He eventually departs out of duty, becomes engaged to another, then learns Mrs. Falconer's husband has died. Gray remains faithful to his betrothed, though his heart lies elsewhere, but "a duty can never set aside a duty."[5]

To his credit, Allen never followed a set formula in his work. As time passed, he experimented with issues and began to deal with the realism and reality of his time. He confronted the conflict of the physical and the spiritual side of people, and, in so doing, "ushered out the South's age of gentility." *The Reign of Law* (1900), for instance, has as its hero a young student expelled from college because of his Darwinist views. *The Mettle of the Pasture* (1903) focuses on the double standard of morality for men and women. His 1909 book, *Bride of the Mistletoe*, suggests the possibility of adultery. And later books continued the trend. But reviewers — and his audience — did not like the new Allen. He had lost his chivalry, replacing it with what *The Nation* termed "a gauze-veiled eroticism." The *Courier-Journal* complained that he had debased marriage and "has smeared with a slime life's loftiest relations." Allen's new world of writing was not his world; he did not have the will or spirit to present the human soul as before and an almost cold prose resulted. His output declined; his fame lessened; his old world was never replaced. Almost a literary outcast, the man who was once called the greatest novelist of his age passed away quietly on 18 February 1925. But the world he chose to remember had died long before.[6]

At almost the same time that Allen's popularity began to fade, a number of other Kentucky writers came to the forefront. They looked at different parts of the commonwealth — Louisville, eastern Kentucky, the western area of the state — and generally received less critical acclaim, though many had popular success between 1900 and 1930.

But one author almost matched Allen's efforts in that era. John Fox, Jr., ironically, was nearly the antithesis in spirit to the elder writer, even though both were born in central Kentucky and both attended present-day Transylvania University. Yet while Allen was austere and humorless, the younger Fox was warm and witty. Author Thomas Nelson Page said the Bourbon countian "drank with zest of the wine of joy of life." Page also described Fox as natural, casual, without any pretension or poise, in contrast to the formal Allen. Moreover, while the elder Allen remained reclusive, Fox sought out company and became friends with Theodore Roosevelt, Mark Twain, and others.[7]

Allen left Kentucky, physically, in the 1890s and wrote many of his works in New York, yet most of his books were set in the Bluegrass State. Fox, on the other hand, departed for schooling at Harvard and for a brief stint as a New York newspaperman, but he could not remain far away from Kentucky. He wrote a friend in 1885, "It is pleasant to get back among hearty whole-souled people whom you understand and who understand you. . . . People of that class always seem to live or have lived in Kentucky." Two years later he told the same friend, "I don't want to write about anything else than Kentucky. . . . I want to be steeped in its history, have its people, their characteristics, their personalities, their modes of life & thoughts in my brain." Then he added, almost laughingly, the touch that delighted people who knew him: "and feed my senses in the beauty & grace of its women." Allen tried to leave Kentucky behind and could not; Fox did not want to try.[8]

On one trip to the mountains, Allen and Fox talked a great deal. Fox — fourteen years younger — wrote that he admired Allen "extravagantly" for his culture, his gentlemanly ways, his sympathy, "his graceful bearing." Walking through the mountains together, the two talked and Fox felt more confident of his own abilities. They wrote, and read aloud their works. And there in the Appalachians, Fox found his literary niche. Allen could have the Bluegrass as his subject; Fox would chronicle the mountain people. Both men tried to portray societies in transition, but only Fox would achieve popular success in doing so.[9]

After a half-dozen books, including *Hell-fer-Sartin and Other Stories*, Fox penned *The Little Shepherd of Kingdom Come* (1903), which sold over a million copies. The book's strength lay more in Fox's writing ability than in the story line, which dealt with mountain and Bluegrass people, with reconciliation, with love. But the words won the audience. In describing the Civil War's beginning, he wrote: "So on a gentle April day, when the great news came, it came like a sword that, with one stroke, slashed the state in twain, shearing the strongest bonds that link one man to another. . . ." Then, at conflict's end, he concluded, "When the war was over, the hatchet in Kentucky was buried at once and buried deep. Son came back to father, brother to brother, neighbor to neighbor . . . and the sundered threads, unraveled by the war, were knitted together fast."[10]

Five years later his even stronger and more realistic novel won further plaudits. *The Trail of the Lonesome Pine* offered old stereotypes and some improbable twists, but its characters symbolized the struggle between the forces of industrialization and tradition then taking place in Fox's beloved mountains. Critical yet sympathetic of both the old cultures and the new, he portrayed in powerful prose a people in transition. Later, Cratis Williams called the book "the best fictional interpretation of mountain life ever achieved." When Fox died at the age of fifty-six in 1919, Appalachian Kentucky lost a friend.[11]

Other writers of the era, such as Charles Neville Buck, Lucy Furman, and Jean Thomas, sought to follow similar themes in their portrayals of Appalachia and had some popular success in doing so, but none presented the conflict and the struggles of the heart of Appalachia as well as did Fox. Buck, for instance, was born in central Kentucky in 1879 and had stints as reporter, cartoonist, and attorney, but gained popularity with a score of novels which featured stock plots and sensational feuds. His books tended to perpetuate mountain stereotypes rather than deal with hill problems. Similarly, Furman left her Henderson home in west Kentucky for education in the Bluegrass, then worked at Hindman Settlement School. In accounts such as *Mothering on Perilous* (1913), she mixed fact and fiction in sympathetic, nostalgic portrayals of the region. Her themes would be taken to extremes later in Jean Thomas's fiction-disguised-as-fact type of weakly plotted, sentimental books, such as *The Traipsin' Woman* (1933). Such efforts kept Appalachia before readers, but only occasionally explored in full the fictional soul of the people.[12]

While the Bluegrass and the mountain regions dominated as local color settings for novels, other parts of the commonwealth were not totally ignored. In northern Kentucky, John Uri Lloyd's *Stringtown on the Pike* (1900) gave that chemist a reputation as a popular writer. By contrasting eastern and northern Kentucky characteristics, Lloyd showed his readers that the state had many faces and oft-conflicting cultures.[13]

In the south-central part of the commonwealth Eliza Calvert Obenchain told of *Aunt Jane of Kentucky* (1907), while in west Kentucky, the multi-talented Irvin S. Cobb did much the same for his region. Journalist, humorist, actor, lecturer, and author, Cobb used his sense of fun and his knowledge of people to craft entertaining (though not always enduring) books about his native state. His "Judge Priest" stories, however, did live on, for in them he presented delightful accounts based on a real-life figure in his hometown of Paducah. Extremely popular as a columnist, as a novelist, and as an actor (*Steamboat Round the Bend*), Cobb simply charmed and captivated. Writing of his time as a combat reporter, he explained, for example, that he had to disguise his fear, for the soldiers had been under artillery fire and assorted bombardments many times, while he had been under fire only "a few times in school elections back home in McCracken County." On another occasion he noted, "I'd rather be an orphan in Kentucky than twins anywhere else." Such wit came from his self-proclaimed "Duke of Paducah," a man who, as he explained, "rarely let dull fact hamper my style." But also from his pen came a memorable literary place and a major fictional character. Cobb's warmth and light style provided a needed balance to the feud-filled accounts emanating from other authors. His was a different Kentucky.[14]

Other than Allen and Fox, many of the authors had grown to adulthood in the same era — several of the Louisville writers, Furman, Cobb, Buck, and Thomas, all were born within fifteen years of the end of the Civil War. Their books focused on different regions, received varying popular acceptance, and used assorted approaches. In the main, they wrote good books for their era. Yet none produced great literature. The next generation of Kentucky authors would change that situation.

In the fifteen years before 1910, an impressive array of writers and critics was born in Kentucky — Caroline Gordon, Allen Tate, Robert Penn Warren, Jesse Stuart, Cleanth Brooks, and Harriette Simpson Arnow, among others. They grew to maturity in the midst of the Black Patch War, World War I, educational change, various reform movements, and a host of other influences. Belonging to that same era were writers born elsewhere but who wrote principally in the state — A. B. Guthrie, Jr., Janice Holt Giles, and James Still. That generation would play an important role in what has been called the rebirth of southern literature, the Southern Renaissance.[15]

By the 1920s, Kentucky did not seem a likely place to look for new major writers. A study based on the number of authors publishing in major presses placed Kentucky at the bottom of the scale in the South. Allen and Fox had passed from the scene by 1925 and other, earlier writers had lost much of their audience. It seemed a nadir.[16]

But Elizabeth Madox Roberts and others soon changed that. She was, however, an unlikely literary savior. Born in 1881, she had lived much of her life in quiet obscurity. Constantly bothered by various, almost incapacitating, health problems — including anemia, tuberculosis, and Hodgkin's disease — Roberts had to overcome much. She was a self-proclaimed rustic and spent most of her life in the small town of Springfield. Teaching in the area for a time, observing her students and her surroundings, she learned the ways of the people. Yet still she did not write. Finally, at age thirty-six, the thoroughly southern Roberts entered the University of Chicago as a first-year student. As she wrote later, "It was about that time the great change came to all places," and the Kentuckian was affected. She met other writers and developed an intellectual confidence.[17]

Following graduation with honors, Roberts came home and began her literary career in earnest. Tall, thin, with a "patrician aloofness" in her manner, she remained almost a recluse. Her prose, however, made her a celebrity. Roberts's first novel appeared in 1926, when she was forty-five; her last came out twelve years after that. But the outpouring in between was major.[18]

In *The Time of Man* (1926), Roberts focused on a people virtually untouched by previous Kentucky writers — the poor whites, the tenant farmers, the voiceless part of the state, a people whose story was one "of hopes ever defeated and ever renewed." That stress on individual will, on the power of the human spirit, on the glory of the commonplace, on agrarian strengths, and on psychological conflicts, would be a constant theme in her work. Roberts's next book, *My Heart and My Flesh* (1927), probed another forbidden subject, miscegenation and social decline. Turning to an earlier time in *The Great Meadow* (1930), she gave readers a less controversial story, one dealing with frontier Kentucky and the inner strengths needed to settle the land. The book remains one of the best fictional treatments of the era. But following that successful work, Roberts's other publications had a decidedly mixed reception. By her death in 1941, she was already somewhat forgotten, and her writing would never regain the status it held in the 1920s and 1930s.[19]

In those years, however, she was proclaimed one of America's greatest novelists. The New York *Times* said of *The Time of Man*: "There has not been a finer first novel published in this country for many years." In the 1930 *Saturday Review of Literature* a writer called Roberts and Ernest Hemingway the best representatives of America's new generation of writers. Mark Van Doren in *English Journal* in 1932 compared her to Theodore Dreiser and Sinclair Lewis and found her "the most distinguished because she is truly personal." That same year another New York *Times* story proclaimed that of all the talented new southern writers, "no star is more brilliantly ascendant than that of Elizabeth Madox Roberts." Critic Ford Madox Ford had earlier called her the greatest writer in America.[20]

Bringing forth such praise was Roberts's sense of history and sense of place. As one author noted, "In her imagination she saw . . . the past and the present as parts of a continuous whole. Of a long succession of seed times and harvests broken again and again by 'the acute moment, the fine and immediate present.'" And her place — Kentucky — operated as "an immense territorial ghost" whose past tied in closely with her present. Writing of the Kentucky that she did not always present sympathetically, she nevertheless recognized her attitude when she said of Kentuckians:

> A pride in the place where they were born stays with them when they go, if they must go, and often they return. . . . Kentucky has form and design and outline both in time and space, in history and geography. Perhaps the strongly marked natural bounds which make it a country within itself are the real causes which give it a history and a pride in something which might be named personality.

Her work went beyond Kentucky in its focus on "that proud ghost, the human spirit," but it was that sense of place which guided her pen till she moved, as her poem proclaimed, "Toward the last holocaust, the infinite merciless first-last unknowing abyss."[21]

In breaking with established patterns, in her agrarian emphasis, Roberts signalled the arrival of the new regionalists in Kentucky writing. Not associated with large urban areas, these writers called home places with names such as Guthrie, Burnside, W-Hollow, and Wolfpen Creek. They chose as subjects not just Bluegrass aristocrats or sugary young urban children but rather a whole variety of peoples. They followed Roberts's lead in bringing Kentucky literature to the forefront.

Best known and most influential of all the new order of writers was Robert Penn Warren. Born into a house and family "full of history," he grew to maturity in west Kentucky, amid violence, segregation, and change. "Red" Warren saw the troops in the Black Patch, read of the region's past, and learned of what he saw as a fatalism in the southern mind. After college with the Agrarians at Vanderbilt University, Warren began to address those matters as he wrote about the human condition, about evil and failure, about confused people in a violent world, about the need for a sense of place, about morality, about guarded greatness, about a people's need to understand their history — and themselves.[22]

Although his career took him outside Kentucky, Warren, in a sense, never left the commonwealth's borders in his mind. Much of his best prose focused on the state, whether it was his first novel *Night Rider* (1939), or *World Enough and Time* (1950), a work based on the Beauchamp-Sharp tragedy, or *Band of Angels* (1955), or *The Cave* (1959), a book tied to the Floyd Collins rescue attempt. His major narrative poem, *Brother to Dragons* (1953), also had a Kentucky setting and historical basis in the Lewis brothers' murder of their slave in 1811. Those book-length efforts, together with *All the King's Men* (1946) and his works of poetry, brought Pulitzer Prizes to Warren in both fiction and poetry, the first person so honored. His naming as the nation's initial poet laureate in 1986 culminated a long series of honors.[23]

Near the end of his career, Warren returned again to his Kentucky past, recalling his early years in *Jefferson Davis Gets His Citizenship Back* (1980) and *Portrait of a Father* (1988). The memories that shaped him remained strong about this place where "In the turpitude of Time/Hope dances on the razor edge." His generation of writers had looked at the hidden heart of their Kentucky and, in so doing, had presented its darker soul.[24]

While Warren captured the kudos of the literary world, many Kentucky readers preferred the softer words of Jesse Stuart. Warren's sometimes tragic vision did not appeal as much as Stuart's sometimes sentimental and often vigorous style. Born within a year of each other, the two men came from very different Kentuckys — Warren from the west, from an education background, Stuart from the east, from a miner/tenant farmer's family. They both were at Vanderbilt at the moment of its great intellectual ferment, although Stuart, a graduate of Lincoln Memorial, had more mixed feelings about his time in Nashville. From college Stuart went back to his home area to teach, to serve as principal — and to write.[25]

Tall and raw-boned, Stuart brought forth descriptions of energy: "He radiates life; he is a seething torrent of poetic vigor." That would be both his strength and his weakness. The energetic Stuart probably wrote too much too fast with too little revision. Some of the resulting weak works brought down his reputation. His successful book of 703 sonnets, *Man With a Bull-Tongue Plow* (1934), set the trend. This was a work of spontaneity and sincerity, of original imagery, from the pen of an American Robert Burns, said some critics. A Chicago reviewer noted both sides of Stuart when he wrote: "His half-rhymes take more liberties with the conventions than a shoe salesman with a party girl. But he's an honest-to-God poet, with . . . gusto and vitality." Others, however, wrote of the mediocrity and crudeness of some verses, calling them "often trite and prosy." Later, another critic summarized Stuart as a rough, raw, vastly talented writer whose work leaves the impression of "much power, poorly controlled."[26]

Throughout his career, Stuart was one of those writers whom people either disliked or liked a great deal. From his W-Hollow farm, he told the varied stories of his hill people. It could be in his humorous and very popular *Taps for Private Tussie* (1943), which angered some who felt the book presented the stereotypical mountaineers as those who "fuss, fight, and fornicate." On the other hand, Stuart's autobiographical writings, *Beyond Dark Hills* (1938), *The Thread That Runs So True* (1949), and *God's Oddling* (1960), and many of his short stories, are strong in their character portrayals, power of language, and mood. He sang the praise of his native land with unabashed love:

> Kentucky is neither southern, northern, eastern or western,
> It is the core of America.
> If these United States can be called a body,
> Kentucky can be called its heart.

Later, in the same poem, he reaffirmed that which shaped him:

> I take with me Kentucky embedded in my brain and heart,
> In my flesh and bones and blood
> Since I am of Kentucky
> And Kentucky is part of me.

In a sense, Stuart represented the raw frontier side of the commonwealth, and, faults and all, he spoke for that part of the people. He gave them a voice and received their support for that.[27]

Living and writing in the eastern Kentucky mountains at the same time as Stuart was another chronicler of that area, but a very different one. James Alexander Still was almost the antithesis of Jesse Hilton Stuart. Although they were born in the same year, attended Lincoln Memorial University at the same time, and went to graduate school at Vanderbilt, most similarities ended there. The Alabama-born Still came to Hindman Settlement School as a librarian in 1932, left there some six years later, and, like Stuart, moved into a log cabin to write. Stuart, a man of strong ego, counted the quantity of his work; the quiet Still, a far less productive author, sought to focus on the quality of his. One was prolific; the other precise.[28]

Still's 1940 book, *River of Earth*, established his reputation as he told the story — like Roberts — of a people of disappointed hopes, though his folk lived amid the coal camps and small farms of Appalachia. Together with two other small volumes, done before World War II began for America, that represented the bulk of Still's literary output for over three decades. In the 1950s and 1960s, he wrote little and was almost forgotten. Then his *Pattern of a Man* (1976) and *The Run for the Elbertas* (1980) appeared, and the man at Wolfpen in Knott County was rediscovered. His works received praise for their simple narratives, strong use of dialect, and spareness of words, but he remained more favored by critics than by book-buyers. Like Warren, he often explored the Kentucky of want, of hunger, of poverty — and of hope — but it was a Kentucky many readers chose to ignore.[29]

Several other writers with Kentucky backgrounds did, like Still, achieve regional or national acclaim, but remained little read in their native area. Caroline Gordon, for instance, was born in Todd County in 1895, not far from where Warren would later live. In books such as *Penhally* (1931), *Aleck Maury, Sportsman* (1934), *None Shall Look Back* (1937), and *Green Centuries* (1941), she focused on the past she knew, the South she saw, and the family world she understood on the Kentucky-Tennessee border. More critically acclaimed than popular successes, her books shared a sense of detachment between author and subject. That and a sometimes complex style brought her more admiration than sales. Gordon's focus on the ideas of decline and historical ruin would be echoed by Warren in his works, though he presented the ideas with more force and verve. That both writers, from the same area, adopted those themes says much about the society in which they grew to maturity.[30]

Gordon's later prose would change and would reflect modification in her own life. For much of that time, her work and her husband's work were often intertwined. Allen Tate, born in Winchester, Kentucky, in 1899, and like so many of the Kentucky writers a product of Vanderbilt, went to visit Warren in Guthrie in 1924. There Tate met Gordon and before the year was out they were married. Until their second (and final) divorce in 1959, they travelled together in Tennessee, New York, and French literary circles and became major influences in American criticism. Tate, as a spokesman for the Agrarians, contributed to *I'll Take My Stand* (1930) and wrote biographies of such southern heroes as Stonewall Jackson and Jefferson Davis, and, in a sense, left Kentucky behind. His poetry and reviews became the staples of his work, and the South as a region continued to be his special literary world. Unlike Warren, Still, Stuart, Gordon, and others in the Vanderbilt/Fugitives circle, he did not return in writing to his home state. Tate remained a fugitive of another sort.[31]

By mid-century, a whole host of other authors was also coming to the forefront. Most had their best literary years ahead of them, but they showed that the literary renaissance in twentieth-century Kentucky was not ready to end. Writers such as Janice Holt Giles, in *The Enduring Hills* (1950), and Harriette

Simpson Arnow, in her book *Hunter's Horn* (1944), dealt with urban-rural conflict and the dilemma of a changing lifestyle in Appalachian Kentucky. At the Abbey of Gethsemani in Nelson County, Trappist monk Thomas Merton started to speak out in print "on behalf of what is best in mankind in one of our worst ages." His autobiographical *Seven Storey Mountain* appeared in 1948 and became a best seller. In the less tranquil setting of Lexington, newspaperman A. B. "Bud" Guthrie, Jr., wrote his studies of the westward movement, *The Big Sky* (1947) and *The Way West* (1949). For the second work, he received the Pulitzer Prize in 1950. In that same city, Elizabeth Hardwick had grown to maturity and had her collegiate schooling. By mid-century she had begun her career as author and distinguished critic. And across the commonwealth, other fledgling authors were starting to put pens to paper; their products would appear in the next half-century.[32]

In short, and for whatever reasons, Kentucky produced a core of strong authors and a host of works of worth between 1900 and 1950. Novelists began to address long-ignored issues, tell the story of all the state's people, and, by doing that, speak to the heart of their America, whether in questioning works of Robert Penn Warren or in the theological ones of Thomas Merton. In literature, Kentucky's cultural evolution was strong and steady.

Music

Few other parts of Kentucky's cultural milieu matched literature in achievement, but neither were other areas cultural wastelands. In the performance of classical music, the state did develop slowly. Of seven professional symphony orchestras established before 1900, none was in the state; of the seventy-three top such groups listed in the 1930s book, *Culture in the South*, no Kentucky name appeared. Finally, in 1937, conductor Robert S. Whitney was hired and what became the Louisville Philharmonic Orchestra commenced. Inaugurating a program of recording commissioned works in the 1940s, it gained an international reputation.[33]

If not the leader in the field of symphony music, the commonwealth was at the forefront in another form of music, one derived more from the folkways of the masses, one called "the music of the damned — not the elect." In country and gospel music, the singers often had a Kentucky accent.[34]

Among the earliest to record country music, in 1922, was a Kentuckian, William B. (Uncle Jim) Houchens of Anderson County. From that modest origin, people from the state took what one author has called a dominating role in the development of the form. Philipine (Fiddlin' Doc) Roberts of Madison County became the most widely recorded and perhaps the most outstanding of all Kentucky fiddlers, for example. But it was with the growth of radio shows, broadcast across the nation, that country music began to reach large numbers. Ironically, the lack of local stations in Kentucky — with only WHAS and, for a time, WLAP providing outlets for talent — meant that the state's

The Louisville Philharmonic Orchestra, shown here in 1947, gained international stature under the direction of Robert Whitney *(lower right).*

music often was broadcast elsewhere. The "talent drain" extended to song.[35]

Radio station WLS in Chicago, with its National Barn Dance, then WSM in Nashville, with the "Grand Ole Opry," became the focal points of country music. In Chicago in the late 1920s, the star was Bradley Kincaid of Garrard County. Taking traditional songs with wide appeal, he sang them with flair and popularized them, then issued songbooks which sold hundreds of thousands of copies in Depression times. Also at Chicago's WLS was Kentuckian John Lair, who was program director and music librarian. He had his own plans, however, and by November 1939 had started the enormously popular Renfro Valley Barn Dance, emanating from a Rockcastle County, Kentucky, locale near where he had been born. From there, from Chicago, from the "Grand Ole Opry," from a few local stations, Kentucky artists found a performing home and a national audience.[36]

The groups included the Pioneer Ramblers string band and Lily May Ledford's Coon Creek Girls, plus individuals such as Louis M. (Grandpa) Jones of Henderson, Clyde Julian (Red) Foley, and Pee Wee King. Foley, born near Berea, would eventually record "Peace in the Valley," the first gospel song to reach a million copies in sales, while King, not a native but Kentucky-based much of his life, would write the most-recorded country music song, "Tennessee Waltz." All three men would be admitted to the Country Music Hall of Fame. (By the 1980s, only Texas had produced more "stars" to country music than had Kentucky.)[37]

Kentucky's other major contribution to country music, besides the indi-

Bill Monroe *(second from left with mandolin)* **and the Original Bluegrass Boys.**

viduals, was a form that had its foundation in old ballads, depended more on acoustic music, and featured improvisation. Bluegrass music has been called "one of Kentucky's most famous exports" and goes back to the Bluegrass Boys of William S. (Bill) Monroe of Ohio County. By 1945, he had gathered what is considered the classic Bluegrass band — Monroe, Lester Flatt, Earl Scruggs, Chubby Wise, and Howard Watts. In time, Bluegrass music would evolve, as rural and mountain folk migrated north and introduced urban themes into the music. But its core, a Kentucky base, would remain. And for those who decry such music, one citizen had a simple answer: "I'd rather listen to Flatt and Scruggs than to Beethoven, and that doesn't mean I'm uncultured. That means I just got different taste."[38]

Numerous Kentuckians appealed to various tastes and made their musical mark in many ways. In Louisville in 1895, the state's best-known jazz artist, Lionel Hampton, published one of the earliest ragtime songs. In other locales, there were singers of opera (Hugh W. Martin or Riccardo Martin), of protests songs (Clay County's Mary Garland or Aunt Molly Jackson), of classical ballads (Jean Ritchie and John Jacob Niles, who by 1940 was averaging fifty recitals a year). And across the commonwealth, in singing schools, in shape-note singing in churches, in conventions attended by thousands, people sang the words of emotional gospel tunes.

In Kentucky, both writers and musicians recorded the change around them, while operating out of a firm heritage they honored and recognized. Whether similar forces produced both the strong literature and the strong musical out-pourings, or whether different influences were at work in each case, the result was the same — a consistent record of achievement.[39]

The Media

Of all the Kentuckians of that era, perhaps the one who influenced the views of more Americans than any other was film director D. W. Griffith. Born in Oldham County, not far from Louisville, this son of a Confederate cavalryman grew to be "self-consciously southern." His contributions to the motion picture industry were legend and major, and his 450 films attest to those strengths. He deserved his title as "Father of Film." However, his best-known work, *The Birth of a Nation*, presented the strong racist stereotypes he never outgrew. It represented the paradox that was Griffith. He could be bigoted or could attack bigotry. He could make powerful antiwar statements or support war. He could be brilliant or show a fatal flaw. After *Intolerance* (1916), the man in the straw hat had less and less success and by the 1930s had returned to his native state, where, forgotten by Hollywood, he died in 1948. Aside from a few exceptions such as Louisville native Charles A. (Tod) Brown-ing, who was Griffith's assistant and himself directed *Dracula* (1931, with Bela Lugosi) and *Freaks* (1932), few Kentuckians made their mark in directing. A few more — Irene Dunn, Una Merkel, Rosemary Clooney, Victor Mature, and Patricia Neal — had success in acting. But all stood small in film history influ-ence compared to Griffith, the man of brilliant talent, strong prejudice, and tragic life.[40]

In another medium touching large numbers of people, a similar situation existed, for one man dominated early twentieth-century journalism. But, as opposed to film, there were many other strong talents always challenging for dominance. The clear leader in Kentucky journalistic circles, and a major player on the national scene, was the man called "the last great personal edi-tor" — Henry Watterson.[41]

Son of a Tennessee congressman, Watterson had served the Confederacy and had, since the 1860s, been editor of the state's most important paper, the Louisville *Courier-Journal*. Irascible, bombastic, extravagant, brilliant, and force-ful, his editorials spoke for the New South, and that, coupled with an appear-ance similar to the stereotypical southern colonel, made him the subject of political cartoons. In his personal life, as in public, Watterson offered many paradoxes. He dressed well and prided himself on his culture, but let down his suspenders and enjoyed a beer and chili for lunch. Often vain, "Marse

Kentucky Historical Society

Although D. W. Griffith's film direction was progressive, the viewpoint he presented in *The Birth of a Nation* was not.

Henry" had been blind in one eye since childhood and tried to hide that, yet had to read galley proofs by holding them only inches from his good eye. Careless in financial matters and with notoriously bad handwriting, Watterson did not let that soften his editorial dealings. One of his reporters recalled how a journeyman printer had tried to decipher Watterson's handwriting and transposed Watterson's "from Alpha to Omega" to "from Alton to Omaha." That move won the printer a quick dismissal.[42]

The twentieth century for Watterson was not so happy as the nineteenth.

Henry Watterson usually posed with his blind right eye concealed from the camera.

One son committed suicide in 1908; another was emotionally unstable. While as editor he won a Pulitzer Prize in 1917, he had increasing conflicts with the paper's management, first with Bruce Haldeman, then later with the new owner, Robert Worth Bingham. The two disagreed over stands taken by Watterson (who opposed woman suffrage and the League of Nations) and brought the old editor to write Bingham that, "too stunned to speak, too pleased to laugh, too brave to cry, he fain would turn his face to the vail and with the psalmist exclaim, 'Now lettest thou thy servant depart in peace.'" In 1919, he left the paper and died two years later.[43]

Over the next three decades, the *Courier-Journal* continued its dominant role in the state and its important place in the national arena, particularly after Barry Bingham became more involved in the 1930s. Bringing in editorial writer Mark Ethridge, he gave the paper a more progressive stance than previously, and in 1946 writer John Gunther called it "one of the best newspapers in the country . . . a splendid liberal force." In fact, the *Courier-Journal* and its afternoon twin, the *Times*, would become a virtual training ground for numerous journalists who became successful elsewhere. (Earlier, Kentucky native Arthur Krock, for instance, had gone from Louisville to the New York *Times*, where he won accolades for his writing.)[44]

But strong writing was not limited to the Falls City. In Lexington Harry Giovannoli of the Republican *Leader* vied editorially with Desha Breckinridge of the Democratic *Herald* for years. Breckinridge was like Watterson in a few ways: he too was a congressman's son, and he too had problems with careless errors. After one such mistake, he wrote, "We took down the Kentucky Statutes to find some section under which we would be justified in killing the proof reader." But mostly the *Herald* and the *Courier-Journal* tended to oppose each other through the 1930s. As the *Courier-Journal* grew more conservative, the *Herald* became the leader in the Progressive Era and in 1932 Virginius Dabney proclaimed that "the liberal leadership in Kentucky journalism has passed to Desha Breckinridge's Lexington *Herald*." Soon after, however, Breckinridge died and that, coupled with Barry Bingham's increasing involvement in the Louisville paper, shifted the equation once more.[45]

Meanwhile, a whole host of other newspapers existed across the commonwealth, some of conservative bent, a few liberal, and some taking no editorial positions at all. The heart and soul of state journalism, in fact, was not the big-city presses and their nationally known editors but rather the county newspapers, which numbered 148 in 1930. Weeklies of perhaps eight pages focused on local news, with columns from various communities that seemed to try to publish as many names as possible. As Thomas D. Clark notes, weather might receive more attention than the sinking of the *Titanic*. And, in a sense, that was their strength, for their limited interests often reflected a large part of the constituency, who had their own confined concerns. In that way, the Kentucky voice often spoke clearest in the small-town press. It also appeared in different form in special-audience newspapers, such as those for the black community, the Louisville *Leader*, founded in 1917, and the Louisville *Defender*, begun in 1933. Older ethnic papers continued for a time — the German-language *Anzeiger* ceased publication just before World War II, while the *Kentucky Irish American* lasted until 1968.[46]

Other Areas of the Arts

For my friend Col R. T. Durrett —
Enid Yandell

Enid Yandell and her assistant posed in the studio before her Daniel Boone statue, which was later placed in Louisville's Cherokee Park.

In other fields, the commonwealth's record was decidedly mixed, with some strong individual work, but no statewide strengths. Sculptor Enid Yandell of Louisville, for instance, achieved some fame early for works such as the Daniel Boone statue dedicated in 1906 in that city's Cherokee Park, but few nationally known sculptors followed her. A 1930s study pointed out that Kentucky, like Tennessee and North Carolina, had no notable center of sculpture and ranked low in that area.[47]

Similarly, in the newer field of photography, the Lexington Camera Club, organized in 1936, would bring together some talented people, including Ralph Eugene Meatyard, but much of its most creative work came after 1950. The strongest contribution in the field in the century's first half may have been from William G. Stuber, who left Louisville to work for Eastman Kodak Company. In 1924, he became president of the company, then chairman of the board.[48]

In art and folk art, the same themes emerged. Paul Sawyier produced watercolors which harkened back to nostalgic, bygone days, and later became treasured examples of Impressionism and Tonalism. More nationally known was the major American painter Frank Duveneck of Covington. Not only a superb artist, he trained many other Kentuckians, including Sawyier, John Bernard Alberts, Paul Plaschke, Dixie Selden, and William Walsh. But Sawyier's death in 1917 and Duveneck's in 1919 left a major void among formal artists. The real strength in the field after that came in folk art, with its visual expressions of personal focus. Yet, in the end, Kentucky's example was not unlike the South's, where historian Charles P. Roland concluded that visual arts were the region's "weakest form of aesthetic outlet."[49]

Architecturally, Kentucky also followed, generally, the southern pattern. Modern inventions, such as elevators, which allowed more vertical construction and were used in a five-story Lexington building in 1899, and air-conditioning, which made lower ceilings more functional, all had an influence on style. But the 118 architects in Kentucky in 1900 (2 were women) and those who followed them tended either to be somewhat free of historical precedents or to rely on historical eclecticism. In the former category, the smaller urban houses of the century's first three decades generally followed the California bungalow style designed for a somewhat similar climate. Just before World War II the ranch-style house began to make its appearance as well. The only prairie-style house in the South is Frank Lloyd Wright's Ziegler House in Frankfort, but art deco with its highly stylized forms appeared sporadically over the state, including several courthouses.[50]

Of the historical revival form, Colonial Revival prevailed in Kentucky until World War II, but Tudor (Luxmond House in Louisville), neo-Italianate (Rostrevor House in Louisville), and Renaissance were common revivals as well. By 1950, preservation of past architectural forms was not yet common, and formless, functional offices replaced that past. Kentucky would have to make an architectural choice as the century wore on. But at mid-century, it varied little from other states' patterns — some excellent examples of individual work, but no challenges to established ways.[51]

In short, while Kentucky received only mixed marks in several areas of the arts, in other forms — including literature and music — the commonwealth scored well. The irony was that what some citizens saw as their own, special,

Kentucky Historical Society

Park Hills, a suburb of Covington, shown in its infancy.

forms of culture — such as country music — were not recognized as legitimate in some circles, where other forms of provincialism prevailed. In literature, virtually all critics recognized the state's strengths, yet Kentucky still could never shove aside existing mass stereotypes of a violent, uneducated people and replace them with images of the commonwealth as a place of literary strength. That positive never was fully stressed in the first half-century, and Kentucky suffered.

Frankfort, Ky. October, 13th, 1915.

In consideration of services performed, I, Parksdale Hamlett, hereby promise and agree if elected to the office of Secretary of State of Kentucky, at the election to be held November 2nd. 1915, to give W. C. Elliston, a clerkship in my office at a salary of not less than Twenty-one Hundred Dollars ($2100.00) per annum, and retain said W. C. Elliston, so long as he shall competently perform the duties of his position, and I further promise and agree to repay to said W. C. Elliston the sum of Two Hundred and Fifty Dollars, ($250.00) if I am defeated for said office of Secretary of State.

All photos, Kentucky Historical Society

Political bosses Percy Haly (top), Billy Klair (right), and Ben Johnson (left) wielded substantial power in Kentucky. Corruption took many forms in Kentucky politics, including vote buying and, as indicated in the letter above, job buying. Apparently, if his candidate became secretary of state, W.C. Elliston would secure a $2,100-per-year job in exchange for the sum of $250 and "services performed."

8

"Politics . . . in Kentucky"

James H. Mulligan stood before a distinguished banquet audience at the Phoenix Hotel in Lexington in February 1902. To that point in a life that began in 1844, he had received only limited contemporary attention in his home state, despite his many strengths. The son of an Irish immigrant, attorney Mulligan had been a minor judge, city editor of a newspaper, and state legislator, but his chief claim to fame had been the fact that he had served two years as consul-general to American Samoa. There he became friends with author Robert Louis Stevenson and was present at his funeral. Mulligan, on his return to the Bluegrass, penned an account of that island, settled into the quiet life of the law, and wrote some verse from his Maxwell Place home.

Now he drew from his pocket a manuscript and, "peering over his glasses with a smile of satisfaction that amounted almost to a leer," began to read a poem, entitled "In Kentucky." Its first verse set the stage.

> The moonlight falls the softest
> In Kentucky;
> The summer days come oftest
> In Kentucky;
> Friendship is the strongest,
> Love's light glows the longest,
> Yet, wrong is always wrongest
> In Kentucky

Five similarly worded verses followed, leading to the final one, which would be endlessly quoted the rest of the century:

> The song birds are the sweetest
> In Kentucky;
> The thoroughbreds are fleetest
> In Kentucky;
> Mountains tower proudest,
> Thunder peals the loudest,
> The landscape is grandest —
> And politics — the damnedest
> In Kentucky[1]

A better-known native son, Irvin S. Cobb, noted similar traits a little over a decade later when he wrote that Kentuckians refer to their state as God's country: "Undeniably it is," he wrote. "Its conformation is heaven-sent; its politics come from the Other Place." Various contemporaries also gave little respect to the political game or those engaged in it. A Bowling Green physician, for example, wrote his legislator in 1916, saying "I trust you are well settled and learning something of politics, graft, and the hungry hands of patriots . . . whose chief aim is to help themselves."[2]

Yet others pointed out the strengths of both the system and its leaders. One observer recalled how people would gather at the Capital Hotel in Frankfort and simply listen as the politicians' informal court took place: "One would tell a story, another a joke, another a reminiscence. The crowd would gradually thicken. . . . Never was there such an entertainment anywhere. . . . They possessed a culture that was rare. . . ." What, then, was Kentucky politics? Was it a hellish, damned system, or a lively, cultured one? Did its leaders lead with little thought of personal gain, or did they resist change, seeking only personal benefit?[3]

The Not-So-Hidden Government

The political system as explained to civics classes included political parties, voting patterns, and local government. It seldom featured what many Kentuckians saw as the dominant, controlling elements in their political life — the power blocs, the bosses, the hidden forces. While in fact the existence of such groups was quite openly known, and while they became issues themselves, still, the power they wielded was not matched by the publicity they received. Throughout the century, various power blocs would form or re-form. Some older groups, such as the ex-Confederates, would fade away, while other elements, such as the *Courier-Journal*, remained constant. Over time, lobbying influences varied from liquor, coal, and racetrack ones, to farm, educational, and, later, Rural Electric blocs. The fact that one group might represent more noble causes — such as education — than another really meant little to politicians who could feel the power of the group at election time.[4]

Symbolic of all the power groups of the early part of the century was the Louisville and Nashville (L & N) Railroad and its strong, enigmatic, and controversial president from 1891 to 1921, Milton Hannibal Smith. A self-made man who shunned publicity and usually hung up the telephone when reporters called him, Smith had a low opinion of politicians and their actions. His well-known views — "all legislative bodies are a menace. In action they are a calamity" — he did little to hide. A candid Social Darwinist, an advocate of no regulation, a man who would not hesitate to fight those in opposition to that view, Smith took steps to protect his position. In the Goebel campaign, the L & N provided free travel passes to allies, pressured laborers to vote the L & N way, and poured massive amounts of money into efforts to defeat the man who had said he would control them. A few years later, when two important political figures began discussions with the L & N, Smith basically agreed to give the men money in order to keep away the regulatory beast: "The two gentlemen named are members of a coterie of blackmailers who have for some time past been endeavoring to extort money from corporations. They have met with some success. . . . They are an unscrupulous gang, but we may rely upon it that they will avoid 'unchaining the dog' as long as there is a possibility that their demands may be complied with."[5]

In truth, the L & N, as the major railroad in the state, had many supporters, and it provided numerous benefits to various communities. But Smith's fears of government caused the line to take actions in the political arena which made the company appear to be the corporate devil its enemies portrayed. The L & N became so powerful that it almost made itself an issue in Kentucky. As a *Harper's Weekly* article noted in 1900: "A man could not be elected justice of the peace or school trustee without the sanction of the Louisville and Nashville politicos. It was a most humiliating political condition." The line had a large number of attorneys on retainer across Kentucky, and many were political leaders and legislators. In 1908, for instance, the list included a past governor, a future one, a future gubernatorial candidate, a future U.S. senator, numerous other important lawyers and legislators, as well as the former chairman of the state railroad commission. L & N money lined the pockets of many Kentucky politicians. By the 1920s, when Smith left, other groups were taking the L & N's place as the major lobbyists in Frankfort, and all in turn would become the focus of attacks on their power. To some degree, the Kentucky political world would always revolve around those influences, which were strong, deep-seated, and powerful.[6]

But politics in Kentucky, more than anything else, focused on individuals. A newspaper in 1906 proclaimed, "Our politics are principally personal," and party factions tended to be tied to individual leaders. Success in campaigning still depended as much on personal strengths as on issues. Aside from these public leaders, two other types held power, both from behind center stage. In the wings the political bosses and the business bosses controlled the main political actors like puppets on a string. One group of bosses would use all their skills and strategies to gain votes and power; the other used their money.[7]

The term business boss can be misleading, for the men of wealth did not necessarily directly control votes. Instead, they used their power indirectly, through contributions, through gifts, through paths to power. From that, such men did not seek office, but rather access to those in office. They preferred to be king-makers rather than rulers.

John C. C. Mayo, for instance, became one of the Democratic Party's major figures, even though he held no office. His liberal contributions and counsel were credited as a major reason the governorship went to J.C.W. Beckham and to James B. McCreary, and he aided several out-of-state politicians who had importance to the coal fields of Appalachia. By 1911 a Louisville paper concluded, "His influence is all pervasive." What did Mayo receive, other than friendship with important figures? During one governor's term, for example, he and others drafted a law that, when passed, gave some questionable land claims validity by granting "squatter's" title to 1.5 million acres of land in the mineral-rich regions of eastern Kentucky. Upheld by the United States Supreme Court, that law proved a major fiscal and political victory for Mayo.[8]

Two of his sometime allies had similar experiences. Rufus H. Vansant of Ashland made his fortune in lumber, and through alliances with Mayo, used that wealth to gain positions of influence. Other than serving in the circuit court clerk's office and as chairman of the State Central and Executive Committee of the Democratic Party, he held no major elected office. Yet to his opponents, he was "the *Big Chief*," a man of power.[9]

Johnson Newlon Camden, Jr., did serve briefly in a major office, as an appointed U.S. senator, but throughout his career he too most often functioned as financial supporter and advisor to governors. Born in West Virginia, where his father would serve as U.S. senator, Camden was well educated, at Phillips Academy, Virginia Military Institute, Columbia Law School, and the University of Virginia. Marriage to a descendant of Kentucky's first governor brought Camden to the Bluegrass, where his "Hartland Stud" at Spring Hill Farm near Versailles became a major thoroughbred center. That activity, plus his interest in banking and in various mining companies, soon made him a millionaire. Born to wealth more than Mayo and Vansant, the reserved and careful Camden formed the third part of the important trio of wealthy business bosses.[10]

More directly concerned in the raw give-and-take of the election game was another set of men, the political bosses. The acknowledged leaders of that group at the turn of the century were the Whallens of Louisville. John H. Whallen and his brother, James, ostensibly were the proprietors of the rather notorious Buckingham Theatre, which to some "was a great stench in the nostrils of decency." One Louisvillian recalled that women passed the theater "with eyes averted and heads held high!" Others described "the Buck" and its burlesque simply as "an unusual show to see." Whatever it was, the theater and its scantily clad chorus girls brought in a great deal of money. When James Whallen died in 1930, he left an estate estimated at a million dollars.[11]

In their lifetimes, the Whallens used their funds to fashion a powerful machine, with its base in the Irish and working-class populations of the city. As one of their workers noted, "The Whallens aid a great many people, like the aged, the orphaned, the hungry, the broke. Cops and firemen, clerks and other city and county workers always have money trouble." Either rent money to minority immigrant groups or thousands of baskets filled with food and clothes would be distributed during the holidays to the needy. At a time when relief was local and sporadic, the Whallens and other bosses provided personal, legitimate aid, if for sometimes illegitimate purposes. In return, they expected the vote of the families served — and they got it.[12]

Master of the large Catholic vote in Louisville, closely allied much of the time to the L & N (and thus opposed to Goebel), tied intimately with the police department that protected them when they used force at the polls, the Whallens dominated Falls City Democratic politics. When later governor A. O. Stanley failed to get that support in 1913, he wrote of "Papa John" Whallen (who died that year): "He is an absolute boss in Louisville. That means the loss of that city, and his defection has caused a panic among my friends." Political fortunes were made or broken by the word of the Whallens.[13]

After the Whallens' demise, the machine was kept intact, first by Michael Joseph ("Mickey") Brennan, then, after his death in 1938, by "Miss Lennie" McLaughlin. While neither would be able to have the complete control of the Whallens, due in part to the emergence of alternate relief sources, both remained formidable power brokers in the Kentucky political game. A similar role in an urban setting was filled by Billy Klair of Lexington. A German Catholic married to a wife of Irish descent, "King Klair" served briefly in the legislature but more often used his insurance company wealth to organize and control key voting areas in the Bluegrass.[14]

Most political bosses in Kentucky, however, operated not from a large urban setting but rather from a smaller regional one. The most important of these, and the boss who wielded the widest statewide influence and power over the century's first three and a half decades, was William Purcell ("Percy") Dennis Haly. A short man who walked with a stoop and whose voice "was like a light fall of gravel," Haly would stand large in politics. Born in Frankfort in 1874, the son of Irish-immigrant parents, he had worked his way up from newsboy, to messenger boy for J.C.S. Blackburn, to sergeant-at-arms in the legislature (when he aided J.C.W. Beckham), to aide to William Goebel. Haly would long admit that the assassinated governor was the most profound influence on his life.[15]

Seizing the Goebel political mantel almost as Goebel fell, Percy Haly became the established power in the faction of the Democratic Party openly led by Beckham. In fact, in some ways he, not Beckham, really dominated. Though not particularly well educated and bothered by an insomnia that kept him awake through many nights, Haly gathered power to him almost magnetically. Never married, he loved the political world most. Appointment as adjutant general when he was in his late twenties gave him the title of General Haly and for the next thirty years, his political army would make him the Warwick of the Democracy. Described as a shrewd and politically ruthless person, a benevolent dictator, "a wonderful organizer who is not a speaker," a likable and not vindictive individual, Haly built a machine funded by his friend Mayo, with Beckham or McCreary as its candidates. It would prove a powerful combination.[16]

Bitterly opposed to that group was a man who brought together elements of the regular politician, the political boss, and the business boss. Ben Johnson of Bardstown, in one way, represented the typical upper-class leader of his time. The son of a large slaveowner and former state senator, attorney Johnson became speaker of the Kentucky house, then a congressman for ten terms. Tall and trim, with white hair and blue eyes contrasting with a ruddy complexion, he was an attractive figure who continued to dress in the style of clothing popular in the nineteenth century.[17]

Yet Johnson was also the business boss, the wealthy man who would use his funds to support local candidates, or to aid the numerous Protestant and Catholic churches in his area, or to help needy people. He also could persuade business allies to withhold bank credit or mortgage renewals to those who opposed him. In such ways his behind-the-scenes operations brought him the power to control votes.[18]

But there was still another Johnson — "Boss Ben," the machine politician. One person described him as a man who "would do almost anything for you if he liked you, but he would destroy you if he didn't." Born in 1858, Johnson had grown up amidst the violence of the postwar era, had killed at least one man in a fight, and had carried a pistol nearly all his life. His temper resulted in several struggles, including one while a member of Congress. As one person recalled, "My God, he was a dangerous S.O.B." The real danger was political, however, for Johnson gained power as he grew older. His time as collector of internal revenue for the commonwealth's fifth district gave him needed knowledge. As congressman he had rewarded allies and they supported him after he left office. Later, he would also become highway commissioner and use the road funds to build more widespread political bases and his own army to counter General Haly.[19]

Nor was Johnson — or Haly, for that matter — fighting alone. "Boss Ben's" son-in-law J. Dan Talbott became a political boss himself, while in Logan County, Thomas S. Rhea gained increasing power, due in part to Haly's support. Allie Young, the so-called "Morehead Manipulator," had a powerful eastern Kentucky base, while in Covington, Republican boss Maurice Galvin ruled. Son of German immigrants and a L & N attorney, Galvin would cross party lines to aid various groups in exchange for their support at other times. And across Kentucky almost every little town had its own version, writ small, of these bosses. A candidate's first move would not be to prepare a platform, or to decide what issues to stress, but rather to go around the region and see what support could be garnered from the bosses. Their decisions might make issues unimportant factors in victory.[20]

Only one matter united many of the bosses. That was their Catholicism. The Whallens, Mickey Brennan, Billy Klair, Percy Haly, Ben Johnson, J. Dan Talbott — all knew that statewide elected office would likely remain out of their reach because of their religion. Johnson in 1911 sought the governorship but dropped out early because of the religious prejudice. Democrat Al Smith's disastrous presidential race in Kentucky in 1928 further accentuated existing conditions. So they remained more the power brokers, wielding power behind the political curtain that separated them from an unsupporting audience.[21]

The System

Winning election in Kentucky meant dealing with numerous matters, of which the bosses were but one. Corrupt voting, black voting, the role of the police, the localism, the apportionment issue, the party factionalism — all these and more made Kentucky politics a complex labyrinth in which even Daedalus might have become lost.

It was a rare election, for example, when each side did not accuse the other of fraud; it was also a rare time when each side was not correct. As one observer noted, "buying votes is as common as buying groceries." Exactly how many votes were bought in any one election is uncertain. A 1909 book surmised that 25 percent of the average county's voters were "floaters," open to purchase. A Wolfe County politician later placed the figure higher in his area: "We used to have to buy 50 percent of the people in this county." He would take several hundred dollars, line up people by a fence, then "sweetened up" the matter with dollar bills to each. They then went about their civic duty.[22]

The price varied with locale and time. In Harlan County, a new voter sold his vote, much later, for four dollars. "I was thoroughly rebuked by my father," he recalled, ". . . for not holding out for the going rate of seven dollars and half a pint of . . . bourbon." A Bath County paper in 1904 noted that votes there were going for twenty dollars in a closely contested primary race. It concluded, correctly: "It is nothing new, and will likely not become an obsolete practice."[23]

Corruption at the polls was not limited to the purchase of votes, for elections could be manipulated various ways. Some voters on the registration lists were suspect, to say the least. As one observer noted of the fraudulent 1905 election in Louisville: "In one case S. D. Guthrie, deceased, was registered from his proper address — the West Jefferson Street Cemetery." Since the counting of ballots did not take place until 10:00 A.M. the next weekday after an election, ample time existed to change the count. One Lawrence County politician related how he voted his eleven-year-old sister once, but often did not need to do that: "You count ever what you want to count. You call up, down at the [party headquarters at] Prestonsburg the next day and ask them how many they need." Non-existent voters suddenly came alive, as elections grew closer. The most famous account — and one which cannot be verified, but which was repeated for twenty years, whenever Beckham ran for office — concerned Bailey's Mill Precinct in Franklin County. In a place with 115 registered voters, so the account went, some 219 votes went to Beckham in the 1903 governor's race, while his opponent received no votes. Republican ex-governor W. O. Bradley explained in a speech four years later the interesting names of those voters: "The fruit was not inactive for A. Apple, P. Plum, P. Pear, and R. Raspberry also voted. . . . The vegetables did their part of the work, for C. Corn, C. Coffee, C. Clover, B. Briar, B. Grass, S. Fern, and B. Beans — I suppose Butter Beans — are all recorded." He recounted a score of other fascinating voter names, the product of either a fertile imagination or a desperate search for labels to attach to votes: F. Fence, R. Road, B. Broom, L.

Log, R. Rock, H. Hog, and so on, even to include H. Old and A. New. Given Percy Haly's Frankfort connections and his ties to Beckham, the story was accepted by many; given the nature of Kentucky voting at the time, it may even have been true.[24]

Later, when Logan County showed a large majority based on the ballots of numerous deceased voters, the political boss of the county noted, with a smile, "We knew all those dead people. . . . We know they were all good Democrats who would have liked to keep on voting for their friends if they could have. We were just carrying out their wishes. . . . A man is not much of a Democrat if he won't help out a dead buddy." Both parties used their clairvoyant powers regarding the dead and their financial ones regarding the living to make the political process more openly corrupt.[25]

That some black voters sold their votes, or voted early and often, was obvious; many white voters did so as well. But efforts at changing the existing situation usually focused on only one of the races. Attempts were made to portray the black vote as more corrupt, and thus needing more restriction. In 1907, a candidate for lieutenant governor urged the disfranchisement of Kentucky blacks, calling them "the scraping of the devil. They are the most fiendish, hellish set on earth." He praised southerners' use of guns to reduce the number of "these black beasts." A newspaper editor, after noting the number of blacks at the polls, told readers, "It is time for the people of Kentucky to consider seriously the elimination of the vote of the ignorant and vicious." Two years later the same paper said the state would not allow "one fourth of the white voters combined with the solid negro [sic] vote to . . . control its destiny."[26]

What seemed particularly troubling to those observers was the fact that blacks voted solidly Republican. In Lexington in 1904, 76 percent of the registered Republicans were black; 91 percent of all blacks so registered. Six years later, the figures had changed little, for the Democratic Party registration was still 96 percent white. Paducah in 1907 had a two-to-one black ratio over whites in its Republican Party. Louisville, in 1921, saw over 26,000 blacks in the G.O.P., with less than 100 in the Democracy. Those statistics made one party the white man's party, and some of its followers would cry out at election time that a vote for Republicans would mean "Negro domination." In actuality, only 13.7 percent of the potential voting population was black in 1900, and the figure would decline over the years. Yet, at election time, such fear tactics were openly used, particularly in the first two decades of the century.[27]

In that time, blacks were further disfranchised across the South. By 1910, all the Confederate states, plus Oklahoma, had followed that restrictive path. Would Kentucky? Various places tried indirect tactics to accomplish that end. Some, such as Danville, gerrymandered voting wards, so blacks were in one only. Others, such as Lexington in 1901, passed a poll tax designed chiefly to eliminate black votes. (It was declared invalid in circuit court.) A few attempts were made in the legislature to pass more major restrictions, but they all failed. Why? Why did Kentucky not follow the South into disfranchisement? Part of the reason was simply that, despite the rhetoric, the black vote was not big enough to be seen as a threat. It was large enough, however, to be important to Republicans, who remained still powerful in the era. With their opposition, together with that of some Democrats, there was not the unanimity to disfranchise as in some other states. And, perhaps most important, the question never really became a major public one. Cries of "Negro domination" would ring out as a tactic, but no leader made disfranchisement his path to power. Blacks continued to vote.[28]

Besides the racial questions, the vote-buying, and the corrupt counting, still other influences controlled election-day voting. The police force, for example, could be an important factor, as the Whallens would show. The Louisville *Post* in 1901 cried out that the police "are not our servants; they are our masters. They are the marching force of the Democratic organization." Nearly a decade later, the same newspaper told how police had so intimidated black voters that as many as 5,000 were unable to cast their ballots. At a different level, control of the state militia was important as well. During the Goebel Affair, each party called out troops commanded by their allies. Two armies, one Democratic, one Republican, had existed. When the Democrats finally gained control of the government, a reorganization — with Haly as adjutant general later — swept away all Republican commanders. When the G.O.P. took the reins of power back in 1907, a reversal followed. The musical-chair effect was seen as necessary, for the militia (after 1912, the National Guard) could be called out as an influence on elections.[29]

But, in the end, it was still politics at the local level that decided most electoral contests. Across Kentucky, the majority of the 120 counties were small in population and rural in outlook. In these "Little Kingdoms," politics was a very intimate, very personal matter. Candidates would stress their kinship ties to others in the county, while reminding voters of what they had done for them, or intended to do when elected. One reporter concluded in 1924, after observing this process for a time: "If one had lost a dear relative, his chances were fair. If in addition his house had burned, and one of his mules had died of colic he must certainly be a runner-up. . . . I remember one man who made specific mention of his mother-in-law in his qualifications, as well as the loss of his other eye. Probably he was elected."[30]

A native of Nicholas County once profiled the county clerk of that place, a man who served in his post from 1909 to 1922 and 1933 to 1957. His story would be typical of Kentucky. The clerk, John F. Sugg of Shakerag, was born in a log cabin, went through the seventh grade, and then began teaching at age eighteen. Subsequently, he took high school courses and one semester of college. In 1904, he won election as county assessor, a job that took him to all corners of the county. As his Boswell recounts, "He got to know the people. He ate with them, slept in their homes, became part of their life." His dining with his hosts was an acknowledgment of equality, a recognition of their importance. With this background, he ran for county clerk and won, again and again, never tasting defeat until the end of his life. Selling licenses, recording deeds or mortgages (all for a fee), Sugg could do "favors" for his constituents; he could be "accommodating." Perhaps half of his time might be spent daily in non-official service to the people — talking to an elderly person, taking a family home in his car, providing a place to sit for a tired visitor to town. That non-bureaucratic feeling provided the human touch to government — and made re-election easier. There was another side to that picture, in Nicholas County and elsewhere. The unchanging, parochial nature of the situation meant that even needed change would come slowly, if at all. The kinship ties fostered nepotism, which also could create various problems, including inefficiency and corruption. The total attention to local matters could mean missing a larger perspective. In essence, Sugg, and other local officials like him, represented — for better or worse — the people they served.[31]

Those citizens elected legislators to serve them also in what seemed to many to be far-off Frankfort. The agrarian society of the state and the existence of so many counties resulted in an unfair apportionment of those seats. By 1940, for instance, a county with a population of 8,500 had the same representation as a county of 63,000. Rural counties benefitted from the tendency, supported by the state constitution, to respect county lines. When counties were placed together in a district, more problems arose, for if one party dominated, then generally a rotation agreement would be made. Each county would provide a representative, on a rotating basis. The system thus hindered legislative stability and underrepresented urban voters.[32]

In fact, looking at state government as it existed at the first decade of the century, some wondered how the offices attracted candidates. The constitution under which it all operated was already being criticized as outdated, even before it was two decades old. The general assembly featured high turnovers and a large number of committees — fifty in the house, forty in the senate — given the limited nature of government at the time. Virtually all departments were understaffed, overworked, and underfunded, with few increases in support over the past two decades. Even the physical facilities were poor. The Governor's "Mansion," built in the 1790s, was described as "an aggregation of ancient sheds . . . and . . . it is difficult to make it a comfortable residence, even by the exercise of almost constant care. In summer it is invaded by dust . . . ; in winter it is hard to heat." The capitol, opened in 1830, was badly overcrowded, with committees meeting in hallways and cloakrooms. Overall, the entire government of the state was made up of about ninety persons, operating in three main buildings.[33]

Yet to go there, to win election, was an eagerly sought-after prize, and both parties fought bitter battles to win the somewhat shoddy laurels of victory. Each group had cores of strength — between 1896 and 1924, some 53 counties went Democratic every presidential election, and 41 went Republican. Adding in those counties that switched allegiances only once, a total of 109 of 120 counties were safely in one column or the other. The battlegrounds were fairly limited, then.[34]

Both parties would find it difficult to approach those electoral conflicts with a united organization, however. The virus of factionalism infected both parties throughout the era and neither could fully find a cure. It was a bit easier for the minority Republicans, who could not win if divided, but even they splintered. While at times the factionalism seemed more personal than anything else, at one level the differences centered over federal patronage and control of it. "Postoffice Republicans" owed their loyalty to federal office-holders, not state ones. Another dividing line was between urban Republicans (in Louisville, Lexington, and Paducah principally) and mountain Republicans.

While many thought Goebel's death would unite the Democratic Party, it did not. Backers of the assassinated governor went to both major factions; both groups had progressive elements; both had political bosses; both had — at different times — power bases across the state. And both factions would be loath to support the other, a situation that would open the way for Republican victories.

All this — personal politics, localism, corrupt elections, power blocs, bosses — suggest that the Kentucky political world was devoid of issues. It was not. The state's political face had many features and all those mentioned were important ones. But so too were issues, for the century's first three decades were fairly fluid ones, politically, in Kentucky, and voters did switch allegiances — or simply did not vote — because of various issue-oriented matters.

Prohibition, for instance, mobilized massive forces for one side or the other. At a time when saloons provided free meals with their drinks, when they served as male meeting places, when breweries delivered bottled beer directly to homes, drinking was a way of life for some. But others looked at drunkenness and its effects on families, at the frequent fights and occasional deaths, and called for change. Religious groups, particularly among the more conservative Protestants, and special organizations, such as the Women's Christian Temperance Union (WCTU) and the Anti-Saloon League, became powerful forces, politically. Though Carry Nation, a native Kentuckian, would visit the state and gather headlines — in 1904 a saloonkeeper in Elizabethtown hit her with a chair after she said he was running "a dirty business" — still it was the massive local group efforts, often led by women, that made the difference. While "Demon Rum" sometimes became a symbol of problems beyond the one issue, attacks on the "Beer Trust" or the "Whiskey Party" became commonplace features of campaigns, and more and more counties voted "dry" — some 82 in 1906 and 100 in 1914. Still, it was a hard fight. Even when a governor's daughter pristinely christened the battleship *Kentucky* with water instead of an alcoholic beverage, as the ship slid away, several in the crowd threw small bottles of whiskey against the ship, christening it properly, to their minds. Prohibition was an emotional, moral issue that would be a major factor in contests.[35]

To some, prohibition of alcoholic drink was a reform that was part of the larger Progressive Era Movement. Others saw it in a different light, as something that diverted attention from deeper economic and social issues. But

Western Kentucky University

Mothers, sons, and daughters marched for temperance.

there was less disagreement about change that was broader, and more diverse, the reforms associated with what was called Progressivism. In a more nebulous way, that too became a political issue, perhaps not so focused as Prohibition, but an important factor in elections as well.

Progressivism was different things to different people. Above all it was a spirit, a faith in progress, an optimistic view of the future. It was limited in its goals in that its primarily upper- and middle-class leaders wanted reform, not revolution. They sought to better their communities, not to change them drastically, to bring modernization, while retaining past values. In one sense, the Progressive Crusade wanted a return to what reformers saw as a better, more moral time, and a reaffirmation of values that would lead the nation to its better future, to its destiny.

While such groups provided a confident, vigorous reform force, there was never an overall consensus on a program; support shifted as specific issues arose. Rural reformers might want very different things than urban ones. Still, in broad terms, Progressivism could mean an appeal for reforms to bring about more direct democracy, to make elected officials more responsible to the public, to bring honesty to government; it could mean better public service, whether in the form of better roads, or better city services, or a new tax system; it could mean more governmental regulation of the economy to control trusts, corporations, and monopolies; it could mean humanitarian social justice, with aid to the poverty-stricken lower class, with child labor laws, and woman suffrage. Progressivism's reactionary side could also mean that immigration would be restricted, or the black vote eliminated, all in the name of reform. Kentucky would be affected by Progressivism, but to what degree would be the important question.[36]

J.C.W. Beckham in his office, ca. 1900.

9

"Politics — The Damnedest — in Kentucky": 1900–1919

The Beckham Years, 1900–1907

The chief executive of Kentucky in 1900 was an accidental governor. John Crepps Wickliffe Beckham, the Democratic candidate for lieutenant governor on the Goebel ticket, found himself at Goebel's death the governor of the state, barely old enough to serve at the age of thirty.

He looked the part, at least. Tall and handsome, "Crepps" Beckham was described as being "especially well bred," a true gentleman. Some, in fact, suspected that he owed his place on the Goebel ticket to that attribute, in order to balance the lower-class origins of the head of the ticket. Beckham had been born in 1869 near Bardstown into a prominent family; his maternal grandfather had been governor and U.S. postmaster general, while one uncle had been governor of Louisiana, another a Florida senator. Serving as school principal did not satisfy Beckham, and he became a lawyer, following his father's path into the state legislature, at age twenty-four. He was elected speaker of the house in 1898 and from that post had accepted second place on his party's ticket.[1]

Now he was governor. It was not the best of times. A few years later, Beckham recalled the situation when he took office: "The civil discord, and I might say, anarchy, the intense bitterness and strife among our people, a bankrupt treasury, a heavy state debt, our finances demoralized, our public institutions in great disorder, and confusion and trouble on every hand." The fiscal situation was not as bad as he suggested — property taxes, fees for licenses and deeds, taxes on banks, billiards, bowling, bulls, cards, circuses, dogs, jacks, pawnbrokers, peddlers, railroads, and thoroughbreds yielded annual receipts of about $4.5 million. But that was still not what was needed, financially. More troubling for Beckham was the political situation. His party remained divided, with many still upset with the Goebel faction's methods. The state, overall, was almost paralyzed by uncertainty over its future.[2]

Beckham, to his credit, did not vacillate. He did take action, though to his critics it was action designed to insure his place in power. First of all, he built a coalition, led by Percy Haly and financed by Mayo, Vansant, and Camden.

Next, Beckham made peace with some powerful enemies, in particular the L & N. Milton Smith recounted later that after he heard from a third party that a truce was desired, he soon agreed to support the Democrats if they "would not abuse corporations." Since the L & N paid 40 percent of the railroad taxes in the state, it was an acceptable deal for both sides. Beckham would be accused of "selling out"; he and Haly, however, had gained a powerful ally. They would need such friends, for a special election would be held in November 1900, to fill the remaining three years of Goebel's term. Beckham had one more card to play in his bid to retain power.[3]

The Goebel Election Law of 1898 had been a major campaign issue in the previous election, for it was blatantly partisan. Several Democrats had deserted the party over that matter. In August 1900, Beckham called a special session to revise the laws and "remove some of the unfortunate bitterness and dissatisfaction that now exists." The resulting act to regulate elections placed the power to appoint local officials back in the county, as it had been earlier. It also removed a potentially damaging issue before the fall elections.[4]

Easily nominated to run for the rest of the term, Beckham tried, with good success, to bring the last of the Populists back into the party, and, with more limited gain, to attract Democrats who had deserted Goebel in 1899. A sizeable number of former party leaders still remained outside the fold, including former U.S. senator William Lindsay, former governor Simon B. Buckner, and former congressmen W.C.P. Breckinridge and W. J. Stone, among others. To unite the party, the Democrats focused on a simple issue. As a historian noted in 1912: "For years after the death of Mr. Goebel, pitiful politicians used his assassination as their stock in trade. . . . Ghoul-like, they metaphorically dig up his remains to excite the populace. . . ."[5]

But would that be enough, given the Democracy's stiil-divided status? One factor favoring the incumbent was that the Republican opposition was not fully united either. Ex-governor William O. Bradley led one faction, while Dr. W. Godfrey "Gumshoe" Hunter opposed him. At the Republican convention, however, some unity prevailed, and the party came together behind a somewhat unknown figure, John W. Yerkes of Danville. Forty-six years old, a professor in the law department at Centre College, Yerkes quickly attacked the Democrats for flying "the black flag of political tyranny." In the campaign he first made the Goebel Election Law the debate and then, when that issue was removed, focused on Beckham's ties to "bossism."[6]

The Goebel election a year earlier had been very close, and apparently the events of the last year had not changed many minds. The official returns gave victory to Beckham by 3,689 votes — 233,052 to 229,363. While Yerkes claimed fraudulent votes denied him the victory, the results basically paralleled earlier ones. Despite the assassination and the ensuing rhetoric, nothing had spurred voters to change very much.[7]

The presidential race that same year, between Republican incumbent William McKinley and Democrat William Jennings Bryan, had been of secondary importance to the governor's contest, and the results varied little from the gubernatorial count. The majority party, as it would in every presidential election until 1924, carried the state. With 86 percent of the eligible voters going to the polls — the third highest figure nationally — Bryan exceeded Beckham's margin and won the commonwealth's electoral vote by a little over 8,000 ballots — 234,899 to 226,801. After that, Beckham could survey the year and see just how much his life had changed. At the start of 1900, he appeared to be a failed lieutenant governor candidate, tied to an unpopular figure. By year's end, he had become governor of the state, had forged a coalition to strengthen his base, had won an election, and had seen his party carry Kentucky in the presidential race. To complete the year, a few weeks after the contest he married Jean R. Fuqua of Owensboro and went on his honeymoon.[8]

By 1902, when Beckham's first regular legislative session began, his political honeymoon had long ended. Already his inaction regarding violence in Breathitt County and his ties to the Hargis faction there was bringing criticism, and that would increase as the Black Patch War flared. Standing before the legislators in 1902, he said little of that. Beckham instead called for retrenchment, indicating that charitable institutions received too much funding, while the state was also "exceedingly generous" in school financing. His message was limited; the general assembly's actions matched that spirit.[9]

On the positive side, the 1902 legislature increased the tax rate in a move that was expected to add a much-needed half-million dollars to state coffers. A child labor law made it illegal to employ those under the age of fourteen in workshops, mills, mines, or factories — though they could so work if a parent gave consent. A state fair was funded, as was the Confederate Home, while Labor Day was proclaimed a holiday. On the other hand, "Boss" Billy Klair of Lexington successfully introduced a law that took the right to vote for school trustees away from women in second-class cities. The general assembly also responded to the situation of a Republican attorney general in a Democratic administration by "ripping" from Clifton J. Pratt the power to appoint his legal assistants and giving that patronage power to the auditor.[10]

The major interest generated in an unmemorable session came from the senatorial contest. Still decided by vote of the general assembly, on joint ballot, the contest in 1902 centered on the incumbent (and the first Republican senator from Kentucky), William J. Deboe of Crittenden County. A compromise choice six years earlier when he had been selected on the 112th ballot, Deboe had not garnered much support since then, even in his own party. A less than friendly critic complained: "He would not know a past participle if he met one in the road, and if some one were to mention a split infinitive in his presence he would want to know 'what district the gentlemen represented.'" Opposing him was the hand-picked choice of Beckham, Haly, and Mayo, the elderly ex-governor and ex-congressman, James B. McCreary. His alliance with that trio further tied the old guard in with the young new leaders. As expected, McCreary won easily by a 95–30 margin, and his election gave Beckham another ally as he sought that rarest of things in a Kentucky gubernatorial race — reelection.[11]

Could Beckham be on the ballot once more, even though the state constitution prohibited consecutive gubernatorial terms? A friendly court decision answered that question by ruling that since he had not served a full first term, he could run again, and the race was on. Earlier, Beckham had barely won, but in the interim he had, with Haly, been building a formidable political machine. Their only real contender within the party had been Henry Watterson, and a temporary alliance of Beckham, Haly, and Allie Young with the Whallens in Louisville took away the *Courier-Journal* editor's base. Beckham won the nomination and opened his campaign in September. Not a strong speaker, he had asked McCreary, Senator J. C. S. Blackburn, and Congressman Ollie James to orate as well, and the group attacked the Republicans as the party of tyrannical martial law, of black rule, of assassination. One of the former Democrats who still supported the GOP commented that "It is pitiful to have William Goebel's wounds torn open at every election and his bones dragged from the grave to secure votes." It may have seemed "pitiful," but it was effective.[12]

The Republicans, once more, had trouble uniting, even though victory seemed possible. Factional leader Godfrey Hunter and former candidate Yerkes backed businessman Morris B. Belknap of Louisville; ex-governor Bradley favored another Louisvillian, attorney Augustus E. Willson. Convention rulings on a contested delegation brought Willson's withdrawal, Bradley's anger, and Belknap's victory on the first ballot. The new candidate did bring good credentials: born in 1856, he had graduated from Yale University, had married the daughter of Democratic governor S. B. Buckner, had served in the Spanish-American War, and had become vice president of the successful W. B. Belknap & Co. firm founded by his father. Running as a businessman-governor, he and his party attacked Beckham for allowing the lawlessness that "fetters enterprise, excludes capital, and handicaps industry," for poor management of charitable and penal institutions, for "odious political machine rule." But, like Beckham, Belknap was not a strong speaker, and his words seemed cold and rehearsed. Handicapped by not being well known outside of Louisville, he generated no real enthusiasm. Even worse, despite the Republicans' attempt to keep dissatisfied Democrats in their ranks by placing one, ex-congressman W. M. Beckner, on their ticket, their vote seemed to be returning to Beckham. The election results confirmed that, for the incumbent garnered 229,014 votes to Belknap's 202,764. For the first time in sixteen years, the Democratic candidate received a majority (54 percent) of all votes cast. In a very short time, the youthful Beckham and Haly had fashioned a political force that would make them dominant figures for another three decades.[13]

At the start of his second regular legislative session, in January 1904, the governor again offered a mild message. After decrying the "irresponsible romances" that portrayed Kentucky as such a dangerous state, and after attacking "irresponsible demagogues" who were stirring up racial hatred by appeals to blacks, Beckham asked for a fiscally conservative approach. The legislature responded with typically parsimonious appropriations to the state

HON. WILLIAM GOEBEL,
OF KENTUCKY.
"OUR MARTYRED GOVERNOR"
DIED FEB 3RD   1900.
"Tell my friends to be brave and fearless and loyal to the great Common people."

Kentucky Historical Society

Democrats evoked William Goebel's "martyrdom" to gain support.

educational and eleemosynary institutions. New funds were given to start construction of a much-needed new capitol and to erect a memorial to Goebel. A State Forestry Commission to encourage timber conservation and a law authorizing county judges to appoint fish and game wardens to protect wildlife both passed easily. Establishment of a School Book Commission and passage of a law allowing the resale of public franchises after a period of years basically completed the major legislation, except for one bill.[14]

The Day Law, segregating all Kentucky schools, also passed during the session, without major voting opposition. Given the overall paucity of accomplishments, that statute identified the legislature with reactionary laws. The failure of an attempt to disfranchise blacks entirely did little to remedy that. At session's close, Beckham was invited to the house floor, where he gave a "happy little talk," praising the general assembly. Perhaps his pleasure came from the creation of Kentucky's 120th county, Beckham County, with its county seat at Olive Hill. Unfortunately, the act clearly violated the state constitution regarding county size and nearness to other county seats, and Beckham County ceased to exist by October of that year. It was a fitting end to the weak 1904 legislative record.[15]

By the time the governor's namesake county was being dissolved, the 1904 presidential race was taking attention away from any unconstitutional laws. The campaign boded well for Democrats, since the nomination of conservative Alton B. Parker brought many once-wayward anti-Bryan party members back to the Democracy, in the national race at least. Election day brought the expected results as Parker carried Kentucky over Theodore Roosevelt, 217,170 to 205,277. Voter turnout was smaller for both parties but at almost 77 percent was still 20 points higher than the national average and third highest in the United States. Democrats carried both Louisville and Lexington, after having lost those votes four years before, and increased their overall majority from 8,000 in 1900 to 12,000. Moreover, the success carried over to the congressional races: of the eleven House seats, Republicans won but two, and one of those by only 44 votes out of 43,000 cast. In contests in which factionalism did not become an issue, the rebuilt Democratic coalition operated well.[16]

But the Democratic union would prove a fragile one, and issues over the next three years would make that very clear. The troubles began in the 1905 Louisville city elections. Two years earlier, in 1903, fraudulent voting had been open and widespread. In response, Republicans had organized a Fusion Party, made up of candidates from both parties. The leaders were lawyers and businessmen, mostly of old-line families. Several had been anti-Goebel Democrats, including the Fusion candidate for mayor, Joseph T. O'Neal. Endorsed by the Louisville Ministerial Association, by the *Journal of Labor*, by the Louisville *Herald* and *Post* newspapers, the Fusionists had a strong base. Opposing them was the regular Democratic organization backed by the Whallens and the *Courier-Journal*, and their candidate, Paul C. Barth.[17]

Election day, 1905, was marked by extensive fraud and use of force. Announced results showed a Fusion defeat by nearly 5,000 votes. The election was contested, but after many intentional delays, the Jefferson County Circuit Court upheld the outcome in a long and complex decision. Appeal to the state's highest court ended differently, however, for on 22 May 1907, it overturned the results. The contest had not been "free and equal," and fraud had been everywhere evident, the court declared in invalidating the election of fifty-two officials. In one example, those stuffing the boxes had apparently used the voter registration books to fill out phony ballots. The ballot stubs thus showed that people voted in straight alphabetical order that election day. (Or, if the count had been short, in reverse order, as more votes were needed.)

Other returns had been signed by non-existent election officers; still more were simply "lost."[18]

Governor Beckham had to appoint interim officials until the November elections and in June named young attorney Robert Worth Bingham as mayor. It would mark the beginning of an alliance that would continue for thirty years. Like Beckham a supporter of temperance, the new mayor began enforcing the Sunday closing laws, an act which did not gain him great popularity. The Fusionists' continued attacks on ex-mayor Barth proved too much, and in August Barth committed suicide. After that, Bingham declined to run for reelection, the Fusionists divided, and the Republicans won the mayoral race. The whole affair had gone on for so many months and had kept the shadow of illegal voting before the populace for so long that it hurt the Democratic image in the state just as another gubernatorial election neared.[19]

The negative effects of that long, drawn-out controversy balanced the more positive ones of the 1906 legislature. While the governor seemed to ignore the Black Patch War, then raging, when he said Kentuckians were "contented and prospering," he was more correct in noting that the federal government's payment of some old Civil War claims had left the state almost free of debt. In that better fiscal climate, the general assembly reversed its recent course and raised judges' salaries, allocated more funds to the construction of a new capitol, and established two normal schools (what would eventually become Eastern Kentucky University and Western Kentucky University). The State Fair was set up, the Office of State Fire Marshal was created, and a Racing Commission was established, which soon permitted pari-mutuel betting instead of betting by bookmakers. The child labor law was amended to prohibit more than sixty hours of work per week, and any labor by those under age fourteen, unless they had no other means of support. It also noted that factory "water closets" (toilets) "shall be kept free [of] obscene writing and marking." The so-called proposed county unit bill, which provided that if a county voted for prohibition then all precincts in the county must be "dry" as well, was amended to exclude most cities in the state from its provisions and, in that form, passed. (A special session, called immediately after the regular one, also approved a tax of one and a quarter cents per gallon of alcoholic liquor.) Prohibition had won the first of many skirmishes on the bigger issue. Other than the establishment of a new Board of Control over eleemosynary institutions (with Percy Haly on it to provide political control over patronage), the session had been a constructive one.[20]

But the unity and positive feelings which could have followed, did not, chiefly because the beast of factionalism had reared its head as well. The 1906 legislature also had to select the U.S. senator and, once more, the process divided the Democracy. The incumbent, Joseph Clay Stiles Blackburn of Versailles, had a strong record of political longevity and had shown a remarkable ability to end up on the winning side — except for his Confederate service. An attorney, "Old Jo" had served ten years in the U.S. House and a dozen more in the Senate before losing that seat in the chaotic politics of the

1890s. He immediately allied with Goebel, previously an enemy, and was reelected to the U.S. Senate. Throughout that time, J.C.S. Blackburn had been a rather typical "Old-School" Southern Democrat with his praise of the Confederacy and attack on federal restrictions. At one time, he cried out regarding federal troops in the South: "He who dallies is a dastard and he who doubts is damned." An excellent speaker with a sonorous voice, he would regale listeners with entertaining stories. One observer spoke to a U.S. Capitol guide and wondered if Blackburn would remember an uncle of his. The guide replied: "If he doesn't know your uncle, you'll never know the difference." On another occasion, Blackburn asked his party to listen to a Republican speaker: "God knows he has a hard enough task to try and defend the Republican party for the angels in Heaven weep and the devils in hell rejoice whenever a Republican gets up to speak."[21]

Now in 1906, "Old Jo" was in trouble. A year earlier, he and Beckham had made clear their opposition to each other: the governor had called for a repudiation of this "professional claim agent," this "discredited" man whose reelection was for sale; Blackburn, in return, had stated: "I have no hesitancy in declaring my contempt for Governor Beckham, his methods, the machine and his conduct of party affairs." But Blackburn could not bring about an alliance with two men who were both his and Beckham's enemies — Watterson and W. B. Haldeman of the *Courier-Journal* — and the contest became a three-man race. With the opposition divided, Haly and Beckham backed a rather innocuous Court of Appeals justice as their candidate. Thomas H. Paynter of Greenup County won the Democratic caucus with 59 votes to Blackburn's 34 and Haldeman's 10. He easily overcame a weak Republican challenge and replaced "Old Jo" as the new senator. The administration had won again but such victories were increasing, rather than decreasing, their number of enemies.[22]

In control of the party machinery, with a string of victories behind them, Haly and Beckham now executed a rather clear power play. In June, they engineered a Democratic primary for November 1906 to select the party nominee for the general election a year away — a rather distant race but perhaps understandable. *And* they included a primary to select the party nominee for the U.S. Senate seat to be chosen by the legislature in 1908. Since that seat would not be vacant until March 1909, the primary was selecting a candidate almost two and a half years before he could go to Washington. The reason for the move was simple: Beckham wanted that nomination, and by running in 1906, he could use the still-potent powers of the governorship to help his chances. Without a primary, he would have to wait and seek party approval under a different administration. In that way, it was a brilliant political move, one that would increase his prospects. But it also meant the introduction of still another factious, factional fight, one that could leave the party further divided on the eve of a gubernatorial race. Beckham and Haly took the gamble that they could win both races by their strategy.

The gubernatorial primary went as expected as state auditor Samuel W.

Hager easily defeated Attorney General N. B. Hays. Hager now had a year to prepare for the governor's race. The senatorial primary proved to be a much more bitter fight. Former governor McCreary, once in the Beckham camp, had allied with Blackburn, Watterson, and others in opposition to the "boy governor." In his talks, McCreary emphasized his experience in dealing with national issues. Beckham, in turn, stressed his youth versus the elderly McCreary, his prohibition stands in opposition to McCreary's more middle-of-the road attitude, and his support for a primary to let the people's will be heard. In passing, the governor called Watterson a "cowardly fighter" who showed evidence "of the decline and decadence of a mind once great." The November 1906 results made Beckham his party's nominee for the 1908 Senate race by an 11,000-vote majority, built chiefly in rural areas. It also gave him more enemies when the 1907 governor's race opened.[23]

The Republicans seemed to sense victory. Almost all the major statewide races of the last dozen years had been very close, and a change of a few thousand votes from recent contests could give them the governorship again. The frontrunner for the nomination was also a strong candidate. Augustus E. Willson, a sixty-year-old Louisville attorney, had been born in Kentucky, but, orphaned young, had spent much of his early life in the North, where he graduated from Harvard University in 1869. His return to the Bluegrass came when he entered the Falls City firm headed by Benjamin H. Bristow and by his mentor, later Supreme Court Justice John Marshall Harlan. A well-read man who liked poetry (and who, in his youth, had met Emerson, Holmes, Lowell, Longfellow, and others in his brother's home), Gus Willson was praised even by the Democratic Lexington *Herald* as "a gentleman of character and ability." That did not mean he was necessarily a good campaigner, however, for he was somewhat colorless and his habit of humming to himself brought him the nickname of "Hummy." Willson had run for numerous offices previously, losing them all to a Democratic majority. Within his own party, he had failed to receive the nomination for governor four years earlier and, in fact, had held no major elective or appointed office by 1907.[24]

Willson had been allied with the Bradley wing of the Republicans, so he first made peace with the opposition faction, a move that brought him the nomination. Next, he began attacks not so much on the Democratic nominee as on Beckham. He criticized the governor's friendly relations with the Breathitt County feudists, his inaction in the Black Patch, his free use of pardons — some 2,103 by one count — his "bossism," his connection to corrupt voting. Willson portrayed himself as the law-and-order candidate, the honest election choice, the county unit advocate, the man who could make Theodore Roosevelt's outburst come true: "Bully, how grand it would be to carry Kentucky."[25]

Democratic gubernatorial nominee Samuel W. Hager bore the burden of being the Beckham-Haly candidate and throughout the campaign had to defend the current administration. He pointed to the accomplishments and attacked the Republicans for the "riot and disorder" of their own governorships. Did Democrats want the centralization, trusts, and mismanagement of the Republicans or "the economical, the safe and conservative policies" of the Beckham years? Taking positive stands, Hager favored stricter child labor laws, more aid to education, antitrust legislation, and fiscal economy. In truth, he was a strong candidate. But he could not discard the Beckham collar he wore, nor could he satisfactorily wash away the prohibition issue. While Willson called the Democrats the "whiskey party" and its leaders "eleventh hour" temperance supporters, Hager seemed to vacillate and was accused of modifying his own "dry" stand in an effort to gain more "wet" votes.[26]

The Republicans carried the election, winning the governor's race with 214,481 votes (51.1 percent) to 196,428 (46.8 percent) for Hager. Victory in the mayor's races in Paducah and Louisville showed the party's urban strength that had made the difference. In fact, half of Willson's 18,000-vote majority came from his hometown of Louisville. But the Democratic loss resulted from more factors than just the urban vote. Blackburn and McCreary, the defeated parties of the year before, plus usual Beckham enemies Watterson and Haldeman, had given only lukewarm support at best to Hager. Democratic "drys" on the liquor issue may have also chosen not to vote — the turnout was down from earlier years — rather than go for their party's nominee. And, finally, there is evidence that Beckham himself made only a half-hearted effort for his one-time protégé. Apparently Haly had a disagreement with Hager, and the gubernatorial nominee, as one person recalled, "always believed, to the day of his death, that Haly knifed him" in the back, politically.[27]

Hager's defeat meant that Beckham had failed in one of his chief goals — to build a united Democratic Party (around himself), one that would be able to defeat the Republicans consistently. Instead, he and Haly had developed a strong political base, which would be a major factor in future races, but not necessarily the controlling factor. They had united a faction, not a party.

Overall, the Beckham administration left a mixed legacy. His ties to the Hargis feudists had kept Beckham from taking action there; his laissez-faire attitude on the Black Patch War had resulted in further inaction by the governor when faced with violence. The formation of the Haly machine and the charges of corrupt voting had cast more dark shadows over Beckham's claim to be a reformer. His quiet alliance with the L & N angered many of the more progressive members of his party. The Day Law and the restriction on woman suffrage had occurred while he was chief executive as well.

On the other hand, his administration had enacted some needed reforms, ranging from physical ones, such as starting construction of a new capitol and establishing two teacher colleges, to legal ones, such as child labor legislation and conservation laws. Still, in the end, Beckham had been more concerned about building and controlling his political base than on enacting great changes in government. He proved a much stronger politician than he did governor.

Kentucky Historical Society

Governor Willson *(seated center)* **hosted a Committee of Governors in 1910.**

The Willson Administration, 1907–1911

Republican electoral success over the last decade had made it so, as Irvin S. Cobb noted, that "the sight of a Republican holding a state office no longer shakes a conservative's belief in the existence of an All-Wise Power." However, it still made Democrats nervous about the hereafter.[28]

Republican Willson faced an immediate dilemma. His party had long been attacked by Democrats for calling out the militia too quickly and, in their eyes, for using force to try to accomplish certain ends. During the Civil War, the Lincoln administration had been unpopular in Kentucky due to the martial law question; in the first Republican governor's term of office, the militia had been called out; during the short-lived Taylor administration military forces had again been present during the Goebel assassination aftermath. Republicans defended the use of the troops as necessary to provide law and order (at a time when there was no state police force). Democrats, however, attacked the actions as an attempt to use centralized force, to use violence, to achieve desired goals. With the Night Riders active, Willson had to decide, once again, whether to call out the militia and feed the Democratic attacks, or to let the violence end on its own. Had he simply activated the troops, that might have been defensible, even to his opposition. But not only did he do that, he also

suggested later that individuals who killed Night Riders would not be perse-
cuted. His law-and-order message seemed diluted by an appeal simply to another form of vigilantism to meet the Night Riders' own version. Still, the
militia did help quell the violence, to a degree — though at the same time
angering the Black Patch farmers who sought relief from the tobacco monopoly and saw Willson as siding with "the trust."[29]

The governor's actions in another area had a similar effect of hardening
party feelings. Symbolically, Goebel's picture was removed from state checks
and documents, to be replaced by either Lincoln, Henry Clay, or John C.
Breckinridge. More controversially, in June 1908, Willson pardoned two of
those implicated in the Goebel assassination. The next year former Governor
Taylor and another man were pardoned as well. The person who had turned
state's evidence and had testified for the Democratic prosecution was not so
treated (and would not be pardoned until much later, in a Democratic administration). All that re-kindled old memories, engendered new debates, and, in
the end, solidified party lines even more.[30]

Governor Willson had a difficult task anyway, for like all Republican administrations in the twentieth century, his party did not control the legislature. Republicans nearly had a majority in the house; Democrats still dominated the senate. All that would be vitally important in the 1908 general
assembly because it was time to elect a U.S. senator.

Beckham, by virtue of his now long-ago primary victory, was the Democratic nominee, but his candidacy still divided the party. The so-called liquor
interests of Kentucky were fighting a losing battle to prohibitionists, but they
did not accept defeat easily. After all, producers of alcoholic beverages were a
major part of Kentucky's manufacturing base. They saw Beckham as a threat
to that industry and used the Senate race to try to defeat that foe.

Republicans buried their factional hatchets long enough to back their most
consistent campaigner, former governor William O. Bradley of Garrard County,
for the post. "Billy O'B," a stocky man with a sharp wit, colorful manner, and
excellent speaking voice, had been the dominant figure in his party for the last
decade. Blacks supported him as the race's "greatest benefactor, counsellor,
and protector" and included him as the only Caucasian in a book of biographical
sketches of Kentucky Negroes. In 1900, he had sought the Senate seat and lost
to Blackburn; now, his prospects were greater and his hopes higher — because
of Democratic divisions.[31]

The anger engendered during the 1906 primary and the 1907 governor's
race still lingered in Democratic ranks. Congressman A. O. Stanley, a "wet"
on the prohibition issue, wrote to his wife about "dry" Crepps Beckham: "He
would sell out the world to go to the Senate. This house is full of squirming
cowardly prohibitionists just like him. They keep full of booze and introduce
bills to punish the man who sells it to them. . . . Beckham is the worst type of
the demogogue and agitator. Some day they will learn that you can not make
men sober by statute." In turn, the Beckham forces pictured their opposition
as corrupt men in the pay of the liquor industry. The deep divisions became

clear when the first ballot for senator was taken in January 1908. Needing a majority of those voting — in that case 69 votes — Beckham received 66, Bradley 64. But seven Democrats had refused to vote for their party's nominee. The reasons given varied — that the primary had been filled with fraud and machine-candidate Beckham was not the legitimate choice, that he was a "dry," and that they simply opposed him.[32] Over the next six weeks, as various votes were taken, the pressure on the renegade Democrats grew immense. Near the end of January Bradley and Beckham tied with 57 votes, while 8 other votes were divided. On the twenty-sixth ballot, nearly a month later, Beckham's 56 votes fell three short of what he needed, as Bradley had 55, and four other people garnered 6 votes. Various Democrats tried to persuade Beckham to withdraw in favor of Mayo or someone else, so the deadlock could be broken and the Democrats could win, but he and Haly refused. Finally, on the twenty-ninth ballot, at the end of February, W. O. Bradley received 64 votes — a majority of one, of those voting — and defeated the Democrat, who had 60. Only then did the visibly shaken Beckham withdraw, but it was too late and a reballot ended similarly. The Republicans had won the Senate seat, and they yelled with glee at their victory.[33]

In the end, four Democrats had voted for Bradley; three were from Louisville, with its heavy liquor industry base, and one was from Danville. (All four would be termed "traitors," would be burned in effigy, and would not be reelected. One was placed on now-Senator Bradley's payroll as his private secretary.) Beckham blamed his defeat on opposition from Watterson's Louisville *Courier-Journal* and from his primary opponents, as well as the "unlimited money" used by the "Whiskey Trust." One newspaper suggested that the "Whiskey Democrats" had gone for Bradley in return for a pledge from Republicans that they would defeat any stronger prohibition bills in the legislature. Still other commentators blamed Beckham for refusing to step aside when it was clear he could not win. Haly was reputed to have said during the balloting: "It's either Beckham or a Republican." The choice had been made.[34]

The rest of Willson's first legislative session in 1908 might have been anticlimactic but it was not. Surprisingly, given the rancor of the Senate race, the two parties united to produce a reasonable semblance of the "square deal" the governor had requested. The major accomplishment of the "Education Legislature" was passage of the educational reform law, establishing high schools in every county and changing various aspects of administration. More money went to the now-renamed State University in Lexington, which was given a bipartisan board, as were the eleemosynary institutions. The general assembly added to its reform image by strengthening the child labor law, the juvenile court system, the mine inspection law, and the school attendance requirements. Off-track betting (usually done by bookies in pool rooms) was prohibited, and abortion was defined as a crime. The county unit proposal strengthening prohibition passed the house, but never got out of a senate committee. A Pure Food and Drug Act received support, as did funding for a tuberculosis sanitorium (though Willson vetoed the latter along with more than a dozen

The 1908 "Education Legislature" in session. This was the last time the General Assembly met in what is today the Old State Capitol.

other bills). Overall, said the Democratic Lexington *Herald*, "it was the best legislature that has assembled in Kentucky in our memory."[35]

Such harmony apparently extended only to the halls of the capitol, for as soon as the session ended, the politics of discord began again. As the fall presidential election loomed, Republicans immediately divided, with Willson supporting William Howard Taft for the nomination while Bradley went with Charles W. Fairbanks. The state convention did not even elect the party's new U.S. senator as a delegate, and the fragile Bradley-Willson alliance was shattered. So too were Republican prospects for victory.[36]

Democrats, meanwhile, were moving the opposite way, as they licked their factional wounds and began the process of political healing. As a Louisville attorney noted, "We have gotten the divided elements of the party together." The *Courier-Journal* called Republican candidate Taft "a mess of pottage and a man of straw," a sentiment apparently shared by the voters, who gave William Jennings Bryan the state's electoral vote by another narrow count — 244,092 to 235,711. The huge turnout of 83 percent of those eligible was second highest nationally and marked Democratic gains in northern and west Kentucky.[37]

By the time Willson's second legislature met, in the recently completed new capitol, the Democratic Party had regained its usual margin in the general assembly, with a 73-27 division in the house and 26-12 one in the senate. In the upper chamber, the solons averaged 45 years of age, generally had been to college or professional school, and were predominantly attorneys (18 of 38). The house members were slightly younger (42), were made up equally of farmers and lawyers, and were less educated. Few differences existed between the parties.[38]

Whatever the make-up, the general assembly passed little in the way of substantive legislation in 1910; a Bureau of Vital Statistics was created; a motor vehicle registration and licensing law passed; the eight-hour day was established for laborers on public works; and electrocution became the legal form of execution. Once again, the county unit extension prohibition bill went down to defeat.[39]

Republicans faced the 1911 gubernatorial race, then, with only a mixed bag of accomplishments to take before the electorate, while they had to defend the controversy surrounding Bradley's election, the use of force in the Black Patch, and the pardons of those implicated in the Goebel assassination. Willson felt comfortable doing so, but when the party's convention met, it did not. The hesitancy in endorsing the administration made Willson "very sore" and very upset with the eventual nominee. The incumbent governor's subsequent contribution to his party's campaign, said one paper, consisted of "canvassing the different golf grounds." Former governor and senator-elect Bradley had not supported the convention's choice either, and he too did little in the race.[40]

The nominee did not fit many typical Republican patterns. Edward C. O'Rear of Mt. Sterling was born in the midst of the Civil War as one of fifteen children, had been largely self-educated, and had become a very successful eastern Kentucky attorney. Elected to the state's highest court, he had ruled in the Berea College/Day Law case in favor of segregation, a fact that alienated many black Republican voters. Fairly tall, with heavy black eyebrows and a dark mustache, O'Rear was an attractive candidate and a good public speaker, but he sometimes declared his stands in ways that made some in his party uncomfortable. Support for the initiative and referendum, for woman suffrage, and the Black Patch farmers made him seem almost radical and placed him closer to Teddy Roosevelt and the Progressives than to the Old Guard. O'Rear had easily won in the convention over E. T. Franks of Owensboro and W. H. Cox of Maysville, but he emerged with a divided party, which never bodes well for the minority forces.[41]

Democrats, however, had their own set of problems, including one dealing with an unexpected issue — religion. In February 1911, a frontrunner for the gubernatorial nomination, Ben Johnson, gave what was termed "one of the most sensational statements ever issued in connection with a political campaign in Kentucky." He withdrew from the canvass, citing the opposition to his Catholicism. Others supported his analysis; party leader Urey Woodson of Owensboro said Johnson had been "hounded and secretly stabbed for months" on the question; a Bowling Green newspaper said a "systematic and insidious" effort had been made to inject religion into the race. The *Baptist World* was quoted: "No Catholic can be elected Governor of Kentucky."[42]

With Johnson gone, the leaders of one faction were down to supporting a fairly unknown "wet" candidate, W. S. Adams of Cynthiana. Despite the aid of Watterson, Whallen, Johnson, Stanley, and others, he lost, in light turnout, by a 62,679 to 40,129 count. (Interestingly, in the race for the lieutenant-governor nomination, Edward J. McDermott, a Louisville Catholic, won.)[43]

The Democratic gubernatorial nominee, once more arisen from the political graveyard, was James B. McCreary of Richmond. It is uncertain whether the man called "Oily Jeems" willingly used his political skills to grease his way into the Beckham-Haly camp, or whether that faction had craftily enticed him back to their side. Either way, the alliance was clear when the party met to adopt a platform. In a "duel of words," "Marse Henry" Watterson had sought to fight the proposed endorsement of the county unit prohibition plank, and Beckham had answered him, defending the proposal. Watterson's "wets" lost 667 to 514. Acknowledging defeat, the editor stood and concluded, "It looks as though I am no longer wanted by my party." Mayo was selected national committeeman, Vansant chairman of the State Central Committee, and the sweep was complete. Once again, a skillful Beckham-Haly arrangement had won, bringing that faction back into control of the Democracy.[44]

And the key to it all had been an alliance formed with a man who was at once a strange political figure and a typical one. McCreary first won statewide office in 1875, when he was elected governor at age thirty-seven. Over the four decades since then he had shown an uncanny ability to take the most popular side, to avoid taking a stand altogether, or to support both groups — a trait that won him the nickname of "Bothsides" McCreary. Stories abounded of his cautiousness. In one, McCreary was observing animals in a nearby field when a friend commented on the beautiful black sheep. "Well, they do appear to be black on this side, at least," concluded McCreary. A vain man at times, "Jeems" seemed to have hair that darkened with age, which brought Watterson's comment about the one-time ally who had left him: "Poor old McCreary! But whatever else could have been expected of a man who dyes his hair at 73?" Yet despite the jokes about him, McCreary was a skilled politician. He had an excellent memory for names and faces, spoke well, and knew where the votes were. As a former Confederate lieutenant colonel, McCreary never played down those ties, nor did he ignore the support gained through the years as governor, congressman, and U.S. senator. Spending his own considerable funds freely, he contributed to numerous local races, further cementing ties across Kentucky. In short, he was a popular, aging, grandfatherly figure, one who might be willing to yield to Haly and Mayo, if they would give him access, once more, to the governorship. The match was made.[45]

After all the political maneuvering on both sides to get the nomination, the election seemed almost anticlimactic. O'Rear supported progressive goals — direct election of U. S. senators, better roads, a non-partisan judiciary, stronger labor legislation, a Public Utilities Commission — but so too, in large part, did McCreary. The Republican stressed the need to cleanse the state of political lobbyists and the liquor interests, but the Democrat was a "dry" as well. Generally, the O'Rear forces were forced to rely on attacks on McCreary as a pawn of Beckham, as a man "rescued from oblivion" simply to run at Haly's bidding.[46]

McCreary responded by criticizing O'Rear's retention of his court seat and salary while running for governor and the apparent support of him by some liquor industries. After pointing to the Republicans' record of "assassination, bloodshed and disregard of law," the Democrat noted that the thrice-convicted and recently pardoned Caleb Powers had run for and been elected to Congress. Turning to the national scene, McCreary blasted the Taft administration's tariff policy and northern Republicans' own "bossism."[47]

It did not hurt McCreary that 1911 was filled with news stories marking the fiftieth anniversary of the Civil War, nor that a statue to Kentucky Confederate John Hunt Morgan was unveiled just before the election. All that rekindled memories of his own Confederate ties. He also was better funded than his opposition and used traditional barbecues, such as a Lexington one that featured 3,000 gallons of burgoo and 140 sheep, as a popular tactic. But new campaign features appeared as well, as both parties used automobiles and motion pictures to reach more voters across the state.[48]

O'Rear's reach was not nearly long enough, and, as expected, McCreary won a decisive victory, with 226,771 (52 percent) votes to 195,435 for O'Rear (45 percent), and 8,718 (2 percent) for Socialist Walter Lanfersiek of Newport. The Democrats basically won across the board — in the cities, in the tobacco belt, and even-better-than-expected in the mountains. The old colonel was back in the political saddle once more.[49]

The McCreary Administration, 1911–1915

Ironically, the elderly new governor represented, in many ways, the transition taking place in Kentucky politics. His inaugural address sounded the usual themes of economy and progress, and Confederate veterans figured prominently in the ceremonies. In that way, he stood for the past, for nostalgic Kentucky. Yet some of the very traits that were his weaknesses would become his strengths in the new administration. Seldom in advance of the public, McCreary was not far removed from the trends either, and the people of the state were ready for change. The fact that the governor was not a strong leader worked to the administration's advantage as well, for McCreary would not stand in the way of progressivism. The old issues of Goebel, "Negro Domination," and Confederatism were dying out as McCreary took the oath of office, and new ones were replacing them. It was not, as some saw it, "the Inauguration of the Era of Good Feelings," for Kentucky politics was too forceful for that, but it would, as it turned out, mark the full emergence of a new era. Progressive political winds would blow across Kentucky — for a time at least.[50]

Irvin S. Cobb once told the story of how a candidate for the bar, on being questioned by a judge, explained that the only law he knew was what he had read in the *Revised Statutes of Kentucky*. Replied the justice: "My son, the trouble with you is that the next legislature is liable to meet and repeal every damn thing you know." McCreary's first legislature seemed ready to make that prediction come true. Despite the opposition of people like the editor of the Louisville *Post* who complained about "restless women" seeking "costly and disturbing" experiments, women were given the suffrage regarding school matters, by 62–25 and 24–11 margins. That action returned to some Kentucky females the vote taken away a decade earlier. In a less progressive action, the general assembly also reversed its recent trend toward bipartisan control of state institutions, by making the Board of Prison Commissioners appointed by the governor. The board's important patronage powers thus remained under the control of the chief executive.[51]

But most legislative actions were new and broad. The three most important laws were ones creating a statewide, compulsory, direct primary system, establishing a Department of Public Roads and creating a Road Fund for it, and, finally, passing the controversial county unit bill which further aided prohibition efforts. Passage of the latter measure by 70–19 and 24–14 margins showed the strength of those seeking such restrictions, and the Democracy's closer agreement on the issue.[52]

While some other acts showed the session's continuing Old South ties — the Jefferson Davis birthplace was purchased and a pension system was established for Confederate soldiers and their widows — the overall tone was still one of progressive actions. New regulatory groups were created, in the form of a State Board of Forestry, a State Insurance Board, and a Department of Banking. Women's labor outside the home was restricted to sixty hours per week as well. And, in what became a notable event as time passed, an exhausted general assembly finally formed the 120th — and last — of the state's counties and honored the governor by naming it McCreary. Few disagreed with the Paducah *Sun*'s summation that the legislature had accomplished more than any "in recent years." It was a good start.[53]

What made it even better for McCreary and the Democrats was that their party had also elected a U.S. senator during the session, and without a bitter factional fight. Earlier, in the July primary the year before, incumbent Senator Thomas Paynter had seen the hopelessness of his cause and had withdrawn before the election. That left the nominee, Ollie Murray James of Crittenden County in west Kentucky, facing Edwin P. Morrow, the nephew of Republican Senator Bradley, in the legislative vote for senator. Democrats, with a large majority, remained united, and they easily won on a joint ballot count of 105–28. As it turned out, it was the last time the legislature elected a U.S. senator.[54]

The new senator was impressive in many ways. At six feet, six inches in

Kentucky Historical Society

The hulking Governor McCreary *(at center with shovel resting on ground)* **seemed ill-suited for "working on road," as claimed in this 1913 image.**

height, and weighing some three hundred pounds, "the Marion Giant" combined that massive physical presence with a booming voice and spellbinding oratory. One listener recalled him as an "enormous man with enormous voice." Something of a demagogue and a man who used racist appeals more than most state politicians of his day, James advocated the Black Patch tobacco farmers' cause, visited racetracks, frequently opposed woman suffrage, and supported the "wets." Originally not allied with Goebel, he had finally joined in his campaign, a move that paid political dividends three years later when at age thirty-one, he sought his first office and won the congressional seat he held at the time of his election as senator. In that position, James had united most frequently with A. O. Stanley to form a state faction that tended to support progressive measures while opposing Beckham's group. Yet Stanley realized the fragile nature of the alliance as he summarized fellow attorney Ollie James: "He knows little . . . [but] he is no fool — winning — tireless — resourceful — . . . a catchy, fluent, magnetic speaker — he is in every way a formidable and dangerous antagonist." James also had a further ally, for his brother-in-law R. Y. Thomas, Jr., of Muhlenberg County represented another Kentucky district in Congress at the same time. But Thomas's 1913 divorce and violent actions — he killed a man in a dispute — lessened his impact. Still, "Big Ollie"

Kentucky Historical Society

Ollie James campaigned for A.O. Stanley on the Old State Capitol grounds in 1915. The banner overhead urges to "Vote Straight Democratic Ticket. Peace — Progress — Prosperity."

had risen steadily up the political ladder and his election as senator marked him as a major new political force.[55]

The so-called Era of Good Feelings for the Democratic Party did not last much beyond the legislative session. Within two months, Beckham's open letter "To the Democrats of Kentucky" brought forth the bitter words and angry accusations that marked the beginning of the presidential contest. Accusing Watterson and Whallen of "secret opposition" to the party's candidates in both the 1907 and 1911 gubernatorial races and "scurrilous abuse" of him personally, the former governor concluded of "Marse Henry": "He has never stood for any good or moral cause in our state. He has invariably appeared as the advocate and champion of the criminal element." Watterson, never one to stand back in the midst of a fight, answered the next day under the headline, "The Fulmination of a Coarse Blackguard and an Illiterate Blatherskite." The editor said he was not surprised that Beckham would lie or that he would use language "that only a drunken vulgarian would use"; what else could be expected, he asked, of such a weak man who "has not character enough to qualify him to hold the lowest office in the land?"[56]

The partial reason for the sudden attacks was the fact that Kentucky Democrats were divided in their support of potential presidential candidates; with Republicans split nationally and with the prospects good for a Democratic president, the various leaders wanted their faction to be in control of the spoils and the power. One candidate was Woodrow Wilson, a man called by Watterson "a New Jersey Crook." In an editorial, he said that "beneath the veneering of scholarly polish lay the coiled serpent of unscrupulous ambition." The fact that Beckham and McCreary went with Wilson did not cause Watterson to soften the blows.[57]

The other faction of the party, led by Watterson, James, and Stanley, supported a native Kentuckian, Champ Clark of Missouri. After expulsion from a Kentucky university his senior year for shooting at a classmate, Clark had gone elsewhere, eventually to become Speaker of the U.S. House of Representatives. Throughout the years away from his native Anderson County, Clark had kept his Kentucky connections, later describing the people as "the most hospitable, the most emotional, the kindest-hearted under the sun." A few other Democrats still supported a third candidate, the old warrior William Jennings Bryan, but even Ollie James, his floor leader in the previous national convention, had turned from him. When the May state convention met to choose delegates, it selected representatives from both factions, but instructed them to vote for Clark. As it turned out, Clark was a frontrunner at the national convention but could not get the two-thirds majority then needed. For forty-five ballots, the Kentuckians remained loyal to Clark, then finally went to winner Wilson on the next and final ballot. James had served as permanent chairman of the entire convention, and when he and his party returned home they were confident of victory.[58]

As well they might be, for Kentucky Republicans, like their national counterparts, were deeply divided between the regular party nominee Taft and the Progressive or "Bull Moose" Party choice Teddy Roosevelt. With former gubernatorial candidate O'Rear, the editors of the Louisville *Post* and the Louisville *Herald*, and several major Republican leaders in the Bull Moose camp, deep splits had occurred. The results showed that. In the lightest presidential vote turnout in twenty years (but still the third highest nationally), Democrats won the state's thirteen electoral votes with 219,584 popular votes (48.5 percent); Republicans, combined, had almost as many — 217,278 (47.7 percent) — but their votes had been equally divided between Taft and Roosevelt. In fact, the third-party Progressives had done exceptionally well in the state, carrying fifteen counties and getting a bigger vote in Louisville than in almost any urban area in the nation. The question now was whether Republicans would unite in a more progressive party, to take into account that faction, or whether they would reject them and become more conservative. Happy Democrats simply celebrated the fact that their party would have a president in Washington for the first time in sixteen years.[59]

By the time McCreary's second legislative session opened in 1914, the sixteenth (income tax) and seventeenth (direct election of senators) amendments to the U.S. Constitution had been ratified. That progressive tone did not carry to the Kentucky general assembly, for the 1914 session was decidedly weak. Watterson commented on "the fool things that were done"; the Lexington *Herald* said the legislature, at its close, "just died an inglorious death"; the Paducah *Sun* said the best move the general assembly made was to adjourn. One of the better actions, a Workman's Compensation Law, was declared unconstitutional later. Woman suffrage had been rejected 51–29 in the house. Otherwise, the solons supported central authority adoption powers through the State Textbook Commission, created an Illiteracy Commission and an office of the Confederate Pension Commission, established a road tax, strengthened the concealed weapons law and the child labor law, and unveiled a new statue of Goebel. Few mourned the session's close.[60]

Part of the reason so little had happened, in contrast to two years earlier, was the void in leadership. Once again, a political race had overshadowed the session, and McCreary's role as one of the candidates removed his administration from any position of strength. In fact, he was one of three major political leaders vying for the party's Senate nomination, to be decided in the August primary. For his part, the governor ran a pleasant race, praising his opponents, pointing out his accomplishments, and reminding voters how he had helped "redeem Kentucky from Republican rule." But few expected him to win and his political impotency was clear. Earlier, he could not have won the governor's race without Beckham and Haly's backing; he did not have that now, and his campaign showed that his support was as temporary as the black dye on his hair.[61]

The race was expected to be between Democratic factional leaders Beckham and Stanley. The frontrunner, the former governor, stressed his "dry" ties, past record, and how he deserved the seat denied him by "whisky Democrats" six years before. Behind the scenes Haly made an alliance with Louisville bosses Whallen and Brennan, and with the L & N — though as Milton Smith of the railroad said, "We don't care who is Senator," noting that if an antagonist was elected, Washington "is as good a place as any to bury him." When a minor fourth candidate, David H. Smith of Hodgenville, withdrew, his vote was expected to go to Beckham as well. Crepps would be hard to beat.[62]

The third major candidate, Stanley, wanted desperately to defeat Beckham, a man he genuinely disliked. Convinced that Haly was pushing "that old fool" McCreary "as a drivelling dupe" to take votes from him, Stanley knew he was fighting the odds: "[Beckham] has a twenty dollar bill for every postage stamp of mine . . . [and] an army of trained and purchased politicians." He told his wife how a L & N representative had approached him, but he had turned him away because he could not give the "assurances" desired. With that corporation, the tobacco trust (which Stanley had attacked), and the wealthy in-state supporters in hand (though Mayo died in May), Beckham had a well-funded campaign.[63]

But Stanley would not yield to "my ancient enemy," Beckham, a man he had earlier termed "a fungus growth on the grave of Goebel," and now called a "Little Lord Fountleroy" who placed his "dimpled hand in the cadaverous clutch of Percy Haly." Though his private letters show that Stanley did not feel confident of victory despite the support of fellow Beckham-haters Watterson and Ben Johnson, he wanted to stay in the race to inflict damage on Beckham, for the future. As an excellent speaker and hard campaigner, he did just that. One typical day he left at eleven one morning and took a train to Winchester, campaigned there till midnight, then caught a 1:00 A.M. train to eastern Kentucky, arriving at 5:30. He electioneered until noon, took another train to a nearby city, spoke for an hour, and then started again. In such talks, Stanley questioned his opponent's temperance stands: "Beckham's as dry in the country as a dusty road; in the cities he's so wet you can . . . wring water out of him." He attacked Beckham as a tool of the corporations and of the bosses and appealed to farmers and coal miners to support him instead. As he told his spouse, "I will do my damnedest to get 'Beckham's goat.'"[64]

Complicating the canvass was one other factor. In May 1914, U.S. Senator W. O. Bradley died, and Governor McCreary appointed Beckham's ally, the wealthy Johnson Camden, to fill the vacancy until the November election of that year. Camden had agreed not to run for the full term that Beckham and the others sought, but did seek election to fill the remainder of Bradley's term, which expired in March 1915. His short-term candidacy was on the ballot as well when the August primary took place. The resulting vote went as expected, as Beckham won the party's nomination by some 7,000 votes, with 72,677 to Stanley's 65,871 and McCreary's weak 20,257. It marked the end of McCreary's career, while loser Stanley still emerged in a strong position. Beckham's future would depend on whether he could finally gain the Senate seat he had long sought.[65]

Three months later the November election decided who would win the full Senate term, and the Republicans had gone through their own divisive selection process. Former congressman and longtime Bradley enemy Godfrey Hunter had first eyed the nomination, then withdrew in favor of Richard P. Ernst of Covington. As soon as that took place, former Republican governor Gus Willson announced his candidacy and was successful in his pursuit of the nomination. But it was to little avail, for the popularity of the Democratic Wilson's presidency at the national level, coupled with the unpopularity of the Republican nominee's own previous administration and the lingering Bull Moose division, gave Democrats the victory. Beckham won by some 32,000 votes and became the state's first popularly elected senator.[66]

The shouting had barely ended before the governor's race in 1915 began. Some half-dozen candidates sought the Democratic party's nomination but one, short-term Senator Camden, declared he would seek no further office. Commissioner of Agriculture John W. Newman of Versailles withdrew in June; State Auditor Henry M. Bosworth of Lexington lasted until August. Lieutenant Governor Edward J. McDermott of Louisville gained McCreary's backing but won little support outside the Falls City. That left two major candidates, each acting for a major faction, each supporting a different side in the explosive prohibition question. Representing the "drys" and advocating statewide prohibition, Superintendent of Public Instruction Harry V. McChesney of Frankfort was forty-six, a good speaker, and a strong candidate. He had the firm backing of Beckham, Haly, state treasurer Tom Rhea, and others. On Newman's withdrawal, McChesney garnered his support as well.[67]

Still, the acknowledged leader in the race was Owsley Stanley of Henderson — the only west Kentucky candidate in the race. Born in the central part of the state in 1867 to an ex-Confederate, preacher father and a mother who was a governor's niece, Stanley had graduated from college, been a teacher, then an attorney, before winning election to Congress in 1902. Well-respected and popular with constituents for his words and actions attacking trusts and monopolies and supporting a Jeffersonian philosophy, Stanley showed his real strength was in his campaigning abilities. On the platform, he would loosen his tie, then as he warmed to his task, throw off his coat, then his vest, all the while giving a flamboyant though often eloquent talk. At the same time, he could be biting in his words. Journalist Arthur Krock remembered how in a congressional debate a Florida representative compared Stanley to a Kentucky mule. Rising, with an actor's hurt look in his eye, Stanley replied, "I would rather be a doorkeeper in the House of the Lord than dwell on a dais in the tents of iniquity. And I would rather be an honest ass than the gentleman from Florida." In another instance, Stanley was touting the pleasantries that resulted from drinking his state's bourbon whiskey — a sensation that at various times in his life, Stanley knew very well. He told, as Krock described it, how that resulted in "a mood of peace toward men, a sense of listening to a great symphony played by a perfect orchestra, a desire to go about the world doing good." But, he asked the House, what followed from drinking some low-class blended whiskey? "Why gentlemen, this unspeakable mixture turns an anchorite into a howling dervish and makes a rabbit spit in a bulldog's eye." It was this man running on themes of progressivism, retrenchment, and reform that swept to victory in the Democratic primary. Supported by Bosworth after he withdrew, Stanley garnered 107,585 votes to McChesney's 69,722 and McDermott's 25,918. Some of the other losers in the primary were notable — bosses Klair (railroad commissioner) and Rhea (auditor) both went down to defeat.[68]

For the Democrats, the primary was not so divisive as was the convention called to prepare a party platform. Senator Beckham, unpopular because of his bipartisan prohibition talks with Republican O'Rear, rose to protest certain actions and was hooted and jeered. Hisses of "Snake in the Grass" were some of the kinder words thrown his way. The resulting platform praised the Woodrow Wilson administration, supported a workman's compensation bill, the county unit law (not statewide prohibition), more powers for the Railroad Commission, revision of the tax code, and "rigid economy." The chief legacy of the gathering, however, was wide dissension and a divided party.[69]

Republicans were delighted. Their nomination process had started as a contest between Godfrey Hunter and Ed Morrow, who with Bradley's death had taken over the leadership of his uncle's faction. But Hunter's withdrawal before the balloting, coupled with his son's presence elsewhere on the ticket, insured a generally united party, though the Bull Moose defection was still a factor. The nominee's strengths, however, made party leaders confident they could bring victory back to the Republican camp.[70]

Edwin Porch Morrow, one of twins born to ex-Union officer Thomas Z. Morrow, a nineteenth-century gubernatorial nominee, was a Spanish-American War veteran, a respected attorney in Somerset, and at age thirty-seven already a long-time campaigner. In fact, he and opponent Stanley were much alike. Like Stanley, Morrow had as his strength his oratory. Later U.S. Senator John Sherman Cooper, also of Somerset, remembered how Morrow had "a kind of emotional quality about his speaking which could make people laugh or make them cry." Popular and witty, "Howdy Ed" Morrow was one of the few people who could match Stanley on the stump. Perhaps it was because the two were so alike that Stanley and Morrow became close. Stanley later recalled: "We were the best of personal friends. I loved Ed as perhaps I have loved no other man." With the Republicans adopting a platform that varied little from the Democratic one, the two campaigns and the two candidates were almost mirror images.[71]

The resulting rollicking race became a part of Kentucky folklore. Stories supported chiefly by oral tradition spread rapidly, telling how the two would go to speaking engagements together, then, on arrival, would verbally rip each other apart, and would thereafter go to a bar together and drink and laugh the night away. The most famous story about the race has two versions. Various present-day Kentuckians will swear that their father was present and told them the story, then others will tell the same account, but reversing the two characters. The most prevalent version tells how Morrow and Stanley were speaking on a hot summer day. Stanley, who had fortified himself with bourbon, grew sick and vomited in front of the entire crowd. Later, when he stepped to the platform, he recovered quickly and replied, solemnly, "Ladies and gentlemen, this just proves what I have been saying all over Kentucky, Ed Morrow plain makes me sick to my stomach."[72]

Even without the stories, the race was colorful enough. In his opening address Morrow first used the tried-and-true ploy of attacking extravagance by the incumbent and promising to remove politics from the system, especially in regard to prisons: "What is needed in Kentucky is less politics and more business; . . . more red pepper and less red tape." In scorning the lobbyists of "the Third House," he averred that "You cannot clean house with a dirty broom; you cannot overthrow a lobby-controlled legislature by returning largely the same members. . . . A new broom and a general housecleaning is needed in Frankfort." Morrow concluded by saying that he wanted to make Kentucky "indeed the fairest land in all the world and that the sun shall shine again upon the Old Kentucky Home." Later he would also advocate repeal of the dog tax. In his final campaign speech, Morrow pledged, "If I could be elected Governor by 500 stolen ballots, I would not accept the office."[73]

Stanley answered with his own attack on "Invisible Government," on Republican pardons of those connected with the Goebel Affair, and on earlier Republican expenses. Other tactics were used; a contemporary account noted that after Stanley went by mule some sixteen miles to a mountain town, he told his listeners that Morrow had refused to go there because he could not arrive by automobile! Lively language continued throughout the canvass, as when Stanley noted, "Ed Morrow's pronouns wander through a wilderness of words searching vainly for their antecedents." In that tone, the campaign ended, the voting began, and the race grew even more interesting.[74]

As the results poured, then trickled, in, both sides claimed victory, and both screamed fraud. For nine days, the decision was uncertain; by 9 November only two places — Louisville and Laurel County — remained out. Eventually the Falls City gave Stanley a majority, but late returns from the Republican mountains seemed to balance that. What was going on behind the scenes was a furious scrambling, as politicians tried to gauge what votes had not been counted and how many votes were needed to be counted for their candidate to win. Both sides engaged in questionable or illegal actions. Later, Stanley pointed to a Pike County "coup" that changed the tide; another observer indicated that a local Republican leader in northern Kentucky had defected to the opposition; still others looked at McCracken County returns in the western part of the state. Whatever the reason, the final vote was announced as Stanley 219,991, Morrow 219,520. By a margin of 471 votes out of nearly 440,000, Stanley had won. In a wise political speech, done with an eye to four years hence, Morrow said he would accept the results and not retard the state's development by challenging them. The fact that Democrats controlled most of the decision-making bodies made his decision easier.[75]

The Stanley Administration, 1915–1919

Despite the governor's whisker-thin victory, the legislature was safely Democratic, by 28–10 and 63–37 margins. It was also freer of factionalism than usual, for Beckham was readying for his stay in Washington. All that, together with Stanley's own reform bent, resulted in a very progressive administration. The 1916 legislature proved personally stormy, for one of the assistant sergeants-at-arms drew a pistol in the House Chamber, as he ordered a representative to sit down. Another conflict was narrowly avoided soon after where angry words were exchanged between representatives over whether the legislator had had a knife in his hand. But other than that, and a failed attempt to segregate Louisville streetcars, the session was chiefly progressive. The general assembly passed a Corrupt Practices Act which, if it had contained enforcement powers and fewer loopholes, would have been more effective. It required candidates to file reports of their expenses, limited the amount to be spent at each level of contest (the governor's race restricted to $10,000 in expenses), and forbade public service corporations from contributing to any campaign. An "anti-pass" law directed at the L & N made it illegal for "common carriers" to offer free passes to state or municipal officials. An anti-trust law prevented "conspiracies and combinations in restraint of trade"; an elec-

Kentucky Historical Society

Governor Stanley posed in 1916 with hat, coat, and cigar.

tive workman's compensation program was set up as well. The legislature
revised the inheritance tax law created a decade earlier, established various
new boards to regulate special groups, and impeached a McCreary County
judge. Its major failure had been the 45–46 vote in the house, rejecting woman
suffrage for Kentucky. Still, the session had been an unusually strong one,
overall.[76]

Stanley was fortunate, as well, for with a sitting Democratic president — a
recent rarity — the party was united going into the 1916 presidential race. In
fact, Kentucky's Ollie James would play a major role in the campaign. He had
apparently gained Wilson's support early, for even though he had favored
Champ Clark for the nomination in 1912, it was James — not the original
Wilson supporters — who had been given the state patronage. Now, four years
later, he was selected as the national convention's permanent chairman and
from that position gave the speech that became the battle cry for the cam-

paign. In his melodious, "pipe-organ" voice James told the delegates: "I can
see the accusing picture of Christ on the battlefield, with the [World War I]
dead and dying all around him, with the scream of shrapnel and the roll of
cannon, and I can hear the Master say to Woodrow Wilson: 'Blessed are the
peacemakers, for they shall be called the children of God.'" Delegates screamed
and shouted their approval. Then James told how Wilson had maintained an
honorable peace, "without orphaning a single American child, without firing
a single gun, without the shedding of a single drop of blood." To cries of
"Repeat it," James did and added that the president had "truly demonstrated
that principle is mightier than force, that diplomacy hath its victories no less
renowned than war." The convention yelled in approval and demonstrated
for twenty minutes. It was James's greatest speech and marked him as a potential presidential candidate in 1920. After that, the Kentucky election results
surprised few. With a turnout of 81.7 percent of the eligible voters (second
highest nationally), Kentucky gave Wilson 269,990 (51.9 percent) votes and
Republican Charles Evans Hughes 241,854 (46.6 percent). The GOP had beaten
back Watterson's attack on Hughes as "the Kaiser candidate," and had healed
most of the old Bull Moose factional wounds, but could not overcome Wilson's
popularity in a state that appeared to be increasingly solidifying its Democratic vote, especially in once-Republican urban areas.[77]

After that victory, Stanley could have continued to do as he had in the
summer of 1916; that is, feed his pheasants, work in his vegetable garden full
of cauliflower, beans, and tomatoes, and stay focused on a job that, as he told
his wife, "demands vigilant, intent, constant watch, care — you must keep *Keen
eyes* open all the time — and then you do not know half that is going on." But
in 1917 he called a special session, one that lasted over two months, in an
effort to deal with the state's revenue problems.[78]

Receipts in 1910 had totalled $6.6 million; by July 1916, the amount had
grown to nearly $9 million. But usually that was not enough, and deficits
tended to run between $100,000 and $700,000. Since the state could not
legally incur a large debt from one fiscal year to the next, a series of warrants
— promises to pay — were issued. By 1913, $80,000 a year was spent on interest
alone on those warrants; the warrants themselves totalled nearly 25 percent of
the state's annual receipts. Even at that, Kentucky was not in particularly bad
shape, comparatively, for its per capita gross debt fell far below the national
average. Similarly, that debt expressed as a percentage of the assessed valua-
tion of taxable property was also about half the national figure. Still, the
system needed changing, for property could not be classified and taxed at
different rates for tax purposes, and in most places property was evaluated at
only one-third to one-half of its fair value. A 1915 amendment to the state
constitution allowed the legislature to change that situation, effective in 1918.
Stanley called the special session to begin the modernization of the Kentucky
revenue system and the general assembly obliged by creating a State Tax Commission, which would be headed by M. M. Logan, the state's attorney general,
who resigned to chair the group.

Changes were drastic: land assessments increased nearly 40 percent, tangible personal property 80 percent, intangible personal property almost 260 percent, and bank deposits some 1,500 percent. Additional taxes were placed on distilled spirits, oil production, race tracks, and corporate licenses. To balance these increases, the session reduced the livestock tax, and the property tax rate went from 55 cents to 40 cents per $100 of property. Overall, the effect would be additional revenues of over $1 million, but the burden of taxation was also shifted from real estate to other forms of wealth. In a sense, Stanley and the solons were helping the state's agrarians. The next year, the legislature also adopted the first real budget system. The two actions improved greatly — but did not solve — Kentucky's revenue situation.[79]

As a result, the 1918 general assembly found itself with more funds to spend and quickly moved to take advantage of the situation. Almost every part of state government, including higher education, received needed additional support. The State Board of Health was given more powers and county health boards were set up. Legislators faced a new concern as well, for by January 1918 American blood was being shed on distant ground in World War I. A state Council of Defense was established and funded, and a state flag adopted. But Governor Stanley did not yield to the passions of the hour as did some of the legislators, and he vetoed the act which prohibited the teaching of German in the schools. But perhaps the most important action of the 1918 session, politically, was one which finally ended the long-divisive fight over prohibition. By agreeing to let the people settle the matter by statewide vote on a proposed amendment to the Kentucky constitution, the legislators and the governor removed that question from their hands. At the same time, by a 94–17 joint ballot vote, Kentucky ratified the eventual Eighteenth Amendment to the U.S. Constitution, establishing national prohibition. Ironically, the home of bourbon became the first "wet" state to so ratify. After two decades, one major fight seemed ended.[80]

Another unexpectedly began in August. Ollie James had easily won his primary for the Senate seat he held, but within weeks, on 18 August 1918, he died at the age of forty-seven, a victim of Bright's disease. The governor quickly appointed attorney George B. Martin of Boyd County to fill the unexpired term and called a meeting of the State Central and Executive Committee of the Democratic Party to select a nominee for the full six-year term. With Stanley's men in leadership positions in the committee, and with Beckham glad to forestall what had been expected to be a Stanley attempt at his seat in 1920 by letting Stanley gain this Senate seat instead, the governor received the nomination. The Republican nominee, Dr. Ben L. Bruner of Louisville, was an almost unknown on the state scene, and Stanley's chances seemed excellent. But the governor's German-language veto and his long-time "wet" views angered some, and a national mood against the Democrats hurt him. Wilson's letter calling for his election may have been the deciding factor in Stanley's narrow 5,590-vote win.[81]

On 19 May 1919, seven months before the conclusion of his regular term as governor, Stanley resigned to take his Senate seat. Lieutenant Governor James D. Black of Knox County became the state's chief executive. Sixty-nine-year-old Black had been a teacher, school superintendent, attorney, legislator, college president, and assistant attorney general before his election as lieutenant governor. Not on the Stanley slate originally, the "dry" Black and the "wet" Stanley did not become allied after their joint election. In one instance, Stanley refused to travel out of state on vacation, leaving Black in charge, for, as he told his wife, "the Good Lord only knows what Black would do with the [patronage] places still unfilled." Now, Black faced the unenviable position of defending a man (Stanley) he did not want to defend, of having been a "dry" in a "wet" administration, of trying to balance Stanley's supporters with his own. It was not a good situation from which to run a campaign.[82]

Black had no legislative assembly during his time in office and, with a party primary taking place within three months after taking office, to be followed by a general election, he spent most of his time campaigning. In the primary, his opponent was Chief Justice John D. Carroll of New Castle, an able man believed to be backed by some Stanley supporters. But, if so, they were not numerous enough; Black defeated Carroll 63,905 to 43,159. He had hurdled one obstacle.[83]

Facing Black in the general election was a well funded and very formidable foe — Ed Morrow. Making some two hundred speeches, "Howdy Ed" used his famous oratorical powers to attack, first, his friend Stanley, then Black. Since his defeat, Morrow reminded his listeners, "the marks of the strangling death grip of the old political order" had tightened around the throat of the state, leaving extravagence, partisan control of state institutions, and more "needless jobs and useless officeholders." Supporting the usual "good" things — good roads, good educational funding, and good controls on utilities — Morrow called on what Walter Baker has termed the Republican coalition "of rich and poor, black and white, town and mountain" to join him in rejecting the Democracy.[84]

In the few matters he had dealt with outside of campaigning, Black had not done well. When the state's highest court had ruled the Textbook Commission's actions illegal, Black had verbally criticized the board but had taken no action. Now, on the eve of the election, he had to answer charges that the Board of Control had contracted to purchase some cloth at twice its regular price, and that some corrupt influences were at work. Trying to be positive in his race, the governor turned to national issues, instead of state ones, in his call for votes. He "unreservedly" supported United States admission to the League of Nations, while Morrow refused to take any stand on the question. Black praised President Wilson and tried to make the race a referendum on him.[85]

But it was all to no avail. Despite the fact that Stanley had left a million-dollar surplus in the treasury and that Stanley, overall, had a good progressive record, that administration was used against Black. The new governor's pro-Wilson stance probably caused some of the usually Democratic urban German vote to go to Morrow, while the president's actions in regard to recent coal strikes further hurt Black with the labor vote. And, finally, it just was not a good time for incumbents, for the chaos of that postwar world seemed to be calling out for change. Ed Morrow, campaigning on the slogan "Right the Wrong of 1915," won the prize denied him four years earlier by swamping Black by a vote of 254,290 (53.8 percent) to 214,114 (45.3 percent). It remains the biggest Republican gubernatorial margin ever in the state. The state prohibition amendment passed by a surprisingly narrow 10,807-vote majority. Together, the two votes marked the beginning of an era of even more political uncertainty.[86]

The old leaders of the nineteenth century were passing from the scene. Ex-governors Buckner and Bradley had died in 1914; former senators Blackburn and McCreary had joined James in death in 1918. And at Maxwell Place, where for a decade old Judge Mulligan had been living a broken man due to family problems, the author of "In Kentucky" had died in 1913. In the political arena little had occurred to change his characterization of state politics as "the damnedest."[87]

Samuel Woodfill posed in 1938 for a mural commemorating his bravery during "The Great War." The caption on the finished mural noted, "Kentucky's Outstanding World War Soldier — Breaking resistance in the Meuse Argonne on Oct. 12, 1918. First Lt. Samuel L. Woodfill, 60th Inf., 5th Div., A.E.F., leading his company personally silenced three machine guns, killed nineteen of their crews, the last two with a pick-mattock, clearing the way for the advance to the objective, for which he was awarded the Congressional Medal of Honor — for conspicuous gallantry and intrepidity, in action, above and beyond the call of duty."

10

"Hard Times Comes A-Knocking at the Door": War, Disease, and Depression

James B. McCreary and A. O. Stanley had been wartime governors. In their administrations, politics had never been adjourned, but the conflict that widened from Europe to the world soon engulfed their commonwealth and even pushed politics out of the limelight. For the first time, Kentuckians became part of a world war.

World War I

When the conflict broke out overseas in 1914, little unanimity existed in Kentucky regarding America's course of action. By far, most approved of the nation's neutrality, but bellicose editors such as Henry Watterson of the Louisville *Courier-Journal* and Desha Breckinridge of the Lexington *Herald* early on supported America's entrance on the side of the Allies. In September 1914, "Marse Henry" concluded an anti-German editorial with the memorable phrase: "To Hell with the Hohenzollerns and the Hapsburgs." Breckinridge later admitted in March 1917, "It looks as if we are drifting toward war . . . and I hope with all my heart we are. I have thought from the first we should be in the war." Both men eagerly advocated American intervention elsewhere as well, and they chided Wilson — with whom both had crossed verbal swords — for not sending soldiers into unsettled Mexico earlier than he did. "Nothing that we can do will help the Mexicans until we absorb them," wrote Watterson. "I am a jingo."[1]

Other Kentuckians had a decidedly different bent, however. While the state did not have a large immigrant population, it did have a vocal one with important people in it. The two largest groups, the Irish and the Germans, also happened to be tied more to the Central Powers than to the Allies, particularly after the 1916 Irish revolts against England. The *Kentucky Irish American* was almost pro-German in some of its editorials, while the *Anzeiger* openly questioned Wilson's actions. Watterson's editorial stance angered Louisville's German-American community and a rival paper, the Louisville *Herald*, supported them, calling Watterson narrow minded and bigoted. In a state where some churches had only recently stopped offering services in German, where German was the language of science, and where some of the best educated in the state had been to schools in Germany, a small but vocal opposition existed.[2]

There was also a broader but quieter opposition, one that feared involvement in any conflict. Such antiwar sentiment lay beneath the surface and would not be voiced often; it could be transferred quickly into at least non-opposition to the conflict. But when the United States formally entered the war on Good Friday, 6 April 1917, not all celebrated. The next month the *Kentucky Woman's Journal* published a warning, amid the patriotic fervor: "The unspeakable pathos of war is that it settles nothing. . . . A stupendous task is ours — to train the new generation that the idea of fighting and killing is not the highest form of patriotic service." Others voiced such feelings openly, particularly in rural areas. A Fulton County observer reported how people there talked about an unpatriotic farmer, while the writer commented, "I longed to smash the soap box orator . . . who aired his views in the country store that we were no freer than Germany." A Kentuckian, reflecting on upcoming American battles in France, wrote in April 1918: "It makes me sick to think of it and so far away and so dreadful."[3]

Yet, in the end, the majority of Kentuckians supported the war effort whole-heartedly. To some, it was simply the transference of the Progressive Crusade to the world. A Kentuckian of the era recalled later how it was done "with some sense of mission. . . . It was a war to end all wars." Reformers of the world, America was fighting for the future fate of all people, said Breckinridge of the *Herald*: "We wage not our own, but humanity's war." Watterson's editorial, "War Has Its Compensations" won him a Pulitzer Prize. Others, particularly the young men, were seized by "the war fever," and they entered into the conflict eager for adventure. They would find that — and much more.[4]

First and foremost, war meant fighting, and Kentuckians soon were part of the Great Crusade. The Kentucky Guard patrolled railroad bridges and public buildings in the state, then on 13 April 1917 were made part of the federal service. Married men were mustered out, their places filled, and the units became part of the 138th Field Artillery, the 38th and the 149th Infantry, and the 137th and 138th Machine Gun Battalions. But unlike in earlier conflicts, state identity was not maintained in newly formed units. Drafted men from Kentucky, Indiana, and Illinois, for instance, made up most of the 84th Division, but Kentuckians generally were spread among various divisions. Two counties in the state apparently did not have to draft anyone to fill their quotas, but those mountain counties of Lee and Breathitt were the exceptions, and about 60 percent of those who served were drafted. Some went to war as one recruit did. A friend noted that the soldier believed the country was wrong — "he feels so strongly against everything" — but that "we are in it now and everyone must do what we can to win." Another Kentuckian recalled later, when asked if his unit was eager to ship out to France: "Anxious to go? Heck no!" Others, however, volunteered eagerly, went willingly, and wrote avidly about this "hum-digger" of a war.[5]

Death came quickly to the commonwealth. On 20 September 1917, a former University of Kentucky student was killed in the conflict; news reached the campus in mid-October. Soon, such information began to arrive across the state. Of the 84,172 who served (12,584 of them black), about half went overseas. Some 890 were killed in action; 1,528 died from accidents or disease; thousands more were wounded or gassed. Jefferson County and Louisville furnished the most soldiers — 17,025 — and suffered the most losses — 353 — and Robertson County the fewest — 3 dead of 150 who served. Henry Watterson's grandson was among those who never returned. In the horror of trench warfare, there were individual heroes — including Medal of Honor winners Samuel Woodfill of Fort Thomas and Willie Sandlin of Buckhorn — and there were troop leaders. At least sixteen generals came from Kentucky, with the highest ranking being Major Generals Henry T. Allen of Sharpsburg (who commanded U.S. troops in postwar Germany), J. Franklin Bell of Shelbyville (a former Army Chief of Staff), George B. Duncan of Lexington, Hugh L. Scott of Danville, W. L. Siebert of Bowling Green (Director of Chemical Warfare), and F. L. Winn of Winchester. From land-locked Kentucky, the Navy had Rear Admirals Robert M. Berry of LaGrange, Carlo M. Brittian of Richmond, and Hugh Rodman of Frankfort. The 1,804 officers from Kentucky included 29 African Americans in the segregated armed forces. For all those troops, black and white, enlisted and officer, combatant and non-combatant, the war came to an end in 1918, on the eleventh hour of the eleventh day of the eleventh month. A Kentucky soldier's words said it all: "I cried because I was so glad it was all over. . . . We heard the last big roar die away and the world seemed quiet."[6]

Back in Kentucky, civilians on the homefront had been part of the war effort as well. Immediately after the declaration of war, patriotic rallies had been held and volunteers had offered their services to the cause. Citizens sacrificed through "Lightless" evenings, and "Fireless" Mondays, "Meatless" Tuesdays, or "Wheatless" Wednesdays, in efforts to conserve items. Scrap drives (which often took park or courthouse fences) or Liberty Loan drives came regularly. With all that appeared a fierce patriotism, one exemplified by the Lexington *Herald*, which said those who did not buy war bonds should be "quickly consigned . . . as enemies of their country" whose "mildest punishment should be deportation." Civil liberties suffered in such an atmosphere: President Wilson signed a law making it illegal to criticize the government or the flag. In Mt. Sterling in February 1918, a man was sentenced to sixty days in jail for cursing the president after he was unable to purchase wheat flour. Three months later another such arrest took place there. In Louisville, the avowed Socialist, German-American Henry Fischer of Fischer Packing Company, criticized the war as a "capitalist scheme," and only his good relations with labor leaders kept charges from being filed against him. A statewide committee, composed of University of Kentucky and University of Louisville professors, was established to censor "all German textbooks."[7]

Kentucky Historical Society

A pumpkin appears as "Kaiser Bill" at a Frankfort Halloween party, ca. 1918.

At the same time, stronger restrictions on morals and morality were established. The Kentucky Derby and horse racing continued much as before, but liquor prohibition came with the war. A 1918 state law "to prevent idleness" also established that if males aged sixteen through sixty did not "regularly" work thirty-six hours per week, they could be declared vagrants and arrested. Houses of prostitution were shut down in Louisville and Lexington, supposedly because of the nearness of army camps. In the Falls City, the "red-light" district had been on Green Street, and the city council patriotically changed the thoroughfare's name to Liberty Street. Lexington's most famous madam, Belle Brezing, reportedly told authorities she would not reopen even if the war ended, for "amateurs" were already taking her business: "All you need now is an automobile and a pint of whiskey."[8]

Across Kentucky, various groups were organized to see that other businesses and people properly aided the war effort. The 1918 legislature gave $50,000 to the Kentucky Council of Defense to coordinate, through numerous committees, the state's work. Charged "to vigilantly guard the interests of the state and report treasonable acts or utterances," the council had subpoena and investigatory powers as well. Through it, county councils, chaired by the county judge, were set up to work with federal food and fuel administrators, Liberty Loan Committees, and the Red Cross, among others. At the school-district level, community councils functioned as smaller versions of the county group. Such councils had to approve any non-war-related construction as well. With all that, with "Four Minute Men" giving talks around the state, with the railroads under government control, people at the local level began, in some ways for the first time, to feel the impact of the federal government in an intimate, daily form.[9]

One thing not well controlled was prices. A study of Lexington showed that a dozen items that cost $53.20 in 1913, a year before the conflict started, cost $138.20 in 1920 — an increase of almost 160 percent. Men's clothing in that period went up 135 percent in Lexington, rents 44 percent, and various sundries, such as shaves, haircuts, cigarettes, taxis, newspapers, and the like, 64 percent. Water rates remained stable and electric rates declined, which meant a 114 percent increase in the cost of living overall. That was much higher than the National Industrial Conference's figures of 71 percent for the United States as a whole. Good statewide figures for Kentucky are not available, but limited statistics indicated that the entire commonwealth at least matched the national average. State land prices doubled between 1914 and 1918 and almost tripled by 1920, for instance. All this was offset, to a degree, by additional revenue. Tobacco, the chief cash crop, went from $12.55 per hundred pounds in 1914 to $40.19 in 1921 — an almost 220 percent rise. Assessed bank deposits, which had been underassessed before 1918, increased from almost $180 million in 1918 to nearly $260 million two years later — a 44 percent movement upward. In short, Kentuckians were grumbling about high prices, but, overall, most probably had prospered and profited during the war years.[10]

Part of the additional monies resulted from the presence of army camps in the commonwealth. Fort Thomas in northern Kentucky served as a concentration point for troops sent elsewhere, as did Camp Stanley near Lexington. But the largest bases were Camp Zachary Taylor in Louisville and the newly purchased Camp Knox, some thirty miles southward. The latter was opened in August 1918 and chiefly used as a firing range for the field artillery school located to the north. On the other hand, Camp Taylor, built at a cost of over $9 million, became a major post, with some two thousand buildings. At one time it housed 63,000 men and, overall, an estimated 125,000–150,000 soldiers trained there (including Wendell Willkie and F. Scott Fitzgerald). After the war its limited space made it expendable, and it was auctioned off piecemeal, while the larger Camp Knox gained the artillery center, eventually became Fort Knox in 1932, and was later named the army's armor school.[11]

Ironically, more soldiers would die at Camp Taylor than there were Kentuckians killed overseas, and the killer was not nearly so combatable. After an extremely cold winter the previous year, the Spanish influenza struck Kentucky in late 1918; at Camp Taylor 11,000 became ill. Sick soldiers lay on the floor, in the absence of available cots; nurses were stricken; doctors died as well. At the base, an estimated 1,500 soldiers passed away. Across the state, "the Spanish Lady" did not respect those not in uniform, either. One person remembered, simply, "It killed people in piles." The governor's own family were stricken but recovered. Others were less fortunate. Paducah had over 2,000 cases, with 24 dead; Lexington nearly 1,500, but with almost 100 deaths. By October the State Board of Health ordered closed all schools, places of amusement, and churches. Political rallies stopped, funeral services were forbidden, and large plants closed their doors. The deserted streets and quiet towns combined with a hog cholera epidemic in west Kentucky, which left hundreds of dead hogs scattered across the countryside, to produce a surrealistic effect. The epidemic was still raging at war's close, and victory celebrations were often muted as a result. Finally, by the first months of 1919, it was over. Official records reported nearly 14,000 deaths directly due to influenza in Kentucky in 1918-19.[12]

In a sense, the flu epidemic's close more accurately reflected the ending of World War I than did the November armistice, for until the influenza ceased, a great shadow still lingered over the people. Only with its passing could they stop and calculate the effects of it all. Some results of the war were surface and obvious: the German Insurance Bank of Louisville became Liberty Insurance Bank while the German-American Bank of Carrollton merged and became First National Bank. Some were transitory, at all levels: sauerkraut became "Liberty cabbage," then sauerkraut again, and while women filled some jobs once held by men, they often lost them when the soldiers returned. In the schools, the number of male teachers had fallen 40 percent from one year to the next, and many never returned to that profession.[13]

In one area — race relations — results were harder to gauge. White America had made a conscious effort to include blacks in the homefront efforts, through segregated groups such as the State Committee on Organization for the Negroes of Kentucky for War Work. Some of the more racist newspaper attacks seemed less prevalent during the 1917-18 period as well. And even where there was segregation, as at Camp Taylor, a few semi-positive signs had occurred. There word spread that white officers were not going to salute a visiting black colonel. Ex-Confederate and former state adjutant general John B. Castleman, an aristocratic son of slaveholders, had a statement published that defused the potential problem: "I shall, of course, salute Colonel Davis, if, as I trust, I shall encounter him. A salute is to the uniform." Simply the fact the African Americans fought for their country was not enough, however, as later college president Rufus B. Atwood found when he returned to his hometown of Hickman in far-west Kentucky. A medal-winning soldier who had served overseas, he was told not to come back in uniform, for the police chief there resented blacks in uniform. That attitude more generally reflected the state's response, and the war had only marginal effects on race relations.[14]

In that regard, things did not seem to change, as a mountain woman noted: "You couldn't tell much difference" in the people's way of life, she recalled. But other Kentuckians saw it differently, ranging from Elizabeth Madox Roberts's view that a "great change" came, to a Louisvillian's conclusion that "Henceforth forever the door was closed on innocence." A Burkesville soldier wrote home, "I would not take a thousand dollars for what I have seen and learned about war," and he spoke for the thousands who returned with a different world view, whether positive or negative. Some saw things they had never before known existed and brought back new ideas to their communities as they sought more modern improvements. Such people became forces for change. Others, however, had seen too much and did not like the results; they retreated from the world, back to the security of their little kingdoms. As historian Larry Hood has noted, some turned away from state Progressivism and inward to their locales. The wartime sacrifices of food, the cold of winter, the news of battle losses, the draft of the young, and, then, finally, the deaths of the influenza epidemic caused a religious people to question whether Providence approved of their course of action. Almost with a sense of resignation, a tired populace mostly tried to go back to their old ways. Yet within them, and around them, seeds of change planted by the war could not stop growing. The result would be conflict, continuing conflict, of a different kind.[15]

A Disturbing Interlude: the 1920s

The passions of war, once released, did not go away easily. The Bolshevik Revolution in Russia brought to the forefront fears of Communism, of radicals, of anarchists, of almost anything alien; the resulting "Red Scare" filled the newspapers with stories of arrests, bombings, and deportations. While only two of the seventy-two cities raided for radicals in 1920 were in the South, one of those two was Louisville. Nationally, some 4,000 alleged Communists were arrested in 1920, and 600 were forced to leave the country; Wall Street was bombed and dozens killed later in the year. All that combined with race riots at home and continuing conflicts abroad to make this new postwar world seem a very unstable place indeed.[16]

With the resulting societal changes nationally in the 1920s — the flappers, "the jazz age," the gangsters, the sexual revolution, the women's vote, the political scandals — came different reactions. Some Kentuckians, particularly in larger urban areas, embraced the age and all it meant; others rejected it entirely, were affected little by it, and went on with life as before. And still others sought, through force, to shape the age to their own view of what was correct and what was not.

The so-called second Ku Klux Klan grew out of such attitudes and became a national organization, with perhaps its greatest strength in Kentucky's neighboring state of Indiana. Not only anti-black, but also anti-immigrant, anti-Catholic, anti-Jewish, and almost anti-modern, the reborn Klan owed part of its reason for being to the popularity of Kentuckian Griffith's racist *Birth of a Nation*. It also appealed to those seeking an America controlled and dominated by white, Anglo-Saxon, Protestants, who would define — and enforce — what they saw as traditional values. In short, it seemed made to appeal to Kentuckians.[17]

Yet, though the Klan had a sizeable presence in the state, it did not domi-nate as it did in other places, North and South, where it elected senators and governors, and, for a time, wielded a major influence. Kentucky seemed likely to follow that path, for the Black Patch War's Night Riders had contained some Klan-like elements and blacks had suffered as a result. In Fulton in 1908, a forerunner of the powerful later Klan had pledged "to preserve the purity of the WHITE RACE . . . AND TO PERPETUATE THE WHITE MAN'S GOVERNMENT." By the 1920s, that attitude had merged with the fear of foreigners and Catholics to bring about a "new" Klan, based on old fears.[18]

Across Kentucky, the organization began to grow. In Caldwell County in west Kentucky an estimated one thousand members paid a ten-dollar fee and became a key factor in county affairs. A Fourth of July parade there in 1924 drew up to 5,000 people, while in Russellville the local paper regularly printed stories favorable to the Klan. Some lawyers in the region lost cases because the KKK had infiltrated or influenced the jurors. Nor was the story different in east Kentucky. The Pond Creek Klan, for example, included among its members a lawyer, dentist, doctor, two deputy sheriffs, and numerous mer-chants and miners. Made up of young (34.3 years of age, on average) and married (85 percent) men, that Klan likely varied little from the norm in the state. Throughout the commonwealth, such groups appealed, as did the War-ren County Klan, for white supremacy and an end to "foreign" (Catholic) rule. In the 1924 book *The Kall of the Klan in Kentucky*, its preacher-author wrote that blacks and aliens were responsible for the "political crookedness" in the nation, while the "mighty host" of immigrants were poor-quality people who threatened to turn the melting pot into a garbage can. Such appeals gained the Klan a 1924-estimated 50,000–200,000 members in the state, but it is doubt-ful its membership ever exceeded 100,000.[19]

For a decade, from 1920 to 1930, the Klan influenced Kentucky life. It was credited with supporting the successful Louisville mayoral candidate in 1921, taking votes from the candidate for Kentucky attorney general two years later, being an important factor in the 1924 Senate race between A. O. Stanley and F. M. Sackett, electing half of the city council in Shelbyville in 1925, defeating a candidate for commonwealth's attorney in Bourbon County two years fol-lowing that, and influencing other such efforts across the state.[20]

Yet, the Klan never become a dominant force in Kentucky and, from the beginning, faced strong opposition. The Warren County Klan was refused the use of the Opera House for meetings, and, despite appeals based on free speech grounds, that story was repeated across Kentucky. Court rulings up-held limitations in Klan activities, and when the author of *The Kall of the Klan* spoke in Lexington and Owensboro he was arrested. Major papers, such as the Lexington *Herald*, agreed that "there is no place in America for a secret organization of this kind." Party platforms officially opposed the Klan, and its political power was at best brief and broken. By 1929, when the national grand dragon of the KKK spoke in Kentucky, the organization was nearly dead, partially by its own violent and corrupt hand. But Kentuckians had

Kentucky Historical Society

Klan members mourn the passing of one of their own in Frankfort, 1925.

never embraced the Klan's call with much eagerness and had opposed it with some energy. Perhaps the memories of the Night Riders were too strong and too recent. For whatever reason, the white hood industry did not find as ready a market in Kentucky as expected.[21]

Lawlessness from a different source became prevalent as well. The advent of national Prohibition resulted in a dilemma for thirsty Kentuckians. Did they obey the law and stop drinking? Or did they continue to fill their cups and break the law by making or purchasing illegal drink? A sizeable number of citizens chose the second alternative. Economically, Prohibition hit Kentucky particularly hard; some towns dependent on the distilling industry, such as Tyrone in Anderson County, virtually disappeared. Larger places saw jobs and tax revenues decline, and Louisville lost some 6,000–8,000 positions. Combined with that were hard times for some farmers. A Clinton County man remembered how his father took his tobacco to sell and ended up owing the warehouse twenty cents: "That after working in the tobacco all year long." The wife in the family, on hearing the news, cried, prayed, then concluded that the only way to get the money they needed to get them through the winter was to make moonshine. Later, "she said the whisky that they made and sold for thirty-two dollars was more money than they had worked out in the three years before." That family stopped producing once they got solvent; other entrepreneurial Kentuckians filled the liquor void by setting up stills in hollows and hidden places across the state. Moonshining — always something of a modified cottage industry in parts of Kentucky — became even more widespread. A mountaineer told a doctor that stills had multiplied tenfold in his area since World War I: "They pay!" In west Kentucky, in the land between the Cumberland and Tennessee Rivers, Golden Pond moonshine became a prime source of whiskey for speakeasies across the Midwest.[22]

All that did not take place without a continuing state and federal effort to prevent it, and battles between moonshiners and the government became almost commonplace. In February 1921, for example, five deputies were wounded in a Carter County raid; the next year after two law officers were killed in a Menifee County raid, some five hundred agents and two armed airplanes searched out the offenders and killed one, while losing another "revenuer" in the process. Leslie County in 1923 saw a deputy sheriff and three bootleggers die in a gun battle, while from nearby Hazard in 1926, officers seized fifteen stills in a week and arrested twenty-eight people without loss of life. Even though the courts filled with defendants, many more went untouched. In some locales the people had for a long time either sanctioned such activities, citing economic need, or at least accepted them. That made the task of finding moonshiners an "us" versus "them" situation, with the community opposed to such efforts. Some places, on the other hand, saw moonshining as a lawless activity which hurt the progressive image they sought to project for their communities and gave little support to either group.[23]

Nor was illegal drink only available in a moonshine jug in a rural area. Irvin S. Cobb said that Prohibition was so strictly enforced in Kentucky that in some places "a thirsty stranger may have to walk all of a half a block to find a place where he can get a drink." Historian J. Winston Coleman, Jr., told of making home brew in his basement during the 1920s, while others in the same city of Lexington recalled later that each family had a favorite bootlegger from whom they got their liquor. In Louisville, when federal agents raided the prestigious Pendennis Club, in the heart of downtown, they seized large quantities of illegal champagne, whiskey, and gin. All classes broke the liquor laws. (Ironically, those who did so were, in one sense at least, not so far removed from the Klan, for it too crossed class lines and it too decided that its illegality transcended state and national law.) For many Kentuckians, it was a joyous day when in April 1933 they could legally buy 3.2 beer, and, in March 1934, all liquor — unless their counties remained "dry," which many did. It would take the bourbon industry years to recover, and the state's economy had much to overcome to get back to earlier levels of production, but at least one form of illegal activity would be slowed. The rationing of sugar and the shortage of copper (for tubing) in World War II would further hurt moonshining; by 1968, the state would rank only eighth in the number of stills seized.[24]

Drought and Depression

While much of America prospered, or seemed to prosper, in the 1920s, Kentucky did not. Later U.S. Senator John Sherman Cooper served as a county judge in the 1930s, but, as he recalled, "people were in trouble even before the Depression." More recently, a student of the era concluded that for eastern Kentucky, the Depression "did not come suddenly like the avenging angel of the night. It was instead a daily condition for at least five years preceding the trauma felt by the rest of the country."[25]

For those Kentuckians whose livelihood was tied to the soil, disaster struck early in the decade. The tobacco market, inflated by the war, went into a sudden decline. A Washington countian remembered 1921 as the start of the Depression there, for tobacco prices fell to one-seventh of the previous level. Later rises could not undo the damage — and the debts incurred. Overall, the state's production went from 504,000,000 pounds in 1919 to 376,000,000 a decade later. And, even though agricultural extension agents were active in most places by the 1920s, farming of all kinds still remained almost unchanged from decades earlier. Kentuckians, for example, spent only 1 percent of their farm income on fertilizer in 1929 (versus 2.3 percent in Indiana) and only 2.8 percent of the farms had a tractor a year later (versus the national average of 13.5 percent). Twelve mountain counties together had a total of seventeen tractors. While the number of farms lighted by electricity doubled in the twenties — from 2.2 percent to 4.3 percent — that figure lagged behind the U.S. percent of 13.4. Only the old options of dealing with an agricultural depression were available, and they were not helping.[26]

Nature itself seemed to be forsaking farming. The 1927 Mississippi River flood washed away much land and virtually the entire town of Columbus, Kentucky. Then in a reversal, an almost unprecedented drought struck the entire commonwealth in 1930 and extended into the next year. In the Bluegrass region the average annual rainfall went from 44 inches to 25 inches (and in summer months fell from 12 inches to 5 inches); the land was so brown that it seemed dead. Mayfield, in west Kentucky, had no rainfall at all for the month of July 1930, when temperatures rose over 100 degrees. Nearby Murray went a month and a half without rain that fall. Across the state, water rationing had to be instituted and ice plants were closed to conserve water. Crops and animals died; people suffered; farms withered away.[27]

Even before the drought, agrarian conditions had not been good, and in one county there had already been an 85 percent increase in requests for aid from a Family Welfare Society in 1928. A year later, even before the stock market crash, a study of another county showed "dozens" of abandoned farms, with more in danger of falling under the auctioneer's gavel. The survey concluded that the situation was getting worse every year. A Laurel County appraisal found farm expenditures at $324 per year and the value of goods and services obtained at only $356. Then came the crash, then the two droughts. The cry of a Morgan County man echoed across Kentucky: "The people are going to starve to death unless something is done soon."[28]

Statistics told only part of the story, but they revealed enough. The value of farm property in Kentucky fell during the decade from $1.5 billion to $1.0 billion; the average value of overall farm property declined from $5,587 to $4,177. Both the number of farms and the agrarian population fell as well — the 270,000 farms in 1920 were 246,000 a decade later, and over 125,000 fewer people lived down on the farm. Kentucky ranked forty-sixth among the states in the average cash farm income gained between 1920 and 1931. Besides the tobacco decline, the acres planted in corn fell by some 20 percent; wheat went from 840,000 acres in 1919 to only 204,000 a decade later. Hog production fell from 1.5 million in 1920 to 1.0 million in 1930, while the thoroughbred fall sales in Lexington went from a $1,411 average in 1929 to a $573 average the next year. Land values in horse-rich Fayette County declined from $50 million in 1920 to $27 million in 1930.[29]

There were a few positive statistics. While the percentage of mortgaged farms had increased slightly, to 24.3 percent of the total, that fell far below the national average of 42 percent and ranked Kentucky third best nationally. Moreover, the percent of farms operated by tenants also rose only a small percentage, to about 36 percent, which also was less than the U.S. average of 42 percent in 1930. In fact, about the only saving grace for the farmers of the commonwealth in the difficult years of the 1920s and the drought years of 1930–31 was the fact that more owned their land than was typical in America. But even for those people, the continuing problems made that an uncertain benefit at best. Agriculture seemed a hard and cruel taskmaster by 1930.[30]

Nor were other parts of the state's economy immune from the problems of the twenties. In addition to Prohibition's killing effect on the liquor industry in the state, coal production had been unstable during those years as well. When the stock market crash occurred in October 1929, it only began to bring to a wider variety of Americans some of the problems Kentuckians had long been experiencing. For citizens of the commonwealth, it added still another chapter to a book of depression that they had been reading too long already.

Despite expressed hopes that the deepening national depression would not affect Kentucky greatly because of the state's lack of large industry, such was not the case. When the governor declared in 1931 that "there is nothing to this so-called business depression," he simply ignored reality. The most obvious business casualty early were the banks of his state. Their financial resources of $385 million in 1929 fell to $231 million by 1933 and would not return to the pre-Depression level until 1943, in the middle of World War II. Money problems resulted in an increasing number of bank closures — 20 in 1930 (double the usual number) and 41 in 1932. By 1933 some 83 banks, out of 345 in the state, were in liquidation. Actually, most investors received some of their deposits and savings back, even from liquidated banks, but the range went from full payment to no payment. The 16 bank liquidations completed in 1936 were fairly typical: 2 banks repaid in full, 4 paid around 90 percent, 6 returned between 50 and 90 percent, while the 4 others gave patrons 30, 20, 5,

R. S. Scott Hardware sought to muster optimism in 1932.

and 0 percent. It was a form of gambling citizens had not sought, and it seemed to Kentuckians almost that fate decided whether they would get 100 percent back, as Maysville citizens did, or 20 percent, as did those in Hickman. Closures took their toll on more than just depositors as well. The head of the First National Bank of Paducah slit his wrists; following that institution's later merger with two other banks, continuing problems culminated in the president's being found floating in a city lake.[31]

The most wide-ranging and devastating failure was that of the state's largest bank — BancoKentucky or the National Bank of Kentucky. Controlled by flamboyant James B. Brown, the Louisville financial institution did as he dictated and his decisions proved particularly unwise. His cavalier attitude regarding funds and his insider loans were bad enough, but Brown then merged the faltering BancoKentucky with the even weaker Tennessee firm of Caldwell and Company — an institution that quickly went into receivership. Knowledgeable corporations quietly withdrew their money from BancoKentucky and in the four-day period before it closed, nearly $7 million was taken out. Directors sold remaining assets at panic prices, but could not stave off bankruptcy. Used as a depository by smaller banks, BancoKentucky took several of them down with it in failure, including two African American banks in Louisville. The state was shaken to its economic roots by the failure.[32]

Other businesses felt the effect of the Depression as well. The L & N railroad, for instance, saw income drop in half by 1931, and it paid no dividends to stockholders for two years. Construction in Louisville declined 50 percent in 1930 and industry after industry began laying off workers. Four years after the start of the Depression, one-half of the state's industrial workers had lost their jobs, and most could not find new ones. In 1932, unemployment in the commonwealth's largest city registered at 23.5 percent for white workers and 37.2 percent for blacks.[33]

But the real cost was not found in the statistics but in the human accounts. Homeless people, living in "Hoovervilles" whenever they could find shelter, passed from town to town, as one Kentuckian recalled, "carrying their few belongings" and seeking work, "but there wasn't any work." In Grayson County, the drought combined with years of agricultural distress, so that "a vast number of people need food and clothing." The Appalachian area saw troops of men looking for jobs before winter. "A state of acute famine" was said to exist. Former coalminer Melvin Profitt, father of two children, worked for a time as a farmhand for a dollar a day in 1930. But that did not long continue, and he concluded, "I didn't intend for my family to starve." All around him in Wolfe County, the money was gone and some were forced to dress in feed sacks or in much-patched clothes: "You seldom ever seen women and children out in public [;] they were practically naked, and had to stay in the hollows." He gave his wife his last five dollars and walked for five days into surrounding counties, trying fruitlessly to locate a job. He returned, treated his blisters, and set out again, finally finding work in the mines for a while. That ended, Profitt came back, farmed, hunted, and survived. He did as a Shelby County farmer said: "We just kept working."[34]

For those without jobs, the prospects for getting help were mixed, at best. Most locales had "poor farms" or almshouses where paupers could live and be given a meal, but those generally were limited in size and scope. A 1929 study of relief for the poor in Kentucky offered the more typical pattern. County courts would hear each person's appeal, then would declare whether the person should receive relief and, if so, whether it would be delivered as cash, food, or services (such as medical care). An order would then be given to the county treasury. The next month, the same process would be repeated for each applicant. The Carnegie Institution survey noted typical cases from Leslie County; amounts ranging from ten to twenty dollars a month were given to such people as a seventy-year-old man, a teacher for his blind uncle, a woman who was caring for the children of a deceased neighbor, an epileptic woman, and a "granny woman" whose son had worms. Refused were appeals from a woman with a crippled son, a woman who sought to help a sick neighbor, and a seventy-six-year-old ex-minister. Over one year that county helped 121 cases at a cost of $3,352. The amount of aid per capita could be very low — 9 cents in one county — and the problems could be great. The survey found, for example, that decisions were often made on political grounds, and that little attention seemed to be given to the recipient's fitness to use the funds. Still, that method provided about the only means of relief in most counties. It was not enough, and desperate Kentuckians sought more. Confederate pensions went up drastically, for example, between 1932 and 1933, but that provided no long-term answer either.[35]

Nor were matters perceived as getting better. Even though tobacco proved a good Depression crop, as usage increased in the 1930s, Kentucky still was, as one editor confessed, in "a damn bad situation." An Inez attorney told a friend in 1932, "things don't look good. There is no employment and times are extremely hard. . . . The people feel that there is something radically wrong. In fact, we all know there is something wrong." And, as a Kentucky governor concluded later, the most tragic thing about the Depression was that the young were beginning to feel defeated, to lose their enthusiasm. They were starting to give up.[36]

Both young and old were also starting to return home. In the previous decade, amidst the hard times, the state had lost by out-migration some 120,000 people. But now, as other areas suffered, sometimes more than Kentucky, the situation reversed. Some of the 850,000 native Kentuckians who lived outside the state now returned. For one of only two times in the twentieth century, the commonwealth's population growth in the decade of 1930 to 1940 exceeded the national average. A reporter captured the spirit of the reverse exodus: "They came home. In creaking old Fords, in the stuffy day coaches of trains and in crowded busses they trickled back, opening up the deserted little cabins, moving in with parents, brothers, sisters. . . ." Rural areas and small towns grew faster than the cities, but the numbers placed an added strain on the state's already weakened economy. Observers feared that the violence of the coal fields, or just the small crime wave in another county, were harbingers of future problems. Answers were needed.[37]

The New Deal

The election of Franklin D. Roosevelt, and actions taken by him as president, began almost immediately to have a positive effect on the people. Something was being done, and the future suddenly seemed brighter for so many of those in distressed situations. Lexington *Herald* editor Desha Breckinridge noted, only three weeks after FDR's inaugural, that "the spirit here really, on the whole is very much better." That reversal of mood may have been the president's greatest achievement.[38]

The "Hundred Days" of the special session of Congress called immediately after Roosevelt was sworn in brought with it a New Deal that provided a wide variety of answers to the problems of relief and recovery. In so doing, it drastically changed, for the rest of the century, the relationship between the people, the state, and the federal government. Tied most intimately to county government, and only tangentially to the state at times, Kentuckians had been little affected by direct national involvement in their lives. Now that all ended. Not their county seat, not Frankfort, but Washington, D.C., became the focal point for help for so many. Some disliked that shift, and others found it hard to modify earlier ways of doing things. Habits of a lifetime died hard, even in the face of the Depression. One woman remembered when her family's situation forced her father to take a job in a new government program: "They didn't make enough to make a living on the farm, and my father went to work with the WPA. It embarrassed him and humiliated him." Another woman explained, "I would not think of accepting charity from anyone. . . . I think I would rather be hungry." To such independently proud people, any such aid, in any circumstance, was a blow to their self-esteem. But inaction, hunger, and poverty were equal destroyers of self-respect.[39]

The resulting array of New Deal programs set up to address the variety of problems seemed almost numberless and dazzling in their coverage to so many Kentuckians. In March 1933, for example, the Civilian Conservation Corps (CCC) established work camps for youths aged eighteen to twenty-five, paid them a monthly salary, and put them to work building lodges and cabins in parks, constructing hiking paths and trails, controlling erosion, and planting new trees. As on offshoot, it also changed the ways people looked at their land. At its peak in 1936–37, the CCC enrolled 30,000 Kentuckians in its work camps, and some 80,000 received jobs during its existence. The funds sent home from paychecks meant much to those at the time; the revitalized and reforested land would mean much to later generations.[40]

Oriented to the land, in another way, were New Deal programs focusing on farming. The Agricultural Adjustment Act (AAA) recognized long-term problems by providing for refinancing farm mortgages through various means, including some 17,000 Farm Credit Administration loans. Its solution to low prices was more controversial. The AAA asked farmers to reduce their production in return for subsidies, and in that way a basic parity price could be maintained. For tobacco that meant crops declined in size 28 percent by 1935, but market income increased $7 million. The slaughter of 48,000 Kentucky hogs had a similar economic impact in the long run, but it had a strong negative effect in some quarters. Whether for crops or animals, the idea of limiting people in what they could produce seemed to some citizens almost an attack on their individualism, on the American dream; for those struggling just to survive, not dream, the higher prices proved a godsend.[41]

Declared unconstitutional in 1936, the AAA was reborn, in modified form, in 1938, set up quotas for tobacco and corn, and stabilized prices. The later as well as the earlier version of AAA had indifferent success in some areas, especially in eastern Kentucky, but, overall, appealed a great deal to the state's farmers. Some allied social experiments, such as Sublimity Farms in Laurel County and Christian-Trigg Farm, proved less successful. In the end, however, Kentucky agriculture was drastically changed by the new policies. Farmers in the commonwealth had always existed in a kind of paradoxical state, for they

Spencer & Wyckoff of Detroit traveled to Dawson Springs to photograph the officers and enlisted men of the 3557ᵗʰ Company CCC Camp SP12.

often lived insular lives, focused on their land and little else, yet, at the same time, had long been affected by national and overseas market conditions. Still, the awareness of those influences often remained murky. Now, however, it was obvious that federal involvement had a clear impact on their lives. Almost by default, some of the isolation ended and an awakening slowly began.[42]

In some ways, the farm problems still took second place to the continuing worry of unemployment. A short-term response, the Federal Emergency Relief Administration (FERA), had provided 100,000 Kentucky families with six to thirteen dollars per month. But more constructive solutions were sought, and a series of different economy-stimulating programs resulted. The Public Works Administration (PWA) spent $49 million on water, river, and sewage projects (as well as a gold depository at Fort Knox), while the shorter-lived Civil Works Administration (CWA) put some 100,000 citizens to work building roads, constructing schools, and surveying historic buildings. Though operational less than a year, CWA and the longer-operating PWA began the transition from straight payments — the dole — to the relief work that left behind more lasting legacies.[43]

The best-known of the New Deal relief agencies was the Works Progress Administration (later called the Works Projects Administration). By then, 18 percent of Kentuckians were already on relief. In several counties the figures exceeded 50 percent. Some $162 million in WPA federal money came into the commonwealth in an attempt to help change those figures, and, at its 1938 peak, the agency employed over 72,000 Kentuckians in a variety of jobs.

George Goodman of Paducah served as state director of a program that, with the PWA, modified the face of Kentucky. As historian George Blakey has noted, the WPA built 14,000 miles of roads, some 73,000 bridges, viaducts, and culverts, and 900 buildings — chiefly schools and fire stations. Other construction projects included sewers and 200 recreational centers.[44]

In some ways, the most imaginative projects received less attention. The WPA, for example, employed up to 3,100 women to work in sewing rooms, where clothes for the needy were made. By 1937, over 2 million such garments had been produced. Surplus food was gathered to use for school lunches for children of families on relief. New libraries were established and older ones revitalized, while pack horses anticipated the later bookmobiles and took reading materials to far-flung homes. Teachers without jobs taught adult illiterates to read, while others conducted vocational classes. Unemployed artists painted, writers wrote, and musicians performed under WPA auspices. Murals were commissioned for public buildings; books, such as *Kentucky: A Guide to the Bluegrass State* (1939), were published; and music projects, such as the Folk Song Festival near Ashland, were supported.[45]

The real story of the WPA was its accomplishments, both for the community and for the people. Though criticized in various ways, the agency left an obvious mark. In Knott County, in Appalachia, for example, it funded 25 miles of road construction, 17 new bridges, 3 school buildings, and 274 sanitary privies. And the story was repeated across Kentucky. The WPA also served as a vehicle for relief, and in 1935 its workers averaged nearly $16 per month (females slightly higher than males). Elsie Welte of Newport was one of those workers. Her husband sick, their savings gone, she had "a hard time getting enough to eat." She started working in a WPA sewing center: "It sure did help because the bills were really getting ahead of us. . . . With this money we are started [*sic*] to get on our feet." Not surprisingly, she concluded: "We believe in W.P.A." The WPA not only broke down isolation and provided better conditions for Kentuckians; it gave them a sense of accomplishment while they received relief.[46]

One part of the WPA also helped a younger group, as it aided needy students by creating part-time jobs so they could remain in school. The National Youth Administration (NYA) began in 1935 and by the next June provided aid to 4,768 students in 122 Kentucky schools. In each year thereafter, up to 10,000 young adults of both sexes, black and white, could type, file, do repair work, improve playgrounds, or perform a variety of other tasks in order to receive paychecks; career counselling, apprenticeships, placement services, and out-of-school aid were also part of the NYA's attempt to give the young people of the state what they had almost lost during the Depression — an opportunity.[47]

At the end of the age spectrum, passage of the Social Security Act in 1935 meant that support for the elderly would not depend on individuals, or on county almshouses, but instead on a federally operated system that would become operative in 1942. Until then, needs would be met by an Old Age Assistance program, funded equally by state and federal dollars. For financially strapped Kentucky that proved difficult, but finally A. Y. Lloyd, director of the new state Division of Public Assistance, began issuing checks in 1936. Within a year and a half 34,000 Kentuckians were receiving an average of $9.56 per month in such aid. Social Security went through a series of controversies as the governor fought the national controls over personnel. But federal involvement that a decade before would have been almost unthinkable now was becoming accepted.[48]

Kentuckians, old and young, rich and poor, black and white, still struggled to shake off the effects of the Depression, even with the aid of the various programs. By 1937, some 143,000 people in the commonwealth remained out of work, while 54,000 more received employment only by virtue of the federal government. Then, to add to the problems, Nature intervened once more. In January of that year rains drenched the Ohio River Valley and Kentucky received eleven inches more than normal for the month. The Great Flood of 1937 resulted. At Louisville flood stage was 28 feet; the river crested at twice that height, at 57.1 feet. For three weeks the waters stayed above flood level. Downriver, at Paducah, where 17.5 inches of rain fell in the month, the flood level of 43 feet was passed as the river rose to 61 feet and remained out of its banks for a month. Freezing rain, sleet, and snow added to the disaster. In the Falls City, two-thirds of area businesses were inundated. Over 200,000 people were evacuated but few died as a result of the flood; some 17,000 animals drowned and their carcasses presented a long-term danger. Author Alice Hegan Rice noted, "the danger of typhus has been great, as dead rats, cats, and dogs float in the streets, and a dead horse has been lying in an alley back of us for days." Her house had not been submerged but she had been without water or electricity for three weeks. Others were less fortunate and sarcastically termed themselves another form of F.F.V. — "Filthy Flood Victims." In Paducah, high water forced the evacuation of some 25,000 people; then fires further damaged the downtown. Influenza struck, and the city was virtually abandoned.[49]

Not until March could a semblance of normality return. Bread lines filled the already-crowded, Depression-era relief locales. In Louisville alone, 33,000 homes had been destroyed or damaged, and property damage was estimated at $52 million for the city and $250 million for the entire state. A similar story had been written up and down the Ohio as small communities suffered proportionally as great or greater than Louisville. In Frankfort, on the Kentucky River, waters had inundated half the downtown, forcing the evacuation and later abandonment of the state prison. On the Ohio River, only Henderson escaped the deluge, and it entered a growth period as a result. The flood-visited cities soon rebuilt and by 1939 Louisville had regained its dominance of Kentucky industry — one-half of the wage earners in manufacturing were employed there at that time. Ironically, a wall of water in a local flood, at Frozen Creek in Breathitt County in July 1939, killed a much larger number — fifty-one people there and over seventy in the area — than did the more mas-

Kentucky Historical Society

A huge runner for one of the generating units is placed at TVA's Kentucky Dam on the lower Tennessee River at Gilbertsville in 1944. Workers rushed construction of the dam to make power available for war industrial use.

sive 1937 one. With that, the state returned to confronting economic instead of natural disasters.[50]

The Tennessee Valley Authority (TVA) dealt with flood control, but also offered cheap and available electricity. Controversial because of its competiveness with private enterprise and its large purchase of land and homes in the areas affected, it joined with the Rural Electrification Administration (REA) to bring electricity to rural Kentucky. Only 4 percent of the state's farms had electric power in the early 1930s; by 1941 some 17 percent did, and the number was growing rapidly.[51]

In 1941, then, after eight years of the New Deal, Kentuckians could look back on what had happened with some amazement. Not all the problems had been solved, for unemployment remained a matter that still demanded attention. And different difficulties had arisen as a result of new programs. Yet, in 1933, the people had been almost without hope, and the state seemed unable to do much about the despair. Things were bad and the future looked bleaker. Now, farms were more secure, more productive, and more profitable. Labor legislation gave workers in the cities and the coal mines more protection, while Social Security offered safeguards for the elderly. All across the state, construction projects had resulted in new roads, desperately needed school buildings, and a myriad of other projects. Conservation work had aided the state's forests and parks. Banks were stable once more. And, most important, a new spirit, a more optimistic one, had emerged. Government cared, and in its caring, offered more protection for workers, for consumers, for citizens of all ages.

All that came at a price, one that created some doubts, even among those who benefited. Local control had both its positive and negative sides, and the pluses risked being lost as control passed to more distant hands. Dangers of too much dependence on federal support might be as great as too little. The funding for the $1 billion in spending in the state in the decade had to be assessed. Yet, in the end, the bottom line for Kentuckians simply was a comparison of where they had been, not only in 1933, but for a decade earlier, versus where they stood in 1941. In most respects, they indicated that their lives were better. The New Deal had changed the rules considerably, but they had adjusted, had accepted most changes, and had moved on to what they hoped would be an even brighter decade in the 1940s.

World War II

For those Kentuckians who followed international events, the news in the 1930s had done little to brighten their outlook. Powerful new armies and navies in Japan and Germany suddenly became expansive; new leaders named Hitler and Mussolini showed themselves to be dangerous dictators; battles in Spain, Ethiopia, and China threatened to grow into wider conflicts. Yet, Kentuckians, like their fellow Americans, seemed optimistic about the nation's ability to remain isolated from the European and Asian dangers. When a poll of Kentucky college students in 1935 asked whether the United States could stay out of war, three of every four answered "yes." The state's congressional delegation generally voted as their fellow lawmakers in regard to neutrality legislation in 1935, 1937, and 1939. Even when the 1939 invasion of Poland widened into a second world war, many Americans and Kentuckians echoed the later remembrances of a then-new West Point graduate, William Buster of Burgin: "It was not our war."[52]

But the tentacles of war began reaching out to embrace more and more of the world. Gradually, America started preparing for a time when it might be engulfed in the conflict. Still, it was a slow, careful, and tardy move, for powerful forces feared any departure from isolationism. The state's senators and representatives in Washington — with the exception of the very conservative mountain Republican leader John M. Robsion — supported actions increasing military appropriations, though such votes may not have accurately reflected the sentiments of their constituents. A peacetime draft began; state National

Guard forces were called to active duty; Kentuckians began to become part of the growing defense effort. In February 1941, Henderson's Husband E. Kimmel became the nation's highest ranking naval officer and succeeded fellow Kentuckian Admiral Claude C. Bloch, as commander of the Pacific Fleet at Pearl Harbor.[53]

Still, life in Kentucky seemed to be moving at its regular pace, as if there were no threat of war in distant places. Adopted Louisvillian Willie Snow Ethridge wrote of people in her town in 1941: "They are forever doing things: riding horseback; cruising and sailing on the wide Ohio; swimming; playing tennis, badminton, golf, and ping pong; going on picnics, short excursions on the river, week ends [sic] in Indiana, and trips to Chicago and New York. Always something." In more rural Kentucky, the December 1941 newspapers told familiar stories: in Hickman County in west Kentucky the Rook club and a spelling contest vied for news; in Harrison County in the central part of the state, an Elks Club celebration grabbed headlines; in Cumberland in eastern Kentucky the page-one story told of the opening of hunting season; and in Burlington in northern Kentucky, the Gayety Theater had a "western" scheduled for showing on Sunday, December 7, following a run of the movie "Dive Bomber."[54]

Jim Hamlin of Harlan County had entered the navy at age twenty-six and on his application form, in response to the question which asked why he wanted to join the service, he had written, "So I can get something to eat." Satisfied with the results and advanced to Fireman 1st Class, he was aboard the battleship USS *California* at Pearl Harbor, when Sunday, December 7, dawned. The Japanese attack came as a total surprise, a shock, and it took time just to fathom what was occurring. His ship took two torpedoes and a bomb and began to list. Hamlin and the crewmen fought the fires and watched numbly as other sailors died. He survived, left the sinking battleship, and transferred to another vessel. Unaware of that, the Navy Department sent a telegram to his father, reporting him dead; a memorial service was held. Then another telegram arrived, telling that Hamlin had survived. Resurrected, he fought on, crying only twice in the wartime years. The last came when, near Pago Pago, he heard a radio playing "My Old Kentucky Home." He was a much different person than the one who had left that home so many years before.[55]

During the Pearl Harbor attack, a naval chaplain from Murray, Kentucky, had uttered the words, "Praise the Lord and pass the ammunition." That rallying cry competed with the confusion and shock felt across the state and the nation. Nor had the bad news ended. In the Philippines, where the American forces had been caught off guard as well, a nationalized Kentucky Guard unit served as Company D, 192nd Tank Battalion. Mostly made up of men from Harrodsburg, the unit had been called to federal service in November 1940 and had arrived in Manila only two weeks before the war began. Low on food, water, equipment, and hope, they fought in the agony of the Bataan Campaign and were part of the general surrender there. That only began what historian Russell Harris has called "the tortures of the damned."[56]

The Stagg Distillery in Frankfort hosted a 1942 rally in support of the war effort.

Kentucky Historical Society

The survivors joined the Bataan Death March, straggled into another death trap at Camp O'Donnell, packed the "Hell Ships" for transportation out of the Philippines, and survived prisoner-of-war camps elsewhere. Of the sixty-six men who had left Harrodsburg, by war's end only thirty-seven lived to return. And those who had survived carried with them the memories, always the memories. One man witnessed a beheading, another saw people buried alive. A soldier could not erase the image of sick men waiting in line for a taste of putrid water and decaying food; another could not forget having to bury POW corpses in graves where the water level floated the bodies to the top. He had to hold the dead down until other bodies would push them to their rest. Those on the "Hell Ships" did not have enough room even to stand, and the absence of ventilation made people die of heat and suffocation. At least two of the prisoners ended the war in camps near enough to see mushroom clouds of the atomic bombs.[57]

Kentuckians knew few of those details during wartime. They only knew that American forces had been attacked in Hawaii, had fought and surrendered in the Philippines, and had suffered as prisoners. The result was an outpouring of patriotism, as the conflict united people as had perhaps no other war in the nation's history. One editor noted, "Where last week we were Democrat and Republican . . . , today we are — Americans all — determined and powerful." Very few questioned why the country fought, or its goals. Those who had gone off to war in 1917 had done so imbued with the stories of Civil War heroism and of sure and quick victory in the Spanish-American War. They had returned hardened, bitter, and sometimes disillusioned. The youth of the World War II generation had grown up with that legacy and went to fight with more realistic expectations. Yet because of Pearl Harbor, they also left with more of a sense of purpose, with more dedication to getting the job done, with more of a sense of the need to protect the nation. In World War I soldiers had fought less for America than for the world. Now they fought for both.

Still, the reasons why individuals entered the service were varied. Henry Giles despaired of "the shame of commodity lines & no jobs but the WPA" and joined the army for economic reasons. Frank Mathias of Carlisle left for the army "with a thrill of adventure," and the boy who had seen no body of water larger than the Ohio River fought in the Pacific Theater. And so from small town to large, as volunteers or draftees, Kentuckians became part of the armed forces. For blacks, they found that they often had to fight not only fascism but racism in the armed forces; for women in the service they too received contradictory signals about their roles. They were part of a time of transition for the military. Of those Kentuckians who served, some achieved fame as enlisted men — Private First Class Franklin R. Sousley of Ewing was one of the Marines raising the flag at Iwo Jima and was killed soon after — others as officers — Lt. General Simon B. "Bull" Buckner, Jr., of Munfordville became the highest-ranking American combat fatality when he was commanding ground forces in the Okinawa invasion. And those who fought in combat and did not die often emerged from the war very changed men. European death camps overwhelmed with the horror of the Holocaust, while Harry Jackson wrote home from Europe, saying that the most frightening thing was not the danger in fighting: "Rather it's the look in men's eyes after they have come out of it — they are the living dead without fear, evil, or comfort."[58]

Change came to the people living in Kentucky during the war years as well. Louisville's Bowman Field airport, whose runways had been concreted in 1938, was taken over by the Army Air Force in August 1940 and became a training base. To the south, at Fort Knox, WPA labor built Godman Field that same year. In fact, much activity was taking place at that base. The 864 buildings at Fort Knox in 1940 had increased to 3,820 by 1943; new land purchases doubled the size of the post to some 106,000 acres; troop numbers increased, then went up again and again. In addition to the gold that had been stored there since 1937, the U.S. Bullion Depository at Fort Knox also received for safekeeping from the Library of Congress the original Declaration of Independence, the signed copy of the Constitution, the autographed manuscript of Abraham Lincoln's Gettysburg Address, and other documents that seemed vulnerable on the east coast. About the time those returned to Washington in 1944, the crown jewels of Hungary arrived to replace them.[59]

The commonwealth took on more of the appearance of an armed camp as another base was established in the state. Camp Breckinridge's 35,000 acres in Henderson, Webster, and Union Counties served as a training ground for some 30,000 infantry, including later baseball star Jackie Robinson. It also housed 1,300 German and Italian prisoners-of-war, who often worked on nearby farms. (Some POWs were also interned in Maysville and other towns during the war.) Besides construction at Camp Breckinridge, Camp Campbell, and Fort Knox, the Louisville District of the Corps of Engineers also aided in building the Ohio River Ordnance works in Henderson, the Bluegrass Ordnance Depot near Richmond, and Nichols General Hospital in Louisville. Whether as training ground, as suppliers of munitions to wage war, or as healer of those scarred by the conflict, Kentucky was playing an increasingly large role in the nation's military effort.[60]

Very quickly, civilian industry in Kentucky converted to a wartime status as well. In Owensboro, for example, Glenmore Distillery Company began to make industrial alcohol for use in gunpowder manufacturing. Louisville's Ford Motor Assembly Plant produced Jeeps and military trucks instead of automobiles, while Hillerich & Bradsby workers crafted gun stocks rather than "Louisville Slugger" bats. A boom-town economy developed in the Falls City, bolstered by new industries, such as a series of chemical plants that transformed Louisville into the world's largest producer of synthetic rubber. By conflict's end, the city ranked eighteenth nationally in the volume of war contracts awarded.[61]

Unfortunately, that prosperity — and the growth of military bases in certain areas — did not translate to huge economic gains statewide. One study indicated that of thirteen southern states, Kentucky ranked tenth in the amount

Ford Motor Company

The Ford Motor Company plant in Louisville converted to Jeep production during the war.

of money gained from wartime government contracts. With few heavy industries outside of Louisville and with no coastline for shipbuilding or for naval bases, the commonwealth was losing economic ground to other southern states. Compared to the prewar period, Kentucky was prospering, yet not as much as needed if it wanted to achieve significant growth.[62]

The possibility and promise of better-paying jobs in the defense industry proved an irresistible lure for Kentuckians of both sexes, black and white, during the war years. The long-time trickle of outmigration began to achieve flood status as a result. A Floyd County youngster remembered the almost changeless pattern of growing up there, "until the war came along and then

. . . it sorta broke all that up. Everyone started the outward migration." Whether to southern Ohio, or Michigan, or some more distant places, Kentuckians — especially from rural areas and small towns — settled into new jobs, making more money than they had ever received. A survey of thirty-three eastern Kentucky counties found that between 1940 and late 1942, some 85,000 people — one-fifth of the population — had migrated. Young, male, and unmarried for the most part, these workers voiced simple reasons for leaving: to get a job, or a better one. At least some had traveled the same migratory path earlier and had worked in the North until the Depression hit. They had then returned to their family farms, in hollows and hills across the region. Now, however, they had left those homes again and this time most would not return during their working years. Another study of an Appalachian community, in Clay County, revealed that of its nearly four hundred residents in 1942, only 57 percent remained just five years later. Across Kentucky, the story was the same. Due to the Depression, the state had been given a second chance to retain those citizens; its economic promises had again failed.[63]

The war transformed the homefront and people's lives in many other ways. Good crop yields, increased wages, and greater personal income combined to give Kentuckians a higher standard of living than most had known before. Increasing numbers of women entered the workforce. A Louisville woman told her army spouse, "You are now the husband of a career woman — just call me your little ship yard Babe!" She experienced that "grand and glorious feeling" of having her own checking and saving accounts for the first time. All that made the shortages and sacrifices easier to take. Rationing of gasoline, meat, coffee, sugar, cheese, butter, and more, victory gardens, blood donations, war bond purchases, scrap drives — such intrusions in daily life reminded people of the war going on and their role in it. Each community was touched; in Boyle County, for example, 1,400 pounds of aluminum were gathered in one early effort, 112,000 pounds of rubber in another drive. People were asked to bring in grease so the glycerin could be used for bullets, and, in one week, the Boyle countians had donated a ton. Tire rationing began in January 1942, shoe rationing a year later (3 pairs of shoes could be purchased annually), and, for the first time, the government began withholding federal income taxes from paychecks. Statewide, almost every county organization aided the war effort in some way, whether it was the various patriotic groups, the churches, the Red Cross, Boy and Girl Scouts, Eastern Star, Rotary, Lions Clubs, Kiwanis, Garden Club, Parent-Teacher Association, National Association for the Advancement of Colored People, or others. People filled defense positions such as air raid warden, auxiliary fire and police, scrap collectors, entertainers for troops, hospital assistants, surgical dressing preparators, teachers for aliens, and clerical assistants. It was a widespread and united effort.[64]

The war also caused the revival of one old tradition and the disruption of another. Hemp had once been the chief cash crop of Kentucky, but by 1929 only five farms grew the fiber. Foreign production had superseded the domestic. However, the Japanese capture of the Philippines created a serious shortage of fiber in the United States, and the government began a program to encourage farmers to grow hemp once more. While some 36,000 acres were planted in 1942, and a plant for processing the fiber was built near Winchester, overall, the program never realized its planned goals. With peace, the legal production of hemp virtually ceased.[65]

Ending in wartime was the State Fair, which did not open in 1942 and 1943, and the Kentucky Derby became simply a "Streetcar Derby" because of the rationing of gasoline and tires. Attendance at motion picture theatres increased greatly but various sports teams, facing a shortage of able bodies, suspended operations. Present-day Western Kentucky University stopped football for the war's duration in 1943; Eastern Kentucky University played no football or basketball schedule in 1943 and 1944; Transylvania University suspended football in 1942 and did not resume it at the end of the conflict. Kentuckians knew matters were serious when their sport teams were affected by war.[66]

It had been one of the state's sporting events, the Derby, that three soldiers had been talking about in 1945. The race was delayed that year until June 9, and they were wondering about the future. The three said "If we live, we'll . . . have a reunion at Churchill Downs." Before that Derby, V-E Day in May 1945 brought a peace of sorts for those fighting in the European Theater. It was hard to believe; Captain Jackson wrote: " I catch myself . . . listening for artillery shells and the sharp crack of rifle fire. . . ." He admitted that "all emotion has dried up in me — and yet moist tears even now treckle [sic] down my cheeks." Those in the Pacific Theater fought on, and died, for months more until the dropping of the atomic bombs hastened the war's end. A Kentucky soldier, stationed at Okinawa, preparing to invade Japan, recalled his fear they would be "slaughtered" in such an invasion, and noted his relief about the bomb: "it saved us." Of the 300,000 Kentuckians who served in the armed forces, over 7,000 did not return. But for Captain Jackson, for the man on Okinawa, for the three soldiers who did rendezvous at the 1946 Derby — for all those who lived, the relief came in knowing it was over at last.[67]

Kentuckians broke into noisy celebrations in August 1945, with the end of the war on V-J Day. In Cynthiana, church bells, sirens, and car horns all formed a din of noise, and an impromptu parade of hundreds marched and cheered. Similar reactions took place over the state. In Harlan, the newspaper editor noted that the loss of life might sober any celebration, and wondered, after the A-bomb, if mankind could "be trusted with the fruit of his scientific wisdom. His record to date is not good." Still, the paper reported that the victory crowds there exceeded any previous celebration in history, and tired citizens stopped only late into the night. They were at peace.[68]

With the end of the fighting, most Kentuckians seemed more interested in trying to move on with their lives than in assessing the effects of the war. A kaleidoscope of occurrences could be recalled: careers, like Pearl Harbor scapegoat Admiral Kimmel's, had been ended; "black markets" had grown up amid the shortages; overcrowded hotels and trains had taxed people's patience; one

Kentucky congressman, Andrew Jackson May of Floyd County, would eventually be convicted of accepting $53,000 in bribes to give an armament maker favorable wartime treatment; migrations had taken away some of the state's most enterprising young; and combat deaths had taken away life itself from thousands of Kentuckians. Those dead would be long remembered by their family and friends.

Yet, like America, the commonwealth had emerged relatively unscathed from a major world war that had devastated and virtually destroyed whole nations. In fact, the commonwealth and its people generally had prospered economically during the conflict. Personal savings had grown, people were more sophisticated in outlook, and conditions were ripe for further change. The soldiers could return to a future that promised them education through the G.I. Bill, or jobs in a successful post-depression economy. Even though the world at peace did not seem so stable a place as most would have expected after the conclusion of a war — with the perceived threat of communism and with the power unleashed by the atomic bomb — still, there was much reason to have a sense of accomplishment and to feel optimistic about the future. Kentuckians had earned the right to celebrate.[69]

Louisville Courier-Journal

Robert Worth Bingham, U.S. ambassador to the Court of St. James's, stands with his daughter, Henrietta *(left)*, and his third wife, Aleen, in 1933.

11

"United We Stand"?
The Politics of Division, 1920–1930

The Morrow Administration, 1919–1923

In the decade of the 1920s, Americans supposedly sought a return to "normalcy." But what was normal now in Kentucky politics? Was it assassination, the use of violence to achieve ends (as in the Black Patch), and bitter political factionalism? Was a two-party system, with Republicans often winning, the norm? All that had been the history of the past two decades. Would the 1920s continue that trend?

New governor Ed Morrow could see all around him signs of change, indicators that things might not be the same. The fact that his twin brother, Charles, was commanding some of the American troops in Siberia fighting Russian Communists, told of a changing world situation. Nearer to home, Morrow's budgets reflected the influence of a new force, crying out for funds. By 1920, 12.7 percent of the state's budget went to highways; a decade earlier, no funds had. Percentage-wise, education suffered from that shift, and its share of state spending fell from 44.7 percent in 1910, to 38 percent ten years later (and 30 percent by 1927, when highways took 45 percent of the budget). Finally, the state had gained some needed new funds as a result of the revised inheritance tax. With a deficit of over $900,000 in 1922, Kentucky showed a large positive balance a year later, chiefly due to payment of an inheritance tax of $2,370,835 by the Bingham estate. That payment was part of a larger story, one that had brought another new political player to the scene.[1]

Robert Worth Bingham, the son of an ex-Confederate educator, had been born in North Carolina in 1871, had married a Kentucky woman in 1896, and had received his law degree from the University of Louisville a year later. Settled in Kentucky, he was elected county attorney, then served briefly as mayor of Louisville, through appointment by Governor J.C.W. Beckham, after the courts had invalidated the regular election. Unsuccessful in two other attempts at office — once as a Republican, once as a Democrat — Bingham had settled into the practice of law until two events changed his life. In 1913, his wife was killed in an automobile accident; three years later, in 1916, Bingham married Mary Kenan Flagler, a wealthy widow worth perhaps $150 million. Her death only eight months later left him with an inheritance of $5 million — and many questions. Rumors circulated immediately, since her family did not know of the handwritten codicil giving Bingham those millions. Whispers of negligence and even murder made the rounds. Yet the best available evidence suggests no criminality. Bingham made unwise, even poor, decisions, but other than that, it appears that his wife died a natural death. The circumstances — his unexpected inheritance, the brief duration of the marriage, the secrecy around certain matters — all kept the rumors alive, especially among his enemies. The wealth Bingham received brought with it large burdens.[2]

Almost instantly, Bingham became a major factor in Kentucky politics. In August 1918, he purchased the *Courier-Journal* and soon reversed Watterson's editorial course on both prohibition and woman suffrage. "Drys" thanked him, while national suffrage leader Ida H. Harper quickly praised Bingham for stopping the paper's "abusive and vindictive" editorials against women's rights. By later placing Percy Haly on the paper's payroll, Bingham also made clear the paper's new loyalties in party factionalism fights. Three men now forged a new triumvirate — Bingham, the publicist; Haly, the planner; and Beckham, the politician. That combination proved a particularly potent one in the Democratic politics of the 1920s.[3]

As a person, Bingham remained something of a paradox. With a net income in 1924 of nearly a hundred thousand dollars and with large amounts still left from the inheritance, he could be extremely generous in aiding friends and select charities — North Carolina newspaperman Josephus Daniels received a $10,000 loan in 1921, charities accepted $40,000 in gifts in 1923, political campaigns constantly garnered large donations. Yet, at the same time, Bingham could be terse and almost hostile when writing to those opposing him. Part of that resulted from a tendency, like those before and after him, to see his course as correct, and his enemies as corrupt. In 1934, he wrote one of his employees: "We are all that stands between the people of Kentucky and the power of those crooked scoundrels to plunder them without restraint." Later Bingham wrote his son Barry, saying, "We must never vary one iota on principle." And the paper often did stand, almost alone, for important principles. Yet, it also often took conservative stances that Bingham did not as readily acknowledge. An overtone of superiority sometimes colored his writings, as when he commented about the Irish-Catholic boss Mickey Brennan: "He belongs to the type which is mainly moved by the emotions," and "People of his type are so passionate and so personal about everything, and so consistently illogical." Part of the paradox of Bingham was that this man who often genuinely spoke for the people was himself an aristocrat through and through. His letters tell of his preoccupation with hunting lodges, full-bred dogs, carefully crafted guns, English genealogy, and "the right people." An avowed Anglophile, Bingham rented a castle in Great Britain and lived like nobility, which brought the opposition to satirize him as "Lord Bing." Aristocrat and democrat; generous and harsh; supporter of good government and ally of political bosses — Bingham was many things, but most of all, he was now a force in Kentucky life.[4]

New leader Bingham also had a new rival to contend with, one from a decidedly different background. James B. Brown had been born in rural Kentucky (a year later than Bingham), had worked his way up from office boy, and had gained the support of the Whallen machine. By 1908 he was president of a Louisville bank; in 1919 he headed the National Bank of Kentucky, reportedly the largest financial institution in the South. He also was a major stockholder in the L & N and Standard Oil of Kentucky. A man who slept by day and conducted much of his business late at night or in the early hours of the morning, Brown — like Bingham — could be generous to friends, usually through stock gifts or through coverage of their gambling losses at his lavish outings to French Lick resort in Indiana. But he and Bingham soon opposed each other both on policy matters — Brown supported pari-mutuel betting and Bingham eventually did not — and on simple questions of political power. To have his own journalistic base to counter the *Courier-Journal*, Brown purchased the Louisville *Herald*, then the *Post*, merged them in 1925, and began a series of circulation wars. Soon two of the richest men in the state faced off, each armed with his own newspaper, each ready to do battle.[5]

The battle lines for Democrats would not be drawn in Governor Morrow's first legislative session, however. Republicans controlled the house, and in the senate where Democrats held a 20–18 margin, one renegade Democrat, C. W. Burton of Grant County, defected and the so-called "Burton Majority" gave Republicans practical control of the general assembly by virtue of the lieutenant governor's tie-breaking powers. Yet, after eight years out of power, and with the legislature virtually under its control, the Republicans' record varied little from previous Democratic ones. The major piece of legislation was a newly constituted Board of Charities and Corrections, which through its bipartisan make-up promised to remove prison and mental hospital positions from patronage fights. A one-cent tax on gasoline was designed to help finance a primary system of highways, while a $2,500 per day tax on race tracks was expected to help support the increased minimum salary of $75/month for teachers. Other education bills, a law restricting free speech, an act removing peace officers who did not protect their prisoners, a law which reduced the likelihood of voting fraud, and a measure "to prohibit grazing on Capitol grounds" were about the most noteworthy of the other actions. It was not a particularly impressive start for Morrow.[6]

Disappointment followed later in the year as well, for in the 1920 campaign for president, most southern border states, including Tennessee, cast their votes for Republican Warren G. Harding — except for Kentucky. In the first election in which women could vote, the commonwealth led the nation in voter participation — 71.2 percent — and, once more, went Democratic, giving James M. Cox a slim majority of only 4,000. Party balance had apparently not been affected by the presence of women, although statistics suggest that Kentucky women voted in larger numbers than expected. The lowest female turnout, not surprisingly, came in isolated, rural, and poorer counties. Overall, the state's voting patterns had changed little, it appeared.[7]

The race for senator seemed to provide a different answer, however. In-cumbent J.C.W. Beckham had introduced no important bills, had attended sessions and committee meetings with typical regularity, and had supported his party on most major issues — in short, a rather usual record for a Kentucky senator. Yet he had not voted on the woman suffrage question and was per-ceived to have been in opposition. Would that prove fatal for his reelection? It did not help that no incumbent Kentucky senator had been reelected in many years. Seeking to continue that trend was a Republican who could claim some part in the Goebel legend as well. Richard P. Ernst had been born in Covington, had been valedictorian at Centre College, and, as an attorney, had successfully defended Goebel in his 1895 shooting of a rival. Together with political boss Maurice Galvin, Ernst controlled northern-Kentucky Republicans, and both men also had ties to Cincinnati leaders across the river. Galvin's brother served as mayor of the Queen City while Ernst had his corporate law office there. The "carpetbagger" label resulted, but Republicans answered that with attacks on Beckham's suffrage views and on the League of Nations. The suffrage issue and the lingering vestiges of factionalism may have been the difference, for 7,000 fewer Democrats voted for Beckham than for presidential candidate Cox, while Ernst garnered nearly 2,000 more than Harding. The result was a reversal of the presidential results, and Ernst defeated the incumbent, 454,226 to 449,244. Democrats pointed to "the steal" of votes at the Lynch precincts in Harlan County; Republican saw the results as the repudiation of Beckham, Haly, and Bingham.[8]

By the time Morrow's second legislature assembled in 1922, the off-year elections had given the Democrats a very small majority in the senate, and a large one of thirty-four votes in the house. Among the new members was the first woman, Mary E. Flanery of Cattlettsburg. She and other Democrats of-ten clashed with the governor and Republican members of the general assem-bly, but a modicum of decent legislation still resulted from the divided legisla-ture. Senate Bill 1 — the so-called Bingham Co-operative Marketing Act — aided hard-pressed tobacco farmers, while the prohibition of convict labor on road-building and other projects removed a much-abused situation. Two new teacher training (normal) schools — later located at Murray and Morehead — were authorized, a Child Welfare Commission was created, and the age of consent was raised. The legislature set up a commission to govern the "My Old Kentucky Home" site and approved construction of a monument to Ken-tucky-born Jefferson Davis. An act prohibiting "the appearance of persons clothed only in a bathing costume upon the public highways" passed, though one allowing for bonds to build those roads did not. In fact, much of the temper of the session can be found in what did not become law. The governor vetoed some $700,000 in appropriations — mostly for higher education and road projects — while the senate passed and the house finally deleted a bill that would set up a board to censor motion pictures shown in the common-wealth. Yet, in the end, the legislature of 1922 would chiefly be identified with one other bill that failed to pass.[9]

In January 1922, three-time presidential nominee William Jennings Bryan appeared before a joint session of the Kentucky General Assembly. The topic of his talk was expected to be the explosive question of evolution. The year before, the Baptist State Board of Missions had appointed a committee to push for enactment of legislation to rid the godless University of Kentucky of the "false and degrading" theory of Darwinian evolution, and the board's newspaper, the *Western Recorder*, had already started a campaign to do just that. Lexington Baptist minister John W. Porter began taking a leadership role in the state anti-evolution struggle and soon published *Evolution – A Menace*, which proclaimed that Jesus Christ "shall not be crucified on the cross of a false philosophy called evolution." His supporters argued that the theory contradicted Biblical authority, eliminated God from the creation, and made humans no different in origin than animals.[10]

As expected, "the Great Commoner" Bryan called for passage of a law forbidding the teaching of evolution. Quickly, bills making it unlawful to teach "Atheism, Agnosticism, or the Theory of Evolution" were introduced in the house and senate as follow-ups to his plea. The fundamentalist forces were ready to fight, and Kentucky would be the ring in which the nation's first major conflict on the issue would occur. It was the beginning of a bitter controversy.[11]

Important opponents faced off against the anti-evolution crusade. Appearing before the legislature, Dr. E. Y. Mullins, the president of the Southern Baptist Theological Seminary in Louisville, took a risky and courageous stand against the bill, and, in so doing, blunted the Baptist attack. He argued that religious bodies should not censor scientific teaching. Various Protestant groups also divided over the issue, but in each influential leaders spoke out against the proposal. Some pointed to the importance of the separation of church and state, as expressed in the First Amendment to the U.S. Constitution; others, such as the *Central Methodist*, spoke for free speech; still more noted that some ministers believed in a qualified, theistic evolutionary process. The Episcopal Diocese of Kentucky protested the bill and declared that curriculum decisions should be left to the schools.[12]

The well-respected (and irregular Presbyterian) Dr. Frank L. McVey, as president of the University of Kentucky, faced the issue squarely. In a February letter, he explained that the school "does teach evolution," but he did not feel that a conflict existed between that theory and Christian beliefs. Should the university shun evolution it would shut itself off from modern thought: "If the history of America has stood for anything, it has stood for freedom of belief, freedom of speech, and tolerance in religious matters." Passage of the bill, he concluded, would be an anti-intellectual attack on all public education.[13]

Strong stands by McVey, Mullins, and Rev. E. L. Powell of Louisville's First Christian Church helped kill the senate evolution bill in committee. But the house version came to a climactic vote on 9 March 1922. A furious five-hour debate saw opponents attack a proposal that "smacks of intolerance and the shadows of the Dark Ages," while supporters said Kentucky's children should

Kentucky Historical Society

University of Kentucky President Frank L. McVey prepares to deliver his monthly talk on "world affairs," as Burnam Pearlman *(right)* **introduces.**

not be exposed to false and misleading theories. One legislator, in a broken voice, told how his son had returned from the university "with his faith destroyed." As the emotional vote was finally taken, a 41–41 tie seemed possible and both sides scrambled to find a friendly absentee vote. "Hard-shell" Baptist Bryce Cundiff of Breathitt County — land of feuds and home of the man who had introduced the Day Law further segregating schools — came to his desk and cast the deciding vote against the legislation. By that single vote, the anti-evolution bill was defeated. As historian William E. Ellis has noted, "the nation's first ballot on legislation to suppress the teaching of evolution had ended."[14]

An analysis of the vote indicates that generalizations are difficult. No particular region supported anti-evolution, and the poorer and less well educated areas were actually evenly divided on the issue. Statistically, it was not a "redneck" religious rebellion. The issue cut across most identifiable lines and divided all Kentuckians.[15]

Nor did it end in the 1922 defeat. Revival preacher Billy Sunday spoke against evolution in the Louisville schools in 1923, and, that same year, Kentucky Wesleyan College suspended five faculty members over their views on the subject. The Anti-Evolution League of America, headed by Kentucky's Reverend Porter, made its national headquarters in the Falls City and from there orchestrated the campaigns that would be successful in other states. Ironically, when national attention focused on the "Monkey Trial" in Dayton, Tennessee, in 1925, it was a University of Kentucky-trained teacher, John T. Scopes, once of Paducah, who was the center of William Jennings Bryan's attacks. More quietly, Scopes's sister would be denied a job by the Paducah school system for her beliefs on evolution. But further attempts to get a vote on anti-evolution legislation failed in 1926 and 1928. Kentucky, together with North Carolina, had been in the forefront in the South in fighting the fundamentalist attacks on evolution.[16]

It has long been argued that Kentucky's citizenry have shown a deep anti-intellectualism and that education has suffered as a result. The fact that the anti-evolution fight went as far as it did supports that view. However, it should be balanced at the same time by the efforts against anti-intellectualism. McVey and Mullins represented the leadership, and the press championed them, but they could not have won — and won again with the failure of bills later — without widespread support for their course of action. In the legislative vote, the poorer and less well educated counties went against the anti-evolutionists as often as they supported them. In short, the evolution controversy showed, once again, the contradictory nature of the Kentucky character.[17]

For a little more than six days after the evolution fight, Kentucky rested. But then still another controversy arose — the 1923 governor's race. Before its close, that race would introduce a major new political player to the statewide scene, would be dominated by divergent issues as few others had been, would force an at least temporary realignment of parties, and would prove to be good political theater.

The players were well suited to the roles they would play in the Democratic primary. Each faction had its candidate. The Stanley group backed J. Campbell Cantrill of Scott County. A fifty-two-year-old veteran legislator and congressman, Cantrill came from a political family, had backed Goebel, but had broken with Beckham early in Cantrill's career. Tall and red-headed, with a sharp mustache dominating a stern face, Cantrill gave an appearance of calmness and dignity, but he could be a harsh enemy. A conservative, "wet," states-rights Democrat who used some racist appeals and opposed woman suffrage, he garnered a great deal of support because of his advocacy of the tobacco farmers in the cooperative fights of the early 1920s. He had a well-organized campaign.[18]

In opposition to Cantrill stood another Democratic congressman, forty-three-year-old Alben W. Barkley of Paducah. More progressive in his stands — he tardily supported prohibition and woman suffrage — Barkley gained his strength from his tremendous energy and powerful speaking voice. An attorney who had heard Stanley, James, Bryan, and other orators proclaimed Barkley the most effective: "He was nearly irresistible. When he got going he carried everything with him, like a windstorm." Another observer noted, later, that Barkley could turn a speech delivered from a hay wagon "into something resembling the sermon on the mount." At times, the candidate liked to talk almost too much, bringing one leader to conclude that Barkley had "no terminal facilities." Once, in what was his fifth speech of the day, Barkley apologized for having to cut his talk to two hours but promised to compress his ideas so all of them could be given. Yet at the same time he won over the crowds that heard him, and many did. His not atypical Union County schedule in 1923 resulted in Barkley's giving eleven speeches there in a single day, beginning at 7:00 A.M. and ending near midnight. This man who had been born in a log cabin and who had worked his way to become an attorney was a formidable, fresh force.[19]

Somewhat belatedly, the Beckham-Haly-Bingham faction embraced Barkley, more because they disliked Cantrill than supported the newcomer. The *Courier-Journal*, in fact, delayed endorsing Barkley until just before the election. But the faction's ties were clear, for Beckham's law partner, Elwood Hamilton, chaired Barkley's campaign, and Haly became a key advisor. In fact, "the General's" advice on issues was taken and the iron-man campaigner, Barkley, soon began calling for a tax on coal deposits and for the elimination of pari-mutuel betting at race tracks. In his opening address, after typical promises to reduce government and taxes, the candidate vehemently lambasted the coal, racetrack, and railroad lobbyists who swarmed on Frankfort, and pledged to lead a new host to the capital city to "redeem the state from all who would despoil her." Soon after, he directly attacked the pari-mutuel betting system.[20]

Those tactics placed many political figures in a quandary, among them Robert Worth Bingham of the *Courier-Journal* and *Times*, and Desha Breckinridge of the Lexington *Herald*. Both men had been active in creating the pari-mutuel system that had replaced bookmakers at Kentucky tracks; both had helped set up the Kentucky Jockey Club; both had worked in the tobacco cooperative fight and cared little for Cantrill; both felt uncomfortable with Barkley as well. Both also probably would have liked to have been governor, but neither sought to campaign for the office. In the end, each went with a different group, and their papers spewed forth a barrage of vindictive words as a result. The Louisville *Times* included the Lexington paper in an editorial entitled "Two Prostitutes," while the *Herald* responded, saying the two Louisville papers, "The Heavenly Twins," attempted to place "the brand of corruption or disservice" on all who failed to heed Haly's call. Those who assume "to speak with the authority of the delphic [*sic*] oracle," should remember, said Breckinridge, that there can be honest disagreements. And what the two editors were experiencing was happening all across the state as forces realigned and re-formed for political combat.[21]

The traditional interpretation of politics in Kentucky in the 1920s suggests that conservative Bourbon Democrats supporting racing and coal merged forces with Republicans holding the same interests to form a corrupt biparti-san combine that dominated the state. Usually, the Bingham-Haly-Beckham faction is pictured as the reform element in this scenario.[22] And there is much to support that view, for Barkley's anti-gambling, anti-race-track campaign harkened to Goebel's earlier anti-monopoly pleas. His stands were the more progressive ones.[23]

Yet there is much wrong with that simplistic picture. The political leader of the Beckham faction had not had a terribly progressive administration as governor, had opposed woman suffrage, and had his own ties to corporations; Haly was a political boss, pure and simple. Bingham — and Beckham — had also united with Republicans in the past as they had sought allies. The KKK probably supported Barkley and opposed Stanley in their races. This does not mean the Beckham faction did not support "good" causes. They often did. At certain times, they deserve accolades. But their opponents were not quite the stereotypical reactionaries as often portrayed (though some certainly were). Some people, like Desha Breckinridge, had been leaders of the Progressive Movement in the state, and Stanley's administration had a liberal record of accomplishments. In short, while the fights of the 1920s are often presented as ones of good versus evil, reformers versus reactionaries, it is dangerous to go very far down that generalization road. Each faction had elements of pro-gressivism and conservatism in it; each had political bosses; each sought some-thing very simple — political power. In the end, each used an issue it thought it could win with — defense of racing, or attacks on gambling.[24]

Supporting Barkley in his race was the Anti-Pari-Mutuel Gambling Com-mission, headed by fundamentalist pastor M. P. Hunt. (Indicative of the strange alliances being formed on the one issue, the strong, anti-Catholic Hunt was partly financed by Catholic leader P. H. Callahan.) That commission por-trayed Cantrill as in league with "the toughs, tauts, and all of the Scarlet women," and with "organized vice and commercialized crime."[25]

Cantrill, in turn, opposed the coal tax as an action that would drive capital from Kentucky and said the betting issue was but a minor one. He called instead for a business administration that would reduce taxes and cut expenses — already an overused argument — and for support of a bond issue that would allow the commonwealth to fund its schools adequately. Meanwhile, support-ers like the youthful A. B. "Happy" Chandler sang ditties that showed that the pari-mutuel question was not so minor, after all:

> Mr. Barkley says that betting is a crime
> He fights the races so
> I think he must have lost some dough
> that he bet upon a losing horse one time.[26]

In bitter opposition to the Anti-Pari-Mutuel Gambling Commission stood Cantrill's staunchest ally, the Kentucky Jockey Club. Founded in 1918, it was in many ways the dangerous lobby its opponents pictured. Some thirty members of the legislature were said to be on its payroll; it spent large amounts of money to defeat its opponents in political races; it crossed party lines as Democrats Jim Brown, Billy Klair, Johnson Camden, and Desha Breckinridge joined forces with the so-called "Stanley Republicans" Maurice Galvin and others, while horsemen Matt Winn and A. B. Hancock stood at the rail, watching. Yet, it also represented a legitimate attempt to defend its turf, when under attack from outside forces with their own well-funded base. The question seemed to be which group could prevail.[27]

The primary election results, at one level, seemed to indicate the strength of issue-oriented regionalism. Backed by eastern Kentucky coal interests and his native central Kentucky racing lobby, Cantrill carried virtually every county east of a line running from Louisville to Cumberland Gap. West Kentucky native Barkley, representing rural interests, carried virtually all the counties west of that line. Cantrill, however, did exceptionally well in the commonwealth's largest urban areas, winning 79, 69, and 64 percent of the vote in Lexington, Covington, and Newport, respectively, while carrying Bingham's hometown by 12,000 votes. Aided by large amounts of Jockey Club money at election time, Cantrill won enough areas to give him a majority of 9,000. Though defeated, Barkley had given a good account of himself in what had been a friendly canvass between the two principals; he came out of the election in a strong position should he seek further office.[28]

Just at the moment of their victory, disaster struck the Cantrill camp. For the last month of the campaign, Cantrill had almost disappeared, due to health problems. It was a testament to his organization that he could win while mostly confined to a bed in Louisville's Seelbach Hotel. But by late August, he was in critical condition with a ruptured appendix, and doctors held "very little hope" for his recovery. On 2 September 1923, J. Campbell Cantrill, Democratic nominee and almost certain victor for governor, died.[29]

With the general election only two months away, there was no time for another primary. Barkley made it known that he did not want the position, since voters had rejected him and his presence would reopen factional wounds. Who would be the nominee? The Democratic State Central and Executive Committees, made up mostly of members of the Stanley faction, met to wrestle with the problem and their selection turned out to be virtually the hand-picked preference of Jim Brown. That fact meant that factionalism would remain an issue and that the nominee would be an anathema to Brown's enemy, Bingham.[30]

Representing the Democratic Party now was William Jason Fields, a forty-eight-year-old, seven-term congressman from Olive Hill. A college graduate who had been a drummer for a grocery, he had turned to politics and had been quietly successful. Although not a strong supporter of America's entry into the world war, Fields otherwise had a rather non-controversial career in

Washington, was not an outstanding speaker, and was not particularly well known across Kentucky. His chief attribute may have been the fact that Brown and others felt they could control Fields, who did not have a reputation as a strong leader.[31]

Once selected, Fields soon took to the campaign trail, and, in his opening speech, attacked the Morrow administration's record on pardons, roads, and expenditures.[32] On the other side, Republicans had not been sanguine of victory going into the race, but Democratic divisions and Cantrill's death had given them new hope. Their nominee now sought to capitalize. Former Attorney General Charles I. Dawson had defeated Superintendent of Public Instruction George Colvin of Washington County, legislator-banker John W. Stoll of Lexington, and Louisville Mayor Huston Quinn for the nomination. Yet, in some ways, he was an unusual pick, for Dawson had first served as a Democratic legislator from Logan County. After moving to Republican Bell County, he was elected county attorney on a fusion ticket, and then reelected as a Republican. Now the leader of that party, he ripped Fields's selection process: "The Democracy . . . has had thrust upon it as its candidate for governor one who today holds his commission by virtue of the fact that he was the choice of a small but determined group." The Democrat was but a supposed Moses, "rescued from the bullrushes by the seven wise men" who chose him.[33]

Mostly the campaign degenerated into a name-calling contest. Fields, who ran as "Honest Bill from Olive Hill," was portrayed by Dawson as "Dodging Bill of Olive Hill, who answers no questions and never will." Fields, in response, called Dawson "Changing Charley," due to his political switches. In that atmosphere, election day drew a smaller turnout than usual, but, otherwise, the results surprised few. Fields and a Democratic ticket that included Secretary of State Emma Guy Cromwell won a sizable victory, 356,045 (53.3 percent) to 306,277 (45.8 percent).[34]

When Morrow left office a few months later, he departed with mixed results. Like all Republican governors of the century, he had not fashioned a strong enough record to bring about victory for a Republican successor, due in part to an inability to control the legislature. His administration had better protected the state's black citizens, had created a bipartisan board of control over prisons, had established two new teacher colleges, and had other important accomplishments, but Morrow had also been financially cautious, and in the anti-evolution fight had not taken a major leadership role. In short, Morrow left behind a solid, and rather typical, record for a Kentucky governor.[35]

The Fields Administration, 1923–1927

Four years after it began, the Fields administration ended "unwept, unhonored, and unsung," according to a historical analysis that appeared two decades later. In less than ten years, another commentator concluded that Fields "met many reverses." More recently, a historian indicated that the administration's record was mixed at best. Going into his term without great expectations of success, it seemed Fields met those expectations.[36]

Part of the governor's problems came from his own actions. He quickly announced there would be a ban on dancing in the Governor's Mansion while he was chief executive and moved an inaugural dance from that building to the rotunda of the Capitol. Even then, he and his wife did not attend the inaugural ball. That moralistic tone in the Roaring Twenties did not carry over to government, however, for the governor's son and other relatives were added to the state payroll. Given his opponents' insistence that Fields was tied to a corrupt bipartisan combine and was controlled by Brown, Klair, and others, such nepotistic actions only supported those views.[37]

Moreover, Fields faced what other governors of that decade did — a fragmented, leaderless legislature, a faction-ridden party, and a strong opposition led by the newspaper with the largest circulation in the commonwealth. A reporter two years earlier concluded of the general assembly that it was "headless, without homogeneity or programs, divided into factions; swayed by partisanship; individually bent on the promotion of special and local petty interests; largely raw in legislative experience" and dominated by lobbyists of the "Invisible Government." Any governor faced problems in leading and taming that beast.[38]

In truth, Fields's administration may warrant greater praise. He came to office under a cloud due to his selection by a small cabal, but, while allied to that faction, was much his own man. A simple and straight-forward person, sometimes criticized for his lack of urbanity, Fields had good intentions and, as it turned out, a key program. His error was not his plans but his inability to translate intentions into reality. The new governor was just not experienced enough and strong enough to mobilize forces to overcome the factionalism that destroyed his hopes and caused him to resort to petty public bickering with opponents.[39]

On New Year's Day 1924, just before Fields's first legislative session, the state-initiated Efficiency Commission of Kentucky presented its two-volume study entitled *The Government of Kentucky*. While a fiscally conservative document, it presented a good guide to improving Kentucky's government.[40] Fields, in his message to the legislature, focused on finances more than governmental reform, however. Strongly stressing the urgency of more funds for education and charitable institutions, he said the university needed classrooms, the "deplorable" prison in Frankfort needed expansion, and blacks needed facilities to care for their poor, just as whites had. The governor called for state tuberculous sanatoria, a reform of asylums that "are a disgrace to our state," and the payment of the $6-million state debt. To make all this happen, as well as to provide a huge amount of money for new roads for the "detour state," he proposed a $75-million bond issue to be paid off by an added gasoline tax, an auto license tax, an increase in the property tax, and other sources of revenue. The next day an impressed Lexington *Herald* editor gave the whole front page to the proposal, calling it "the beginning of a new era."[41]

Kentucky Historical Society

Governor Fields signs a 1926 bill into law as Mrs. Fields, former Governor Edwin Morrow *(to his left)*, and others look on.

Not all agreed, and a powerful opposition soon arose. Some Republicans, such as former governor Willson, the Lexington *Leader*, and that party's members of the Efficiency Commission, opposed the proposal as too expensive. Fields's factional opponents and the Louisville *Courier-Journal* also came out against the plan, for the same reasons. Even though the immediate state debt would be paid off, they argued that the bond issue would commit Kentucky to a larger debt. Left unaddressed was whether the proposed sources of revenue would be sufficient to cover that. Actually, the bond proposal was a solid one that would provide needed funds for the state. But the real source of opposition was not just the fiscal conservatism; it was also a matter of trust. Viewing Fields as a creature of a faction that the opposition pictured as corrupt, Bingham and others did not trust him — or want him — to spend the money that would result from passage of the bond. They saw it as a massive fund for corruption.[42]

Fields and some of his allies seemed almost stunned by the fierceness of the opposition, and both sides responded with unwise words. After a *Courier-Journal* editorial, "Reject the Bond Bill," said that the proposal would bring "a lifetime burden of taxation," Fields answered with a public letter to Bingham, accusing him of opposition for partisan purposes. Had he consulted Haly and Bingham beforehand, sneered Fields, perhaps they would have been more favorable. Bingham, in turn, replied a few days later with his own letter. The bipartisan machine, manipulated by Klair and Galvin, controlled Fields and kept Kentucky in "political mud," said Bingham, and he had to oppose them. That same day, a Fields ally, Breckinridge of the *Herald*, wrote that he regretted that the governor had dignified "the nominal editor of the Courier-Journal" with a letter: "Once the *Courier-Journal* was a real Kentuckian, owned and edited by real men. . . . We, with all others who love their state . . . range ourselves alongside the Kentuckian who is governor and his own master in any contest with one who is neither Kentuckian nor his own master." With that exchange, the two Democratic papers were almost irrevocably divided. Some of those Republicans who were in opposition quietly and gleefully watched as the administration split apart.[43]

Fields had proposed passage of the bond issue and its submission to the voters for approval. In the legislature, many rural interests (including Republican ones) supported the road-building that would bring highways to their communities, while those in locales affected by the education and charitable parts of the issue also advocated the proposal. By a 52–45 vote in the house (with 31 Democrats and 21 Republicans for, and 35 Democrats and 9 Republicans opposed), and a 22–16 vote in the senate, the bond issue passed and was placed on the ballot. But Kentucky's storied fiscal conservatism, backed by strong newspaper editorials, won out in the end, and, in the fall elections, the issue went down to a 374,328 to 275,863 defeat. Urban and central Bluegrass areas opposed it the most; the road-poor mountains had given it the greatest support. Overall, the state had clearly opted for a "pay as you go" philosophy which, as one governor said three decades later, "meant that we didn't go far." An opportunity for advancement had been missed.[44]

At almost the same time Governor Fields was trying to get approval for the bond issue that would aid prisons and other state institutions, actions were taking place within the legislature which seemed to make a mockery of his reform agenda. Political boss and Fields's advisor Allie Young proposed to overturn the existing bipartisan system of control over prisons and charitable institutions and oust the head of the board — moves that brought politics, once more, back into the system.

The state's penal system had long been an embarrassment. In 1901, the commonwealth's two prisons, at Frankfort and Eddyville, had housed some 1,700 inmates, with over a thousand of them black — testament to the dual justice system still operating. Some 60 percent of those incarcerated were illiterate, 300 cases of syphilis were treated in just one of the institutions, and 42 people died that year. The parole system had been instituted in 1900 (for first offenders only) and fifty-three people had been released under its provisions; however, the overriding outlook still was that expressed by the Eddyville warden: prisoners should not, he said, be "regarded as 'unfortunates' and petted and coaxed" but rather as violators of the law. Among those violators were young boys — a fourteen-year-old arrived on a murder conviction — and a few women — 54 in Frankfort. One warden reported that with 414 cells and 530 prisoners, "bestial practices and new lessons in every kind of crime are being daily taught." Over the next decade, news stories and reports told a depressingly familiar story. By 1905, more people were in prison, in the same number of cells, with more deaths, and with about the same number of pa-

Kentucky Historical Society

Prisoners crowd into the dining room at the state reformatory in Frankfort.

roles, annually. Of the 1,900 inmates, some 360 were under the age of twenty, nearly 300 were serving life sentences, and at least 60 had tuberculosis. Virtually all suffered from poor treatment and poor food — one story noted rats in the milk, mice in the hash, and bugs in the bread and in the beds.[45]

By 1910, "hardened" criminals were separated from others and placed solely at Eddyville, and two years later the Board of Prison Commissioners instituted reforms that gave prisoners some of the money they had earned by their labor, brought better sanitary practices into the institutions, and abolished prolonged whipping. By 1918, that board had been merged with the Board of Control for Charitable Institutions — which supervised the three "Asylums for the Insane," the School for Training "feeble-minded children," the two "Houses of Reform," schools for the blind and for "deaf-mutes," the "Home for Incurables," and the Kentucky Confederate Home. Then, under the Morrow administration, that merged board had been made bipartisan in an attempt to remove politics even more from its deliberations.[46]

The newly constituted Board of Charities and Corrections selected Joseph P. Byers, the general secretary of the American Prison Association, as commissioner, and it appeared the correction system was well on its way to a needed professionalization. Still, troubling problems continued. In 1922 Commissioner Byers replaced the warden at Eddyville, citing his political involvement; the next year that same prison saw a "shoot-out" erupt which left three guards and three inmates dead. In that atmosphere, Senator Young made his attack on Byers, the bipartisan board, and state institutions in general. The governor did not openly oppose or support his ally's attempt to give the administration more control over the system.[47]

The conflict was political, personal, and professional. At the personal level, Byers had replaced the provider of fire insurance for the state institutions, causing that particular person to lose a half-million dollars in premiums each year. His opposition came quickly. The commissioner's refusal to hire the friends of politicians for guard jobs further alienated important people. At the more professional level, the board had called for an end to corporal punishment and had stressed rehabilitation efforts in the prisons. A 1922 investigating committee had disagreed openly with that emphasis. Now, two years later, another committee heard testimony — almost solely from witnesses friendly to their viewpoint — and issued its findings. Not surprisingly, the so-called Young Report recommended more Kentuckians in positions of responsibility (Byers was from Pennsylvania), called for abolishment of the commissioner's office, asked that wardens and superintendents be appointed by the governor (instead of by the board), and supported a return to what would be a more partisan arrangement. The existing board correctly characterized the report as one which sought "the establishment of a pure political machine, perfect in its detail for partisan spoils."[48]

Strange allies combined to defend the bipartisan board concept and Byers. The urban press generally, and the *Courier-Journal* and Lexington *Herald* in particular, strongly opposed the Young Report and the bills to place its recommendation into law. Breckinridge wrote of his shame that politicians sought to return Kentucky to the Dark Ages of corrections, when self-interest reigned rampant. The editor was "astounded" that his Democratic Party could even think of making "so heinous a mistake." Service, not spoils, should be the guidelines now.[49]

Young's Senate bill made it clear on which side he stood. His draft legislation also asked that the new board be given authority to fire all current employees and hire new ones if desired — a huge patronage power — and required that all hired superintendents "must be residents of Kentucky." By a 22–15 vote, with the parties evenly divided, the bill passed the senate and went to the house. There, by a 46–48 margin, the bill was finally defeated. But it was too late, in many ways. The power grab had further alienated those opposed to Fields and the bond issue; it convinced his enemies he was but a tool of the bosses; and it proved too close a vote for Byers. When the governor refused to reappoint certain board members the next year, Byers resigned as commissioner. He was replaced by a Kentuckian, who lived not too far from William J. Fields.[50]

The bond issue and the xenophobic Board of Charities and Corrections fights dominated the session, but other matters gained attention as well. Despite Barkley's election defeat on the question of ending pari-mutuel betting, that issue was resurrected in the legislature and passed the house by a wide 56–38 margin. But the senate killed by a 14–24 count an attempt to move the bill past a first reading. Another Barkley issue, the coal tax, also died in committee. What did pass, in addition to placing the bond issue on the fall ballot, were bills which increased the gasoline tax and shifted the tax burden from real estate to personal property. Commissions were established for Real Estate, Crippled Children, and State Parks. In the end, those bills that passed chiefly were ones supported by Fields in his modest programs. Even then, had the bond issue been successful in the fall, the session would have been ruled an important one. As it was, the general assembly gained its most praise for what it did not do — dismantle the Board of Charities and Corrections.[51]

That weak legislative record and the divided party that emerged from the 1924 general assembly session did not brighten Democratic hopes for victory in the general elections. Not only was it a presidential election year, but incumbent A. O. Stanley sought to do what had not been done by Kentucky senators for over forty years — win reelection. Furnishing the opposition was a relative newcomer to the Kentucky political scene. Frederic Mosley Sackett, Jr., had been born in Rhode Island, educated at Brown University and Harvard Law School, practiced his profession in Ohio for some years, then had moved to Louisville, the hometown of his wife, Olive Speed. Quitting his law practice, Sackett had taken over some of the Speed family interests, had become president of the Louisville Cement Company and of the Gas Company, and had soon moved into coal production. During World War I, he had served as federal food administrator for the state. A youthful-looking, handsome, fifty-three-year-old millionaire, Sackett led the Louisville and urban Republican branch of his party and now sought to make that the base for his victory.[52]

In his opening campaign address, Sackett praised Republican prosperity for the nation, endorsed the national tariff policy of his party, and indicated his full support for Prohibition. In short, he would skirt divisive state issues, make a plea to the "drys" who distrusted the old "wet" Stanley, and hope that Democratic divisions would give him the election. Even though Sackett apparently had his own private liquor stock, the Anti-Saloon League soon announced their support for the Republican, and Bingham, who called fellow upper-class Louisvillian Sackett "one of the best men I know," gave the *Courier-Journal*'s endorsement as well.[53]

Stanley found himself without many allies. The fact that he read the following into the *Congressional Record* did not endear him to the "wets":

> My country tis of thee
> Land of home breweries
> Thy brew I love
> I love thy booze and thrills
> and thy illicit still,
> the moonshine runs in rills
> from high above.

Kentucky Historical Society

Law officers sit before the booty (lining the rock shelter entrance) from a moonshine raid in Boyd County, ca. 1928.

Governor Fields, who was a "dry," had not been an enthusiastic supporter to begin with; now Stanley opposed the bond issue and that meant even less aid from the sitting administration. The incumbent senator sought to present a different Republican administration than did Sackett, for Stanley painted a national picture of "depression, bankruptcy, and ruin," of corruption, of a "stand pat oligarchy in the Senate." Behind the scenes, his campaign attacked this "wealthy New Englander." But also covertly, Ku Klux Klan followers opposed Stanley. The siphoning of "drys," Klan supporters, Fields's allies, and the Bingham factions from the Democratic Party meant trouble for Stanley. The results showed that, as Sackett won 406,141 to 381,623. At Sackett's swearing-in as senator in March 1925, Kentucky would have two Republican senators for the first time in its history.[54]

And on top of that, Republicans carried Kentucky in the presidential election by about the same margin. Democratic apathy, which lowered voter participation by 100,000 from 71.2 percent in 1920 to 60.5 percent; the presence of a third-party candidate, the Progressive Robert M. La Follette, who took his 38,000 votes heavily from Democratic areas; and the Democracy's choice of a candidate widely perceived as a "Wall Street lawyer" — all these doomed John W. Davis's candidacy and gave "Silent Cal" Coolidge a quiet victory. The Republicans won 48.8 percent of the vote (396,758), the Democrats 46 percent (374,543), and the La Follette Progressives an important 4.7 percent, with a strong showing in northern Kentucky (38,465). About the only positive sign for Democrats was that they had held on to Fields's former congressional seat, with the election to a full term of political newcomer Fred M. Vinson of Louisa. Otherwise, it had been a disastrous election.[55]

Republicans stumbled a bit over the next year, however, for their election of a mayor in Louisville in 1925 was later overturned by the courts due to ballot stuffing, and Governor Fields appointed the defeated Democrat as acting mayor. Somewhat more troubling was the status of ten-term Republican Congressman John W. Langley of Pike County. A former teacher and state legislator before winning his seat in Congress, "Pork Barrel John" had been convicted in 1924 of "conspiracy to violate the Prohibition Act" through trying to sell 1,400 bottles of whiskey. By January 1926, he had exhausted his appeals when the U.S. Supreme Court affirmed his sentence. Langley resigned his seat and went to federal prison in Atlanta. Paroled the day after Christmas in 1926, and pardoned two years later, Langley told his side of the story in his *They Tried to Crucify Me*; he also eventually saw his wife successfully win his old seat in November 1926. Thirty-eight-year-old Katherine Gudger Langley, mother of three and the daughter of a North Carolina congressman, served from 1927 to 1931 as Kentucky's first female representative and the eighth nationally.[56]

All the Langley actions were going on as the 1926 general assembly opened. It became clear very quickly that neither Fields nor his opponents were willing to let old issues die. Pari-mutuel and coal tax bills made headway, but once more, were defeated. The governor tried again to get a bond issue approved, this time reducing the size and breaking the question into separate issues. One bond, designed to help university funding, was defeated in the legislature, in various forms. Two other bond issues, to reduce the state's debt and to provide $5 million for penal, charitable, and correctional institutions, made it to voters, only to be defeated there. With the pet issues of both factions out of the way, the legislature followed Fields's recommendations to institute some of the Efficiency Commission's findings. While governmental reorganization died in committee, a Budget Commission, state budget officer position, and uniform budget system were all created, as was a centralized state purchasing system. Another suggestion, the lifting of the constitutional limitation on salaries, passed the general assembly but was easily defeated by parsimonious voters in the fall. The solons also passed an increase in the gasoline tax, a forestry bill to help reforestation, and over a hundred road bills of specific nature ("there shall be added . . . the following road project: From the highway near John T. Noffsinger to Hannah's bridge on Pond river, in the county of Muhlenberg . . ."). And in a burst of activity, the legislature made Robert E. Lee's birthday a legal holiday, adopted the cardinal as the state bird and the goldenrod as the state flower, and rejected a proposed child labor amendment to the U.S. Constitution. Fields vetoed a bill to make the office of county school superintendent elective, but his veto of another bill — one that would allow baseball to be played on Sunday — was overridden. Active in pushing his overall program with good results, Fields had seen his key projects defeated by the voters. It all meant a rather regular record — some accomplishments, but no great change.[57]

Great change, however, seemed likely in the 1926 race for United States senator. Incumbent Ernst had money but little personal following and faced important obstacles in his bid to achieve that most elusive of Kentucky political goals in the Senate — reelection. Within his own party, Ernst had done little to prevent Representative Langley from going to prison, and mountain Republicans were lukewarm in their support as a result.[58] But Ernst's greatest obstacle to reelection was his Democratic opposition, Alben Barkley. In the three years since his defeat for governor, the west Kentuckian had broken free, in a sense, from both of his party's factions. He told a friend how Haly and he had disagreed: "The General . . . is a wonderful fellow, with one of the most attractive personalities I have ever known, and it has been a matter of great regret to me that my course since the Governor's race has not met his entire approval." That course included a compromise with the Fields forces, one in which, it was rumored, Barkley would not push the pari-mutuel issue if elected. Jim Brown gave money and support to Barkley as well. And so the nominee entered the race with the support — albeit reluctant at times — of both factions.[59]

In the campaign, the youthful "Iron Man" contrasted with the sixty-eight-year-old Ernst, who used Ed Morrow to do much of his speaking for him. Barkley ripped the Republicans for their party's national scandals, particularly Ernst for his votes on pension bills, and, more crucially, a soldiers' bonus for World War I veterans. Ernst, in turn, tried to fuel the factional flames by pointing to Barkley's coal tax, bond issue, and pari-mutuel stands. His stress on the tariff issue and Coolidge prosperity, however, proved a mistake, for Kentucky's economy was already hurting. Aided by his campaign manager Fred Vinson, Barkley ran a wise race, and, in the end, his personality and the issues brought victory by a 286,997 to 266,657 count. Even though he had carried Louisville and done adequately in the mountains, an incumbent senator had lost once more. Seemingly, removal to Washington made it difficult to keep all the contacts necessary for reelection. Barkley had six years to see if he could change the trend.[60]

There was also, for Democrats, another disturbing trend, and that was frequent Republican victories in races for governor. In the last five gubernatorial contests, each party had easily won twice, and the other election (the Stanley-Morrow race) had been a virtual dead heat. Now with Fields unpopular and Democrats feuding over the governor's contest, Republicans saw an excellent opportunity for victory. Whenever that happened, the party's factions began to come alive. In 1927, it was a classic division for the party, for the urban branch put forth thirty-nine-year-old attorney and Collector for Internal Revenue for Kentucky, Robert H. Lucas of Louisville. Backing him were two fellow Louisvillians, Senator Sackett and boss Chesley Searcy, the recently defeated Ernst, and the Lexington *Leader*. In opposition stood the mountain Republican candidate Flem D. Sampson of Barbourville. The fifty-two-year-old Sampson, one of ten children, had worked his way to success, serving as teacher, city attorney, college roommate of and law partner with Caleb Powers (the accused accessory in the Goebel case), bank president, and then chief justice of the state's highest court. Now he and mountain Republican congressman John Marshall Robsion controlled the eastern area and joined with northern Kentucky boss Maurice Galvin to form a strong combination. Lucas attacked Galvin and the Republican Party's ties to racing and the L & N, but Sampson basically ignored that issue. He spoke only in general terms of supporting schools and roads and opposing a coal tax. The primary showed a clear pattern: Lucas carried the five congressional districts in the west (including Louisville), while Sampson swept all six in the east. Since Republican strength was in Sampson's area, he won nearly 60 percent of the vote and now faced the Democratic nominee.[61]

The presence of J.C.W. Beckham as a candidate for governor insured that the Democratic primary would be bitter, for factional feelings would only intensify. With Logan County boss Tom Rhea serving as his chairman, Beckham once more made the abolition of pari-mutuel betting his key issue. Backing him in that stand were Bingham, Haly, and — miracle of miracles — his old enemy A. O. Stanley. Blaming his recent senatorial defeat on the lack of support by Fields, Stanley took new allies: "There is one funny thing about beds, we often have to take them, not as we would make them, but as *they are made for us*, and . . . I shall certainly enjoy the good company of my new bed-fellow."[62]

Under the other factional sheets lay the Fields forces, with its usual bedfellows of Camden, Klair, Breckinridge, and Jim Brown, joined by recently retired congressman and Beckham-hater Ben Johnson and Barkley ally Seldon Glenn (known as "Ferryboat" Glenn since he went from side to side). Their candidate was not particularly well known across the state and would have significant barriers to overcome. State Auditor and former House Speaker Robert T. Crowe of Oldham County proved to be only an average campaigner (as was Beckham), so the question came down to how much each side could control various voting blocs.[63]

Basically, the Beckham-Bingham forces did a better job of "selling" their candidate's argument that a corrupt, bipartisan combine controlled the state and the commonwealth could only be freed through elimination of racetrack betting. Both sides had to fend off questions that they had not always been loyal to the party (they had not); both had to answer charges that their candidate was only the front for other controlling interests; both attacked previous administrations — Fields's versus Beckham's — as corrupt; both resorted to personal critiques. Crowe, who was born in Canada but was a naturalized citizen, was criticized for that by the paper that had taken the opposite stand regarding Byers and the prisons. Charges that the Jockey Club had given large sums of money to the Lexington *Herald* for campaign purposes both in the past and present were refuted by an audit of the books. Governor Fields, in turn, wrote another open letter to the *Courier-Journal* accusing that paper of dragging journalism "through the slums of political chicanery." While Fields used the highway commission to help Crowe, and the State Federation of Labor backed that faction as well, the perception of corruption, coupled with Beckham's greater name recognition and the Canadian-immigrant versus the Kentucky-aristocrat issue, proved the difference. Though losing the urban areas by big margins, Beckham still defeated Crowe by nearly 24,000 votes, not only carrying the same areas Barkley had in his primary race four years earlier, but also making some inroads in central Kentucky. Those votes won it for Beckham, and his allies, such as the Paducah *News-Democrat*, proclaimed it the "greatest moral victory . . . in a quarter of a century."[64]

It was now Beckham or betting. It was also a question of whether party loyalty would prove stronger than the pari-mutuel issue. On the second matter, it soon became clear how each party responded. The Republican anti-racing candidate Lucas immediately supported Sampson; Democrats Crowe, Fields, Johnson, Brown, Klair, and others actively worked against Beckham in the general election. Did the pari-mutuel issue have the widespread appeal necessary to overcome that? Did it have enough to defeat both the Republicans and a sizeable part of one Democratic faction? Would the home of the thoroughbred reject racing?[65]

In what the national press was calling "Kentucky's Race-Horse Election," strange — or perhaps some not-so-strange — alliances were being forged. The Women's Christian Temperance Union (WCTU) supported the "dry" Beckham who was allied with the "wet" Stanley, while "dry" Fields opposed them. Leading Democratic papers, the Lexington *Herald* and the Louisville *Herald-Post*, bitterly opposed their party's gubernatorial nominee while the Republican Lexington *Leader* wrote decidedly nicer words about him. The Jockey Club, to which Bingham once had major ties, now was his enemy. Normally Republican-voting blacks questioned their party's Klan connections and threatened to bolt. The New York *Times* noted that not for three decades "has such topsy-turvydom existed in Kentucky."[66]

Republican nominee Sampson continued to ignore the pari-mutuel issue most of the time, since those opposed to Beckham because of that issue would vote for Sampson anyway. Instead he talked of free textbooks and appealed to labor, picturing Beckham as an aristocrat while he had grown up poor: "I'm just plain old Flem. When I'm elected Governor of Kentucky, come into my office and sit down and say 'Howdy Flem.'" Sampson and his allies also used the xenophobia so prevalent in Kentucky politics against Bingham — whose papers had criticized Crowe's Canadian ties. Turning the tables, the *Herald-Post* printed satires from the disloyal "Lord Bing," writing to "Prince Haly" and "Duke Beckham." Editorial cartoons showed "The Four Horsemen of the Apologies" — Bingham, Haly, Beckham, and Stanley — while it was left to the

Kentucky Historical Society

Odds are posted over the clubhouse gardens at Churchill Downs on Derby Day 1933.

old orator Ed Morrow to add his distinctive touch to that image. Here, he intoned, were four horsemen on their hobby horse, "armed with spears of 'the issue' . . . dashing wildly over the highways and by-ways . . . crying aloud, 'Show us the Pari-Mutuel Dragon . . . Yet will we slay him . . . and we long for dragon meat and office.'" What a strange group this was, he added — Haly was Beckham's "Sancho Panza," Bingham was "of foreign clime," yet was involved here, while Stanley, his friend Stanley — alas for years he "slept side by side, nay, in the very arms of the dragon."[67]

Beckham, the subject of that outburst, showed that he possessed a sharp tongue as well, as he called Sampson "Flem-Flam-Flem." Friendly newspapers printed cartoons that showed the bipartisan combine as an octopus, reaching out to grab all the power it could. Did Kentuckians want the Jockey Club lobby to control the state? It was in those tones that the campaign came to an end. In truth, the one issue of betting had become almost cartoonish, while other serious state concerns — educational funding, economic matters, prison reform, and the like — were virtually ignored. The issue may have been clear-cut and the race colorful, but it did little to help solve the state's long-term problems.[68]

Election day dawned cold and damp, traditionally no help to mountain Republicans. But on that wet track, Sampson won, though every other member of his ticket placed. Some very strange results suggested either careful planning by leaders or some fraud, for Beckham had been soundly defeated 399,700 (52.1 percent) to 367,567 (47.9 percent). But the 32,000-vote margin did not apply to the rest of the Republicans, all of whom lost. Unprecedented ticket-splitting, probably encouraged by Jockey Club funds, had occurred, and the possibility of some kind of deal seemed evident. Betting had won out over Beckham. The Derby had been more important than the Democratic leader. It did require a real scramble for voters to insure that all the rest of the Democrats did win, however, for Lieutenant Governor James Breathitt, Jr., was finally declared the winner over E. E. Nelson by only 159 votes, out of over 700,000 cast. Overall, Sampson had carried the normally Republican areas, as well as those won by Cantrill and Crowe in the previous Democratic primaries. The congressional district Fields had once represented went for Sampson in a 20,000-vote turnaround. Louisville, Covington, Newport, and Lexington all gave the Republican large margins, ones that more than offset Beckham's ballots in rural west Kentucky. Still, the whole affair had so tarnished Kentucky's image that the New York *Times* concluded that "students of democracy will find little to encourage them." It was not the commonwealth's brightest hour.[69]

It was perhaps a fitting conclusion to Fields's four-year fling with fame. A little-known congressman before his election as party nominee, he had entered office expecting to bring factions together behind a program that he genuinely believed was good for the state. And it probably was. Yet the bitterness of the factionalism and the strong personalities on both sides seemed to overwhelm him. He did not fully understand how his moral stands, his nepotism, his ties to the bosses, and his public feuds with the *Courier-Journal* all hurt his ability to lead the party. As a result, his became the first Democratic administration to lose not only a Senate seat but also a presidential election and the next governorship (although in the latter case, Fields seemed happy at the outcome of the election). Defeat of his bond issues had meant that instead of being praised for a constructive administration, "Honest Bill" would leave office a bitter and disappointed man. After he failed in his attempt to regain his seat in Congress, Fields generally remained out of politics. Given what he had experienced as governor, he did not appear too unhappy over that situation.[70]

The Sampson Administration, 1927–1931

Sampson seemed destined for political disaster, and his destiny was fulfilled. Democrats controlled the legislature and all the other elective offices; they, quite rightly, felt responsible for his election and expected him to recognize that as well. Sampson thus had two choices — he could work with the Democrats and get what he could out of the situation, or he could try to rally one of the Democratic factions to his side, and, in combination with the Republicans, become dominant. The new governor tried the second option, but his own personality, his unwise choice of issues, and his lack of constructive leadership doomed that course. The result would be four years of bitterness and drift.

The governor's first legislative session told what could be expected — very little. Evolution and pari-mutuel bills were defeated; the legislature did create a Kentucky Progress Commission with a $50,000 budget, revised the marriage laws (raising the ages to sixteen for boys and fourteen for girls), and made "My Old Kentucky Home" the state song. Sampson's key project, a free textbook bill, passed, but the solons provided no revenue to enact its provisions. In short, it had been almost a "do-nothing" session.[71]

Much more interest in politics came in the fall of 1928, when the campaign for president swept into full force. The Democrats' nomination of New Yorker Al Smith created immediate problems for Kentucky party leaders and they knew it. Editor Desha Breckinridge wrote a friend in May indicating there was "very strong opposition to Smith, both because of his being classed a wet and because he is a Catholic. . . . Kentucky is also burdened with quite virulent religious fanaticism." A few months later, his analysis had not changed: "It is going to be a hell of a job to carry Kentucky for Smith. Many men and more women now intend to remain away from the polls or to vote for Hoover because Smith is a Catholic." While the big-city, "wet" image of Smith brought opposition from the WCTU and Anti-Saloon League, the issue that he could not overcome was religion. Governor Sampson — who had only recently been indicted and then acquitted for taking gifts from textbook firms — took to the campaign trail for Republican Herbert Hoover, and the governor and Robsion apparently used the religious issue as their base. In a speech at Harlan, Sampson was reported to have said, "If you want to preserve the churches and continue the public schools, you will vote for Herbert Hoover, because if Governor Smith is elected he will destroy the churches and schools." When asked if reports of his talk were incorrect, he did not respond.[72]

He did not need to, for election day brought Republicans their greatest electoral victory ever. Despite Barkley's speech seconding Smith's nomination, the New Yorker had gained little Kentucky support. With lower-than-usual Democratic turnout, but high levels of Republican voting, Hoover carried 93 of the 120 counties and won by a huge margin — 558,064 (59.3 percent) to 381,070 (40.5 percent). The victors had won Kentucky by a greater margin than they did nationally. On that 177,000-vote majority, numerous Republicans rode Hoover's coattails to victory in other campaigns. In the eleven races for Congress, Republicans won nine and defeated major Democrats such as Brent Spence, Virgil Chapman, and Fred Vinson. The Kentucky *Irish American* concluded that the state's motto should be "No Catholic Need Apply" and the state's nickname should change to "dark and bigoted ground." The 1928 election had been such a disaster for Democrats that it at least briefly united them, after the fact, to oppose the Republican governor even more.[73]

Sampson's next battle took place in the highway commission, for it controlled more money and more people than any other agency of state government. Moreover, it had become the major dispenser of patronage. Those who administered the highway funds could offer not only jobs but livelihood for destitute relatives of influential men, grateful men who in turn would be expected to repay the favor. The promise of a road could be dangled before the eyes of every community, for that meant jobs for local contractors, increased business for merchants (now closer to their customers), and the hope of success for farmers who had seen perishables ruined by slow transportation. A decision on state contracts and sinecures could mean prosperity or failure for large numbers of Kentuckians who would have even fewer alternatives when the Great Depression hit. When there was little relief in the form of public employment, there was the highway department. In return it asked for only two things: just like the old bosses, it wanted people's loyalty and their votes.[74]

As election time drew nearer, both became more important. Observers noted that weeds and grass that had grown all summer now suddenly required workers. According to Thomas D. Clark, "In some states, cutting weeds along the road . . . often has more political significance than a genuine promise of reform. As a matter of fact, a good crop of carefully chosen weed-cutters . . . might well hold a balance of power in a hotly contested election." It is little wonder that those who studied the systems concluded that the highway program had become "the most politically significant function of state government."[75]

Governor Fields chose retired congressman Ben Johnson to head that department in an attempt to defeat Beckham. As part of the understanding that apparently existed with Sampson, the newly elected governor kept Johnson on in 1927. But "Flem-Flam-Flem" understood the power the commission could wield and did not trust some kind of bipartisan combine to elect another Republican. He sought to build his own political base. Increasingly by-passed in the decision making, Johnson gathered proof of his allegation of partisanship and questionable financial dealing, but saw much of the documentation go up in smoke when a fire in the Old Capitol Annex destroyed many records. Arson was suspected, but not proven. Finally, in December 1929, Sampson dismissed Johnson. That only intensified the political war.[76]

At the beginning of the 1930 session of the general assembly, Senator Allie Young presented a proposal to reorganize the highway department. As later amended, it gave the governor, lieutenant governor, and attorney general the power to make appointments to the commission. Since two of the three were Democrats, Sampson lost control. After a new governor (presumably Democratic) was selected in 1931, the bill stated, the power of appointment would rest solely with him. The *Courier-Journal* found itself allied with old enemy Sampson as it correctly criticized the bill as pure "ripper" legislation. But Democrats united enough to push the legislation through by 53-42 and 22-15 votes. Sampson vetoed the ripper, calling it "unprovoked, unsportsmanlike [!], unprogressive, unnecessary, unreasonable, unfair, unjust, undignified,

Congressman John M. Robsion *(left)* **and Governor Flem D. Sampson** *(right)* **survey the possibilities at Cumberland Falls, 10 October 1929.**

unpatriotic, destructive, spiteful, reactionary and backward." The veto was easily overridden. As then-state senator Happy Chandler later recalled: "We put Mr. Ben back in."[77]

Ben Johnson became a virtual dictator. The *Courier-Journal* said that if the chairman continued in power, the commission "will be a bold, imperious machine, manned by politicians . . . dictating policies of government, commanding the fear of the electorate that want roads"; in fact, that was exactly what Johnson sought. By 1930, some 10,000 people were employed on the roads. Overall, highway funds constituted 47.6 percent of the state's budget, and those funds were not controlled by Governor Sampson but by his opposition. He had lost another battle.[78]

It was not his last loss. Next on his list of passion-inducing issues was the Cumberland Falls question. Not yet developed, this so-called "Second Niagara" featured a "Moonbow," as well as much scenic beauty. It also provided the water force that could drive a company's utilities. Would a nature trust or a power trust dominate? Would Kentucky want to hear the roar of water or the hum of electric generators?

Sampson and fellow mountain Republican Robsion had come out in favor of "industrial expansion" years before. The governor had already pledged to support the powerful and controversial Samuel Insull and his bid to develop the site as a hydroelectric project through his Cumberland River Power Company. The company had taken options on the land and sought to get support for their power dam concept in the 1930 general assembly.[79]

A well-organized and grass-roots opposition stood against the plan. Led by Tom Wallace of the Louisville *Times*, a strong conservation movement pushed a second option. In 1927, the Kentucky-born senator from Delaware, T. Coleman duPont, had offered to buy the Cumberland Falls land and donate it to the commonwealth as a state park. One study showed that sixty-nine of seventy-three newspapers in Kentucky opposed the Sampson-Insull plan and favored the duPont offer. A large pro-conservation dinner attracted all but three legislators, and a bill soon passed which gave the state park commission the right of eminent domain so the Insull interests could be bought out. Next, the more controversial and so-called duPont Bill, which put into place the philanthropic option, came up for a vote. By 63–30 and 21–16 margins, it too passed. Stubborn to the end, Governor Sampson vetoed the action, calling it an obstruction to industrial development. With no Democrat supporting him, the veto was easily overridden in the house, but in the senate, the fight went longer, and the constitutional requirement of twenty votes was barely gained. By that one-vote margin, the veto was overridden, the duPont offer accepted, and Cumberland Falls preserved. It was significant that at a time when industrial development seemed almost the Holy Grail that all states sought, often with few thoughts as to the consequences, Kentucky followed another vision, one that valued conservation more. The question for the future would be whether the unity shown on the Falls issue could be transferred to other, similar concerns, such as forests and mining.[80]

For the present, Sampson had suffered another major defeat, one that grieved few, even in his own party. At the start of the session, the governor had called for funding for free textbooks, sterilization of the mentally impaired, and restrictions on chain stores. His program had been submerged in the highway reorganization and Falls fights, never to resurface. Instead, the legislature went its own way, ripping further gubernatorial powers — including the power to appoint members of the textbook commission — and funding additional projects — including the purchase of land for a Mammoth Cave park. It passed a revised election law, a driver's license law, and a new gross sales tax on retail stores. A furious chief executive vetoed a dozen acts; eleven times the legislature overrode him. The summary of the session was reasonably unanimous from one end of the state to the other. The Ashland *Daily Independent* indicated that no real progress had been made toward solving the state's problems, while the Owensboro *Messenger* concluded that "there has never been a governor of Kentucky so discredited, so little trusted . . . as Flem Sampson after two years of bungling manipulation of the state's public agencies." As various papers commented, Sampson had been shorn of his locks.[81]

Republicans grew increasingly powerless. In January, President Hoover appointed Kentucky Senator Sackett as ambassador to Germany. Sampson selected his ally Robsion to fill the vacancy. The congressman described as a "fire-eating fundamentalist" sought election for the rest of the term, as well as for a full term beginning in March 1931. Since Sackett's reelection chances had not been good, due in part to the deepening national Depression, that turn of events did not hurt the Republicans greatly. Democrats countered with one of those strange nominations that sometimes take place for major office. With numerous ex-governors and congressmen available, the party selected instead a rather second-level politician as the nominee.[82]

Forty-six-year-old Marvel M. Logan of Edmonson County and Bowling Green had been an L & N attorney, county judge, and state attorney general. Serving, as Sampson had at the time of his nomination, as a justice on the state's highest court, Logan was a rotund, pleasing person who was not identified with any faction or any major controversy. That was his strength, and he quietly campaigned on the issue of the national economy, trusting that to take him to victory. Robsion tried all the "r" issues — rippers, "Rum, Rome" and roads — and sought to identify the Democrats with "wet" Al Smith, Catholicism, and bosses. The *Courier-Journal*, often supporting urban Republicans, disavowed mountain leader Robsion, calling him a "thorough-going demagogue, [and] habitual practitioner of the shady arts of practical politics." That description apparently matched voter reaction, for the Democrats swept the day. In the race to fill the three-month short term, Robsion lost to Ben Williamson of Boyd County; for the six-year term he lost to Logan 336,735 to 309,182. Republican congressmen could not duplicate the victories of the Al Smith year, as Democrats won nine of the eleven seats there. The Democracy had redeemed virtually all the state's delegation to D.C. Could they do the same for the governorship?[83]

There the issue was more uncertain, for factional politics would not go away. The Republicans selected an attractive forty-two-year-old candidate, Louisville mayor William B. Harrison, and, rather true to recent form, the *Courier-Journal* went with the urban Republican. Part of the paper's reason for their action was due to what occurred in the Democratic convention. There W. B. Ardery of Paris and James Breathitt, Jr., of Hopkinsville had lost out to Ruby Laffoon of Madisonville, the candidate supported by most of the major bosses. At age sixty-two, Laffoon was considerably older than his opponent and had enjoyed a decidedly more complex career. Born in a log cabin, the Democratic nominee had worked as a messenger, then took law classes and passed the bar exam in 1890. After attorney Laffoon had represented both the Night Riders and the L & N, he sought state office in 1907. He lost that year running for state treasurer and again in a primary race for auditor four years later. Four years after that, he was defeated in the primary for the post of commonwealth's attorney. Finally, the resilient candidate won election as circuit court judge and from that position ran for governor. The portly, cigar-smoking Laffoon, bothered by a limp as a result of an early accident that left one leg an inch and a half shorter than the other, was known as a jovial, old-style orator who could stir an audience. However, he probably owed his selection more to the fact that his cousin, a minor boss named Polk Laffoon, Jr., had talked other leaders into going for Ruby. They likely saw him in much the same light as they had Fields — that he would be a candidate amenable to their controls. Like Fields, he would prove them wrong.[84]

The only real contested nomination for the Democrats had been for the position of lieutenant governor, but that would prove to be a significant fight. Rising leader Fred Vinson supported fellow eastern Kentuckian Jack Howard of Prestonsburg, while Camden, Johnson, and Klair went with the central Kentuckian, State Senator Happy Chandler. In a very tight fight that further alienated Vinson and his young opponent, the difference proved to be Micky Brennan's eventual support. Backed by the bosses, Chandler became the nominee.[85]

Laffoon and Chandler took to the campaign trail, and in the gubernatorial candidate's opening speech he set the tone for the race. The issues were "Hoover, Harrison, . . . and Hard Times" and Democrats must be elected to restore confidence. Reforms were needed in the penal institutions and in schools, Laffoon argued, and "Little Boy Blue" Harrison was not the person to do that.[86] Meanwhile, "Billy the Kid" insisted that he was indeed the man for the job. In factual, detailed, and unexciting talks, Harrison hit hard at Johnson, the highway commission, and the bipartisan combine idea. Election of Laffoon would turn over power to the bosses, just when reform was needed, he stressed. As for his opponent, Harrison concluded: "We've had in Kentucky the great pacificator, Henry Clay; the Great Emancipator, Abraham Lincoln; and now we have the great promiser, Ruby Laffoon."[87]

But promises were what people wanted in the dreary Depression days of 1931. Hoover at the national level and Sampson at the state seemed utter failures, and Republican attempts to divert attention from that simply did not work. Despite a few party defections (notably Bingham) and the presence of something less than a major candidate at the head of the ticket, the Democrats won by the largest margin since 1868. Harrison carried Louisville and some of the mountain counties, but even in eastern Kentucky the coal ones were turning Democrat. Harrison won in few other places, losing by a 446,301 (54.4 percent) to 374,239 (45.6 percent) count. Constantly competitive and successful over the past dozen years, the Republicans now faced a dark future. The Democratic faction of Beckham, Bingham, and Haly likewise looked forward with little hope, for they had been unsuccessful once more. And what of the administration of the new governor? The past two chief executives had done poorly. Could Laffoon, cast out of the same political mold, do any better, particularly in the midst of a depression? Very uncertain political prospects loomed on the horizon.[88]

Kentucky Historical Society

"Hoover presses button which starts flow of gas from Kentucky to Washington, D.C." This show of prosperity for Kentucky through Republican leadership was not enough to sway voters in 1931.

Governor Ruby Laffoon, standing behind the Democratic rooster, and Lieutenant Governor A. B. Chandler take the oath of office, administered by Chief Justice Richard P. Dietzman. J. Dan Talbott faces the camera at left.

12

Old Deal, New Deal, or Misdeal?
Politics, 1931–1939

The Laffoon Administration, 1931–1935

Some governors are fortunate. They enter office in a time of national prosperity or when state income is increasing. Such chief executives can fashion a plan of action and find funds to implement it. Even a mediocre person might show a good record of achievements in such situations. On the other hand, some governors are simply unlucky. They enter the capitol and find shortages and problems awaiting them at every turn. They have to deal with crisis after crisis, and their options are to raise money through a new source — usually higher taxes — or to cut spending drastically, or to do both and still have to pare the programs the governor sought in the heady days of the campaign. And then there are some governors who either add to their fortune or misfortune as a result of their administrative actions.

Ruby Laffoon was unlucky and made his situation worse. Facing a depression, with a drought just over, and with the coal fields in a "war," he did not have good prospects to start with; to his credit, he took some needed steps to change all that. But the coupling of economic problems and factional infighting proved too much, and some unwise decisions regarding both doomed his administration to turbulence and chaos.[1]

The new governor had two sides, which confused both friends and allies. At one instance, as at his inaugural, he could tell, with much emotion, of his dreams to be governor so he could help the people. He asked for more funds for charitable and penal institutions, for children, for roads to aid the rural poor. Yet the other Ruby Laffoon was the machine politician who listened closely to the advice of his cousin Polk Laffoon, Jr., a power in the utilities field and in the Jockey Club, and, at other times, to different bosses. Ben Johnson had given thousands of dollars in depressed times to Ruby Laffoon and was rewarded with a return to the highway commission. Johnson's son-in-law, J. Dan Talbott, served as state auditor. Billy Klair guided the governor's programs, as did Allie Young.[2]

Yet, the fragile coalition that had helped secure Laffoon's election did not long survive the stresses of dividing the spoils. A post-election meeting at

French Lick, Indiana, had left those present believing Laffoon would support the candidacy of John Y. Brown for speaker of the house. Brown was only thirty-one, the namesake of a former governor but was not related to him, and had risen from being the son of a tenant farmer to become an attorney. But as the occasion approached, Laffoon supported another candidate, supposedly because Cousin Polk had made a commitment to him. Young, Talbott, and others remained with Brown, and defeat was so clear that the governor's man never was nominated. It was not an auspicious start.[3]

Blessed with a 26 to 12 and 74 to 26 Democratic majority in the legislature, but cursed with factionalism in the ranks, Laffoon had a disastrous first session in 1932. Seeking first a 2 percent sales tax, then, when that went nowhere, a 1 percent tax, he made numerous enemies. Lieutenant Governor Happy Chandler, bosses Young, Johnson, and Talbott, and others refused to support the tax. In March a rally against the bill ended with a mob of a hundred people storming the Governor's Mansion, breaking furniture, and damaging a carpet in the process. Thanks to Senator Young's efforts, the sales tax died in the upper house. More supported were spoils bills — the Board of Charities was made partisan, the highway commission was reorganized since a Democratic governor again held the appointee reins, and the Fish and Game Commission was removed more from the control of sportsmen. Appropriations had been made with the expectation of sales tax revenue. Without that, and with the accompanying reduction of the real estate tax, the budget far exceeded revenues. Laffoon vetoed the real estate measure, cut millions from the budget (particularly in higher education) through more vetoes, and generally made few people happy. The opposition *Courier-Journal* called it "about the worst legislative session in Kentucky's history"; the Republican Lexington *Leader* suggested that the governor in less than four months had lost control of his party "and has been definitely discredited." Papers friendly to Laffoon remained discreetly silent.[4]

By the fall of 1932, the Democratic Party's bright prospects in the November elections had helped relieve the despondency following that first legislative session. With the Depression deepening, and Herbert Hoover's popularity falling as fast as the autumn temperatures, Republican wins were in doubt at all levels. A strange set of events regarding congressional seats made Democratic chances even better in Kentucky. The 1930 census figures forced a reduction in the state's number of House seats from eleven to nine. The legislature's subsequent efforts to redistrict the commonwealth were invalidated by both state and federal courts, but too late for a new plan to take effect. As a result, all candidates ran at large, with the nine receiving the most votes statewide being declared winners. Such a decision greatly favored the Democrats, who generally carried the state and were expected to do so overwhelmingly in 1932. And that is exactly what occurred. When the votes were counted, Democrats won every congressional seat, with between 573,000 to 575,000 votes per candidate, to the Republicans' totals of 389,000 to 391,000. Since geography had not been a factor, Virgil Chapman and newcomer John

Y. Brown — who normally would have been in the same congressional district — were both elected. Republicans, who generally had one or two "safe" districts, now had none, and lost every race.[5]

Democrats made a clean sweep of other major races, for incumbent Alben W. Barkley became the first Kentucky senator in forty-two years to be reelected. At the Republican convention which selected as his opponent former congressman Maurice H. Thatcher of Louisville, a minister had concluded his prayer, saying, "God Almighty is a Republican." If so, He scratched the ticket in 1932, for Hoover and the Depression dominated the campaign and Barkley won handily by a vote of 575,077 to 393,865.[6]

There were no surprises in the race for president either. A Kentuckian summed up the situation clearly: "The people here in this county will vote almost to a man, not for Roosevelt, but against Hoover. They are dazed with their problems. Many families have not had any gainful employment for two years or more. Farmers could not pay a debt last fall. The result is that they are grousing about anything and everything." Those attitudes carried over to the voting, and Franklin D. Roosevelt won 95 of the state's 120 counties, 59.1 percent of the ballots, and the popular vote by a 580,574 to 394,716 margin. The GOP lost votes in every county over the previous presidential race, and Democrats made significant gains in all urban areas and the coal fields of both western and eastern Kentucky. The once-Republican-controlled coal vote was moving out from under the owners' dominance, as labor unions began to make gains. A new Democratic coalition was emerging.[7]

With the first Democratic president in twelve years, a reelected senator, and control of all nine House seats, the Kentucky Democracy was absolutely supreme at the national levels. But in the "dark and bloody ground" of Kentucky politics, that national situation did not extend to internal party matters — as Ruby Laffoon quickly found out.

The problems had started in the 1932 general assembly when disagreements over policy matters (the sales tax) and over the division of spoils had created deep divisions among Laffoon's erstwhile supporters. Those divisions became unbreachable chasms by 1933, and the battleground was in the highway commission. The reorganization of that body by the 1932 legislature left each commissioner with a great deal of discretionary power over his little fiefdom. Then and later, that power could be used politically — "the State Highway work here is being used extensively to further the interests of the Democratic party in Pike County, even going so far as to require local contractors to consult Mr. Zack Justice before employing common laborers" — or for personal gain — "I will Pay you for your trouble [.] I will Give you $50.00 to get me on . . . and Pay you "$10.00 Per month[.] I have family to take care of and no crop to Fall Back on."[8]

The governor had rewarded Ben Johnson and some of his supporters with appointments to the commission, but the majority were staunch Laffoon allies. By a 5 to 4 vote, they began to give the governor more and more control over the highways. The district headquarters were moved from Morganfield to Laffoon's hometown of Madisonville, where the commission purchased land from the governor for $15,000. His vacant house was leased to the commission for $600 a year. By executive order Laffoon then required that all state contracts and purchases be approved by him. Johnson had three men carry highway materials to the governor; state business ground to a halt as thousands of requisitions backed up in the chief executive's office. Defeated, Laffoon modified the order. But he fought on.[9]

Nothing seemed to go Laffoon's way. Figures in 1933 showed that state government had incurred a deficit of $2 million the previous year. Faced with that and with the need to provide matching funds in order to receive certain New Deal programs, the governor called a special legislative session to begin in August. His remedy for the revenue problem — a sales tax — was still bitterly opposed by a now fairly united opposition. Ben Johnson, Allie Young, Happy Chandler, and John Y. Brown were termed by Laffoon "the most insidious lobby that ever infected the Capitol," but his words could not defeat them. Federal Relief Administrator Harry L. Hopkins spoke to the general assembly regarding relief funds. But in the end the sales tax bill was defeated in a nonpartisan vote. Hundreds of unemployed marched on the capital and called for relief; Laffoon ordered them fed and housed in state warehouses.[10]

In that atmosphere, a bitter Ruby Laffoon struck out at almost everyone. Several sources indicated that the governor had said opposition to his tax program was financed by "a bunch of New York Jews." Turning to the *Courier-Journal*, Laffoon called it "that filthy, dirty sheet," a paper that was a "menace to the good interests of Kentucky." Later, Liberty Bank, whose largest stockholder was Bingham, found itself the subject of frequent state bank examiners sent by Laffoon. The man from Madisonville concluded that "God Almighty is walking by my side today as he has walked with me through my life." The Louisville paper noted the establishment of "the New Firm of Me & God." The special session ended without sufficient funds for relief being granted.[11]

Given all the bitterness and factionalism, it would be surprising if the 1934 general assembly did anything; that it accomplished what it did was almost amazing and showed Laffoon's organizational prowess. With the legislature one-third Republican, one-third Laffoon Democrats, and one-third anti-Laffoon Democrats, deadlock seemed likely. But using the bait of roads, the governor made a deal with the minority and together the Republicans and Laffoon faction had a working majority. To deal with his enemies, Laffoon got approval for a law that "ripped" various offices from Auditor J. Dan Talbott, and another that allowed the governor to remove any appointive officer for cause. Using that "fire at will" clause, he soon removed Ben Johnson and his allies from the highway commission. The coalition in the senate stripped Lieutenant Governor Chandler of his powers there as well. It was pretty raw power politics; it was also pretty effective.[12]

In fiscal matters, the legislature increased the tax on manufactured whiskey from two to five cents per gallon, but offset that additional revenue by cutting the property tax from thirty cents to five cents per one hundred dol-

Governor Laffoon proposed a sales tax at the 1933 special legislative session. The measure went down to defeat.

lars. That meant $2.5 million less in funds, and the decision to give $250,000 to help make Mammoth Cave a national park further tightened the budget noose. To its credit, the general assembly passed significant laws regarding government and education. A reorganization bill reduced commissions and departments from sixty-nine to twenty-four in number and abolished several officers, while the fiscal system was reformed through establishment of an executive budget system and state budget officer. A Public Service Commission was created as well.[13]

The 1934 school code modernized the system in certain ways, setting up a Council on Public Higher Education, a school term of six "or more" months, and mandatory attendance to age sixteen. The bill had its negative sides as well, however, for it abolished the boards governing the two black schools and gave governance over them to the State Board of Education. White colleges and universities retained their own boards. The general assembly also provided for submission of two amendments — one to repeal state prohibition and one to allow the enactment of old age pension laws — and spent considerable time debating a nudist colony law that eventually passed. That act required a twenty-foot wall around the premises and indicated that the attorney general shall inspect "said colony . . . at such time as may be deemed necessary." Whether the state's law enforcement officer made frequent or infrequent surprise inspections is unknown.[14]

The 1934 regular session concluded with a resolution requesting the governor to call a special session to deal with the continuing fiscal problems. He soon complied, called another meeting of the general assembly in May, and began an offensive against his opponents. In a radio address, Laffoon termed the *Courier-Journal* "the Dillinger of the Press," and later cried to a cheering crowd, "To hell with Haly. . . . To hell with the *Courier-Journal*." John Y. Brown answered with attacks on the ripper bills and the bosses backing Laffoon; Chandler decried the proposed sales tax as a "millstone about the necks of the people of Kentucky"; Johnson pointed to corruption in the highway department and got a court injunction which delayed (but did not stop) his removal. But Laffoon's opposition did not have the votes. Some seventeen legislators were either on the state payroll or had a family member who was, and all were in the Laffoon pocket. The coalition with the Republicans continued as the special session opened.[15]

In a disorganized, defensive, and almost sad address to the general assembly, Governor Laffoon apologized "for talking to you in this rambling way, for I haven't had time to sleep, or eat, much less write a speech." He then called for a 3 percent sales tax, an income tax, and other measures to help the fiscal situation. The atmosphere in Frankfort grew even tenser a week later when a hundred unemployed men, calling for relief, marched on the Governor's Mansion. In response to death threats on the chief executive's life, National Guardsmen surrounded the building. While that occurred, the legislature debated. Defeated initially, the sales tax finally passed by the minimal constitutional requirements — 51 to 47 and 20 to 17. Soon after the session concluded, an exhausted governor entered a sanatorium. His health did not get much better the rest of his term, and in 1935 he had surgery for an appendicitis attack. Meanwhile, the sales tax brought forth a children's chant:

> "Hippity-hop to the toy shop
> "To buy a red balloon.
> "A penny for you, a penny for me,
> "A penny for Ruby Laffoon."

Ridiculed by the youth, suffering from poor health, under attack from his political opposition, Laffoon could at least take some satisfaction, perhaps, in the fact that he was finally defeating the factional enemies that so bedeviled him. In the congressional elections of 1934, another foe was vanquished. With redistricting in effect, incumbents John Y. Brown and Virgil Chapman were both in the same district. Laffoon supported Chapman and used levies on state officeholders to raise a reported $100,000 to finance that race, while Bingham and his friends backed Brown. In the battle of factions, Chapman won out by some 8,000 votes. But could the Laffoon victories carry over to the

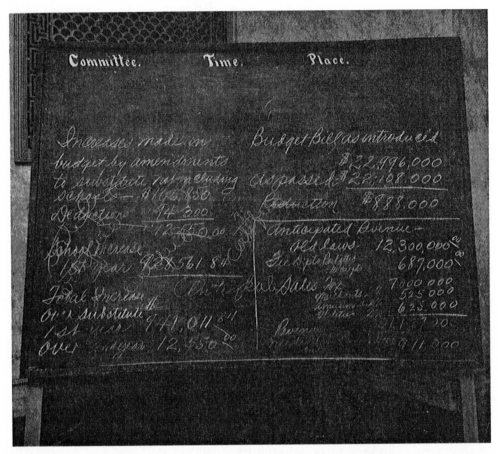

Committee.   Time.   Place.

A blackboard reflected the status of budget deliberations in the legislature at 12:45 P.M., 15 February 1935. Anticipated revenue *(lower right corner)* **included income from a 2 percent sales tax. "Increases made in budget by amendments . . ." included a school increase of $928,561.84 the first year of the budget.**

greater prize to be won in 1935, the governor's race?[16]

In control of the party machinery, the Laffoon faction ignored pleas by Barkley and President Roosevelt for an open primary and approved gubernatorial nomination through a closed party convention — the only one for Democrats in the century, after 1903. And so it appeared the opposition was again thwarted. But Kentucky's archaic constitution rose to the rescue. Under one of its provisions, whenever the governor left the boundaries of the state, he lost all powers to govern. Laffoon took such a trip, to Washington, D.C., to discuss relief measures, and Lieutenant Governor Chandler was informed by the governor's secretary that he was acting governor. Chandler talked to Talbott and Zack Justice, took out a legal pad and wrote something on it, and gave it to a *Courier-Journal* reporter. The next day, headlines told of his convening of a special legislative session for the purpose of enacting a primary law. A furious

Laffoon rushed home and proclaimed the action illegal, but the state's high-est court, by a 4–3 vote, supported the constitutionality of the call, and said it could not be reversed. Subsequently, the general assembly did pass a primary law, but the Laffoon forces added a requirement for a second runoff primary should no candidate receive a majority. The second primary was supposedly added because it would take its toll on the expected opposition candidate, the aging J.C.W. Beckham.[17]

The stage was set. Now it was time to determine who the actors were in what might become either a farce or a drama. The definite outsider was Billy Klair's candidate Frederick A. Wallis of Bourbon County. He garnered little support and was viewed more as a "spoiler" in the primary. The Laffoon faction's choice was clearcut as well, with Fred Vinson and the Louisville bosses Brennan and McLaughlin all backing Tom Rhea of Russellville.[18]

But who would represent the anti-Laffoon forces? Bingham and Haly wanted their old ally, former governor Beckham, to make one more attempt. Calling the Laffoon forces "ruffians and robbers," Bingham promised $25,000 to aid that bid. But the death of Beckham's only son in late 1934 left the family devastated and his wife strongly opposed to another race. His April decision not to run had the faction scrambling for a suitable candidate. Sometime-enemy, sometime-ally Ben Johnson, together with Dan Talbott, was already pushing Happy Chandler, and, more and more, he became appealing to Haly and Bingham as well. The newspaperman did not know Chandler personally, and Haly expressed little private confidence in him, but both concluded "he is certainly better than most of the others." The choice was made; Chandler would be the one.[19]

The newly anointed factional savior hardly hesitated, and he took his exu-berant, emotional campaign all over the state. Born in 1898 in Henderson County in west Kentucky, Albert Benjamin Chandler had seen his parents sepa-rate when he was young. Graduation from Transylvania College in Lexington, a brief stay at Harvard, some coaching, then a law degree from the University of Kentucky, were followed by a legal practice in Versailles, and then a state senate seat and the lieutenant governorship. At age thirty-seven, he stood poised to reach a major goal.[20]

But the real Chandler story was not his career; it was the man himself. Young and personable, he brought a different campaign style to the stump, one far removed from the long and flowery oratorical efforts of the past. His shorter talks might feature the candidate's singing, quoting from the Bible and Shakespeare, calling people by name in the crowd, and engaging in a verbal give-and-take with the voters. "You know that's the truth, don't you Billy-Boy Morgan?" he would cry out. His fans would answer with, "Tell it, Happy boy! Oh, tell it." Happy would respond with Horatio Alger-type sto-ries of his hard times as a youth, sing songs, and weep with emotion. As historian Charles P. Roland notes, "the gathering then began to take on a spell like those of an evangelical revival meeting." Chandler was fresh; he was fun; he was different. And in the still-dark Depression days of the 1930s, he made a tremendous impression on the voters who wanted someone new and sought a change from the old politics of despair.[21]

The issues almost took second place to the person before them. Happy would promise to redeem the state from "Ruby, Rhea, and Ruin," and would rail out endlessly at Laffoon and his candidate, calling Rhea "Sales Tax Tom." He ridiculed the bipartisan combine and bossism. Yet in the end his campaign was himself. The opposition might make jokes about his readiness "to sing a syrupy song," or to kiss a baby, or exaggerate a point, but he looked like the future when compared to the dreary campaigning of Tom Rhea.[22]

Rhea was mismatched. If he had been nominated by convention as his faction had sought, he might well have been governor, for he was a shrewd, superb organizer, and the so-called "Gray Fox of Russellville" could have gotten the Democracy behind his bid. But in a popular primary, his weaknesses were magnified. As a legislator from the era recalled later, "Tom Rhea . . . was a king maker and not a king. He had not a great deal of personality and was a very mediocre speaker running against a young fellow with lots of charisma, lots of energy." Sixty-three years old — twenty-six older than Chandler — Rhea was brother of an ex-congressman and had been Logan County sheriff, state treasurer, and highway commissioner. Once a McCreary and Beckham leader, he had moved to Laffoon and had brought in a strong young organizer, Earle Clements, to be his campaign manager. Backed by the state government employee assessments, by highway fund control, and by a strong statewide organization, he still had a good opportunity for victory. Attacking Chandler as "the Shadow Man" for boss Ben Johnson, he supported a "business-like" administration and fiscal reform. But would that be enough to overcome a popular young upstart?[23]

Rhea won the primary. Unfortunately for him, he did not win an outright majority, and a second primary would be necessary. He had gained 203,010 votes, Chandler 189,575, and several other candidates the critical 57,000. Now, in a monthlong run-off race it would be just Tom and Happy. Chandler immediately gained two advantages. First of all, boss Billy Klair, with his candidate Wallis out of the race, set up his tent in the Chandler camp. Then news of what happened in Harlan worked to the benefit of the young challenger. Governor Laffoon had sent in troops in an effort to help Rhea, since the coal operators still controlled the miners' votes, and the operators were pro-Chandler. A grand jury would indict the soldiers for interfering in the election, and, in the second primary, the Harlan vote would become even more pro-Chandler.[24]

When the results of the second primary were known, Chandler had won, with 260,573 votes to Rhea's 234,124. The two-primary strategy had backfired. It was a huge turnout with some major turnabouts. Klair's Fayette County went from 36 percent for Chandler to 63 percent; of Chandler's 26,000-vote majority, one fourth of that came from Harlan, where the Verda coal camp went 335–4 and the Yancy one 550–3 for Chandler. Those and other totals more than balanced the large vote numbers in Rhea's Logan County, where he gained 10,127 out of 10,908 votes cast, even though only 4,654 had voted there in the 1927 primary. Overall, Rhea carried the western and eastern counties, and Chandler the central and northern Kentucky ones. Viewed only a year earlier as a "well-meaning up-start playboy" who was but a 20–1 long shot to unseat the 8–5 gubernatorial favorite Tom Rhea, Chandler had kept gaining ground in the race, and, in a second heat, had overcome the odds. Now he had one more race to run in order to seize the biggest stakes — the governorship.[25]

The only obstacle in Chandler's path was the easy winner of the Republican primary, King Swope of Lexington. Like Chandler, he was young (forty-two), a native Kentuckian, an attorney, and an excellent speaker; unlike Happy, he had briefly served in Congress and was a circuit court judge at the time of his nomination. His campaign presented him as a tough, no-nonsense candidate and boasted that Swope had never recommended a parole or pardon for anyone convicted in his court. At the same time, the Republicans and some Democrats again allied, as Governor Laffoon and many highway commissioners came out against Chandler. The New York *Times* noted that defeated Democratic candidate Rhea openly supported Swope and had attacked Chandler for his alliances with Johnson, Talbott, Klair, Haly, and all "the militant forces of the Roman Catholic Church."[26]

In his opening address, Swope had earlier sought to tie Chandler to the bosses, saying that "It may be the voice of Happy, but the hands are the hands of Ben Johnson." Politics, he said, remained as the chief state problem: "Kentucky . . . has been betrayed by the kiss of glowing but violated promises. Lashed by the scorpion of factionalism and stung by the adder of partisanship, she presents a pitiful and appalling picture of political servitude and degradation." Other than a later attack on Chandler's exaggeration of his service record, Swope kept to those themes.[27]

The platforms of the two candidates really differed little. Chandler brought in enough of the Laffoon faction, including Fred Vinson and Mickey Brennan, to counter that threat. So, in the end, it came down to the candidates and in that, Happy had the advantage. Turning the Republican argument of the stern judge on its head, he capitalized on Swope's caustic, aloof, and temperamental attitude. Chandler, ever-smiling, ever the showman, portrayed his opponent as an unfeeling judge, an unmerciful dictator, a hard man, a cold king. As journalist John Ed Pearce noted later, "the staid, traditional King Swope was an aging carriage horse facing Man O' War" and the results showed that. It is doubtful any Republican could have won in 1935, given the popularity of the New Deal, but Swope also faced the burden of opposing a formidable Democrat. On a rainy day, the largest number of voters ever to cast their ballots in Kentucky gave Chandler a 556,262 to 461,104 win, as he carried 77 counties in gaining a 95,000-vote margin. The Democratic Party made some inroads in the black vote, and in the growing labor vote in the mountains, but that coalition was still developing. In the end, it was an individual's victory —

Governor Chandler signs a 1936 bill with members of the Kentucky Bankers Association looking on. A prominently displayed photo seems to invoke FDR's presence.

and he was just beginning.[28]

The Chandler Administration, 1935–1939

Chandler was firmly convinced that he was "destiny's darling," and events in the early years of his term seemed to confirm that. In one sense, he was lucky, for the New Deal programs affecting the people of Kentucky could be identified with a new "Boy Governor" as well. Politically, he also benefitted from a decline in factionalism and bossism, in part because the Laffoon faction lost strength, in part due to the absence of leaders. Death claimed some of both factions, and in the half-decade after 1935, Beckham, Bingham, Haly, Klair, Young, Brennan, and Galvin would all die. In Bingham's case, his urbane successor, son Barry, made the paper better but proved much less blatantly political than his father. But in most situations, there was no immediate replacement for the leaders, and that power vacuum allowed Chandler to build his own political base. And, finally, he helped destiny by recognizing that government was so technical that experts were needed. He brought in young professionals, like James Martin, who helped remake government, in a manner similar to the Washington, D.C., "Brain Trust" of FDR.

Chandler's administrative actions reflected the man. He could be warm and charming; he could also hold grudges and take revenge. His term contained both elements. Chandler would bring about genuine reform regarding administration and the public debt, yet, whether intentionally or not, those same actions displaced all but his political allies in government and centralized more power in the governor's hands. A combination of populist and fiscal conservative, Chandler would also guide what some called "Kentucky's Little New Deal," yet his political model was not FDR but rather the oft-time Roosevelt critic Harry F. Byrd of Virginia (who was godfather to a Chandler child). In fact, much of what Happy proposed came straight from actions taken earlier by his conservative mentor Byrd. But whatever he was, reformer or reactionary or both, Chandler certainly hesitated little and certainly made things happen.[29]

Before his first legislative session began in 1936, Chandler removed some 3,500 state government employees. He then adopted the strategy of dealing with major matters — reorganization, the budget, and revenues — through three special sessions, covering a two-and-a-half-month period. Since the general assembly could only deal with issues specified by the governor in his call to the special sessions, such sessions gave more control over deliberations to the chief executive. In the combination of the briefer-than-usual regular session and the special ones, Chandler got many of his programs passed. The Rhea primary law, for instance, was replaced with a one-primary law, mandatory for each party in every election. A needed statewide voter registration act was passed as well. To deal with overcrowded prisons, an initial appropriation for a new penitentiary at LaGrange was approved, as was a liberalization of the probation and parole system. On the law-and-order side, a Kentucky Highway Patrol was established. Two double standards were retained, for the redefined divorce law still set different rules for men and women, while the Anderson-Myer Act provided up to $175 per year for blacks to attend out-of-state colleges in order to take courses closed to them by constitutional requirements — segregation — in Kentucky. The man behind that law was newly elected Republican Charles W. Anderson, Jr., of Louisville, the first Negro to sit in the previously all-Caucasian general assembly, and the first black legislator to serve in a southern state since the turn of the century.[30]

The major achievements of the various legislative sessions, however, dealt with revenue and reorganization. Chandler and his allies opposed the sales tax Laffoon had finally pushed through, and quickly repealed that. To replace the lost revenue, taxes were imposed on whiskey, beer, and cigarettes, and new individual and corporate levies were set up as well. The repeal of statewide prohibition brought about the withdrawal of stored liquor and a one-time fiscal tax bonanza resulted for the fortunate governor. With the state debt being reduced and the budget once more balanced, Chandler had achieved the financial stability he sought.[31]

Almost every southern state went through some kind of governmental reorganization between 1927 and 1940, including Byrd's Virginia. In 1934, Ruby Laffoon had made a good start in Kentucky, one for which he got too little credit due to the partisanship of the times. But a 1933 study of state government, the Griffenhagen Report, had proposed change beyond that imposed by Laffoon's somewhat haphazard moves the next year, and now the general assembly took that further. Basically, the Reorganization Act grouped administrative functions under a smaller number of departments, reduced the authority of secondary elected officials, set up more direct lines of command, and generally placed more power in the governor's hands. Critics noted provisions which allowed the governor to remove, without cause, the members of the State Board of Education, while enemies called the law an attempt by a dictator to create "an invincible political machine." In fact, Chandler got the best of both political worlds in the Reorganization Act, for it was a needed reform which would establish the basic structure of state government for over three decades, *and* he received more political power as well. All in all, the 1936 legislative sessions had been wildly successful ones for the "Boy Governor."[32]

Chandler was not so successful in mollifying his allies after the session. Haly, Beckham, and Bingham, and their former enemies, Johnson and Talbott, had been the forces behind Chandler's rapid ascension. Each thought he could control an untested young politician. But now it was slowly becoming clear that the governor was growing stronger than his creators. Those who could take a secondary place to him would remain as allies; those who could not became enemies. The first to go was Ben Johnson. Repaid for his support by being named chairman of the highway commission, "Old Ben" began rewarding friends, usually with little appeal to Happy. But by April 1936, he began complaining of Chandler's political involvement in decision making, and a bitter "Boss Ben" later released a letter in which he called the governor "an official corruptionist." In less than eight months, Johnson had gone from key advisor to bitter outsider, as he rejected a lesser appointment on a reorganized commission.[33]

But there was more to the story than just a disagreement between two powerful politicians. Johnson's son-in-law Dan Talbott served as insurance commissioner and had become Chandler's key advisor. As the chief patronage man and "unseen governor," Talbott wielded great power, which could have worked to his father-in-law's benefit. But nearly four years earlier, Johnson had written his daughter's husband that "Henceforth I shall have nothing whatever to do with you," and time had only partially healed the deep wounds. They were reopened in July 1936, when Johnson wrote a Catholic priest about Talbott's "wild infatuation" with another woman, a charge that his son-in-law denied. Whether true or false, something — the rumors, or just power politics — created a rift that further separated the two men. Months earlier, Talbott had already turned to Johnson's old enemies, met with Haly, and, as Barry

Bingham wrote, "they are working out a plan whereby Ben Johnson can be dropped out . . . and Dan Talbott is right with them on that." Johnson's king-making days soon ended.[34]

Ironically, with Robert Worth Bingham's and Percy Haly's deaths by 1937, the other part of Chandler's ring of support was gone as well. Talbott reported to the governor in 1937 how he had met with Barry Bingham, had "criticized his editors" to him, and had said that further "insulting" attacks would be viewed by the administration "as coming from an enemy and not a friend." While the *Courier-Journal* remained in the Chandler camp through 1937, it soon would turn away as well.[35]

The number of Chandler allies-turned-enemy grew by one as a result of the 1936 U.S. Senate race. Incumbent Democrat M. M. Logan was widely viewed as vulnerable, and Chandler and his then-loyal *Courier-Journal* both backed their old friend J. C. W. Beckham as the challenger. To John Y. Brown, however, that action was a betrayal, for he clearly believed that in exchange for his support in the governor's race in 1935, Chandler had promised to back him in the 1936 Senate contest. Ambitious and angry, Brown entered the race, thus dividing the anti-Logan vote and incurring the wrath of the Binghams, who called him "stubborn and foolish." Nevertheless, Brown played the role of spoiler well, as Logan defeated both him and Beckham in what was the former governor's last race. Brown became a bitter and long-time opponent of Chandler. Whether by circumstances or political action, Happy had shed himself of those who had sought to control him and had become stronger than they. He was his own man — but at what future political cost?[36]

Such divisions hardly caused the Democratic Party to blink before the Republican challenge in the fall 1936 elections. Senator Logan handily defeated former Progressive and now Louisville Republican leader Robert H. Lucas, by a 539,968 to 365,850 count. Democratic congressmen easily won eight of the nine seats, and widely popular Franklin D. Roosevelt carried 86 counties in receiving 58.4 percent of the vote. The incumbent president's 541,944 to 369,702 victory showed the changing coalitions of the party. Once rural-based, the Democrats had carried all the commonwealth's major urban areas; once a minority in the eastern mountains, the party now carried a majority (17 of 32) of the counties, chiefly due to the labor vote; once a "white man's party," the Democracy won a majority of the votes in the black wards of Louisville. The transformation was not yet complete, for the black vote would remain divided for years to come. But increasingly the Republicans were being reduced to some wealthy urban conservatives, some rural mountain farmers, and little else. Delighted Democrats saw only continued political victories on the political horizon.[37]

The rest of Chandler's legislative actions seemed anticlimactic following the great changes of 1936. In a twenty-day special session that started on 23 December 1936, then in a regular session in 1938, followed by two more special sessions that went into late May, the accomplishments were limited.[38] Not a great deal of attention was paid to such legislative doings, for the state was

Kentucky Historical Society

Old pro Senator Alben Barkley serves burgoo at a Jessamine County political rally.

instead watching with fascination as a battle of political giants unfolded. In 1938 incumbent Senator Barkley faced reelection, and he was backed by the formidable combination of the federal administration generally and President Roosevelt personally. Kentucky, in fact, had not had such a place of political prominence in Washington for two decades. Early on, FDR had appointed Robert W. Bingham ambassador to the Court of St. James's, and he served four years in England before his death. Barkley himself became Senate majority leader in 1938; at the Supreme Court native Kentuckians Louis D. Brandeis and James C. McReynolds were joined by Stanley Reed of Maysville. More behind the scenes, presidential secretary Marvin McIntyre and rising-star Edward F. Prichard, Jr., of Paris were key advisors, while Fred Vinson gained influence as the years passed. To oppose a man supported by such a bloc of powerful figures seemed suicidal.[39]

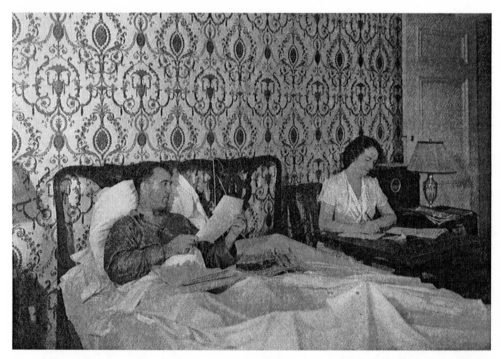

Kentucky Historical Society

Governor Chandler was shown in bed at the Governor's Mansion on 26 July 1938, following his claim that he had been poisoned.

But Happy Chandler had overcome great odds before. Convinced that he was destined to be president, perhaps believing himself almost invincible following his string of successes, certainly confident that he could out-campaign "Old Alben," Chandler took on the sixty-year-old incumbent and announced his candidacy in February. The young governor had tried to avoid such a confrontation, for he had asked Roosevelt to appoint the other senator, M. M. Logan, to a vacant Supreme Court position, which would have allowed Chandler to take that Senate seat. But the president had followed Barkley's recommendation instead and had appointed Reed to the court. Chandler, as one journalist wrote, "likes to run for office, but doesn't care much for serving in it." In fact, he would be absent from the state 20 percent of the days he served as governor. Impatient, Chandler could not wait any longer on destiny. He entered the fray.[40]

Chandler ran on his record as governor and on his personality. He noted achievements such as governmental reorganization, debt reduction, and old-age assistance, and presented Barkley as an aging, outdated politico who had done little. Singing "Sonny Boy" and shaking hands with seemingly everyone, the colorful Chandler made the race one all America watched. Columnist Joseph Alsop called Happy "a political Holy Roller, religiously convinced that . . . he can set the whole state to speaking in tongues." He continued: "If you don't like extroverts, Chandler would send you shuddering into a dark closet, but they seem to admire extroverts in Kentucky. The people went wild over him." *Time* pictured Chandler as "a brassy colt" challenging Barkley, "the plodding champion."[41]

Political thoroughbred that he was, Barkley knew he faced a challenge and put everything into his stretch run. He called out a variety of allies, ranging from Tom Rhea and Earle Clements of the old Laffoon faction to the Louisville bosses, to Fred Vinson and John Y. Brown, to the *Courier-Journal*. Barkley also belied Chandler's charge that he was old and tired by matching Chandler's energy on the election trail. Traveling an average of 4,500 miles a week, making dozens of speeches, Barkley was, in his own way, as effective a campaigner as Happy. One July incident pointed that out clearly. The Chandler campaign claimed an illness that had kept the governor from electioneering for several days was the result of a deliberate poisoning of some water, indirectly suggesting that someone in the Barkley camp was behind it all. Few took the charge seriously, and the man called "Old Alben" made it a centerpiece of his talks. Indicating he would place an "ice water guard" in his camp, Barkley would pause in the middle of a talk, start to take a drink of water, then stop, eye the glass warily, and laughingly put it aside. The crowd roared. The whole matter did make Chandler seem more affected by the long, rigorous race than the older Barkley.[42]

In those speeches, Barkley would invoke the aid of two entities that he considered to have about equal support in Kentucky — God and FDR. And if he could not conclusively show that the first was on his side, he could clearly claim the second. President Roosevelt came to the commonwealth in July to campaign for Barkley's reelection, for two reasons. First of all, Barkley was his hand-picked choice for majority leader, and repudiation of him would be a defeat for the administration. But more than that, Roosevelt also saw Chandler as a potential challenger, a populist, Huey Long-type of Democrat who did not support the New Deal with much enthusiasm. At Latonia Race Track, Roosevelt diplomatically said Chandler would make a good senator, but made it clear that his choice was Barkley — "that son of Kentucky of whom the whole nation is proud." The president repeated the message to huge crowds in a railroad swing across the state. Chandler's challenge was in trouble.[43]

Other than the question of youth versus experience, the only real election issue centered around tactics. There was little question that Chandler would use his administration's powers to support a candidate — in this case, himself — for virtually every twentieth-century governor had done that. State funds printed pro-Chandler material; state control of old-age pension checks was used by the governor; employee assessments were done to raise funds; road projects were initiated and people hired to help the campaign. The real question was whether federal workers and the recipients of the vast network of federal aid would be asked to do the same for Barkley. For the first time there was a large force available to counter the state one. Would Roosevelt, Barkley, and the WPA use that power?[44]

Special Collections & Archives, Eastern Kentucky University

The Keen Johnson Building, on the campus of Eastern Kentucky University, survives as an impressive example of WPA construction.

Years later, Barkley wrote that charges of WPA involvement in the 1938 Senate race were "untrue"; at the time, the state administrator of the Works Progress Administration indicated, "there is not a semblance of truth in this charge." There was. George H. Goodman, head of the WPA in Kentucky, was a Barkley friend, and his files show that federal workers did surveys on how the senator was doing in each county. WPA employees were asked to vote for Barkley; their offices had his campaign materials in them. A district director reported on various county situations with notations such as "the WPA is giving 100% cooperation." He also noted the Chandler administration's use of highway and old-age funds for similar purposes.[45]

Newspaper reporter Thomas L. Stokes won a Pulitzer Prize for a series that concluded that "the WPA . . . was deep in politics" in Kentucky. Later a Senate committee found that federal officials, though often not in their official capacity, worked hard for Barkley. One person raised $24,000 from federal employees. Such findings would lead to congressional passage of the Hatch

Act, restricting such involvement in the future. The same investigating committee also found, however, that Chandler's allies had raised $10,000 from state employees. It was clear that no one's hands were free of guilt. Involved in a desperate fight, each side used whatever resources it could command.[46]

In the end, the state and federal forces nullified each other. Chandler's gamble that his campaigning could overcome Barkley's lead was negated by the incumbent's own strong canvass. With those two key advantages taken away, Chandler was left defenseless before the appeals of a popular president, a popular incumbent, and a popular New Deal. He lost the primary by a large margin, 294,391 to 223,149. Barkley won Louisville, the rural areas, the labor vote, and west Kentucky by sizeable majorities, carrying 74 of the 120 counties. Such a loss was hard for the until-then-unbeaten Chandler to take, and he blamed it on the WPA influence. He could not accept that he had been beaten; privately, to his dying day, he would remain very bitter toward both Barkley and Roosevelt. They were more popular than he was; they had defeated destiny.[47]

Or had they? Almost providentially for Chandler, the other Kentucky senator, M. M. Logan, suddenly died on 3 October 1939, and Happy, through a prearranged agreement, resigned the governorship and was immediately appointed U. S. senator by new governor Keen Johnson. He had become senator after all, only nine months later than had he defeated Barkley. As he left the governorship, Chandler could look back with pride on major accomplishments. At the same time his repudiation of Brown in 1936, his break with the Binghams, his opposition to Barkley in 1938, his coolness to Roosevelt all had turned away potential allies. Chandler's personal style of politics had transcended party, and thus while he had had the opportunity to unite the Democratic factions, in a transitional time he had instead divided the party once again. That curse of a new factionalism would remain with the Democrats for decades more.[48]

The magazine rack at Frankfort Office Equipment was stocked to fill Kentuckians's thirst for crime detection, "true stories," movie stars, comic books, and romance in 1940.

13

Wartime Politics, 1940–1950

The Johnson Administration, 1939–1943

The new chief executive's first order of business was to get reelected for a full term. The last person in such a situation, James D. Black, had failed in that task and had served a grand total of seven months as governor. Keen Johnson did not want history to repeat itself.

In many ways, Johnson varied from the typical political candidate of his generation, particularly in his background in journalism. Born in 1896 in Lyon County, Johnson was the son of a circuit-riding Methodist preacher, had served in World War I, and, after college, had become editor of the Richmond *Daily Register* in 1925. From that post, he had been elected lieutenant governor a decade later.[1]

For a time, Johnson had been the political ugly duckling in the Chandler administration, for he was not one of them, and in fact had been on the other side. In the 1927 primary he had favored Crowe over Chandler friend Beckham. Then in 1935, Johnson had been in the Rhea faction opposing Chandler. The vagaries of the electorate had carried the two men from different factions — Chandler and Johnson — into office together, and an uneasy truce had existed. But Johnson worked closely with Dan Talbott, mended political fences, and by 1939, when no strong Chandlerite seemed a candidate, gained Happy's support in the primary. Former factional enemies Chandler and Johnson joined in a strange alliance brought about by confused circumstances.[2]

Chandler's decision was made much easier when it became clear who the other major Democratic challenger would be. Avowed administration critic John Y. Brown's entry into the race, and support of him by Chandler enemies Laffoon, Rhea, Clements, and Barkley, brought out the full power of the Chandler forces for Johnson. Backed by John L. Lewis and the United Mine Workers and with the aid of a grateful Barkley (whom Brown had aided in the 1938 Senate race), Brown made a strong bid. But when the August primary rolled around, it was not enough. Brown carried Barkley's west Kentucky and the labor-oriented eastern mountains, but could not do the same in the urban centers, nor in Chandler's Bluegrass strongholds. With over a 33,000-vote margin, Keen Johnson won the nomination.[3]

Opposing him in the general election was a familiar face, 1935 loser King Swope. In the Republican primary political boss Galvin had joined with some young Republicans in an attempt to bring fresh candidates to the forefront. Newcomer John Sherman Cooper of Pulaski County had too much to overcome, however, and lost by a 121,297 to 73,305 margin. Mountain Republicans Robsion and Sampson, together with Louisville leader Jouett Ross Todd, had brought Swope to the forefront once more. But it was all to little avail. The Republican's attacks on "excessive spending" were matched by Johnson's promises to be "a saving, thrifty, frugal governor." Swope's call for a black college in west Kentucky was an attempt to keep the old Republican coalition together, but that faltered before continued New Deal programs that aided blacks as well. Johnson countered with a presentation of American peace — with war breaking out in Europe — and prosperity — in contrast to the Republican years: "homes are happy; fear is a stranger; children laugh." He pointed to the popularity of the state and national administrations and warned of changing leaders with a war raging. Swope could not match that appeal. Though there was a much lower voter turnout than four years earlier, Swope lost by a larger margin, one of over 100,000. Johnson's 460,834 (56.5 percent) to 354,704 (43.5 percent) win came from carrying two of every three counties and all urban areas except the Republican's hometown. Johnson had reached one goal — retention of the governorship. Now he could turn to the business of governing.[4]

Given the factional and party turmoil and infighting that had characterized recent administrations, Johnson's initially seemed like a sea of calm amid post-political storms. The governor's chief goal seemed to be the operation of an economical government, and he met that goal. On a personal level, he typed many of his own letters; administratively he stressed thrift in Frankfort, and by 1942 the last of the state's guaranteed debt, as expressed in warrants, was paid off. But the tight budgets and stress on frugality did not satisfy all of his party, some of whom saw Johnson as parsimonious: "Old Keen," said one, "frugaled here and he frugaled there till he damn near frugaled us to death."[5]

In another sense, the relative calm hurt Johnson, for the past factional fight had provided constant copy for the press and had kept political leaders busy. Now, Johnson's ambitious attorney general used his office to publicize his governmental concerns (and, not coincidentally, to gain from the publicity), while political correspondents such as Howard Henderson of the *Courier-Journal* wrote various exposés, including a significant one regarding laundry contracts. It is doubtful whether Johnson's administration had any more political scandal than others, but the publicity made it appear that way. The press was not kind to one of their own.[6]

Johnson's first legislative session, in 1940, amended numerous acts and, in one statute, repealed a large number of obsolete laws, as recommended by a State Bar Association Committee. Otherwise its record was rather typical. One measure provided pensions for justices of the highest court; another provided funds to make an earlier-authorized teacher retirement plan finally op-

Governor Johnson *(right)* appeared at the opening of a Western Union line for Eastern Airlines in 1940.

erational; a third devoted $1 million more each year for old-age assistance. Soil Conservation Districts were established, a Kentucky Aeronautics Commission and a Farm Tenancy Commission created, and the sale of "cannabis" prohibited. Although Johnson took a much lower-key approach to the general assembly than did Chandler, it basically followed his lead entirely. The result was a moderately successful, quietly uneventful session. It matched the temper of the times and of the governor.[7]

Kentuckians appeared more interested in the upcoming presidential race than any legislative assembly. The question of Roosevelt's running for a third term brought diverse opinions. One Newport woman explained why she supported that unheard-of step: "I think he can get in, because he and the party have helped many people and they are not going to forget it." Others, however, saw Roosevelt's decision to seek another term in decidedly more negative terms. The fact that Republican challenger Wendell Willkie's brother Fred was a leading Kentucky distiller added still another element to the blend.

But with memories of the New Deal and with the shadows of war hanging over them, Kentuckians did not repudiate FDR and gave him a vote greater than the national average. His 557,322 (57.4 percent) votes overwhelmed Willkie's 410,384 (42.3 percent). Once again, the president's party won eight of the nine congressional seats. Democrats remained in the ascendancy.[8]

The next year, 1941, brought Pearl Harbor and war. Thus, when the general assembly met in its regular session less than a month later, attention was understandably more focused on the war than on legislation. A State Defense Council was established, "Special Police" were authorized to guard crucial locations, and all national holiday observances, except three, were suspended for the duration of the conflict. In non-wartime acts, the almost faction-free legislature — which was firmly controlled by the governor — passed a Tennessee Valley Authority enabling bill and allowed for submission to the voters of a constitutional amendment which would void the existing $5,000 limit on governmental salaries. A special session enacted the first significant legislative redistricting in half a century. Ironically, in the midst of war, Kentucky had one of its quietest and most conflict-free sessions.[9]

But the state was not yet free of internecine politics, as the 1942 Senate race showed. Incumbent Chandler expected no primary opposition, for all the major political figures had lined up behind him. Then, just before the deadline, John Y. Brown filed for the office, despite the fact that he had little organization or backing. That State Senator Earle Clements served as Brown's campaign manager solidified the break between Clements and Chandler; Clements's skills and Brown's sharp oratory meant that the underdog would wage at least an interesting campaign. In fact, Brown discovered a lively issue, for Chandler had accepted a gift of a sixty-foot swimming pool from a contractor and an oil company executive. While that in itself could bring out Brown attacks, the issue intensified since construction had started after the War Production Board had ordered a halt to non-war-related building. Although the board later stated that the project did not violate their orders, Brown ads cried out: "For others, blood, sweat and tears. For a U. S. Senator a free steel-girded swimming pool." The Republican Lexington *Leader* noted the incumbent's presence on the Military Affairs Committee and one donor's wartime contracts, and called it all "highly improper." The *Courier-Journal* termed Chandler's acceptance of the pool "a stupid and improper performance." The pool matter proved a good issue for Brown, but he had little else — no organization, scant political support, few allies. As in his 1936 Senate race, Brown seemed as interested in attacking Chandler as he did in winning the election. To the surprise of few, Chandler won handily; his challenger garnered but 28 percent of the ballots. Still, it was a Pyrrhic victory for the Democracy, for the party bitterness, hidden for a time, now would grow once it reappeared publicly.[10]

That fact was clearly evident the next year, during the 1943 governor's race. There were signs warning the Democrats that it might require a united party to win. In Chandler's general-election Senate race versus a virtual un-

FOR OTHERS
BLOOD, TOIL, SWEAT AND TEARS
FOR A U. S. SENATOR
A FREE STEEL-GIRDED SWIMMING POOL

THERE'S FUN AT CHANDLER'S STEEL SUPPORTED PLUNGE . . . . BUT
KENTUCKIANS DIE FOR LACK OF STEEL ON FAR-FLUNG BATTLEFIELDS.

THE FACTS— On May 1, four months and twenty-four days after Pearl Harbor, Ben H. Collings started the construction of a swimming pool in Senator A. B. Chandler's backyard at Versailles.

A standard pool of this type requires no less than 9,000 pounds of steel, in addition to incidental tubing and brass accessories.

Steel, as well as these incidental metals, is an urgent war-time need. Most people can't get it, because the government needs it so much.

Mr. Collings is a Louisville war contractor, who has been and is engaged on big contracts.

Senator Chandler is a member of the Senate Military Affairs Committee, which passes on legislation for the department that authorizes war contracts.

Mr. Collings and Senator Chandler agree that the pool was a personal gift to the senator, a token of friendship for which, incidentally, another citizen would have had to pay about $5,000.00.

THE BACKGROUND—All of us are being called upon to sacrifice these days. We donate our scrap metal. We bring in our scrap rubber. We buy war bonds. Some have lost their businesses and some their jobs in the face of national necessity. Many have sons in the armed services, in camps here and far across the waters. Some of these sons are "missing in action." Some of them we shall never see again.

THE QUESTIONS— What then of one who chisels on the national effort?

What of a high official who uses steel for fun, while for want of it the blood of Kentucky boys stains foreign shores and the oceans in between?

What of a senator, in this supreme and tragic hour, who accepts a costly present from a man whom he is in position to favor?

THE CONCLUSION— There is just one issue in this election. Just one issue in America. Just one issue in the world.

With Americans, with fathers and mothers and wives and sisters and brothers and sweethearts of men who are offering their lives for our freedom at stations all around the globe, that issue cannot be political or partisan. It is all-American. It is freedom. It is life. It is victory for those principles without which all patriots would choose to be dead.

No one reluctant to sacrifice, no one indifferent to the common burden of effort and hardship and anxiety and grief, no one who puts personal pleasure above national need has a place in America today—and least of all does such a one have a place in the high ranks of government.

EXPLANATION—It is out of these convictions that John Young Brown has become a candidate for the Democratic nomination to the United States Senate. We invite support, not for him but for a sentiment, for a cause to which Americans have pledged their lives, their fortunes and their sacred honor.

★

VOTE FOR JOHN YOUNG BROWN!

[THIS ADVERTISEMENT PAID FOR BY A GROUP OF FARMERS WHO RECALL THAT JOHN YOUNG BROWN, AS CONGRESSMAN-AT-LARGE FROM THE STATE IN 1933-1934, WAS ONE OF THE FIRST SUPPORTERS OF PRESIDENT ROOSEVELT IN HIS AGRICULTURAL PROGRAM.]

Kentucky Historical Society

John Young Brown's ad attacked Chandler, claiming "There's fun at Chandler's steel supported plunge. . . . but Kentuckians die for lack of steel on far-flung battlefields."

known Republican, Richard J. Colbert, the incumbent had won by over 40,000 votes, but that was smaller than expected. Moreover, wartime inflation and Governor Johnson's tight fiscal policies left several groups, particularly teachers and government employees, suffering financially. The legislative redistricting bill had caused several rural areas to lose seats in the general assembly, and blame for that unfairly fell on the Johnson administration as well. The vitriolic, muckraking attacks of the governor's own attorney general, coupled with unfavorable newspaper stories, made it appear that corruption and scandal were more a part of the Johnson years than they in fact were. None of that boded well for the Democrats, but they had not lost a governor's race in twelve years, after all. If nothing else, the party expected the shadow of FDR would hide their blemishes and allow victory.[11]

They would need that, for the party was clearly divided in the primary. Johnson's lieutenant governor, Rodes K. Myers of Bowling Green, had broken with the administration and stood in opposition, but had only secondary support. More of a challenger was Ben Kilgore of Franklin. With aid from the *Courier-Journal*, and strong ties to the Rural Electric Association and to the Farm Bureau (where he had been executive secretary), Kilgore had powerful blocs on his side. Both Myers and Kilgore also had potent opposition, chiefly the administration of Keen Johnson. The governor in a scourging speech called Kilgore a carpetbagger from North Carolina, "a political adventurer, and a phony farmer," while ridiculing Myers's whole campaign. Johnson's support made the difference in the primary: both Myers and Kilgore lost.[12]

Democratic hopes for victory now lay with the winner, J. Lyter Donaldson of Carrollton. Attorney, bank president, and former chairman of the highway commission, the nominee had served as Johnson's campaign manager and was the governor's obvious choice. That also meant that he would be identified with the administration and would have to defend it as if it were his own. The nominee for lieutenant governor, William H. May of Prestonsburg – a congressman's nephew and later a major behind-the-scenes politico – represented a different faction, and that did not help. Nor did the fact that no one on the Democratic ticket came from the party's stronghold of west Kentucky. Donaldson had a hard fight ahead.[13]

In opposition stood a tall, white-haired, sixty-three-year-old former state court of appeals judge. Born in Ohio with an ex-Union soldier as father, Simeon Willis had come to Kentucky as a boy, had taught school, then had become a respected attorney in Ashland on the Ohio River. He had experienced various successes and failures in politics and had not been in office for a decade. That would prove a strength, for he was a fresh figure, with little of a political track record to hinder him. On the stump, Willis presented calm, well-reasoned talks, in the main, as he stressed three themes. First, he dealt with the question of changing parties in wartime, and, second, sought to show that such a transformation was needed due to the "bossism" of the incumbents: "Mr. Donaldson professes to fear the psychological effect of my election upon the successful prosecution of the war. . . . What Mr. Donaldson really fears is the devastating effect of my election upon his political machine." By arguing that soldiers must return to find a better state than the one they left, Willis negated, in part at least, the wartime question. But it was his third theme that attracted most attention. The Republican took the familiar path for state politicians in advocating tax relief, and went one step further, calling for a total repeal of the income tax. The *Courier-Journal*, while praising Willis's "thoughtful and well-rounded program," termed his advocacy for repeal "weird unreality."[14]

Donaldson, to his credit, did not try to match that promise and frankly said that government could not run as it should if such a repeal took place. Trying to turn attention to national matters, the Democrat stressed instead the past history of the "reactionary" Republicans following World War I and called for Democratic leadership to win the peace in the Second World War. Like Willis, he supported more funds for roads, education, and old-age assistance. And, like Willis, he failed to generate great enthusiasm. It was a quiet race, more like the two attorneys arguing their briefs before the electorate. In particular, Donaldson was perceived to be running a "very leisurely," almost lackadaisical, campaign, as if his party was invincible.[15]

It was not. The official returns gave Simeon Willis over an 8,000-vote majority and a 279,144 to 270,525 win. The combination of his personality and judicial approach with his attacks on the so-called Democratic machine had been a factor, obviously, but the income tax issue may have been even more significant. Yet at another level the victory owed just as much to two other matters. Willis had stopped Democratic inroads into the black vote, particularly in Louisville, and had regained many of those ballots. At the same time, his campaign had benefitted from Democratic factionalism. Senator Chandler had little enthusiasm for Johnson's man Donaldson and his forces had not been particularly active for the party. The Democratic attorney general even wrote Willis, telling him that if he attacked "the state machine," he could win: "I won't cry a bit if you succeed." In the end, then, no one thing defeated Donaldson, but rather a whole series of them — Willis's personality, the Democratic divisions, apathy, Donaldson's weak campaigning, unrest in the coal fields, the income tax issue, the black vote, and the corruption issue. Each took some normally Democratic votes away. Together they brought what surprised Democrats had not expected — a Republican as governor.[16]

The Willis Administration, 1943–1947

The new administration took office on 7 December 1943. Outgoing Governor Johnson in his witty farewell address noted the fact that it was the second anniversary of Pearl Harbor:

> The Republicans today drive the Democrats from the state Capitol just as the Japs made Pearl Harbor untenable. . . . The brave defenders of Pearl Harbor were not expecting such a cowardly blow. . . . But we Democrats knew that

a state of political warfare existed between us and the Republicans. We even knew the zero hour. It was to be 6 A.M. on November 2. . . .

Then came the dawn! Came the attack! And what an attack! Swarms of well-armed Kentuckians quickly mounted the offensive against us in every front. Our men fought bravely. . . .

But still the enemy pressed forward. He brought up fresh reserves at unexpected intervals. He was out to beat the Democrats. And beat us he did.

Johnson then noted that his party's was but a "temporary exodus" and warned his successor: "In Kentucky we swear in a governor and then start swearing at him."[17]

The Democratic counterattack started immediately. Republican election successes had not extended to the legislature, which remained Democratic by 56–44 and 23–15 margins. Moreover, two powerful rising politicians — Clements and Harry Lee Waterfield — would lead each house, and each man sought to use his position as a steppingstone to the governor's mansion. Nor could Willis count on a united Republican Party to back him, for his lieutenant governor, attorney general, and superintendent of public instruction all would have public disagreements with the chief executive. The governor's hesitancy to "clean house," particularly with the wartime shortages of experienced people, alienated other Republicans who sought more spoils in office. And on top of all that, Willis was serving with wartime restrictions and limitations all around him. Prospects were not promising.[18]

The problems became quickly apparent. In a strict party vote the senate stripped Lieutenant Governor Kenneth Tuggle of his powers. Then the fight over the budget became so acrimonious that the matter had to be decided by special session. Despite that, accomplishments did occur. The corrupt practices act was strengthened, a Tuberculous Sanatoria Commission was created to plan TB hospitals, and some decentralization of agencies took place. Willis had backed off his income tax stance, indicating that conditions were not yet favorable for that, and an attempt to repeal the tax failed anyway. Also not gaining passage was a bill allowing blacks to attend previously all-white professional schools. That measure passed the house, but failed in the senate.[19]

But the session ended in stalemate, without an enacted budget. Finally, two months later, the governor called a special session to deal only with educational items in the budget. Once together, the legislators prepared a full budget, similar to the earlier Democratic version. Republican leaders called on Willis to accept the results; he refused but continued the discussion. At issue was whether the governor or the legislature would control what appeared to be a sizable budget surplus. Winning that point, the governor forged a compromise with the legislature and a $66-million budget was passed. But that action was probably invalid, since it had not been part of the original call to the session, so a second session was immediately called. Finally, by 16 June 1944, Kentucky had a budget, one that provided new funds for schools, charitable institutions, and the needy. Democrats had not let Willis be as fiscally conservative as he wanted; the governor had not let his opposition spend as

Kentucky Historical Society

Governor Willis supported disabled American veterans by participating in the Forget-Me-Not Sale, 1946.

freely as they sought. The result was a generally good budget that showed that conflict could be resolved positively for the commonwealth.[20]

The fall 1944 elections were so predictable that few new political wounds were opened, for a change. Up for reelection, Senate Majority Leader Barkley had proved against Chandler six years earlier that he was virtually unbeatable in Kentucky, and his Republican opposition, James Park of Lexington, became the most recent sacrificial electoral lamb. Barkley won with 464,053 votes

(54.8 percent) to Park's 380,425 (44.9 percent). At the presidential level, an equally unbeatable candidate — FDR — sought a fourth term, this time against New Yorker Thomas E. Dewey. One question would be how precincts with a heavy black registration would go. The year before, Willis had easily outdistanced Donaldson in Louisville in those wards. Now, in 1944, the trend reversed once again, and areas that had given the Republican candidate a 1,758-vote majority in 1943 gave Roosevelt a 2,688 margin a year later. Overall, Roosevelt and Dewey evenly divided the black ballot in Louisville. That added vote proved helpful, for the president received his lowest totals ever from the commonwealth. However, he still won by over 80,000 votes, with 472,589 (54.5 percent) to 392,448 (45.2 percent) for Dewey. Election of eight Democrats — including newly elected Earle Clements — out of nine congressional seats continued the Democratic sweep of presidential elections under Roosevelt. The Willis victory a year earlier seemed more and more a personal win, an aberration, rather than a trend to Republicans.[21]

The year between legislative sessions is normally a quiet one for the governor. However, 1945 proved an exception. The state's prosecution of the Southern Pacific Railroad, which for tax purposes had its headquarters (but no rails) in Kentucky, continued and would end the next year with a $4-million payment of back taxes on bonds. While the commonwealth gained unexpected funds, the company soon moved its headquarters elsewhere. In April, the governor called another special session to deal with the increased funding needs of the public assistance program. Fortunately, revenues were 7 percent higher than expected, and a ready surplus existed to fund that need. August saw the end of World War II and the start of the process of postwar adjustment. Then, effective 1 November 1945, Senator Chandler resigned his post to serve as commissioner of baseball. Governor Willis appointed William A. Stanfill of Hazard to serve until the next general election — a year away — and since Stanfill would not seek to win election for the two additional years remaining in Chandler's term, candidates quickly began preparing for the open Senate seat available in 1946. Chandler's resignation also removed him further from a place of influence in state politics, a void which would allow one of his enemies to build his own powerful faction.[22]

With the Senate election in the fall, and the governor's race the next year, the 1946 legislative session seemed as much a setting for political deal-making for the future as it was for bill-drafting. Minor contests took on more meaning as a result. In the selection of the Democratic floor leader in the house, forces opposing John Y. Brown — who was expected to run for the U.S. Senate — caused his defeat for floor leader by one vote. In the state senate, the Clements camp more successfully kept the control there by electing Richard P. Moloney of Lexington to the same post. The Democratic factions were solidifying their positions. Governor Willis, with even fewer Republicans in the legislature than two years earlier, requested repeal of the income tax, but his own party was split on that issue, and the question lost 36–60 in a parliamentary vote. By session's end, the mine safety laws were improved and better funded, the permissible tax rate for schools was raised, black education was given significant financial increases, the concealed weapons law was strengthened, and a call for a new constitution was approved for submission to the voters. The budget as enacted was based on several new sources of income as a result of the war's end (taxes on new automobiles, for instance), and was a great deal larger. Even at that, a surplus of more than $18 million existed near the end of Willis' term. The state's financial outlook seemed promising.[23]

Both parties claimed credit for the constructive aspects of the session; both had high hopes of winning the 1946 Senate race as well. Democrats, who had controlled both Senate seats for fifteen years, did not bring forth as many strong candidates as had been expected. Some of the young hopefuls still were tied to Washington, while others, such as Clements and Waterfield, preferred to focus on the governorship. As a result, John Y. Brown was the best known of the Democratic possibilities, but he carried with him the stigma of a string of defeats, ranging from the congressional race, to two tries for the Senate, to, only recently, the floor leader fight. He did have labor support and Barkley backing; he also had, as usual, opposition from the *Courier-Journal* and Chandler. Brown's chief challenge came from Philip A. Ardery of Paris, a young attorney from an old Kentucky family, but a man without a great deal of political experience and only recently returned from the war. In a light turnout, Brown became the Democratic nominee by a margin of nearly 13,000 votes.[24]

Republican hopes rested on another war veteran, John Sherman Cooper of Somerset. He was both a typical and an atypical Kentucky politician. In one sense Cooper's road to the nomination varied little from other figures of the time. Born in 1901, he grew up in a political family with his father and uncle each serving as county judge. At age twenty-six, Cooper was elected to the legislature; two years later he too became county judge, although the Depression years proved difficult ones for such positions. In 1939, Cooper sought the Republican nomination for governor but lost in the primary. He then entered the U.S. Army in World War II and at conflict's end was elected circuit judge. All that seemed fairly typical for a Kentucky political figure.[25]

But John Sherman Cooper was different. A tall, handsome man, he excelled at sports, both in high school and college, yet was also class poet. The Kentuckian would be voted the most popular member of his class at Yale. He did well in Harvard Law School before his father's health caused him to return home. Debts left by his father's subsequent death burdened Cooper for years. That, plus the poverty and problems he had to deal with as county judge, may have contributed to the nervous breakdown he suffered (and, interestingly, a part of his past not used openly against him in later races). Cooper recovered and continued to be the kind of person who could be at home talking to people in a country cabin or in an Ivy League-dominated board room. His college connections brought him into friendship with leaders like later Missouri senator Stuart Symington and the brother-in-law of later Kentucky senator Thruston Morton; his family ties gave him access to local

PHILIPPINES

University of Kentucky Special Collections

John Sherman Cooper *(right)* **lost his 1948 bid for the Senate, but went on to serve capably as U.S. delegate to the U.N. General Assembly in 1949, the first of six State Department assignments.**

machines and state Republican leaders. He was a liberal and a Republican. Yet, what most observers first commented on about Cooper as a politician was not his background, but rather his campaign style. Quite simply, as newspaperman Allan Grant noted, "He was everything a politician is not." Habitually late, sometimes forgetful, Cooper spoke in a halting, slow, soft manner, with "no polish, no flourish whatever." At a time when Barkley's long-winded, colorful oratory or Chandler's short, folksy style each were popular, Cooper was far from either of those standards. He was sincere, often blunt, and could be effective on occasion. But if he violated most of the oratorical rules, it only seemed to endear him to his audience. They saw him as a smart, decent, simple man, trying hard, and they appeared to like his differences from the norm.[26]

The Cooper image sometimes obscured the fact that he was also a shrewd practical politician. Friendly with Brown's enemy Chandler, he got Happy's support in the general election. Cooper's ties to Morton and the Binghams brought him the endorsement of the usually Democratic *Courier-Journal*. Hitting Brown for an earlier vote regarding veterans' bonuses, ex-soldier Cooper worked hard to secure that bloc. Using demagogic words, he indicated that a vote for Democrats would be a vote for "left-wingers, Pinks, PACs, and Communists." In short, there might be what one journalist called a "Jesus Image" about Cooper, but he did not ignore the political underworld necessary for election. In combination, the two were hard to beat and Cooper won handily, 327,652 to 285,829. Brown's once-bright political star was shooting off into obscurity, while Cooper's was on the ascendancy.[27]

As the governor's race approached in 1947, Republicans should have been hopeful. Their party had won a U.S. Senate seat and Governor Willis's administration had forged a good record, given the fact that the legislature was Democratically controlled and the agenda restricted by the war. Fiscally, the per capita appropriation to schools had doubled, old-age assistance and aid to dependent children payments had gone up over 65 percent, teachers' pay had increased twofold, and five new TB hospitals were funded. Tolls on twelve of the thirteen toll bridges had been removed and park revenue had expanded. Some of that resulted from inflationary pressures, some from Democratic budget initiatives, but it had all occurred under a Republican administration, one virtually free from scandal.[28]

But there were deep factional chinks in the Republican shining armor. After failing to persuade his first two choices to run for governor — one was Thruston Morton — Willis and his supporters reluctantly aided his superintendent of public instruction, John Fred Williams of Johnson County. An urban-rural alliance, backed by Willis's lieutenant governor Tuggle, supported another member of the administration, fifty-year-old attorney general Eldon S. Dummit of Lexington. Both candidates supported the usual causes — education, parks, roads — and their races were chiefly distinguished by Dummit's more anti-administration stance. That apparently had more attraction, for he won the primary by a 68,755 (52.0 percent) to 60,345 (45.6 percent) margin. Party factionalism had, in a sense, repudiated the Republicans' own administration. Already-confident Democrats were delighted.[29]

On the Democratic side, their typical factionalism appeared less prevalent. Chandler had developed a personal following, but with him as baseball commissioner, the future of that faction was unclear. It put forth no candidates in 1947. Barkley remained powerful and popular but had never built up the kind of organization that offered and controlled candidates as earlier factions had done. He remained neutral in the race. In short, the time was one of transition, and two rising politicians sought to fill the existing political leadership vacuum. Thirty-six-year-old Harry Lee Waterfield represented the Democratic Gilbraltar, the Jackson Purchase region of Kentucky, and became first known there as a Hickman County newspaperman. In 1942, he had been president of the Kentucky Press Association; two years later, he was speaker of the Kentucky house. Personable and capable, he gained the support of 1943's defeated candidates, Donaldson and Kilgore, 1946-Senate-primary-loser Ardery, and the *Courier-Journal*. Viewed as a progressive candidate, he had widespread support.[30]

His opponent, fifty-year-old Earle Chester Clements of Morganfield in west Kentucky, looked like the former athlete he was. At six feet tall and two hundred and twenty pounds, Clements could be physically dominating, and, on occasion, showed that. But his chief strength was not his presence, was certainly not his oratory, but was his organization skills. From a political family, Clements had served as a football coach (with Johnson's later lieutenant governor Rodes Myers as one of his assistants) and then had won election as sheriff, county clerk, and county judge. Like Cooper, he had held the latter post in the midst of the Depression. From that base, he had been elected to the legislature and then to Congress. Clements now sought statewide office.[31]

If victory came to Clements, it would be because of his methodical and systematic approach. Energetic, honest, and pragmatic, he was remembered by one veteran journalist as "the most accomplished political operator that I know." Forging compromises and filling the factional void, "he out-organized everyone else." Clements united the regions; he gained the support of the old Rhea machine in west Kentucky, now led by Emerson "Doc" Beauchamp; he allied with the Louisville group controlled by "Miss Lennie"; he selected Lexington *Herald* editor and horseracing advocate Tom Underwood as campaign manager to solidify central Kentucky; and he tied in with rising urban leaders such as Lawrence Wetherby and rural ones such as Carl Perkins. It was not his personality that drew these people to Clements, for he could be short-tempered, secretive, sometimes cold, often taciturn, and occasionally ruthless. But Clements liked playing the political game. "He enjoys it as a spectator sport," one journalist intoned. And if he was cautious in his commitments, if he preferred to make certain he had gathered all the supporters he could on his team, if he methodically considered the results before making a decision, once he committed to a course of action, once he told someone his conclusion, Clements remained firm. Because of his personality, he was not a man who had many close friends, but he was a person who had many allies — and votes. John Ed Pearce concluded that Clements "may have been the greatest political intellect of this century in Kentucky."[32]

He was certainly a formidable foe for another capable politician, Harry Lee Waterfield. Only two real issues surfaced during their Democratic primary. Waterfield favored a pari-mutuel tax, while Clements did not, and

Waterfield supported the development of electric power through public means, while Clements, supported by a strong Kentucky Utilities bloc, favored private interests. Well-financed and well-organized, the Clements campaign also hit at Waterfield's 4-F war status and gained more labor support through John Y. Brown's late endorsement of Clements. On election day, all that translated to a 159,012 to 124,104 Clements win, in which he carried seven of nine congressional districts, including Louisville, where the organization's support apparently meant more votes than the *Courier-Journal* endorsement of Waterfield.[33]

The furious Democratic primary did not result in what had been in the past an often-fatal factional split, where the losing group supported the Republican candidate. Instead, the party stayed basically united, which meant that Republican nominee Eldon Dummit had a very difficult task, particularly since his own party was far from harmonious. In the primary Dummit's attacks on the Republican administration and its candidate had brought victory but killed whatever chance he had to win in the general election. Some other issues were discussed, such as Clements's opposition in Congress to the Taft-Hartley Act restricting labor unions, but with little effect. When Dummit's campaign manager in the primary (who had since been replaced) turned against the candidate late in the race and said that his promises "are insincere and will not be fulfilled," it was simply the last nail in Dummit's long-constructed political coffin. Clements won handily, 387,795 (57.2 percent) to 287,756 (42.5 percent). It was the beginning of two decades of uninterrupted Democratic control of the governorship. It also marked the establishment of a new Democratic faction led by Earle Clements.[34]

The Clements Administration, 1947–1950

New governors in Kentucky often have less than a month between the time they take the oath of office and the start of their first legislative session. Clements's previous experience as senate majority leader helped him plan his program in that short time; his strong will and 75-25 and 28-9 Democratic majorities in the general assembly helped him carry it out.[35]

By session's end, opposition papers were writing how the governor "crushed all opposition" with the "Clements steamrollers." They noted his frequent presence by the speaker, watching a vote, gesturing to members who seemed ready to defy him. But the more supportive press noted that Clements got almost everything passed that he sought and was "a post graduate of parliamentary politics." They praised his organizational skills.[36]

By whatever method, Clements did have a productive legislative session. Lower taxes on stocks and bonds and a reduction in the inheritance tax were designed to help attract business; the lost revenue from that was more than offset by an increased tax on distilled spirits and by a 40 percent rise in the gasoline tax. The latter funds would go to an extensive road-building program, which could be used selectively by the governor as a reward to support-

Kentucky Historical Society

"Queen Sally Baker, club Queen of America" paid a visit to Governor Clements *(center)* **and Lieutenant Governor Wetherby** *(at podium)***. Note the portrait of Governor Goebel presiding over the Senate.**

ive legislators. Despite his campaign stance opposing a pari-mutuel tax, Clements supported one of 3 percent, reportedly because he and Underwood believed a larger one was likely if they did not propose their own. It too passed and added funds to the state coffers. The new monies went to a variety of projects, including a $3-million retroactive pay raise for teachers and an increase in state park funds. A Legislative Council (later called the Legislative Research Commission) was created, to be operated by a professional staff, while the highway patrol, which had limited powers and tended to get involved in politics, was replaced by a stronger state police force. In a quiet move that was almost not reported in some of the press, the general assembly amended the Day Law, which segregated schools. The new act introduced by Charles Anderson of Louisville allowed blacks to receive nursing and medical instruction in previously all-white professional schools and hospitals. Without publicity or fanfare, "Cautious Clements" had made the first successful legislative attack on the state's segregation code. While the governor did fail to get a centralized board to govern all Kentucky colleges and could not get limits placed on strip mining, his had been a strong first session, overall.[37]

Democrats needed such a showing if they wanted to win the state for their party in the fall elections. Incumbent Harry S. Truman was a decided underdog nationally to Republican Thomas Dewey going into the nominating conventions. Alben Barkley in a roaring, attacking, enthusiastically received keynote speech at the Democratic gathering set the tone for the Truman race that followed and received the nod as the candidate for vice-president. The presence of a native son on the ticket obviously helped the party in Kentucky, and it would need that stimulus. The States Rights or Dixiecrat Party, with Strom Thurmond of South Carolina as its presidential candidate, vied for votes in the commonwealth as well, running in opposition to the civil rights plank in the national Democratic Party platform. A split party could cost the Democrats, as it had the Republicans in 1912. But "Old Alben" had stayed with Truman, whose family had Kentucky ties as well. Old "Give 'Em Hell Harry" did his part, speaking to thirteen groups in Kentucky over a twenty-five-hour period. Together, they won a larger percentage than had FDR four years before and secured Kentucky for the Democrats once more. Truman and Barkley carried 92 of 120 counties, polling 466,756 votes (56.7 percent) to Dewey's 341,210 (41.5 percent), to Dixiecrat Thurmond's small 10,411 (1.3 percent). The Democratic victory had resulted despite an apparent move by blacks back to the Republican Party, even though the Democrats had a more favorable platform than ever before. The Dixiecrat identification apparently caused Louisville black wards, which had split in 1944, to go 63 to 36 percent in favor of the Republicans in 1948. The black shift nationally to the Democratic Party was moving slowly in Kentucky.[38]

When U.S. Senator John Sherman Cooper heard Barkley's keynote address, he told his mother he would likely lose his bid for election to a full term because he felt Barkley would win the vice-presidential nomination, and, with him on the ticket, Democrats would sweep the state. He proved a good prophet on all counts. Cooper had several advantages — he had a solid record in Congress, he was the incumbent, and he had, once more, the endorsement of the *Courier-Journal*. Moreover, his Democratic opponent had several weaknesses.[39]

Virgil M. Chapman of Bourbon County had faced the now-almost-perennial candidate John Y. Brown in the Democratic primary. Despite the opposition of organized labor and Waterfield, Chapman had won a 12,000-vote victory, chiefly through his ties to Lexington *Herald* editor Underwood and to Governor Clements. Now he faced Cooper. But for a man who had served in Congress for over two decades and who was known as "Mr. Tobacco" because of his support of that interest, Chapman brought many liabilities to the political table. Chandler opposed him and went for Cooper; Barkley was reluctant to speak for Chapman due to the candidate's opposition to the national Democratic platform on labor and civil rights. Described as "a lone-wolf-type-of-politician" who had a drinking problem, Chapman had much to overcome in his bid to unseat the incumbent. But Cooper had been right. Although his margin was nearly 100,000 different from the Republican presidential candidate's, it was still not enough and, in something of a surprise, Chapman won with 408,256 votes (51.4 percent) to 383,776 (48.3 percent). The Barkley vice-presidential bandwagon had carried the Democrats back into a Senate seat and Cooper out of office.[40]

Only one event marred the Democratic success of 1948, but it had all the elements of a Greek Tragedy. Edward F. Prichard, Jr., of Bourbon County, was widely viewed as the party's fastest rising star. Described as "a child prodigy . . . , the top of his class at Princeton, a celebrity as a law student at Harvard . . . , assistant to famed Supreme Court Justice Felix Frankfurter, advisor to President Franklin D. Roosevelt, and 'boy wonder of the New Deal' by the time he was 24 years old," "Sonny" Prichard was all that and more. Sometimes raw and irresponsible, usually brilliant and bold, he did not look the part of the politician, for he was overweight and not always dapper. But he was a witty, insightful speaker with a photographic memory, and despite some politicians' resentments over his rapid rise, almost all expected him to run for governor in the next campaign, to win, and to have a liberal administration. In 1948, he was but thirty-three years old. Then what he later called a "moral blind spot" brought him, for whatever reason — and several were mentioned over the years — to help stuff a precinct ballot box. Indictment, then conviction, came in 1949, and the appeal went to the U.S. Supreme Court, where four justices disqualified themselves due to their friendship with "Prich" and the appeal was not heard. Five months into the two-year federal prison term, he was pardoned by President Truman. After that, Prichard returned to Kentucky, to face a future that would now hold no political office. How would this brilliant man cope with the dark defeat of his bright ambitions? It would be years before that question was answered.[41]

Other than the Prichard matter, Governor Clements and Kentucky enjoyed a good 1949. "The Veep" Barkley was serving as vice-president; three Supreme Court justices had Kentucky ties, with Vinson as chief justice; Cooper was appointed to represent the United States at the United Nations; the University of Kentucky won a second consecutive national basketball championship; Happy Chandler was heading baseball where Kentucky's "Pee Wee" Reese starred; Robert Penn Warren's recent Pulitzer Prize-winning book was made into an Oscar-winning motion picture; Lexington's A. B. Guthrie published a novel which won a Pulitzer the next year; Carolyn Conn Moore was elected as the first woman in the state senate; a constitutional amendment was passed that raised the salary limit for statewide officers from $5,000 to $12,000; a successful special session took place; Bowling Green's Duncan Hines was governing the nation's food tastes; Arthur Krock was running the Washington office of the New York *Times*; and seventy-one-year-old Barkley wed thirty-seven-year-old Jane Hadley, to much publicity.[42]

And the year 1950 would prove to be even better for Earle Clements personally. When Barkley took the oath of office as vice-president in January 1949, his Senate seat became vacant. The governor had appointed his friend and highway commissioner, sixty-four-year-old Garrett L. Withers of Webster

County, to serve the remainder of Barkley's term. But the full-term election would be in the fall of 1950, and Clements sought that seat.[43]

In the interim, two things happened that affected that race. The 1950 legislative session proved more notable for what did not pass than for what did. Solons defeated Clements's attempt to regulate strip mining, to install a merit system for state workers, and to institute a retirement system. A proposal to enact a sales tax or a lottery tied to the Kentucky Derby in order to provide a bonus for veterans passed each house, but in a different form. The two versions could not be reconciled by the conference committee and the measure died there. About the only significant actions were passage of a further modification of the Day Law, one allowing blacks to attend previously all-white colleges, if black schools did not offer courses in a particular area; an increase in the income tax; enactment of a senate resolution that supported even greater integration; and a fight between two legislators on the house floor which resulted in the sergeant-at-arms' drawing a pistol. A critical *Courier-Journal* called the session "the most ruthlessly operated in anybody's memory" and used terms such as "high-handed and repressive" and "government by manipulation." The other matter which had significance in the Senate race was the invasion of South Korea in June, and America's entry into the Korean War. Soon, Kentuckians were dying overseas. The effect of that on politics was as yet uncertain.[44]

As it turned out, the presence of Kentucky Democrats in the national administration, together with the strengths of an already-formidable Clements organization, made the Senate race predictable. The Republicans nominated a man defeated for governor twenty-seven years earlier, the conservative former federal judge Charles I. Dawson, now of Louisville. He failed to generate much enthusiasm or to find important issues, and Clements won easily, 334,249 to 278,368. A few weeks later, on 27 November 1950, Clements was sworn in as U.S. senator, and after only a year in Washington, he would be selected assistant majority leader under Lyndon B. Johnson. Kentucky had another major political figure at the national level. Forty-two-year-old Lieutenant Governor Lawrence W. Wetherby became governor and a new administration began, once more, in Frankfort.[45]

Although mid-century Kentuckians looked toward a future of challenge and promise, this stretch of road near Natural Bridge displayed a more fatalistic vision.

14

Mid-century: Moment of Decision

"We are at the end of an epoch . . . Kentucky's true greatness lies ahead." So read the 1945 introduction to *Kentucky: Designs for Her Future*, the first of three studies planned to portray Kentucky as it was and as it should be in the era that followed World War II. It was a time when men and women realized that great technological, economic, and social changes loomed on the horizon. Military victory brought with it the hope that a new and better world would emerge in the peace. It was a moment of decision.[1]

Kentucky stood with America at that crossroad, and its people looked at which turn to take. *Kentucky: Designs for Her Future*, edited by sociologist Howard W. Beers, was one attempt to provide a guide for that decision — if indeed there was a decision to be made. A compilation of some thirty radio addresses given by University of Kentucky faculty, the book proved more a presentation of Kentucky's current status than a blueprint for the future, but the three hundred pages of studies did suggest how the commonwealth should utilize its human and material resources in the decades ahead. Some of the dozens of suggestions for positive change were specific: write a new constitution, have fewer names on the ballot, increase teachers' salaries, reduce the number of "emergency" teachers, improve access to public libraries, increase the number of hospital beds (where the state ranked forty-sixth), do a better job of caring for the mentally ill, and find more effective ways to deal with the difference in school district property assessments (which ranged from $238 per pupil in one county to $11,074 in another). Other comments were more general: choose leaders not out of personal consideration but impersonal ones; rid yourself of a tendency to tolerate inefficiency rather than risk change; and restore wildlife, fish, and forests to create a "new frontier" for Kentucky. Beers and other professors concluded that citizens had too much "complacency, smugness, and satisfaction with things as they are." Now was their opportunity to "prepare a greater heritage for their descendants than was received from their ancestors." If they would do that, then an almost unlimited future loomed ahead in the new world of postwar Kentucky.[2]

Receiving more attention since they represented state government's contribution to planning were a series of eleven reports, totalling over 320 pages, issued between February and July 1945. The Postwar Advisory Planning Commission, created by Governor Willis and chaired by H. F. Willkie of Louisville, went beyond the university-dominated Beers study and included educators such as Herman L. Donovan and Rufus Atwood, businessmen such as Paul Blazer, newspaperman Tom Wallace, and political figures such as past Louisville mayor William B. Harrison. But it did not include any women, and only one of its original twenty-five members represented Democratically controlled west Kentucky. Still, its "Program of Action for Kentucky" had a distribution of 100,000, and its recommendations were numerous and varied.[3]

In education, the Planning Commission suggested that school districts be consolidated across county lines, if necessary; that teachers be required to take four years of college, rather than the current two; that teachers' salaries be increased (since only seven states had lower averages); that reciprocal agreements with other states should be developed regarding schools of architecture, veterinary medicine, and medicine; that all state institutions of higher learning be placed under an administrative board; that the school term be lengthened (since the state stood forty-eighth and last in that category); and that a better method of school financing be found – the U.S. average was $94.03 per student in 1940 versus the Kentucky average of $48.09.[4]

Regarding government, the group recommended: a new state constitution; the creation of a State Planning Agency; a Building Code Council; Kentucky State House Commission (to deal with the 177,000 substandard non-farm dwellings); an Area and Planning and Zoning Commission; a full-time legislative research bureau; an office for coordinating veterans' affairs; more funding for roads and airports; and a stronger State Highway Patrol. In health care, the commission asked that health offices be extended to the sixteen counties without such aid, while in environmental matters, it suggested controls on water pollution, called for reforestation of stripped coal lands, and advocated the creation of more parks. Kentucky should conduct a study of labor conditions and take whatever corrective action was required, establish a state chamber of commerce, increase the minimum wage, and diversify industrially, since half of the state's industrial development was in Louisville. Agriculturally, the commonwealth must develop new strains of tobacco and stress modern farming techniques. The commission also added that the introduction of new plants, "such as kudzu, is of first importance." If not always prescient, the group had, nevertheless, given the state a good listing of problems, needs, and possible answers.[5]

The Committee for Kentucky represented the private sector's equivalent of the government-created Postwar Advisory Planning Commission. Headed by the energetic president of Louisville's Kaufman-Straus Company, Harry W. Schaeter, the Committee for Kentucky had as its main core a mix of representatives from business and higher education, but included, as well, people from the black community, labor, journalism, women's groups, the Parent Teachers Association, and other such organizations. It too issued a series of reports, spread out over several years, and by 1950, the dozen summaries totalled over four hundred pages of suggestions for change. Those reports had three advantages over the previous studies, for they were more colorfully designed, were spread out over several years so the idea remained before the public, and were periodically updated with new statistics, which brought further publicity. Unlike the other plans, the Committee for Kentucky reports also included a price tag on what was being proposed — $51 million per year in new revenue and $100 million additional in capital expenditures — and some options on how to raise the money — higher current taxes and possibly a new sales or severance tax. Overall, the committee repeated many of the findings of the other two groups, and included many of the same people — seven of the twelve reports were written wholly or in part by University of Kentucky faculty. Its recommendations added still another pillar to those calling for a temple of change.[6]

Noting that "there is an amazingly high degree of correlation between what a state invests in education and the standard of living of its people," the committee found Kentucky very deficient in that regard. The commonwealth stood forty-seventh in the level of education of its populace, and in one county only 0.4 percent of the people were high school graduates. Lengthen the school term, said the committee, increase teachers' salaries, provide more funds per pupil, consolidate school districts, offer more public library services, and — in a departure — examine the whole question of segregation of schools and the "waste and inefficiency" of that system.[7]

Looking at government, the group called for a constitutional convention to reexamine a document they variously described as "static," "restrictive," and "anachronistic"; they also asked for more funds for public welfare, workmen's compensation, and the geological survey, requested an emphasis on geographic and historic sites for tourism, supported the inclusion of more state employees under a merit system, and recommended creation of a State Building Code and a State Housing Commission. The committee stressed the need to reduce the tenancy rate on farms, to build more rural highways (only 20 percent of farms were reached by hard-surfaced roads), to provide sanitary water sources, and to bring electricity and telephones to more agrarian areas. Combined, the Committee for Kentucky *Reports*, the Postwar Advisory Planning Commission *Final Report*, and *Kentucky: Designs for Her Future* had over a seven-year period given the state a detailed blueprint for the future. But would anyone follow those guidelines? Would the plans sit, ignored on some dusty shelf, or would they lead, as one said, "to Kentucky's true greatness"?[8]

Despite the often-gloomy spirit of the various reports, there was also much to build on in the future. The state's political leadership held key positions in the nation's capital while at home the destructive party factionalism had lessened. The commonwealth's literary strengths, built in a half-century of tradition, remained strong. The labor wars appeared ended, at least in their most destructive form. And Kentucky had quietly taken significant steps to integrate its black citizens into more of the everyday life of the entire people. Overall, the state had sometimes attempted fundamental change and had succeeded, as in the woman suffrage struggle. In other areas, transformations

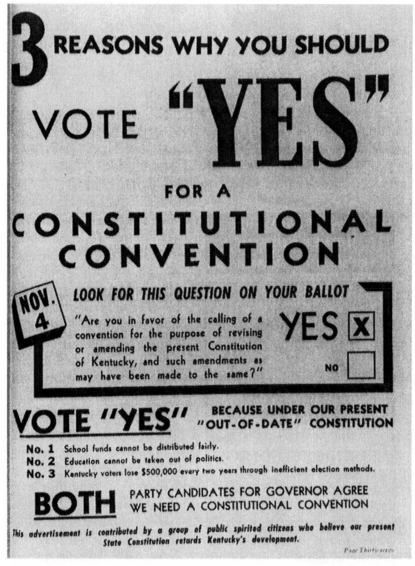

**Most plans for Kentucky's future recommended constitutional reform.
This 1947 campaign for change, along with other twentieth-century
bids, proved unsuccessful.**

had taken place almost despite citizen efforts. The tobacco growers, for instance, fought fruitlessly almost in the first decade of the century and again in
1920 to effect fundamental marketing change but had largely failed. The New
Deal agricultural revolution finally provided them the security so long sought.
By 1950, then, the people of Kentucky had embraced some of the greatest
change any generation had ever experienced. There were numerous people
living then who had been young adults in 1900. Looking back they could

scarcely believe how their world had been modified. They had seen automobiles, airplanes, radios, motion pictures, electrical appliances, and so much more become commonplace. Jets and television were inching into that consciousness now as well. Health care had increased drastically and people lived longer. The years since 1900 had been good ones; despite the worries of war and rapid change, much hope existed.

At mid-century, then, Kentuckians had much information given them and numerous options as they had to decide what course to follow. Fifty years earlier, the commonwealth had been an important state in the national picture. It was then emerging from a difficult period, as were other states. But the courses followed, the choices made, when coupled with other circumstances, had not always been the ones Kentucky needed to retain its relative position. In many areas the half-century since 1900 had not been a good one for Kentuckians. They shared in America's woes of two world wars, an influenza epidemic, a national depression, and now yet another conflict, in Korea. Part of the naiveté of citizens had disappeared in the gas attacks and trench warfare of World War I; part of the soul of the twentieth-century Kentuckians died when the soldiers saw the concentration camps of another war. The struggle to survive disease, or hunger, or joblessness had left its mark on generations as well. But, beyond that, Kentuckians had to live with even more — additional violence in feuds, the Black Patch War, and the Harlan Coal Wars, and additional economic problems in an agricultural depression of the twenties and the drought of 1930. For the thousands of individual stories of achievement and hope, there were others of tragedy and despair.

At the national level some dynamic leaders, such as Teddy Roosevelt, Woodrow Wilson, and Franklin D. Roosevelt, had left major legacies affecting people's lives. In Kentucky, seldom did such leadership emerge. If defeat disciplines the soul, then Republicans had the best-trained souls in the state. Their opponents in turn were so often torn apart by bitter factionalism that a united Democratic Party seemed only a political theorist's dream. All the political groups seemed more interested in searching for power and forging election coalitions than in formulating policy; a policy of drift was safer than one of challenges to be met. As a result, leaders appeared more interested in defeating a rival than in winning legislative victories. That internecine attitude left little time to nurture a spirit of progress.

But did the people of Kentucky even want progress, however defined? In general, most change had come slowly to the state, and that was exactly what its citizens seemed to desire. Correctly, they saw their traditions, their folkways, their past as strengths that should not be cast aside. Those elements provided needed stability and anchors from which to face the uncertain future. But problems arose when Kentuckians worshipped the old ways to the exclusion of any modification. That false god made them often forget that one great constant of their past had been change — from a frontier lifestyle to a settled one, from a slave system to a free one, from an agrarian world to an industrial one. Each generation had lived and thought in different ways than its predecessor; each also kept with it, at the same time, a vitally important common memory, shared with earlier generations. The debate was not whether the people would change, for they would. Instead, the debate was whether they would advocate and embrace new ways, or whether they would fight them. Would theirs be a policy of drift or one of foresight? Their answers would determine the state's future in the second fifty years of the twentieth century.

At mid-century, then, Kentuckians remained uncertain about their state and nation, their future, and their lives. Women had seen men returning from the war, going to school on the G.I. Bill and becoming better educated, and they asked if their own status would ever change. Blacks had seen cracks appear in the wall of inequality and segregation, but they knew also just how firmly planted those foundations were. People of both sexes and races saw their educational system near the bottom nationally. No great crusade for learning seemed on the horizon. Those living on limited incomes, existing in poverty or dependant on outside forces for jobs and their livelihood, recognized that Kentucky's economy rose and fell on such volatile parts as coal, whiskey, and tobacco. For many, migration outside the state appeared the only alternative to poverty. As one person in a small community explained, "It seemed at Possum Trot that the living go and the dead return." A college professor expressed it simply: "Youth is Kentucky's major export product." Would that continue? Would the state's hopes and its best future go elsewhere?[9]

For those who stayed, the small communities of Kentucky remained the heart of the state in 1950. There people had changed since 1900, for many now left homes lighted by electricity, drove an automobile to town on a Saturday, and perhaps joined friends in watching a motion picture at a packed matinee. But much remained similar to earlier times. Those courthouse squares would be filled with people, eager to shop, renew acquaintances, make new friends, or just talk. Those cars might be the new mode of transportation, but as one person from Jessamine County recalled, you left the doors unlocked, so people could sit down and rest. He remembered returning on several occasions to find total strangers sitting there. It did not bother people, for "I never heard of anyone who had anything stolen from his car under those circumstances." Manners required that doors be left unlocked. Besides, he noted, "You knew almost all people by name or . . . by family. But you spoke whether you knew them or not because it was the thing to do." That spirit of hospitality and trust the people did not want to leave behind as the years passed.[10]

Elements almost of frontier times lived on in a world of expanding technology. There was still another Kentucky, peopled by different outlooks, propelled by different forces, pushed by different items of importance. Harlan and Anna Hubbard built a ten-foot houseboat in northern Kentucky in 1944, and two years later began to drift down the Ohio River, stopping to spend two summers growing a garden. Theirs marked a return to a time when early settlers in flatboats made their way down the river, in search of new homes. For the Hubbards they sought not homes, but a return to that less complex lifestyle. Estranged from urban society, comfortable in their solitude and simpler tastes, they caught fish, raised vegetables in summer gardens, bartered with river people, and lived off what they had. They read aloud to each other, as had earlier generations, they played music together, they worked daily. Once when their shantyboat was iced in near Owensboro, some people from the area helped to get it out. Wrote Hubbard: "[They] offered their services so freely that I knew they would accept no money in payment. I asked Uncle Bill what to do. He said country people are accustomed to turning out and helping one another, so we must thank them heartily, and when the opportunity came, help them or another, a stranger perhaps, and expect no reward. His philosophy might have come from someone's Utopia, yet here it was, practiced in Daviess County, Kentucky, in the year 1948." That it did reflected the continuing aspects of another time still present across the commonwealth. Harlan Hubbard may have been, as author Wendell Berry writes, "an exile from his century" but he and his wife connected the two centuries in their lifestyles. They showed that the future many Kentuckians sought was not the goal of all of those in the state. Kentucky still could not fully reconcile reform and change with tradition.[11]

The newspaper editors of the small towns spoke for their fellow citizens as they looked toward the years beyond 1950. They were optimistic and expected better days ahead, but at the same time they could not shake off the fear that things might not improve after all, that the brave new world ahead might be a foreboding one. The Corbin *Times* noted that the sad record of the forties "was a story of war, of many dying, of a bomb." But the years also brought the soldiers home, "to hunt their dreams," and to build a better community in a still-uncertain time: "the outlook is not all good, but it is better." In Glasgow, the editor's wife concluded that "Our nation is well fed, secure, full of assurance based on experience." She pointed to the great scientific progress of the past half-century and "the social revolution . . . in our thinking." Hopeful, she said that the last half of the century "could very well be used in the development of the kind of maturity that would make full use of our scientific and social progress." At the Cynthiana *Democrat*, the more pessimistic editor pointed to the last fifty years and its record of two bloody world wars. "But despite obstacles . . . mankind's progress has been the greatest ever recorded." Still, he was uncertain, for "misunderstanding among nations and intolerance between races seem to be just as much a part of the picture today as they were a century ago. . . . The year 1950 offers another new challenge toward molding our destiny. . . ." And, as he could have said, so too did the years beyond 1950.[12]

In the first half of the twentieth century, Kentucky had been forced to face many challenges. The commonwealth could have taken different and more effective steps to end violence; it could have followed the educational reform movement of the first decade of the century and have built on that. The state could have passed and supported additional acts of reform. That it did not doomed Kentucky, all too often, to retrenchment or retreat while too many

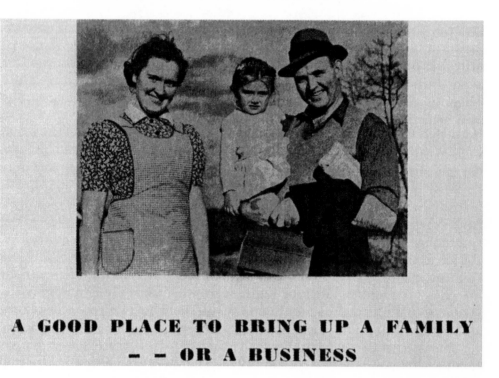

A GOOD PLACE TO BRING UP A FAMILY
— — OR A BUSINESS

With this 1948 ad, the Union Light, Heat & Power Co. voiced a "strong faith in the future" of Kentucky.

other rivals were advancing. Now, in 1950, the studies told people what needed to be done. Once more plans offered answers to problems. Kentucky still had the ability to reverse — at least in part — the negative trends of a half-century. It had strengths to build on and the commonwealth could decide for itself whether that future promise would be realized or squandered. Would the rest of the century be a new story of bright achievement or an old one of lost opportunities?

Notes

1. "The Sun Shines Bright in The Old Kentucky Home"

1. Alice C. Hegan, *Mrs. Wiggs of the Cabbage Patch* (1901), 153.

2. Annie Fellows Johnston, *The Little Colonel* (1895), 113.

3. William S. Ward, *A Literary History of Kentucky* (1988), 52, 122, 139.

4. Abby M. Roach, "The Authors Club of Louisville . . . ," *Filson Club History Quarterly* (hereafter *FCHQ*) 31 (1957): 28-37; Louisville *Courier-Journal Magazine*, 22 February 1959; William S. Ward, "Anni Mirabiles: Kentucky Literature at the Turn of the Century," *Kentucky Review* 5 (1985): 41-43. Mrs. Johnston was generally absent from Kentucky after 1901 until 1910.

5. Roach, "Authors Club," 36-37, 32; New York *Times*, 14 January 1934; George H. Yater, *Two Hundred Years at the Falls of the Ohio: A History of Louisville and Jefferson County* (1979), 153.

6. "Alice Hegan Rice," *The Centurion* (March 1918), 1; Melville W. Otter Briney Diary and Memory Book, 24 April, 12 June, 3 July 1915, Filson Club; Roach, "Authors Club," 33-34; New York *Times*, 3 October 1920; Miriam Gaines, ". . . George Madden Martin," *Kentucky Women's Journal* 1 (1916): 8; Louisville *Herald-Post*, 5 October 1931; Thomas D. Clark in Mary C. Browning, *Kentucky Authors: A History of Kentucky Literature* (1968), xii; Cale Young Rice, *Bridging the Years* (1939), 48.

7. John H. Ellis, *Medicine in Kentucky* (1977), 57; Steven C. Wheatley, *The Politics of Philanthropy: Abraham Flexner and Medical Education* (1988), passim; Melvin I. Urofsky, *Louis D. Brandeis and the Progressive Tradition* (1981).

8. Marguerita Gifford, *St. James Court in Retrospect* (1966), 1; Melville O. Briney, *Fond Recollection: Sketches of Old Louisville* (1955), 135; "19 St. James Court" and other reminiscences, R. M. Hughes Collection, Photographic Archives, Kentucky Historical Society; Rice, *Bridging the Years*, 80-81; Yater, *Two Hundred Years*, 162.

9. *Louisville Blue Book of Selected Names . . . For the Year Ending 1904* (1902), passim. Some 8,000 people were listed in this work (3 percent of the county's population). Generally, they are considered the upper-class elite, for purposes of this discussion.

10. Louisville *Courier-Journal*, 1 April 1903; Federal Writers' Project, *Kentucky: A Guide to the Bluegrass State* (1939), 348; quoted in Sue Lynn McGuire, "The Little Colonel: A Phenomenon in Popular Literary Culture," *Register of the Kentucky Historical Society* (hereafter *Register*) 89 (1991): 122; Louisville *Courier-Journal*, 3 May 1920; Alice Hegan Rice, *The Inky Way* (1940), 95. See also Lester F. Keys, ed., *Historic Jefferson County* (1992), passim.

11. Arthur P. Dudden, "Nostalgia and the American," *Journal of the History of Ideas* 22 (1961): 516, 528-29. The analysis in the preceding two paragraphs results from examination of selected Louisville diaries, letters, and newspaper accounts from the first decade of the twentieth century.

12. On 1860-1900 Louisville, see Robert E. McDowell, *City of Conflict: Louisville in the Civil War, 1861-1865* (1926); Hambleton Tapp and James C. Klotter, *Kentucky: Decades of Discord,*

1865-1900 (1977), 63, 96-100, 307-8; and Yater, *Two Hundred Years*, passim. Most surveys include Kentucky as a southern state. See, for instance, John Shelton Reed, *The Enduring South* (1975), 14, 18, 115.

13. Kentucky *Acts* (1902), 61-64, 208-9; (1910), 220; (1912), 41-46, 220-21; (1926), 278; Lexington *Leader*, 18 October 1911; Lexington *Herald*, 6 January 1926. In *Bosworth v. Harp*, 154 Kentucky 559, the state's highest court ruled that the Confederate pension was legal.

14. Louisville *Courier-Journal*, 30 May 1900; R. C. Riebel, *Louisville Panorama* (1954), 147; "Memorable Reunion at Owensboro," *Confederate Veteran* 10 (1902): 343-44.

15. Author's Interview with Hambleton Tapp, 5 April 1978; Omer Carmichael and Weldon James, *The Louisville Story* (1957), 12-13; Charles Reagan Wilson, *Baptized in Blood: The Religion of the Lost Cause, 1865-1920* (1980), 36, 168, 178; Thomas D. Clark, *Helm Bruce, Public Defender* (1973), v, 19.

16. Jefferson County, the unit of which Louisville is part, had 232,549 people — 10.8 percent of the state's population — in 1900. Kentucky's urban population, overall, was 423,646 (19.7 percent of the population). See Thomas R. Ford, *Health and Demography in Kentucky* (1964), 12, and Dewey W. Grantham, *Southern Progressivism: The Reconciliation of Progress and Tradition* (1983), 6, 277. Additional parts of the Louisville urban landscape lay across the river in Indiana suburbs and are not included in this study.

17. Grantham, *Southern Progressivism*, 7; Clark, *Helm Bruce*, v; Charles D. Warner, *Studies in the South and West* (1889), 279, 281; *I Remember: The Autobiography of Abraham Flexner* (1940), 19; Yater, *Two Hundred Years*, 130; C. W. Johnston, *The Sunny South and Its People* (1918), 95. See also *A History of the Jews of Louisville, Ky.* (1902).

18. Author's Interview with William Chescheir, 12 September 1980; *Louisville Blue Book*, 156-57.

19. Yater, *Two Hundred Years*, 129; George H. Yater, "Notes to Two Hundred Years at the Falls . . ." (1982), note to p. 129; Clark, *Helm Bruce*, 19. Hill is perhaps best known as a coauthor of what became the song "Happy Birthday to You."

20. George R. Leighton, *Five Cities: The Story of Their Youth and Old Age* (1939), 68. Generalization in this and the preceding paragraph came from a reading of biographical volumes in works such as Temple Bodley and Samuel M. Wilson, *History of Kentucky* (4 vols., 1928) and E. Polk Johnson, *A History of Kentucky and Kentuckians* (3 vols., 1912), plus H. Levin, *Lawyers and Lawmakers of Kentucky* (1897), and W. T. Owens, comp., *Who's Who in Louisville* (1926).

21. *Louisville Blue Book*, 183-93, passim; Louisville *Courier-Journal*, 5 April 1903, 12 December 1934; Yater, *Two Hundred Years*, 135, 161; Abby M. Roach, "Then — Girlhood in Louisville in the Nineties," *FCHQ* 37 (1963): 139-41. See also Virginia Fitzpatrick, "Frederick Law Olmsted and the Louisville Park System," *FCHQ* 59 (1985): 54-65.

22. Yater, *Two Hundred Years*, 137; Louisville *Courier-Journal*, 11 July 1909.

23. W. Jefferson, "Education and Educators in Kentucky at the Turn of the Century," *FCHQ* 30 (1956): 3-4; Elizabeth A. Perkins, "The Forgotten Victorians: Louisville's Domestic Servants, 1880-1920," *Register* 85 (1987): 116, 123.

24. Allen J. Share, *Cities in the Commonwealth: Two Centuries of Urban Life in Kentucky* (1982), 93; Browning, *Kentucky Authors*, 131; Louisville *Herald*, 26 October 1919.

25. Johnston, *Sunny South*, 105; Lawrence H. Larsen, *The Rise of the Urban South* (1985), 140; William E. Cummings, "Pomp, Pandemonium, and Paramours: The G.A.R. Convention of 1895," *Register* 81 (1983): 283-86; Yater, "Notes," note to p. 162.

26. *Twelfth United States Census* (1900), vol. II, pt. 2, clxxviii; Yater, *Two Hundred Years*, 153-57, 163; Larsen, *Rise of the Urban South*, 118, 121-24; William E. Ellis, "Tenement House Reform:

Another Episode in Kentucky Progressivism," *FCHQ* 55 (1981) 1: 378-82. The General Assembly in 1910 passed a law regulating tenements.

27. Gifford, *St. James Court*, 43; Rice, *Inky Way*, 40-41, 45; *Who's Who in Louisville*, 146; Mary Boewe, "Back to the Cabbage Patch: The Characters of Mrs. Wiggs," *FCHQ* 59 (1985): 194-95.

28. Boewe, "Back to the Cabbage Patch," 201-2; Rice, *Inky Way*, 71.

29. Rice, *Inky Way*, 221-23; Boewe, "Back to the Cabbage Patch," 188.

30. Otto A. Rothert, *The Story of a Poet: Madison Cawein* (1921), 69-70, 403. The name is pronounced KAH-WINE.

31. *Ibid.*, 77, 80, 91, 68, 306, 159, 274.

32. Ward, *Literary History*, 95-97; New York *Times*, 23 January 1915; Rothert, *Story of a Poet*, 262, 310-12, 151, 156, 144, 450 (poem); Boston *Transcript*, 19 December 1914; Louisville *Times*, 8 December 1914. See also John W. Townsend, "Has Kentucky Produced a Poet?" *Register* 4 (1906): 23-30, and Edwin C. Litsey, "Lesser Literary Center of America: Louisville, Kentucky," *Book News* 24 (1906): 535.

33. William H. Turner, "The Demography of Black Appalachia: Past and Present," in Turner and Edward J. Cabbell, eds., *Blacks in Appalachia* (1985), 240; D. H. Schockel, "Changing Conditions in the Kentucky Mountains," *Scientific Monthly* 3 (1916): 119. Appalachian Kentucky is defined different ways. The statistics used are those of the authors cited, and the counties included may vary slightly from author to author.

34. James C. Klotter, "Little Shepherds, Little Colonels, and Little Kingdoms: A Selective Review of Kentucky Writing, 1784-1950," *Journal of Kentucky Studies* 3 (1986): 65-66; Ward, *Literary History*, 76-82; John Fox to Michajah Fible, 13 May 1887, Manuscript Department, University of Virginia.

35. Cratis D. Williams, "The Southern Mountaineer in Fact and Fiction," *Appalachian Journal* 3 (1976): 211-22 (quotation on 219); Fox, *The Trail of the Lonesome Pine* (1984; orig. pub. 1908); Anne Gabbard Shelby, "Appalachian Literature and American Myth: A Study of Fiction from the Southern Mountains" (M.A. thesis, University of Kentucky, 1981), 20-27; R. Gerald Alvey, "Cultural Conflicts in Kentucky Literature" (University of Kentucky College of Agriculture Cooperative Extension Service Publication H.E. 1-321), 2 (hereafter UK Extension Service).

36. Quotation from William G. Frost, "Our Contemporary Ancestors in the Southern Mountains," *Atlantic Monthly* 83 (1899): 311. The same term appeared later in Horace Kephart, *Our Southern Highlanders* (1913), 373. For general views of the Appalachian image in this era, see Henry D. Shapiro, *Appalachia on Our Mind* (1978); Williams, "Southern Mountaineer," 8-61, 100-162, 186-261, 334-92; and James C. Klotter, "The Black South and White Appalachia," *Journal of American History* 66 (1980): 832-49.

37. Klotter, "Black South and White Appalachia," 840; Josiah H. Combs, "The Kentucky Highlands," in William R. Thomas, *Life Among the Hills and Mountains of Kentucky* (1926), 100; Ellen Churchill Semple, "The Anglo-Saxons of the Kentucky Mountains," *Bulletin of the American Geographical Society* 42 (1910): 566; Mrs. S. M. Davis, "The 'Mountain Whites' of America," *Missionary Review of the World*, N.S. 8 (1895): 423.

38. William G. Frost, "New England in Kentucky," *Advance* (6 June 1895), 1285; Frost, "Appalachian America," *Ladies Home Companion* 23 (September 1896), 4.

39. On the stereotypes, see the sources in note 36, as well as R. Gerald Alvey, "Cultural Stereotypes in Kentucky Literature" (UK Extension Service Publication 3M-3-82), 2.

40. John W. Raine, *The Land of Saddle-Bags: A Study of the Mountain People of Appalachia* (1924), 5; William A. Bradley, "The Folk Culture of the Kentucky Cumberlands," *Dial* (31 Janu-

ary 1918), 97-98; Jack Temple Kirby, *Media-Made Dixie: The South in the American Imagination* (rev. ed., 1986), 15-16.

41. Henderson Daingerfield, "Social Settlement and Educational Work in the Kentucky Mountains," *Journal of Social Science* 39 (1901): 176; T. J. Manning to W. G. Frost, 24 July 1903, Appalachian Feuds Collection, Southern Appalachian Archives, Berea College Library; Louisville *Post*, 17 February 1922; Louisville *Herald*, 8 August 1922; Campbell quoted in Williams, "Southern Mountaineer," 19.

42. Frank Waldo, "Among the Southern Appalachians," *New England Magazine* N.S. 24 (1901): 243; Schockel, "Conditions in the Kentucky Mountains," 128; Mary Breckinridge to "Elizabeth," 23 September 1926 (copy), Frontier Nursing Service Administrative Records, University of Kentucky Library; Transcript of Interview with Mardi Bemis Perry and Susan Morse Putnam, 25 January 1979, Frontier Nursing Service Oral History Project, University of Kentucky Library (hereinafter FNSOHP).

43. Ronald D Eller, *Miners, Millhands, and Mountaineers: Industrialization of the Appalachian South, 1880-1930* (1982), xviii; G. S. Dickerman, "The Mountain People in Eastern Kentucky," *Berea Quarterly* 7 (May 1903): 28, 19, 26; Daniel Tysen Smith, "Appalachian's Last One-Room School: A Case Study" (Ed.D. dissertation, University of Kentucky, 1988), 19; Springfield *Sun*, 27 September 1911.

44. Kephart, *Our Southern Highlanders*, 21; William H. Haney, *The Mountain People of Kentucky* (1906), 40; S. S. MacClintock, "The Kentucky Mountains and Their Feuds," *American Journal of Sociology* 7 (1901): 3, 13; Mabel Green Condon, *A History of Harlan County* (1962), 11-12.

45. I. A. Bowles, *History of Letcher County* (1949), 73; Laurel Shackelford and Bill Weinberg, eds., *Our Appalachia: An Oral History* (1977), 37n; Transcript of Interview with John Caldwell, 6 July 1978, FNSOHP; Jack Temple Kirby, *Rural Worlds Lost: The American South, 1920-1960* (1987), 48.

46. On the isolation, see, for example, Kephart, *Our Southern Highlanders*, 23; Semple, "Anglo-Saxons," 565; C. T. Revere, "Beyond the Gap: The Breeding Ground of Feuds," *The Outing Magazine* (February 1907), 612.

47. E. L. Noble, *Bloody Breathitt's Feuds* (4 vols., 1936-47), 4:48; Author's Interview with Mike Gabbard, 11 May 1980; Transcript of Interview with Sophia Couch, 22 August 1978, FNSOHP; Eller, *Miners, Millhands, and Mountaineers*, 7, 23; John C. Campbell, *The Southern Highlander & His Homeland* (1969; orig. pub. 1921), 91; Semple, "Anglo-Saxons," 580; Shackelford and Weinberg, eds., *Our Appalachia*, 84.

48. Mary Verhoeff, *The Kentucky Mountains: Transportation and Commerce, 1750 to 1911* (1911), 89-90; Campbell, *Southern Highlander*, 227; Thomas, *Life Among the Hills*, 16; John F. Day, *Bloody Ground* (1981; orig. pub. 1941), 321; Gilbert C. Fite, *Cotton Fields No More: Southern Agriculture, 1865-1980* (1984), 30.

49. Grace F. Ryan, "The Highlands of Kentucky," *The Outlook* 58 (1898): 363; Arthur W. Spaulding, *The Men of the Mountains* (1915), 67-68; Nellie Ballou, "Politics in Moonshine Land," New York *Times Magazine*, 8 June 1924; Alfreda Withington, "The Mountain Doctor," *Atlantic Monthly* 150 (1932): 474-75; Transcript of Interview with James Parton, 25 May 1979, FNSOHP; Louise Chapman, "A Cadet in Scalf Hollow," *Quarterly Bulletin of the Frontier Nursing Service*, 20 (1944): 41.

50. Charles E. Martin, *Hollybush: Folk Building and Social Change in an Appalachian Community* (1984), 29-30, 89; David E. Whisnant, *All That is Native and Fine: The Politics of Culture in an American Region* (1983), 121-22; Samuel W. Thomas, ed., *Dawn Comes to the Mountains* (1981), 97.

51. *Thirteenth Census of the United States . . . 1910: Abstract . . . With Supplement for Kentucky* (1913), 585-87; Transcript of Interviews with Perry and Putnam, Mr. and Mrs. Charlie Rice, 30

October 1978, and Wilma D. Whittlesey, 30 November 1979, all in FNSOHP; *The Trail of the Pioneer* (1927 film, videotape in FNS Collection).

52. Transcript of Interview with Brooke Alexander, 24 September 1979, FNSOHP; Rice Interview; Transcript of Interview with Hallie Maggard, 20 November 1978, FNSOHP; Otto J. Scott, *The Exception: The Story of Ashland Oil & Refining Company* (1968), 20; Sophonisba P. Breckinridge, *Madeline McDowell Breckinridge: A Leader in the New South* (1921), 233.

53. Thomas A. Arcury and Julia D. Porter, "Household Composition in Appalachian Kentucky in 1900," *Journal of Family History* 10 (1985): 187-93.

54. Louisville *Courier-Journal*, 6 April 1924; Noble, *Bloody Breathitt's Feuds*, 2: 86; Elizabeth R. Hooker, *Religion in the Highlands* (1933), 67.

55. Transcripts of Interviews with Felix Sheppard, 11 September 1978, and Molly Lee, 6 February 1979, both in FNSOHP; Martin, *Hollybush*, 86; Withington, "Mountain Doctor," 768; Howard W. Odum, *Southern Regions of the United States* (1936), 27; G. C. Jones, *Growing Up Hard in Harlan County* (1985), 1-2, ix; Ercel Stidham Eaton, *Appalachian Yesterdays* (1982), 8, 13.

56. Tom Eversole, "Memories About This and That" (typescript, Kentucky Historical Society), 50; Eller, *Miners, Millhands, and Mountaineers*, 93; Day, *Bloody Ground*, 194.

57. Thomas D. Clark, *The Kentucky* (rev. ed., 1969), 334-45; James C. Klotter and Henry C. Mayer, *A Century of Banking: The Story of Farmers Bank and Banking in Owsley County, 1890-1990* (1989), 9-11; Thomas D. Clark, "Kentucky Logmen," *Journal of Forest History* 25 (1981): 149-50, 157.

58. Clark, *The Kentucky*, 335-42; *History and Programs Commemorating the Founding of the City of Catlettsburg, Kentucky* (1949), 30-31.

59. Eunice T. Johnson, comp., *History of Perry County, Kentucky* (1953), 47; Day, *Bloody Ground*, 191-92; Clark, *The Kentucky*, 345; Thomas, ed., *Dawn Comes to the Mountains*, 109.

60. Albert E. Cowdrey, *This Land, This South: An Environmental History* (1983), 103; Day, *Bloody Ground*, 194-95; Thomas D. Clark, *The Greening of the South: The Recovery of Land and Forest* (1984), 24; Kentucky *Bureau of Agriculture, Labor, and Statistics Report 1904-05*, 16; Kentucky *Bureau of Agriculture, Labor, and Statistics Report* (1910-11), 13, 145-46; Edward F. Seiller, comp., *Kentucky Natural Resources, Industrial Statistics* (1930), 6.

61. Seiller, comp., *Kentucky Resources*, 7; Joseph L. McConnell, "Growth of Manufacturing in Kentucky, 1904 to 1929" (M. A. thesis, University of Kentucky, 1932), 60; Thomas D. Clark, *Kentucky: Land of Contrast* (1968), 272-73; Hazel and Kelly Morgan, *History of Clay County, Kentucky 1767-1976* (n.d.), 167; Day, *Bloody Ground*, 191.

62. *Labor History in Kentucky* (1986), sect. IV, 35.

63. Randall G. Lawrence, "Appalachian Metamorphosis: Industrializing Society in the Central Appalachian Plateau, 1860-1913" (Ph.D. diss., Duke University, 1983), 65, 70; Shackelford and Weinberg, eds., *Our Appalachia*, 145 (J.C.C. Mayo, Jr. interview); Ronald D Eller, "The Coal Barons of the Appalachian South, 1880-1930," *Appalachian Journal* 4 (1977): 197.

64. On Mayo see a *FCHQ* article (1977) by Harry M. Caudill, virtually all of which is included in his *Theirs Be The Power: The Moguls of Eastern Kentucky* (1983), 59-83; Shackelford and Weinberg, eds., *Our Appalachia*, 148; and C. C. Turner and C. H. Traum, *John C. C. Mayo* (1983).

65. Caudill, *Theirs Be The Power*, 61-84; Eller, *Miners, Millhands, and Mountaineers*, 53-55, 60, 63; Shackelford and Weinberg, eds., *Our Appalachia*, 149-51; Lexington *Herald*, 4 January 1911; New York *Times*, 12 May 1914. Mayo's son said his father's estate was valued at only $600,000, but other estimates placed its real value as high as $20 million. The court decisions can be found in 127 Kentucky 667-722 and 219 U.S. 140.

66. Eller, *Miners, Millhands, and Mountaineers*, 60, 63; Helen M. Lewis, Linda Johnson, and Donald Askins, eds., *Colonialism in Modern America: The Appalachian Case* (1978), passim; D. H. Stigall, "The Mountain Problem: How It May Be Solved" (undergraduate thesis, Eastern Kentucky State Normal School, 1913), 4.

67. Quoted in David E. Whisnant, *Modernizing the Mountaineer* (1980), 9.

68. Judge Watson, "The Economic and Cultural Development of Eastern Kentucky From 1900 to the Present" (Ph.D. diss., Indiana University, 1963), 50-52; Mabel Brown Ellis, "Children of the Kentucky Coal Fields," *The American Child* 1 (1920): 289.

69. Willard Rouse Jillson, *The Coal Industry in Kentucky* (2d ed., 1924), 38, 27; Henry C. Mayer, "A Brief History of the Kentucky Coal Industry," in Forrest Cameron, ed., *The Kentucky Underground Coal Mine Handbook* (1985), 173-74; Claude E. Pickard, "The Western Kentucky Coal Fields: The Influence of Coal Mining in the Settlement Patterns, Forms, and Functions" (Ph.D. diss., University of Nebraska, 1969), 47; Paul Camplin, *A New History of Muhlenberg County* (1984), 25; Springfield *Sun*, 12 July 1911; Transcript of Interview with Buck Layne, 10 March 1976, Knott County Central High School Oral History Project.

70. Pete Browning, "You Can't Quit," *Mountain Review* 2 (1976): 9; Interview with J. Jake Jordan, Eastern Kentucky University Oral History Center; Transcripts of Interviews with Ed Morgan, 7 July 1978, and Dan Young, 28 August 1978, both in FNSOHP; Shackelford and Weinberg, eds., *Our Appalachia*, 218; Lawrence, "Appalachian Metamorphosis," 80, 88.

71. Watson, "Development of Eastern Kentucky," 47; Whisnant, *Modernizing the Mountaineer*, 258-59; Eller, *Miners, Millhands, and Mountaineers*, 190; Breckinridge, *M. M. Breckinridge*, 224; Bodley and Wilson, *History of Kentucky*, 2: 642.

72. Thomas A. Keleman, "A History of Lynch, Kentucky, 1917-1930," *FCHQ* 48 (1974): 156-76; Ellis, "Children of Coal Fields," 333.

73. Michael S. Armour, "A Tribute to Wheelwright," *Mantrip* 4 (1989): 5-6; Shackelford and Weinberg, eds., *Our Appalachia*, 218-19; Lawrence, "Appalachian Metamorphosis," 80.

74. Ellis, "Children of Coal Fields," 317; Bruce Crawford, "The Coal Miner," in W. T. Couch, ed., *Culture in the South* (1934), 363; Lawrence, "Appalachian Metamorphosis," 155; Eller, *Miners, Millhands, and Mountaineers*, 184, 190; Henry P. Scalf, *Kentucky's Last Frontier* (2d ed., 1972), 329-30; Ellis, "Children of Coal Fields," 329, 324.

75. Hooker, *Religion in the Highlands*, 99.

76. Pete Daniel, *Standing at the Crossroads: Southern Life Since 1900* (1986), 18; Thomas, *Life Among the Hills*, 24; Shackelford and Weinberg, eds., *Our Appalachia*, 222; Hooker, *Religion in the Highlands*, 100; Sally Maggard, "From Farmers to Miners: The Decline of Agriculture in Eastern Kentucky," in Lawrence Busch, *Science and Agricultural Development* (1981), 39.

77. Doug Cantrell, "Immigrants and Community in Harlan County, 1910-1930," *Register* 86 (1988): 121-32, 137-41. Overall, industrialization had virtually no effect on family life characteristics between 1880 and 1910 except coal families split from parental household earlier. See Thomas A. Arcury, "Industrialization and Household Family Life Characteristics: Appalachian Kentucky Young Adults in 1880 and 1910," *Journal of Family History* 15 (1990): 308-10.

78. Ellis, "Children of Coal Fields," 342-45; Joe D. Carr, "Labor Conflict in the Eastern Kentucky Coal Fields," *FCHQ* 47 (1973): 180; Crawford, "Coal Miner," 361; "'They Let the Black Man Go So Long Before They Ever Done Anything For Him'. . . An Interview with Hilton Garrett," *Mantrip* 4 (1980): 21.

79. Paul F. Cressey, "Social Disorganization and Reorganization in Harlan County, Kentucky," *American Sociological Review* 14 (1949): 390; Transcript of Interview with Tempie Young, August 29, 1978, FNSOHP.

80. Keleman, "Lynch," 175; Ronald D Eller, "Industrialization and Social Change in Appalachia, 1880-1930," in Lewis, Johnson, and Askins, *Colonialism in Modern America*, 41.

81. Ellis, "Children of the Coal Fields," 310, 313; Harry M. Caudill, *Night Comes to the Cumberlands* (1963), 115, 175; Martin, *Hollybush*, 87; Thomas, *Life Among the Hills*, 61.

82. Margaret Ripley Wolfe, "The Appalachian Reality: Ethnic and Class Diversity," *East Tennessee Historical Society Publications* 52 and 53 (1981-82): 40-42, 47-49, 52-53, 60; Lawrence, "Appalachian Metamorphosis," 46, 63.

83. Jean Ritchie, *Singing Family of the Cumberlands* (1988; orig. pub. 1955), 3-4, 8, 72, 119, 180-81, 244-54; Charles K. Wolfe, *Kentucky Country: Folk and Country Music of Kentucky* (1982), 152.

84. Loretta Lynn, with George Vecsey, *Loretta Lynn: Coal Miner's Daughter* (1976), 5, 10-12, 22, 2, 60, 106, 30, 14. For an examination of Lynn and Ritchie as musicians, see Wolfe, *Kentucky Country*, 166-67.

85. C. Ray Hall, "Kentucky by the Numbers," Louisville *Courier-Journal Magazine*, 27 November 1988. The universities had different names at the time.

86. Lexington *Herald*, 22 July 1906.

87. *Ibid.*, 26 July 1925; Louisville *Courier-Journal*, 24 November 1938, 25 November 1940; Allen, *A Kentucky Cardinal* (1968; orig. pub. 1895), 43-44; Fox, *The Little Shepherd of Kingdom Come* (1973; orig. pub. 1903), 63.

88. Campbell, *Southern Highlander*, 340, 361. He includes 34 Kentucky counties in Appalachia.

89. *Twelfth Census* (1900), vol. 1: *Population*, pt. 1, xviii, xxiv; P. P. Karan and Cotton Mather, *Atlas of Kentucky* (1977), 16; *Abstract of the Thirteenth Census* (1910), 23-24.

90. Springfield *Sun*, 14 December 1910; *Abstract of the Thirteenth Census* (1910), 38; Pickard, "The Western Kentucky Coal Fields," 26; Jasper B. Shannon, *Fifty Years of Population Trends in Kentucky by Geographic Regions* (1938), 4.

91. Merton Oyler, "Natural Increase and Migration of Kentucky Population: 1920 to 1935," *Kentucky Agricultural Experiment Station Bulletin* No. 395 (1939), 271; *Abstract of the Thirteenth Census* (1910), 82; William E. Connelley and E. Merton Coulter, *History of Kentucky* (5 vols., 1922), 2: 996; *Fifteenth Census* (1930), vol. 3: *Population*, pt. 1, 24.

92. Leonard E. Meece, "Negro Education in Kentucky," *Bulletin of the Bureau of School Service* [University of Kentucky] 10 (March 1938): 23; *Twelfth Census* (1900), vol. 1: *Population*, pt. 1, cxix, cxxii; *The Crisis* 4 (September 1912): 218.

93. Meece, "Negro Education," 24-27, 31-32; *Fifteenth Census* (1930), vol. 3: *Population*, pt. 1, 913-20.

94. *Twelfth Census* (1900), vol. 1: *Population*, pt. 1, cxxxii, cxlix, clix; Oyler, "Natural Increase," 256-57; *Abstract of the Thirteenth Census* (1910), 175.

95. *Twelfth Census* (1900), vol. 1: *Population*, pt. 1, civ, xcix, cvii-cix; Louisville Genealogical Society *Lines and By-Lines* 5 (1990): 2; Stanley Ousley, "The Kentucky Irish American," *FCHQ* 53 (1979): 195; Harriette Simpson Arnow, *Seedtime on the Cumberland* (1983; orig. pub. 1960), 5.

96. Harold U. Faulkner, *The Quest for Social Justice, 1898-1914* (1931), 16; *Abstract of the Thirteenth Census* (1910), 83, 86, 206-7, 217; *Fifteenth Census* (1930), vol. 3: *Population*, pt. 1, 28.

97. Ford, *Health and Demography*, 16; *Twelfth Census* (1900), vol. 1: *Population*, pt. 1, lxxxiv; *1980 Census of Population*, vol. 1, pt. 19, 19-7; *Fifteenth Census* (1930), vol 3: *Population*, pt. 1, 29.

98. *Twelfth Census* (1900), vol. 1: *Population*, pt. 1, lxix-xx; *Abstract of the Thirteenth Census*

(1910), 63, 56, 68.

99. *Abstract of the Thirteenth Census* (1910), 95-96.

100. *Twelfth Census* (1900), vol. 1: *Population*, pt. 1, clx, vol. 3: *Vital Statistics*, pt. 1, liv; *Abstract of the Thirteenth Census* (1910), 101, 260; Mary C. Erwin, "The Vicious Circle: A Study of the Effects of the Depression and New Deal Relief Programs in Eastern Kentucky" (M.A. thesis, University of Louisville, 1968), 37; *1970 Census of Population: Age at First Marriage*, 78; John Modell, Frank F. Furstenberg, and Douglas Strong, "The Timing of Marriage in the Transition to Adulthood . . . 1860-1975," in John Demos and Sorane S. Boocock, eds., *Turning Points: Historical and Sociological Essays on the Family* (1978), 122-43; Graham B. Sparrier and Paul C. Glick, "The Life Cycle of American Families: An Extended Analysis," *Journal of Family History* 5 (1980): 98-112.

101. Louisville *Courier-Journal*, 26 September 1931; H. H. Mitchell, "Health," in *Child Welfare in Kentucky* (1919), 22, 20; Lexington *Herald*, 28 October 1915; Breckinridge, *M. M. Breckinridge*, 153, 132; Kentucky *Acts* (1912), 353-72; (1944), 174-79; "Vital Statistics Report . . . ," *Bulletin of the Department of Health* 17 (August 1944): 2; *Kentucky 1973 Vital Statistics* (n.d.), 18; Committee for Kentucky, *A Report on Health* (1945), 4.

102. Mitchell, "Health," 24-25; Ellis, "Children of Coal Fields," 300; Grace M. Hatch, "The Hindman Settlement School," *Kentucky Magazine* 1 (1917): 389; Frederick Eberson, *Portraits: Kentucky Pioneers in Community Health and Medicine* (1968), 101-10; Ellis, *Medicine in Kentucky*, 72; D. Anthony Smith and Arthur H. Kenney, "Linda Neville . . . ," *FCHQ* 64 (1990): 360-76; 67 (1993): 467-81. See also Judy Gail Cornett, "Angel for the Blind: The Public Triumphs and Private Tragedy of Linda Neville" (Ph.D. diss., University of Kentucky, 1993).

103. Mitchell, "Health," 26-27; Lexington *Annual Report* (1916), 7; Joseph J. Eisenbeis, "Recollections of Louisville, Kentucky, 1890-1930" (typescript, Filson Club); Eversole, "Memories," 20; Mary T. Brewer, *Rugged Trail to Appalachia: A History of Leslie County* . . . (1978), 4; John Clement, *Kentucky Facts* (1990), 215, 294, 319; Daniel E. McClure, Jr., *Two Centuries in Elizabethtown and Hardin County, Kentucky* (1979), 421; Kentucky *Acts* (1912), 213-14; *Abstract of the Twelfth Census* (1900), 178, 208-13, 186, 190; Report of the Efficiency Commission, *The Government of Kentucky* (2 vols., 1924), 2: 623. Sewers came to these communities at these times: Mt. Sterling (1909), Benton (1930), Lancaster (1938), Somerset (1940), and Carlisle (1965).

104. Committee for Kentucky, *Report on Health*, 3; James T. Patterson, *America's Struggle Against Poverty, 1900-1980* (1981), 15; Mark Sullivan, *Our Times* (6 vols., 1926-35), 1: 473.

105. Sullivan, *Our Times*, 2: 515; Louisville *Courier-Journal*, 2, 5 April 1903; Lexington *Herald*, 24 February 1905; Hickman *Courier*, 3 October 1912; Thomas D. Clark, *The Southern Country Editor* (1948), 68-69; Thomas Sugrue, *There is a River* (1942), passim; Vince Staten, "The Prophet from Kentucky," Louisville *Courier-Journal*, 5 March 1994.

106. Lexington *Daily Leader*, 15 March 1901; Lexington *Herald*, 21 July 1910; Clifford Amyx, "The Death of a Railroad Town: Boyhood Memories," *Appalachian Heritage* 17 (1989): 53-54; Louisville *Courier-Journal*, 12 April 1903; Hazel Green *Herald*, 6 January 1910.

107. Kentucky *Board of Health Report* (1908-09), 67, 136.

108. Margaret Ripley Wolfe, "The Agricultural Experiment Station and Food and Drug Control: Another Look at Kentucky Progressivism, 1898-1916," *FCHQ* 49 (1975): 325-28, 335-38; Kentucky *Acts* (1908), 10-22; *Report of the Kentucky Agricultural Experiment Station on the Enforcement of the Pure Food Law*, in *Kentucky Documents* (1903), 4-5, 25; Louisville *Courier-Journal*, 25 February 1910; Sullivan, *Our Times*, 2: 518, 527, 530-50; James H. Young, *Pure Food: Securing the Federal Food and Drugs Act of 1906* (1989), 179-80.

109. Frederic D. Ogden, ed., *The Public Papers of Governor Keen Johnson, 1939-1943* (1982), 218; Grantham, *Southern Progressivism*, 311; Kentucky *Acts* (1904), 100-106, 86; (1914), 52-59; (1918), 290-353; Mitchell, "Health," 16; Ellis, *Medicine in Kentucky*, 74; Irwin T. Sanders, "Health

and Welfare," in Howard W. Beers, ed., *Kentucky: Designs for Her Future* (1945), 254. See also Robert L. Spraw and Edward B. Gernert, *History of Kentucky Dentistry* (1960), 120.

110. Kentucky *Board of Health Report* (1908-09), 67; Federal Writers' Project, *A Centennial History of the University of Louisville* (1939), 65, 81-88; Dolores Smith, "Medical Education in Kentucky . . . 1817-1920" (E.S. thesis, University of Louisville, 1976), 36, 95.

111. J. S. Chambers and Harry R. Lynn, "Medical Service in Kentucky," *University of Kentucky Studies in Medical Science* 1 (1931): 5-9, 15, 29, 32, 39-41; Joyce Wilson, *This Was Yesterday: A Romantic History of Owsley County* (1977), 16, 18.

112. Charles M. Meacham, *A History of Christian County Kentucky* (1930), 234.

113. Morton Keller, *Affairs of State: Public Life in Late Nineteenth Century America* (1977), 599-600; Richard G. Stone, Jr., *Kentucky Fighting Men, 1861-1945* (1982), 35; Ruth Perkins, "Green County Obituaries . . . ," *Green County Review* 12 (1988-89): 25; Williamstown *Courier*, 21 February 1901; Lexington *Daily Leader*, 20 March 1901; Columbia *Adair County News*, 3 July 1901; Lexington *Morning Herald*, 1 January 1901.

114. Quoted in James Larry Hood, "The Collapse of Zion: Rural Progressivism in Nelson and Washington Counties, Kentucky" (Ph.D. diss., University of Kentucky, 1980), 138; Carl N. Degler, *Out of Our Past: The Forces that Shaped Modern America* (1962), 316-17, 329.

115. Louisville *Courier-Journal*, 24 January, 13 February, 17 April, 22 May, 23 June, 25 May, 1 June, 14, 19 March, 28 April, 24 May, 5 June, 24 March 1901. For a full listing of events of 1901 see a printed index to that year's *Courier-Journal*, copy available at the Kentucky Historical Society.

116. Robert Penn Warren, *Portrait of a Father* (1988), 49; Dudden, "Nostalgia and the American," 516-17, 527-28; Thomas D. Clark and Albert D. Kirwan, *The South Since Appamottox* (1967), 10; Fox, *Little Shepherd*, 139; Thomas D. Clark, *Agrarian Kentucky* (1977), viii-x.

117. Thomas A. Knight and Nancy Lewis Greene, *Country Estates of the Blue Grass* (1905), [6].

118. Clark, *Kentucky: Land of Contrast*, 238-39; Odum, *Southern Regions*, 13; Thomas D. Clark, "Rural Life," in Charles Reagan Wilson and William Ferris, eds., *Encyclopedia of Southern Culture* (1989), 9, 11; Wendell Berry, *A Continuous Harmony: Essays Cultural and Agricultural* (1970), 79.

119. Louisville *Courier-Journal*, 11-17 June 1906.

2. *"Divided We Fall"*: Violence in Kentucky

1. James C. Klotter, "Feuds in Appalachia: An Overview," *FCHQ* 56 (1982): 291-94; idem, *William Goebel: The Politics of Wrath* (1977), 126; unidentified clipping, 5 February 1900, in Goebel Collection held by Charles Atcher, Lexington; Cleveland *Plain Dealer*, 8 May 1905, in Bradley Family Papers, University of Kentucky Library.

2. New York *Times*, 13 September 1879, 9 July 1885; Chicago *Tribune*, 23 July 1885; Henry D. Shapiro, *Appalachia on Our Mind: The Southern Mountains and Mountaineers in the American Consciousness* (1978), passim.

3. "Kentucky's Political Anarchy," *Harper's Weekly* (10 February 1900), 126; Klotter, *Goebel*, 103-14; Isaac F. Marcosson, *Adventures in Interviewing* (1919), 22.

4. See, for example, Lexington *Leader*, 31 August 1910.

5. Klotter, *Goebel*, 115-25; Francis X. Busch, *They Escaped the Hangman* (1953), 13-100; L. F. Johnson, *Famous Kentucky Tragedies and Trials* (1972; orig. pub. 1916), 308-19. See also R. E. Hughes, F. W. Schaefer, and E. L. Williams, *That Kentucky Campaign* (1900), Urey Woodson, *The*

First New Dealer (1939), 73-138, 255-73, and Caleb Powers, *My Own Story* (1905), 155-490.

6. Klotter, *Goebel*, 123-25.

7. Virgil Carrington Jones, *The Hatfields and the McCoys* (1948), 223, 229, 222; Altina L. Waller, *Feud: Hatfields, McCoys, and Social Changes in Appalachia, 1860-1900* (1988), 6, 238-43; Otis K. Rice, *The Hatfields and the McCoys* (1978), 121-22; "In the Land of the Great French-Eversole War," *Kentucky Explorer* 4 (1990): 48; Hazard *Herald*, 30 April 1926; Hartley Davis and Clifford Smyth, "The Land of Feuds," *Munsey's Magazine* 30 (1903): 165; Louisville *Courier-Journal*, 16 June 1918.

8. John F. Day, *Bloody Ground* (1981; orig. pub. 1941), 116-17; E. Carl Litsey, "Kentucky Feuds and Their Causes," *Frank Leslie's Popular Monthly* 53 (1902): 284, 287; Davis and Smyth, "Land of Feuds," 162, 172; William H. Haney, *The Mountain People of Kentucky* (1906) 72-73, 76. See Klotter, "Feuds in Appalachia," for a fuller discussion of feud causation.

9. Waller, *Feud*, 6-12, 232-33, 249; Gordon B. McKinney, *Southern Mountain Republicans, 1865-1900* (1978), 126-28; John Alexander Williams, *West Virginia* (1976), 97.

10. Klotter, "Feuds in Appalachia," 311-14; I. J. Schwartz, *Kentucky*, trans. by Gertrude W. Dubrovsky (1990), 54; Ronald D Eller, *Miners, Millhands, and Mountaineers: Industrialization of the Appalachian South, 1880-1930* (1982), 30; J. Wayne Flynt, *Dixie's Forgotten People: The South's Poor Whites* (1979), 128. See also John C. Campbell, *The Southern Highlander & His Homeland* (1969; orig. pub. 1921), 111, and James W. Raine, *The Land of Saddle-bags* (1924), 141-43.

11. E. L. Noble, *Bloody Breathitt's Feuds* (4 vols., 1936-47), 3: 8, 15; New York *Times*, 5 May 1903; Lexington *Herald*, 7-8 February 1908.

12. Johnson, *Tragedies and Trials*, 320-36; Kelly Kash, "Feud Days in Breathitt County," *FCHQ* 28 (1954): 343; Noble, *Breathitt*, 3: 11-13; New York *Times*, 7 November 1909; "Marcum Assassination . . . ," *Kentucky Explorer* 4 (1989): 16; William Dinwiddie, "The 'Feud' in Jackson, Kentucky" (typescript, copy in author's possession), 7. Kash, Noble, and Dinwiddie all were eyewitnesses to many of the events described herein. Cockrill is sometimes spelled Cockrell in the accounts.

13. Kash, "Feud Days," 344; Noble, *Breathitt*, 3: 35-37, 41; Dinwiddie, "Feud in Jackson," 9-10; "Marcum Assassination," 20; Louisville *Courier-Journal*, 13 June 1906. Jett was also related to the Cockrills of the other faction.

14. Thomas D. Clark, *The Kentucky* (1969; orig. pub. 1942), 19; New York *Times*, 15 August 1903; Lexington *Herald*, 9 November 1902; R. L. McClure, "The Mazes of a Kentucky Feud," *The Independent* (17 September 1903), 2218; Davis and Smyth, "Land of Feuds," 170.

15. Dinwiddie, "Feud in Jackson," 11-12; "The Great Hargis-Marcum Feud," *Kentucky Explorer* 4 (1989): 61; New York *Times*, 5 May 1903; Noble, *Breathitt*, 3: 55-58; Kash, "Feud Days," 346-47; *History of the First Regiment of Infantry, Kentucky State Guard-Louisville Legion* (n.d.), 163.

16. New York *Times*, 23 May, 20 June, 15 August, 23 September 1903; Johnson, *Tragedies and Trials*, 327-32; Lexington *Leader*, 14 August 1903; Bernice C. Caudill, *Pioneers of Eastern Kentucky, Their Feuds and Settlements* (1969), 95-96; Meriel D. Harris, "Two Famous Kentucky Feuds and Their Causes" (M. A. thesis, University of Kentucky, 1940), 92; New York *Times*, 3 April, 16 May 1904; Louisville *Courier-Journal*, 13 June 1906; Noble, *Breathitt*, 3: 116-18.

17. Lexington *Herald*, 24 May 1907, 7-8 February, 31 May 1908; Johnson, *Tragedies and Trials*, 333-36; Noble, *Breathitt*, 3: 109-10; Hazel Green *Herald*, 7 October 1909; Kash, "Feud Days," 350-52. The Lexington *Herald*, 8 February 1908, gave Beach's full name as Beauchamp Cooper Hargis; George W. Noble, *Behold He Cometh In the Clouds* (1912), 156, says the name was Henry Ward Beecher Hargis.

18. *Post* quoted in Lexington *Leader*, 2 August 1903; Hazel Green *Herald*, 23 September 1909; Charles K. Wolfe, *Kentucky Country: Folk and Country Music of Kentucky* (1982), 155; Louis-

ville *Courier-Journal*, 1 May 1927.

19. John C. Miller, *The Black Patch War* (1936), 3-9, describes the process in the Black Patch. Little had changed since cultivation in colonial times. See T. H. Breen, *Tobacco Culture* (1985), 46-51.

20. Tracy A. Campbell, "The Politics of Despair: The Tobacco Wars of Kentucky and Tennessee" (Ph.D. diss., Duke University, 1988), 30-32; Marie Taylor, "Night Riders in the Black Patch" (M. A. thesis, University of Kentucky, 1934), 7; James O. Nall, *The Tobacco Night Riders of Kentucky and Tennessee, 1905-1909* (1939), 7-8.
See also Suzanne Marshall, *Violence in the Black Patch of Kentucky and Tennessee* (1994), Rick S. Gregory, "Desperate Farmers: The Dark Tobacco District Planters' Protective Association of Kentucky and Tennessee, 1904-1914" (Ph.D. diss., Vanderbilt University, 1989), and Christopher Waldrep, "The Night Riders and the Law in Kentucky and Tennessee, 1870-1911" (Ph.D. diss., Ohio State University, 1990). The Campbell dissertation was published in revised form as the *Politics of Despair: Power and Resistance in the Tobacco Wars* (1993) and the Waldrep one as *Night Riders: Defending Community in the Black Patch, 1890-1915* (1993).

21. W. F. Axton, *Tobacco and Kentucky* (1975), 83, 87; Campbell, "Politics of Despair," 35, 38, 42; Christopher Waldrep, "Tobacco Farmers, The Tobacco 'Trust,' and the Federal Government," *Journal of Kentucky Studies* 1 (1984): 188-91.

22. Campbell, "Politics of Despair," 46, 70; Waldrep, *Night Riders*, 7; Nall, *Tobacco Night Riders*, 22, 36; New York *Times*, 23 June 1914. The organization originally had another name.

23. Dewey W. Grantham, Jr., "Black Patch War: The Story of the Kentucky and Tennessee Night Riders, 1905-1909," *South Atlantic Quarterly* 59 (1960): 216-17; Arthur Krock, *Memoirs* (1968), 35; Nall, *Tobacco Night Riders*, 19, 35; Campbell, "Politics of Despair," 76, 108; Marie Taylor, "Night Riders in the Black Patch," *Register* 61 (1963): 295; "The Night Riders," *The Outlook* (29 February 1908), 483; Waldrep, *Night Riders*, 47-48.

24. Taylor, "Night Riders" (article), 296; Nall, *Tobacco Night Riders*, 28; Theodore Saloutos, "The American Society of Equity in Kentucky: A Recent Attempt in Agrarian Reform," *Journal of Southern History* 5 (1939): 361-62.

25. Nall, *Tobacco Night Riders*, 43-45; Charles M. Meacham, *A History of Christian County, Kentucky* (1930), 345; Clauscine R. Baker, *First History of Caldwell County Kentucky* (1936), 141.

26. Miller, *Black Patch War*, 18-22.

27. Meacham, *Christian County*, 347; Taylor, "Night Riders" (article), 297.

28. Forrest C. Pogue, Jr., "The Life and Work of Senator Ollie Murray James" (M.A. thesis, University of Kentucky, 1932), 30; F. S. Ewing to A. O. Stanley, 18 June, 8 December 1909, A. O. Stanley Papers, General File, Box I, University of Kentucky Library; Wayne E. Cabral, "Night Riding: A Study in Economic and Social Disruption" (M. A. thesis, Eastern Kentucky University, 1972), 71-72; John L. Mathews, "The Farmers' Union and the Tobacco Pool," *Atlantic Monthly* (October 1908), 488; Campbell, "Politics of Despair," 188, 195.

29. Grantham, "Black Patch War," 219; Miller, *Black Patch War*, 21, 42, 50, 58. See W. O. Mers to the author, 13 March 1980, for a description of one fortified home.
On the constitutional issue, see *Franks* v. *Smith* 134 S. W. 484; Mary H. Miller, *A Citizen's Guide to the Kentucky Constitution*, LRC Research Report No. 137 (1981), 38; and Christopher Waldrep, "Augustus E. Willson and the Night Riders," *FCHQ* 58 (1984): 242.

30. Bill Cunningham, *On Bended Knees: The Night Rider Story* (1983) 28-36; Nall, *Tobacco Night Riders*, 57, 60; Taylor, "Night Riders" (thesis), 27-28; Campbell, "Politics of Despair," 141.

31. Campbell, "Politics of Despair," 144, 124-25, 136, 153; Hickman *Courier*, 19 November 1908.

32. Temple Bodley and Samuel M. Wilson, *History of Kentucky* (4 vols., 1928), 2: 710; Campbell, "Politics of Despair," 159; Taylor "Night Riders" (thesis), 35-36, 42-43; Cunningham, *On Bended Knee*, 104-6; Nall, *Tobacco Night Riders*, 75-81; Waldrep, *Night Riders*, 83, 86-88, 97-98. See also William H. Henderson, "The Night Riders Raid on Hopkinsville," *FCHQ* 24 (1950): 346-58, and William M. Boden, "The Nightriders Invade Hopkinsville," *Register* 55 (1957): 345-46.

33. Bill Cunningham, "The Black Patch War," *Rural Kentuckian* 36 (December 1982): 8; Waldrep, *Night Riders*, 100, 121; Nall, *Tobacco Night Riders*, 79-81, 109, 137-38. Almost any Kentucky newspaper for 1908 covers the various attacks. See, for example, Paducah *Weekly News-Democrat*, 9 January, 13, 20 February, 26 March, 16 April 1908. See Tylene McNeill to author, 7 January 1980, for an eyewitness's recollection of the Eddyville raid.

34. Nall, *Tobacco Night Riders*, 38, 141-43; Campbell, "Politics of Despair," 179-81; Owensboro *Inquirer*, 20 February 1908; George C. Wright, "The forced removal of Afro-Americans from rural Kentucky," *Reflections: Occasional Papers on Research in Kentucky Public Records* 1 (1990): 3-4; Paducah *Weekly News-Democrat*, 12 March, 8 October 1908; Cabral, "Night Riding," 76.

35. "Resolution passed in a meeting of the Board of Directors of the Planters Protective Association . . . July 25, 1907," and F. G. Ewing to [A. E. Willson], 7 January 1908, both in Preston-Johnston Papers, P. P. Johnston I, Series VII, Box 1, University of Kentucky Library; Meacham, *Christian County*, 354-55.

36. L. W. Kenney to Willson, 14 December 1907, Charles M. Meacham, James Breathitt, and John C. Duffy to Willson, 14 December 1907, Homer B. Bryson to Willson, 30 September 1907, A. E. Willson Papers, Filson Club; Waldrep, "Willson and Night Riders," 239.

37. Willson to Charles L. Gray, 17 September 1910 (copy), Willson Papers; Nall, *Tobacco Night Riders*, 160; Lexington *Herald*, 23 August 1908; L. F. Johnson, *The History of Franklin County, Ky.* (1912), 236-37; John Stites to Willson, 2 January 1910, Willson Papers.

38. Richard G. Stone, Jr., *A Brittle Sword: The Kentucky Militia, 1776-1912* (1977), 97; Christopher R. Waldrep, "The Law, The Night Riders, and Community Consensus: The Prosecution of Dr. David Amoss," *Register* 82 (1984): 235-56; idem, "'Human Wolves': The Night Riders and the Killing of Axiom Cooper," *ibid.* 81 (1983): 407-24; Waldrep, *Night Riders*, 125, 167, 178-81; Miller, *Black Patch War*, 72.

39. Paducah *Weekly News-Democrat*, 3 December 1908; Campbell, "Politics of Despair," 231-33, 222, 165; Campbell, *Politics of Despair*, 107-33; Axton, *Tobacco and Kentucky*, 94-95; Lexington *Leader*, 5 November 1915.

40. Axton, *Tobacco and Kentucky*, 86; Bodley and Wilson, *History of Kentucky*, 2: 34.

41. William E. Connelley and E. M. Coulter, *History of Kentucky* (5 vols., 1922), 2: 1014; Nall, *Tobacco Night Riders*, 119; New York *Times*, 26 August 1915; "The Willson Landscape or Hager's Dream" (pamphlet), W. O. Bradley Scrapbooks, 1907, University of Kentucky Library; Paducah *Weekly News-Democrat*, 27 February 1908.

42. George C. Wright, *Racial Violence in Kentucky, 1865-1940* (1990), 118-19, 112-13; Lexington *Herald*, 17-18 October 1916. Lynchings as used herein may also refer to mob murders of blacks in ways other than by hanging. See, for instance, Lexington *Herald*, 1 June 1908.

43. Wright, *Racial Violence*, 71, 7-8, 10; Edward L. Ayers, *Vengeance and Justice: Crime and Punishment in the 19th-Century American South* (1984), 241.

44. Wright, *Racial Violence*, 4, 64, 320-23.

45. *Ibid.*, 222, 294-301; Johnson, *History of Franklin County*, 164.

46. Wright, *Racial Violence*, 287-90; *Hale* v. *Commonwealth*, 269 Kentucky Reports 743; 303 U.S. 613 (1938).

47. Wright, *Racial Violence*, 227, 251-55.

48. *Ibid.*, 256-58; Lexington *Herald*, 28 August 1925, 20-23 January, 3 February, 5-6 March 1926, 26 November 1927, 18 June 1932; New York *Times*, 6 March 1926; Lee A. Dew, "The Hanging of Rainey Bethea," *Daviess County Historical Quarterly* 2 (1984): 51-59.

49. Lexington *Leader*, 31 October 1919; New York *Times*, 1 November 1919; Lexington *Herald*, 1 November 1919; Wright, *Racial Violence*, 145-47. At Dix River in 1924, whites tried to force black workers from a construction site, but through the efforts of the construction company and the National Guard, the black workers were able to return. See Lexington *Herald*, 10-15 November 1924. *The Crisis* 21 (April 1921), reported that the leader of the Corbin mob had been convicted and sent to jail for a two-year term. People interviewed about the event in 1977 had varied and often conflicting recollections. See transcripts in the Sue Bennett College Library.

50. Wright, *Racial Violence*, 180-82, 202-4, 211; Lexington *Herald*, 25 June 1926. See also A. E. Willson to Ralph Gilbert, 18 January 1911, Willson Papers.

51. A. O. Stanley to Sue Soaper Stanley, 2, 8 April 1908, Box 2, Stanley Papers; Lexington *Herald*, 12 January 1917; Wright, *Racial Violence*, 193-94, 199.

52. Mt. Vernon (Ky.) *Signal*, 23 August 1901; Kentucky *Adjutant General's Report* (1904), 21; Wright, *Racial Violence*, 189; *The Crisis* 19 (April 1920): 298.

53. On Lockett, see John D. Wright, Jr., "Lexington's Suppression of the 1920 Will Lockett Lynch Mob," *Register* 84 (1986): 263-79; J. Winston Coleman, Jr., "Death at the Court-House" (pamphlet, 1952), 1-28; Joe Jordan, "Lynchers Don't Like Lead," *Atlantic Quarterly* 177 (February 1946): 103-8; Lexington *Herald*, 10-16 February, 11 March 1920; New York *Times*, 10 February 1920; St. Louis *Post-Dispatch*, 15 February 1920.

54. H. C. Bearly, "The Pattern of Violence," in W. T. Couch, ed., *Culture in the South* (1934), 679; Henry A. Ploski and Roscoe C. Brown, eds., *The Negro Almanac* (1967), 213.

55. George L. Willis, *Kentucky Democracy* (3 vols., 1935), 1: 421; Harry M. Caudill, *Night Comes to the Cumberlands* (1963), 135; New York *Times*, 10 November 1921, 8 November 1933.

56. William E. Ellis, H. E. Everman, and Richard D. Sears, *Madison County: 200 Years in Retrospect* (1985), 273-74; Joyce Wilson, *This Was Yesterday: A Romantic History of Owsley County* (1977), 74; William E. Ellis, "'The Harvest Moon was Shinin' on the Streets of Shelbyville': Southern Honor and the Death of General Henry H. Denhardt, 1937," *Register* 84 (1986): 361-96; John Ed Pearce, "Murder Most Mysterious," Louisville *Courier-Journal Magazine*, 8 December 1985, 14-18, 52-58; New York *Sunday News*, 3 October 1937.

57. Pete Daniel, *Standing at the Crossroads: Southern Life Since 1900* (1986), 51; William Lynwood Montell, *Killings: Folk Justice in the Upper South* (1986), xv, 151; Raymond D. Gastil, "Homicide and a Regional Culture of Violence," *American Sociological Review* 36 (1971): 412; Ayers, *Vengeance and Justice*, 270.

58. Montell, *Killings*, 130-32.

59. Williamstown *Courier*, 3 January 1901; "Changing Faces, Common Walls: History of Corrections in Kentucky" (10th ed., 1985), 10; Federal Bureau of Investigation, *Uniform Crime Reports* 4 (October 1933): 9; 16 (1945): 92.

60. *Bulletin of the State Board of Health of Kentucky* 6 (June 1934): 29-30; *1955 Kentucky Vital Statistics Report* (1956), 2; Gestil, "Homicide," 415; *Vital Statistics of the United States, 1976: Mortality*, Part B (1979), 459-65; Vince Staten, "Is Kentucky Southern?" Louisville *Courier-Journal Magazine*, 29 November 1987, 7; FBI *Uniform Crime Reports* (1989), 50; (1977), 44-53.

61. Louisville *Courier-Journal*, 19 January 1906; Lexington *Herald*, 11 October 1908; Springfield *Sun*, 14 December 1910; clipping dated 24 January 1911, Appalachian Feuds Collection,

Southern Appalachian Archives, Berea College Library; E. Polk Johnson, *A History of Kentucky and Kentuckians* (3 vols., 1912), 1: 130; Irvin S. Cobb, *Kentucky* (1924), 26.

3. "All Happy and Bright": Life in Kentucky

1. Ercel S. Eaton, *Appalachian Yesterdays* (1982), 9; Alben W. Barkley, *That Reminds Me* (1954), 43, 48; Fred W. Peel, "Growing up in Central Ky.," 48 (typescript, Kentucky Historical Society); William Lynwood Montell, *Don't Go Up Kettle Creek: Verbal Legacy of the Upper Cumberland* (1983), 173; James A. Stevens, "Home in Boone County: Life on the Farm, 1917-1937," n.p.; Arthur Krock, *Myself When Young* (1973), 11; Mabel Green Condon, *A History of Harlan County* (1962), 154.

2. Elizabeth Madox Roberts, *The Time of Man* (1982; orig. pub. 1926), 277, 240; L. L. Miles to Robert W. Bingham, 24 July 1933, Papers of Robert Worth Bingham, Manuscript Division, Library of Congress.

3. Metcalfe County Inventory Book, Reel 2920, Box 26, Special Collections, University of Kentucky Library, 278-305, 290-91; Manuscript Census (1900), Metcalfe County, Kentucky; *Metcalfe County, Kentucky Cemetery Records*, Vol. I (1983), 175.

4. Metcalfe County Inventory Book, 298-99; Manuscript Census (1900), Metcalfe County, Kentucky.

5. Transcript of Interview with Rev. and Mrs. Edward Coffman, 16 September 1977, Kentucky Oral History Commission (hereafter KOHC), Kentucky Historical Society; Joseph Jacob Eisenbeis, "Recollections of Louisville, Kentucky, 1890-1930," [4-5] (typescript, Filson Club); Tom Eversole, "Memories About This and That," 15, 24 (typescript, Kentucky Historical Society); "The Jones Family History," *Green County Review* 2 (1979): 54.

6. Harriette Simpson Arnow, *Old Burnside* (1977), 36; Eversole, "Memories," preface; James W. Broaddus, "The Coffey Family, Father and Son, Rockcastle County, Kentucky, 1880-1957: Oral History and Material Culture with a Small Focus," *Kentucky Folklore Record* 30 (1984): 3.

7. Robert Penn Warren, *Portrait of a Father* (1988), 46; Josiah H. Combs, *Combs: A Study in Comparative Philology and Genealogy* (1976), xiv; Louisville *Courier-Journal*, 12 April 1903.

8. Author's Interview with Arch Mainous, 1988; "Jones Family History," 54; Helen Congleton Breckinridge, *Memories of Cannel City, Kentucky* (1993), 26.

9. Barkley, *That Reminds Me*, 44; Diary, Vol. I, 3, Chester C. Travelstead Collection, Kentucky Library, Western Kentucky University.

10. Peel, "Growing Up," 26, 24; Paul Camplin, *A New History of Muhlenberg County* (1984), 63; Mark Sullivan, *Our Times: The United States, 1900-1925* (6 vols., 1926-35), 1: 404; Irvin S. Cobb, *Exit Laughing* (1941), 50; Barkley, *That Reminds Me*, 16.

11. Peel, "Growing Up," 23; Owensboro *Messenger-Inquirer*, 15 September 1986 (Corinne Taylor Gregory); Louisville *Courier-Journal*, 7 January 1906; Paducah *Weekly Sun*, 20 April, 30 March 1910; Sullivan, *Our Times*, 1: 390, 388; Harold U. Faulkner, *The Quest for Social Justice, 1898-1914* (1931), 170; Sallie C. D. Isaac, *The Story of Drakesboro and Its Founder* (1952), 43; Margaret W. Preston Diary, 1 January 1909, Box 40, Preston-Johnston Papers, University of Kentucky Library; Lexington *Herald*, 20 January 1905.

12. M. B. Morton, *Kentuckians Are Different* (1938), 123; Peel, "Growing Up," 22; Faulkner, *Quest for Social Justice*, 170; Sullivan, *Our Times*, 1: 392.

13. Burton Rascoe, *Before I Forget* (1937), 39; Broaddus, "Coffey Family," 2-3; Peel, "Growing Up," 111; James T. Stewart, "Recollections of Life in Western Hart County During the Early 1900's," *Hart County Historical Society Quarterly* 23 (1991): 10-11.

14. Alfreda Witherington, "The Mountain Doctor," *Atlantic Monthly* 150 (1932): 768; Fred Lewis, "A Story About My Life," *Frontier Nursing Service Quarterly Bulletin* 62 (Autumn 1986): 7; S. S. MacClintock, "The Kentucky Mountains and Their Feuds," *American Journal of Sociology* 7 (July 1901): 12; Arthur W. Spaulding, *The Men of the Mountains* (1915), 69-70; Stevens, "Home in Boone County," Chap. I; "Unique Kentuckian Gives Rare View of Mountain Life of Yesteryear," *Kentucky Explorer* 6 (April 1992): 74; William Lynwood Montell, *Killings: Folk Justice in the Upper South* (1986), 69.

15. Transcript of Interview with Frank Bowling, 31 July 1978, Frontier Nursing Service Oral History Project; Author's Interview with Mike Gabbard, 11 May 1980; Barkley, *That Reminds Me*, 45.

16. *I Remember: The Autobiography of Abraham Flexner* (1940), 23; Louis J. Hebel, "This is the Way it Was," 8-9 (typescript, Filson Club); Stevens, "Home in Boone County," "Summer" chap.; Eisenbeis, "Recollection of Louisville," 27-28; Eaton, *Appalachian Yesterdays*, 59; Author's Interview with Marjorie Gabbard, 11 May 1980; Peel, "Growing Up," 168; J. Marcus Whitler, *Memories of My Youth, 1926-1933, in Breckinridge County, Kentucky* (n.d.), 179-80.

17. Eversole, "Memories," 10; Hebel, "Way It Was," 6; Eisenbeis, "Recollections of Louisville," [46-47]; William E. Ellis, H. E. Everman, and Richard D. Sears, *Madison County: 200 Years in Retrospect* (1985), 260; Sullivan, *Our Times*, 1: 63; Frederich F. Thwing Diary, 19 July 1912, Kentucky Library, Western Kentucky University.

18. John Fox, Jr., *Blue-Grass and Rhododendron: Outdoors in Old Kentucky* (1901), 11; Eversole, "Memories," 38; Charles E. Martin, *Hollybush: Folk Building and Social Change in an Appalachian Community* (1984), 9.

19. Wayne E. Fuller, "Rural Free Delivery," in *Encyclopedia of Southern Culture* (1989), 45; Charles M. Meacham, *A History of Christian County Kentucky* (1930), 234; Cale Young Rice, *Bridging the Years* (1939), 12; Warren, *Portrait of a Father*, 57; Thwing Diary, passim; Rascoe, *Before I Forget*, 48.

20. Owensboro *Messenger-Inquirer*, 22 September 1986 (Dora Landrum, Mittie Dore, Irene Taylor). General statements regarding the time electricity reached towns are based on the author's readings of most printed Kentucky county histories.

21. "Nathan B. Stubblefield and the Vagaries of Success," *Bulletin of the Kentucky Historical Society* 11 (April 1985): 1; Louisville *Courier-Journal*, 7 May 1991; J. Winston Coleman, Jr., *Nathan B. Stubblefield: The Father of Radio* (1982), 7-15.

22. Terry L. Birdwhistell, "WHAS Radio and the Development of Broadcasting in Kentucky, 1922-1942," *Register* 79 (1981): 333, 343-46; George T. Blakey, *Hard Times and New Deal in Kentucky, 1929-1939* (1986), 5; Elmer G. Sulzer, "Mountain Communities Listen In," *Mountain Life and Work* 12 (1937): 15-17; Harry W. Schacter, *Kentucky on the March* (1949), 41; *Purchase Remembrances* (rev. ed., 1982), 63.

23. See Whitler, *Breckinridge Co. Memories*, 417, 442, 496-97, for unusually frank recollections of sexual practices in that era, and Mount Vernon *Signal*, 4 January, 22 March 1901, for advertisements. Kentucky *Acts* (1918), 686-87, forbade ads relating to "a venereal disease . . . or condition of the sexual organs caused by sexual vice."

24. Peel, "Growing Up," 117, 6; Sullivan, *Our Times*, 4: 165; Jennie J. Ashby, "My Story" (typescript copy in author's possession).

25. Ruby Yancey to author, 4 February 1980; *Remembering Barry Bingham* (1990), 15; "If you kicked too much . . . : An Interview with Joe Branham," in *Labor History in Kentucky* (1986), v-31; Albert E. Cowdrey, *This Land, This South* (1983), 6-7.

26. Rascoe, *Before I Forget*, 64; Whitler, *Breckinridge Co. Memories*, 253, 3-4.

27. Gordon Wilson, *Fidelity Folks: A Visit to a Self-Sufficient Kentucky Village* (1946), 6-7;

MacClintock, "Kentucky Mountains," 18; Bowling interview.

28. Senior Honors English, 1988, "Teenage Times in Calloway County, 1900-1987," in *Recollections* (n.d.), 255-56; Whitler, *Breckinridge Co. Memories*, 15; Lewis, "A Story About My Life," 8; Wilson, *Fidelity Folks*, 102, 105; Owensboro *Messenger-Inquirer*, 15 September 1986 (Corinne Gregory); James Larry Hood, "The Collapse of Zion: Rural Progressivism in Nelson and Washington Counties, Kentucky" (Ph.D. diss., University of Kentucky, 1980), 117-18, 171, 243, 305; Lexington *Herald*, 9 February 1930.

29. Camplin, *Muhlenberg County*, 129; Arnow, *Old Burnsides*, 49; Peel, "Growing Up," 61.

30. Daniel E. McClure, *Two Centuries in Elizabethtown and Hardin County, Kentucky, 1776-1976* (1979), 422; Transcript of Interview with W. E. Crutcher, 8 January 1975, 14, Fred Vinson Oral History Project, University of Kentucky Library; Thomas D. Clark, *Pills, Petticoats and Plows: The Southern Country Store* (1944), 37, 22-23, passim; Peel, "Growing Up," 60; Henry May, *The End of American Innocence* (1959), 95.

31. Joan W. Conley, comp., *History of Nicholas County* (1976), 167; H. A. Sommers, *History of Elizabethtown, 1869-1921* (1981), 154; Transcript of Interview with Noel M. Williams, 19 December 1977, KOHC; Thomas D. Clark, *Kentucky: Land of Contrast* (1968), 240.

32. J. Winston Coleman, Jr., *The Squire's Memoirs* (1975), 87; Eleanor B. Chalkley, *Magic Casements* (1982), 68; Lexington *Daily Leader*, 12 December 1900; Lexington *Herald*, 7 January 1923; Thomas D. Clark, *A History of Laurel County* (1989), 309.

33. Judith J. Phillips, "Enlightenment, Education and Entertainment: A Study of the Chautauqua Movement in Kentucky" (M.A. thesis, University of Louisville, 1985), 18; Shelia E. Brown Heflin, "Owensboro's Chautauqua Years, 1902-1932," *Daviess County Historical Quarterly* 1 (1983): 3-11; Paducah *Weekly News-Democrat*, 20 May, 17 June 1909.

34. Heflin, "Owensboro's Chautauqua Years," 7-11; Coffman Interview; Ellis et al., *Madison County*, 312; Phillips, "Enlightenment, Education, and Entertainment," 66-69.

35. *History and Program Commemorating the Founding of the City of Catlettsburg, Kentucky* (1949), 31; Frances M. Marsh, "When I Was a Child in Maysville" (typescript in author's possession), [1]; Hawesville *Hancock Clarion*, 2 October 1986. Kentucky *Acts* (1922), 397-98, prohibited appearances of "persons clothed only in bathing costumes" on roads or city streets.

36. Stephanie Dew, "Vaudeville in Owensboro; 1900-1910," *Daviess County Historical Quarterly* 1 (1983): 56-62; Hebel, "Way It Was," 19-20; Gregory A. Waller, "Introducing the 'Marvellous Inventions' to the Provinces: Film Exhibition in Lexington, Kentucky, 1896-1897," *Film History* 3 (1989): 223; idem, "Situating Motion Pictures in the Prenickelodeon Period: Lexington, Kentucky, 1897-1906," *Velvet Light Trap* 25 (1990): 15, 21; Lexington *Herald*, 16 August 1925; Mabel Brown Ellis, "Children of the Kentucky Coal Fields," *The American Child* 1 (1920): 368; Louisville *Courier-Journal*, 2 January 1910; Lexington *Herald*, 8 March 1916. Estimates of dates when theaters were present in various areas is based on data from the city and county histories cited in this work, as well as other uncited ones.

37. Julian Reveles, "Kentucky in Reel Life," Louisville *Courier-Journal Magazine* (15 July 1979), 9-15; J. W. Williamson, *Southern Mountaineers in Silent Films* (1994), 3-4, 8, 13-18, 37; Edward D. C. Campbell, *The Celluloid South* (1981), passim.
See also "Narrative Films About Kentucky," a list prepared by Joseph Millichap, and Louisville *Courier-Journal*, 6 September 1992.

38. See, for example, Paducah *Weekly News-Democrat*, 5 July 1906, and "Memory Book, 1912-1913," in Melville W. O. Briney Papers, Filson Club.

39. Kentucky *Acts* (1902), 243-44; Hazel Green *Herald*, 19 August 1909; Hopkinsville *Kentuckian*, 4 November 1911; Burkesville *Banner*, 26 July 1912.

40. *Child Welfare in Kentucky* (1919), 123-24; Hopkinsville *Kentuckian*, 9 March 1911; Ken-

tucky *Acts* (1910), 189-90; (1914), 104-6; (1918), 184-89; (1934), 562-63.

41. Mt. Vernon *Signal*, 11 January 1901; May, *End of American Innocence*, 338; Lexington *Herald*, 19 September 1915; Briney Diary, 4 June 1915; *Child Welfare in Kentucky*, 121; Diary of Margaret Simpson, 21 February 1927, William C. Wineland Papers, Filson Club; Lowell H. Harrison, *Western Kentucky University* (1987), 80; Wilson, *Fidelity Folks*, 105.

42. John Modell, *Into One's Own: From Youth to Adulthood in the United States, 1920-1975* (1989), passim.

43. R. C. Riebel, *Louisville's Panorama* (1954), 140, 147. On the dates of clubs across Kentucky, see note 36 explanation.

44. Transcript of Interview with Elizabeth Stagner, 15 November 1977, KOHC; Martin, *Hollybush*, 97; N. V. Witherspoon Diary, 16 June, 21 August 1914, Kentucky Historical Society Library.

45. Marsh, "Child in Maysville," 5-7.

46. Preston Diary, 14 June, 11 September, 12 February 1900.

47. *Ibid.*, 5 July, 21 April 1907, 22 June 1910, 24 September, 11 October 1912, all Box 40; Margaret Preston to P. P. Johnston, Jr. [9 February 1914], 22 February [1914], 1 March [1914], series VIII, Box 3, Preston-Johnston Papers.

48. Transcript of Interview with Robert W. Thompson, KOHC; J. T. Gooch, ed., *Just The Other Day: A History of Madisonville, Kentucky* (1981), 22; Wade Hall, *The Kentucky Book* (1979), 195; Lexington *Daily Leader*, 5 July 1900; Woman's Club, *Early and Modern History of Wolfe County* ([1956]), 17-20; Bob Smith, "Kentucky Foothills Once Boasted Famed Resorts . . . ," *Kentucky Explorer* 4 (June 1989): 11. The hotel burned in 1927 and the railroad was abandoned in 1942. The Commonwealth took title to Natural Bridge in 1942.

49. Lexington *Herald-Leader*, 15 July 1990; Montell, *Don't Go Up Kettle Creek*, 138; Thomas D. Clark, "Growing Up With the Frontier," *Western Historical Quarterly* 3 (1972): 361; Peel, "Growing Up," 84; Transcript of Interview with A. H. Barber, 1988, copy in author's possession; Eversole, "Memories," 31.

50. J. W. Wells, *History of Cumberland County* (1947), 132; Woodrow Allen, "History of Somerset, Kentucky" (M.A. thesis, University of Kentucky, 1951), 57; Kentucky *Bureau of Agriculture, Labor, and Statistics Report* (1914-15), 13-57; "Shepherdsville," in John E. Kleber, ed., *The Kentucky Encyclopedia* (1992), 818; Diary, Vol. I, 5, in Travelstead Collection; Kentucky *Progress Commission Report* (1929), 46.

51. Millard Dee Grubb, *The 4 Keys to Kentucky* (1949), 162; James Duane Bolin, "From Mules to Motors: The Street Railway System in Lexington, Kentucky, 1882-1938," *Register* 87 (1989): 130, 141; William S. Oxendine, "A History of Barbourville, Kentucky" (M. A. thesis, University of Kentucky, 1954), 37; Alma Owens Tibbels, *A History of Pulaski County Kentucky* (1952), 169; Frieda J. Dannheiser, ed., *The History of Henderson County, Kentucky* (1980), 172; *Founding of Catlettsburg*, 19.

52. Bolin, "From Mules to Motors," 134-35; Dannheiser, ed., *Henderson County*, 172-74.

53. Faulkner, *Quest for Social Justice*, 136; John D. Hicks, *Republican Ascendancy, 1921-1933* (1960), 169; George B. Tindall, *The Emergence of the New South, 1913-1945* (1967), 257; Charles Reagan Wilson, "Automobile," in *Encyclopedia of Southern Culture*, 598; Hazard *Herald*, 8 October 1926.

54. Laurel Shackelford and Bill Weinberg, eds., *Our Appalachia* (1977), 37n; John W. Hevener, *Which Side Are You On?* (1978), 1; D. Trabue Davis, *Story of Mayfield Through a Century, 1823-1923* (1923), 38; Lewis W. McKee and Lydia K. Bond, *A History of Anderson County, 1780-1936* (1936), 217; Wells, *Cumberland County*, 307; Lexington *Herald*, 15 January 1922, 11 January 1928.

Kentucky's first state-produced automobile was apparently "The Dewabout," a four horse-power machine that went twenty-five m.p.h. and was made by Thomas B. Dewhurst of Lexington. Lexington *Daily Leader*, 24 February 1901; Lexington *Herald*, 2 April 1911.

55. Leon L. Freeman and Edward C. Olds, *The History of Marshall County, Kentucky* (1933), 166; Peel, "Growing Up," 76; Hebel, "Way It Was," 11; Clay Lancaster, *Vestiges of the Venerable City* (1978), 147; Paducah *Weekly Sun*, 4 May 1910.

56. Tindall, *Emergence of the New South*, 256; Kentucky *Department of Public Roads . . . Report* (1912-13), 5, 16, 27; Kentucky *Acts* (1914), 440-41; Efficiency Commission, *The Government of Kentucky* (2 vols., 1924), 1: 617, 611; Mary T. Brewer, *Rugged Trail to Appalachia: A History of Leslie County . . . 1878-1978* (1978), 56; Kentucky *Department of Public Roads . . . Report* (1915), 4; Louisville *Times*, 19 September 1931.

57. Louis S. Schafer, "Early Engines," *Kentucky Living* 47 (February 1993): 14-15; Lexington *Herald*, 6 December 1904; Paducah *Weekly News-Democrat*, 4 October 1906; Kentucky *Acts* (1904), 303-6; (1910), 242-49; (1918), 62-65.

58. Paducah *Weekly News-Democrat*, 4 June 1908; Richard Wright, "Air Transportation in Kentucky," in Grubb, *4 Keys*, 602; "Bowman Field," in Dianne Wells and Mary Lou S. Madigan, comps., *Update: Guide to Kentucky Historical Society Highway Markers* (3d ed., 1989), 1676; Kentucky *Acts* (1926), 341; (1932), 27-33; "Certified Pilots," (Kentucky), in Civil Aeronautics Commission Report, 6 August 1940, in Transportation folder, Box 88, Project Files, Records of Works Progress Administration, Kentucky Department for Libraries and Archives.

59. Thomas D. Clark, *The Kentucky* (rev. ed., 1969), 118; Krock, *Myself When Young*, 54-55; Fox, *Blue Grass and Rhododendron*, 184, 186; Cowdrey, *This Land, This South*, 139; Kentucky *Acts* (1904), 150-51, (1912), 153-70; "Kentucky's Department of Fish and Wildlife Resources" (n.d.), [1-2].

60. Lexington *Leader*, 22 October 1900, 14 June 1919; *Young & Co.'s Business and Professional Directory of the Cities and Towns of Kentucky* [1906-07] (n.d.), 664; Isaac, *Story of Drakesboro*, 43.

61. Ronnie Peach, "Kentucky Diamonds Produced Major League Gems," *Back Home in Kentucky* 4 (July/August 1981): 13-15; Henry Mayer, "Kentucky's All-Time All Stars," *Rural Kentuckian* 42 (April 1988): 28-30; Hopkinsville *Kentuckian*, 18 May 1911; Hebel, "Way it Was," 21a.

62. Lexington *Herald*, 23, 28 November 1904, 29 October 1900; John S. Watterson, "Inventing Modern Football," *American Heritage* 39 (September/October 1988): 106; John Y. Brown, Sr., *The Legend of the Praying Colonels* (n.d.), 139, 5, 22, 25, 47, 52-54, 109-10.

63. Milton D. Feinstein, "History and Development of Football at the University of Kentucky, 1877-1920" (M. A. thesis, University of Kentucky, 1941), 49, 52-55, 64-65, 75, 86, 119; Watterson, "Modern Football," 110; Thwing Diary, 19 March 1912; Louisville *Courier-Journal*, 15 October 1941; Bob Hill and C. Ray Hall, "Rivalry," Louisville *Courier-Journal Magazine*, 1 November 1987, 4. See also Gregory Kent Stanley, "'Not Condusive to the Best Interests of this Institution': President James Kennedy Patterson, the Board of Trustees, and University of Kentucky Athletics, 1890-1910," *FCHQ* 69 (1995): 159-70.

64. Bert Nelli, *The Winning Tradition: A History of Kentucky Wildcat Basketball* (1984), ix, 5, 15, 29, 33, 37; Lexington *Herald*, 17 February 1907, 22 March 1905, 18 March 1928, 3 June 1977; [Eastern Kentucky University Archives] *Inventories . . . Kentucky High School Athletic Association Records* (1988), viii; Freeman and Olds, *Marshall County*, 159; Terry Birdwhistell, "An Educated Difference: Women at the University of Kentucky Through the Second World War" (Ed.D. diss., University of Kentucky, 1994), 135-36; Harrison, *Western Kentucky University*, 83-86; Allen Guttman, *A Whole New Ball Game: An Interpretation of American Sports* (1988), 70; Tom Rankin, "Basketball," in *Encyclopedia of Southern Culture*, 1214.

65. Ralph W. Clark, "The Legal Regulation of Organized Racing in Kentucky" (M.A. thesis, University of Kentucky, 1941), 18, 23-27, 37, 48-51; Lexington *Herald*, 19 September 1908; Ed-

ward L. Bowen, "Kentucky Thoroughbred Racing in the Twentieth Century," in Mary W. Wharton and Edward L. Bowen, *The Horse World of the Bluegrass* (1980), 47-53; Bob Gorham, ed., *Churchill Downs: 100th Kentucky Derby* (1973), 6, 64, 106; Ed. Fountaine, "More Than Just a Race," *Daily Racing Form* 97 (4 May 1991): 13.

The Lexington *Herald*, 8 March 1908, reported the first polo match played in that city had taken place the day before.

4. "Weep No More My Lady": Majorities and Minorities

1. Arthur Krock, *Myself When Young* (1973), 20; Sarah Young to E. G. Young, 2 February 1916, Papers of E. G. Young, Kentucky Library, Western Kentucky University; Opal Cline Crabb Interview, Owensboro *Messenger-Inquirer*, 15 September 1986.

2. Sara M. Evans, *Born for Liberty: A History of Women in America* (1987), 68-70, 96, 138, 160; Scott C. Osborn, "A Study and Contrast of the Kentucky Mountaineer and the Bluegrass Aristocrat in the Works of John Fox, Jr." (M. A. thesis, University of Kentucky, 1939), 51.

3. David B. Jenks, "A Study of the Adoption of a State Mandated Citizenship Education in Kentucky" (Ed.D diss., University of Kentucky, 1982), 144n; Thomas D. Clark, *The Rural Press and the New South* (1948), 60-61.

4. Josephine K. Henry, "The New Woman of the New South," *Arena* 63 (1895): 353-54.

5. A. O. Stanley to Sue Stanley, [17 February 1905], Box 1 (Supplement), A. O. Stanley Papers, University of Kentucky Library; Lexington *Herald*, 21 March 1914; Carol Guethlein, "Women in Louisville: Moving Toward Equal Rights," *FCHQ* 55 (1981): 158; Leonard Niel Plummer, "Political Leadership of Henry Watterson" (Ph.D. diss., University of Wisconsin, 1940), 52; Ed. M. Wallace to Henry Martin, 31 July 1920, H. L. Martin Papers, Kentucky Historical Society.

6. James Lane Allen, *Flute and Violin* (1891), 202; Allen, *Summer in Arcady* (1896), 59.

7. D. H. Schockel, "Changing Conditions in the Kentucky Mountains," *Scientific Monthly* 3 (1916): 128; James W. Raine, *The Land of Saddle-bags* (1924), 226; Josiah H. Combs, "The Kentucky Highlands," in William R. Thomas, *Life Among the Hills and Mountains of Kentucky* (1983; orig. pub. 1926), 87; Samuel W. Thomas, ed., *Dawn Comes to the Mountains* (1981), 110; Transcript of Interviews with Grace Reeder, 25 January 1977, and Helen E. Browne, 27 March 1979, both in FNSOHP.

8. Jack Temple Kirby, *Rural Worlds Lost: The American South, 1920-1960* (1987), 164; Fred Lewis, "A Story About My Life," *Frontier Nursing Service Quarterly Bulletin* 62 (Autumn 1986): 8; Transcript of Interview with Marvin B. Patterson, 13 May 1978, FNSOHP.

9. A. S. Elliott, "The Ky. Mountaineer," *Bibliotheca Sacra* 63 (1906): 492; Morehead *Independent*, October 1934, and Oneida *Mountaineer*, n. d., both in "Mountains" clipping file, Kentucky, Louisville Free Public Library; Pauline Myers, "Mountain Mothers of Kentucky," *Hygeia* 7 (1929): 353.

10. J. Marcus Whitler, *Memories of My Youth, 1926-1933 in Breckinridge County, Kentucky* (n.d.), 708; Kentucky *Labor Inspectors Report* (1903), 28-65, (1904-05), 18; Kentucky *Bureau of Labor Report* (1918-19), 26; Patricia M. Hummer, *The Decade of Elusive Promise: Professional Women in the United States, 1920-1930* (1979), 14.

11. Morton Keller, *Affairs of State* (1977), 472; *Child Welfare in Kentucky* (1919), 261, 272-73; Mary Bronaugh to Mrs. Samuel Wilson, 26 November 1921, in Samuel Wilson Collection, University of Kentucky Library; Kentucky *Acts* (1926), 63-65; "The Legal Status of Women in the United States of America, January 1, 1938, Report for Kentucky," *Bulletin of the Woman's Bureau* no. 157-16 (1938), 10; Kentucky *Acts* (1950), 639-41.

12. On suffrage in Kentucky, see Claudia Knott, "The Woman Suffrage Movement in Kentucky, 1879-1920" (Ph.D. diss., University of Kentucky, 1989); Carol Crowe-Carraco, "Women's Quest for Reform," in James C. Klotter, ed., *Our Kentucky: A Study of the Bluegrass State* (1992), 188-96; Helen D. Irvin, *Women in Kentucky* (1979), 89-104; Paul E. Fuller, "Women's Suffrage," in John E. Kleber, ed., *Kentucky Encyclopedia* (1992), 965-66; idem, *Laura Clay and the Woman's Rights Movement* (1975), passim; and Hambleton Tapp and James C. Klotter, *Kentucky: Decades of Discord, 1865-1900* (1977), 86-90. See also Linnie Rice, "The Emancipation of Womanhood" (undergraduate thesis, Eastern Kentucky State Normal School, 1914).

13. Fuller, *Clay*, 1-12, 25, 29, 51-55, 80, 92-93, 110, 154-55; Rebecca E. Averrill to Laura Clay, 7 November 1906, Box 3, Laura Clay Papers, University of Kentucky Library; Lexington *Herald*, 6 June 1919. More critical views of Clay's stance on the racial question appear in Aileen S. Kraditor, *The Ideas of the Woman Suffrage Movement, 1890-1920* (1965), 151-56, and Irvin, *Women in Kentucky*, 103. See also Clay to Anna Shaw (10 May 1907), and Alice Blackwell (22 September and 14 October 1907), Box 3, Clay Papers.

14. On Madeline M. Breckinridge's life, see Melba Porter Hay, "Madeline McDowell Breckinridge" (Ph.D. diss., University of Kentucky, 1980); idem, "Madeline McDowell Breckinridge," *Register* 72 (1974): 342-63; Sophonisba P. Breckinridge, *Madeline McDowell Breckinridge* (1921); James C. Klotter, *The Breckinridges of Kentucky* (1986), 213-16, 230; the Madeline McDowell Breckinridge Papers and the Henry Clay Estate Foundation Papers, University of Kentucky Library; and Lexington *Herald*, 26-28 November 1920.

15. Porter [Hay], "M. M. Breckinridge," 345; Breckinridge, *M. M. Breckinridge*, 212; Fuller, *Clay*, 132, 147-59; Crowe-Carraco, "Women's Quest," 194-96; Lexington *Herald*, 16, 22, 25 February 1919; Anne Firor Scott, *The Southern Lady: From Pedestal to Politics, 1830-1930* (1970), 184.

16. Lexington *Herald*, 27 November 1920; Fuller, *Clay*, 162-66, 22-41.

17. Isabella M. Pettus, "The Legal Education of Women," *Journal of Social Science* 38 (1900): 243; Kleber, ed., *Kentucky Encyclopedia*, 323-24, 243, 964-65, 810; John D. Wright, Jr., *Lexington: Heart of the Bluegrass* (1982), 170; Anne Harrison, comp., *Women in Kentucky State Government, 1940-1980* (1981), [ii]; Kentucky *Superintendent of Public Instruction Report* (1905-07), 91-183; Irvin, *Women in Kentucky*, 110-12, 116-19; Crowe-Carraco, "Women's Quest," 199-200.

18. Carol Crowe-Carraco, "Kentucky's New Woman and the Years of Yearning, 1889-1914," in *Corsets, Croquet and Crusades* (1989), 5; James R. McGovern, "The American Woman's Pre-World War I Freedom in Manners and Morals," *Journal of American History* 55 (1968): 318; S. B. Lott to "Nannie and children," 10 January [1914], Lott Family Letters, University of Kentucky Library; Judy Yount Lyons, "Remembering" (copy in author's possession), n.p.; Irvin, *Women in Kentucky*, 123; Paula S. Fass, *The Damned and the Beautiful: American Youth in the 1920s* (1977), 16, 25, 77.

19. Scott, *Southern Lady*, 230-31; Diary entry, 26 March 1914, in Melville W. O. Briney Papers, Filson Club.

20. Wade Hall, *The Rest of the Dream: The Black Odyssey of Lyman Johnson* (1988), 111, 125; Nancy J. Weiss, *Whitney M. Young, Jr. and the Struggle for Civil Rights* (1990), 7.

21. George C. Wright, *History of Blacks in Kentucky* (1992), 2: 54, 62; Lexington *Herald*, 2 August 1925; George C. Wright, *Life Behind a Veil: Blacks in Louisville, Kentucky, 1865-1930* (1985), 60; William B. Strother, "Negro Culture in Lexington, Kentucky" (M.A. thesis, University of Kentucky, 1939), 84; Lexington *Herald-Leader*, 26 April 1992.

22. Tapp and Klotter, *Decades of Discord*, 328; New York *Times*, 20 April 1920; Walker D. Hines to W. J. Dickinson, 5 November 1903 (copy), H. Walters to Milton H. Smith, 28 July 1904 (copy), and W. L. M. to M. H. S. [Smith], 30 July 1904 (copy), all in Box 10, Louisville and Nashville Railroad Co. Papers, University of Louisville Archives.

23. Marjorie Norris, "An Early Instance of Non-Violence: The Louisville Demonstrations of

1870-71," *Journal of Southern History* 32 (1966): 487-504.

24. Wright, *Life Behind a Veil*, 53-54; George C. Wright, "Black Political Insurgency in Louisville, Kentucky: The Lincoln Independent Party of 1921," *Journal of Negro History* 68 (1983): 9; Kentucky *House Journal* (1910), 239; "Along the Color Line," *The Crisis* 36 (May 1929): 163; Lexington *Herald*, 19 February 1911; Wright, *History of Blacks*, 2: 53.

25. *The Crisis* 6 (June 1913): 71; 8 (October 1914): 273; 9 (November 1914): 11; Wright, *Life Behind a Veil*, 62, 277; Omer Carmichael and Weldon James, *The Louisville Story* (1957), 21; Wright, *History of Blacks*, 2: 56, 58.

26. Lexington *Herald*, 19 August 1919; Kentucky *Institution for the Education of the Blind. . . . Report* (1900), 16; Kentucky *Prison Commission Report* (1900), 38; (1912-13), 58.

27. See, for example, Herbert A. Thomas, "Victims of Circumstance: Negroes in a Southern Town, 1865-1880," *Register* 71 (1973): 253-71; John Kellogg, "The Formation of Black Residential Areas in Lexington, Kentucky, 1865-1887," *Journal of Southern History* 48 (1982): 21-52.

28. Arthur Krock, comp., *The Editorials of Henry Watterson* (1923), 97; James Larry Hood, "The Collapse of Zion: Rural Progressivism in Nelson and Washington Counties, Kentucky" (Ph.D. diss., University of Kentucky, 1980), 275; E. Polk Johnson, *History of Kentucky* (3 vols., 1912), 1: 181, 398; Kentucky *Superintendent of Public Instruction Report* (1905-07), 131.

29. Krock, *Myself When Young*, 79; Hall, *The Rest of the Dream*, 59. See also Claude H. Nolen, *The Negro's Image in the South* (1967).

30. Gerald L. Smith, "Blacks in Lexington, Kentucky: The Struggle for Civil Rights, 1945-1980" (M. A. thesis, University of Kentucky, 1983), 38.

31. Dewey W. Grantham, *Southern Progressivism* (1983), 113-14.

32. *The Crisis* 7 (November 1913): 333; 9 (January 1915): 125-26; A. M. E. *Church Review* 31 (January 1915): 313.

33. Wright, *Life Behind a Veil*, 162-66, 200-202; idem, "William Henry Steward: Moderate Approach to Black Leadership," in Leon Litwack and August Meier, eds., *Black Leaders of the Nineteenth Century* (1988), 275-89.

34. Wright, *Life Behind a Veil*, 120-22; Florette Henri, *Black Migration: Movement North, 1900-1920* (1975), 81; *The Crisis* 8 (September 1914): 236; 10 (August 1915): 198-99; 35 (January 1928): 24; Allen F. Davis, *Spearheads for Reform* (1967), 99, 140-41; Louisville *Courier-Journal*, 15 September 1987.

35. Louisville *Courier-Journal*, 14, 21 January 1906; A. O. Stanley to Sue S. Stanley, 7 March 1906, Box 1, Stanley Papers; Kentucky *Acts* (1906), 315; Gregory A. Waller, "Another Audience: Black Moviegoing, 1907-16," *Cinema Journal* 31 (1992): 6-7, 23; Lexington *Herald*, 6, 7 July 1910; *The Crisis* 17 (April 1919): 283; Wright, *Life Behind a Veil*, 239.

36. C. W. Johnston, *The Sunny South and Its People* (1918), 106; Bill C. Malone, *Southern Music, American Music* (1979), 19.

37. Charles M. Meacham, *A History of Christian County, Kentucky* (1930), 228; unidentified clipping, 9 November 1913, in Cromwell Scrapbook, University of Kentucky Library; Carl B. Boyd, Jr., and Hazel Mason Boyd, *A History of Mt. Sterling, Kentucky, 1792-1918* (1984), 83; Tom Owen, comp., "History" in *The Louisville Board of Aldermen, 1976-7* (1976) n.p.; Wright, "Black Political Insurgency," 9; *The Crisis* 21 (January 1921): 117-18; Wright, *Life Behind a Veil*, 208-9, 271-72.

38. *Kentucky's Black Heritage* (1971), 73; Howard K. Beers and Catherine P. Heflin, *The Negro Population of Kentucky* (1946), 3; William H. Turner, "Blacks in Appalachian America . . . ," *Phylon* 44 (1983): 203; Wright, *Life Behind a Veil*, 83, 85-88, 136, 91-92; William E. Ellis, H. E. Everman, and Richard D. Sears, *Madison County* (1985), 249; Elizabeth A. Perkins, "The Forgot-

ten Victorians: Louisville's Domestic Servants, 1880-1920," *Register* 85 (1987): 118.

39. C. Vann Woodward, *The Strange Career of Jim Crow* (3d rev. ed., 1974) 207; W. D. Johnson, *Biographical Sketches of Prominent Negro Men and Women of Kentucky* (1897); J. Stoddard Johnston, *The Commercial History of the Southern States: Kentucky* (1903); Lawrence Harris, *The Negro Population of Lexington* . . . ([1907]); Smith, "Blacks in Lexington," 13. Often the black community had its own badges of segregation, for blacks with light skin could form a kind of black elite, as pointed out in Ted Poston, *The Dark Side of Hopkinsville* (1991), passim.

40. Johnston, *Commercial History*, n.p.; Charles K. Wolfe, *Kentucky Country* (1982), 111-13; Alice A. Dunnigan, *The Fascinating Story of Black Kentuckians* (1982), 312; Wright, *Life Behind a Veil*, 118.

41. Federal Writers' Project, *Kentucky: A Guide to the Bluegrass State* (1939), 178; Ernest Collins, "The Political Behavior of the Negroes in Cincinnati, Ohio and Louisville, Kentucky" (Ph.D. diss., University of Kentucky, 1950), 56; Zane L. Miller, "Urban Blacks in the South, 1865-1920 . . . ," in Leo F. Schnore, ed., *The New Urban History* (1975), 201.

42. Interview with John Sherman Cooper, 13 May 1979, Cooper Oral History Project, University of Kentucky; Interview with Robert W. Thompson, 20 October 1977, KOHC; Gordon Wilson, *Fidelity Folks: A Visit to a Self-Sufficient Kentucky Village* (1946), 73; Eleanor B. Chalkley, *Magic Casements* (1982), 44.

43. Quoted in Wright, *Life Behind a Veil*, 6.

5. "The Corn Top's Ripe": Agriculture, Industry, and Labor

1. Harriette Simpson Arnow, *Seedtime on the Cumberland* (1960), 8; Jack Temple Kirby, *Rural Worlds Lost: The American South, 1920-1960* (1987), 120-21; Paul Camplin, *A New History of Muhlenberg County* (1984), 63; M. B. Morton, *Kentuckians Are Different* (1938), 136; William Lynwood Montell, *Monroe County History, 1820-1970* (2d ed., 1970), 11-12.

2. James W. Broaddus, "The Coffey Family, Father and Son, Rockcastle County, Kentucky, 1880-1957 . . . ," *Kentucky Folklore Record* 30 (1984): 11-13.

3. H. C. Northcott Diary, January-June 1905, Series I, Box 2, Northcott Collection, Kentucky Library, Western Kentucky University; Virginia Cary Hudson, *O Ye Jigs & Juleps* (1962), 11.

4. Charles E. Martin, *Hollybush: Folk Building and Social Change in an Appalachian Community* (1984), 85; William Lynwood Montell, *Don't Go Up Kettle Creek: Verbal Legacy of the Upper Cumberland* (1983), 51; Thomas D. Clark, "Rural Life," in *Encyclopedia of Southern Culture* (1989), 11.

5. Alben Barkley, *That Reminds Me* (1954), 43; *The Nation* (12 July 1947), 41; Tracy A. Campbell, "The Politics of Despair: The Tobacco Wars of Kentucky and Tennessee (Ph.D. diss., Duke University, 1988), 28.

6. Louisville *Courier-Journal*, 1 March 1906; Kentucky *Bureau of Agriculture, Labor and Statistics Report* (1904-05), iv-v, (1910-11), 6; Gilbert C. Fite, *Cotton Fields No More: Southern Agriculture, 1865-1980* (1984), 87; Donald B. Dodd and Wynelle S. Dodd, *Historical Statistics of the South, 1790-1970* (1973), 23.

7. *Twelfth Census* (1900), v, pt. 1, lxix; Dodd and Dodd, *Historical Statistics*, 23.

8. *Twelfth Census* (1900), v, pt. 1, 2-3; *Abstract of the Thirteenth Census* (1910), 280; *1984-1985 Kentucky Agricultural Statistics* (1985), 106.

9. *Twelfth Census* (1900), v, pt. 1, lxxi, xciii, 8, cx; Fite, *Cotton Fields No More*, 34; Efficiency Commission, *The Government of Kentucky* (2 vols., 1924), 2: 247; *Abstract of the Thirteenth Census* (1910), 294.

10. *Twelfth Census* (1900), v, pt. 1, ciii, cix; Efficiency Commission, *Government of Kentucky*, 2: 247.

11. *Twelfth Census* (1900), v, pt. 1, cxxiii; Dodd and Dodd, *Historical Statistics*, 22; Kentucky *Bureau of Agriculture Report* (1904-05), 89; *1984-1985 Kentucky Agricultural Statistics*, 10; Temple Bodley and Samuel M. Wilson, *History of Kentucky* (4 vols., 1928), 2: 36-37.

12. *1984-1985 Kentucky Agricultural Statistics*, 10; Kentucky *Agriculture Report* (1904-05), 89; *Abstract of the Thirteenth Census* (1910), 381, 383, 397; J. J. Hornback, "Economic Development in Kentucky Since 1860" (Ph.D. diss., University of Michigan, 1932), 136. In 1900, Kentucky farmers spent an average of $4 per year on fertilizer; the U.S. average was $10. *Twelfth Census* (1900), v, pt. 1, cxli.

13. Owensboro *Messenger-Enquirer*, 15 September 1986.

14. Quoted in Wade Hall, *The Kentucky Book* (1979), 178.

15. W. F. Axton, *Tobacco and Kentucky* (1975), 51, 102; *Abstract of the Thirteenth Census* (1910), 403; Kentucky *Bureau of Agriculture Report* (1904-05), 89; George D. Hagan, "Kentucky's Part in the World War" (M.A. thesis, University of Kentucky, 1926), 10-11; *1984-1985 Kentucky Agricultural Statistics*, 10; J. Campbell Cantrill to C. C. Bagby, 26 November 1918 (copy); H. F. Bryant to Cantrill, 8 March 1919, both in J. Campbell Cantrill Papers, microfilm, Special Collections, University of Kentucky Library.

16. Thomas D. Clark, *A History of Kentucky* (rev. ed., 1960), 391.

17. New York *Times*, 4 January 1921; James McNally to J. Campbell Cantrill, 3 January 1921; Otto Smither to Cantrill, 4 January 1921; Thomas B. Cromwell to Cantrill [5 January 1921?], all in Cantrill Papers; Lexington *Leader*, 4 January 1921; Axton, *Tobacco and Kentucky*, 103-6; Ralph M. Barker to Cantrill, 16 November 1921, Cantrill Papers; New York *Times*, 8, 16, 24, 28 January 1921; Campbell, "Politics of Despair," 242. See also "Kentucky Tobacco Rebellion," *Literary Digest* 68 (29 January 1921): 14; Howard Beers, ed., *Kentucky: Designs for Her Future* (1945), 56.

18. *Twelfth Census* (1900), v, pt. 1, cxlvi, cxciv, cci, ccxiv, ccxxi; Paducah *Weekly News-Democrat*, 25 January 1906.

19. Judge Watson, "The Economic and Cultural Development of Eastern Kentucky From 1900 to the Present" (Ph.D. diss., Indiana University, 1963), 15; Kirby, *Rural Worlds Lost*, 87; James E. Wallace, "Cattle Industry," in John E. Kleber, ed., *Kentucky Encyclopedia* (1992), 172.

20. Montell, *Don't Go Up Kettle Creek*, 39; Joyce Wilson, *This Was Yesterday: A Romantic History of Owsley County* (1977), 5; Fred W. Peel, "Growing Up in Central Kentucky" (typescript, Kentucky Historical Society), 1, 78; Interview with C. W. Murphy, Eastern Kentucky University Oral History Center.

21. *Abstract of the Twelfth Census* (1900), 332; Joseph L. McConnell, "Growth of Manufacturing in Kentucky, 1904 to 1929" (M. A. thesis, University of Kentucky, 1932), 18-22.

22. McConnell, "Manufacturing in Kentucky," 12, 17, 11.

23. Robert W. Bingham to Barry Bingham, 8 March [1935] (copy), Papers of Robert Worth Bingham, Manuscript Division, Library of Congress; Louisville *Courier-Journal*, 19 January 1906.

24. McConnell, "Manufacturing in Kentucky," 93, 19, 88.

25. Maxwell Ferguson, *State Regulation of Railroads in the South* (1916), 127, 120-21, 53, 39. See also 195, 207-8. For a national decision aiding one Kentucky town, see Lee A. Dew, "Henderson, Kentucky, and the Fight for Equitable Freight Rates, 1906-1918," *Register* 76 (1978): 34-44.

26. Louisville *Courier-Journal*, 24-27 September 1930. McConnell, "Manufacturing in Kentucky," 97, sees freight rates as an influential but not crucial factor.

27. Broadus Mitchell, "A Survey of Industry," in W. T. Couch, ed., *Culture in the South* (1934), 89; Kentucky *Bureau of Agriculture Report* (1904-5), 466; Kentucky *Progress Commission Report* (1929), 20-21.

28. McConnell, "Manufacturing in Kentucky," 34, 41-42, 47, 87; Kentucky *Bureau of Agriculture Report* (1904-05), 471; William E. Ellis, *Patrick Henry Callahan* (1989), 67-70; Kentucky *Labor Inspectors Report* (1903), 28-65; *Louisville: Nineteen Hundred and Five* (n.d.), n.p.; Ellen C. Semple, "Louisville: A Study in Economic Geography," *Journal of School Geography* 4 (1900): 367-69; Louisville *Courier-Journal*, 14 April 1992; *Illustrated Industrial Souvenir of Owensboro, Ky.* [1904], 33; Paducah *Weekly Sun*, 7 December 1910.

29. Joseph L. Massie, *Blazer and Ashland Oil: A Study in Management* (1960), 2, 5, 7, 9, 45, 169; Otto J. Scott, *The Exception: The Story of Ashland Oil & Refining Company* (1968), 35, 111, 118, 123.

30. Kentucky *Railroad Commission Report* (1908-09), 359, 376; Steven A. Channing, *Kentucky* (1977), 143; Dewey W. Grantham, *Southern Progressivism* (1983), 4; Maude W. Lafferty, *The Lure of Kentucky* (1939), 341; Thomas D. Clark, "A Historical Perspective on Education in Kentucky" (paper given to Shakertown Roundtable, 1985, copy in author's possession), 9.

31. Carl Ryant, "Kentucky and the Movement to Regulate Chain Stores, 1925-1945," *FCHQ* 57 (1983): 274-75, 283, 276-82. See also Ryant, "New Merchandizing in the New Era: Change in the Kentucky Retail Trade During the 1920s," *Journal of Kentucky Studies* 1 (1984): 202-10.

32. Kentucky *Inspector of Mines Report* (1900), 7, 24, 66.

33. *Ibid.* (1912), 7; Willard R. Jillson, "A History of the Coal Industry in Kentucky," *Register* 20 (1922): 40, 45. See also idem, *The Coal Industry in Kentucky* (1924).

34. Howard W. Odum, *Southern Regions of the United States* (1936), 36; *Mines and Quarries: 1929* (1933), 255; Kentucky *Inspector of Mines Report* (1900), 26.

35. William R. Thomas, *Life Among the Hills and Mountains of Kentucky* (1930), 42-43; Willard R. Jillson, "The Re-born Oil Fields of Kentucky," *Register* 18 (1920): 36, 39; Columbia *Adair County News*, 26 June 1901; Hornback, "Economic Development," 140; Bodley and Wilson, *History of Kentucky*, 2: 89, 91. See also Jillson, *New Oil Horizons in Kentucky* (1948), 8-9.

36. Center for Labor Education, *Labor History in Kentucky* (1986), iv-26, iv-27; Herbert Finch, "Organized Labor in Louisville, 1880-1914" (Ph.D. diss., University of Kentucky, 1965), 220, 218, 222; Louisville *Kentucky Irish American*, 22 March 1902; Kentucky *Acts* (1902), 44-45, 49; (1914), 212-16; Kentucky *Labor Inspectors Report* (1903), 134.

37. Kentucky *Labor Inspectors Report* (1903), 18, 17, 156. In 1910, Kentucky provided that laborers on public projects would work an eight-hour day. See Kentucky *Acts* (1910), 344-45.

38. Kentucky *Labor Inspectors Report* (1904-05), 200-204; Jasper B. Shannon and Ruth McQuown, *Presidential Politics in Kentucky, 1824-1948* (1950), 88; Lexington *Herald*, 17 October 1919; New York *Times*, 17 October 1919.

39. New York *Times*, 2 January, 3-6, 28 February 1922; Cincinnati *Times-Star*, 17 January 1922; John E. L. Robertson, *Paducah* (1980), 81; *Labor History in Kentucky*, iv-29, iv-30.

40. Kentucky *Adjutant General Report* (1901), 28-36.

41. Kentucky *Inspector of Mines Report* (1901-02), 36-37.

42. Columbia *Adair County News*, 6 November 1901; Paducah *Weekly News-Democrat*, 26 July 1906; Lexington *Herald*, 26 December 1906; J. D. Bolin "'An Air of Tenseness': Labor Strife and Tragedy in Kentucky's Western Coal Field, 1930-1939" (paper in author's possession), 9-11.

43. Paul F. Cressey, "Social Disorganization and Reorganization in Harlan County, Kentucky," *American Sociological Review* 14 (1949): 389-93; Harry M. Caudill, "Harlan County, Ken-

tucky," in Charles Reagan Wilson and William Ferris, eds., *Encyclopedia of Southern Culture* (1989), 1482-83.

44. F. Ray Marshall, *Labor in the South* (1967), 76-79; Curtis Seltzer, *Fire in the Hole: Miners and Managers in the American Coal Industry* (1985), 18-22; Maier B. Fox, *United We Stand: The United Mine Workers of America, 1890-1990* (1990), 263; John Gaventa, *Power and Powerlessness* (1980), 96; Stuart Sprague, "Hard Times in Bell and Harlan," *Mountain Review* 2 (July 1976): 19; John W. Hevener, *Which Side Are You On? The Harlan County Coal Miners, 1931-39* (1978), 3, 5, 9.

45. Hevener, *Which Side*, 19, 10; Gaventa, *Power and Powerlessness*, 88-89.

46. Paul F. Taylor, *Bloody Harlan: The United Mine Workers of America in Harlan County, Kentucky, 1931-1941* (1990), 14-17, 164-70; Hevener, *Which Side*, 39-40, 106-7.

47. Taylor, *Bloody Harlan*, 12-18; Hevener, *Which Side*, 33-50; Bruce Crawford, "The Coal Miner," in Couch, ed., *Culture in the South*, 369-70; "Which Side Are You On?" by Florence Reece, cited in Hevener, *Which Side*, x.

48. Hevener, *Which Side*, 63-69, 81-83, 28-29; Taylor, *Bloody Harlan*, 27-28.

49. Hevener, *Which Side*, 56-71; Taylor, *Bloody Harlan*, 27, 31; National Committee for the Defense of Political Prisoners, *Harlan Miners Speak* (1932).

50. Gaventa, *Power and Powerlessness*, 102-3; Tony Bubka, "The Harlan County Coal Strike of 1931," *Labor History* 11 (1970): 55; Taylor, *Bloody Harlan*, and Hevener, *Which Side*, passim; Frances C. Jones "Harlan County Kentucky As I Know It" (typescript in possession of Sarah Jones Rutherford, copy in author's possession); Alessandro Portelli, "History-Telling and Time: An Example from Kentucky," *Oral History Review* 20 (1992): 61. See also George J. Titler, *Hell in Harlan* (n.d.).

51. Hevener, *Which Side*, 138, 139-72; Taylor, *Bloody Harlan*, 162-201, 215-28; U. S. Senate, *Violation of Free Speech and Rights of Labor Hearings*, 75th Cong., 1st Sess. (1937), passim; Louisville *Courier-Journal*, 25-26 January 1938; G. C. Jones, *Growing Up Hard in Harlan County* (1985), 50.

52. Taylor, *Bloody Harlan*, 238; Cressey, "Social Disorganization," 393; Louisville *Courier-Journal*, 4 November 1991.

6. *"The Young Folks"*: Education

1. Dewey Grantham, *Southern Progressivism* (1983), 258.

2. Fred A. Engle, Jr., "The Superintendents and the Issues: A Study of the Superintendents of Public Instruction in Kentucky, 1891-1943" (Ed.D. diss., University of Kentucky, 1966), 61-66, 241-43; Barksdale Hamlett, *History of Education in Kentucky* (1914), 177-78, 185-86, 193-94, 223-25, 233-35, 271-73, 206; Lexington *Leader*, 22 September 1915.

3. Moses E. Ligon, *History of Public Education in Kentucky* (1942), 121-23; Kentucky *Superintendent of Public Instruction Report* (1919-21), 7.

4. Lexington *Herald*, 11 March 1912; Kentucky *Superintendent of Public Instruction Report* (1905-07), 91-183; S. P. Breckinridge, *Madeline McDowell Breckinridge* (1921), 184-85; Chapter 2 in manuscript text, 42, in Ellis Hartford Collection, Kentucky Library, Western Kentucky University; Paul E. Fuller, *Laura Clay and the Woman's Rights Movement* (1975), 47, 93.

5. Ligon, *Public Education*, 118; Kentucky Education Commission, *Public Education in Kentucky* (1921), 27-28; Henry P. Scalf, *Kentucky's Last Frontier* (2d ed., 1972), 397-98; Laurel Shackelford and Bill Weinberg, eds., *Our Appalachia* (1977), 54.

6. Ligon, *Public Education*, 118; Hamlett, *History of Education*, 198; James Still, *The Wolfpen*

Notebooks (1991), 98.

7. Kentucky *Superintendent of Public Instruction Report* (1905-07), 9, 110, 151.

8. Hamlett, *History of Education*, 180, 191; Ligon, *Public Education*, 165-67; Vance Armentrout, *An Inventory of Kentucky* (1922), 7; Kentucky *Acts* (1928), 183-88.

9. Morton Keller, *Affairs of State* (1977), 482; Kentucky *Acts* (1904), 200-201; (1908), 198-205; (1912), 279-81; Hamlett, *History of Education*, 240; Engle, "Superintendents and Issues," 139, 260-61; T. J. Coates to Stanley Committee, 19 October 1915, in Box III, General File, A. O. Stanley Papers, University of Kentucky Library.

10. C. Vann Woodward, *Origins of the New South, 1877-1913* (1951), 399; Lexington *Daily Leader*, 17 February 1901; Kentucky *Superintendent of Public Instruction Report* (1905-07), 22; *Taxation* 2 (October 1919): 12-13.

11. Kentucky *House Journal* (1902), 29; Nollie O. Taff, *History of State Revenue and Taxation in Kentucky* (1931), 79; Hamlett, *History of Education*, 190; Kentucky *Superintendent of Public Instruction Report* (1917-19), ix; *Taxation* 2 (October 1919), 9. The Lexington *Leader*, 5 January 1913, reported that the Russell Sage Foundation placed Kentucky fortieth among the forty-eight states in expenditures per child.

12. Kentucky *Superintendent of Public Instruction Report* (1905-07), 411; *Abstract of the Thirteenth Census* (1910), 245.

13. J. A. Sullivan to A. E. Willson, 25 December 1907, A. E. Willson Papers, Filson Club; Allen W. Moger, *Virginia: Bourbonism to Byrd, 1870-1925* (1968), 245, 251.

14. Hamlett, *History of Education*, 193, 197; Engle, "Superintendents and Issues," 63; J. G. Crabbe to A. E. Willson, 14 December 1907, Willson Papers. For a general critique of the reform movement, see Keith C. Barton, "The Gates Shut Quickly: Education and Reform in Kentucky, 1903-1908" (microfilm, University of Kentucky Library).

15. Hamlett, *History of Education*, 204-5.

16. Nancy K. Forderhase, "'The Clear Call of Thoroughbred Women': The Kentucky Federation of Women's Clubs and the Crusade for Educational Reform 1903-1909," *Register* 83 (1985): 29; Kentucky *Acts* (1908), 133-43; Hamlett, *History of Education*, 203-10; Engle, "Superintendents and Issues," 220-21; Ligon, *Public Education*, 142, Hartford ms. history, Chapter 2, 4-5.

17. Hamlett, *History of Education*, 200-201; Forderhase, "Clear Call of Thoroughbred Women," 32.

18. Hartford ms. history, Chapter 5, 8-9; Kentucky *Superintendent of Public Instruction Report* (1921-23), 25; Ligon, *Public Education*, 213-14; Howard K. Odum, *Southern Regions of the United States* (1936), 100.

19. Louise Combs and Kern Alexander, "The Development of the Kentucky State Department of Education" (typescript, copy in author's possession), 53, 23-24, 34-35; Kentucky *Superintendent of Public Instruction Report* (1917-19), x; (1925-27), 11; Ligon, *Public Education*, 160; Legislative Research Commission, *A Guide to the Kentucky Reform Act of 1990* (1990), 1. See also Anna Youngman, "The Revenue System of Kentucky: A Study in State Finance," *Quarterly Journal of Economics* 32 (1917): 202.

20. Ligon, *Public Education*, 150, 170, 154-55; Thomas D. Clark, *History of Kentucky* (rev. ed., 1960), 241; Kentucky *Superintendent of Public Instruction Report* (1925-27), 9; Combs and Alexander, "State Department of Education," 17, 19, 27.

21. Grantham, *Southern Progressivism*, 258.

22. Kentucky *Superintendent of Public Instruction Report* (1919-21), 5; Kentucky Education Commission, *Public Education*, 3-4, 109, 116, 140.

23. Efficiency Commission of Kentucky, *The Government of Kentucky* (2 vols., 1924), 2: 243-427; Odum, *Southern Regions*, 240, 232; Louisville *Courier-Journal,*19 September 1943; Postwar Advisory Planning Commission of Kentucky, *Final Report* (1945), 72, 66, 61.

24. Taff, *State Revenue and Taxation*, 122, 124; Kentucky *Auditor of Public Accounts Report* (1926-27), 15; (1930-31), 12; (1934-35), 12; Truman M. Pierce et al., *White and Negro Schools in the South* (1955), 327.

25. *Officers, Committees and Members of the Kentucky Legislature* (1904), 37; Kentucky *House Journal* (1904), 73, 294, 524-27; clipping, Louisville *Herald,*11 October 1907, in Scrapbook "1907-08," in W. O. Bradley Papers, University of Kentucky Library; Richard A. Heckman and Betty J. Hall, "Berea College and the Day Law," *Register* 66 (1968): 39, 41; Kentucky *Acts* (1904), 13; Kentucky *House Journal* (1906), 7-8.

26. James C. Klotter, "The Black South and White Appalachia," *Journal of American History* 66 (1980): 843-49. See also Paul David Nelson, "Experiment in Interracial Education at Berea College, 1858-1908," *Journal of Negro History* 59 (1974): 13-37 and Jacqueline G. Burnside, "Suspicion Versus Faith: Negro Criticisms of Berea College in the Nineteenth Century," *Register* 83 (1985): 237-66.

27. Kentucky *Senate Journal* (1904), 1051-53; Kentucky *Acts* (1904), 181-82; Louisville *Courier-Journal*, 12 March 1904; Lexington *Herald*, 18 February 1905; Louisville *Courier-Journal*, 13 June 1906; Heckman and Hall, "Berea College," 45-49. On Frost's views, public and private, see Berea *Citizen*, 17, 24 March 1904, and Frost to William B. Smith, 4 February 1904, to James Speed, 6 February 1904, and to R. N. Roark, 12 February 1904 (copies), all in William G. Frost Papers, Berea College Library.

28. Hickman *Courier*, 24 March 1910; George C. Wright, "The Founding of Lincoln Institute," *FCHQ* 49 (1975): 63-68; Kentucky Commission on Human Rights, *Kentucky's Black Heritage* (1971), 64-65; Louisville *Courier-Journal*, 24 August 1975.

29. Kentucky *Superintendent of Public Instruction Report* (1925-27), 42; Efficiency Commission, *Government of Kentucky*, 2: 277.

30. Elizabeth B. Newhall, "Schools," in *Child Welfare in Kentucky* (1919), 79; Leonard E. Meece, "Negro Education in Kentucky," *Bulletin of the Bureau of School Services* [University of Kentucky] 10 (1938): 69, 71, 78; R. B. Atwood, "Financing Schools for Negro Children from State School Funds in Kentucky," *Journal of Negro Education* 8 (1939): 665; Arthur Graham, "The Civil Rights Struggle in Lexington: An Interview with Audrey L. Grevious," *Kentucky Review* 10 (1990): 62.

31. Kentucky *Superintendent of Public Instruction Reports* (1917-19), 196-97; (1925-27), 43; (1919-21), 38; (1923-25), 35; Myrtle K. Phillips, "The Origin, Development, and Present Status of Public Secondary Education for Negroes in Kentucky," *Journal of Negro Education* 1 (1932): 419-20.

32. Kentucky *Superintendent of Public Instruction* (1903-05), 310-11; Department of the Interior, *Negro Education: A Study of the Private and Higher School for Colored People in the United States* (2 vols., 1917), 2: 259, 1: 34; Atwood, "Financing Schools for Negroes," 665; Lexington *Herald*, 3 June 1977; "Improved Conditions for Negroes in Louisville," *Monthly Labor Review* 61 (1945): 727. See also Meece, "Negro Education," 124.

33. Efficiency Commission, *Government of Kentucky*, 2: 262; Kentucky *Superintendent of Public Instruction Report* (1917-19), 200; Phillips, "Secondary Education for Negroes," 422; William H. Fouse, "Educational History of the Negroes of Lexington, Kentucky" (M. A. thesis, University of Cincinnati, 1937), 134; Meece, "Negro Education," 86, 92, 94; Graham, "Civil Rights Struggle," 62.

34. James D. Anderson, *The Education of Blacks in the South, 1860-1935* (1988), 151, 182; Kentucky *Superintendent of Public Instruction Report* (1903-05), 322; (1921-23), 33.

35. Dept. of Interior, *Negro Education*, 2: 267-68; Efficiency Commission, *Government of Kentucky*, 2: 390, 399, 404-8; Gerald L. Smith, "'Mr. Kentucky State' A Biography of Rufus Ballard Atwood" (Ph.D. diss., University of Kentucky, 1988), 112; Ligon, *Public Education*, 258-63; Kentucky *Acts* (1926), 304-5; (1934), 217-18, 317; Atwood, "Financing Schools for Negroes," 665. The Smith dissertation recently appeared in book form under the title *A Black Educator in the Segregated South*.

36. *Kentucky's Black Heritage*, 41-42; James B. Hudson, "The History of Louisville Municipal College" (Ed.D. diss., University of Kentucky, 1981), 1, 31, 38, 42-43, 47-48.

37. Kentucky *Acts* (1936), 110-12; (1948), 18. One state superintendent wrote that he feared out-of-state, northern education "gives Negroes false ideas." Quoted in George C. Wright, *Life Behind a Veil: Blacks in Louisville, Kentucky, 1865-1930* (1985), 263.

38. George C. Wright, *A History of Blacks in Kentucky* (1992), 2: 170-86; New York *Times*, 22 June 1949; Pete Daniel, *Standing at the Crossroads: Southern Life Since 1900* (1986), 161.

39. *Child Welfare in Kentucky*, 52; Postwar Planning Commission *Report*, 70; Ligon, *Public Education*, 138.

40. Kentucky Education Commission, *Public Education*, 72; *Child Welfare in Kentucky*, 72; William T. Congleton II Interview with Stella C. Atkinson, November 1988, in Helen Congleton Breckinridge, *Memories of Cannel City, Kentucky* (1993), 27; S. S. MacClintock, "The Kentucky Mountains and Their Feuds," *American Journal of Sociology* 7 (July 1901): 17; Gordon Wilson, *Fidelity Folks* (1946), 135.

41. Kentucky *Superintendent of Public Instruction Report* (1905-1907), 85; Fred W. Peel, "Growing Up in Central Kentucky" (typescript, Kentucky Historical Society), 134; Pierce et al., *White and Negro Schools*, 191; Arthur W. Spaulding, *The Men of the Mountains* (1915),71; Kentucky Education Commission, *Public Education*, 90, 92.

42. Kentucky Education Commission, *Public Education*, 74, 73; Carye Abell, in Owensboro *Messenger-Inquirer*, 1 September 1986.

43. Kentucky Education Commission, *Public Education*, 75-76; Fred Lewis, "A Story About My Life . . . ," *Frontier Nursing Service Quarterly Bulletin* 62 (Autumn 1986): 6; Peel, "Growing Up," 127; Mabel B. Ellis, "Children of the Kentucky Coal Fields," *The American Child* 1 (1920): 354-57.

44. Kentucky *Superintendent of Public Instruction Report* (1903-05), 24; Louisville *Courier-Journal*, 26 April 1932.

45. Kentucky *Superintendent of Public Instruction Report* (1905-07), 160, 161; (1917-19), xvi; (1919-21), 12; Paducah *Weekly News-Democrat*, 13 June 1907.

46. Paducah *Weekly News-Democrat*, 13 June 1907; Hickman *Courier*, 5 September 1912; Hamlett, *History of Education*, 196; Kentucky *Superintendent of Public Instruction Report* (1905-07), 422-26; Breckinridge, *Cannel City Memories*, 28.

47. Kentucky *Superintendent of Public Instruction Report* (1919-21), 11; Harry W. Schacter, *Kentucky on the March* (1949), 6; Postwar Planning Commission, *Report*, 70; Frank L. McVey, *The Gates Open Slowly: A History of Education in Kentucky* (1949), 272; Louisville *Courier-Journal*, 18 September 1943.

48. Louisville *Courier-Journal*, 17 December 1989; *Child Welfare in Kentucky*, 55; Combs and Alexander, "State Department of Education," 28, 46.

49. Kentucky *Superintendent of Public Instruction Report* (1905-07), 6, 104; Efficiency Commission, *Government of Kentucky*, 2: 284; Hamlett, *History of Education*, 179, 250; Fred C. Kelly, "In the Blue Grass Country," *Current History* 43 (1936): 362; Kentucky Education Commission, *Public Education*, 36, 59; Combs and Alexander, "State Department of Education," 44; Kentucky

Superintendent of Public Instruction Report (1919-21), 4.

50. Engle, "Superintendents and Issues," 251; T. J. Coates, "The Educational Awakening in Kentucky," in *United States Bureau of Education Bulletin* 30 (1913): 56; Kentucky *Acts* (1940), 742-50; (1942), 537-46; (1954), 147-48; Louisville *Courier-Journal*, 29 March 1946.

51. Kentucky *Superintendent of Public Instruction Report* (1919-21), 12; (1905-07), 430-31; Kentucky Education Commission, *Public Education*, 55; Woodbridge Spears, "Elizabeth Madox Roberts: A Biographical and Critical Study" (Ph.D. diss., University of Kentucky, 1953), 81.

52. Ellis "Children of Coal Fields," 347; Kentucky *Superintendent of Public Instruction Reports* (1917-19), 58; (1919-21), 12; Louisville *Courier-Journal*, 19 September 1943; Kentucky *Acts* (1944), 110-11; James C. Klotter, ed., *The Public Papers of Governor Simeon Willis* (1988), 5. Pierce et al., *White and Negro Schools*, 207; John E. Kleber, ed., *The Public Papers of Governor Lawrence W. Wetherby* (1983), 27.

53. Thomas D. Clark, "A Historical Perspective on Education in Kentucky" (paper presented to Shakertown Roundtable, 1985), 17; Robert Penn Warren, *Portrait of a Father* (1988), 64-65; Ercel S. Eaton, *Appalachian Yesterdays* (1982), 67.

54. Berea College, *Guide to the Hindman Settlement School Collection* (1982), 1-3; "Settlement Institutions in Appalachia," *Appalachia* 5 (May-June 1972): 32; William S. Cornett, "Untying Some Knots in Knott County," in Wilson Somerville, *Appalachia/America* (1981), 183-85; Cratis Williams, "The Appalachian Experience," *Appalachian Heritage* 7 (1979): 10.

55. David E. Whisnant, *All That is Native & Fine* (1983), 90; Ronald D Eller, *Miners, Millhands, and Mountaineers* (1982), xviii; Nancy K. Forderhase, "Eve Returns to the Garden: Women Reformers in Appalachian Kentucky in the Early Twentieth Century," *Register* 85 (1987): 240, 245, 247, 261.

56. *Twelfth Census* (1900), vol. II, pt. II, c; Ellis, "Children of Coal Fields," 302; *Kentucky Documents* (1901), 41.

57. Louisville *Courier-Journal*, 12 April 1903.

58. Willie E. Nelms, Jr., "Cora Wilson Stewart and the Crusade Against Illiteracy in Kentucky," *Register* 74 (1976): 12-15, 20, 24; 82 (1984), 154, 164-67, 169; Kentucky *Superintendent of Public Instruction Report* (1917-19), 423; Kentucky *Acts* (1916), 602-3; (1918), 154-56; *The Nation* (12 July 1947), 41.

59. Lexington *Herald*, 8 January 1922.

60. Kentucky *Superintendent of Public Instruction Report* (1905-07), 191; Kentucky *Acts* (1908), 5; Hamlett, *History of Education*, 281; Charles G.. Talbert, *The University of Kentucky: The Maturing Years* (1965), 31.

61. Grantham, *Southern Progressivism*, 272; Kentucky *Superintendent of Public Instruction Report* (1917-19), 290, 249; Talbert, *University of Kentucky*, 87; Thomas G. Dyer, "Education," in Charles R. Wilson and William Ferris, eds., *Encyclopedia of Southern Culture* (1989), 239; Lexington *Herald*, 30 March 1932; H. L. Donovan, "The Evolution of a University," *FCHQ* 21 (1947): 217; Hamlett, *History of Education*, 294, 302.

62. H. Clarence Nixon, "Colleges and Universities," in W. T. Couch, ed., *Culture in the South* (1934), 232; Kentucky *Acts* (1906) 393-404; (1922), 51-53; Lexington *Herald*, 30 April 1915, 8 April 1919; Klotter, ed., *Public Papers of Governor Willis*, 153-56.

63. "Public Higher Education in Kentucky," *Kentucky Legislative Research Commission Research Publication No. 25* (Old Series)(1951), 7, 17, 100; George E. Harris, "The Drain of Talent Out of Ohio and Kentucky" (M.A. thesis, Kentucky State University, 1956), 71.

7. "We Will Sing One Song": Kentucky's Cultural Milieu

1. John W. Townsend, "A History of Kentucky Literature Since 1913," *FCHQ* 13 (1939): 36; Lawrence S. Thompson, "Books at the University of Kentucky," *ibid.* 24 (1950): 58; Howard W. Beers, ed., *Kentucky: Designs on Her Future* (1945), 250.

2. Lexington *Herald-Leader*, 31 December 1978.

3. On Allen generally, see William S. Ward, *A Literary History of Kentucky* (1988), 40-47; James C. Klotter, "Little Shepherds, Little Colonels, and Little Kingdoms: A Selective Review of Kentucky Writing, 1784-1950," *Journal of Kentucky Studies* 3 (1986): 64-65; William K. Bottorff, *James Lane Allen* (1964); and Grant C. Knight, *James Lane Allen and the Genteel Tradition* (1935). Quotation from Allen, *Summer in Arcady* (1896), ix.

4. Allen, *Flute and Violin and Other Kentucky Tales and Romances* (1897; orig. pub. 1891), 99-100, 119.

5. Allen, *The Choir Invisible* (1974, orig. pub. 1897), 135, 191. Summaries of the story line for many of the books mentioned in this chapter can be found in Ward, *Literary History*, and in Lawrence S. Thompson and Algernon D. Thompson, *The Kentucky Novel* (1953).

6. Bottorff, *Allen*, 151; Thomas D. Clark and A. D. Kirwan, *The South Since Appomattox* (1967), 217; Knight, *Allen*, 128, 161; Ward, *Literary History*, 44, 43; Louisville *Courier-Journal*, 11 September 1909. See also James Lane Allen to Cale Rice, 18 June 1909, 26 April 1915, 6 May [1915], Rice Collection, Kentucky Library, Western Kentucky University.

7. Thomas Nelson Page, "John Fox," *Scribner's Magazine* 66 (1919): 675, 674, 678; Jack Temple Kirby, *Media-Made Dixie* (rev. ed., 1986), 40. On Fox generally see Ward, *Literary History*, 76-83; Mary C. Browning, *Kentucky Authors* (1968), 244-45; Klotter, "Little Shepherds," 65-66; Harriet R. Holman, ed., *John Fox and Tom Page as They Were* (1970); Cratis Williams, "The Southern Mountaineer in Fact and Fiction," *Appalachian Journal* 3 (1975-76): 211-22; Elizabeth Fox Moore, *John Fox, Jr.: Personal and Family Letters and Papers* (1955); and Warren I. Titus, *John Fox, Jr.* (1971).

8. John Fox, Jr., to Michajah Fible, 4 March 1885, 13 May 1887, John Fox, Jr., Collection, University of Virginia Library.

9. Moore, *Fox*, 37-38.

10. Fox, *Little Shepherd of Kingdom Come* (1973; orig. pub. 1903), 153, 247.

11. Williams, "Southern Mountaineer," 219. See also Anne Gabbard Shelby, "Appalachian Literature and American Myth: A Study of Fiction From the Southern Mountains" (M. A. thesis, University of Kentucky, 1981), 20-27.

12. Ward, *Literary History*, 83-84, 86-88; Williams, "Southern Mountaineers," 226-34, 359-61; Julia Neal, "Lucy Furman; Life and Works" (M. A. thesis, Western Kentucky University, 1933), 3-11; "Jean (Bell) Thomas," in John E. Kleber, ed., *The Kentucky Encyclopedia* (1992), 879-80. Neal (iv) notes that Furman was born in 1869, not 1870, as was often given.

13. Ward, *Literary History*, 62-64; R. Gerald Alvey, "Cultural Conflicts in Kentucky Literature" (University of Kentucky College of Agriculture Cooperative Extension Service Pamphlet H. E. 1-321), 3; Michael A. Flannery, "The Local Color of John Uri Lloyd," *Register* 91 (1993): 24-50. Lloyd won pharmacy's highest award in 1920.

14. Ward, *Literary History*, 57-61; Harry S. Caudill, *Slender is the Thread: Tales from a Country Law Office* (1987), 71; Anita Lawson, *Irvin S. Cobb* (1984), passim; "Humor," in Kleber, ed., *Kentucky Encyclopedia*, 446; Irvin S. Cobb, *Exit Laughing* (1941), 96. For some authors' problems, see Lida Calvert Obenchain to Margaret Calvert, 14 May 1911, Calvert-Obenchain-Younglove Collection, Series II, Box 1, Kentucky Library, Western Kentucky University.

15. Wade Hall, "Literature," in James C. Klotter, ed., *Our Kentucky: A Study of the Bluegrass*

State (1992), 224; Richard H. King, *A Southern Renaissance . . . 1930-1955* (1980), 7.

16. Howard W. Odum, *Southern Regions of the United States* (1936), 560-61.

17. Harry M. Campbell and Ruel E. Foster, *Elizabeth Madox Roberts* (1956), 66, 19, 21, 28-29; Louisville *Courier-Journal*, 24 February 1929; Ward, *Literary History*, 155; Andrew J. Beeler, Jr., "Elizabeth Madox Roberts . . ." (M.A. thesis, University of Louisville, 1940), 3, 6; Woodbridge Spears, "Elizabeth Madox Roberts . . ." (Ph.D. diss., University of Kentucky, 1953), 81, 34; Earl H. Rovit, *Herald to Chaos: The Novels of Elizabeth Madox Roberts* (1960), 2-4.

18. Campbell and Foster, *Roberts*, 51; Beeler, "Roberts," 19; Ward, *Literary History*, 151.

19. Beeler, "Roberts," 106, 116; F. Lamar Janney, "Elizabeth Madox Roberts," *Sewanee Review* 45 (1937): 391; Rovit, *Herald to Chaos*, 25; Ward, *Literary History*, 152-58; Mary E. Nilles, "The Rise and Decline of a Literary Reputation: Vagaries in the Career of Elizabeth Madox Roberts" (Ph.D. diss., New York University, 1972), 3-4. Edith Summers Kelley (1884-1956) had dealt with sharecropping in her almost forgotten novel, *Weeds* (1923).

20. New York *Times*, 5 December 1926; *Saturday Review of Literature*, 25 January 1930; Mark Van Doren, "Elizabeth Madox Roberts: Her Mind and Style," *English Journal* 21 (1932): 522; New York *Times*, 20 November 1932; Louisville *Courier-Journal*, 24 February 1929. See also J. Donald Adams, "Elizabeth Madox Roberts," *Virginia Quarterly Review* 12 (1936): 80, 86, 90 and William H. Slavick, "Elizabeth Modox Roberts," in Joseph M. Flora and Robert Bain, eds., *Fifty Southern Writers After 1900* (1987), 411-21.

21. Janney, "Roberts," 389, 409; Glenway Wescott, "Elizabeth Madox Roberts: A Personal Note," *The Bookman* 71 (March 1930): 13; Campbell and Foster, *Roberts*, 22; Nilles, "Rise and Decline of a Reputation," 55. See also Wade Hall, "Place in the Short Fiction of Elizabeth Madox Roberts," *Kentucky Review* 6 (1986): 5.

22. Interview with Robert Penn Warren, 6 October 1977, Warren Oral History Project, University of Kentucky Library; Robert Penn Warren, *Portrait of a Father* (1988), 53; Marshall Walker, "Robert Penn Warren," *Journal of American Studies* 8 (1974): 232; Ward, *Literary History*, 184-85. On Warren generally see, as examples, Leonard Cooper, *Robert Penn Warren* (1960); Victor H. Strandberg, *A Colder Fire: The Poetry of Robert Penn Warren* (1965); William Bedford Clark, *The American Vision of Robert Penn Warren* (1991); and James H. Justus, *The Achievement of Robert Penn Warren* (1981).

23. Ward, *Literary History*, 167-86; Clark, *American Vision*, xi.

24. Quotation in Warren, *Portrait of a Father*, [88].

25. H. Edward Richardson, *Jesse: The Biography of an American Writer, Jesse Hilton Stuart* (1984), 1-2, 139, 148, 155-66. Richardson notes that Stuart was born in 1906, not 1907 as is often given. *Ibid.*, 485. On Stuart, see also Everetta Love Blair, *Jesse Stuart* (1967); Ruel E. Foster, *Jesse Stuart* (1968); J. R. Lemaster and Mary Washington Clarke, eds., *Jesse Stuart: Essays on His Work* (1977); and J. R. Lemaster, *Jesse Stuart* (1980).

26. Vergil Leon Sturgill, "Genius of W-Hollow," *Southern Literary Messenger* 2 (1940): 155; Federal Writers' Project, *Kentucky: A Guide to the Bluegrass State* (1939), 124; Richardson, *Jesse*, 216, 219; Dayton Kohler, "Jesse Stuart and James Still: Mountain Regionalists," *College English* 3 (1942): 525, 528.

27. R. Gerald Alvey, "Cultural Stereotypes in Kentucky Literature" (University of Kentucky College of Agriculture Cooperative Extension Service Pamphlet 3M-3-82), 5; Williams, "Southern Mountaineer," 243; Ward, *Literary History*, 234-45; Richardson, *Jesse*, 328-29, 308-9; Kohler, "Stuart and Still," 525.

28. Ward, *Literary History*, 223; Kohler, "Stuart and Still," 523, 529.

29. Shelby, "Appalachian Literature," 38; Ward, *Literary History*, 224-32; Lexington *Herald-*

Leader, 21 July 1991.

30. Ashley Brown, "Caroline Gordon," in Flora and Bain, eds., *Fifty Southern Writers*, 215-24; Ward, *Literary History*, 189-96.

31. Ward, *Literary History*, 159-67; William Pratt, "Allen Tate," in Charles R. Wilson and William Ferris, eds., *Encyclopedia of Southern Culture* (1989), 897; Joy Bale Boone, "Allen Tate," in Kleber, ed., *Kentucky Encyclopedia*, 867.

32. Williams, "Southern Mountaineer," 380-90; Glenda Kay Hobbs, "Harriette Arnow's Literary Journey" (Ph.D. diss., Harvard University, 1975), preface, 5, 81, 108; "A Thomas Merton Symposium," *Kentucky Review* 7 (1987): 58, 5-145; Ward, *Literary History*, 272-78, 216-23, 332-37, 266-72, 322-25, 380-85. See also David J. Harkness, "Literary Profiles of the Southern States: Kentucky," *Southern Observer* 1 (1953): 18-23; Dorothy Edwards Townsend, *Kentucky in American Letters, 1913-1975* (1976), passim; and Ish Ritchey, *Kentucky Literature, 1784-1963* (1963), passim.

33. Irving Soblosky, *American Music* (1969), 94; W. T. Couch, ed., *Culture in the South* (1934), 291; Carol C. Birkhead, "The History of the Orchestra in Louisville" (M. A. thesis, University of Louisville, 1977), iii; Robert Bruce French, "Music," in Kleber, ed., *Kentucky Encyclopedia*, 665.

34. Pete Daniel, *Standing at the Crossroad* (1986), 99.

35. Charles F. Faber, "Country Music," in Kleber, ed., *Kentucky Encyclopedia*, 231-32; Charles K. Wolfe, *Kentucky Country* (1982), 29, 46-47.

36. Wolfe, *Kentucky Country*, 47-48, 52, 77; Betty B. Ellison, "Renfro Valley Barn Dance," in Kleber, ed., *Kentucky Encyclopedia*, 767. On Kincaid, see Kelly Thurman, "Bradley Kincaid: Music from the Mountains in the 1920s," *Register* 80 (1982): 170-82, and Loyal Jones, *Radio's Kentucky Mountain Boy, Bradley Kincaid* (1980).

37. Wolfe, *Kentucky Country*, 56, 80, 92, 95, 171. See also individual entries on Ledford, Jones, Foley, and King in Kleber, ed., *Kentucky Encyclopedia*, passim.

38. Gail King, "Bluegrass Music," in Kleber, ed., *Kentucky Encyclopedia*, 90-91; Wolfe, *Kentucky Country*, 97, 102; Laurel Shackelford and Bill Weinberg, eds., *Our Appalachia* (1977), 358.

39. French, "Music," 665-66; Bill C. Malone, *Southern Music, American Music* (1979), 80; Thurman, "Kincaid," 171; William Lynwood Montell, *Singing the Glory Down: Amateur Gospel Music in South Central Kentucky, 1900-1990* (1991), 18, 25, 27, 44-45.

40. Gregory A. Waller, "David Wark Griffith," and Thomas M. House, "Charles Albert Browning," both in Kleber, ed., *Kentucky Encyclopedia*, 392-93, 132; Louisville *Courier-Journal*, 7 November 1982; Kirby, *Media-Made Dixie*, 3.

41. Joseph F. Wall, *Henry Watterson* (1956), xiii.

42. *Ibid.*, passim; Arthur Krock, *Myself When Young* (1973), 110-11; Malcolm Boyley, "In Memory of 'Marse Henry,'" *Louisville Magazine* 30 (December 1979): 20-22.

43. Wall, *Watterson*, 291, 306, 310-15; Hopkinsville *Kentuckian*, 9 February 1911; Henry Watterson to Robert W. Bingham, 3 March, 22 March 1919, Papers of Robert Worth Bingham, Manuscript Division, Library of Congress.

44. Samuel W. Thomas, "George Barry Bingham, Sr.," and Robert Shulman, "Courier-Journal," both in Kleber, ed., *Kentucky Encyclopedia*, 79, 233; Louisville *Courier-Journal*, 9 May 1935; Ronald T. Farrer, "County Newspapers," in Wilson and Ferris, eds., *Encyclopedia of Southern Culture*, 937.

45. James C. Klotter, *The Breckinridges of Kentucky* (1986), 208-43; Lexington *Herald*, 15 October 1908; New York *Age*, 20 April 1905, 16 March 1915; Virginius Dabney, *Liberalism in the South* (1932), 410.

46. Odum, *Southern Regions*, 224; Thomas D. Clark, *Southern Country Editor* (1948), 81-82;

idem, *The Rural Press and the New South* (1948), 11-13, 70; Herndon J. Evans, *The Newspaper Press in Kentucky* (1976), 26-41, 103-16; and "Louisville Defender," "Louisville Leader," and "Kentucky Irish American" entries in Kleber, ed., *Kentucky Encyclopedia*, 582-83, 505. See also Urey Woodson, *"The Good Old Days," Being Some Newspaper Reminiscences . . .* (1931), 7-23.

47. Nancy D. Baird, "Enid Yandell," *FCHQ* 62 (1988): 5-32; Ula M. Gregory, "The Fine Arts," in Couch, *Culture in the South*, 277.

48. Robert C. May, "The Lexington Camera Club," *Kentucky Review* 9 (1989): 3-47; James C. Anderson, "Photography," in Kleber, ed., *Kentucky Encyclopedia*, 720.

49. Arthur F. Jones, *The Art of Paul Sawyier* (1976), 1, 37, 86; John W. Townsend, "Paul Sawyier: Kentucky Artist, Some Recollections of Him," *FCHQ* 33 (1959): 310-13; Robert Neuhaus, *Unsuspected Genius: The Art and Life of Frank Duveneck* (1987), passim; Lynn Renau and Harriet Fowler, "Art and Artists," in Kleber, ed., *Kentucky Encyclopedia*, 34; Charles P. Roland, *The Improbable Era: The South Since World War II* (1975), 161.

50. Clay Lancaster, *Vestiges of the Venerable City: A Chronicle of Lexington, Kentucky* (1976), 148, 165, 171; John Shelton Reed, *The Enduring South* (1974), 2; C. Julian Oberwarth, *A History of the Profession of Architecture in Kentucky* (1987), 20; Robert J. Cangelosi, "Residential 20th-Century Architecture," in Wilson and Ferris, eds., *Encyclopedia of Southern Culture*, 101-2; William B. Scott, Jr., "Architecture," in Kleber, ed., *Kentucky Encyclopedia*, 30.

51. Cangelosi, "20th-Century Architecture," 102; Roland, *Improbable Era*, 158; Scott, "Architecture," 30-31.

8. "Politics . . . in Kentucky"

1. Unidentified clipping, "James H. Mulligan" Vertical File, Kentucky Historical Society Library; John W. Townsend, *Kentucky in American Letters, 1784-1912* (2 vols., 1913), 1: 348-51; Lexington *Herald*, 12 February 1902. See also E. I. "Buddy" Thompson, "The Mulligans of Maxwell Place," in *Lexington – As It Was* (1981), 508.

2. Lexington *Leader*, 14 April 1916; James O. Carson to E. G. Young, 9 January 1916, Papers of E. G. Young, Kentucky Library, Western Kentucky University.

3. Marmaduke B. Morton, *Kentuckians Are Different* (1938), 45.

4. John H. Fenton, *Politics in the Border States* (1957), 14.

5. Mary K. Bonsteel Tachau, "The Making of a Railroad President: Milton Hannibal Smith and the L & N," *FCHQ* 43 (1969): 125-43; Morton, *Kentuckians Are Different*, 86; George R. Leighton, *Five Cities* (1939), 77; James C. Klotter, *William Goebel* (1977), 20-21, 71-74; Milton H. Smith to H. Walters, 29 September 1903 (copy), Chairman's Correspondence File, Box 34, Louisville and Nashville Railroad Co. Records, University of Louisville Archives.

6. John G. Speed, "The Kentucky Insurrection," *Harper's Weekly* (17 February 1900), 135; *Law Department, Louisville & Nashville R. R. Co., List of Attorneys, December 1, 1908* (1908), 3-4, in Box 17, File 614, L & N Records.

7. Lexington *Herald*, 6 November 1906.

8. New York *Times*, 12 May 1914; John E. Buckingham, "Sketch of the Life of John C. C. Mayo" (typescript copy, Kentucky Historical Society), 10; Louisville *Courier-Journal*, 14 November 1911; Lexington *Herald*, 8 February, 4 January 1911; Louisa *Big Sandy News*, 2 July, 20 August 1926.

9. Lexington *Herald*, 10 June 1908, 1 September 1915; Lexington *Leader*, 21 July 1911; A. O. Stanley to Sue Soaper Stanley, 18 January 1914, Box 3, A. O. Stanley Papers, University of

Kentucky Library.

10. Lexington *Leader*, 31 December 1933; typescript sketch of Camden, in Johnson Newlon Camden Papers (microfilm), University of Kentucky Library; A. O. Stanley to Sue Stanley, 28 August 1914, Box 3, Stanley Papers.

11. M. P. Hunt, *The Story of My Life* (1941), 164; John Jacob Eisenbeis, "Recollections of Louisville, Kentucky, 1890-1930" (typescript, Filson Club), [55]; Louis J. Hebel, "This is the way it was" (typescript, Filson Club), 30; Lexington *Herald*, 16 March 1930. See also Sarah R. Yates and Karen R. Gray, "When Politics was a Girlie Show," *Louisville Today* (June 1981): 18-21, 52-55.

12. John Erie Davis, "When the Whallens Were Kings," *Louisville* 30 (November 1979): 18-19; Carolyn L. Denning, "The Louisville (Kentucky) Democratic Party: Political Times of 'Miss Lennie' McLaughlin" (M. A. thesis, University of Louisville, 1981), 23.

13. A. O. Stanley to Sue Stanley, 14 April 1913, Box 3, Stanley Papers.

14. "Michael Joseph Brennan," "Lennie Lee (Wallis) McLaughlin," and "William Frederick Klair," in John E. Kleber, ed., *The Kentucky Encyclopedia* (1992), 122, 598-99, 520-21; Denning, "'Miss Lennie,'" passim; Louisville *Courier-Journal*, 11 May 1988; John D. Wright, Jr., *Lexington: Heart of the Bluegrass* (1982), 130; Nancy C. Graves, "William Frederick Klair" (seminar paper, Transylvania College, 1953; microfilm, University of Kentucky), passim; James Duane Bolin, "Bossism and Reform: Politics in Lexington, Kentucky, 1880-1940" (Ph.D. diss., University of Kentucky, 1988), 49-62.

15. Thomas H. Appleton, Jr., "William Purcell Dennis Haly," in Kleber, ed., *Kentucky Encyclopedia*, 399-400; Arthur Krock, *Myself When Young* (1973), 179; Cincinnati *Enquirer*, 3 January 1915; Lexington *Herald*, 7 July 1927; Danville *Messenger*, 22 June 1917; Louisville *Times*, 17 February 1937.

16. Marie Brenner, *House of Dreams: The Bingham Family* . . . (1988), 134; Author's Interview with Tom Waller of Paducah, 1974, Kentucky Oral History Commission Collection, Kentucky Historical Society; Cincinnati *Enquirer*, 3 January 1915; Ashland *Independent*, 21 July 1910. See also Percy Haly to Justus Goebel, 6 April 1900, Goebel Family Papers (microfilm), and Percy Haly Scrapbooks (microfilm), both in University of Kentucky Library.

17. On Johnson, generally, see James C. Klotter and John W. Muir, "Boss Ben Johnson, the Highway Commission, and Kentucky Politics, 1927-1937," *Register* 84 (1986): 18-50; Ben Johnson Collection, Kentucky Historical Society; Temple Bodley and Samuel M. Wilson, *History of Kentucky* (4 vols., 1928), 3: 244-46; Sarah B. Smith, *Historic Nelson County* (1971), 384-88.

18. Klotter and Muir, "Boss Ben Johnson," 19, 32; 1906 clipping, Springfield *Sun*, Scrapbook II; David W. Gaddie to C. A. Johnston, 7 October 1908, Scrapbook, both in Johnson Collection.

19. Fenton, *Politics in the Border States*, 18; unpublished biography of Johnson by John W. Muir (copy in author's possession); Klotter and Muir, "Boss Ben Johnson," 19, 22, 31-46; Author's Interview with George W. Chinn, 1976.

20. Klotter and Muir, "Boss Ben Johnson," 32-33. See also entries on the various people in Kleber, ed., *Kentucky Encyclopedia*.

21. Klotter and Muir, "Boss Ben Johnson," 22, 33. Catholicism did not mean election could not take place — Paducah and Lexington, for instance, had a Catholic mayor, and Johnson won congressional races. But religion was a factor, especially the higher up the political ladder one climbed.

22. Elizabeth R. Hooker, *Religion in the Highlands* (1933), 60; H. C. Kennedy, *A Damphool in the Kentucky Legislature* (1909), 47; Interview with C. W. Murphy, 3 September 1977, Eastern Kentucky University (EKU) Oral History Center.

23. Paul Browning letter, in *Appalachian Notes* 3 (1975): 13; J. A. Richards, *A History of Bath County, Kentucky* (1961), 352.

24. George P. Metcalf, "The Fusion Movement in Louisville, 1905-1907" (M. A. thesis, Murray State University, 1969), 43; John W. Manning, "The Government of Kentucky" (typescript, 1940, University of Kentucky Library), 58n; Interview with J. Jake Jordan, 18 April 1980, EKU Oral History Center; E. A. Jonas, *A History of the Republican Party in Kentucky* (1929), 40; Bradley talk, 5 October 1907, in W. O. Bradley Scrapbooks, "1907," University of Kentucky Library.

25. Harry M. Caudill, *Slender is the Thread: Tales from a Country Law Office* (1987), 104. Seldom were offenders punished. In 1915 in Pike County, one of every six voters was indicted for bribery; the state's highest court threw out the resulting convictions due to improper admission of evidence. See Lexington *Herald*, 14 February 1915, and Kentucky *Attorney General's . . . Report* (1914-15), 10-11.

26. London (Ky.) *Sentinel*, 24 October 1907; Lexington *Herald*, 6 November 1907, 5 November 1909. See also Rezin C. Davis to John J. Davis, 10 August 1908, 30 August 1909, in John J. Davis Papers, West Virginia University Library.

27. Precinct Books, 1903-04, Democratic Party Papers, Samuel M. Wilson Collection, University of Kentucky Library; Lexington *Leader*, 19 October 1910; George C. Wright, "Black Political Insurgency in Louisville, Kentucky: The Lincoln Independent Party of 1921," *Journal of Negro History* 68 (1983): 9; *Twelfth Census* (1900): *Population*, I, part 1, cci. See also Paducah *Weekly News-Democrat*, 3 October 1907; Louisville *Kentucky Irish American*, 28 August, 30 October 1907; Lexington *Herald*, 5 November 1911.

28. Richard W. Griffin, *Newspaper Story of a Town: A History of Danville, Kentucky* (1965), 17; Lexington *Daily Leader*, 29 January, 15 March 1901. See also George C. Wright, *Life Behind a Veil* (1985), 157.

29. Louisville *Post*, 4 October 1901; *The Crisis* 1 (December 1910): 15; Richard G. Stone, *A Brittle Sword* (1977), 95; Louisville *Courier-Journal*, 24 February 1910.

30. Robert M. Ireland, *Little Kingdoms: The Counties of Kentucky, 1860-1891* (1977), 142-50; Thomas D. Clark, "Kentuckians," in Federal Writers' Project, *Kentucky: A Guide to the Bluegrass State* (1939), 4-5; Nellie Ballou, "Politics in Moonshineland," New York *Times Magazine*, 8 June 1924.

31. J. B. Shannon, "How to Stay Elected: A Story of Local Political Success," *Register* 79 (1981): 162-74. Sugg was defeated for office in 1957 and died four years later.

32. Manning, "Government of Kentucky," 75; Mary Helen Miller, *Citizens Guide to the Kentucky Constitution*, LRC Research Report No. 137 (1981), 15-16.

33. E. Polk Johnson, *History of Kentucky and Kentuckians* (3 vols., 1912), 1: 166; *Officers, Committees, and Members of the Kentucky Legislature* (1904), 3-34; *Kentucky Documents* (1904-05), passim; *Report of the Custodian of Public Buildings* (1902), 4-8.

34. Malcolm E. Jewell and Everett W. Cunningham, *Kentucky Politics* (1968), 9.

35. Carry Nation to W. H. Polk, in Lexington *Daily Leader*, 19 February 1901; Elizabethtown *News*, 29 July 1904; Paul Kleppner, *The Third Electoral System* (1979), 211; Paducah *Weekly News-Democrat*, 11 October 1906; Lexington *Herald*, 24 September 1914; John S. Gillig, "The Predreadnaught Battleship USS *Kentucky*," *Register* 88 (1990): 55, 55n. See also Mabel Crowder, "The Liquor Problem" (undergraduate thesis, Eastern Kentucky State Normal School, 1913). An excellent survey of the pre-1900 background can be found in Thomas H. Appleton, Jr., "'Like Banquo's Ghost': The Emergence of the Prohibition Issue in Kentucky Politics" (Ph.D. diss., University of Kentucky, 1981), 1-59.

36. On Progressivism, see for example: James Larry Hood, "The Collapse of Zion: Rural Progressivism in Nelson and Washington Counties, Kentucky" (Ph.D. diss., University of Ken-

tucky, 1980); Dewey W. Grantham, *Southern Progressivism* (1983); idem, *The Democratic South* (1963), 56; George B. Tindall, *The Persistent Tradition in the New South* (1975), 53-57; William A. Link, *The Paradox of Southern Progressivism* (1992); Lewis L. Gould, ed., *The Progressive Era* (1974), 2-10; Robert H. Bremner, *From the Depths: The Discovery of Poverty in the United States* (1956), 131-203; and Jack T. Kirby, *Darkness at the Dawning: Race and Reform in the Progressive South* (1972).

9. *"Politics—The Damnedest—in Kentucky": 1900-1919*

1. Arthur Krock, *Myself When Young* (1973), 174; George L. Willis, *Kentucky Democracy* (3 vols., 1935), 1: 415; E. A. Jonas, *Once Upon a Time* (1942), 110-11; G. Glenn Clift, *Governors of Kentucky, 1792-1942* (1942), 109-11; Lowell H. Harrison, ed., *Kentucky's Governors, 1792-1985* (1985), 115-18.

2. J. C. W. Beckham to W. A. Williams, 12 December 1912, in W. A. Williams Collection, Kentucky Historical Society; Kentucky *Auditor's Report* (1900-1901), iii-v, 130, 213.

3. Louisville *Herald-Post*, 14 October 1927; Interview with Milton Smith by C. P. Connolly, 6 October 1913 (typescript copy, Kentucky Historical Society), 54; Kentucky *Auditor's Report* (1900-1901), 168-69.

4. Lexington *Daily Leader*, 15, 28 August 1900; Kentucky *Acts* (Extraordinary Session, 1900), 6-23. See also Lexington *Daily Leader*, 12 January 1901, and G. Glenn Clift, "Kentucky Politics, 1900-1953," *Southern Observer* 2 (1954): 47.

5. Gaye Keller Bland, "Populism in Kentucky, 1887-1896" (Ph.D. diss., University of Kentucky, 1979), 171; Lexington *Daily Leader*, 15 August, 19 July, 27 September, 19 October, 3, 5 November 1900; E. Polk Johnson, *History of Kentucky and Kentuckians* (3 vols., 1912), 1: 515.

6. Columbia *Adair County News*, 9 January 1901; unidentified clippings, 4 May, 14 July 1904 in W. O. Bradley Scrapbooks, "1904-1906"; Lexington *Daily Leader*, 17 July, 3 September, 7 October 1900. On Yerkes, see H. Levin, ed., *Lawyers and Lawmakers of Kentucky* (1897), 509-10.

7. Lexington *Daily Leader*, 5 December 1900, 5 November 1915. See also Franklin T. Lambert, "The Kentucky Democracy in the 1890's" (M. A. thesis, University of Louisville, 1977), 206-7, and W. C. P. Breckinridge to Sophonisba Breckinridge, 9 November 1900, vol. 509, Breckinridge Family Papers, Library of Congress.

8. Jasper B. Shannon and Ruth McQuown, *Presidential Politics in Kentucky, 1824-1948* (1950), 74; Lexington *Daily Leader*, 22 November 1900.

9. Kentucky *House Journal* (1902), 20-35.

10. Kentucky *Acts* (1902), 281-392, 44-45, 243-44, 61-64, 49; Lexington *Herald*, 19 March 1902; Louisville *Courier-Journal*, 20 March 1902; Laura Clay to Ida H. Harper, Laura Clay Papers, University of Kentucky Library.
Pratt, the Republican, had taken his appeal in the contested 1899 election to the courts, and their favorable decision in 1901 had unseated Democrat Robert J. Breckinridge. See Mt. Vernon *Signal*, 22 November 1901, *Pratt* v. *Breckinridge*, 112 Kentucky Reports 1-28, and Hambleton Tapp, ed., *A Sesqui-Centennial History of Kentucky* (4 vols., 1946), 2: 726.

11. Hambleton Tapp and James C. Klotter, *Kentucky: Decades of Discord, 1865-1900* (1977), 365; Columbia *Adair County News*, 1 May 1901; Kentucky *House Journal* (1902), 147.

12. Louisville *Herald*, 6 July 1903; *Democratic Campaign Book, 1903* (1903) 40, 48; Lexington *Leader*, 6, 20 September 1903.

13. Mt. Vernon *Signal*, 20 December 1901; Jonas, *History of Republican Party*, 34; Lexington *Leader*, 15-19 July, 5 August, 13 September 1903; Ben LaBree, ed., *Press Reference Book of Prominent Kentuckians* (1916), 201; *Democratic Campaign Book, 1903*, 15, 61; Lexington *Herald*, 23

August 1907; Alex P. Humphrey to John T. Shelby, 23 October 1903, Box 215, Craig-Shelby Papers, University of Kentucky Library; Lexington *Morning Democrat*, 19 December 1903. See also Bodley to T. M. Green, 31 October 1903, in Thomas Marshall Green Papers (microfilm), University of Kentucky Library.

14. New York *Times*, 6 January 1904; Kentucky *Acts* (1904), 6-9, 283-84, 150-52, 10-26; Louisville *Courier-Journal*, 16, 19, 26 March 1904.

15. Kentucky *Senate Journal* (1904), 1051-53; George C. Wright, "William Henry Steward: Moderate Approach to Black Leadership," in Leon Litwack and August Meier, eds., *Black Leaders of the Nineteenth Century* (1988), 285; Louisville *Courier-Journal*, 16 March 1904; Kentucky *Acts* (1904), 27-30; Gerald R. Toner and Ellen Cox Call, "Three Cases That Shaped Kentucky's History," *Kentucky Bench & Bar* 56 (Winter 1992): 18-21; Martha J. Birchfield, "Beckham County, Kentucky," *FCHQ* 64 (1990): 60-70.

16. Lexington *Morning Democrat*, 14 December 1904; Shannon and McQuown, *Presidential Politics in Kentucky*, 78-81.

17. George P. Metcalf, "The Fusion Movement in Louisville, 1905-1907" (M.A. thesis, Murray State University, 1969), 25-38; George H. Yater, *Two Hundred Years at the Falls of the Ohio* (1979), 148-50.

18. Thomas D. Clark, *Helm Bruce, Public Defender* (1973), 43-50; Metcalf, "Fusion Movement," 51-71; Lexington *Herald*, 23 May 1907; Percy N. Booth, "The Louisville Contested Election Cases," *The Green Bag* 10 (1908): 81-83, 88. See also Peyton H. Hoge, "Letter to the Editor," *The Outlook* (30 November 1907).

19. Yater, *Two Hundred Years*, 150; Jonas, *Republican Party*, 40-41.

20. Kentucky *House Journal* (1906), 22, 24; Paducah *Weekly News-Democrat*, 15 March 1906; Kentucky *Acts* (1906), 365-66, 393-404, 466-69, 297-99, 60-77; Appleton, "Banquo's Ghost," 68-85.

21. Arthur Wallace Dunn, *From Harrison to Harding: A Personal Narrative . . . 1888-1921* (2 vols., 1992), 1: 167, 2: 36; Klotter, *Goebel*, 35, 92, 96; O. O. Stealey, *Twenty Years in the Press Gallery* (1906), 211, 215; Louisville *Courier-Journal*, 13 September 1918, 17 October 1943.

22. Lexington *Herald*, 17 January 1905, 3-4 January 1906; Jonas, *History of Republican Party*, 38; Willis, *Kentucky Democracy*, 1: 583-84. Paynter had defeated William Goebel for the Court of Appeals seat.

23. Louisville *Courier-Journal*, 21 November 1906; Lexington *Herald*, 21 November 1906; Paducah *Weekly News-Democrat*, 1 November 1906; Appleton, "Banquo's Ghost," 101-20.

24. Harrison, ed., *Kentucky's Governors*, 118-19; Loren P. Beth, *John Marshall Harlan* (1992), 83; Jonas, *Once Upon a Time*, 110; Robert K. Foster, "Augustus E. Willson and the Republican Party of Kentucky" (M. A. thesis, University of Louisville, 1956), vii-ix, 11-12, 42, 46; Krock, *Myself When Young*, 181; Lexington *Herald*, 21 August 1907.

25. Lexington *Herald*, 26 February, 14 November 1907; George A. Newman to A. E. Willson, 5 March 1907, Willson to John W. Yerkes, 10, 21 March 1907 (copies), Yerkes to Willson, 30 March 1907, Willson to John M. Harlan, 17 April 1907 (copy), all in Augustus E. Willson Papers, Filson Club; clipping "Pardons Etc. by Governor Beckham," in W. O. Bradley Scrapbooks, 1907; Louisville *Courier-Journal*, 8 November 1907; Lexington *Leader*, 23 June 1907; J. M. Harlan to Willson, 16 May 1907, Willson Papers.

26. Paducah *Weekly News-Democrat*, 5, 19 September, 30 October 1907; Lexington *Herald*, 1, 21 September 1907; Louisville *Courier-Journal*, 11 June 1907, Lexington *Leader*, 23 June 1907; Willson draft speech, 1907, Willson Papers; Appleton, "Banquo's Ghost," 123-55; Harrison, ed., *Kentucky's Governors*, 120. See also *Democratic Campaign Hand-Book, 1907* (1907), 6-15, 129.

27. Roy R. Glashan, comp., *American Governors and Gubernatorial Elections, 1775-1978* (1979), 108; Metcalf, "Fusion Movement," 84-86; Paducah *Weekly News-Democrat*, 7 November 1907; Harrison, ed., *Kentucky's Governors*, 120; Louisville *Herald-Post*, 13 October 1927; Louisville *Courier-Journal*, 19 April 1927; Appleton, "Banquo's Ghost," 155-59; typescript, Milton Board folder, Box 27, Thomas R. Underwood Papers, University of Kentucky Library; Author's Interview with Lawrence Hager of Owensboro (son of S. W. Hager), 1974, Kentucky Oral History Commission Collection, Kentucky Historical Society.

28. Irvin S. Cobb, *Kentucky* (1924), 23.

29. Tapp and Klotter, *Decades of Discord*, 12, 259-60, 449; Lexington *Herald*, 23 August 1908, 5 October 1909; Louisville *Courier-Journal*, 24 February 1910; Foster, "Willson," 61, 70.

30. Jackson *Breathitt County News*, 17 January 1908; Lexington *Herald*, 9 January, 14 June 1908; Paducah *Weekly News-Democrat*, 29 April 1909; Taylor Pardon, 23 April 1909, in William S. Taylor Papers (microfilm), University of Kentucky Library.

31. W. D. Johnson, *Biographical Sketches of Prominent Negro Men and Women of Kentucky* (1897), 11. On Bradley, see Maurice H. Thatcher, *Stories and Sketches of William O. Bradley* (1916), and Harrison, ed., *Kentucky's Governors*, 110.

32. A. O. Stanley to Sue Stanley, 17 February 1908, Box 2, Stanley Papers; Louisville *Herald*, 15 January 1908; Paducah *Weekly News-Democrat*, 19 March 1908.

33. Paducah *Weekly News-Democrat*, 19 January, 27 February 1908; Lexington *Herald*, 29 February 1908; New York *Tribune*, 29 February 1908.

34. Louisville *Herald*, 29 February, 13 March 1908; Frankfort *State Journal*, 29 February 1908; Cincinnati *Enquirer*, 31 May 1914; "Speech of J. C. W. Beckham . . . on March 12, 1908 . . . ," in Democratic Party Papers, Wilson Collection; unidentified clipping, "1907-08," Bradley Scrapbooks; Orval W. Baylor, *J. Dan Talbott* (1942), 67.

35. Kentucky *House Journal* (1908), 50; Kentucky *Acts* (1908), 133-43, 22-32, 72-79, 172-81, 198-205, 145-52, 119-21, 10-22, 44-49; Lexington *Herald*, 18, 27, 28, 19 March 1908. See also Louisville *Courier-Journal*, 18 March 1908; Owensboro *Daily Messenger*, 21 March 1908.

36. Cincinnati *Enquirer*, 10 May 1908; Louisville *Times*, 8 May 1908; Lexington *Herald*, 8 May 1908.

37. Lexington *Herald*, 11-12 June 1908; Frankfort *State Journal*, 11 November 1908; Rezin C. Davis to J. J. Davis, 10 August 1908, Box 2, Davis Papers; Louisville *Courier-Journal*, 20 June 1908; Shannon and McQuown, *Presidential Politics*, 82-83.

38. Hazel Green *Herald*, 25 November 1909; *1910 Legislative History*, passim.

39. Kentucky *Acts* (1910), 96-110, 242-49, 344-45, 111-13, 357-58; Louisville *Courier-Journal*, 17 March 1910; Lexington *Leader*, 16 March 1910.

40. J. A. Sullivan to Henry Watterson, 22 July 1911, Vol. 11, Henry Watterson Papers, Manuscript Division, Library of Congress; Louisville *Kentucky Irish American*, 2 September 1911; Lexington *Leader*, 6 June, 13, 16 July 1911. See also W. O. Bradley to Ed Morrow, 28 March 1911, Edwin Porch Morrow Papers (microfilm), University of Kentucky Library.

41. Lexington *Daily Leader*, 18 October 1900; Lexington *Leader*, 6 August, 12 July 1911; Frankfort *State Journal*, 12 September 1961; Louisville *Courier-Journal*, 6 September 1953; Lexington *Herald*, 14 February 1907, 29 March 1911; Louisville *Courier-Journal*, 24 May 1912.

42. Louisville *Herald*, 4 February 1911; unidentified clipping, 5 February 1911, in Scrapbook III, Johnson Collection; Bowling Green *Messenger*, 6 February 1911; Louisville *Kentucky Irish American*, 11 February 1911.

43. Lexington *Leader*, 14, 18 June, 2, 20 July 1911; Louisville *Kentucky Irish American*, 24

June, 1 July 1911.

44. Lexington *Leader*, 20, 16 August 1911; Springfield *Sun*, 23 August 1911; Louisville *Courier-Journal*, 20 May 1911.

45. Harrison, ed., *Kentucky's Governors*, 88-92; Joe Creason, *Joe Creason's Kentucky* (1972), 55; Henry Watterson to Desha Breckinridge, 22 August 1911, Vol. 12, Watterson Papers; Lexington *Leader*, 5 March 1933; Confederate Veteran Association of Kentucky, *Constitution, By-Laws and List of Membership* (5th ed., 1895), passim; C. E. Woods to J. T. Dorris, 30 August 1936, Box 6, William L. Wallace Collection, Eastern Kentucky University Archives. See also a handwritten sketch of McCreary's life in James B. McCreary Papers, University of Kentucky Library.

46. *Democratic Campaign Hand Book 1911* (1911), passim; Lexington *Leader*, 14, 28 August 1911.

47. Hopkinsville *Kentuckian*, 7 September 1911; Lexington *Leader*, 18 September 1911; Louisville *Times*, 19 September 1911.

48. Lexington *Leader*, 1, 18 October, 5 November 1911; Lexington *Herald*, 16 September, 30 October 1911.

49. Louisville *Courier-Journal*, 29 November 1911; Lexington *Leader*, 8 November 1911; Hopkinsville *Kentuckian*, 9 November 1911; Springfield *Sun*, 8, 15 November 1911; Glashan, comp., *American Governors*, 108-9. See also Randall A. Haines, "Walter Lanfersiek, Socialist from Cincinnati," *Cincinnati Historical Society Bulletin* 40 (1982): 125-42.
McDermott's victory as lieutenant-governor marked the highest statewide office held by a Catholic to that date. Louisville *Kentucky Irish American*, 10 December 1911.

50. Lexington *Herald*, 15 November, 13, 14 December 1911.

51. Irvin S. Cobb, *A Laugh A Day Keeps the Doctor Away* (1923), 53; Lexington *Herald*, 22, 14 March, 26 January 1912; Melba Porter Hay, "Madeline McDowell Breckinridge" (Ph.D. diss., University of Kentucky, 1980), 131; Kentucky *Acts* (1912), 193-94, 201-5.

52. Kentucky *Acts* (1912), 47-77, 96-100; Lexington *Herald*, 20, 26 January 1912.

53. Kentucky *Acts* (1912), 220-21, 41-46, 529-41, 28-40, 8-27, 232-35, 184-92; Paducah *Sun*, 13 March 1912.

54. Lexington *Leader*, 25 June 1911; John E. Kleber, *The Kentucky Encyclopedia* (1992), 463.

55. Krock, *Myself When Young*, 183-84; Arthur Krock, *The Consent of the Governed and Other Deceits* (1971), 6-9; Cincinnati *Enquirer*, 18 June 1916, 31 August 1913; Author's Interview with Tom Waller, Paducah, 1974, Kentucky Oral History Commission, Kentucky Historical Society; Louisville *Courier-Journal*, 27 January 1900; Lexington *Herald*, 4 March 1916; A. O. Stanley to Sue Stanley, undated [1910], Box 2, Stanley Papers; Paul Camplin, *A New History of Muhlenberg County* (1984), 173-74.
On James overall, see three master's theses: Forrest C. Pogue, Jr., "The Life and Work of Senator Ollie Murray James" (University of Kentucky, 1932); Virginia M. McCalister, "The Political Career of Ollie M. James" (Indiana University, 1933); Thaddeus M. Smith, "Ollie Murray James" (Eastern Kentucky University, 1973).
James lived on the opposite corner of the street from former Republican U.S. Senator Deboe in the small town of Marion.

56. Louisville *Evening Post*, 1 May 1912; Louisville *Courier-Journal*, 2 May 1912.

57. Louisville *Courier-Journal*, 2 May, 21 February 1912.

58. Champ Clark, *My Quarter Century of American Politics* (2 vols., 1920), 1: 95-97, 78; A. O. Stanley to Sue Stanley, [July 1912?], Box 2, Stanley Papers; Pogue, "Ollie James," 34; Louisville *Courier-Journal*, 30 May 1912; *Congressional Quarterly's Guide to U. S. Elections* (1975), 148; Willis, *Kentucky Democracy*, 1: 423; Cincinnati *Enquirer*, 4 August 1912.

59. Lexington *Herald*, 4 April 1912; Lexington *Leader*, 12 January 1913; Shannon and McQuown, *Presidential Politics in Kentucky*, 86-90; Carl Washburn to author, 26 January 1976, in author's possession; Lowell Harrison, "Kentucky and the Presidential Elections, 1912-1948," *FCHQ* 26 (1952): 320-21.

60. Louisville *Courier-Journal*, 19 March 1914; Lexington *Herald*, 19 March 1914; Paducah *Sun*, 18 March 1914; Mary Helen Miller, *Citizen's Guide to Kentucky Constitution*, *LRC* Research Report No. 137 (1981), 25; Kentucky *Acts* (1914), 226-63, 34-46, 101-4, 440-41, 88-89, 212-26; Owensboro *Messenger*, 19 March 1914; Cincinnati *Enquirer*, 13 March 1914; Lexington *Herald*, 7 March 1914.

61. Lexington *Herald*, 18 March, 7 April 1914; Louisa *Big Sandy News*, 13 June 1913.

62. Louisville *Herald-Post*, 14 October 1927; Connolly Interview with Milton Smith, 31-32; Cincinnati *Enquirer*, 26 April 1914.

63. A. O. Stanley to Sue Stanley, 18 April 1913, Box 3; undated [1912], Box 2; [January 1913], Box 3; 5 February 1913, Box 3, Stanley Papers.

64. A. O. Stanley to Sue Stanley, 16, 14 April 1913, 10 February 1914, [January 1913], Box 3, Stanley Papers; Thomas W. Ramage, "Augustus Owsley Stanley" (Ph.D. diss., University of Kentucky, 1968), 30; Bardstown *Kentucky Standard*, 16 July 1914; Lexington *Herald*, 27 January, 4 February 1914; Appleton, "Banquo's Ghost," 214; A. O. Stanley to Sue Stanley, [January 1913], Box 3, Stanley Papers.

65. Lexington *Herald*, 24 May, 4 June, 13 August 1914.

66. Cincinnati *Enquirer*, 26 April, 17 May, 7, 14, 28 June, 8 November 1914; Harrison, ed., *Kentucky's Governors*, 118, 122.

67. Lexington *Herald*, 2, 6 March, 6 January, 24 June, 3 August, 24, 28 July 1915; A. O. Stanley to Sue Stanley, 28 August, 7 September 1914, Box 3, Stanley Papers; Cincinnati *Enquirer*, 7 March 1915.

68. Ramage, "Stanley," 1-28; Thomas W. Ramage, "Augustus Owsley Stanley," in James C. Klotter and Peter J. Sehlinger, eds., *Kentucky Profiles* (1982), 155-57; Eleanor B. Chalkley, *Magic Casements* (1982), 74; Jonas, *Once Upon a Time*, 112-13; Krock, *Consent of the Governed*, 10-11; A. O. Stanley to John B. Finn, 5 February 1915, General File, Box III, Stanley Papers; Louisville *Courier-Journal*, 22 August 1915. See also Henderson *Daily Gleaner*, 30 April 1903, regarding Stanley's wife and her political ties.

69. Lexington *Leader*, 1, 2, 10 September 1915; Owensboro *Daily Messenger*, 2, 4 September 1915; Lexington *Herald*, 1-3 September 1915.

70. Cincinnati *Enquirer*, 31 January 1915, 7 June 1914, 16 June 1915; Lexington *Leader*, 28 July 1915; Ramage, "Stanley," 177-78.

71. Willard Rouse Jillson, *Edwin P. Morrow - Kentuckian* (1921), 21-35; *Campaign Hand Book of the Republican Party 1915* (1915), 6-7; Transcript of Interview with John Sherman Cooper, 13 May 1979, Cooper Oral History Project, University of Kentucky Library; Lexington *Leader*, 16 June, 29 August 1915; Lexington *Herald*, 16-17 June 1915; Louisville *Courier-Journal Magazine*, 25 June 1950.

72. Creason, *Creason's Kentucky*, 51; Ramage, "Stanley," in Klotter and Sehlinger, eds., *Kentucky Profiles*, 168; Thomas D. Clark, *The Kentucky* (1942), 370; Bill Cunningham, *Kentucky's Clark* (1987), 82-83. The author has heard the Morrow-Stanley stories from nearly a score of present-day citizens.

73. Lexington *Leader*, 7 September 1915; Louisville *Herald*, 2 November 1915.

74. Lexington *Leader*, 20 September 1915; Cincinnati *Enquirer*, 10 October 1915; Clark, *The Kentucky*, 371. It is unclear exactly when the last comment was made by Stanley, but the most

likely time would be 1915.

75. Lexington *Herald* and *Leader*, 4-12, 23 November 1915; Louisville *Herald*, 3-5 November 1915; Ramage "Stanley," 189; Lucien Beckner, "Drifting Sands of Politics, 1900-1944," in Tapp, ed., *History of Kentucky*, 2: 738. Democrats won the other races, with the exception of secretary of state, where James P. Lewis defeated Barksdale Hamlett by 188 votes. Hamlett had been the subject of many Republican attacks for expenses he incurred while superintendent of public instruction. Lexington *Herald*, 9 December 1915.

76. Will S. Kaltenbacher, comp., *Who's Who in the Kentucky General Assembly Session 1916* (n.d.), 9; Louisville *Courier-Journal*, 14 March 1916; Wright, *Life Behind a Veil*, 191; Kentucky *Acts* (1916), 53-73, 1-7, 74-84, 354-408; Joel Goldstein, ed., *Kentucky Government and Politics* (1984), 170; *Legislative Record* 9 (April 1991): 1; Lexington *Herald*, 11, 15 March 1916.

77. Arthur S. Link, *Wilson: The New Freedom* (1956), 161; New York *Times*, 16 June 1916; Smith, "James," 78-79; Pogue, "James," 91, 98, 93; Shannon and McQuown, *Presidential Politics in Kentucky*, 91-94; Harrison, "Kentucky and Presidential Elections," 321; Arthur Krock, ed., *The Editorials of Henry Watterson* (1923), 125.

78. A. O. Stanley to Sue Stanley, 24 July, undated, August, all in 1916, Box 3, Stanley Papers.

79. Kentucky *Auditors Reports* (1910-11), (1911-12), (1912-13), (1916-17), passim; Daniel W. Lynch, *The Development of State and Local Debt in Kentucky: 1890-1962* (1966), 40-45; idem, "The Development of State and Local Debt in Kentucky; 1890-1962" (Ph.D. diss., University of Kentucky, 1965), 229-31; *Taxation: A Magazine Published by the Kentucky Tax Reform Association* ... 2 (October 1919): 4, 1, 5; Nollie O. Taff, *History of State Revenue and Taxation in Kentucky* (1931), 83, 89; Anna Youngman, "The Revenue System of Kentucky," *Quarterly Journal of Economics* 32 (1917): 143, 180-86; Kentucky *Auditor's Report* (1916-17), x-xi; Kentucky *State Tax Commission Report* (1917), 11-14.

80. Lexington *Leader*, 21 March 1918; Owensboro *Messenger*, 22 March 1918; Kentucky *Acts* (1918), 290-353, 24-30, 126; New York *Times*, 31 March 1918; Lexington *Herald*, 15 January, 24 March 1918; Harrison, ed., *Kentucky's Governors*, 124-25.

81. Ramage, "Stanley," 217-23; Pogue, "James," 111-12; Lexington *Herald*, 31 January 1919.

82. Lexington *Herald*, 9 May 1919; Harrison, *Kentucky's Governors*, 126-27; A. O. Stanley to Sue Stanley, August 1916, Box 3, Stanley Papers.

83. Tapp, ed., *History of Kentucky*, 2: 739; Lexington *Leader*, 17 August 1919.

84. Jillson, *Morrow*, 41, 46, 80; Lexington *Leader*, 10 October 1919; Lexington *Herald*, 15-16 May 1919; Walter A. Baker, "The GOP in Kentucky: A History of the Kentucky Republican Party, 1919-1956" (B. A. thesis, Harvard College, 1958), 7, 12-15.

85. Harrison, ed., *Kentucky's Governors*, 127-28; Lexington *Leader*, 17, 29 October, 1, 2 November 1919; "Democratic Platform ... 1919," in General File, Box IV, Stanley Papers; Lexington *Herald*, 7 October, 21 September 1919.

86. Kentucky *Auditor's Report* (1918-19), [iii]; Lexington *Herald*, 16 September 1919; Louisville *Evening Post*, 6 November 1919; Lexington *Leader*, 9 October, 6, 22-23 November 1919; Gleshan, comp., *American Governors*, 108; Appleton, "Banquo's Ghost," 227.

87. Thompson, "The Mulligans," 8-10.

10. "Hard Times Comes A-Knocking at the Door": War, Disease, and Depression

1. Ronald R. Alexander, "Henry Watterson and World War I," *Journal of the West Virginia Historical Association* 1 (1977): 17, 15; Desha Breckinridge to Curry Breckinridge, 12 March

1917, "1907-1918 Correspondence of Currie [sic] D. Breckinridge," Breckinridge Family Papers, Library of Congress.

2. Stanley Ousley, "The Kentucky Irish American," *FCHQ* 53 (1979): 186-87; Clyde F. Crews, "Over Here: Louisville Faces World War I," *Louisville* (August 1989): 13-14; Alexander, "Watterson," 18; Summers Davis to John J. Davis, [December 1914], Box 2, John J. Davis Papers, West Virginia University Library.

3. "The President's Page," *Kentucky Woman's Journal* 2 (May 1917): 4; David B. Danbom, "The Agricultural Extension System and the First World War," *The Historian* 41 (1979): 319; S. D. Martin Diary, 15 April 1918, in B. F. Buckner Papers, University of Kentucky Library.

4. James Larry Hood, "The Collapse of Zion: Rural Progressivism in Nelson and Washington Counties, Kentucky" (Ph.D. diss., University of Kentucky, 1980), 170-71; Mr. and Mrs. Kelly Morgan, *History of Clay County, Kentucky, 1767-1976* (n.d.), 183; Lexington *Herald*, 8 April 1917; Alexander, "Watterson," 22; E. G. Young to wife, 6 April 1917, Edward G. Young Papers, Kentucky Library, Western Kentucky University.

5. Federal Writers' Project, *Military History of Kentucky* (1939), 327-36; *Historical Annual, National Guard of the Commonwealth of Kentucky, 1938* (1938), 37; Temple Bodley and Samuel M. Wilson, *History of Kentucky* (4 vols., 1928), 2: 714-15; Lee Kincaid, "Draft Not Needed in Lee County in WWI," *Lee County Historical and Genealogical Society Newsletter* (October-November 1986): [3]; Martin Diary, 19 May 1918; James W. Hammack, Jr., "The Eagle and the Ground Hog: Differing Perspectives on World War I," 12, 5 (paper in author's possession); Burkesville *Cary's Weekly*, 17 January 1919.

6. Lexington *Kentucky Kernel*, 11 October 1917; James Russell Harris, "At War, 1776-1991," in James C. Klotter, ed., *Our Kentucky: A Study of the Bluegrass State* (1992), 149; Bodley and Wilson, *History of Kentucky*, 2: 682, 697, 676, 536, 528; George D. Hagan, "Kentucky's Part in the World War" (M.A. thesis, University of Kentucky, 1916), 36-50; George H. Yater, *Two Hundred Years at the Falls of the Ohio* (1979), 168; Federal Writers' Project, *Military History*, 337-42; Richard G. Stone, Jr., *Kentucky Fighting Men, 1861-1945* (1982), 53.

7. Leon L. Freeman and Edward C. Olds, *The History of Marshall County Kentucky* (1933), 31; Jean B. Tachau, "A Story" (typescript, 1970), 1; Interview with Feral H. Bloodworth, 20 October 1977, Logan County, Kentucky Oral History Commission (hereafter KOHC), Kentucky Historical Society Library; John D. Wright, Jr., *Lexington* (1982), 163; Martin Diary, 4 February 1918; Lexington *Herald*, 6 April 1918; John A. Garraty, *Woodrow Wilson* (1956), 127; Carl B. Boyd, Jr., and Hazel Mason Boyd, *A History of Mt. Sterling, Kentucky, 1792-1918* (1984), 98-99; Yater, *Two Hundred Years*, 167; Kentucky *Council of Defense Report* (1919), 9. See also David M. Kennedy, *Over Here: The First World War and American Society* (1980).

8. Louisville *Courier-Journal*, 26 April 1992; Kentucky *Acts* (1918): 697-700; Yater, *Two Hundred Years*, 166 and *Notes to "Two Hundred Years"* (1982), 170; James Duane Bolin, "Bossism and Reform: Politics in Lexington, Kentucky, 1880-1940" (Ph.D. diss., University of Kentucky, 1988), 107-8; Buddy Thompson, *Madam Belle Brezing* (1983), 129.

9. Kentucky *Council of Defense Report* (1919), 3-27; Hagan, "Kentucky's Part in World War," 1-7; Hood, "Collapse of Zion," 193-94.

10. Leon Wise, "The Cost of Living in Lexington, 1913-1920" (B.A. thesis, University of Kentucky, 1920), 9, 14, 17, 28, 22, 29; Hagan, "Kentucky's Part in World War," 10-11; Kentucky *State Tax Commission Report* (1919), 7. See also Joseph L. McConnell, "Growth of Manufacturing in Kentucky, 1904 to 1929" (M.A. thesis, University of Kentucky, 1932), 8.

11. Hagan, "Kentucky's Part in World War," 23-28; Yater, *Two Hundred Years*, 207; John P. Meyer, "History and Neighborhood Analysis of Camp Taylor" (M.A. thesis, University of Louisville, 1981), 18-20, 35, 39-41; Louisville *Courier-Journal*, 16 August 1977.

12. Yater, *Two Hundred Years*, 169; Alice Hegan Rice, *The Inky Way* (1940), 210; Transcript of

Interview with Tempie Young, 6 September 1978, FNSOHP, University of Kentucky Library; Nancy D. Baird, "The 'Spanish Lady' in Kentucky, 1918-1919," *FCHQ* 50 (1976): 293-300; John E. L. Robertson, *The History of Citizens Bank and Trust Company of Paducah, Kentucky* (1988), 22; *Annual Reports of The City of Lexington, Ky. for the Year 1918* ([1919]), 15; Gregory K. Culver, "The Impact of the 1918 Influenza Epidemic on the Jackson Purchase Region" (M.A. thesis, Murray State University, 1978), 34-36, 41. One doctor reported losing few patients. His remedy: Kentucky Bourbon. Hawesville *Hancock Clarion* (Supplement), 29 June 1989.

13. Yater, *Two Hundred Years*, 168; Kentucky *Banking Commissioner Report* (1916), v; Kentucky *Bureau of Labor Report* (1918-19), 84-91; Kentucky *Superintendent of Public Instruction Report* (1918-19), vii.

14. Kentucky *Council of Defense Report* (1919), 15, 27; Boyd and Boyd, *Mount Sterling*, 96; Arthur Krock, *Myself When Young* (1973), 196-97; Gerald L. Smith, "'Mr. Kentucky State': A Biography of Rufus Ballard Atwood" (Ph.D. diss., University of Kentucky, 1988), 24-27. See also Arthur E. Borbeau, *The Unknown Solder: Black American Troops in World War I* (1974).

15. Transcript of Interview with Mrs. Jaily Sizemore, 26 July 1978, FNSOHP; Woodridge Spears, "Elizabeth Madox Roberts" (Ph.D. diss., University of Kentucky, 1953), 34; Louis J. Hebel, "This is the Way it Was," 29 (typescript, Filson Club); Burkesville *Cary's Weekly*, 24 June 1919; Lela G. McConnell, *The Pauline Ministry In the Kentucky Mountains* (4th ed. [c. 1943]), 55; Hood, "Collapse of Zion," 230-31, 243, 269; William E. Leuchtenburg, *The Perils of Prosperity, 1914-32* (1958), 8, 47.

16. Blaine A. Brownell, *The Urban Ethos in the South, 1920-1930* (1975), 85; Leuchtenburg, *Perils of Prosperity*, 80.

17. David M. Chalmers, *Hooded Americanism: The History of the Ku Klux Klan* (1968), 2, 26, 33; Arnold S. Rice, *The Ku Klux Klan in American Politics* (1962), 13-16.

18. David M. Chalmers, "The Ku Klux Klan in the Politics of the 1920's," *Mississippi Quarterly* 18 (1965): 235-40; Ouida Jewell, *Backward Glance* (2 vols., 1973), 1: 43-44.

19. Chalmers, *Hooded Americanism*, 154-55; Clausine R. Baker, *First History of Caldwell County* (1936), 142-44; Thomas D. Matijasic, "The Ku Klux Klan in the Big Sandy Valley of Kentucky," *Journal of Kentucky Studies* 10 (1993): 75; Edward Coffman, *The Story of Logan County* (1962), 217; Author's Interview with James G. Wheeler, Paducah, 1974, KOHC; Ku Klux Klan, Pond Creek, Ky. Membership Roll, 1926-1927 (microfilm), University of Kentucky Library; "Ku Klux Klan, Warren County Klan, Realm of Ky., Notice," Kentucky Library, Western Kentucky University; E. H. Lougher, *The Kall of the Klan in Kentucky* (1924), 48, 13-14; Stanley Frost, *The Challenge of the Klan* (1924), 8.

20. Louisville *Kentucky Irish American*, 3 November 1928, 9 July 1927; Lexington *Herald*, 7 November 1923; A. O. Stanley to Sue Stanley, 8 September 1924, Box 3, A. O. Stanley Papers, University of Kentucky; Chalmers, "KKK in 20's," 237; "Shelby County" entry, 1947, Box 227, Earle Clements Collection, University of Kentucky Library; A. B. Chandler to Raymond Cornell, 16 August 1927 (copy), Box 1, A. B. Chandler Papers, University of Kentucky Library.

21. Warren County KKK Notice; Louisville *Kentucky Irish American*, 1 September 1928; Rice, *KKK in Politics*, 41-42, 113; Lexington *Herald*, 8, 12, 4, 23 August, 7 June, 9 September, 4 October 1923; Coffman, *Logan County*, 243; Chalmers, *Hooded Americanism*, 155, 292-96. See also H. Boyce Taylor, *Bible Briefs Against Hurtful Heresies*, 36, a Murray, Kentucky, book that portrayed the Klan as anti-American.

22. John E. Kleber, ed., *The Kentucky Encyclopedia* (1992), 22, 577; William Lynwood Montell, *Don't Go Up Kettle Creek: Verbal Legacy of the Upper Cumberland* (1983), 182-83; Alfreda Withington, "The Mountain Doctor," *Atlantic Monthly* 150 (1932): 773; "Golden Pond Moonshine" (pamphlet, n.d.), [1].

23. New York *Times*, 17 February 1921, 13, 16-17 December 1922; Lexington *Herald*, 29

March 1923; Hazard *Herald,* 19 February, 2 April 1926; Kleber, ed., *Kentucky Encyclopedia,* 646-47.

24. Irvin S. Cobb, *Kentucky* (1924), 59; J. Winston Coleman, Jr., *The Squire's Memoirs* (1975), 22; Comments made to author by Scott D. Breckinridge and Burton Milward, Lexington, May 1992; Louisville *Courier-Journal,* 10 August 1930; Lexington *Herald,* 7 April 1933; Bill Samuels, "The Bourbon Industry," in Cabinet for Economic Development, *Kentucky: 200 Years, Business and Industry Highlights* (1992), 16; Kleber, ed., *Kentucky Encyclopedia,* 647; Charles R. Wilson and William Ferris, eds., *Encyclopedia of Southern Culture* (1989), 707.

By 1937, the state's distilleries produced 43 percent of the nation's distilled liquor. See Federal Writers' Project, *Kentucky: A Guide to the Bluegrass State* (1939), 63.

25. Transcript of Interview with John Sherman Cooper, 13 May 1979, John Sherman Cooper Oral History Project, University of Kentucky Library; Mary C. Erwin, "The Vicious Circle: A Study of the Effects of the Depression and New Deal Relief Programs in Eastern Kentucky" (M.A. thesis, University of Louisville, 1968), 69.

26. Transcript of Interview by Arthur Kelly with A. H. Barker, 1988 (copy in author's possession); *United States Census (1930): Agriculture,* II, Part 2, 91, 55-56, 855-65; Howard W. Odum, *Southern Regions of the United States* (1936), 66.

27. Joseph R. Schwendeman, *Geography of Kentucky* (5th ed., 1979), 45; Nan E. Woodruff, *As Rare as Rain: Federal Relief in the Great Southern Drought of 1930-31* (1985) 22, 5; Lorine L. Butler, "The Home of America's Finest Horses," *Travel* 67 (August 1936): 20; Kleber, ed., *Kentucky Encyclopedia,* 207; Lewis W. McKee and Lydia K. Boyd, *History of Anderson County* (1975; orig. pub. 1937), 155. See also Kevin J. Ruhl, "Kentucky Floods and Droughts," U.S. Geological Survey Water-Supply Paper 2375.

28. Lexington *Herald,* 7 October 1928; Kentucky *Progress Commission Report* (1929), 24; Judge Watson, "The Economic and Cultural Development of Eastern Kentucky from 1900 to the Present" (Ph.D., Indiana University, 1963), 16-17; Woodruff, *As Rare as Rain,* 144.

29. *U.S. Census (1930): Agriculture,* II, part 2, 38, 40, 746, 22-23; Odum, *Southern Regions,* 20; Watson, "Development of Eastern Kentucky," 16; Joseph M. Porter, "The Kentucky Jockey Club" (M.A. thesis, Eastern Kentucky University, 1969), 76-77; James Duane Bolin, "The Human Side: Politics, the Great Depression, and the New Deal in Lexington, Ky., 1929-35," *Register* 90 (1992): 270.

30. *U.S. Census (1930): Agriculture,* II, part 2, 47, 31.

31. Louisville *Courier-Journal,* 15 October 1930, 18 June 1931; Kentucky *Division of Banking Report* (1972), [n.p.]; Kentucky *Banking Commissioner Annual Report* (1926 through 1935), passim; Kentucky *Director of Banks, Annual Report* (1936 through 1942), passim; Robertson, *History of Citizens Bank,* 29-31. A Louisville tailor saw a once-wealthy customer come in his store, go to the restroom, and shoot himself. See Lexington *Herald-Leader,* 28 October 1979.

32. Robert Fugate, "The BancoKentucky Story," *FCHQ* 50 (1976): 29-46; Yater, *Two Hundred Years,* 192.

33. Louisville *Courier-Journal,* 2 April 1931, 19 January 1934; Yater, *Two Hundred Years,* 192-94; George T. Blakey, *Hard Times and New Deal in Kentucky, 1929-1939* (1986), 11. See also *United States Census (1930): Unemployment,* I, 19.

34. Barber interview; Woodruff, *As Rare as Rain,* 15; Mary Breckinridge, "The Corn-Bread Line," *The Survey* 64 (15 August 1930): 423; *Quarterly Bulletin of the Kentucky Committee for Mothers and Babies* 6 (Winter 1931): 3; Laurel Schackelford, ed., "Folks of the Wolfe County Hills," *Adena* 2 (1977): 57-62; Louisville *Courier-Journal,* 28 October 1979.

35. Jack Foster, *So It's Been Told: Footnotes to Hancock County History* (1992), 4; Arthur H. Estabrook, "Poor Relief in Kentucky," *Social Science Review* 3 (1929): 224-42; Kentucky *Auditor's*

Report (1932-33), 214.

36. Federal Writers' Project, *Kentucky* (1939), 183-84; Desha Breckinridge to Breckinridge Long, 7 December 1931, Box 95, Breckinridge Long Papers, Manuscript Division, Library of Congress; William R. McCoy to Simeon Willis, Box 1, Simeon Willis Papers, University of Kentucky Library; Frederic D. Ogden, ed., *The Public Papers of Keen Johnson, 1939-1943* (1982), 136.

37. Merton Oyler, "Natural Increase and Migration of Kentucky Population: 1920 to 1935," *Kentucky Agricultural Experiment Station Bulletin No. 395* (1939), 256-57; P. P. Karan and Cotton Mather, eds., *Atlas of Kentucky* (1977), 16-17; Louisville *Courier-Journal*, 21 November 1940; George A. Hillery, Jr., "Population Growth in Kentucky, 1820-1960," *Agricultural Experiment Station Bulletin No. 705* (1966), 13; Henry P. Scalf, *Kentucky's Last Frontier* (1977), 393.

38. Desha Breckinridge to Henry Breckinridge, 25 March 1933, Box 2, Henry Breckinridge Papers, Manuscript Division, Library of Congress.

39. Mary Fitts, in Owensboro *Messenger-Inquirer*, 27 September 1986; Lillian DeMyer Interview, Work Projects Administration Files, Kentucky Department for Libraries and Archives.

40. Blakey, *Hard Times and New Deal*, 78-88; Thomas D. Clark, *The Greening of the South* (1984), 811.

41. Blakey, *Hard Times and New Deal*, 32, 105-15. See also Gilbert C. Fite, *Cotton Fields No More: Southern Agriculture, 1865-1980* (1984).

42. Blakey, *Hard Times and New Deal*, 117-30; Erwin, "Vicious Circle," 111, 138; John H. Fenton, *Politics in the Border States* (1957), 73.

43. Blakey, *Hard Times and New Deal*, 72-77, 46-58. See also Joseph E. Brent, "The Civil Works Administration in Western Kentucky," *FCHQ* 67 (1993): 259-76.

44. Blakey, *Hard Times and New Deal*, 58-62; Erwin, "Vicious Circle," 90; Wayne T. Gray, "Mountain Dilemmas," *Mountain Life & Work* 12 (1936): 1; Watson, "Development of Eastern Kentucky," 23; Bill Cunningham, *Kentucky's Clark* (1987), 101; Louisville *Courier-Journal*, 18 December 1934. The latter source indicated an estimated 550,000 Kentuckians were on federal relief.

45. "Physical Accomplishments on WPA Projects Through October 1, 1937," Reference File, Box 4, Records of the WPA in Kentucky, Kentucky Department for Libraries and Archives; Blakey, *Hard Times and New Deal*, 61-71.

46. John F. Day, *Bloody Ground* (1981; orig. pub. 1941), 173; Average Monthly Rate, Table 17, Reference File, Box 4, WPA Records; Bill and Elsie Welte Interview, *ibid.*; Erwin, "Vicious Circle," 143.

47. Blakey, *Hard Times and New Deal*, 91-103; June 1936 NYA Statistics, Reference File, Box 4, WPA Records. The NYA later was transferred to agencies other than the WPA.

48. Blakey, *Hard Times and New Deal*, 36-44; "Statistical and Informational Releases," Old Age Assistance, Box 5, WPA Records.

49. "Unemployment Census, 1937," Box IX, Alben W. Barkley Collection, University of Kentucky Library; Kleber, ed. *Kentucky Encyclopedia*, 327-28; Gustave A. Breaux, "1937 Flood at Louisville," *FCHQ* 11 (1937): 111-16; Forrest C. Pogue Oral History Institute, *Purchase Remembrances* (rev. ed., 1982), 70-71; Paducah *Sun-Democrat*, 7 March 1937; Rice, *Inky Way*, 257-58.

50. "A History of Louisville," Louisville *Courier-Journal*, 17 February 1963; Kleber, ed., *Kentucky Encyclopedia*, 327-28, 423; Howard W. Beers, ed., *Kentucky: Designs for Her Future* (1945), 141; Claribel H. Phillips, *150 Years of Lewisport and Its People* (1987), 43; Thomas D. Clark, *The Kentucky* (1942), 28; Lexington *Leader*, 7-10 July 1939. See also Ruhle, "Kentucky Floods and Droughts."

51. Blakey, *Hard Times and New Deal*, 132-42.

52. "The League Holds Slim Lead in College Poll," *Literary Digest* (2 February 1935): 6; Heinz H. Seelbach, "The Attitude of Kentucky Congressmen Toward Foreign Relations From 1935 to Pearl Harbor" (M.A. thesis, University of Kentucky, 1943), 10, 13-15, 23-26, 51, 82; William R. Buster, "Remarks at Founder's Day Dinner - 1991" (copy in author's possession).

53. Seelbach, "Attitude of Kentucky Congressmen," 21, 24, 50-51, 64-65; Harris, "At War," in Klotter, ed., *Our Kentucky*, 150; Bill Weaver, "Kentuckians Under Fire: Admiral Kimmel and the Pearl Harbor Controversy," *FCHQ* 57 (1983): 151-52.

54. Ethridge quoted in Wade Hall, *The Kentucky Book* (1979), 128; Clinton *Hickman County Gazette*, 27 November 1941; Cynthiana *Democrat*, 4 December 1941; Cumberland *Tri-City News*, 4 December 1941; Burlington *Boone County Recorder*, 4 December 1941.

55. C. Ray Hall, "The Survivors," Louisville *Courier-Journal*, 7 December 1991. Edwin L. Puckett of Glendale and Clyde Creech of Cumberland were listed among the dead at Pearl Harbor. Harris, "At War," in Klotter, ed., *Our Kentucky*, 151 and Cumberland *Tri-City News*, 11 December 1941.

56. Lewis N. Hughes, "Back to Bataan" (typescript, copy in author's possession); James Russell Harris, "The Harrodsburg Tankers: Bataan, Prison, and the Bonds of Community," *Register* 86 (1988): 230-48.

57. Harris, "Harrodsburg Tankers," 249-77. Sources for the Harris article include oral interviews in the Veterans of World War II Oral History Project, University of Kentucky Library, and in the Kentucky National Guard Oral History Project.

58. Richmond *Daily Register*, 8 December 1941; Louisville *Courier-Journal*, 10 December 1941; Dianne Watkins, ed., *Hello Janice: The Wartime Letters of Henry Giles* (1992), xi; Frank F. Mathias, *G. I. Jive: An Army Bandsman in World War II* (1982), ix, 56; Louisville *Courier-Journal Magazine*, 3 December 1989; Stone, *Kentucky Fighting Men*, 102, 107, 85; James Russell Harris, "In Uniform," in *Praise the Lord and Pass the Ammunition: Kentuckians and World War II* (1994), 2-11. Buckner was the son of a Kentucky governor. See Lloyd J. Graybar, "The Buckners of Kentucky," *FCHQ* 58 (1984): 202-18.

59. Charles Parrish, "The Louisville Engineer District," in Barry W. Fowle, ed., *Builders and Fighters: U.S. Army Engineers in World War II* (1992), 137-45; Kleber, ed., *Kentucky Encyclopedia*, 107, 346, 910.

60. Kleber, ed., *Kentucky Encyclopedia*, 157, 408, 969; Foster, *So It's Been Told*, 5; Jean Calvert and John Klee, *The Towns of Mason County* (1986), 163; Parrish, "Louisville Engineers," 142-44.

61. James D. Cockrum, "Owensboro Goes to War," *Daviess County Historical Quarterly* 2 (1984): 6; Yater, *Two Hundred Years*, 211, 207-8; "A History of Louisville," Louisville *Courier-Journal*, 17 February 1963; Kleber, ed., *Kentucky Encyclopedia*, 342, 577, 969.

62. Beers, *Kentucky*, 141.

63. Klotter, ed., *Our Kentucky*, 72; Wayne T. Gray, "Population Movements in the Kentucky Mountains," *Rural Sociology* 10 (1945): 380-86; Olaf F. Larson, "Wartime Migrations and the Manpower Reserve on Farms in Eastern Kentucky," *Rural Sociology* 8 (1943): 151-53; Harry K. Schwarzweller, James S. Brown, and J. J. Mangalam, *Mountain Families in Transition* (1971), 76.

64. Richard C. Brown, *A History of Danville and Boyle County, Kentucky, 1774-1992* (1992), 119-21; Boxes 154-56, WPA Records; Elizabeth Perkins, "The Home Front," in *Praise the Lord*, 14-21, and Judy B. Litoff and David C. Smith, eds., *Since You Went Away: Letters from American Women on the Home Front* (1991). Information in this paragraph is also based on various newspapers 1941-45, and numerous county histories. For a brief, general survey of the national scene, see John P. Diggins, *The Proud Decades* (1989), 144-53, and John M. Blum, *V Was for Victory: Politics and American Culture During World War II* (1976).

65. James F. Hopkins, *A History of the Hemp Industry in Kentucky* (1951), 210-13; Kleber, ed., *Kentucky Encyclopedia*, 422.

66. Kentucky *Department of Agriculture* (1944-45), 46; Louisville *Courier-Journal*, 26 April 1992; Lowell H. Harrison, *Western Kentucky University* (1987), 119; J. T. Dorris, ed., *Five Decades of Progress: Eastern Kentucky State College 1906-1957* (1957), 154, 202; John D. Wright, Jr., *Transylvania* (1975), 384. All national holidays, except the Fourth of July, Labor Day, and Christmas, were suspended by the legislature. Kentucky *Acts* (1942), 627-28.

67. Louisville *Courier-Journal*, 26 April 1992; Baird, "Letters to Harry Jackson," 313; Thomas Hamilton, in Owensboro *Messenger-Inquirer*, 29 September 1986; Kleber, ed., *Kentucky Encyclopedia*, 496, 969; War Department Bureau of Public Relations, *World War II Honor List of Dead and Missing: State of Kentucky* (1946), i-iii; James Russell Harris, "Kentuckians in World War II: Numbers and Losses" (typescript in author's possession).

68. Harlan *Daily Enterprise*, 15, 10, 12 August 1945; Cynthiana *Democrat*, 16 August 1945; Greta Whitehead, in Owensboro *Messenger-Inquirer*, 31 August 1986.

69. Weaver, "Admiral Kimmel," 154-74; Lexington *Herald-Leader*, 7 December 1992; "A History of Louisville," Louisville *Courier-Journal*, 17 February 1963; New York *Times*, 4 July 1947; Lexington *Herald*, 4 July 1947; Diggins, *Proud Decades*, 99; Montell, *Don't Go Up Kettle Creek*, 191; Stephen E. Ambrose, "The War on the Home Front," *Timeline* 10 (Nov.-Dec. 1993), 2-4, 6. See also James Still, *The Wolfpen Notebooks* (1991), 27.

11. "United We Stand"? The Politics of Division, 1920-1930

1. Temple Bodley and Samuel M. Wilson, *History of Kentucky* (4 vols., 1928), 2: 687, 691, 694; N. O. Taff, *History of State Revenue and Taxation in Kentucky* (1931), 122-24; Kentucky *Auditor's Report* (1922-23), 3. See also John W. Manning, *The Government of Kentucky* (1940), 145; Daniel W. Lynch, *The Development of State and Local Debt in Kentucky: 1890-1962* (1966), 40-42. The inheritance tax had been enacted in 1906 and revised a decade later.

2. On Bingham, there are brief overviews in John E. Kleber, ed., *Kentucky Encyclopedia* (1992), 80, and W. T. Owens, comp., *Who's Who in Louisville* (1926), 29. Of the several book-length works which focus heavily on his life, the best is William E. Ellis, "Robert Worth Bingham and the Southern Mystique" (typescript). David L. Chandler and Mary V. Chandler, *The Binghams of Louisville* (1987), contains many errors, as well as some questionable interpretations. For an extended critique, see the articles by Samuel W. Thomas and James J. Holmberg in *FCHQ* 63 (1989): 307-85. Other examinations of Bingham can be found in Ellis, "The Bingham Family," *ibid.* 61 (1987): 5-33; idem, "Robert Worth Bingham and the Crisis of Cooperative Marketing in the Twenties," *Agricultural History* 56 (1932): 99-116; and idem, "Robert Worth Bingham and Louisville Progressivism, 1905-1910," *FCHQ* 54 (1980): 169-95; Marie Brenner, *House of Dreams: The Bingham Family of Louisville* (1988), 22, 81-137, 156; Sallie Bingham, *Passion and Prejudice* (1989); and Susan E. Tifft and Alex S. Jones, *The Patriarch* (1991).

3. Joseph F. Wall, *Henry Watterson* (1956), 320-21; Henry Watterson to R. W. Bingham, 22 March 1919; Ida H. Harper to Bingham, 28 August 1918, both in Robert Worth Bingham Papers (microfilm, Filson Club, Louisville); Orval W. Baylor, *J. Dan Talbott* (1942), 81.

4. Robert W. Bingham to H. J. Graham, 19 November 1924 (copy), Box 11; Josephus Daniels to Bingham, 8 January 1926, Box 8; Bingham to A. Y. Ford, 9 July 1923 (copy), Box 10; Bingham to W. W. Davies, 27 October 1920 (copy), Box 8; Bingham to Emanuel Levi, 20 July 1934 (copy), 19 September 1934 (copy), both Box 15; Bingham to Barry Bingham, 1 October 1934 (copy), Box 1; Bingham to Emanuel Levi, 19 October 1934 (copy), Box 15, and passim, all in Papers of Robert Worth Bingham, Manuscript Division, Library of Congress; Louisville *Herald-Post*, 19 October 1927.

5. On Brown, see Owens, comp., *Who's Who in Louisville*, 28; George R. Leighton, *Five Cities* (1939), 90-91; Michael Lesy, *Real Life: Louisville in the Twenties* (1976), 69; Lexington *Herald*, 18 January 1924; George H. Yater, *Two Hundred Years at the Falls of the Ohio* (1979), 188-89; Robert F. Sexton, "Kentucky Politics and Society, 1919-1932" (Ph.D. diss., University of Washington, 1970), 76.

6. W. R. Jillson, *Edwin P. Morrow - Kentuckian* (1921), 55-57; Lexington *Herald*, 11, 18-19, 21 March 1920; Louisville *Courier-Journal*, 18 March 1920; Vance Armentrout, *An Inventory of Kentucky* (1922), 38-40. See also Lexington *Leader*, 18 March 1920, and Owensboro *Messenger*, 18 March 1920.

7. Jasper B. Shannon and Ruth McQuown, *Presidential Politics in Kentucky, 1824-1948* (1950), 95-99, 99n; Lowell H. Harrison, "Kentucky and Presidential Elections, 1912-1948," *FCHQ* 26 (1952): 321-22.

8. George W. Summer to Thomas R. Underwood, "Record of Senator J. C. W. Beckham in U. S. Senate" (undated), Box 27, Thomas Rust Underwood Papers, University of Kentucky Library; unidentified clipping, June 1914, in Thomas Cromwell Scrapbooks, University of Kentucky Library; Louisville *Courier-Journal*, 13 April 1895; George L. Willis, *Kentucky Democracy* (3 vols., 1935), 1: 456; L. V. Armentrout to R. W. Bingham, 4 August 1920, Box 3, Bingham Papers; Glenn Finch, "The Election of United States Senators in Kentucky - The Beckham Period," *FCHQ* 44 (1970): 40-42, 50; Hazard *Herald*, 12 November 1926; Louisville *Courier-Journal*, 12 July 1936; *Statistics of the Presidential and Congressional Elections, 1920-1962* (1963), 6.

9. Lexington *Herald*,1, 3 January, 26 February, 16-22, 26 March 1922; Kentucky *Acts* (1922), 1-23, 132-34, 51-53, 281-82, 97-102, 397-98. In the Senate, Democrats averaged 54.3 years of age, Republicans 49.7, with business the most popular occupation, followed by farming, and the law. It was a reasonably well-educated group with 74 percent of the Democrats and 44.4 percent of the Republicans noting attendance at a college. See *Kentucky Directory* (1922).

10. William E. Ellis, "The Fundamentalist — Moderate Schism Over Evolution in the 1920's," *Register* 74 (1976): 112-13; Alonzo W. Fortune, "The Kentucky Campaign Against the Teaching of Evolution," *Journal of Religion* 2 (1922): 227, 230-31; L. Beatrice Simms, "The Anti-Evolution Conflict in the 1920s" (M.A. thesis, University of Kentucky, 1953), 6-7. See also Paducah *Weekly News-Democrat*, 17 June 1909, for an example of Bryan's earlier anti-evolution talks.

11. Milo Martin Meadows, Jr., "Fundamentalist Thought and Its Impact in Kentucky, 1900-1928" (Ph.D. diss., Syracuse University, 1972), 168-70.

12. Meadows, "Fundamentalist Thought," 104; William E. Ellis, *E. Y. Mullins and the Crisis of Moderate Southern Baptist Leadership* (1985), 151, 154-68; Ellis, "Fundamentalist — Moderate Schism," 116-20; Simms, "Anti-Evolution Conflict," 17.

13. William E. Ellis, "Frank LeRond McVey: His Defense of Academic Freedom," *Register* 67 (1969): 37-50; Meadows, "Fundamentalist Thought," 184-86; Frank L. McVey, *The Gates Open Slowly* (1949), 231-32.

14. Simms, "Anti-Evolution Conflict," 34; McVey, *Gates Open Slowly*, 232-33; R. Halliburton, Jr., "Kentucky's Anti-Evolution Controversy," *Register* 66 (1968): 103; Norman E. Furniss, *The Fundamentalist Controversy, 1918-1931* (1954), 82; William E. Ellis, "Recurring Crisis: The Evolution/Creation Controversy in Kentucky," *Journal of Kentucky Studies* 1 (1984): 131.

15. Meadows, "Fundamentalist Thought," 210-12.

16. *Ibid.*, 220, 230-31; Furniss, *Fundamentalist Controversy*, 82; Bill L. Weaver, "Kentucky Baptists' Reaction to the National Evolution Controversy, 1922-26," *FCHQ* 49 (1975): 269, 272n, 275; William E. Ellis, "John Thomas Scopes: A Kentuckian and the Trial of the Century," *Bulletin of the Kentucky Historical Society* 15 (June 1989): 1, 5; Halliburton, "Anti-Evolution Controversy," 104-6; Ray Ginger, *Six Days or Forever?* (1958), 59-60, 74; Thomas D. Clark and Albert D. Kirwan, *The South Since Appomattox* (1967), 196. See also Lexington *Herald*, 11 June 1926. Miss

Scopes was subsequently offered a position in the Louisville schools.

17. Meadows, "Fundamentalist Thought," 5, 103, 210-12; McVey, *Gates Open Slowly*, 236.

18. Lexington *Leader*, 13 May 1963; George W. Robinson, "The Making of a Kentucky Senator: Alben W. Barkley and the Gubernatorial Primary of 1923," *FCHQ* 40 (1966): 124-26, 133n; "Scrapbook 1910-1913," "Scrapbook . . . 1914," and passim, James Campbell Cantrill Papers (microfilm), University of Kentucky Library.

19. James K. Libbey, *Dear Alben* (1979), 1-12; Author's Interview with Tom Waller, 1974, Kentucky Oral History Commission, Kentucky Historical Society; David Brinkley, *Washington Goes to War* (1988), 209; Donald A. Ritchie, "Alben W. Barkley: The President's Man," in Richard A. Baker and Roger H. Davidson, eds., *First Among Equals: Outstanding Senate Leaders of the Twentieth Century* (1991), 139; Louisville *Courier-Journal*, 16 October 1963; Alben W. Barkley, *That Reminds Me* (1954), 24-27.

20. Robinson, "Making of a Senator," 127-29; Lexington *Herald*, 20 February 1923. See also P. H. Callahan to T. O. Turner, 11 August 1922, Thomas O. Turner Papers, University of Kentucky Library; Libbey, *Dear Alben*, 40-41.

21. Ralph W. Clark, "The Legal Regulation of Organized Racing in Kentucky" (M.A. thesis, University of Kentucky, 1941), 32, 60; Joseph M. Porter, "The Kentucky Jockey Club: Political Involvement in the Twenties" (M.A. thesis, Eastern Kentucky University, 1969), 9-10; Lexington *Herald*, 13 May, 22 July 1923. See also James C. Klotter, *The Breckinridges of Kentucky* (1986), 234-36.

22. See, for example, Dewey W. Grantham, *The Life and Death of the Solid South: A Political History* (1988), 95-96.

23. Robert F. Sexton, "The Crusade Against Pari-Mutuel Gambling in Kentucky," *FCHQ* 50 (1976): 49.

24. *Ibid.*, 54; Klotter, *Breckinridges*, 215-18.

25. Sexton, "Crusade Against Gambling," 50-54; William E. Ellis, *Patrick Henry Callahan* (1989), 48-49; Porter, "Kentucky Jockey Club," 29; M. P. Hunt, *The Story of My Life* (1941), 113-19, 162-63.

26. Lexington *Herald*, 8 April, 12 June 1923.

27. Porter, "Kentucky Jockey Club," 33; Lexington *Herald*, 20 October 1920; Jackson *Times*, 10 April 1925. For the Barkley campaign's view of corruption in his opposition see statements of Elwood Hamilton, 16 March 1923, in a typescript labelled "For Judge Bingham from Platt," Box 20, Bingham Papers.

28. John H. Fenton, *Politics in the Border States* (1957), figure 8; Sexton, "Crusade Against Gambling," 55; Robinson, "Making of a Senator," 131, 123; copy of unsigned letter to Urey Woodson, 11 July 1938, Box 78, Homer Stille Cummings Papers, University of Virginia Library.

29. Lexington *Herald*, 27 June, 10 July, 29-31 August, 2-3 September 1923; George L. Willis, *Kentucky Democracy* (3 vols., 1935), 1: 462.

30. Libbey, *Dear Alben*, 42-43; Baylor, *J. Dan Talbott*, 82.

31. William E. Ellis, "William Jason Fields," in Lowell H. Harrison, ed., *Kentucky's Governors, 1792-1985* (1985), 132-33; Louisville *Courier-Journal*, 22 October 1954; Lexington *Leader*, 13 May 1963.

32. Lexington *Herald*, 23 September 1923; Libbey, *Dear Alben*, 43.

33. Lucian Beckner, "Drifting Sands of Politics, 1900-1944," in Hambleton Tapp, ed., *A Sesqui-Centennial History of Kentucky* (4 vols., 1945), 2: 740; Lexington *Herald*, 10 May, 9, 12, 24, 27 June 1923; E. A. Jonas, *A History of the Republican Party in Kentucky* (1929), 65; Owens, comp.,

Who's Who in Louisville, 46; Publicity Director to Frank Tracy, 21 September [1923], Box 30, Underwood Papers; Jasper B. Shannon, *Presidential Politics in Kentucky, 1952* (1954), 8-9; Lexington *Herald*, 13-14 September, 25 October, 27 June 1923; Emma Guy Cromwell, *Woman in Politics* (1939), 78-80.

34. Louisville *Courier-Journal*, 25 October 1923; Lexington *Herald*, 25-26 October 1923; Lawrence A. Burdon, "A Statistical Study of Kentucky Elections, 1920-1948" (M. A. thesis, University of Louisville, 1950), 48; Roy R. Glashan, comp., *American Governors and Gubernatorial Elections, 1775-1978* (1979), 168.

35. See "Accomplishments" (typescript), Edwin Porch Morrow Papers (microfilm), University of Kentucky Library; Jillson, *Morrow*, passim; and Melba Porter Hay, "Edwin Porch Morrow," in Harrison, ed., *Kentucky's Governors*, 130-31.

36. Beckner, in Tapp, ed., *Sesqui-Centennial History*, 2: 741; G. Glenn Clift, "Kentucky Politics, 1900-1953," *Southern Observer* 2 (March 1954): 48; Ellis, "Fields," in Harrison, ed., *Kentucky's Governors*, 134.

37. Lexington *Herald*, 24 November 1923; New York *Times*, 26 November 1923; Ellis, "Fields," in Harrison, ed., *Kentucky's Governors*, 133; Louisville *Kentucky Irish American*, 7 May 1927.

38. Armentrout, *Inventory of Kentucky*, 23.

39. On Fields's interests, see Desha Breckinridge to Thomas R. Underwood, 8 August 1930, Box 34, Underwood Papers, and Owensboro *Messenger*, 20 March 1924.

40. *The Government of Kentucky: Report of the Efficiency Commission of Kentucky* (2 vols., 1924), 1: 393, 12, 128, 155, 185, 50, 427, 419, 608, 577, 640, 233; 2: 408, 300, 453.

41. Lexington *Herald*, 9 January 1924.

42. *Ibid.*, 20, 26 October, 24 February, 25 January 1924.

43. Louisville *Courier-Journal*, 19, 22-29 February 1924; Lexington *Herald*, 22, 28-29 February 1924. A. O. Stanley told his wife in a 16 August 1924 letter, "One good thing — the Courier Journal hates fields [*sic*] perhaps worse than even me." Box 3, Stanley Papers.

44. Lexington *Herald*, 9 February, 5 March, 5, 25 November 1924; Kentucky *House Journal* (1924), 414-15; Kentucky *Senate Journal* (1924), 1772; John E. Kleber, ed., *The Papers of Governor Lawrence W. Wetherby, 1950-1955* (1983), 131.

45. Kentucky *Prison Commissioners' Report* (1901), 26, 70, 33, 73, 41, 46, 26, 47, 22, 23, 56; Kentucky *Acts* (1900), 77-80; Mt. Vernon *Signal*, 8 March 1901; Kentucky *Prison Commissioners' Report* (1905), 6, 40, 54, 8, 31-32, 66-67, 38; Lexington *Herald*, 28 July 1927.

46. Robert G. Crawford, "A History of the Kentucky Penitentiary System, 1865-1937" (Ph.D. diss., University of Kentucky, 1955), 78-84; Armentrout, *Inventory of Kentucky*, 46-47; Kentucky *Prison Commissioner's Report* (1912-13), 6-7. The law giving prisoners some of their earnings was declared unconstitutional. See Kentucky *Prison Commissioners' Report* (1913-15), 12.
For example of a beating in one of the asylums, see Lexington *Herald*, 17, 27-29 September 1906.

47. Crawford, "History of Penitentiary System," 84; Kyle Ellison, "Changing Faces, Common Walls: A History of Corrections in Kentucky" (10th ed., 1985), 8-9; Federal Writers' Project, *Military History of Kentucky* (1939), 350-51; Bill Cunningham, "Castle on the Cumberland," *Rural Kentuckian* 39 (May 1985): 11-12; Louisville *Courier-Journal*, 21 March 1924.

48. Crawford, "History of Penitentiary System," 85-88; Lexington *Herald*, 29 February, 5-6 March 1924. See also Joseph P. Byers, "Parole in Kentucky," *Journal of Social Forces* 1 (1923): 135-36.

49. Lexington *Herald*, 12, 14 March 1924.

50. *Ibid.*, 5, 16, 18, 20 March 1924, 27 March 1925; Crawford, "History of Penitentiary System," 90-91.

51. Lexington *Herald*, 14, 22, 27 February 1924; Kentucky *Acts* (1924), 108-9, 595-607, 468-83, 20-25, 13-14; Louisville *Courier-Journal*, 20-21 March 1924.

52. Bernard V. Burke, "Senator and Diplomat: The Public Career of Frederic M. Sackett," *FCHQ* 61 (1987): 85-86; Owens, comp., *Who's Who in Louisville*, 153; Kleber, ed., *Kentucky Encyclopedia*, 791; Sexton, "Kentucky Politics," 94-95.

53. Lexington *Herald*, 7 September, 14 August 1924; Paducah *Kentucky Citizen*, 3 October 1924; Lexington *Leader*, 31 October 1924; Sexton, "Kentucky Politics," 95, 102; R. W. Bingham to Wayne B. Wheeler, 12 November 1924 (copy), Box 26, Bingham Papers. Sackett defeated B. J. Bethurman of Lexington in the Republican primary; Stanley won out over John J. Howe of Carrollton. Lexington *Herald*, 3 August 1924.

54. Sexton, "Kentucky Politics," 93, 99, 105; Lexington *Herald*, 7 September 1924; Walter A. Baker, "The GOP in Kentucky" (B.A. thesis, Harvard College, 1958), 28-29; Finch, "The Election of Senators in Kentucky," 46-47; Clift, "Kentucky Politics," 48; Thomas W. Ramage, "Augustus Owsley Stanley" (Ph.D. diss., University of Kentucky, 1968), 259-61; Willis, *Kentucky Democracy*, 1: 465, 472. The Lexington *Herald*, 25 November 1924, presented the results in the text as the official count. Different numbers are in *Statistics of the Presidential Elections*, 7.

55. Harrison, "Presidential Elections," 322-23; Clift, "Kentucky Politics," 48-49; Shannon and McQuown, *Presidential Politics*, 100-103; Malcolm E. Jewell, *Kentucky Votes* (3 vols., 1963), 3: 13. Slightly different vote counts appear in Harrison, Shannon and McQuown, and Svend Peterson, *A Statistical History of the American Presidential Elections* (1968), 132.

56. Sexton, "Kentucky Politics," 110-13; Jonas, *History of the Republican Party*, 68-69, 72; John W. Langley, *They Tried to Crucify Me* (1929), 106-16, 15, 73, 58; Louisville *Courier-Journal*, 18 January 1932; Lexington *Herald*, 12 January 1926, 18 January 1932; Kleber, ed., *Kentucky Encyclopedia*, 535-36; Hazard *Herald*, 23 July, 20 August 1926. See also David R. Castleman, "Louisville Election Frauds In Court and Out," *National Municipal Review* 16 (1927): 761-69.

57. Porter, "Jockey Club," 59-60; Taff, *Taxation in Kentucky*, 145; Hazard *Herald*, 26 November 1926; Lexington *Herald*, 22 January, 6, 11, 17, 28 February, 11-12, 17-19 March, 23 November 1926; Lexington *Leader*, 18 March 1926; Kentucky *Acts* (1926), 764-807, 851-61, 756-64, 878, 1021-22, 1025-26, 1014-15, 182-83; Bodley and Wilson, *History of Kentucky*, 2: 137; Henry B. Simpson, "The General Assembly of 1926" (M.A. thesis, University of Kentucky, 1926), 32-33, 10, 8, 22. Simpson, 1-3, 40, noted that there were 66 House and 39 Senate committees, that 21 of 38 senators and 55 of 100 representatives were either lawyers or farmers, and that one-third of the Senate and one-fourth of the House were college graduates. Of the 138 legislators, 30 were Methodists, 29 Baptists, 24 Church of Christ members, and 10 Catholics.

58. W. V. Gregory to Alben Barkley, 22 February 1926, J. C. Hopkins to Barkley, 10 August 1926, both in Box IV, Political File, Alben W. Barkley Collection, University of Kentucky Library; New York *Times*, 24 October 1926; Louisa *Big Sandy News*, 22 October 1926.

59. Alben Barkley to Garth Ferguson, 16 February 1926 (copy), Ferguson to Barkley, 16 January, 27 February 1926, Box IV, Barkley Collection; New York *Times*, 24 October 1926.

60. Glenn Finch, "The Election of United States Senators in Kentucky: The Barkley Period," *FCHQ* 45 (1971): 288-89; Hazard *Herald*, 15, 22 October, 26 November 1926; Libbey, *Dear Alben*, 47-48; Lexington *Leader*, 16, 22 October 1926; Lexington *Herald*, 1, 3, 23 November 1926.

61. Owens, comp., *Who's Who in Louisville*, 107; Burke, "Sackett," 194; James B. Skaggs, "The Rise and Fall of Flem D. Sampson, 1927-1931" (M.A. thesis, Eastern Kentucky University 1976), 17-18; Louisville *Kentucky Irish American*, 12, 26 March, 16 April 1927; Sexton, "Kentucky Politics," 145, 147; Frances S. Wagner, "The Kentucky Gubernatorial Election of 1927" (M.A. thesis, University of Louisville, 1969), 81-87, 92-94; Flem D. Sampson to D. M. Calvert, 16 Sep-

tember 1954 (copy), Box 214, A. B. Chandler Papers, University of Kentucky Library; Lexington *Herald*, 3 July 1927.

Sampson had been impeached when circuit judge, but had not been convicted. See Wagner, "Election of 1927," 81-82, 83n.

62. Louisville *Courier-Journal*, 25 July 1927; Ramage, "Stanley," 276; A. O. Stanley to Thomas Underwood, 7 October 1927, Box 33, Underwood Papers. See also Louisville *Times*, 29 May 1927, and A. O. Stanley to H. H. Tye, [26 August 1927], Box V, Stanley Papers.

63. Louisville *Kentucky Irish American*, 30 April 1927; James C. Klotter and John W. Muir, "Boss Ben Johnson, The Highway Commission, and Kentucky Politics, 1927-1937," *Register* 84 (1986): 22-24; Wagner, "Election of 1927," 36; comment made to author by George Chinn, 26 February 1980; Lexington *Herald*, 2 July, 12 November 1927; Sexton, "Kentucky Politics," 141; Skaggs, "Rise and Fall of Sampson," 5, 10.

64. Sexton, "Crusade Against Gambling," 56; Louisville *Courier-Journal*, 19 April, 1 July 1927; Louisville *Kentucky Irish American*, 23 April, 7 May 1927; Lexington *Herald*, 13, 14, 18-21, 24, 28-29 July, 3, 8-9, 20 August 1927; Wagner, "Election of 1927," 49-50, 57-72; Sexton, "Kentucky Politics," 148; "Kentucky to Choose Between Beckham and Betting," *Literary Digest* (27 August 1927), 13.

65. Skaggs, "Rise and Fall of Sampson," 27; Finch, "Election of Senators," 43; Klotter and Muir, "Boss Ben Johnson," 24; Sexton, "Crusade Against Gambling," 56.

66. "Kentucky's Race-Horse Election," *Literary Digest* (19 November 1927), 10; Porter, "Jockey Club," 35; New York *Times*, 26 October 1927; Louisville *Kentucky Irish American*, 29 October 1927.

67. Skaggs, "Rise and Fall of Sampson," 34-38; Louisa *Lawrence County Recorder*, 22 September 1927; Louisville *Herald-Post*, 18-19 October 1927; Lexington *Herald*, 16 October 1927.

68. Sexton, "Crusade Against Gambling," 56-57; Lexington *Herald*, 12 November 1927.

69. Louisa *Lawrence County Recorder*, 10 November 1927; Lexington *Herald*, 8-12, 22 November 1927; "Kentucky's Race-Horse Election," 10; Sexton, "Kentucky Politics," 155-56; Louisville *Kentucky Irish American*, 12 November 1927; Louisville *Courier-Journal*, 2 December 1927; Robert F. Sexton, "Flem D. Sampson," in Harrison, ed., *Kentucky's Governors*, 137. In a letter from Forrest Pogue to the author, 20 June 1988, Pogue, who worked for Mickey Brennan at one time, wrote: "Mickey Brennan . . . regaled me with stories of how he helped count Beckham out in the Governor's Race."

70. Ellis, "Fields," in Harrison, ed., *Kentucky's Governors*, 135.

71. Owensboro *Messenger*, 16 March 1978; Kentucky *Acts* (1928), 546-50, 534-35, 851-52, 183-88; Lexington *Herald*, 9, 22 February, 16 March 1928; Lexington *Leader*, 16 March 1928; Paducah *Evening Sun*, 16 March 1928.

72. Desha Breckinridge to W. H. Claggett (copy), 1 May 1928, Box 88, Breckinridge Long Papers; Breckinridge to Henry Breckinridge, 7 September 1928, Box 2, Henry Breckinridge Papers, both in Manuscript Division, Library of Congress; Fred Allen Engle, "The Free Textbook Controversy in Kentucky," *FCHQ* 52 (1978): 334-35; Lexington *Herald*, 3, 5 November 1928. See also New York *Times*, 20 September, 3 October 1929; Louisville *Courier-Journal*, 27 September 1929, 2 November 1928.

73. Willis, *Kentucky Democracy*, 1: 491; Shannon and McQuown, *Presidential Politics*, 104-8; Jewell, *Kentucky Votes*, 3: 22-25; Harrison, "Presidential Elections," 323-24; Sexton, "Kentucky Politics," 201; Louisville *Kentucky Irish American*, 10 November 1928.

74. Klotter and Muir, "Boss Ben Johnson," 35; unidentified clipping, 6 March 1930, Ben Johnson Papers, Kentucky Historical Society; Neal R. Pierce, *The Border South States* (1975), 220.

75. Jessie I. Smith, "A Kentucky Political Election," *American Mercury* 90 (1960): 120; Thomas D. Clark, *The Emerging South* (2d ed., 1968), 133; J. B. Shannon et al., *A Decade of Change in Kentucky Government and Politics* (1943), 8.

76. Klotter and Muir, "Boss Ben Johnson," 23-27; *Ben Johnson* v. *Flem D. Sampson . . . Brief for Plaintiff* (1930), 2-17. An appeal of Sampson's decision went to the state's highest court. See *Opinions of the Attorney General of Kentucky for the Year 1928* (1928), 192-93, and *Johnson* v. *Sampson*, 232 *Kentucky Reports* 648 (1930).

77. Klotter and Muir, "Boss Ben Johnson," 27-30; Louisville *Courier-Journal*, 18 January, 4, 24 February, 7 March 1930; Lexington *Herald*, 18, 22 February 1930; A. B. Chandler Interview, 4 April 1973, Chandler Oral History Project, University of Kentucky Library.

78. Klotter and Muir, "Boss Ben Johnson," 30-33, 36, 38; Kentucky *Auditor of Public Accounts Report* (1930-31), 124; Harrodsburg *Herald*, 15 September 1933.

79. George W. Robinson, "Conservation in Kentucky: The Fight to Save Cumberland Falls, 1926-1931," *Register* 81 (1983): 39-40.

80. *Ibid.*," 29-31, 30n, 46, 51-58; Lexington *Herald*, 4-5 January, 19 February 1930; Louisville *Courier-Journal*, 22 January, 26 February, 8, 11 March 1930; Tom Wallace, "Caught in the Power Net," *The Survey* (1 July 1929), 389-94, 416-17. Happy Chandler in a 4 April 1973 interview (University of Kentucky Library) said, "My vote saved Cumberland Falls from the Insull people. . . . It passed by only one vote." In the Senate, the vote was 20-11, and the failure of any one of the 20 to vote for the bill would have defeated it, for the state constitution required 20 votes to override a veto.

81. Lexington *Herald*, 15 January, 21-22 March 1930; Skaggs, "Flem Sampson," 76-77; Ashland *Daily Independent*, 21, 23 March 1930; Owensboro *Messenger*, 21, 23 March 1930; John Ed Pearce, *Divide and Dissent* (1987), 27.

82. Burke, "Senator Sackett," 198-99; Lexington *Herald*, 8, 10, 17 January 1930; Louisville *Courier-Journal*, 10 January 1930.

83. Kleber, ed., *Kentucky Encyclopedia*, 567-68, 777; Sexton, "Kentucky Politics," 221; Willis, *Kentucky Democracy*, 1: 466-67; "Law Department, Louisville & Nashville R.R. Co. List of Attorneys March 1, 1906," Box 17, Louisville and Nashville Railroad Co. Records, University of Louisville; Louisville *Courier-Journal*, 19, 25, 23 October, 13 November 1930; Jewell, *Kentucky Votes*, 3: 28-30.

84. Campaign Booklet, 1931, Johnson Papers; Lexington *Herald*, 2 July 1931; Louisville *Courier-Journal*, 2-3 July, 21 October 1931; Beckner, in Tapp, *Sesqui-Centennial History*, 2: 744; Cincinnati *Enquirer*, 14 May 1931; New York *Times*, 14 May 1931; Vernon Gipson, *Ruby Laffoon* (1978), 3n, 3-14, 21-30, 41; Marie Taylor, "Night Riders in the Black Patch," *Register* 62 (1964): 33; "Law Department, Louisville & Nashville R. R. Co. List of Attorneys May 1, 1915," L & N Papers; Lexington *Herald*, 24 January 1932.

85. Interview with John Y. Brown, Sr., 9 March 1976, Fred M. Vinson Oral History Project, University of Kentucky Library; Chandler Interview; W. E. Crutcher Interview, Vinson Project; Frenchburg *Menifee County Journal*, 22 November 1962.

86. Klotter and Muir, "Boss Ben Johnson," 39; Louisville *Courier-Journal*, 13 September 1931; Louisville *Kentucky Irish American*, 24 September 1927.

87. Louisville *Courier-Journal*, 20, 26 September, 11 October, 23 September 1931; Sexton, "Kentucky Politics," 224. The issue of Catholicism still was a factor. See J. M. Gilbert to H. M. Frakes, 26 October 1931 (copy) and Mrs. J. B. Adams to Ann Guillian, 13 October 1931, Johnson Papers.

88. Louisville *Kentucky Irish American*, 31 October, 7 November 1931; Louisville *Courier-*

Journal, 7, 21 November 1931; Lexington *Herald*, 21 November 1931; Sexton, "Kentucky Politics," 227. The figures in the text appeared in newspapers at the time as the official count. Different figures appear in Glashan, *American Governors*, 108.

12. *"United We Stand"?: The Politics of Division, 1920-1930*

1. Lucien Beckner, "Drifting Sands of Politics, 1900-1944," in Hambleton Tapp, ed., *A Sesqui-Centennial History of Kentucky* (4 vols., 1945), 2: 746.

2. *Ibid.*; Vernon Gipson, *Ruby Laffoon* (1978), 42: Louisville *Courier-Journal*, 9 March 1932; Orval W. Baylor, *J. Dan Talbott* (1942), 167-71; Transcript of Interview with A. B. Chandler, Chandler Oral History Project, University of Kentucky Library.

3. Baylor, *Talbott*, 165-68; Louisville *Courier-Journal*, 24 January 1932; Lexington *Herald*, 5 January 1932.

4. Robert B. Stewart, "The 1932 House of Representatives of Kentucky" (M.A. thesis, University of Kentucky, 1932), 1-6; Gipson, *Laffoon*, 77-78; George T. Blakey, *Hard Times and New Deal in Kentucky, 1929-1939* (1986), 20; Beckner, in Tapp, *Sesqui-Centennial History*, 2: 747; Kentucky *Acts* (1932), 268-83, 622; Lexington *Herald*, 16-18 March 1932; Owensboro *Messenger*, 18 March 1932; Louisville *Courier-Journal*, 2 April 1932; Lexington *Leader*, 20 March 1932.

5. Malcolm E. Jewell, *Kentucky Votes* (3 vols., 1963), 3: 30.

6. Louisville *Courier-Journal*, 8 September, 26-30 October, 29 November 1932.

7. "Your Son" to J. D. Atkinson, 7 July 1932 (copy), Box 1, Simeon Willis Papers, University of Kentucky Library; Lowell H. Harrison, "Kentucky and the Presidential Elections, 1912-1948," *FCHQ* 26 (1952): 324; Jasper B. Shannon and Ruth McQuown, *Presidential Politics in Kentucky, 1824-1948* (1950), 109-11. See also Bill Weaver, "The Campaign of 1932 and the New Deal Relief Program in Kentucky" (M.A. thesis, Western Kentucky University, 1964), 14.

8. James C. Klotter and John W. Muir, "Boss Ben Johnson, the Highway Commission, and Kentucky Politics, 1927-1937," *Register* 84 (1986): 40; Louisville *Times*, 27 July 1933; J. L. Morgan to R. W. Hunter, 16 August 1932, Box 1, Willis Papers; O. Patterson to T. O. Turner, 26 December 1935, Thomas O. Turner Papers, University of Kentucky Library.

9. Klotter and Muir, "Boss Ben Johnson," 41, 43n, 44n; Gipson, *Laffoon*, 74, 91.

10. Kentucky *Auditor's Report* (1932-33), 3, 12, 134; Louisville *Courier-Journal*, 1 March, 17-18, 30 August, 5, 14 September 1933; Louisville *Herald-Post*, 14 September 1933; Louisville *Democrat*, 2, 7 September 1933; Blakey, *Hard Times and New Deal*, 49.

11. Louisville *Courier-Journal*, 23 August, 5-7 September 1933, 19 September 1993.

12. Owensboro *Messenger-Inquirer*, 15 March 1934; Baylor, *Talbott*, 251, 255-59; Louisville *Courier-Journal*, 3 January, 16 March 1934; Louisville *Herald-Post*, 21 April 1934.

13. Ashland *Daily Independent*, 18 March 1934; Louisville *Courier-Journal*, 16 March 1934; Lexington *Herald*, 18 March 1934; New York *Times*, 25 February 1934; Kentucky *Acts* (1934), 679-714, 70-109, 540; Daniel W. Lynch, *The Development of State and Local Debt in Kentucky, 1890-1962* (1966), 46.

14. Kentucky *Acts* (1934), 197-347, 527; John W. Manning, *The Government of Kentucky* (1940), 172; Louisville *Courier-Journal*, 16 March 1934.

15. Kentucky *Acts* (1934), 1048-55; Louisville *Courier-Journal*, 26, 12 March, 14, 22 April, 18 May, 12, 24 June, 14 November 1934; Louisville *Times*, 21 May 1934.

16. Louisville *Courier-Journal*, 10, 30 May, 16 June, 3 July 1934; Baylor, *Talbott*, 268-70; Blakey,

Hard Times and New Deal, 52, 174; notes of conversation with Robert B. Kinnaird, Frankfort, 24 April 1978; Gipson, *Laffoon*, 134; Transcript of Interview with John Y. Brown, Sr., 9 March 1976, Fred M. Vinson Oral History Project, University of Kentucky Library; Robert W. Bingham to Emanuel Levi, 20 July 1934 (copy), Box 15, John Y. Brown to Bingham, 27 August 1934, Box 5, Papers of Robert Worth Bingham, Manuscript Division, Library of Congress; Louisville *Courier-Journal*, 7 August 1934.

17. Gipson, *Laffoon*, 141, 147; Chandler Interview; Paul Hughes, "Life Has Been Good to the Boy Wonder," Louisville *Courier-Journal Magazine*, 16 July 1950. See also *Royster* v. *Brock*, 79 S.W. 2d 707.

18. Robert W. Bingham to R. P. Taylor, 3 July 1935 (copy), Box 1, Bingham Papers; Lexington *Herald*, 22 September 1935; Cincinnati *Enquirer*, 6 October 1935.

19. Robert W. Bingham to Barry Bingham, 8 March [1935] (copy), 24 April 1935 (copy), 25 April 1935, 10 May 1935, all in Box 1; R. W. Bingham to Ulrich Bell, 8 November 1934 (copy), Box 4; R. W. Bingham to Tom Wallace, 25 September 1935 (copy), Box 26; Barry Bingham to R. W. Bingham, 12 June [1935], Box 1, all in Bingham Papers.

20. On Chandler's career see Charles P. Roland, "Albert Benjamin Chandler," in Lowell H. Harrison, ed., *Kentucky's Governors* (1985), 142-50; Louisville *Courier-Journal*, 16 June 1991; and Chandler's autobiography, *Heroes, Plain Folks, and Skunks: The Life and Times of Happy Chandler* (1989).

21. Stephen D. Boyd, "The Campaign Speaking of A. B. Chandler," *Register* 79 (1981): 227-39; Charles P. Roland, "Happy Chandler," *ibid.* 85 (1987): 155; Louisville *Courier-Journal*, 16 June 1991.

22. Ben Johnson to S. H. Holland, 8 May 1935, Box 7, A. B. Chandler Papers, University of Kentucky Library; 1935 campaign speech, typed copy in Turner Papers; Lexington *Leader*, 11 December 1935.

23. Chandler Interview; Louisville *Herald-Post*, 28 December, 27 August 1935; Interview with Tyler Munford, 18 September 1975, Earle C. Clements Oral History Project, University of Kentucky Library; Louisville *Courier-Journal*, 17 April 1946, 30 June 1935; "Thomas Stockdale Rhea," in John E. Kleber, ed., *Kentucky Encyclopedia* (1992), 768-69; Springfield *Sun*, 12 April 1911; unidentified clipping, 14 February 1935, in Johnson Papers.

24. Lexington *Leader*, 18 August 1935; Covington *Kentucky Times-Star*, 3 September 1935; Chandler Interview; Paul F. Taylor, *Bloody Harlan* (1990), 108-12.

25. Election Results (photostat), 7 September 1935, Box 9, Chandler Papers; Nancy C. Graves, "William Frederick Klair" (microfilm, University of Kentucky Library), 34; Taylor, *Bloody Harlan*, 115-19; unidentified clipping, Democratic Party Papers, Samuel M. Wilson Collection, University of Kentucky Library; John H. Fenton, *Politics in the Border States* (1957), 30-35; Louisville *Courier-Journal*, 8 August 1935; Lexington *Leader*, 11 December 1935; Cincinnati *Enquirer*, 14 October 1934.

26. Lexington *Leader*, 18 August 1935; Lexington *Herald*, 25 September 1935; Kleber, ed., *Kentucky Encyclopedia*, 864; Central City *Messenger*, 12 September 1935; Harlan *Daily Enterprise*, 15 August 1935; New York *Times*, 29 September, 13 October, 5 November 1935.

27. Louisville *Times*, 21 September 1935; Lexington *Herald*, 22 September 1935; Walter A. Baker, "The GOP in Kentucky" (B. A. thesis, Harvard College, 1958), 57-58. On the Chandler military record issue, see clippings in Scrapbook, "Vol. 7 (1935)," King Swope Collection, University of Kentucky Library, particularly in the 10-11 October period; and R. V. Lee, "Official Statement of the Military Service of Albert Benjamin Chandler," Box 409, Chandler Papers.

28. Louisville *Courier-Journal*, 9 October, 3 September, 3 October 1935; Cincinnati *Enquirer*, 6 October 1935; A. B. Guthrie, Jr., to Donald McWain, undated, 1935, in Box 2, Bingham Papers; Lexington *Herald*, 13-14, 8 October 1935; John Ed Pearce, *Divide and Dissent* (1987), 41;

Roy R. Glashan, comp., *American Governors and Gubernatorial Elections, 1775-1978* (1979), 108; Olivia M. Frederick, "Kentucky's 1935 Gubernatorial Election" (M.A. thesis, University of Louisville, 1967), 131-40.

29. Blakey, *Hard Times and New Deal*, 180-81; Pearce, *Divide and Dissent*, 42-44. On the Chandler-Byrd connections see A. B. Chandler to Harry Byrd, 4 December 1935, Box 132, and passim, Harry F. Byrd Papers, University of Virginia Library; J. Harvie Wilkinson III, *Harry Byrd* (1968), 7, 39; Chandler Interview transcript, 11.

30. Beckner, in Tapp, *Sesqui-Centennial History*, 2: 750, Kentucky *Acts* (1936), 149-51, 63-65, 10-12; J. B. Shannon, J. E. Reeves, Harry R. Lynn, and H. Clyde Reeves, *A Decade of Change in Kentucky Government and Politics* (1943), 12, 15; Kyle Ellison, "Changing Faces, Common Walls: History of Corrections in Kentucky" (10th ed., 1985), 11; Kleber, ed., *Kentucky Encyclopedia*, 513; Louis C. Kesselman, "Negro Voting in a Border Community: Louisville, Kentucky," *Journal of Negro Education* 26 (1957): 274; Louisville *Courier-Journal*, 19 September 1943.

31. G. Glenn Clift, "Kentucky Politics, 1900-1953," *Southern Observer* 2 (March 1954): 50; Louisville *Courier-Journal*, 16 June 1991; Kentucky *Acts* (3d Special Session, 1936), passim.

32. Edward M. Wheat, "The Bureaucratization of the South," in James F. Lee, ed., *Contemporary Southern Politics* (1988), 268; J. H. Bradford to A. B. Chandler, 6 July 1932, Box 102, Byrd Papers; Shannon et al., *Decade of Change*, 21; Manning, *Government of Kentucky*, 100, 114-18; Howard W. Beers, ed., *Kentucky: Designs for Her Future* (1945), 230; Clinton *Hickman County Gazette*, 20 August 1936; William T. Strunk, "The Background of the Kentucky Merit System" (typescript, copy in author's possession), 19, 22-23.

33. Klotter and Muir, "Boss Ben Johnson," 47-49; Ben Johnson to A. B. Chandler, 20 April, 5 May, 9 June, all in Box 69, Chandler Papers; Louisville *Herald-Post*, 25 July 1936; Ben Johnson to William Wilson, 18 December 1936, Johnson Papers.

34. Unidentified clipping, possibly 17 April 1940, in Howard Henderson Papers, University of Kentucky Library; Louisville *Herald-Post*, 22 June 1936; Ben Johnson to Dan Talbott, 8 November 1932 (copy), Ben Johnson to Frederick M. Dunne, 27 July 1936 (copy), both in Johnson Papers; Pearce, *Divide and Dissent*, 40; Barry Bingham to R. W. Bingham, 12 November [1935], Box 2, Bingham Papers. See also Joe Muir to Henry Muir, 14 May 1936, Ben Johnson to John J. O'Connor, 18 December 1936 (copy), and Ben Johnson to James Farley, 3 June 1937 (copy), all in Johnson Papers.

35. Dan Talbott to A. B. Chandler, 1 April 1937, Box 19, Chandler Collection.

36. Glenn Finch, "The Election of United States Senators in Kentucky: The Beckham Period," *FCHQ* 44 (1970): 44; Brown Interview; Thomas H. Syvertsen, "Earle Chester Clements and the Democratic Party, 1920-1950" (Ph.D diss., University of Kentucky, 1982), 40: Robert W. Bingham to Guthrie Coke, 14 September 1936 (copy), Box 7; R. W. Bingham to Lee L. Miles, 29 September 1936 (copy), Box 17, both in Bingham Papers.

37. *Statistics of the Presidential and Congressional Elections, 1920-1962* (1963), 11; Cincinnati *Enquirer*, 12 March 1916; Jewell, *Kentucky Votes*, 3: 41-42; Harrison, "Presidential Elections," 325; Shannon and McQuown, *Presidential Politics*, 114-17; Lawrence A. Burdon, "A Statistical Study of Kentucky Presidential Elections, 1920-1948" (M.A. thesis, University of Louisville, 1950), 28-32; Mary C. Erwin, "The Vicious Circle: A Study of the Effects of the Depression and New Deal Relief Programs in Eastern Kentucky" (M.A. thesis, University of Louisville, 1968), 160-62; Ernest Collins, "The Political Behavior of the Negroes in Cincinnati, Ohio, and Louisville, Kentucky" (Ph.D. diss., University of Kentucky, 1950), 80-87, Table VI; Louisville *Democrat*, 14 November 1936; Baker, "GOP," 59-60.

38. Kentucky *Acts* (Extraordinary Session, 1936-37), (1938), (First Extraordinary Session, 1938), (Second Extraordinary Session, 1938), all passim.

39. Markeeta Vincent Wood, "Robert Worth Bingham, American Ambassador to the Court

of St. James, 1933-1934" (M.A. thesis, Western Kentucky University, 1978), passim; Blakey, *Hard Times and New Deal*, 173; Calvin P. Jones, "Kentucky's Irascible Conservative: Supreme Court Justice James Clark McReynolds," *FCHQ* 57 (1983); Kelly Kash, "Feud Days in Breathitt County," *FCHQ* 28 (1954): 348. See also videotaped interviews with Edward F. Prichard, Jr., University of Kentucky Library.

40. Roland, "Happy Chandler," 146-49; James K. Libbey, *Dear Alben: Mr. Barkley of Kentucky* (1979), 78; Walter L. Hixson, "The 1938 Kentucky Senate Election: Alben W. Barkley, Happy Chandler and the New Deal," *Register* 80 (1982): 312-14; unidentified clipping, "A. B. (Happy) Chandler" vertical file, Kentucky Library, Western Kentucky University; Louisville *Courier-Journal*, 16 April 1939.

41. Walter Davenport, "Happy Couldn't Wait," *Collier's* (16 July 1938), 12-13, 50-51; unidentified clipping, Box 78, Homer Stille Cummings Papers, University of Virginia Library; "Roosevelt Handicap," *Time* (1 August 1938), 9-12.

42. H. S. Cummings to Tom Rhea, 7 August 1938; Rhea to Cummings, 8 August 1938, both in Box 147, Cummings Papers; Henry Ward to Alben Barkley, 15 June 1938, Box IX, Political File, Alben W. Barkley Collection, University of Kentucky Library; Crutcher Interview Transcript, 61; Owensboro *Inquirer*, 29 July 1938; Louisville *Courier-Journal*, 1 July 1938; *Time* (1 August 1938), 9-12; Alben W. Barkley, *That Reminds Me* (1954), 164; Hixson, "1938 Senate Election," 324-25. Henry Ward told Hugh S. Johnson in a 30 November 1938 letter (Box 51, Chandler Collection) that Chandler's "publicity man since has confessed to me that it [poisoning charge] was just that" — a publicity stunt.

43. *Time* (1 August 1938), 9-12; Hixson, "1938 Senate Election," 321-23; Blakey, *Hard Times and New Deal*, 183.

44. *Kentucky Welfare* (March 1938); Ben Johnson to Alben Barkley, 16 April 1938 (copy), Johnson Papers; Cecil T. Williams to "Dear Friend," undated, Box IX, Political File, Barkley Collection; unidentified clipping, Box 3, Goodman-Paxton Papers, University of Kentucky Library; New York *Times*, 4 January 1939; Hixson, "1938 Senate Election," 318-19. See also R. P. Taylor to R. W. Bingham, 8 August 1936, Box 24, Bingham Papers.

45. Barkley, *That Reminds Me*, 166; "Statement by George H. Goodman . . . , " Box IX, Political File, Barkley Collection; "Political Analysis 1938," Box 2, Goodman-Paxton Papers; Ernest Rowe to George Goodman, 16 June 1938 (copy), Box IX, Barkley Collection.

46. Hixson, "1938 Senate Election," 317-20; Washington *Daily News*, 1 July 1938; New York *Times*, 4 January 1939; John Henry Hatcher, "Alben W. Barkley, Politics in Relief, and The Hatch Act," *FCHQ* 40 (1966): 251-52; Erwin, "Vicious Circle," 178. See also Harry L. Hopkins to all WPA Workers, 5 May 1938, Box 2, Goodman-Paxton Papers.

47. Hixson, "1938 Senate Election," 326-27; 1938 Primary Results, Box IX, Political File, Barkley Collection; A. B. Chandler to Harry F. Byrd, 20 September 1938 (copy), Box 51, Chandler Collection; Fourth and Fifth Chandler Interview Transcripts; Pearce, *Divide and Dissent*, 45-46; Louisville *Courier-Journal*, 16 June 1991; Blakey, *Hard Times and New Deal*, 188. Different vote totals than those cited are given in Jewell, *Kentucky Votes*, 1: 30-31.

Barkley went on to defeat Republican John P. Haswell, a Louisville banker, 346,735 to 212,266 in the 1938 general election. Official vote, Box IX, Barkley Collection.

48. Frederic D. Ogden, ed., *The Public Papers of Governor Keen Johnson, 1939-1943* (1982), 2; Harrison, ed., *Kentucky's Governors*, 146-47.

13. Wartime Politics, 1940-1950

1. Frederic D. Ogden, ed., *The Public Papers of Governor Keen Johnson, 1939-1943* (1982), 1-3;

Frederic D. Ogden, "Keen Johnson," in Lowell H. Harrison, ed., *Kentucky's Governors* (1985), 150.

2. Keen Johnson to "Dear Sir," 15 July 1927, W. A. Williams Collection, Kentucky Historical Society; Louisville *Courier-Journal and Times*, February 1970; Transcript of Interview with A. B. Chandler, Chandler Oral History Project, University of Kentucky Library, 30.

3. Thomas H. Syvertsen, "Earle Chester Clements and the Democratic Party, 1920-1950" (Ph.D. diss., University of Kentucky, 1982), 51; Ogden, ed., *Keen Johnson*, 522-23, 527; Glenn Finch, "The Election of United States Senators in Kentucky — The Barkley Period," *FCHQ* 45 (1971): 296-97; New York *Times*, 13 August 1939; Ogden, ed., *Keen Johnson*, 2.

4. Walter A. Baker, "The GOP in Kentucky" (B.A. thesis, Harvard College, 1958), 61-63; Ogden, ed., *Keen Johnson*, 532-49; Richard C. Smoot, "John Sherman Cooper: The Paradox of a Liberal Republican in Kentucky Politics" (Ph.D. diss., University of Kentucky, 1988), 62, 68, 76-77; Roy R. Glashan, comp., *American Governors and Gubernatorial Elections* (1979), 108.

5. Louisville *Courier-Journal Magazine*, 23 July 1950; Beckner, in Hambleton Tapp, ed., *A Sesqui-Centennial History of Kentucky* (4 vols., 1945), 2: 752; Daniel W. Lynch, *The Development of State and Local Debt in Kentucky* (1966), 51; John Ed Pearce, *Divide and Dissent* (1987), 47. The state still had nonguaranteed revenue bond debt obligations of several million dollars, however.

6. Beckner, in Tapp, ed., *Sesqui-Centennial History*, 2: 752. See Ogden, ed., *Keen Johnson*, 94, 94-95n, 101n, 101-2, 102n, 103, 103n, 108, 110-11n.

7. Lexington *Herald-Leader*, 17 March 1940; Paducah *Sun-Democrat*, 15 March 1940; Kentucky *Acts* (1940), 742-50, 90-91, 672-80, 37-71, 1-10, 79-81; Louisville *Courier-Journal*, 15-16 March 1940.

8. Interview with Elsie and Bill Welte, Work Projects Administration Files, Kentucky Department for Libraries and Archives; *The Nation* (12 July 1947), 41; Lowell H. Harrison "Kentucky and the Presidential Elections, 1912-1948," *FCHQ* 26 (1952): 325-26; Jasper B. Shannon and Ruth McQuown, *Presidential Politics in Kentucky, 1824-1948* (1950), 118-21; Malcolm E. Jewell, *Kentucky Votes* (3 vols., 1963), 3: 51-55.

9. Kentucky *Acts* (1942), 62-67, 109-11, 627-28, 537-46; Lexington *Herald*, 1 March 1942; Kentucky *Acts* (Special Session, 1942), 1021-50; *Kentucky Government, 1939-1943* (n.d.), 7. A new state office building, begun under Chandler, was also completed during the Johnson administration.
The salary amendment was defeated 121,797 to 94,765. Ogden, ed., *Keen Johnson*, 112.

10. Finch, "Election of Senators — Barkley Period," 297-98; Syvertsen, "Clements," 52, 57-58, 61; "Politics, No. I 1942 - July 25, 1943" Scrapbook, King Swope Collection, University of Kentucky Library; Louisville *Courier-Journal*, 25-26 June, 5, 7, 14 July 1942; Mt. Sterling *Gazette and Kentucky Courier*, 3 July 1942; Lexington *Leader*, 26 June 1942.

11. Beckner, in Tapp, ed., *Sesqui-Centennial History*, 2: 752; G. Glenn Clift, "Kentucky Politics, 1900-1953," *Southern Observer* 2 (March 1954): 51.

12. Ogden, ed., *Keen Johnson*, 505-8; Philip H. Losey, "The Election and Administration of Governor Simeon Willis, 1942-1947" (M.A. thesis, Eastern Kentucky University, 1978), 10-11; Louisville *Courier-Journal*, 1, 8, 30 August 1943; Syvertsen, "Clements," 90.

13. "This is the Story of a Candidate" (pamphlet, 1943) in author's possession; Louisville *Courier-Journal*, 1, 12, 14 August 1943, 28 March 1960, 17 October 1986.

14. James C. Klotter, ed., *The Public Papers of Simeon Willis, 1943-1947* (1988), 1-23; W. R. Jillson, "Governor Simeon S. Willis," *Register* 42 (1944): 3-5; Louisville *Courier-Journal*, 17 August, 30 September, 1, 3, 5, 21 October 1943. The Kentucky Tax Research Association in July 1943 had stated that the seven-year-old income tax was not needed, since the state's debt had been retired.

15. Louisville *Courier-Journal*, 7, 26, 1, 3, 30, 12 October, 26 September, 29 August 1943; Glenn Lane to Harry Lee Waterfield, 26 January 1945, Box 3, Harry Lee Waterfield Papers, Murray State University; Interview with Tyler Munford, 18 September 1975, Earle C. Clement Oral History Project, University of Kentucky Library.

16. Klotter, ed., *Simeon Willis*, 3; Louisville *Courier-Journal* 26, 31 October, 14 November 1943; *Time* (15 November 1943), 22; Ernest Collins, "The Political Behavior of the Negroes in Cincinnati, Ohio and Louisville, Kentucky" (Ph.D. diss., University of Kentucky, 1950), 92-94; William Clark Spragens, "The 1947 Kentucky Gubernatorial Election" (M.A. thesis, University of Kentucky, 1941), 3, 12; New York *Times*, 24 October 1943; Covington *Kentucky Post*, 12 January 1944; Meredith to Simeon Willis, 13 August 1943, copy in author's possession. See also Mrs. Frederick Wallis to "Anne," 16 November 1943, in possession of Henry and Sally Meigs, Louisville.

All the Republican ticket was elected, except secretary of state candidate Mary L. Cave, who lost by 5,000 votes to Charles O'Connell.

17. Ogden, ed., *Keen Johnson*, 511-13.

18. Klotter, ed., *Simeon Willis*, 3-4.

19. Kentucky *Senate Journal* (1944), 15-19, 42-43; Louisville *Courier-Journal*, 10, 19 March 1944; Kentucky *Acts* (1944), 174-79; Klotter, ed., *Simeon Willis*, 38; Losey, "Administration of Willis," 42-44.

20. Klotter, ed., *Simeon Willis*, 46n, 52, 56, 62-64, 73n, 72-73, 78-79; Louisville *Courier-Journal*, 9, 25 May 1944; Losey, "Administration of Willis," 51-58.

21. Jewell, *Kentucky Votes*, 1: 49, 3: 63-65; Louisville *Courier-Journal*, 31 October 1944; Collins, "Political Behavior," 83, 87, 90-94; Louis C. Kesselman, "Negro Voting in a Border Community: Louisville, Kentucky," *Journal of Negro Education* 26 (1957): 276; Shannon and McQuown, *Presidential Politics*, 122-25; Harrison, "Presidential Elections," 326-27. See also "Kentucky: Border State," *Life* (18 September 1944).

22. Klotter, ed., *Simeon Willis*, 330n, 96-97, 97n, 255-56, 238-39, 239n; Covington *Kentucky Post*, 4 April 1947; Executive Order, 24 April 1946, 19 November 1945, Secretary of State's Records, Box 67, Kentucky Department for Libraries and Archives; Kentucky *Acts* (1945), 7-8.

23. Louisville *Courier-Journal*, 6, 8, 25, 27 January, 22, 24, 29 March 1946; Klotter, ed., *Simeon Willis*, 308-9; Kentucky *Commissioner of Finance Report* (1947), 143-47.

24. Finch, "Election of Senators – Barkley Period," 298; Clift, "Kentucky Politics," 51; Jewell, *Kentucky Votes*, 1: 51-55. There were seven other candidates in the primary race. The overall vote was 55,297 for Brown, 42,423 for Ardery, and 29,978 for the others.

25. Smoot, "Cooper," 1-49, 62-77, 87; Transcript of Interview with John Sherman Cooper, 13 May 1979, 18 November 1979, John Sherman Cooper Oral History Project (JSCOHP), University of Kentucky Library. Cooper noted that his 1939 primary loss gave him the statewide contacts he needed in 1946.

26. Smoot, "Cooper," 13-26, 53-55; Cooper Interviews; John Ed Pearce, "Mr. Cooper Says Farewell," Louisville *Courier-Journal Magazine*, 5 March 1972; Lexington *Herald-Leader*, 23 February 1991; Louisville *Courier-Journal*, 1 March 1991; Bill Cooper, "John Sherman Cooper: A Senator and His Constituents," *Register* 84 (1986): 208-10.

27. Henry Ward to John B. Breckinridge, 5 May 1955, John B. Breckinridge Papers, University of Kentucky Library; Smoot, "Cooper," 96-102; Syvertsen, "Clements," 228; Transcript of Interview with Robert L. Riggs, Thruston B. Morton Oral History Project, University of Kentucky Library; Cooper Interviews; Cooper, "Cooper," 200; Jewell, *Kentucky Votes*, 1: 55.

28. Klotter, ed., *Simeon Willis*, 4-6; Simeon Willis to Paul Hughes, 20 July 1950, Box 5, Simeon Willis Papers, University of Kentucky Library; *Your Kentucky Government, 1943-1947*, 77, 23, 10,

48, 29.

During Willis's administration, the state went to a five-day workweek for the first time. Ashland *Daily Independent*, 27 August 1947; Paducah *Sun-Democrat*, 2 October 1947.

29. Spragens, "1947 Election," 19, 40; Clarence Bartlett to J. B. Lawton, 25 June 1947, Box 2, Eldon S. Dummit Collection, University of Kentucky Library; Dummit Campaign Flyer; Cincinnati *Enquirer* (Kentucky Edition), 8 December 1946, 30 April, 4 May 1947; Transcript of Interview with Thruston Morton, 14 October 1974; Transcript of Interview with Kenneth H. Tuggle, 19 August 1974, both in Thruston B. Morton Oral History Project, University of Kentucky Library; "Opening Campaign Address by John Fred Williams," copy in author's possession; "Address of Eldon S. Dummit . . . July 5, 1947," Box 2, Dummit Collection; Jewell, *Kentucky Votes*, 2: 33.

30. Cincinnati *Enquirer*, 8 December 1946; Versailles *Woodford Sun*, 24 July 1947; Syvertsen, "Clements," 236, 253, 264; Allan M. Trout, "The Diversified Career of Harry Lee Waterfield" (pamphlet, n.d.) in Vertical Files, Kentucky Historical Society; Spragens, "1947 Election," 48; Carolyn L. Denning, "The Louisville (Kentucky) Democratic Party's 'Miss Lennie' McLaughlin" (M.A. thesis, University of Louisville, 1981), 111.

31. Syvertsen, "Clements," 2-11; Syvertsen, "Earle Clements," in Harrison, ed., *Kentucky's Governors*, 157-58.

32. Pearce, *Divide and Dissent*, 49, 48, 59, 227; Transcript of Interview with Robert L. Riggs, 15 March 1976, Earle C. Clements Oral History Project (ECCOHP), University of Kentucky Library, 3, 22, 24; Bowling Green *Park City Daily News*, 13 March 1985; Louisville *Courier-Journal*, 8 May 1983, 26 November 1950; Syvertsen, "Clements," 18, 21-24, 248, 234; Transcript of Interview with Frank B. Dryden, 11 November 1975, ECCOHP, University of Kentucky Library, 6, 16-17; Transcript of Interview with J. Thaxter Sims, 15 March 1976, ECCOHP, University of Kentucky Library, 2, 4.

33. Spragens, "1947 Election," 68-73, 82-83, 164-65, 192-97; "Who Owns the Clements Camp?" (pamphlet, 1947), Breckinridge Papers; Jewell, *Kentucky Votes*, 2: 31; Syvertsen, "Clements," 281-82.

34. Syvertsen, "Clements," 308-10; Spragens, "1947 Election," 89-90, 179, 103-4, 109-15, 143-44, 153-55; Louisville *Times*, 12 August 1947; Louisville *Courier-Journal*, 30 October, 2 November 1947; Jewell, *Kentucky Votes*, 2: 35.

35. Louisville *Courier-Journal*, 4 January 1948.

36. Lexington *Leader*, 23 March 1948; Covington *Kentucky Times-Star*, 20 March 1948; Malcolm E. Jewell and Penny M. Miller, *The Kentucky Legislature* (1988), 229; Louisville *Courier-Journal*, 18 February 1980; Ashland *Daily Independent*, 21 March 1948; Lexington *Herald*, 20 March 1948.

37. Owensboro *Messenger*, 23 March 1948; Paducah *Sun-Democrat*, 19-22 March 1948; "A Summary of the 1948 Kentucky Legislature," Box 129, Earle C. Clements Collection, University of Kentucky Library; Kentucky *Acts* (1948), 1-37, 59-62, 172-84; Syvertsen, "Clements," 390-93, 415-16, 439; Louisville *Courier-Journal*, 19 August 1979, 11 December 1949; Riggs Interview Transcript, 10.

Prior to the session a study showed that Kentuckians paid 6.1 percent of their average income to taxes, versus a 6.7 percent national average. Committee for Kentucky, *Blue-Print for a Greater Kentucky* (1949), 82.

38. Harrison, "Presidential Elections," 327-28; James K. Libbey, *Dear Alben: Mr. Barkley of Kentucky* (1979), 94-96; Shannon and McQuown, *Presidential Politics*, 126-29; Philip A. Grant, Jr., "The Presidential Election of 1948 in Kentucky," *Journal of Kentucky Studies* 6 (1989): 86-91; Collins, "Political Behavior," 99, 101, 92, 83.

39. Cooper, "Cooper," 196.

40. Finch, "Election of Senators - Barkley Period," 300-301; Paris *Kentuckian-Citizen*, 6 March 1951; Robert Bendiner, "Tour of the Border States: Kentucky," *The Nation* (16 October 1948), 424-25; Glenn Finch, "The Election of United States Senators in Kentucky — The Cooper Period," *FCHQ* 46 (1972): 164-65; Tom Raney to Herndon Evans, 25 February 1966, "People - Senator Letters," File, John B. Breckinridge Papers; Smoot, "Cooper," 116-21; Baker, "GOP in Kentucky," 80-83.

41. On Prichard's career, see Arthur Schlesinger, Jr., "'Prich': A New Deal Memoir," *New York Review of Books* (18 March 1985), 21-26; John Ed Pearce, "The Man Who Might Have Been President," Louisville *Courier-Journal Magazine*, 24, 31 October 1976; Neal R. Pierce, *The Border South States* (1975), 224-25; Louisville *Courier-Journal*, 20 January 1985; Lexington *Herald*, 29 November 1979; Lexington *Herald-Leader*, 24, 28 December 1984; Kleber, ed., *Kentucky Encyclopedia*, 740-41. See also Ben Kilgore to H. L. Waterfield, [October 1945], Box 3, Waterfield Papers; Louisville *Courier-Journal*, 16 January 1946.

42. C. Ray Hall, in Louisville *Courier-Journal*, 1 June 1991; Mrs. W. B. Ardery et al., *Kentucky in Retrospect . . . 1792-1967* (1967), 128-29; John E. Reeves, *Kentucky Government* (1966), 20.

43. Typed biography, Box 1, Garrett L. Withers Collection, University of Kentucky Library; Kleber, ed., *Kentucky Encyclopedia*, 961-62.

44. Paducah *Sun-Democrat*, 19-20 March 1950; Covington *Kentucky Times-Star*, 20 March 1950; Owensboro *Messenger*, 19 March 1950; Lexington *Leader*, 17 March 1950; Kentucky *Acts* (1950), 851; Louisville *Courier-Journal*, 17, 19 March 1950; Kentucky *Adjutant-General's Report* (1957-60), 49-50.

45. Harrison, ed., *Kentucky's Governors*, 161; Kleber, ed., *Kentucky Encyclopedia*, 257; Clift, "Kentucky Politics," 52.

14. Mid-Century: Moment of Decision

1. Howard W. Beers, ed., *Kentucky: Designs for Her Future* (1945), v.

2. *Ibid.*, passim, quotations on 127, 282, 288.

3. Postwar Advisory Planning Commission of Kentucky, *Final Report* (1945), v-x; "Press Release," in author's possession.

4. Planning Commission *Final Report*, 3, 7, 13, 11, 58-59, 65-66, 72-75.

5. *Ibid.*, passim, quotation on 43.

6. *Reports of Committee for Kentucky, 1943-1950* (n.d.), passim. Each of the twelve reports was issued separately, with separate pagination. All were bound together in volumes with the above title.

7. "Blueprint for a Greater Kentucky" in *Reports of Committee for Kentucky*, 93, 17, 16; "A Report on Education," in *ibid.*, 6, 25-28.

8. *Ibid.*, passim, quotations in "Report on the Constitution," in *ibid.*, 18-19, and Beers, ed., *Kentucky*, v.

9. Jack Temple Kirby, *Rural Worlds Lost: The American South, 1920-1960* (1987), 115; Beers, ed., *Kentucky*, 42.

10. Lexington *Herald-Leader*, 14 October 1985.

11. Harlan Hubbard, *Shantyboat Journal*, Don Wallis, ed. (1994), 3-240, 205 (quotation); Wendell Berry, *Harlan Hubbard, Life and Work* (1990), 2-3, 10, 62 (quotation). See also Vincent Kohler and David F. Ward, eds., *Harlan Hubbard Journals, 1929-1944* (1987).

12. Corbin *Times*, 1 January 1950; Glasgow *Times*, 5 January 1950; Cynthiana *Democrat*, 29 December 1949.

Photo Credits

All photos are from the Kentucky Historical Society Photograph Collections, unless otherwise noted.

Cover

(clockwise from top right) Donna Flaugher, Ohio River Portrait Coll.; Dunn Coll.; Dunn Coll.; Jane Fink, Ohio River Portrait Coll.; Carol Yates Bennett, Ohio River Portrait Coll.; Rev. Joseph & Rev. William Zahner, Ohio River Portrait Coll.

1. "The Sun Shines Bright in The Old Kentucky Home"

p. 2 Dunn Collection; p. 6 *Art Work of Louisville, Ky.* (Louisville, 1903); p. 9 Dunn Coll.; p. 12 James E. Quinn, Sr., Ohio River Portrait Coll.; p. 14 Caufield & Shook photo, *Press Reference Book of Prominent Kentuckians* (Louisville, 1916); p. 16 John Chadwick, E. Matthams Coll.; p. 19 Louisville *Courier-Journal*; p. 22 Robert Burns Stone Coll.; p. 25 Post Card Coll.; p. 30 Consolidation Coal Co. Coll.; p. 32 Alice Lloyd College Archives; p. 35 Dunn Coll.; p. 36 Whitlock Studio, Dunn Coll.; p. 38 Jillson Coll.; p. 40 Dunn Coll.; p. 43 KHS Manuscripts Coll.; p. 46 Louis G. Gutermuth, Jr., Ohio River Portrait Coll.; p. 49 Post Card Coll.

2. "Divided We Fall": Violence in Kentucky

p. 50 Kraemer Art Co. Coll.; p. 54 Ethel B. Miller Coll.; p. 57 Jillson Coll.; p. 62 Wolff, Gretter, Cusick, Hill Coll.; p. 69 J. Winston Coleman Coll., Transylvania University; p. 71 Donna Flaugher, Ohio River Portrait Coll.; p. 73 *That Kentucky Campaign . . .* , by R.E. Hughes, F. W. Schaefer, and E. L. Williams (Cincinnati, 1900).

3. "All Happy and Bright": Life in Kentucky

p. 74 *(top)* Kathleen Rollins, Ohio River Portrait Coll.; *(center left)* Goupille Family/Laurel County Coll.; *(center right)* Harry R. Bright, Ohio River Portrait Coll.; *(bottom)* Wolff, Gretter, Cusick, Hill Coll.; p. 82 Robert B. Stone Coll.; p. 85 Robert B. Stone Coll.; p. 87 Rev. Joseph and Rev. William Zahner, Ohio River Portrait Coll.; p. 95 Wolff, Gretter, Cusick, Hill Coll.; p. 98 *(top)* Jean Clark Smoot, Ohio River Portrait Coll.; p. 98 *(bottom)* Dunn Coll.; p. 102 Post Card Coll.

4. "Weep No More, My Lady": Majorities and Minorities

p. 104 *Kentucky Progress Magazine* (August 1932); p. 107 Dorothy Wehry, Ohio River Portrait Coll.; p. 111 Wolff, Gretter, Cusick, Hill Coll.; p. 114 Wolff, Gretter, Cusick, Hill Coll.; p. 118 Wolff, Gretter, Cusick, Hill Coll.; p. 120 T. T. Wendell Coll.

5. "The Corn Top's Ripe": Agriculture, Industry, and Labor

p. 122 *Kentucky Progress Magazine* (November 1928); p. 124 Elizabeth Parker, Ohio River Portrait Coll.; p. 128 Susan Ijames Bonnell, Ohio River Portrait Coll.; p. 130 Kentucky Agriculture and Natural Resources Coll.; p. 136 Dunn Coll.; p. 138 Harry Boone Nicholson, Sr., Ohio River Portrait Coll.; p. 141 University of Kentucky Special Coll.

6. "The Young Folks": Education

p. 144 Dunn Coll.; p. 151 *Kentucky Progress Magazine* (August 1932); p. 153 Berea College; p.

156 Wolff, Gretter, Cusick, Hill Coll.; p. 163 Berea College; p. 165 *Kentucky Progress Magazine* (June 1929).

7. "We Will Sing One Song": Kentucky's Cultural Milieu

p. 168 *(clockwise from top left)* Franklin Marion Gentry II, James Lane Allen Coll.; Harris & Ewing photo, General Portrait File; Jay Te Winburn photo, General Portrait File; Center for Robert Penn Warren Studies, Western Kentucky University; Dey photo, General Portrait File; Jesse Stuart Foundation; p. 179 *In Kentucky* (Winter 1947), No. 4; p. 180 General Portrait File; p. 182 "D.W. Griffith's 'The Birth of a Nation'" Souvenir Program, KHS Library; p. 183 General Portrait File; p. 185 The Filson Club Historical Society; p. 187 Dunn Coll.

8. "Politics . . . in Kentucky"

p. 188 *(clockwise from top)* Wolff, Gretter, Cusick, Hill Coll.; Wolff, Gretter, Cusick, Hill Coll.; Wolff, Gretter, Cusick, Hill Coll.; *Kentucky Progress Magazine* (Winter 1933); p. 200 Western Kentucky University.

9. "Politics–The Damnedest–in Kentucky": 1900-1919

p. 202 Beckham Coll.; p. 207 KHS Manuscripts Coll.; p. 213 Wolff, Gretter, Cusick, Hill Coll.; p. 216 General Picture File; p. 221 Wolff, Gretter, Cusick, Hill Coll.; p. 222 Wolff, Gretter, Cusick, Hill Coll.; p. 229 Wolff, Gretter, Cusick, Hill Coll.

10. "Hard Times Comes A-Knocking at the Door": War, Disease, and Depression

pp. 234, 238, 243, 247 Wolff, Gretter, Cusick, Hill Coll.; p. 251 Melba Porter Hay, General Picture File; p. 254 *In Kentucky* (Autumn 1944); p. 257 Wolff, Gretter, Cusick, Hill Coll.; p. 260 Ford Motor Company.

11. "United We Stand"? The Politics of Division, 1920-1930

p. 264 Louisville *Courier-Journal*; p. 270 Dunn Coll.; p. 277 Wolff, Gretter, Cusick, Hill Coll.; p. 279 Mrs. Augusta Roach, General Picture File; p. 282 Harry Boone Nicholson, Sr., Ohio River Portrait Coll.; p. 287 Caufield & Shook photo, Dunn Coll.; p. 291 Dunn Coll.; p. 295 Harris & Ewing photo, General Picture File.

12. Old Deal, New Deal, or Misdeal? Politics, 1931-1989

p. 296 Dunn Coll.; pp. 301, 303, 307 Wolff, Gretter, Cusick, Hill Coll.; p. 311 *In Kentucky* (Winter 1946); p. 312 Wolff, Gretter, Cusick, Hill Coll.; p. 314 Special Collections & Archives, Eastern Kentucky University.

13. Wartime Politics, 1940-1950

pp. 316, 319 Wolff, Gretter, Cusick, Hill Coll.; p. 321 *Kentucky Farmer's Home Journal* (July-August 1942), KHS Manuscripts Coll.; p. 325 Wolff, Gretter, Cusick, Hill Coll.; p. 328 University of Kentucky Special Collections; p. 332 Wolff, Gretter, Cusick, Hill Coll.

14. Mid-Century: Moment of Decision

p. 336 Dunn Coll.; p. 340 *In Kentucky* (Autumn 1947); p. 344 *In Kentucky* (Summer 1948).

Index